"Required reading for anyone who wants to understand the events that rocked the nation in 1968 and their enduring impact on American life."

—Senator Edward Kennedy

"Witcover has written an important book about an important truth: that 1968 was the critical watershed year of late-twentieth-century politics."

—Kevin Phillips, author of *The Politics of Rich and Poor*

"A dramatic and extraordinarily well-documented narrative of one of the decisive years of the century—a year that none of us who lived through it will ever forget. Jules Witcover brings it back in vivid detail."

—David Broder, syndicated columnist

"It is impossible to read *The Year the Dream Died*, Jules Witcover's excellent account of 1968, without triggering personal memories....Illuminating commentary."

—Larry Williams, *Philadelphia Inquirer*

"A rich and compelling narrative of the time. Highly recommended."

—*Library Journal*

"Recaptures the drama....Witcover was on the scene for many of the events he describes and apparently kept his old notebooks. That gives his scenes an immediacy that few historians could match."

—*Baltimore Sun*

"Witcover gives us what Johnson said. How McCarthy sulked. How Spiro Agnew ran his mouth. How Nixon couldn't figure out what to say to Witcover's little girl. What it was like, second by second, in the hotel kitchen where Kennedy was shot, because the author was there....The quotes, the eyewitness descriptions, the factualness, are its unique hallmarks....This is a selfless account, blessedly free of theory."

—Carolyn See, *Washington Post Book World*

"Excellent...illluminating commentary."

—Fort Worth *Star-Telegram*

"History at its best...a powerful, cautionary tale well worth pondering by all who want to understand how and why their country changed so profoundly and disturbingly."

—Haynes Johnson, author of *The System*

"This important year finally has the book it deserves—and, no surprise to those of us who have followed his career, Jules Witcover has written it."

—Richard Cohen, *Washington Post*

Also by Jules Witcover

85 Days: The Last Campaign of Robert Kennedy

The Resurrection of Richard Nixon

White Knight: The Rise of Spiro Agnew

A Heartbeat Away: The Investigation and Resignation of Vice President
Spiro T. Agnew (with Richard M. Cohen)

Marathon: The Pursuit of the Presidency, 1972–1976

The Main Chance (a novel)

Blue Smoke and Mirrors: How Reagan Won and Why Carter Lost the
Election of 1980 (with Jack W. Germond)

Wake Us When It's Over: Presidential Politics of 1984 (with Germond)

Sabotage at Black Tom: Imperial Germany's Secret War in America,
1914–1917

Whose Broad Stripes and Bright Stars?: The Trivial Pursuit of the
Presidency, 1988 (with Germond)

Crapshoot: Rolling the Dice on the Vice Presidency

Mad As Hell: Revolt at the Ballot Box, 1992 (with Germond)

JULES WITCOVER writes the only nationally syndicated column devoted
exclusively to national politics, based at the *Baltimore Sun*, as well as a
weekly column for the *National Journal*. He has authored or co-authored
five consecutive books on the presidential campaigns and eight books on
American politics and history, including *85 Days: The Last Campaign of
Robert Kennedy, The Resurrection of Richard Nixon, Marathon, Whose Broad
Stripes & Bright Stars, Crapshoot: Rolling the Dice on the Vice Presidency,* and
Mad as Hell. He lives in Washington, D.C.

THE YEAR THE DREAM DIED

REVISITING 1968 IN AMERICA

JULES WITCOVER

WARNER BOOKS

A Time Warner Company

Warner Books, Inc., 1271 Avenue of the Americas, New York, NY 10020
Visit our Web site at http://warnerbooks.com

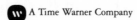 A Time Warner Company

Printed in the United States of America
First Trade Printing: June 1998
10 9 8 7 6 5 4 3 2 1

Library of Congress Cataloging-in-Publication Data
Witcover, Jules.
    The year the dream died : revisiting 1968 in America / Jules Witcover
      p.   cm.
    ISBN 0-446-67471-0
    1. United States—History—1961–1969.   2. Nineteen sixty-eight, A.D.
3. United States—Politics and government—1963–1969.   4. United
States—Social Conditions—1960–1980.   I. Title.   II. Title: Nineteen
sixty-eight.
E846.W55   1997
973.92—DC20   96-42017
                                                                          CIP

Book design by Giorgetta B. McRee

To Marion Elizabeth

I have a dream, that one day every valley shall be
exalted, every hill and mountain shall be made low,
the rough places will be made plains and the crooked
places will be made straight. . . .

Martin Luther King Jr.

Some men see things as they are and say, "Why?" I
dream things that never were and say, "Why not?"

Robert F. Kennedy

CONTENTS

FOREWORD

It was one of those extraordinary benchmark years: it seemed to signify that the country, under the ferocious pressure of rapid technological change (most particularly, the nightly delivery of televised news into each home), the growing pain of an unwinnable war in a distant Asian society, plus bitter, increasingly explosive racial division, was on the verge of a national nervous breakdown. The year had begun with the stunning North Vietnamese assault upon American forces in Vietnam at the time of Tet, an assault that robbed an already embattled administration of its little surviving credibility and the validity of its pronouncements that victory was just around the corner. It speeded up immediately with two challenges to the sitting president by two members of his own party, Eugene McCarthy and Robert Kennedy, challenges that put in play a children's army of student dissenters, and that turned the Democratic primaries into a de facto referendum on the war. If in the past American political divisions had been primarily based on region and class and ethnicity, a new ingredient had now been added, profound generational differences, not just region by region, but remarkably and often quite painfully, house by house. Those who had suffered through the Depression and fought in World War II and who tended to accept the word of the existing leadership were on one side, their children, raised in a more affluent and more iconoclastic age, were on the other.

Nineteen sixty-eight was the year in which politics seemed to begin with violent events in a small country 12,000 miles away, to go into the streets at home, and finally to reach the conventions themselves. It was a year marked by two shattering assassinations, the murders of Martin Luther King and Robert Kennedy. In that year, one sometimes had a sense that violence begat violence. All kinds of different forces were at work: the year marked a collision of the politics of the old, for better and for worse, with the politics of the new, for better and for worse. It came a little more than a decade into the full era of politics by television, the entire nation sitting at home watching the news in its living rooms on a medium that seemed to need and demand ever more action, for television news loved action, because action provided film. Nothing had done more to expedite the jarring domestic political events of 1968 than the jarring nightly reports from Vietnam, what the writer Michael Arlen eventually called The Living Room War. In a way the events of 1968 reflect the culmination of an age; the dissenters kept going into the street, until at the central moment of the political year, the Democratic convention in Chicago, the most important events were outside the convention hall in the streets rather than inside on the podium.

No one captured the politics of that year at the time better than Jules Witcover, one of our best and most careful political writers. In *The Year the Dream Died* he has set down with great skill and precision the political events that reflected a year in which the nation itself seemed on the edge of unraveling. To read this book is to be brought back to that frenetic, moving, painful, bittersweet time.

—David Halberstam, February 1997

INTRODUCTION

Most Americans, reflecting on which single event in the half century since World War II most changed the course of the nation's history, are likely to focus on the assassination of President John F. Kennedy on November 22, 1963. Certainly that grim episode was the most traumatic of the time. The incredible, sickening news jolted Americans in all walks of life as they were going about their routine business on a bright and balmy autumn afternoon. Then came a bizarre aftershock: the nation's mourning harshly interrupted by the shooting of the accused assassin in full view of millions of television watchers.

According to historian Arthur M. Schlesinger Jr. in his epic *A Thousand Days: John F. Kennedy in the White House*, the young president's sudden death led columnist Mary McGrory to remark to fellow Irishman Daniel Patrick Moynihan, then the assistant secretary of labor, that "we'll never laugh again." To which Moynihan replied: "We'll laugh again. It's just that we'll never be young again."

In the national spirit, that may have been true for many Americans. But the fact was that the man who succeeded Kennedy as president, Vice President Lyndon B. Johnson, dedicated himself to carrying on the New Frontier agenda of the fallen leader, fortifying the shaken nation's courage and will with a stirring exhortation to sustain JFK's vision.

Kennedy in his inauguration address had laid out a challenge for a renewed America of domestic equality and tranquillity and of international leadership. He had noted in eerily prophetic terms that "all this will not be finished in the first hundred days. Nor will it be finished in the first thousand days, nor in the life of this administration, nor even perhaps in our lifetime on this planet. But let us begin." Johnson, playing on that phrase in his first major speech as president, urged Congress: "Let us continue." And continue President Johnson and Congress did. Not merely that; they expanded far beyond Kennedy's vision of a challenging New Frontier, to a quest for Johnson's own dream of a Great Society: the riches of the nation, both spiritual and material, would be bestowed in ever greater measure upon all its citizens.

In time, the intrusion of the war in Vietnam, and Johnson's determination to continue the pursuit of his ambitious domestic agenda while expanding the American military commitment and direct involvement in Southeast Asia, subverted both the Kennedy vision and the Johnson dream. But it was not until the unfolding of the events of 1968 that both the vision and the dream were truly shattered, and the nation detoured onto a much more demoralizing and ultimately destructive course. The two great protest movements of the time—for racial equality and justice at home and for the end of a senseless and, in many minds, immoral war abroad—lost their most prominent and charismatic leaders when more assassins' bullets cut down Dr. Martin Luther King Jr. in Memphis in early April and Senator Robert F. Kennedy in Los Angeles in early June of that momentous year.

These and other events unleashed rioting, repression and assaults on the sensibilities of average Americans that turned generations, races, classes and lifestyles against one another in social and cultural divisions that persist in the nation's politics to the present time.

In the process, a generation of younger, liberal Americans was robbed of hope and, eventually, of trust in its government. A conservatism that only four years earlier had been emphatically rejected in the presidential candidacy of Republican Barry M. Goldwater started to take root. It was grounded in public revulsion against the perceived excesses of the protest against the war, and in public weariness toward the continued demands of black Americans. Having achieved great progress in the realm of equal rights, black Americans pressed on in a pursuit of economic justice that was threatening to many white workers, who began to see protection not in their traditional allegiance to the Democratic Party, but in a Republican Party that seemed to appreciate their economic—and cultural—fears.

Then, rising from the ashes of 1968 was a national administration that proved itself unworthy of the people who elected it, and contemptuous of them and their most cherished national institutions. Wholesale abuse and arrogance of power produced a president and a government of deceit and corruption on a scale seldom if ever seen before in the nation's history, culminating in the infamous Watergate affair. For the first time in the nearly two centuries of the American republic, a vice president and then a president—Spiro T. Agnew and Richard M. Nixon—were forced from office in what the successor in the White House—Gerald R. Ford Jr., the country's first unelected vice president and president—aptly labeled "our long national nightmare."

The chapters that follow revisit with the perspective of nearly three decades this cataclysmic year of 1968. It was a year when the sensitivities and nerve ends of millions of Americans were assaulted almost beyond bearing, and the hopes of other millions were buried beneath a wave of violence, deception and collective trauma unmatched in any previous January through December in the nation's memory. For still other millions, however, 1968 presented an opportunity to set the country on an entirely different course—of retrenchment in social welfare and the role of the federal government. For all these millions taken together, the year was truly a watershed.

The journey back into 1968 as portrayed here is in part personal, from the eyes, files and recollections of one who witnessed firsthand many of the pivotal events of the year and observed at close range the principals involved in them. But this account also builds upon the observations and writings of many others, and on the public record that documents the triumphs and tragedies of that momentous year. The following were particularly helpful with their recollections of the events and issues of 1968 and their assessments of the significance, then and now, of that stormy year:

Vice President Al Gore; 1968 presidential candidates Eugene J. McCarthy and George McGovern; Speaker of the House Newt Gingrich; Senators Edward M. Kennedy and Bob Kerrey; Representatives Barney Frank, Joseph P. Kennedy II and John Lewis; Ambassador to Mexico James Jones; California State Senator Tom Hayden; former Senators Howard Baker, Gary Hart and Harris Wofford; former Secretary of Defense Melvin R. Laird; former Secretary of Education William Bennett; former South Vietnamese Ambassador to the United States Bui Diem; also Taylor Branch, Alan Brinkley, Patrick Buchanan, William P. Bundy, Anna Chennault, Cartha DeLoach, Fred Dutton, Peter Edelman, John Ehrlichman, Albert Eisele, Jerry Eller, John Kenneth Galbraith, Curtis Gans, Jack Germond, Todd Gitlin, Doris Kearns Goodwin, Richard Goodwin, Tom Johnson, Frank Mankiewicz, John Mashek, Harry McPherson, Tom Ottenad, David Riesman, Walt W. Rostow, William Safire, Jerrold Schecter, Arthur M. Schlesinger Jr., Daniel Schorr, John Sears, Rick Stearns, Ted Van Dyk, Ben Wattenberg, Curtis Wilkie and Garry Wills. Also most valuable were oral accounts from David Hoeh, the late Erwin Knoll, the late Allard K. Lowenstein, David Mixner and Donald Peterson in the McCarthy Historical Project Archive at the

Georgetown University Library and from Clark Clifford, the late Bryce Harlow and the late Lawrence F. O'Brien in the Oral History Collection at the Lyndon B. Johnson Library, observations by Bennett, Buchanan and Ron Walters in the C-SPAN series *1968: The Year and Its Legacy*, and research assistance from Harry Middleton, John Wilson, Regina Greenwell and Linda Hanson at the LBJ Library.

I am also indebted to my fiancée, Marion Elizabeth Rodgers, whose buoyant spirit and understanding, as a writer, of the tribulations of seeing a book through to publication greatly lightened the burden; to my diligent agent and friend, David Black; to Melody Miller; and to Nelson Schwartz and the rest of the library staff of the *Baltimore Sun* Washington Bureau for research assistance. Finally, I thank especially my son, Paul, and daughters, Amy and Julie, for their perceptions as filtered through the prism of their own generation, whose future was greatly affected by the year when, for so many, the dream of a nobler, optimistic America died, and the reality of a skeptical, conservative America began to fill the void.

—March 1997

THE YEAR
THE DREAM DIED

CHAPTER 1

Ring Out the Old, Ring in the New

On the eve of the new year 1968, Americans faced a somber outlook, judging from what greeted them in their daily newspapers and on their network television screens. A holiday truce in the Vietnam War had been marred by incidents of violence on both sides, offering little promise that the mayhem of 1967 in Southeast Asia—and the protests against the war at home—would diminish substantially in the new year.

President Lyndon Baines Johnson seemed determined to press on with his prosecution of the war. According to a Harris Survey, 61 percent of Americans still supported their country's involvement, though with considerable reservations. But only 39 percent in a Gallup Poll approved of Johnson's handling of the conflict and a growing and more demonstrative minority, particularly on college campuses, sought to get all U.S. forces withdrawn from the stalemate and brought home. The effort was driven in part by altruism, in part by self-preservation, among principally the better-heeled members of the 50 million baby boomers born into security in the decade after the end of World War II.

Comfortable but restless and ultimately rebellious against what they saw as an increasingly homogenized and self-centered society, the oldest of them were only age twenty-two in 1967. With the threat of nuclear war ever-present, many navigated adolescence with an abandon often punctuated by experimentation with drugs. In some polls most of the baby boomers surveyed said they believed nuclear war would occur in their shortened lifetime, and many of them lived accordingly.

And then there was the trauma of the assassination of John Kennedy. He was the one political figure who, by appearance, wit and attitude, had demonstrated affinity toward their adventurous generation and had preached that one man could make a difference. If the world, and their own lives, were to be saved, many of the baby boomers thought, the task could not be left to the rigid elders who were responsible for the existing sorry state of affairs at home and abroad.

Most specifically, through the medium of television that was a baby-sitter for many of them through their formative years, these young Americans saw the Vietnam War up close and they despised it—or basically just didn't want to fight it.

The year just concluding had seen a major escalation of American engagement in the fight to defend the South Vietnamese regime in Saigon against the tenacious insurgency of the indigenous Vietcong and their North Vietnamese sponsors. Johnson in April of 1967 had elected to send American bombers over the North Vietnamese capital of Hanoi and its principal port of Haiphong, in an effort not only to staunch the flow of armaments and foodstuffs to the Vietcong guerrillas but also to strike a psychological blow at the communist enemy. Both objectives had failed in those purposes, and instead they increased opposition to the war, and to LBJ's tactics, at home.

After nearly four years of insisting that the country could pay for the conduct of the war and for his domestic Great Society at the same time, Johnson in August 1967 asked Congress for a 10 percent surcharge tax. It was an open acknowledgment that his earlier insistence that Americans could afford both guns and butter had been seriously mistaken. American leaders in business and finance, supporters of Johnson's war efforts up to this point, began to express severe reservations. The *New York Times* editorially warned that Vietnam was "a bottomless pit" and feared that "the rebuilding of slums and other domestic tasks" at the heart of the Great Society agenda "are being sacrificed to the necessity for spending upward of $2 billion a month to feed the Vietnam conflict."

More conspicuously, the American intensification of the war had ignited campuses from New England and New York to California. It triggered scores of protest marches and the public burning of thousands of draft cards by students demonstrating their commitment to stop the fighting, even at the risk of government prosecution. Many wore their hair long, dressed in hippie garb and used marijuana or stronger drugs, to the annoyance and often open hostility of their sedate elders and blue-collar, "straight" contemporaries. The nonviolent ones were called "flower children" who preached love as the ultimate answer to every problem. (But there were haters, too, like George Lincoln Rockwell, a forty-nine-year-old racist who in 1958 had founded the

American Nazi Party. In August 1967 a disgruntled party member shot and killed him.)

David Miller, the first protester to be prosecuted as a draft card burner, was sentenced to two and a half years in federal prison. The judge said he understood Miller's position against the war but "I must be concerned for the thousands of our men in Vietnam, many of whom, I am sure, are just as opposed to this war, philosophically, as you are."

The sentencing did not stop the card-burnings. An organization in San Francisco that called itself The Resistance mobilized draft-age men to turn in their cards at rallies around the country later in the year. Hundreds of cards were presented to a high Justice Department official in Washington in a direct act of defiance and challenge.

A leading force in the campus protest was Students for a Democratic Society (SDS), formed at Ann Arbor in the spring of 1960 by a group of serious-minded University of Michigan undergraduates including Tom Hayden. In 1962, he was the principal architect of what was called the Port Huron Statement, named after the SDS retreat at which it was written.

"We are people of this generation, bred in at least modest comfort, housed in universities, looking uncomfortably to the world we inherit," it said. "Our work is guided by the sense that we may be the last generation in the experiment with living. . . . We would replace power rooted in possession, privilege or circumstances by power rooted in love, reflectiveness, reason and creativity. As a social system, we seek the establishment of a democracy of individual participation. . . . If we appear to seek the unattainable . . . then let it be known we do so to avoid the unimaginable."

Hayden became a civil rights activist in the South and a community organizer in Newark, New Jersey, before focusing more intently on protest against the Vietnam war. "Johnson, unlike Kennedy, really believed he could do everything—guns and butter," Hayden said later. "He also was a New Deal, World War II politician and more likely to see communism behind every civil war and insurrection."

Also spurring the protest were other serious intellectuals of the American left. Marcus Raskin and Arthur Waskow in 1967 drafted a "Call to Resist Illegitimate Authority," insisting that if American participation in the war was to continue, legalities should be adhered to, including a declaration of war and imposition of the Nuremberg judgments on war crimes in Vietnam. Such intellectuals organized to assist conscientious objectors against this particular war. "If in good conscience you objected to the war and decided not to go," Raskin recalled later, "we would help defend you." Some 2,000 protesters from the clergy and academia signed the call.

At the same time, freelancing radicals of theatrical bent such as Jerry Rubin and Abbie Hoffman administered political shock treatment to the establishment and coalesced in what came to be known as the Yippie movement (for Youth International Party). What was called the New Left raised a much more strident, radical voice than the opposition voiced by older, more cautious liberals still committed to the basic political establishment, and it moved beyond voice to disruptive action. The nation found itself with a cultural and lifestyle rebellion on its hands—a "counterculture"—that had been building all through the early 1960s.

Youth dominated this new culture, although it did not have exclusive domain, and the rock music of the young was its signature, disdained as it often was by the older generations, especially uncomprehending parents. "The only real loyalty that exists in the American teenager today is to his music," rock artist Frank Zappa was quoted as telling the *New York Times*. "He doesn't give an actual damn about his country or his mother or his government or his religion. He has more actual patriotism in terms of how he feels about his music than in anything else." But much of rock music by now had become an integral part of the protest against the war in Vietnam, and was greatly influential in shaping young minds and attitudes about the war.

Todd Gitlin, onetime SDS leader and professor of sociology at Berkeley, wrote in his excellent book *Sixties: Years of Hope, Days of Rage:* "One impulse for confrontation came from the desperate feeling of having exhausted the procedures of conventional politics. A second line of radical thinking was that militancy could coax moderates along, and actually widen the antiwar coalition. A third was that the war was soon to be settled by the rational wing of the Establishment; radicals should therefore return to the issue that most requires radicals, the issue of the race. The conclusions were the same: turn up the militancy.

"Beneath the blur of strategic institutions," Gitlin went on, "something else was stirring. In the spreading cross-hatch where the student movement and the counterculture intersected, a youth identity said, in effect: To be young and American is to have been betrayed; to be alive is to be outraged. The same demonstrations which were driven by strategic purpose were also insurgent youth culture's way of strutting its stuff, or, as it might have preferred to say, staking out room to breathe in an alien land. . . . What evolved from the blur of strategy and identity was a movement that was, in a sense, its own program. It did not merely want you to support a position; it wanted you to dive in, and the more total the immersion, the better."

The disclosure in March 1967 in *Ramparts* magazine that the National Student Association had been secretly funded by the Central Intelligence

Agency had a particularly poisoning effect on the attitudes of the young toward their government and the war it was waging in Vietnam. So did further reports of other educational institutions being similarly financed. "The effect of these disclosures was profound," Thomas Powers wrote later in his book *The War at Home*. "The entire country was revealed as something like an engine of the Cold War."

Dr. Martin Luther King Jr., the most prominent and influential civil rights leader of the era, had begun by this time to speak out forcefully against the Vietnam War as well as against racial injustice at home. His linking of the two protests was a critical milestone in each of them.

On March 25, King led his first antiwar march, declaring that "we must combine the fervor of the civil rights movement with the peace movement." And on April 4, speaking at Riverside Church in New York, he identified a central rationale for the linkage. Professing that for a time he had been "perplexed" about what role to play toward the war, King said it finally "came clear to me that the war was doing far more than devastating the hopes of the poor at home. It was sending their sons and their brothers and their husbands to fight and die in extraordinarily high proportions relative to the rest of the population. I could not be silent in the face of such cruel manipulation of the poor." Notably, King made this observation in terms of economic class rather than of race.

King declared that "the Great Society has been shot down on the battlefields of Vietnam. . . . It would be inconsistent for me to teach and preach nonviolence in this situation and then applaud violence when thousands and thousands of people, both adults and children, are being maimed and mutilated and many killed in this war; so that I still feel and live by the principle 'Thou shalt not kill.' "

King led another huge peace demonstration and march in midtown New York on April 15, along with peace activist Dr. Benjamin Spock, black power advocate Stokely Carmichael and others, underscoring the increasing coming together of the civil rights and antiwar movements. Organizers claimed the turnout was the largest ever in the history of the peace movement; city officials sought to minimize it. There was no doubt, however, that the protest was gaining more and more public momentum. A similar, smaller demonstration took place on the same day in San Francisco, the center for antiwar activity on the West Coast.

Hundreds of young Americans, white and black, refused induction into the armed forces out of religious conviction or as a personal testimony against what they, like King, considered an unjust war fought disproportionately by American black men. Among them was Muhammad Ali, the heavyweight boxing champion of the world and devout disciple of the Nation of Islam or, as its members were popularly known, the Black Muslims. Ali sought an exemption as a conscientious objector but his statements made clear he also had political objections.

"Why should they ask me and other so-called Negroes to put on a uniform and go ten thousand miles from home and drop bombs and bullets on brown people in Vietnam," he asked, "while so-called Negro people in Louisville [his hometown] are treated like dogs and denied simple human rights? I am not going to help murder and kill and burn other people simply to help continue the domination of the white slavemasters over the dark people the world over. This is the day and age when such evil injustice must come to an end."

Ali was stripped of his boxing titles, convicted of draft evasion and sentenced to five years in prison and a $10,000 fine. (Ali remained free on bond pending appeals, and four years later, the Supreme Court ruled in effect that he had been wrongfully denied conscientious objector status, and his conviction was overturned.)

Other young Americans of draft age, including many who had been active in the civil rights movement, fled to Canada, where large communities of them formed in Toronto and other cities and often worked in the antiwar movement. At the headquarters of the Student Union for Peace Action near the University of Toronto, Americans who had already made the decision to leave the country of their birth rather than fight a war in which they did not believe busied themselves answering mail from would-be defectors. They passed on advice such as where it was easiest to cross over into Canada.

A twenty-year-old from Wichita Falls, Texas, named Mark Satin made a typical observation when I encountered him one day at the Toronto office: "I feel as though a great weight has been lifted from my shoulders. It's colder here, but you feel warm because you know you're not trying to kill people."

* * *

Hand in hand with the war protest were racial tensions generated by joblessness and squalid living conditions in inner cities. In May, about thirty heavily armed members of the fledgling Black Panther Party marched into the California State Capitol in Sacramento and denounced a gun control bill then under consideration. It was, party chairman Bobby Seale charged, "aimed at keeping the black people disarmed and powerless at the very same time that racist police agencies throughout the country are intensifying the terror, brutality, murder and repression of black people." Five months later, Black Panthers engaged in a shoot-out with Oakland police in which one officer was killed and Panther leader Huey Newton was arrested and charged with murder.

In June, rioting erupted in the predominantly black section of the Boston suburb of Roxbury, and in July inner-city riots and fires broke out in sweltering, overwhelmingly black, sections of Kansas City, Newark, Detroit and other urban centers, with widespread looting by rampaging marauders. In Detroit, the toll was forty deaths and more than a billion dollars in damages as Johnson dispatched 4,800 federal troops to restore order. Another twenty-six perished in Newark as the summer heat combined with hopelessness, frustration and the tinder of heavy drug traffic in what commonly came to be known as the nation's ghettos.

The Republican Coordinating Committee, then the GOP's unofficial ruling body, met and charged that the nation was "rapidly approaching a state of anarchy," laying the fault at Johnson's feet, saying he "has totally failed to recognize the problem." The Republicans professed to see "organized planning and execution on a national scale" to create the disorders, and House Minority Leader Gerald R. Ford Jr. singled out Carmichael, recently resigned chairman of the Student Nonviolent Coordinating Committee (SNCC). "The Republican Party firmly believes in the cause of civil rights and condemns those who betray it whether they be in high office or on the streets," the party leadership group said in proposing new antiriot legislation.

Even such a level-headed moderate as Senator Mark Hatfield of Oregon told an audience back home that civil rights leaders had "sowed the seeds" of the riots, "Martin Luther King included," by preaching civil disobedience to achieve desired ends. Earlier, King, the Georgia Baptist minister who as head of the Southern Christian Leadership Conference (SCLC) was the generally recognized leader of the civil rights protest, had warned that he would "stir up trouble" in major Northern cities over the summer. But he had specified that demonstrations would be "righteous causes" that would be "an alternative to violence."

Nevertheless, leading moderate voices in the black community had criticized him as lending his "mantle of respectability" to groups with communist ties. That charge came in a position paper by the liberal Freedom House in New York, whose trustees included Roy Wilkins, executive of the National Association for the Advancement of Colored People (NAACP), and the Senate's only black member, Edward W. Brooke of Massachusetts, a Republican. King, the paper charged, had "emerged as the public spear-carrier of a civil disobedience program that is demagogic and irresponsible in its attacks on our government."

H. Rap Brown, who had succeeded Carmichael as head of SNCC and was wanted in Cambridge, Maryland, on charges of inciting a riot, also fueled such views with a speech to blacks arguing that "if Washington, D.C., don't come around [on black power demands], Washington should be burned down." Announcing a program to mobilize draft-age black men to oppose the Vietnam War, he declared: "We see no reason for black men, who are daily murdered physically and mentally in this country, to go and kill yellow people abroad, who have done nothing to us and are, in fact, victims of the same oppression our brothers in Vietnam suffer."

Johnson's response to the Republican criticism was creation of a blue-ribbon commission to investigate the causes of civil disorder, headed by Democratic Governor Otto Kerner of Illinois and Republican Mayor John V. Lindsay of New York. But the critics charged that the commission was merely an excuse to stall and do nothing.

Later in the year there were more racial explosions in East St. Louis, Chicago, Hartford, Dayton and other cities. Such tragedies drove home the reality of what the Kerner Commission study would later say was the increasing existence of two Americas; one white, one black, differentiated not merely by skin color but by income, job opportunity, education and family structure. Many blacks were drafted out of the dismal ghetto life into the armed forces and sent to Vietnam; many others voluntarily swapped the hell at home they knew for the hell they didn't know in distant Southeast Asia.

* * *

At the same time, the struggle for equal rights for black Americans—they were still widely referred to as Negroes in accepted discourse—pressed ahead. Although substantial victories had been won throughout the early and mid-1960s in the American South where segregation had been most blatant and entrenched, there remained many battles to be fought, North and South. King, the most prominent leader in the fight, had begun linking the discrimination against blacks and their lack of economic opportunity at home with the heavy burden they were bearing in the Vietnam War—to the chagrin of many whites who were sympathetic to the first complaint but did not so energetically share the second.

At an SCLC conference in Louisville, King threatened to lead "civil disobedience to further arouse the conscience of the nation." He called on men of draft age, white and black, to boycott the war in Vietnam by declaring themselves conscientious objectors. It was, he said, a "dishonorable and unjust" war where blacks were "dying in disproportionate numbers." The linkage of the war and civil rights drew sharp criticism from, among others, Dr. Ralph Bunche, who as undersecretary of the United Nations and a director of the NAACP was among the most respected black voices in the country. King, he said, should realize that his opposition to the American role in the war "is bound to alienate many friends and supporters of the civil rights movement and greatly weaken it."

In many cities, however, King's call for a coalition of civil rights and anti-war activists to bring the war to an end was being answered. Hundreds of thousands marched in New York and San Francisco and hundreds burned their draft cards. The protests intensified with the American bombings of Hanoi and Haiphong, and violence continued to erupt on American campuses.

The marriage of antiwar activists and black rights advocates was a stormy one from the start. Carmichael, who was a militant new voice for black power on the American left, echoed King's words at a Black Power Conference in Newark from which white reporters were barred, only days after the riots that had ravaged that city. But several resolutions were adopted calling for an independent course for blacks in the country.

At a National Conference on New Politics in Chicago in late August and early September, a black-white split over priorities and roles could not be avoided. Floyd McKissick, head of the Congress of Racial Equality (CORE), proclaimed: "No longer can the black message be a plank in someone else's platform." The venom of some radical black voices poisoned the prospects of cooperation. Rap Brown at one point called Johnson "Hitler's illegitimate child" and FBI director J. Edgar Hoover's "sister." Such comments played into the hands of prominent racist politicians like Governor George C. Wallace of Alabama, who continued to use the race card to build on the surprising strength he had demonstrated in a failed bid for the 1964 Democratic presidential nomination.

* * *

The turmoil at home and abroad together made the country a cauldron of disaffection and dissent from the national leadership as the next presidential election year approached. Both within and without Johnson's ruling Democratic Party, politicians driven by their opposition to the war and their concern about conditions at home, or their personal ambition, weighed the prospects and perils of challenging an incumbent president.

LBJ, for all the criticism he faced, remained the most formidable figure in American public life: tough, commanding, dogged. He was a man who wore power as if it were custom-made for him, and he wielded it with an authority that brooked no argument. The subordinates around him, many of them strong-willed in their own right, often cowed in his presence, or even just in the contemplation of his possible disfavor.

A single anecdote illustrates his imperial manner. Once, when President Johnson was visiting an American military base in the Far East, a young serviceman tentatively directed him to his awaiting transportation. "This is your helicopter, sir," he explained. "Son," the president replied majestically, gesturing to a fleet of them, "they're *all* my helicopters."

Johnson's reputation as a power-wielder was compounded by his record as one of Washington's most relentless, and effective, political operators, with a range of persuasive talents that went from imploring to arm-twisting and head-knocking. In a particularly impolitic but accurate recitation of LBJ's political vulnerabilities, Democratic National Chairman John Bailey told a meeting of the Democratic National Committee in March of 1967 that "the opinion polls tell us that the president's popularity suffers because the public may think of him as a 'wheeler-dealer' or a 'professional politician.' At the same time, the president's actions themselves are of the highest order and far from 'political' in character. So that is the cross we bear, we who are the working politicians of the Democratic Party."

That, however, was not the heaviest cross on the shoulders of the Democrats, and of Johnson. It was, indisputably, the war, the growing impression that the United States was bogged down in Vietnam and that Johnson did not have the slightest inclination to withdraw short of victory. Two months after Bailey's speech I spent several days in two distinctly different areas of the country, each of which had been an LBJ stronghold in his 1964 landslide over Republican nominee Barry Goldwater. The first was Knott County, Kentucky, whose 90.8 percent vote for Johnson was the highest for any county in the nation. The second was New Haven County, Connecticut, whose 73.1 percent support led all urban counties.

In the Kentucky hills, where voting Democratic was almost a religion going back to the days of Franklin D. Roosevelt, the fifty lengthy interviews I conducted found that tradition holding firm. Forty-six of the fifty voters said they still supported the president. Typical was a woman living up a hollow (pronounced "holler" there) behind the county courthouse: "I'm against the war, but I feel we've gotten involved. We have to stay there. Sure I'll vote for Johnson. I think he's trying to end it. Besides, we're just people who vote Democratic."

In the suburban New Haven neighborhood of predominantly but not exclusively white middle-income voters, the contrast was stark. Of one hundred interviewed, forty-four said they did not intend to vote for LBJ in 1968, compared to eighty-four of the hundred who said they had in 1964. Typical was R.C. Smith: "I've always been a Democrat and I was for him last time—still am for him in everything but that [the war]. We have to get out of there. If there's a necessity in staying there other than national pride, he's failed to make clear what it is. . . . I'd cast a protest vote even if they ran Barry Goldwater again, that's how bad it is with me."

The Republicans, obviously, had no intention of wasting their next nomination on the sharp-tongued Arizonan again. Rather, the GOP was gearing up for what it hoped and anticipated would be a serious challenge to the Democratic incumbent with a formidable opponent this time. The combination of an increasingly unpopular war abroad and burning cities and racial conflict at home persuaded the Republicans that in spite of the political fiasco that had undone them only four years earlier—the landslide defeat of archconservative Goldwater at the hands of Johnson—they had a fair chance to elect one of their own to the White House in 1968.

* * *

In the 1966 off-year congressional, gubernatorial and state legislative elections, the Republicans had recovered from the 1964 debacle with surprising speed and strength, making the most of the growing public disfavor toward LBJ. With a private citizen named Richard Milhous Nixon leading the charge in an exhausting round of campaign appearances in behalf of Republican candidates, the Grand Old Party had captured forty-seven additional seats in the House of Representatives, three in the Senate, eight governorships and 540 state legislative seats. Of eighty-six candidates for various offices for whom Nixon had campaigned, fifty-nine won, including forty-four House members.

Nixon at the time had been widely regarded as beyond redemption for national leadership after his 1960 defeat by John F. Kennedy, and particularly after his humiliating rejection for governor of California two years later. But he set himself on a course of political resurrection in casting himself in 1966 as the selfless party warrior traveling from state to state virtually alone to advance the GOP banner.

With Nixon's political fortune still in eclipse at the time, it was easy for a young reporter like myself to hitch a ride with him for more than a week to examine what he had in mind. As always, he was personally courteous but privately suspicious of members of a national press corps that he believed had been his undoing. He declined to say little more than "Good morning" to me each day and "Good night" each evening over that period. But each night he would interrogate a single aide—first it was press secretary Patrick J. Buchanan, later former Congressman Pat Hillings, who had placed Nixon in the House from California—about what I was after.

In spite of the paucity of conversation, the trip with Nixon was very revealing. What I saw up close was a political athlete in training for a comeback. He obviously was determined to live down his reputation as a

press-hater after his famous 1962 "last press conference" in which he announced to reporters that "you won't have Nixon to kick around anymore."
He worked single-mindedly to be friendly, cordial and above all cooperative
with every reporter, photographer and television technician he encountered
on his daily political rounds. He apologized if he was late for a press conference or for making their jobs more difficult ("You'll have to cover me live. I'm
not equipped with staff for texts."). At a stop in Michigan, when a local reporter asked him whether there was going to be a contest between Governor
George Romney and himself for the 1968 Republican nomination, he at first
called the question "somewhat naive," then hastily added: "Not on your part.
But the 1966 election will furnish the stable [of candidates]."

One morning, leaving Birmingham, Alabama, I misunderstood the departure time and raced to the airport in a taxi. There I found Nixon's small jet
waiting on the runway. I climbed aboard, apologizing to him for causing the
delay. He smiled and waved off further explanations to save me more embarrassment, for which I was grateful. Later I learned that aides had wanted to
leave without me but he had insisted on waiting because, he told them, "he's
the only reporter we've got."

But still there was no more than casual conversation between us, and from
time to time during his speeches and press conferences I would catch his eye
shooting a quick, nervous glance my way as if to see what I was up to. He never
seemed to grasp that such attempts at the surreptitious were in vain, or that the
television camera caught them as easily as did the naked eye.

Often, in his speeches, Nixon would make a point of complimenting the
opposition on something or other before attacking them. ("It's a device, of
course," he told me in a later interview, "to show I'm fair-minded.") And he
would deflect with a smile and mild disclaimer all questions about another
presidential candidacy in 1968: "If I were concerned only about '68, why
would I be making three fund-raising speeches in Michigan today?" The
question went unanswered by him, but no answer was necessary.

Only on the final leg of the trip, flying from Roanoke, Virginia, to
Washington, D.C., in an old propeller plane, did Nixon agree to talk to me
at length, and then the conversation was generally philosophical. He seemed
to go out of his way to cast himself as a deep thinker, revealing a self-portrait
quite in conflict with his public persona.

"In order to make a decision," he lectured at one point, "an individual
should sit on his rear end and dig into the books. Very few executives do it.
They listen to this side and that, but they don't go to the sources. In this respect I'm like [Adlai] Stevenson." And if that comparison wasn't surprising
enough, a few minutes later he insisted that "I'm not one of those guys who

reads his press clippings. I believe in never being affected by reports about me. . . . I don't ever want to develop those phony, self-conscious, contrived things," said this most transparently self-conscious of public men. "One thing I have to be is always be myself." And a few more minutes later: "I like the press guys, because I'm basically like them, because of my inquisitiveness." This last was a startling, and unnerving, comparison for a reporter who saw Nixon as unlike himself and his colleagues as he could imagine.

Through all this, Nixon disclosed nothing whatever specific about his own political plans. But it didn't take a mind reader at the time to figure out his objective in working like a trouper to elect Republicans and resurrect his party two years after the Goldwater debacle.

With such campaigning, Nixon had not only achieved that end but also rehabilitated his own political future in the process. In the final days of the off-year campaign, in a deft bit of Johnson-baiting, he had attacked the president for agreeing at a meeting in Manila with South Vietnamese Premier Nguyen Cao Ky to offer the North Vietnamese a mutual troop withdrawal in six months. Nixon implied such a move would be an abandonment. The attack dovetailed with Nixon's strategy of making the off-year elections a referendum on LBJ, and himself the conspicuous architect of it. Johnson then cooperated by lashing out at Nixon in a contentious press conference.

"I do not want to get into a debate on a foreign policy meeting in Manila with a chronic campaigner like Mr. Nixon," he said with dripping sarcasm. "It is his problem to find fault with his country and with his government during a period of October every two years." Nixon, LBJ said, "doesn't serve his country well" by trying to leave the impression that the president would abandon an ally "in the hope that he can pick up a precinct or two, or a ward or two."

In thus singling Nixon out, Johnson had raised his critic's stature as the voice of the Republican Party, and as such Nixon became the chief personal beneficiary of the Republican election victories that ensued. Immediately Nixon, after his 1960 and 1962 losses, was back in business as a 1968 presidential prospect.

According to Joseph Califano, at the time LBJ's chief White House aide on domestic affairs, Johnson's boost to Nixon was intentional, designed to elevate the one Republican LBJ thought would be easiest to beat. "When Johnson returned to his office [after the press conference] and saw the wire-service tickers lead with his characterization of Nixon as a 'a chronic campaigner,'" Califano wrote later in *The Triumph and Tragedy of Lyndon Johnson*, "he chortled, 'That ought to put him out front!'"

* * *

Still, Nixon's record as a two-time loser continued to cloud his prospects
and encouraged other Republicans to consider contesting for their party's
nomination. Most prominent were two governors reelected in the same 1966
off-year elections—Romney of Michigan and Nelson Rockefeller of New
York. Also elected to a first term was movie-actor-turned-politician Ronald
Reagan in California, seen at the time as little more than a glamorous new
face in the party, and a fluke.

Rockefeller, who had failed in an earlier bid for the GOP nomination in
1964, said in June of 1967 that he would not try again and instead threw his
support behind Romney. Most other Republican governors, however,
dragged their feet on endorsing Romney as Nixon aggressively moved to reinstate himself as a viable candidate with impressive speeches on foreign
policy.

Romney was an extremely likable but occasionally hot-tempered self-made
man who had jumped from the auto industry, where he shook up Detroit
with the Rambler compact car, into politics. A devout Mormon, he personified the rewards of hard work and clean living. And he played as he worked.
One frigid winter morning I showed up at his Bloomfield Hills home shortly
after daybreak for an interview. As the price of it, I was first obliged to jog
several miles with him. An avid if wayward golfer whose choppy swing resembled a man trying to kill a snake, Romney dealt with the time problem
of covering eighteen holes by playing six holes using three balls—and running from one to the other. Accompanying him on this mad dash could also
be the price of an interview.

But hard work and hard play did not solve Romney's political problems.
He was particularly vulnerable to charges of indecisiveness and was forever
making observations off the cuff that later had to be "clarified" to get himself
out of hot water. One of my regular traveling companions on the campaign
trail, Jack Germond, then of the Gannett Newspapers and later my partner
in column-writing, finally declared that he was going to have a special key
installed on his portable typewriter that, when struck, would print out:
"Romney later explained."

One of Romney's great political difficulties had been articulating a clear-
cut position on what the United States should do about the quagmire of
Vietnam. Once supportive of the American presence, he had backed off in a
blur of fuzziness. And on the last day of August 1967 he committed one of
those fatal gaffes that can bring a candidacy to ruin.

Asked in a television interview in Detroit about his inconsistency, Romney
told of a visit to Vietnam two years earlier, observing that he had received

"the greatest brainwashing that anybody can get when you go over to Vietnam. Not only by the generals but also by the diplomatic corps over there, and they do a very thorough job." After further study, he said, "I have changed my mind . . . I no longer believe that it was necessary for us to get involved in South Vietnam to stop Communist aggression."

He was already struggling with a public impression that he was a businessman out of his element in politics, and the "confession" of having been brainwashed in Vietnam cemented that image. As often happens in politics, the remark made Romney the brunt of endless jokes. He plunged in the polls, dropping sixteen points in the Harris Survey and inspiring an editorial in one home-state newspaper, the *Detroit News*, that called on him to "get out of the presidential race."

Noting that two years had elapsed since his visit to Saigon, during which he had supported the war most of the time, the newspaper asked: "How long does a brainwashing linger?" Democratic Senator Eugene J. McCarthy of Minnesota, known for his biting tongue, observed of Romney's much-demeaned intellect: "I would have thought a light rinse would have done it."

Romney, however, doggedly continued his campaign in the fall of 1967, conducting a tour of urban centers in a very public effort to identify the causes of the inflammatory conditions there. The trip, with a phalanx of national political reporters in tow, was a disaster. Again he was a fish out of water, best illustrated when he and his wife, Lenore, visited a community of hippies in a park in San Francisco's Haight-Ashbury section. They were met with an avalanche of questions about Vietnam from bearded and sandaled love children, often articulated in profanities to which the Romneys were distinctly not accustomed. Even we reporters accompanying him winced at some of the language used in addressing the two very devout Mormons. The abashed candidate promised to send his long-haired critics copies of his latest speech on the war, an arid offer that only triggered more complaints from the hippies who wanted the visitors, in the mode of Haight-Ashbury, to get in touch with their feelings.

As Romney slipped, freshman Governor Reagan began working what he liked to call "the mashed potatoes circuit," drawing turnaway crowds to Republican fund-raising events. In the process, he ignited speculation that he might be presidential timber in spite of the fact he had been in office in Sacramento less than a year. Reagan insisted he was just another favorite-son governor, but his activities raised political eyebrows, including those of Nixon and his strategists.

Nixon, obviously hoping to capitalize on Romney's weakness on the Vietnam issue, began to talk about how a new Republican administration could "shorten the war" by better "orchestration" of American military, economic and diplomatic policies. But he stopped short of promising a quick end to the war if he became a candidate and was elected. His sure-footedness, contrasted with Romney's seeming uncertainty, bolstered Nixon's reputation as an experienced leader in the realm of foreign affairs. In short order he was outdistancing Romney in the polls.

At the same time, pressure from anti-Nixon Republicans mounted on Rockefeller to abandon the beleaguered Romney and declare his own candidacy. *Time* magazine speculated on its cover about a "dream ticket" of Rockefeller and Reagan, and the notion generated much talk, especially among the nation's governors as they gathered in New York for their annual conference.

In what perhaps was the all-time political junket, a luxury cruise ship, the S.S. *Independence*, was chartered to take them and wives, children, assorted aides, political hangers-on and reporters to the Virgin Islands and back. Rockefeller, Reagan and Romney were all aboard, as well as Republican Governor Spiro T. Agnew of Maryland, who had set himself up as a one-man draft-Rockefeller campaign.

En route to the islands, Germond and I corralled Rockefeller on the ship's sundeck and asked him what he thought of the *Time* cover. "I wouldn't be human if I didn't appreciate a nice remark," he said, "but I'm not a candidate, and I don't want to be president." We weren't sure we had heard him correctly. Saying he wouldn't run was one thing; saying he didn't *want* the most important job in the world was quite another, for any politician. "You heard me loud and clear," he said when we pressed him. Well, did he mean that if nominated by his party he would reject the nomination? "I said [with some irritation] I don't want to be president," he insisted.

We broke away before Rockefeller changed his mind and went off to find Romney and Agnew. Romney was heartened by what his chief supporter had told us but Agnew doggedly refused to quit on the New Yorker. "I still say if he's drafted it would take a pretty emphatic individual to turn down a genuine draft," Agnew said. "Indeed, I can't conceive of it." We raced off to file our stories over the shipboard wireless.

Heading into 1968, however, no such Rockefeller draft seemed to be in the cards. If Nixon was to be stopped for the Republican nomination, it appeared that it would have to be Romney to stop him, or nobody. The nation's GOP governors, who in November had won their twenty-sixth state house, had hoped to have a dominant voice in selecting the nominee—perhaps one of their own. But fellow-governor Romney was looking weaker by the day and Rockefeller was sticking doggedly behind him.

At a meeting in Palm Beach, Florida, while insisting Rockefeller would be the party's strongest nominee, the Republican governors seemed resigned already to swallowing Nixon. With Lyndon Johnson still bearing the brunt of criticism for the conduct of the war and the disorder in the streets of America's cities, that nomination began to look more and more attractive, and especially in light of one other major political development—talk of rebellion against LBJ within the Democratic Party itself.

* * *

The results of the 1966 off-year elections had important ramifications for Johnson and his party as well. A month after the Democrats had sustained the heavy setbacks of those elections, the nation's Democratic governors caucused behind closed doors at the Greenbriar resort in White Sulphur Springs, West Virginia. For three hours, they blistered the Democratic National Committee, its chairman, John Bailey of Connecticut, a John Kennedy holdover, and the Johnson White House for failing to give the state parties adequate support in the recent elections. And when they came out, they freely aired their gripes to the awaiting press, to make sure their message got through to its intended target—LBJ himself.

Governor Harold E. Hughes of Iowa, the caucus chairman, told us there was a consensus that an "anti-administration" trend had contributed importantly to the Democratic losses across the country. Johnson, he said, would face a "very tough" fight for reelection unless he addressed the political organizational problems unmasked by those defeats. One caucus participant, Governor Warren E. Hearnes of Missouri, went so far as to suggest that the party "might be better off with someone else" as its 1968 presidential candidate if Johnson "will not honestly re-evaluate his political operations and make changes."

Johnson, however, was preoccupied all through 1967 with Vietnam and the poisonous atmosphere that was intensifying on the campuses and in the cities at home. The only political matter of great concern to him within the Democratic Party at the beginning of the year was the increasingly vocal voice of his old nemesis, Senator Robert F. Kennedy, on the wisdom and morality of the American involvement in Southeast Asia.

Kennedy, rejected by Johnson as his running mate in favor of Senator Hubert H. Humphrey in 1964, had resigned as LBJ's holdover attorney general in that year, had run and was elected to the Senate from New York. From the start, he showed no reluctance to take issue with Johnson's policies on Vietnam, while largely supporting his domestic agenda, pointing out that it was in important respects a continuation of his late brother's.

In the 1966 election campaign, Kennedy had traveled diligently around the country in behalf of Democratic candidates, many of whom had been supporters of his brother's New Frontier legislation. While he did not fare nearly as well as Nixon did for fellow Republicans—fewer than half of Kennedy's campaign beneficiaries won—he did speak out in support of the Johnson administration generally. He specifically stated that he intended to back the ticket of Johnson and Vice President Humphrey for reelection in 1968.

Yet Robert Kennedy was a political phenomenon whose presence on the campaign trail ignited yearnings for a return to Camelot, inevitably fueling speculation of a presidential candidacy of his own. On one long September 1966 weekend trip through four states in the Midwest, his exhortations in his Massachusetts accent to screaming crowds pressing in on him that "we can do better" refreshed memories of the late president. Teenage girls and grown women screeched at his presence, many grabbing at his clothing for souvenirs.

His own references to Johnson nearly always were in the context of his role as the temporary caretaker of John Kennedy's vision. Recalling his brother's domestic agenda at the Carthage College fieldhouse in Kenosha, Wisconsin, he observed that "that's what we began with President Kennedy and was continued so ably by President Johnson." He called for visionary leadership by his fellow Democrats "if we're going to play the kind of role that was foreseen by President Kennedy in 1960 and by President Johnson in 1964."

Kennedy pointedly cast himself as a team player, but repeatedly the matter of his own political future came up. At a rally at the University of Wisconsin at Milwaukee, a young boy asked: "Are you running for president, and how much are you going to win by?" When his reply was lost in the crowd's cheers, he told those who hadn't heard it, with a grin: "I modestly but realistically answered I wasn't." The suggestive answer brought even more cheers. At the Cincinnati airport, someone held aloft a sign that said: RETURN TOUCH FOOTBALL TO THE WHITE HOUSE. Another in Milwaukee, borrowing from the 1964 Johnson slogan, "All the Way with LBJ," said ALL THE WAY WITH RFK—although Kennedy was not running for anything that year.

A few weeks later, at Sacramento City College, Kennedy was campaigning for Governor Edmund G. "Pat" Brown against the challenge from Ronald Reagan when the crowd began to chant: "Kennedy for President!" When the cheers had subsided, he said, playfully: "I'm pleased to come here and accept your nomination. However, there's one person I want to make sure you don't tell . . . that's my younger brother!"

More often than not, though, exhortations to Kennedy to run for president were at this juncture in the context of an anticipated second term for Johnson. In the question-and-answer period in Sacramento, a student asked him for "some assurance that you will run for president in 1972." Kennedy replied, in a serious vein that brought a hush to the raucous crowd: "Oh. Well, I . . . just quite frankly don't know what the future brings. I think one cannot plan that far in advance. . . . I'm going to continue, as long as I'm around on this globe . . . I'm going to continue in public life in some way. I don't know when that man way up there is going to take me, so I can't . . ." His voice trailed off. Then he added: "That's not a very satisfactory answer but it's the best I can do."

Later the same day, Kennedy made a major speech on civil rights at the University of California at Berkeley. It was the eve of Johnson's conference in Manila with Premier Ky and in response to a question Kennedy said he didn't believe the people of South Vietnam wanted Ky as their leader. The answer took the press play away from the civil rights speech that was weeks in preparation as reporters wrote that Kennedy, who clearly had no love for Johnson, was undercutting the president at a critical time.

Kennedy was mortified, because he had also said in response to a question that he would not "dissociate" himself from LBJ on Vietnam. He came into the press room at Berkeley, where he insisted to David Broder of the *Washington Post* that his civil rights remarks deserved featuring, not the answer on Ky. But once again the uneasy relationship between Kennedy and Johnson colored the coverage.

For all of Kennedy's disavowals of immediate presidential ambition and statements of support for Johnson, his differences with LBJ on Vietnam could not be papered over. And as the war dragged on, American casualties mounted and his own distress intensified, Kennedy gave up trying. As early as February 1966, Kennedy had said that the National Liberation Front, the political arm of the Vietcong, would have to be part of any negotiation to end the war. The United States, he said, would have to start thinking about the possibility of a coalition government in Saigon in which the NLF would play some role. That observation had been likened by Humphrey to letting "a fox in the chicken coop," but Kennedy continued to call on the Johnson administration to halt the bombing of North Vietnam and enter into peace talks.

Kennedy's reservations about the war were compounded by what he saw, in harmony with King, as the unfair burden of fighting it that was borne by the poor, the uneducated and the blacks in American society. He was particularly distressed by the attitude of college students who were either critical of the war or supportive of it and yet accepted student deferments that kept them safe from its greatest risks.

On his Western campaign swing in the fall of 1966, for example, Kennedy asked at Everett, Washington, Junior College for a show of hands on how many of the students supported an escalation of the war. A majority went up. "How many of you who are in favor of escalating the war," he then asked, "are in favor of college deferments?" Hands shot up again, and then many were sheepishly withdrawn as they got the point of his second question.

Kennedy's position for negotiation with the NLF was deeply felt and held, grounded in his belief that it was the only way to extricate the United States from Vietnam with some semblance of honor. But because there existed the well-known history of personal dislike between himself and LBJ, that position was not always received by the public as more than an aspect of that mutual animosity. Nor were his increasing criticisms of conditions in the inner cities at home.

Kennedy, aware of this public perception, agonized over it, not wanting his opposition to the war, or to the domestic distress, to be demeaned by the impression that it was nothing more than ill-feeling toward Johnson. So he often went to some lengths to give reassurances to the contrary. And beyond that, he needed to convince himself that his opposition was worthier than any personal pique for past slights or injustices—including, most notably, Johnson's succession to the presidency as a result of John Kennedy's death, which Robert Kennedy deplored.

Of the reality of the bad will between the two men, there was no doubt. Robert Kennedy never wanted his brother to choose LBJ as his running mate in 1960 and had tried to talk him out of it. In the Kennedy White House, he treated Johnson as an unwanted intruder. And, after the Texan had become president, Kennedy seethed privately when LBJ in 1964 used the ruse of disqualifying all his cabinet members from consideration for the Democratic vice presidential nomination as the way to avoid having to consider him.

In a face-to-face meeting at the White House, Johnson told Kennedy his reasons for rejecting him. He used a speakerphone on his desk to record his words and later printed them in his memoir, *The Vantage Point*. They offered only geographical rationales for bypassing Kennedy, in light of the nomination by the Republicans of Barry Goldwater. "I believe strongly that the Democratic ticket must be constituted so as to have as much appeal as possible in the Middle West and the Border States," Johnson informed him. "Also it should be so constituted as to create as little an adverse reaction as possible upon the Southern States," where Kennedy's strong civil rights actions as attorney general had left deep wounds among many white voters.

Nowhere in the statement was there any mention of the imperative of keeping the cabinet intact and out of the political campaign. Kennedy joked at the time that his only regret was that "I had to take so many good men over the side with me," but his resentment was real.

At the Democratic National Convention in Atlantic City, Kennedy aides tried to persuade him to go to the convention floor in what they calculated might create a stampede for his nomination for vice president regardless of Johnson's wishes. Kennedy thought long and hard about it, prowling his hotel suite, head down and his hands thrust in his trouser pockets. But in the end he declined and confined his appearance to the presentation of an emotional film on the life of his slain brother, John. When he appeared on the platform, the hall erupted in a din of cheers and applause. For a full twelve minutes, he stood silently, occasionally letting a forlorn half-smile break onto his face as the adulation rolled over him.

When he finally was able to speak, the conventioneers listened with rapt attention and many wet eyes as he talked of his departed brother in the lines from Shakespeare: "When he shall die, take him and cut him out in little stars, and he will make the face of heaven so fine that all the world will be in love with night, and pay no worship to the garish sun." As he finished, the convention again erupted in minute after minute of applause and cheers. The message was not lost on Johnson; he may have ascended to and held the presidency, and his party was dutifully renominating him. But its heart, at least at this moment in this place, belonged to the brother of his presidential predecessor, and Johnson's own resentment was real as well.

The LBJ-RFK "feud" was, however, an oversimplification for Kennedy's dissent from Johnson's war policies, and in his mind and justification unworthy of himself. "He couldn't look at Lyndon Johnson without the eyes of the country trained on him," Fred Dutton, one of his chief political strategists, said sometime later. "And he felt it more acutely because it [the feud] had some basis in truth."

Also, there always was Kennedy's own reputation as "ruthless" to contend with. In earlier days, when I first met him as a Senate Labor Committee aide and then as his brother John's chief "no man" and campaign manager in the 1960 West Virginia presidential primary, he had felt obliged to be tough and curt. As he became a public man in his own right, however, he learned to be less brusque and even joked about his reputation for ruthlessness. But it clung, and was another element that would make it more difficult for his honest, heartfelt differences with LBJ's policies to be accepted on their merits.

As a result, Kennedy often bent over backward to avoid perceptions of intentional slights toward Johnson that might be drawn from his statements or actions. But Johnson for his part was always ready to see Kennedy's words and deeds in a negative, personal light. In February of 1967, Kennedy went to Paris for talks with the French foreign office. *Newsweek* magazine reported that he had received a peace feeler from North Vietnam. Johnson was hopping mad and called Kennedy on the carpet at the White House. After a stormy forty-five-minute meeting, Kennedy emerged and denied he had ever suggested he had received such a feeler. He added that he believed Johnson "is making a diligent effort to obtain peace." But that observation didn't stop the speculation that "the feud" continued to be at the core of the two men's differences on Vietnam.

Time reported afterward that Johnson had warned Kennedy that if he continued his criticism of the Vietnam policy "you won't have a political future in this country within six months," and that "the blood of American boys will be on your hands." Kennedy dismissed the reported quotes as "wholly inaccurate." But little he said or could say could erase the picture of the two feuding Democrats at an irreconcilable impasse over Vietnam policy—and their deep personal animosity toward each other.

A week later, I happened to accompany Kennedy on a flight to Chicago where he was to address a conference on China at the University of Chicago. Another reporter also was along and to accommodate us because of early deadlines and a tight travel schedule, Kennedy's office gave us copies of his speech so we could write before boarding the plane. As we prepared our accounts in our offices, Kennedy and his aides reviewed the text and decided to insert a phrase absolving any one president for policy failures in dealing with China—an obvious effort to keep the focus on the substance of the criticism and not on "the feud." We were so advised of the change, which would be incorporated in the text as distributed to other members of the press.

Driving out to Dulles International Airport, Kennedy asked the other reporter, from the *Washington Post*, what he had found in the speech to write about. He replied that he had written that Kennedy had attacked the Johnson China policy and then had inserted a last-minute softener. It was true that Kennedy had done so, but the first draft had been given to us as a courtesy and it did not represent what the press at large would receive as the official text. Kennedy groaned. "Is that all you could find in there?" he complained, turning from the car's front seat on the passenger side. "Wasn't there anything in there about China worth writing about?"

As Kennedy continued to complain, the reporter agreed to call a correction into the *Washington Post* from Dulles before the plane left. But when we got to Chicago, a Kennedy aide had a copy of the story as first filed over the *Washington Post–Los Angeles Times* syndicate wire. Kennedy started complaining all over again as we walked through high snowdrifts to the university auditorium. "It will go out all over the country as only another attack on Johnson," he wailed.

With this prospect in mind, Kennedy in the question-and-answer period after the China speech took pains to speak well of LBJ. He said, in one response, that it would be "very unfair" to saddle the president with all the blame for the Vietnam War. But to his dismay the next day many stories featured his differences with the president of his own party.

Kennedy continued to be peppered with questions about "the feud" at every turn. Marching in New York's St. Patrick's Day parade, he told reporters: "I have great admiration for what the president has done here in the United States and in our relationships with countries overseas. I think it's natural that there would be some differences. . . . He has been an outstanding President of the United States and I look forward to campaigning for him in 1968."

* * *

At the same time, however, two other young Democrats, alumni of the University of North Carolina and the National Student Association, were considering a totally opposite course, and hoping to recruit Robert Kennedy to lead them. Allard Lowenstein, thirty-eight at the time, and Curtis Gans, then thirty, got it into their heads that Johnson, in their view repudiated in the 1966 congressional elections, could be beaten in 1968—not simply by a Republican in the general election but denied the Democratic nomination. Lowenstein took upon himself the direct approaches to prospective challengers to Johnson and became the more visible of the Dump Johnson architects. But Gans, a former editor of the ADA (Americans for Democratic Action) *News* who quit the ADA in protest of its support of Johnson on the war, was equally involved, and convinced that the feat could be accomplished.

It was not a novel idea. As early as March of 1967, the liberal California Democratic Council voted to run an antiwar slate for delegates to the 1968 national convention if the war wasn't at least approaching an end in six months. And in May, leaders of the Reform Democrats in New York pledged to "work for the nomination in 1968 of a candidate other than Lyndon Johnson."

Also, two young Harvard graduate students in government, Doris Kearns and Sanford Levinson, wrote an article in *The New Republic* entitled "How to Remove LBJ in 1968." Protest marches against the Vietnam War were all well and good, they said, "but the longer the marchers sit around in coffee houses and tell each other how great it was, the less likely is a viable political strategy to convert into a meaningful political voice the wide base of support for peace that was demonstrated at the march [in New York in April]. What's needed is hard thinking on how to organize a third party . . . to compete for the presidency in 1968."

(Kearns, it so happened, was a White House fellow at the time, and the article drew some national attention when, at a White House reception, she danced with the president she wanted to depose. Instead of kicking her out of the fellowship program, Johnson took her under his wing, determined to win her over on the war. He failed, but later Kearns helped him write his memoirs and wrote her own assessment of the LBJ years, *Lyndon Johnson and the American Dream.*)

Around the same time, Senator McCarthy of Minnesota, at a dinner in New York with friends and old supporters of Adlai Stevenson, suggested that the only thing that might alter Johnson's Vietnam policy would be, as he put it much later, "to take it to the people"—a challenge to his renomination. He might even make it himself, he said, according to one of his dinner companions, but that was as far as it went then.

McCarthy was particularly disturbed, he said later, by the dismal failure of an effort to have the Vietnam policy debated by the Senate. A proposal to that effect by Democratic Senator Wayne Morse had garnered only five votes—his own and McCarthy's included, but not Robert Kennedy's. The final straw for him, McCarthy said later, was testimony before the Senate Foreign Relations Committee in August 1967, when Undersecretary of State Nicholas Katzenbach defended the Gulf of Tonkin Resolution as giving LBJ a blank check on his Vietnam policy and compelling Congress to go along. McCarthy had yet to conclude, however, that he was the one to make the challenge.

Amid such musings, it was Lowenstein and Gans who pursued a specific plan. In January of 1967, Lowenstein as a leader of the National Student Association had talked with National Security Adviser Walt Rostow at the White House and had come away dismayed, he reported later, by "all the worst little blandnesses of the administration, little arrogancies, many big ones." He urged Vice President Humphrey to break with the administration on the war and talked to Dr. King and socialist leader Norman Thomas about the possibilities of running an independent candidate in 1968.

According to Gans later, in a comment reflecting a continuing tension and conflict between himself and Lowenstein, "the idea of dumping Johnson was mine; he [Lowenstein] wanted a third party headed by Martin Luther King." Lowenstein indeed had explored the possibility of a third party led by Dr. King but abandoned it as he believed increasingly with Gans that Johnson could be denied the Democratic nomination.

"My position was always that we had to take [over] the Democratic Party," Lowenstein said later. "It was considered to be a sellout position by the radicals, and a rather naive stupidity by the liberals." Nevertheless, Lowenstein said later, "the base, it seemed to me, had to be in the Democratic Party because a third party would be ineffective. It had to be broad enough so that it would include more than just the traditional peace groups and so-called liberals, and it had to have, since it would have no money and at least from the beginning none of the organized bases of support, namely the civil rights movement or the labor movement, it would have to have a new base . . . and that base would be the students, who had traditionally been discounted in American politics.

"The first months of this effort," he went on, "were filled with efforts by both the radical establishment and the liberal establishment to discourage it. The radicals by and large took the position that this was a trick to destroy the peace movement; that we would show how weak we were and this would give strength to the notion that the war was popular, so that it would be extended."

As a New Yorker, Lowenstein knew Kennedy and began exploring with him a challenge to the incumbent of his own party. The idea did not come to Kennedy out of the blue. One of his young staff aides, Adam Walinsky, a speechwriter, had written him a memo right after the 1966 elections urging him to take on LBJ, and why. During Kennedy's campaign swings in that election cycle, his crowds were so large and so enthusiastic that Walinsky, already thinking of "retaking" the White House, climbed aboard the plane after one stop and proclaimed to his man: "The hell with 1968! Let's go *now!*"

Kennedy, obviously, did not need reasons for wanting Johnson out of the presidency, but there were just as obviously strong political and personal reasons for him to decline. The power of the incumbency and the danger to party unity were political realities to face. How such a challenge would feed his own image as ruthless and how it would be perceived as no more than a personal vendetta were major personal considerations to weigh. And at the time Kennedy was only forty-one; he would have plenty of time later to make a bid for the White House and the restoration of Camelot without taking on a sitting president of his own party. So he told Lowenstein he would have to find someone else.

"He took it as seriously as the idea of a priest in Bogotá deposing the pope," Lowenstein told me later. Still, Lowenstein kept pressing. On a flight to California for a political dinner that summer, he laid out to Kennedy how Johnson could be beaten. Marshaling a resounding anti-Johnson vote in liberal, antiwar Wisconsin was one way, he said; running a peace slate in California was another. Still Kennedy declined. "I did not urge him to make the race," Lowenstein said later. "At that time it would have been foolish, because he didn't need me to urge him. If he was going to run, he didn't need me to make him a case."

Kennedy also squelched a draft-Kennedy effort by some political amateurs who wanted to run him in the New Hampshire primary. Unfazed, they opened an "RFK in '68" office in the state anyway, under the leadership of Eugene Daniell, a sixty-three-year-old former mayor of the town of Franklin. "We are not out to dump Johnson," he said, "but there is an overwhelming feeling among thinking Democrats that Johnson should be put out to pasture. We want to create a situation in which a man of his ego would decide that his health would not take the strain of another campaign. What that means is, he knows he's going to be licked." But there was no indication whatever that the president was reading any such message in anything said or done by any of the dissident Democrats.

Lowenstein persevered. At a Congress of the National Student Association at the University of Maryland in August, he called for formation of Nonpartisans Against the President, insisting that "this Congress can be a launching pad for a decision to make 1968 the year when students help change a society almost everyone agrees is headed for disaster." Among those who heard him was Mary McCarthy, daughter of the senior senator from Minnesota and a student at Radcliffe, who broached the subject with her father.

Others jumped into the Dump Johnson activity. Sam Brown, a young student at the Harvard Divinity School, called for creation of an Alternative Candidate Task Force (ACT '68). Nothing came of it, but Brown and others eventually joined the Lowenstein effort.

Among those who picketed Lowenstein's speech at the University of Maryland was SDS. "The notion that the students that supported the campaign—the Dump Johnson, then the McCarthy, then the Kennedy—were sort of bearded figures that shaved off their radicalism to work is, of course, also myth," Lowenstein said later. "For every person that worked the campaign who was a radical giving the system a dubious last chance, there were a hundred who were fraternity men or Smith girls . . . there were very few beards, who bitterly opposed the war and Johnson, but who had not gone to the radicals at that time. Which is the reason the campaign was effective. It would not have been effective if it had been the radical fringe."

While disavowing interest himself in any such undertaking, Kennedy did ask Lowenstein who was next on his target list. The fledgling Dump Johnson guerrilla said he was going to approach retired Army General James M. Gavin, who was pushing the concept of maintaining an American "enclave" in South Vietnam while negotiating peace. "If you can get him, you're really in the ball game," Lowenstein recalled Kennedy saying. But Gavin told him he was a Republican, and that was that.

Next, Lowenstein tried John Kenneth Galbraith, the Harvard economist, but Galbraith informed him that he had been born in Canada of Canadian parents, and that ruled him out constitutionally. Shopping the idea around, other Democrats put forward two other names from the Senate: George McGovern of South Dakota and McCarthy. McGovern seemed interested but was focused on his reelection to the Senate in 1968 and feared a presidential run would be detrimental in South Dakota. Lowenstein volunteered to explore the mood in the state and reported back to McGovern that he was probably right; South Dakotans were not in arms over the war as, for example, neighboring Minnesotans were. McGovern suggested McCarthy, a Catholic who would be less vulnerable to allegations of being "soft on communism." When Lowenstein approached him, though, McCarthy told him: "I think Bobby should do it."

Through all this, the widespread assumption continued that Johnson had clear sailing for renomination. Some nervous party regulars began talking of imposing a loyalty oath—a pledge to support the party's nominee—on all convention delegates as a way of reining in anti-Johnson sentiment during the widely televised party gathering the following summer in Chicago. Instead, procedures were adopted to shunt any challenges to the convention credentials committee where, it was hoped, they could be dealt with largely beyond the reach of the television cameras.

But the pressure for more aggressive political action against the war, and Johnson, was mounting. In late August, the left wing of American politics opened its largest convention since 1948 in Chicago. Its leaders hoped to harness its many divergent and independent-minded factions into an effective force for the 1968 presidential election, possibly as a third party.

At this National Conference for New Politics there was some talk of wedding the civil rights and antiwar movements by running a ticket of Martin Luther King and Benjamin Spock. But many radical participants, like members of SDS and longtime peace activist Staughton Lynd, were too soured on elective politics at the national level. They argued that their cause would be best served by going home and concentrating on grassroots organizing and protest. A pivotal question was whether advocates of black power, led by Rap Brown, would agree to work with white civil rights and antiwar activists in pursuit of common goals.

King quickly made clear he was not interested in heading a third-party ticket. In a keynote address, he called for "a radical revolution of values" that would destroy "the giant triplets of racism, materialism and militarism." The 1968 election, he said, had to be made "a referendum on the war" in Vietnam. "The American people must have the opportunity," he said, "to vote into oblivion those who cannot detach themselves from militarism, those who lead us not to a new world but drag us to the brink of a dead world."

King's words did not, however, placate many of the black radicals, who complained that he did not speak for them. About eighty of the three hundred members of the black caucus walked out and did not return until their caucus was given a voting strength at the convention beyond its numerical presence. The move did not sit well with many white delegates. "If you think you're going to ease your consciences by licking black boots," one shouted, "you're crazy." But another said: "Blacks are in the vanguard of this revolution and we have to go along." The upshot was a flood of ill feeling and stalemate on the third-party idea, but continued determination somehow to end American participation in the war.

In late September, Lowenstein met in Pittsburgh with leaders of self-starting Kennedy-for-President committees. Persuaded by Kennedy himself that he would not run, Lowenstein urged them to keep an open mind about a candidate, saying there still was time to find one. Daniell, the New Hampshire Kennedyite, disagreed. "It would be the absolute death of this movement if we tried to fight Johnson with nobody," he told the *New York Times*. "Lowenstein is asking us to commit suicide."

By October, Lowenstein still didn't have a candidate. But by this time the general proposition of challenging Johnson had taken on thrust among the party's left. At a Conference of Concerned Democrats in Chicago co-chaired by Lowenstein, McGovern and McCarthy were again mentioned, along with two other senators, Frank Church of Idaho and Vance Hartke of Indiana. None of these was well known, but Lowenstein was determined to get someone. He also approached Congressman Don Edwards of California, to no avail.

Now, however, McCarthy began to sound interested. "The way he said he would do it," Lowenstein recalled later, ". . . I remember the first question he asked me, that made me just roll with joy. He said something like, 'Well, how would we do in Wisconsin? Should we go in there?' " The conversations quickly turned from entreaties to tactics. On the Senate floor one day afterward, McCarthy turned to McGovern and said: "You know those people you sent over to me? I may just do that."

Lowenstein was not the only one who had been pressuring McCarthy to run. His daughter, Mary, phoned home repeatedly with pleas. Abigail McCarthy, the senator's wife, wrote in her book, *Private Faces/Public Places*, that she had said to her daughter at one point: "Mary, I know that somebody should challenge the president. Something has to be done. But does your father have to be the one to do it?" To which Mary McCarthy replied, her mother wrote: "Mother, that is the most immoral thing you ever said."

Liberal Washington lawyer Joseph Rauh also was pushing McCarthy to run and he enlisted Ken Galbraith to join his effort. After a speech at Harvard around this time, McCarthy sat in his living room in Cambridge, Galbraith recalled much later, and told him he had decided to make the challenge to Johnson.

*   *   *

Through all this, the Vietnam War was a shroud draped over Johnson. The voices of criticism and dissent were growing ever louder within his own party and he began to apply the famous LBJ strong-arm methods to counter them with expressions of political support from influential leaders in both parties. That effort produced perhaps the most bizarre political scene of the year in mid-October. It occurred aboard the same "Ship of Fools" that took the nation's junketing governors to the Virgin Islands, and on which Rockefeller had declared not only that he was not going to run for president but that he didn't want the job.

A couple of nights out of New York, the voyage had been a total lark, devoid of substance. As a result, the trip was developing into what amounted to an all-expenses-paid vacation for the scores of reporters who had shipped out. In lieu of news to report, our fraternity whiled away the hours basking on deck and, as the sun headed for the horizon, shifting our operations to one of the several ship's bars.

With the vessel now in international waters, all drinks were tax-free and hence ridiculously cheap. While on the surface this may have seemed a boon to low-paid reporters, it created another, more long-range problem. Green-eyeshade accountants back at our newspapers, unsophisticated travelers as we imagined them to be, would raise eyebrows at the suddenly modest expense accounts and remember, for the next time.

Veterans among us reminded brethren of the reporters' expense-account axiom: Don't cheapen the beat. That is, never submit an expense account that conveyed in any way that politics could be covered on a shoestring. Thus reminded, we occupied ourselves, while downing the tax-free booze, with creating chargeable items that would make our expense accounts respectable. The best was "lighterage," which was the charge to rent a tugboat or other small vessel to take one out to the ship if one was left on the dock at departure. The going rate was about $50. If the green-eyeshade types of the various newspapers had ever gotten their heads together, they would have imagined a veritable fleet of tugboats heading out to the *Independence* from St. Thomas or St. Croix, the voyage's two ports of call.

In due time, however, we were jolted from our expense-account fantasies by the call of controversy, and hence by work to do. Taking a break from their frolicking, the Republican governors caucused and for the first time in three years voted to reject a Democratic-sponsored resolution supporting Johnson on his conduct of the war. The move, blasted by the Democrats as a precampaign political plot to embarrass Johnson, was hailed as a victory by the supporters of Romney. He had been calling such resolutions, approved by the Republican governors in 1965 and 1966, "blank checks" giving LBJ a free hand to conduct the war as he saw fit. Now Romney argued that another Republican endorsement would be used by Johnson "to whitewash the president's mishandling of the Vietnam War."

A total of twenty-one Republicans opposed the resolution, half the number of governors on the cruise, and with thirty-two needed to approve under the governors' association rules, the vote appeared to kill it. Governor John B. Connally of Texas, Johnson's close friend, ally and spokesman for the Democratic governors on the issue, said he would have to consider whether to press for a vote anyway or drop it.

Reagan, asked whether he thought the resolution was being pushed by LBJ from shore, replied: "This is like a small boy with a boat in a pond. There's a string between boy and boat." It wasn't long before the accuracy of that remark was established.

That night, as the assorted governors, wives and political aides swayed to Latin rhythms on the promenade deck of the *Independence*, a Reagan staff person, Lyn Nofziger, happened by the ship's radio shack in the solarium on the top deck. There, he came upon a cable just sent in Morse code from Marvin Watson, Johnson's White House political adviser, to former Texas governor Price Daniel of Texas, head of the White House Office of Emergency Planning newly assigned to function as LBJ's goodwill ambassador to the governors.

The cable instructed Daniel in distinctly undiplomatic terms to lean on the Republicans, and particularly James Rhodes of Ohio, to support the Vietnam resolution. It referred to the similar governors' resolutions of support in the two previous years, and noted that the Ohio governor had expressed support for the war effort on seven separate occasions. "He did all of this on his own without prompting by anybody," Watson reminded Daniel in the cable. "He should be asked whether he is now running out on his former position."

The ship's radio officer dispatched to Daniel in a sealed envelope what clearly had been intended as a private message from the White House. But Nofziger, with what later came to be known as "the purloined telegram," took a copy to Reagan, who read it and gave it back. At a caucus of the Republican governors, Reagan casually mentioned the cable and somebody suggested the copy be released to the press. Nofziger, a former Washington reporter, didn't need written instructions. He showed it to a few reporters, who copied it on a duplicating machine in the ship's press room and began passing it around to various Republican governors for their comment.

It was a scene right out of a Marx Brothers movie as Republicans displayed or feigned outrage and Democrats dove for cover. Romney, who in his younger days had belonged to a dancing club in Washington, sported a huge straw slouch hat, native beads and a bright multicolored tropical shirt as he gyrated to the Latin rhythms on the dance floor of the ship's Boat and Bottle Bar with the wife of Republican Governor Dan Evans of Washington. When reporters cut in to show him the Watson cable, he glowed with vindication. It was another example, he proclaimed, of "news manipulation, snow job, hogwash and attempts at brainwashing."

Romney was biting back with a happy vengeance at the dog that had bitten him a few weeks earlier. Reagan, sitting with his adoring wife, Nancy, at a table at the edge of the dance floor, sipped crème de menthe through a straw and played straight man on how he had gotten hold of the message from the White House. He was enjoying the role immensely.

Connally took refuge in his cabin and instructed the ship's phone operator not to send him any calls. At the same time, Lady Bird Johnson's press secretary, Texan Elizabeth Carpenter, was assigned the task of persuading reporters they were overreacting, but the task was too much for her. Daniel called Watson over the ship's radio and informed him of the leak. "Keep up the good work," a disgusted Watson told him, Daniel confessed later.

The upshot of the whole farce was the end of the Vietnam resolution, and of a prospective trip by Johnson to the Virgin Islands to address the governors' conference. The president suddenly had a schedule conflict. Increasingly now, his public appearances and travel plans were being dictated by the need to keep a lid on dissension over the war.

* * *

While the governors were frolicking aboard the *Independence* and in the Virgin Islands, the street protest against the war reached a peak with a massive march on Washington that had both peaceful and violent aspects. The two veins represented the growing split in the antiwar movement between predominantly older traditional liberals who hoped their sheer numbers would speak persuasively for them, and the younger radicals who believed only physical, disruptive action could impede "the war machine."

Many tens of thousands of all ages from a variety of antiwar groups, organized by the National Mobilization Committee to End the War in Vietnam (formed a year earlier and known in the antiwar movement as "The Mobe"), demonstrated in an orderly fashion at the Lincoln Memorial. Among them were many students from Washington area colleges, including Georgetown,

where a senior in the School of Foreign Service named Bill Clinton also opposed the war but did not take part in the protest. He was working at the
time on Capitol Hill for the senior senator from his home state of Arkansas,
J. William Fulbright, and shared the senator's strong anti–Vietnam War
views.

At the demonstration, however, were Mary McCarthy and other children
of prominent Washington politicians, including some in the Johnson administration. The Mobe estimated the crowd at 150,000; police put it at a third
as many. Then as many as 35,000 marched across the Memorial Bridge con-
necting Washington with suburban Arlington, Virginia, and over to the
Pentagon, where they conducted a vigil that night and all the next day, into
the night.

As part of the protest, more than 300 draft-age males turned in their
Selective Service cards. Then they were handed to a flustered associate attorney general at the Justice Department by William Sloane Coffin, the chaplain
of Yale University, Dr. Spock, antiwar activists Raskin and Waskow and others. Raskin told the official that the people who should be prosecuted were
those who were violating the law in conducting the war in Vietnam, like the
Joint Chiefs of Staff, Secretary of Defense Robert McNamara and Secretary of
State Dean Rusk.

At the Pentagon the next day, many protesters clung to nonviolent tactics
that included placing flowers in the rifle muzzles of troops guarding the
building against any intrusion. Nevertheless, clashes broke out as other
groups attempted to storm the building. Amid exploding tear gas canisters,
about thirty demonstrators managed to get inside but were quickly ejected
by soldiers and club-wielding federal marshals. Before the siege was over,
thirteen marshals, ten soldiers and twenty-four demonstrators had been injured as blood splattered on the Pentagon steps. Some 681 persons were arrested, mostly outside the Pentagon for refusing to disperse after the march's
two-day permit had expired, and were later released. Johnson lauded the military and law enforcement troops for their restraint; Mobe leader David
Dellinger, a disciple of nonviolence, announced that the protest was moving
from peaceful parades to "confrontations" with the government like the
Pentagon sit-in.

The "siege" of the headquarters of "the war machine," though easily re-
pulsed, marked a milestone in the developing tactics of the war protest. From
then on, at least as far as the younger, more militant in the ranks were concerned, it would be less talk and more action. They were determined that
guerrilla warfare, which continued to frustrate the American military in
Vietnam, would increasingly plague the American government at home.

Stiff efforts to shut down military conscription offices culminated in "Stop the Draft Week" demonstrations in late 1967 in Oakland, California, especially, and in New York and elsewhere. At the University of Wisconsin in Madison, students occupied a building where the Dow Chemical Company, which manufactured napalm for use in Vietnam, was engaged in campus recruiting. Police used tear gas to extricate the protesters, triggering a campus-wide strike.

It was not only the young, however, who were determined to throw a monkey wrench into the war machine. Philip Berrigan, an antiwar Catholic priest, and three other men in an openly defiant act of civil disobedience in October poured animal blood on draft records kept at the U.S. Customs House in Baltimore. They were arrested on four felony charges and immediately became lionized within the antiwar movement as the Baltimore Four.

*   *   *

Around the time of the march on the Pentagon, a young college teacher in New Hampshire named David Hoeh was stirring himself to do something about the war in his own state. Hoeh had some local political experience and, observing what seemed to him a very amateurish and disorganized draft-Kennedy effort in the hands of Gene Daniell, decided he would persuade Daniell to let him take over the operation. "I was just about ready to move on that," Hoeh said later, "when I was visited by Curt Gans." Gans, pursuing the Dump Johnson effort, had obtained Hoeh's name from another antiwar New Hampshirite. Hoeh counseled Gans to put together a core of political people rather than academics, gave him the names of about fifteen of them— and then phoned McCarthy aide Jerry Eller in Washington to find out whether Gans was legitimate. Eller told him he was.

Gans, meanwhile, was in contact with a Democratic congressional district chairman named Don Peterson in Wisconsin who shared his concerns about LBJ and the war. Gans suggested that Peterson call on McCarthy in St. Paul, and Peterson did so, in the company of fellow Wisconsin Democrat Karl Anderson. "When I talked to him [McCarthy] in the living room of his home in St. Paul in the late fall of 1967," Peterson said later, "I felt in my heart and mind that I was talking to a man who had committed himself to see that the American people had an opportunity to make a decision about this war. We went back to Wisconsin feeling confident that we had a candidate. And he asked us at that time . . . to invite him to come into Wisconsin and take part in the primary. This we did, as the Concerned Democrats of Wisconsin."

*   *   *

Kennedy, for all his stated lack of interest in challenging LBJ, against this backdrop was taking private soundings of his own among members of his family, groups of old Kennedy supporters and eager-beaver staffers like Walinsky, legislative researcher Peter Edelman, press secretary Frank Mankiewicz and another young speechwriter named Jeff Greenfield. One night at his home in suburban northern Virginia, Kennedy listened to a debate of sorts pitting Lowenstein, JFK alumnus Richard Goodwin and New York writer Jack Newfield, all for a Kennedy challenge, against historian Arthur Schlesinger Jr., who favored a campaign to impose a peace plank on the Democratic National Convention the next year. Finally, Kennedy broke in. "Arthur," he asked, "when was the last time you heard of millions of people rallying to a plank?"

The talks continued, but Kennedy was not interested in tilting at windmills, and that's what a challenge to an incumbent president appeared at this point to be. Reinforcing that view was a private poll in New Hampshire: Johnson 57 percent, Kennedy 27. A public poll by Louis Harris had Kennedy ahead, 51–32, but Harris had begun to have a reputation as a liberal Democratic cheerleader who seldom brought bad news to his friends. The older political hands around the Kennedys met and the consensus was: No go.

Around this time, Kennedy asked Goodwin to write a long memo making the case for running. Goodwin complied, telling Kennedy that he was hurting himself politically by not being himself. "Your position has worsened," he wrote, "because you can't say what you think . . . and people know it. . . . If you were to come out in open opposition [to Johnson] . . . if you represent what the American people want—and I think you do—then they'll go for you. . . . If I am right about this, then you can win the primaries. I have, in fact, little doubt that you can beat Johnson almost everywhere. . . . If you can't beat LBJ in 1968, then whom can you beat? . . . You may well be hurt more by supporting LBJ, since you will have to say a lot of things you don't believe. . . ." Kennedy was troubled by the memo, but still not moved to action.

It was now November. Vice President Humphrey had just returned from Vietnam observing that "we are winning this struggle. I don't say it has been won. I say we are winning it." Johnson in a press conference denounced "storm-trooper bullying" and "rowdyism" by the war protesters and vowed to press on. United Nations Ambassador Arthur J. Goldberg reported, however, that the United States would "not stand in the way" of participation by the National Liberation Front in peace talks in Geneva.

And there was serious leakage aboard the ship of state. Secretary of Defense McNamara, the Ford Motor Company executive who was brought to the Pentagon by John F. Kennedy in 1961 to harness the free-spending military and wound up overseeing the most modern war machine ever assembled in a seemingly endless war, was totally disillusioned about Johnson's mindless pursuit of victory and told him so. In a memo sent to the president on November 1, McNamara recommended a bombing halt by the end of the year, a stabilizing of U.S. forces in Vietnam and a gradual turnover of military responsibilities to the South Vietnamese.

McNamara's memo, published more than twenty-seven years later in his memoir *In Retrospect: The Tragedy and Lessons of Vietnam*, informed Johnson he was convinced that "continuing on our present course will not bring us by the end of 1968 enough closer to success, in the eyes of the American public, to prevent the continued erosion of popular support for our involvement in Vietnam." Yet in persevering, McNamara wrote, the administration would be "faced with requests for additional ground forces requiring an increased draft and/or call-up of reserves" that, as he wrote later in the memoir, "would lead to a doubling of U.S. casualties in 1968." The memo to Johnson estimated there would be as many as "15,000 additional American dead and 30,000 to 45,000 additional wounded requiring hospitalization."

Breaking the North Vietnamese will to fight on, McNamara told the president, was not likely unless the American public's own willingness to persevere indefinitely was persuasive to the enemy. "And the American public, frustrated by the slow rate of progress, fearing continued escalation and doubting that all the approaches to peace have been seriously probed," he wrote, "does not give the appearance of having the will to persist. As the months go by, there will be both increasing pressure for widening the war and continued loss of support for American participation in the struggle. There will be increasing calls for American withdrawal. There is, in my opinion, a very real question whether under these circumstances it will be possible to maintain our efforts in South Vietnam for the time necessary to accomplish our objectives there."

(McNamara's acknowledgment in his memoir that he had been "terribly wrong" in his role in pursuing the war in Vietnam brought him little praise for his candor. Instead great criticism rained down on him for having not spoken out at the time, or in the more than six succeeding years when Americans continued to fight and die there.)

Johnson, convinced by this memorandum and McNamara's close personal relationship with Robert Kennedy that his defense secretary was under the influence of Kennedy regarding his negative views about the war, decided to dump him. He nominated McNamara to be head of the World Bank, where after years of managing destruction in Vietnam he could turn to rebuilding elsewhere around the globe.

Among those Johnson considered as a replacement at the Pentagon upon McNamara's departure was the fabled Clark Clifford, senior adviser of presidents going back to Harry Truman. Clifford, previously asked by Johnson about McNamara's recommendations, had warned that they would "retard the possibility of concluding the conflict rather than accelerating it" and "would be interpreted . . . [as] a resigned and discouraged effort to find a way out of a conflict for which we had lost our will and dedication." So Johnson had ample grounds to expect that Clifford as McNamara's successor would support the existing Vietnam War policy.

(The only member of the old foreign policy establishment called on by Johnson to evaluate the situation who had any reputation for having reservations about the policy was George Ball, the former undersecretary of state. According to Walter Isaacson and Evan Thomas in *The Wise Men*, after attending a White House meeting of the old establishment with Johnson on November 2, Ball told the others: "I've been watching you across the table. You're like a flock of buzzards sitting on a fence, sending the young men off to be killed. You ought to be ashamed of yourselves." But he didn't break with Johnson.

(Much later, McCarthy characterized Ball as a member of "the Nicodemus Society. Nicodemus was the biblical character who came to see Christ after dark and left before morning." The contempt was mutual. Ball told veteran Minnesota newspaperman Albert Eisele several years later that he thought McCarthy "would be regarded as one of those odd footnotes in American history, a kind of eccentric political figure who appears for a very brief time but then disappears, leaving very little behind. I can't think of anything that anybody's going to say in the future, looking back, representing any solid achievement of Gene McCarthy.")

*   *   *

McCarthy for his part had heard enough to persuade him that there would be no change in Johnson's war policy. He contacted Kennedy and told him he was going to be the candidate of the Dump Johnson movement. Some McCarthy aides said later that McCarthy had indicated he would not do so if Kennedy would run, but that Kennedy again had declined. McCarthy told me later he never asked Kennedy directly to run. But in any event the way was now cleared for McCarthy to be that candidate, or so it seemed then.

Two weeks before McCarthy announced his candidacy, the prospect was enough to inspire Ted Kennedy, at a Democratic testimonial dinner in New Hampshire, to use it to tweak the Johnson forces. Speaking in mock solemnity, he intoned: "I would like to discuss for a moment the political situation as we find it in the nation today. And I would like to say a few words about one man who has suddenly emerged as a figure to be reckoned with. I refer to a man who comes not from New England but from Minnesota. He has held high public office. He has just let it be known that he is a candidate for the presidency. He has said that he will enter the New Hampshire primary. And he has made it clear that he is running not because of personal ambition but simply because he is discouraged and dismayed by the war in Vietnam.

"I respect his candidacy and his right to run for the presidency," Kennedy said. "But if there is one man that I will never support and whom no good Democrat would ever support, it is that man from Minnesota—Harold Stassen." And then, after a pause: "I'll bet you thought I was going to say 'Hubert Humphrey.' "

David Hoeh recalled: "When he came out with Harold Stassen the place broke up, and it was just beautiful. The tension came off and everyone relaxed and realized that he was not going to take off on Gene McCarthy, and the faces on the podium—the senators, the governor, the state chairman, the national committeeman—all of them got pretty long. He had made it quite clear to them that there would not be any ringing endorsement of Lyndon Johnson in this hall."

Ted Kennedy went on: "Before I came to New Hampshire I went to my brother Bobby and I said, 'Do you want me to file your disclaimer [of candidacy]?' And he said, 'You mind your own business.' "

There was more laughter, Hoeh remembered, as Ted Kennedy told about Bobby sending each of his children to a separate primary state and telling each one, "I don't want anyone to write in the name of Robert Kennedy—spelled R-o-b-e-r-t." Kennedy, Hoeh said, "was making very light of the fact that this was a [Kennedy] write-in movement in New Hampshire, but he was also reinforcing it. . . . When he did mention Lyndon Johnson's name just in the history of the party, there was no applause at all." The party regulars, he said, "had not gotten the kind of endorsement they wanted [for Johnson] from Ted Kennedy and he was going to go away leaving them holding the bag."

In declaring his candidacy on November 30, 1967, McCarthy took note of "growing evidence of a deepening moral crisis in America; discontent and frustration, and a disposition to take extra-legal—if not illegal—action to manifest protest. I am hopeful that this challenge I am making," he said, ". . . may alleviate to at least some degree this sense of political helplessness, and restore to many people a belief in the process of American politics and of American government."

McCarthy expressed the hope that "on the college campuses . . . and among adult, thoughtful Americans it may counter the growing sense of alienation from politics which I think is currently reflected in a tendency to withdraw from political action and talk of non-partisan efforts; to become

cynical and make threats for third parties or other irregular political movements."

McCarthy made a point of observing that he had waited "a decent period
of time for others to indicate" that they would take Johnson on. "I would have
been glad to have had [Kennedy] move early," he said. "I think if he had,
there would have been no need for me to do anything."

What if Kennedy entered the race in the event McCarthy made "a significant showing?" a reporter asked. "Well, I don't know," McCarthy said be-
nignly. "He might. It would certainly be nothing illegal or contrary to
American politics if he or someone else were to take advantage of whatever I
might do, or what might happen in consequence of what I'm doing. . . .
There's no commitment from him to stand aside all the way and it certainly
would be in order for him, and only proper it seems to me, within the rules
of American politics, for him to make that kind of move."

Again the question came. Would he step aside if Kennedy came in? "That's
projecting things a long way ahead," he said. "I don't see that as a problem
right now." It might not be a matter of "stepping aside," he said wryly. "It
might be . . . less voluntary than that. But I don't see that as a great disaster,
let me tell you, if it should happen that way." If Kennedy chose to view those
remarks as a green light from McCarthy should he decide later to enter the
race, he could not have been blamed.

(Years later, long after he had left the Senate voluntarily, McCarthy told me
that a major reason he had decided to challenge the president of his own
party, beyond the issue of the war, was that "Johnson was abusing the Senate."
His own whole career, McCarthy said, "had been concerned with the function
of institutions in government." LBJ, he said, took to dealing with the more
malleable House of Representatives on a par with the Senate on foreign policy, which had a greater constitutional responsibility in the field. Johnson,
Rusk and McNamara were contemptuous of the Senate in their misleading
statements about the progress of the war, McCarthy said, and the Senate itself failed to face up to the war.

("There were a lot of guys hiding, fifteen or twenty, who were kind of
against the war but weren't prepared to have a real confrontation with the administration," he recalled. "I was frustrated. You couldn't get the Senate to
do anything, which is where the battle should have been fought, primarily.
. . . The Senate was being pushed around, the country was being pushed
around, the press wasn't telling the truth."

(The news media were reporting what had come from administration officials, he said, but "these guys [Rusk and McNamara] didn't know what they
were up to, and they were killing not just Americans but Vietnamese, in a kind

of hopeless cause." Had there been a full-scale debate on the war in the Senate, he mused, he might not have had to run. But absent such a debate, he said, "we had to save them from what they were doing, and I thought the only way to do that was to go into the primaries.")

* * *

Johnson greeted the challenge with a condescending wit that drew laughter from the group of state party leaders to whom he was talking. "We haven't had our primaries," he said. "We haven't had our convention. So there's really no way of guessing who the candidate might be. But I do want to say this: I fully intend to support him. I believe we already have several volunteers for next year's ticket. I like to stay out of these internal party matters."

McCarthy's candidacy certainly did not seem very promising at the start. A few days after his announcement, he was the featured speaker at a Conference of Concerned Democrats in Chicago. The new group, organized by Lowenstein and Gans, was already active in five of the fourteen states that would hold presidential primaries in 1968, including New Hampshire.

The California Democratic Council, as the largest state group called itself, had decided in September to run a peace slate against the regular party slate pledged to Johnson in the California primary the following June. Another conference delegate was the former Michigan Democratic Party chairman, Zolton Ferency, who shortly before had called for LBJ to be replaced on the party ticket nationally and promptly was forced himself to resign from his state post.

Several thousand antiwar, anti-Johnson Democrats jammed the ballroom of the Conrad Hilton to hear McCarthy speak. While awaiting the tardy senator, Lowenstein began to warm up the crowd with a fire-and-brimstone harangue against LBJ that got hotter the more he talked. The audience responded in kind and was worked up to a lather by the time McCarthy arrived. Lowenstein ranted on as the candidate stood at the rear of the hall, steaming. Finally, Gans ran up to the platform and told him. Lowenstein insisted later that he had no idea McCarthy had arrived and "as soon as I had word that he was in the hall I stopped, literally in mid-thought, and he was introduced."

McCarthy's obvious anger was seen by many at the time as pique at being obliged to wait. But confidants said later he felt Lowenstein's highly emotional and personally confrontational speech struck exactly the wrong tone for the kind of campaign he intended to run against the incumbent president. Rather, they said, he wanted to make his case in reasoned voice on more lofty themes of national morality and purpose, and the preservation of the

American spirit, not a personal assault on LBJ himself. And although many in the new Dump Johnson movement thought they were on the ground floor of a revolution, the staid McCarthy had never been a revolutionary and certainly did not see himself as one now.

In the speech and a question-and-answer session, McCarthy was witty, cool, gracious—and flat. The consensus appeared to be that while the dissident Democrats at last had a horse to ride, he was no Seabiscuit. He made no mention of Johnson, disappointing the expectations raised by Lowenstein's offerings of oratorical red meat. He seemed to many in attendance more willing to follow their lead than to lead them. He offered no firm tactical road map, and as a result delegates from states with primaries pressed him to run in theirs. Some forty-two states were represented at the conference, the bulk of which would choose their national convention delegates in state caucuses and conventions traditionally dominated by elected officials, who were keeping a distinct distance from the developing insurgency.

McCarthy himself suggested it might be preferable that favorite sons run in some state primaries and he mentioned Hartke in Indiana and McGovern in South Dakota as examples. Senator Stephen Young of Ohio, another war critic, announced that he intended to do so in his state. Many delegates to the conference urged McCarthy to bypass the nation's first primary in New Hampshire, in March. The threat of a draft-Kennedy effort there posed the risk of splitting the anti-LBJ vote, and some Massachusetts dissidents asked him to start his challenge there. Don Peterson and others wanted him to make his first challenge three weeks later in Wisconsin, an antiwar hotbed, especially in Madison and other college communities, where the Concerned Democrats of Wisconsin had already enlisted some local elected officials opposed to Johnson. A new election law in the state provided that citizens could vote "No" rather than support a candidate, and McCarthy could be expected to be the beneficiary of that provision. "This was a godsend to us," Peterson said later, "because we could say that we would in effect be having a referendum on the president and on his policies and participation in the war in Vietnam." A "Committee to Vote No" was formed.

The upshot of all the talk was that the Concerned Democrats pledged their support but did not convert into a formal McCarthy-for-President organization. The hedge left the door open for a diplomatic retreat in the event McCarthy fizzled, as many present reluctantly expected, or if Robert Kennedy, the candidate many really wanted, relented and decided to run. One view expressed was that McCarthy might at least weaken LBJ sufficiently to encourage Kennedy to take the plunge.

Lowenstein, while still ecstatic that McCarthy had agreed to run, was beginning to have qualms about him as a result of his behavior at the Chicago conference. The turnout had been so unexpectedly large that several thousand people had to listen in an overflow hall. "It was very cold," Lowenstein remembered. "People had waited in line a long time, and you must understand, nobody had ever heard of McCarthy. . . . So there was a considerable amount of work that had gone into getting people interested in coming. What did disturb me was that he refused to go to the other hall to wave at people who had heard the speech. . . ."

To him, Lowenstein said, McCarthy was being asked for "a simple act you do, not as a political obligation, but as an act of human beings. And we had to pretend he didn't know they were there, and I wasn't comfortable with that pretense. And that left me feeling queasy." On subsequent occasions, he said, "we had to conceal what he had not done. We had to say things about why he didn't do things which were not connected to why he didn't do them."

Also, Lowenstein recalled, McCarthy dissembled in a major way when he announced shortly afterward that he would enter the Massachusetts primary. "He said that he'd been put under such pressure by the Massachusetts delegation at the convention in Chicago that he felt he had to give them what they'd asked," Lowenstein said, "which in fact was the reverse of what happened." That delegation "was one of the weakest delegations there," he said, because Massachusetts was the Kennedys' bailiwick. "The one request that the Kennedys had made was that McCarthy should not enter Massachusetts," he said, "which was not an unreasonable request. . . . It seems quite obvious . . . why he announced it: precisely because the Kennedys had not asked him to go in. . . . He felt compelled to make that decision and blame it on the Massachusetts delegation in Chicago."

McCarthy, however, was still maintaining the position that his fight was with Johnson, not Kennedy. On CBS News's *Face the Nation* on December 10, Martin Agronsky asked him: "If you are not successful in the primaries and your support does gain some momentum, but the time were to come when it was clear that you couldn't make it and Senator Kennedy could, would you then support Senator Kennedy?" McCarthy replied: "Well, I have gone so far as to say that I didn't think it would be a national disaster if that situation arose and I might be moved to support him. I think we will wait until the convention to settle that, or somewhere along the way."

When Roger Mudd told him that "the White House thinks you're drawing the cloak of Kennedy around your shoulders and they now suspect the worst, that all you really are is just a front man," McCarthy broke in. "Well, I don't mind them worrying about that," he said. "If this is one of the specters that is haunting the White House, why, I will let it run."

* * *

In mid-December, two separate meetings of Kennedy insiders were held to assess the situation once again. By this time, with the little-known McCarthy having donned the mantle of the anti-Johnson cause and being given little chance of succeeding, Kennedy was in inner turmoil. Schlesinger by now had come around. Kennedy strategist Fred Dutton reported later that Schlesinger now took the lead in arguing that Kennedy had to run. "He argued that maybe it couldn't be done as a practical matter," Dutton said, "but the war was terrible and Johnson was no good, so Kennedy had to put personal considerations aside. He said historic things were happening and Bob owed it to the kids to get in."

When somebody suggested that Kennedy would be risking his political future, he snapped: "My future is not the issue. The issue is whether the country can survive four more years of Lyndon Johnson. If by declaring myself a candidate I could end this war any sooner, I'd feel an obligation to run. . . . I'm against the war, but if I get in I want to have influence. What will Johnson's reaction be? Escalate the bombing? And everybody will believe I'm waging a personal vendetta."

Kennedy said he didn't think McCarthy had the political wherewithal to knock off LBJ, but the odds also seemed very high against himself. The veterans in politics around him agreed. And there was also the distinct possibility that a more serious, effective challenge to the Democratic incumbent from within his party would clear the path for the election of a Republican—in all probability the despised Nixon. After all was said and done, Kennedy could not convince himself that this was his time.

* * *

Up in New Hampshire, David Hoeh was ready to abandon the draft-Kennedy approach for a live candidate, but up to now McCarthy had not indicated an interest in competing in the New Hampshire primary. Hoeh had passed the word of Gans's late October visit to other antiwar Democrats and, looking for a way to lure him into the state, arranged for McCarthy to give an ostensibly noncampaign lecture in Manchester on civil rights in December. Afterward, McCarthy was taken to the home of party activist Sylvia Chaplain to meet some prospective supporters. "This looks like a government in exile," he said on entering, Hoeh remembered.

They talked, with McCarthy inquiring about the draft-Kennedy effort. He was assured that the overwhelming number of those involved would prefer a live candidate, but that a decision would be made by December 28 whether to proceed on the Kennedy draft. "Well, I'd better leave," McCarthy said finally, Hoeh remembered. "I might do something rash if I stay here much longer."

When CBS News anchorman Walter Cronkite subsequently reported McCarthy saying he probably would not enter New Hampshire, Hoeh got a hurried phone call from Blair Clark, McCarthy's just-named campaign manager. He assured Hoeh that the candidate "has not made a final decision with respect to New Hampshire" and asked whether the December 28 date to shut off the Kennedy draft still applied. Hoeh told him it did, but said he could get it held off if "you send me a telegram which confirms this telephone conversation that Senator McCarthy has not made a final decision." The telegram was sent.

On New Year's Eve, as Hoeh and his wife, Sandy, were preparing to go out, he got another call from Clark asking if a meeting could be arranged for the next day, New Year's Day. Hoeh said that was too soon but they could meet on January 2. The meeting was set, for the Sheraton-Wayfarer Hotel in Bedford, just outside Manchester, and the Hoehs went off to ring out the old year and ring in the new.

*   *   *

The year 1967 ended as it had begun—stormy and ominous. In December, war protesters David Dellinger and SDSers Tom Hayden and Rennie Davis met to plot their moves for the new year, already focusing on the Democratic Convention the following August in Chicago. On December 31, the *Chicago Tribune* quoted Dick Gregory, the Chicago-based stand-up comic and civil rights activist, as warning Lyndon Johnson that unless racial injustice in his city was addressed, he would lead demonstrations that would make it possible to hold the convention there only "over my dead body."

At a New Year's Eve party at the Greenwich Village apartment of Abbie Hoffman, he along with Jerry Rubin and other self-styled revolutionaries talked of how they would confront the establishment, and the war, in the year ahead. Hoffman later, to a federal investigator, described the birth of the Yippie Party this way: "There we were, all stoned, rolling around the floor . . . Yippie! Somebody says 'Oink,' and that's it, pig [the Yippie label for police]. . . . And so Yippie was born, the Youth International Party. What about if we create a myth, program it into the media. . . . When that myth goes in, it's always connected to [the] Chicago [Democratic convention]. . . . Come and do your thing—excitement, bullshit, everything, anything . . . commitment, engagement, Democrats, pigs, the whole thing. All you do is change the H in Hippie for a Y in Yippie, and you got it. . . . New phenomena [sic], a new thing on the American scene. . . . You know as long as we can make up a story about it that's exciting, full of shit, mystical, magical, you have to accuse us of going to Chicago to perform magic."

Beyond all the unrest at home, the year 1967 had seen comparable turmoil abroad. Some 15,000 Americans had perished in Vietnam by this time, an estimated 9,000 in 1967 alone, as well as uncounted thousands more of Vietnamese. Demonstrations against the war had erupted overseas, in London and other major Western cities. Rumblings of revolt against communist repression were first heard in Prague; revolutionary Che Guevara was slain in Bolivia; Israel routed its Arab neighbors in the Six-Day War; the bloody Cultural Revolution raged on in China.

The year 1968 was dawning with the outlook bleak for ending the war in Southeast Asia, and no better for calming the troubled seas at home. So, many Americans looked elsewhere for optimism, or at least diversion, on that first day of January.

Some picked up the morning newspaper, turned to the sports section and read how the Green Bay Packers, coached by the legendary Vince Lombardi, had won the National Football League championship over the Dallas Cowboys, 21–17, on a quarterback sneak by Bart Starr in frigid minus-12-degree temperature. Sports fans settled down in the afternoon to watch the college bowl games, including Southern California's 14–3 victory over Indiana, highlighted by the running of one O.J. Simpson.

Others heard President Johnson's first 1968 news conference over their radios from his ranch in Texas; he announced fiscal policies aimed at curbing investment and tourism abroad and spoke optimistically about the year ahead. Still others along the East Coast and in parts of the Midwest took advantage of a heavy snow to sled or go ice skating with the kids, or ventured out for New Year's Day open houses in the neighborhood.

For non–sports fans weathered in, there were the current television favorites —*Gunsmoke, Andy Griffith* and *Truth or Consequences*—to help pass a languorous day. Kids could occupy themselves with the comics in vogue—*Terry and the Pirates, Moon Mullins, Joe Palooka, Winnie Winkle, Li'l Abner* and *Gasoline Alley*—and their folks could catch such first-run movies as *The Graduate, Valley of the Dolls, Camelot, The Happiest Millionaire* and *Thoroughly Modern Millie.*

In New York, an off-Broadway musical called *Hair* celebrated a new sexual freedom with displays of frontal nudity, and the airwaves were pummeled by the oftentimes jarring (to elder ears anyhow) music of Jimi Hendrix, Jim Morrison and the Doors, Jefferson Airplane and other innovative rock groups.

It was a new year and life would go on. At the highest levels of government, there was little time for such diversions. But in Home Town, America, New Year's Day was always a time to pause, reflect a bit and take stock before getting back to the grind of everyday problems and burdens. Nineteen sixty-seven had been nothing to brag about. Nineteen sixty-eight surely would be better.

Lyndon Johnson, with his passion for the presidency, obviously would do all within his power to achieve what would assure his reelection. That would require an end to the Vietnam War and real progress in his drive to build the Great Society at home, free of unemployment, poverty and hunger, and of racial tensions among his fellow Americans. And if he failed, there would be a fresh start with a new president by this time the next year, and that could only be for the better. Or so it seemed to many on January 1, 1968.

CHAPTER 2

January: The Volcano Rumbles

Jan. 2 Sugar Ray Robinson elected to Boxing Hall of fame; 4 live-virus vaccine for mumps licensed; 6 Mike Kasperak receives world's fourth heart transplant; 11 National Farmers Organization withholds grain crops to raise prices; 14 Green Bay beats Oakland, 33–14, in Super Bowl; 15 Supreme Court upholds no bail for court-martialed antiwar Army officer; 17 Air Force sends secret satellite into polar orbit; 18 comedian Bert Wheeler, 72, dies; 21 Food and Drug Administration finds IUDs "safe and effective"; 21 Kasperak dies; 22 NBA franchises awarded to Milwaukee, Phoenix; 23 Joe (Ducky) Medwick elected to Baseball Hall of Fame; 24 *The Good, the Bad and the Ugly* released starring Clint Eastwood; 25 Bob Seagren of USC sets world indoor pole vault record at 17 feet, 4 ¼ inches; 26 low-yield underground nuclear test conducted in Nevada; 29 three human skeletons found buried in crude wooden coffins at state prison farm in Arkansas; Gore Vidal's *Myra Breckinridge* published.

As President Johnson enjoyed a leisurely New Year's Day on his ranch in Texas, the eyes of the nation, and the world, remained fixed on Vietnam. Even as Pope Paul VI in his annual address from St. Peter's Basilica was calling for New Year's Day as a day of peace and exhorting the warring powers "to attempt every possible means that could lead to an honorable solution of the sorrowful dispute," the holiday cease-fire was being seriously breached at Tay Ninh, sixty miles northwest of Saigon near the Cambodian border.

In what U.S. authorities called "the worst truce ever," six hours before the shooting was to resume twenty-three American troops were killed and 153 wounded in a major enemy attack. The American side reported that 355 North Vietnamese and Vietcong troops were killed and five captured in the same engagement, a customary claim that the enemy had been made to pay a fearful price.

But it was the American causalities that had impact at home. In all, the U.S. authorities reported, there were 170 separate enemy-initiated violations of the cease-fire, in which twenty-seven Americans in uniform died to forty-five South Vietnamese and 553 of the enemy. By this time, however, the concept of victory by body count had paled to American audiences. The raw numbers of U.S. casualties were what distressed the wives and husbands, the mothers and fathers and the children of those serving in some godforsaken distant corner of the world. These figures desperately concerned Lyndon Johnson as well. But he was determined to press on, still convinced that the might of the globe's greatest military power—there were now 486,000 American troops in Vietnam—ultimately could not be denied.

The voices from Hanoi, however, continued to insist otherwise. North Vietnamese President Ho Chi Minh, in his own New Year's message, proclaimed that "this year the United States aggressors will find themselves less able than ever to take the initiative, and will be more confused than ever, while our armed forces . . . will certainly win many more and still greater victories." At the same time, though, Ho's foreign minister, Nguyen Duy Trinh, said over Hanoi radio that his government would enter talks if the United States would "first unconditionally cease bombing and all other acts of war" against North Vietnam.

At home, pressures were increasingly building on Johnson to do just that. Robert Kennedy in a speech in San Francisco three days later argued that "it would make some sense to go to the negotiating table and see if we can resolve the conflict. It is possible we can go to the negotiating table and they will not be genuinely interested in finding a solution . . . [but] we have to at least take the first step."

The hawks would have none of it. Chairman L. Mendel Rivers of the House Armed Services Committee urged Johnson "to consider no cessation of bombing unless Hanoi agrees immediately to exchange of American prisoners, or at very least inspection of prisoners by the International Red Cross." And William P. Bundy, the assistant secretary of state for Far Eastern affairs, threw cold water on the idea. "I am not sure that they are anywhere near the point of being ready to yield," he said in a television interview. In the Hanoi statement, he said, there was "no mention of whether they themselves would ex-

ercise any kind of restraint." The danger, he warned, was that the enemy
could "take advantage of things and pour down more divisions, and play the
thing as what they call . . . fighting while negotiating."

And so there was no bombing halt. Instead, LBJ sent his ambassador to
India, Chester Bowles, to Phnom Penh to discuss with the Cambodian chief
of state, Prince Norodom Sihanouk, the possibility of American "hot pursuit"
over the Cambodian border. Vietcong and North Vietnamese forces were suspected of using Cambodia as a sanctuary. Sihanouk in an earlier interview had
indicated he would permit such raids under certain circumstances. But in his
conversations with Bowles he resisted the idea and instead joined the call for
a halt in bombing North Vietnam.

LBJ's most prominent journalistic cheerleader in his conduct of the war,
columnist Joseph Alsop, had already predicted Sihanouk's agreement to permit hot pursuit and labeled it a major turning point. He wrote in the first
days of January that this was so in spite of "the kind of people who fight a
perpetual rear-guard action against the facts [who] say it does not mean very
much. . . . All Asia has no more astute bandwagon-watcher, nor any more
agile bandwagon-leaper, than Prince Sihanouk. And when such a man climbs
half-aboard your wagon, it is time to conclude that you really are going
places."

Aside from Alsop's voice of endless optimism, however, Johnson was increasingly being isolated in the world of public opinion. Shortly before the
new year, he had visited the pope at the Vatican. *Newsweek* in its first issue of
1968 reported that LBJ's efforts to limit the conversation to pleasantries had
been abruptly cut off by his host, urging him to suspend the bombing indefinitely. When Johnson the legendary stroker said how pleased he was that his
daughter Luci had just converted to the Catholic faith, the pope ignored the
comment and proceeded to read from a ten-page memorandum dealing critically with Vietnam.

Nor could the president escape criticism even in being proclaimed *Time*'s
"Man of the Year." The issue's cover, by artist David Levine, showed him as
King Lear being hounded by members of his own political family, conspicuously including Robert Kennedy. "More than ever before in an era of well-
being," *Time* intoned, "the nation's discontent was focused upon its president.
The man in the White House is at once the chief repository of the nation's aspirations and the supreme scapegoat for its frustrations. As such, Lyndon
Johnson was the topic of TV talk shows and cocktail-party conversations, the
obsession of pundits and politicians at home and abroad of businessmen and
scholars, cartoonists and ordinary citizens throughout 1967. Inescapably, he
was the Man of the Year."

From Saigon, *Washington Post* reporter Lee Lescaze wrote on January 2 of the military outlook: "More and more [American] troops have arrived. The enemy main force has been forced out of many populated areas and a balance has been reached in which an allied defeat is no longer possible. But the enemy continues to fight well and his ability to launch major attacks is by no means ended. . . . When the enemy fights, he has what he needs for the battle." Even when there are military successes against the enemy, Lescaze wrote, "Vietnamese hearts and minds have not flocked to the Saigon government." That was at the core of the problem that no amount of pounding of North Vietnamese targets could solve.

Johnson's obduracy on the bombing nagged at Kennedy, making it impossible for him to put the option of a 1968 presidential candidacy completely behind him. His brother Ted returned from a trip to South Vietnam to investigate the refugee problem and reported it to be, like the war itself, a fiasco. On Robert Kennedy's trip to California, Speaker Jesse Unruh of the state assembly got his ear. Unruh was considering a race for the United States Senate and was commissioning a poll to assess his chances. He said he was going to include questions about Kennedy's popularity in the state and urged him to hold the door open on a presidential candidacy until the results were in. California would have 174 delegates to the Democratic National Convention in Chicago in August and together with New York's 190 would give Kennedy a very strong base of support for the nomination. Kennedy was noncommittal.

But the presumptive heir to Camelot was feeling other pressures. Eugene Daniell in the "RFK in '68" office in New Hampshire was backed after a fashion by a New York doctor, Martin Shepard, calling himself a national coordinator of a draft-RFK effort. In the unlikely event that Kennedy might go to New Hampshire and campaign for Johnson, Shepard said, he would turn to some other critic of the war, and of LBJ—McCarthy or possibly Senator Fulbright. "Either with him [Kennedy] or without him, we're going ahead," Daniell said. "Even if he denounces us as infidels."

* * *

Gene McCarthy at first seemed persuaded to duck New Hampshire. In part it was because of the threat of the draft-RFK effort competing for the anti-Johnson, antiwar vote, in part because LBJ had the state Democratic organization strongly on his side. McCarthy backers outside New Hampshire, citing McCarthy's relative obscurity, warned that this combination would cripple his challenge before it got off the ground. But inside the state, his supporters pointed to the heavy national news coverage drawn by the year's first presidential primary. They argued that it offered a golden opportunity to embarrass the sitting president.

McCarthy had already told a Minnesota radio station that the New Hampshire primary was "not a particularly significant test." It was clear, however, that he needed an early opportunity outside of Minnesota to establish himself as a serious challenger to Johnson. He acknowledged that he was "a little disappointed" with unnamed fellow-Democrats who opposed the war for failing to endorse him, using "the excuse that I am not a serious candidate."

Johnson himself was standing aloof from the developing presidential campaign, making no plans to go to New Hampshire to solicit votes for convention delegates. He had the state's chief Democrats, Governor John W. King and Senator Thomas McIntyre, in his corner, heading a pack of blue-ribbon delegates. At first there was consideration of having McIntyre run as a stand-in for LBJ in the preferential primary. That approach made McCarthy reluctant to compete, apparently out of fear that it would blur the competition as a referendum on Johnson's conduct of the war. Eventually, however, it was decided to run a write-in campaign for the president himself in the primary—a much more attractive inducement to McCarthy to enter New Hampshire.

David Hoeh was now telling McCarthy he would win as much as one third of the primary vote, enough to jolt the incumbent and receive favorable national publicity. But others outside New Hampshire continued to argue that McCarthy needed to begin his campaign with an outright victory over LBJ. He should look elsewhere, they said, such as his own neighboring state of Wisconsin, where liberal protesters against the war were strong and organized.

On January 2, Blair Clark met with David and Sally Hoeh and Gerry Studds, another local teacher, at the Wayfarer, presumably to discuss again the pros and cons of McCarthy entering the primary there. They were just sitting down in the dining room when a phone call came in for David. It was McCarthy. "Dave, I've decided to come into the New Hampshire primary," he said, unceremoniously. Hoeh returned to the table, smiling, and announced to Clark: "That was your boss." Hoeh told him the news. "Blair's face dropped into his soup," Hoeh recalled of his introduction to communication, McCarthy style.

Clark and Hoeh worked up a press release and the next day McCarthy announced he was canceling a planned trip to Vietnam and Europe in February and would enter that state's primary after all. The very fact a write-in campaign was being organized there for Johnson, he said, was a "major factor" in his decision. It gave him, he said, "the kind of confrontation on basic issues we wanted." McCarthy by this time had already said he would enter the Democratic primaries in Massachusetts, Wisconsin, Oregon and California. Not only that; he vowed that he was in the race to stay, no matter what Kennedy ultimately did. Concerning New Hampshire, he said, "I intend to go on no matter what happens there, to the other primaries I'm committed to."

At the same time, McCarthy began to ridicule Kennedy's reluctance to take on Johnson. In a speech in New York cheered by about 2,000 anti-LBJ Democrats, he observed that "there seems to be a disposition to wait for a kind of latter-day salvation—like four years from now." Without mentioning Kennedy by name, he noted that there are "some at the highest levels of government and politics who have not yet spoken as their minds and consciences dictate. In some cases, they have not done so for reasons of personal or political convenience." He warned that "four years is too long to wait. Judgment and action are needed now." Later, McCarthy insisted with a straight face that he wasn't trying to needle Kennedy. "I don't know what his plans are," he said. "I just kind of state the case."

Kennedy squirmed under such comments but lamely clung to his position that he had no choice but to support the president of his party. "I have to analyze how I can accomplish more good and be the most useful," he told students at Manhattan Community College. "My judgment is at the moment that I don't further the cause" of peace by backing McCarthy's long-shot challenge.

Another LBJ apologist and cheerleader, conservative columnist William S. White, wrote: "All across the national political scene a process of separating the men from the boys is now going on . . . [and] the grownups are running away with the game. . . . Sen. Robert F. Kennedy has plainly decided to quit while he is no farther behind and so to put the chill on the limping presidential candidacy of an anti-Vietnam war associate, Sen. Eugene McCarthy."

* * *

White's comments were, to say the least, not clairvoyant. Kennedy in fact continued to dither, while other prominent Americans were putting themselves on the line against Johnson's war policies—or being brought into court to answer for their actions in opposing them. On January 5, Spock, Coffin, Raskin and Mitchell Goodman, a novelist, and a Harvard graduate student named Michael Ferber who had helped collect the draft cards they had defiantly left at the Justice Department in October, were indicted by a federal grand jury in Boston on charges of conspiracy to encourage violations of the draft laws.

The indictment was part of a new Johnson administration get-tough pol-

icy against those who were counseling draft-age men to turn in their draft
cards and refuse induction, and were attempting to disrupt the Selective
Service system. General Lewis B. Hershey, its gruff and outspoken director,
said of the indictment: "It's a time for exultation." But the action only
fanned the resentment and steeled the determination of a growing number
of Americans, especially on college campuses, to opt out of what they called
Johnson's war, and to do what they could to force American withdrawal
from it.

Spock defended draft resistance as "a very patriotic endeavor requiring
enormous amounts of courage [and] the most effective way of opposing the
war." He cited the Nuremberg war crimes trials as establishing the obligation for citizens to act when "your government is up to crimes against humanity." He said he was no pacifist and had supported the war against Hitler
and the American involvement in Korea, "but in this war we went in there
to steal Vietnam."

On the same day of the indictment, FBI director Hoover reported that his
agency had arrested more than 600 young men in 1967 on charges of draft
evasion. He charged that the Communist Party in the United States had
"helped plan" the antiwar demonstrations in San Francisco and New York in
the previous April and the Mobilization march and protests in Washington
in October. Hoover also charged that the concept of black power had "created
a climate of unrest and has come to mean to many Negroes the 'power' to riot,
burn, loot and kill." Stokely Carmichael, Rap Brown and others, he said, had
"sowed the seeds of discord, and hope to reap in 1968 a year filled with explosive racial unrest." As Hoover's report was issued, Black Panther poet and
playwright LeRoi Jones had just been sentenced to up to three years in prison
and a $1,000 fine for illegal possession of firearms during riots in Newark the
previous July.

The unrest at home was being fueled more, however, by the increasingly
somber news from Vietnam. The lead headline in the *Washington Post* on the
morning of January 7 announced: U.S. FORCE DECIMATED IN AMBUSH. The dispatch from Saigon reported that a company of 103 American infantrymen
had been trapped in the Queson Valley north of the capital and that all but
twenty-four of them had been killed, wounded or captured. Another district
capital near Saigon was overrun and four American jet fighter-bombers were
shot down over North Vietnam.

If such news was fanning the war protest at home, that protest was having
its own effect in Vietnam. Colonel Louis Gelling, commander of the 196th
Light Infantry Brigade whose company had been ambushed, said of his men
cut down in the encounter: "They met a force easily two and a half times the

size of a company. There was not one man who did not show he was an American. . . . There are no draft-card burners in this crew."

* * *

America was being torn in two, and the Democratic Party particularly. Yet the political peril to Lyndon Johnson, the man caught in the middle, was seen at this point to come principally from the Republicans, engaged in a much blander contest for the right to carry the political contest to him. A Gallup Poll on January 6 had him running ahead of Richard Nixon as the presidential choice of those surveyed, 39 percent to 30, with McCarthy at 12 percent as an independent peace candidate and George Wallace at 11. The only Democrat who might have had a chance to beat Johnson was thought to be Kennedy, and he was continuing to say he expected to support the president for the party's nomination.

Wallace, also a Democrat, was planning to run as an independent. In the first week of January, he reported that his new American Independent Party had produced 107,000 signatures on petitions in only six weeks to qualify the party for a place on the California ballot in November. But he was seen widely as no more than a nuisance candidate.

Not only that; his wife, Lurleen, who had replaced him as governor of Alabama when he could no longer under state law succeed himself, was seriously ill, undergoing outpatient treatment at the Texas Medical Center for a third cancer malignancy. The Wallaces and a teenage daughter were staying in a gaudy motel just across the street from the medical center while she was being treated. They ate quiet dinners together in the motel coffee shop as Alabama plainclothes bodyguards watched over them. Wallace greeted steady streams of well-wishers at the table, and fidgeted. He was making occasional day trips on political campaign business but had been forced to cancel a planned fact-finding trip to Saigon.

One night when I stopped by, he dismissed the speculation that he was aiming for a stalemated race that would force the election into the House of Representatives. He confided how he was going to be a plurality winner in enough states to gain an electoral college victory outright. "The experts," he said, had insisted he couldn't quality for the ballot in California. They would be wrong again, he said, with all this talk about the election being thrown into the House.

Few fellow Democrats believed him. If a serious challenge would be made to Johnson, they believed, it would come from one of the competing Republicans, Nixon or Romney.

* * *

Nixon, who in his failed 1960 presidential race against John Kennedy had campaigned frenetically, foolishly pledging to visit every state and nearly killing himself doing it, had studied that failure microscopically over the ensuing years. He and his political aides concluded that quality of campaigning was infinitely more important than quantity. So he was determined to pace himself this time around, not wearing out his welcome with an electorate that polls said had never really warmed to him anyway.

His first big challenge was to dispose of his image as a political loser, fashioned by his narrow 1960 setback and more so by his humiliating defeat at the hands of Democrat Pat Brown in his ill-considered campaign for governor of California. His 1962 election night promise to the press that "you won't have Nixon to kick around anymore" was taken widely as his swan song in politics. But after a dark, brooding period of rehabilitation he had quietly set his sights on another presidential try. New Hampshire would make or break him; if he could win the nation's first 1968 primary, he reasoned, he couldn't be called a loser any longer.

Rockefeller, his longtime foe, figured at the outset to be a serious threat to the achievement of that objective. But when he stepped aside in favor of the oft-bumbling Romney, it seemed much more possible. Indeed, as Romney struggled against his own negative image as a man uncertain of what he was doing and easily "brainwashed," and polls indicated he was going nowhere, Nixon grew more confident that a laid-back strategy was the answer for him.

All through January, therefore, Nixon stayed away from New Hampshire. He spent leisurely days in places like Virginia, Texas and Oklahoma, distinctly friendly territory, leaving the political line of fire to Romney to face daily in the nation's first primary state. In several interviews, Nixon referred to "these miserable primaries" that took so much out of candidates. But they seemed never far from his calculating mind. At Washington and Lee University in Lexington, Virginia, when asked whether he thought black militants Rap Brown and Stokely Carmichael "had crossed the line of treason," Nixon said no, he didn't think the constitutional definition of treason applied to Brown and "Stokely Primary."

Romney's candidacy in New Hampshire meanwhile, not visibly helped by another fact-finding trip to Vietnam, was already taking on the character of a sinking ship. David Broder reported from the state in the *Washington Post* of January 2 that Romney was "hanging by a thread" there.

"It will take an extraordinary performance—some of his own people would say 'a miracle'—for the Michigan governor to escape a drubbing at the hands of Richard M. Nixon," he wrote. "The rout could be so one-sided that it might not only finish off Romney's already wobbly bid for the Republican nomination, but propel Nixon into so commanding a lead that not even Nelson Rockefeller could later overcome it." Broder wrote of a Romney poll that found him running worse against Nixon after months of campaigning than he had been in the spring of 1967, when he trailed the former vice president by two to one.

In an effort to stanch the bleeding, Rockefeller flew to New Hampshire. There, he tried to buck up the Romney supporters—and convince the press once more that the Michigan governor was not simply a stalking horse for a candidacy of his own. "I am not a candidate, I am not going to be a candidate," was the way Rockefeller began his remarks at a press conference. But he undid the effort by observing later to a question about a draft that "if it came, then I would have to face it." He also tried to downgrade the importance of the New Hampshire primary, saying Romney didn't have to win it to stay in the race.

Still, the leakage continued. Republican Senator Jacob K. Javits of New York, Rockefeller's close ally, declared a few days later that while he continued to support Romney he would switch to Rockefeller if "the signs are clear that he [Romney] can't make it." Romney tried to remain upbeat when he opened his campaign in New Hampshire on January 12. He insisted the contest for the Republican nomination was going to be between himself and Nixon and he challenged Nixon to debate—an improbable event considering Nixon's huge lead in the polls.

Romney in New Hampshire was nothing if not grittily determined. On his first day of campaigning as a declared candidate, he rose before sunrise and went into the bitter cold blackness to a gate outside Sanders Associates, an electronics plant in Nashua. For nearly two hours in temperatures of 10 degrees below zero, he stood bare-headed, his lionlike white mane standing out in a canvas storm coat among reporters shuddering under wool and fur caps. Doggedly, he intercepted frigid workers bent only on getting into the heated plant. As he shook their hands and introduced himself, many looked at him as though he were out of his mind, if they looked at him at all. Others gave him a friendly smile for his fortitude as he stood there, his ears turned crimson from the cold.

Romney visited four other towns across southern New Hampshire that first day, seemingly oblivious to the polls that now had him running as much as three to one behind Nixon, who had not yet even declared his candidacy. That reality, however, was at the core of his challenge to Nixon to debate—and at the core of Nixon's steadfast refusal to do so. Romney's strategists, well aware that they could not compete with Nixon in the foreign policy realm, especially when their man was not coming through clearly on Vietnam, pressed

the argument of his record and stature as a man of high integrity and morality. Rented billboards across the state proclaimed: ROMNEY FIGHTS MORAL
DECAY—until it was decided the ads made him sound like toothpaste, and
they were discontinued.

The Michigan governor also made much of his robust health and zest for
outdoor exercise. On his second day in New Hampshire, between campaign
speeches, he sandwiched in a ski run down a beginners' slope in good style—
until the end, when he fell. But he was nothing if not perseverant. The first
time he ever tried to ski, he reported, he fell down thirty-seven times.

That perseverance was demonstrated anew in a stop-by at a bowling alley
in Franklin a few days later. Members of a women's league were bowling
duckpins, smaller than regulation tenpins. A player had three turns with a
ball much smaller than a regulation bowling ball to try to knock down all ten
pins, rather than two turns with the large ball used in regular tenpin bowling. Romney gamely tried his hand before a large audience of local bowlers,
traveling reporters and television cameramen. After his three allotted tries,
seven pins were still standing. So he kept trying—and trying. On his eighth
try, only one pin was still standing. Gritting his teeth, he went after it again
and again and again, with the ball rolling into the gutter each time.
Amusement among the bystanders turned to embarrassment for Romney.
Still he pressed on—until he finally knocked over the final pin—with his
thirty-fourth ball! The episode was a metaphor for George Romney, the man
who never knew when he was licked.

Romney finally tackled his Vietnam problem in a major speech at Keene
State College, unveiling a plan for a "guaranteed neutralization" of the country, and of Laos and Cambodia as well, through a negotiated settlement between the Saigon government and the National Liberation Front. Part of the
plan, he said, would be agreement among the "great powers"—the United
States, the Soviet Union and "hopefully" China—to leave the region while
guaranteeing peace and stability there. Saigon would be obliged to grant
"amnesty and open participation in the political processes of the south for
members of the Viet Cong" and Hanoi would be called on to "renounce terror and coercion as its way of achieving political goals." Reunification of the
two Vietnams would be left for them to resolve.

Romney's proposal seemed to be a clear step beyond his earlier flat opposition to the possibility of a coalition government. But it remained to be seen
whether he would be able to articulate it consistently and persuasively
enough to satisfy and convince his critics that he knew what he was talking
about. After the speech, a student needled him about his most recent trip to
Vietnam: "Were you brainwashed this time?" Romney, fire in his eyes, shot

back: "I know I wasn't given the full facts when I visited South Vietnam in 1965, and that's what I referred to. I know this time I dug into it and I got the picture, and I gave it to you here tonight." Most of the audience applauded, but there were snickers too.

The next day Romney held a press conference in Concord and sowed more confusion. He insisted he never meant to call for any coalition in which the leaders of the Saigon regime and of the NLF would make a deal without the approval of the South Vietnamese people. And so it went. It was another opportunity for Germond to strike his imaginary typewriter key that printed "Romney later explained."

Still, the candidate persisted. When Leonard Hall, the old Eisenhower political adviser who was heading his campaign, told him one night in his New Hampshire motel bedroom that the effort was going nowhere, Romney gave him a pep talk. Shortly afterward, Hall and another aide brought him an internal poll showing no movement and warned him that a write-in vote for Rockefeller, then being considered by local supporters, conceivably could push him back to a humiliating third place. On other occasions, such a suggestion might have been expected to cause a Romney eruption. Instead, he merely nodded—and went out the next day just as determined as before. Shaking off the frigid temperatures as he stood hatless for hours at a time, he greeted workers decked in ski masks and earmuffs as we accompanying reporters huddled in our parkas and overcoats and shook our heads.

* * *

Some others in opposition to Johnson's Vietnam policy were burdened by neither the confusion of Romney nor the timidity of Kennedy. On January 15, foes of the war staged another protest in Washington, led by former Representative Jeannette Rankin of Montana, the first woman to serve in Congress, and joined by the Senate's two strongest opponents of the war, Ernest Gruening of Alaska and Wayne Morse of Oregon. The next day, more than 3,000 Harvard and Radcliffe undergraduates and more than half the Harvard faculty signed a statement calling on Johnson to de-escalate the war.

Johnson, however, was not backing down. In his State of the Union address on January 17, he continued to accent the positive. "Since I reported to you last January," he said, "three elections have been held in Vietnam—in the midst of war and under the constant threat of violence. A president, vice president, a House and Senate and village officials have been chosen by popular, contested ballot. The enemy has been defeated in battle after battle. The number of South Vietnamese living in areas under government protection has grown by more than a million since January of last year. These are marks of progress."

Johnson acknowledged that "the enemy continues to pour men and material across frontiers and into battle, despite his continuous heavy losses," and that "he continues to hope that America's will to persevere can be broken. Well," the president told Congress, "he is wrong. America will persevere. Our patience and our perseverance will match our power. Aggression will never prevail." He insisted that peace was being diligently pursued. But for a growing number of Americans, the pursuit lacked sufficient urgency, because they believed the war was poisoning a whole generation of young Americans.

One of those who felt that way was Eartha Kitt, the celebrated black singer. At a White House luncheon for fifty women leaders hosted by Lady Bird Johnson to discuss juvenile delinquency, Kitt confronted the first lady directly on the war. "The young people are angry and parents are angry because they are being highly taxed and there's a war going on and Americans don't know why," she said. "Boys I know across the nation feel it doesn't pay to be a good guy. They figure with a [criminal] record they don't have to go off to Vietnam."

Herself the mother of a six-year-old daughter, Kitt said to Mrs. Johnson: "You are a mother too, although you have had daughters and not sons. I am a mother and I know the feeling of having a baby come out of my gut. I have a baby and then you send him off to war. No wonder the kids rebel and take pot. And Mrs. Johnson, in case you don't know the lingo, that's marijuana. . . . They don't want to go to school because they're going to be snatched from their mothers to be shot in Vietnam."

The flustered first lady replied defensively. "I cannot identify as much as I should," she said. "I have not lived the background you have nor can I speak as passionately and well. But we must keep our eyes and our hearts and our energies fixed on constructive areas and try to do something that will make this a happier, healthier, better educated land."

* * *

In the face of such manifestations of home-front disquiet, LBJ on January 19 announced that Clark Clifford, a man of great reputation for probity and wisdom inside and out of government, would take over as secretary of defense upon McNamara's departure. Johnson, in light of Clifford's earlier criticism of McNamara's proposals to "stabilize" U.S. efforts in Vietnam and start shifting the prime burden of the war to the South Vietnamese, had every reason to expect that Clifford would shore up his conviction that the war could be won, and reinforce his determination to persevere. There seemed little doubt that the American commitment would continue full speed ahead. On the same day Clifford was nominated, the Pentagon reported that the military draft call for 1968 would be 302,000 men, compared to 230,000 drafted in 1967.

On the ground in Vietnam, the outlook remained grim. An important American base at Khe Sanh came under siege with dire though exaggerated claims that it could be "another Dien Bien Phu," the French outpost whose loss had signaled the French defeat in Indochina. American incursions into Laos and Cambodia were bringing protests and threats from China. And in the midst of all this, two other foreign policy crises erupted demanding Johnson's immediate attention.

* * *

The first occurred on Sunday night, January 21, when an Air Force B-52 bomber laden with four hydrogen bombs crashed and sank in North Star Bay, seven miles off the western coast of Greenland. The Pentagon was quick to insist that the bombs were unarmed and there was no danger of nuclear explosion. But the notion that the four bombs were lying there under seven feet of ice was immediately unnerving. The crash also triggered a diplomatic row with Denmark, which owned the vast landmass and whose laws prohibited the overflight of any American planes carrying nuclear weapons. The temperature was so cold that it was reported that soon after the plane broke through the ice, the ice formed again over the wreckage.

Within days there were reports of radiation leakage from the site and the discovery of parts of the nuclear bombs, and again the Pentagon insisted the threat to life was negligible. The incident, however, served to remind the world of the perils of the nuclear age.

As that search went on, the second new crisis suddenly confronted Johnson. On January 23, off the coast of North Korea, patrol boats from that communist country seized the USS *Pueblo*, a United States Navy intelligence-gathering ship, with eighty-three crewmen aboard. American authorities insisted that North Korean sailors had boarded the ship at gunpoint sixteen miles off the coast in international waters, but the North Koreans said the *Pueblo* had violated their country's twelve-mile territorial limit. The *Pueblo*, armed, did not fire to defend itself and the ship's captain, thirty-eight-year-old Navy Commander Lloyd M. Bucher, surrendered and, in contradiction to Navy tradition, adhered to orders to follow the patrol boats to the North Korea port of Wonsan.

The uproar in Congress was immediate, with Senator Richard B. Russell of Georgia, chairman of the Senate Armed Services Committee, calling the seizure "almost an act of war." The action was compounded with the release by the North Koreans of a purported confession from Bucher saying he and his shipmates had committed "a criminal act which flagrantly violated the armistice agreement" between North and South Korea. The Pentagon branded the statement "a fabrication" and flatly denied that the ship had violated North Korea's territorial limits. The White House demanded the release of the ship and crew, but to no avail.

When diplomatic overtures yielded nothing, Johnson called up nearly 15,000 air reservists amid movement of strong American naval forces off the North Korean coast. It was the first call-up of reserves since the Cuban Missile Crisis in 1962. At the same time, however, military sources acknowledged that the *Pueblo* as a "spy ship" had been under orders to move off rather than fire its guns—a revelation that caused more consternation on Capitol Hill. Six days after the seizure, LBJ warned North Korea that its action "cannot be accepted" and took the case to the United Nations Security Council, but again to no avail. The crisis was destined to hang on for many months, further plaguing the embattled president.

Nixon, playing the aloof statesman up to this time, finally could not resist. He dubbed the *Pueblo* incident "an incredible blunder" by the Johnson administration for having failed to provide adequate protection for the ship. Nevertheless, he counseled only "firm diplomacy" rather than "rash action." Not yet a declared candidate, he was on cruise control as Romney struggled to keep his own campaign afloat. The Gallup Poll had Nixon comfortably ahead; the only hint of potential trouble was increasing support for Rockefeller despite his insistence that he would not be a candidate.

* * *

As troublesome as the *Pueblo* seizure was, it could not take the spotlight from Vietnam. Hanoi continued to demand that all American bombing of North Vietnam end unconditionally before peace negotiations could start. The enemy assault on Khe Sanh intensified and at home so did the political assault on LBJ's war policies.

In New York in late January, Tom Hayden, now a community organizer and antiwar activist, and longtime colleague Rennie Davis met with lawyers to consider how to conduct the most effective antiwar protest at the Democratic National Convention in Chicago in August. They weighed how best to approach Chicago city officials for permits for a major march and a "Festival of Life" conceived by the Yippies, and the organizing of legal volunteers to obtain bail for protesters the organizers expected would be arrested at the events.

Hayden and Davis as old SDS veterans were, in the watchful eyes of the FBI, indisputably "radicals." Within SDS, however, they were seen, according to Hayden in his book *Reunion: A Memoir*, "as old guard, or perhaps older sibling rivals, of the new leadership," some of which had taken on a distinctly

Marxist radical aspect. The new SDS leaders viewed with deep suspicion any activity regarding the Democratic Party, even in protest of it, preferring a wholesale assault on the political status quo. But the kind of march Hayden and Davis envisioned would be a black eye to Johnson, whom they assumed would be nominated at the Chicago convention.

On January 25, McCarthy began his campaigning for the New Hampshire primary in earnest—in his fashion. He struck fear in few pro-Johnson hearts. He brought to the state the same laid-back manner that had marked his speech at the Chicago anti-Johnson conference, as if he were on a college lecture tour. Where other candidates expressed their desire or even eagerness to be elected, he talked of his willingness to serve. He seldom raised his voice, and sometimes was so obscure in his references that he seemed to be telling private jokes to himself. He showed himself to be among the most dignified of candidates, not only in his refusal to take part in the traditional baby-kissing and other publicity stunts, but also in refusing to be particularly impressed by the notion of his challenge to a sitting president of his own party.

McCarthy seemed indifferent to organization, responding to reporters' questions about how he would staff and finance the New Hampshire and subsequent primaries by saying he would "live off the land"—which turned out to be not far from the truth. "The real problem," he said characteristically at one point, "is to get a good man to drive your car." Blair Clark, a onetime broadcasting executive out of Harvard who for a brief time had run a newspaper in New Hampshire with a fledgling reporter named Ben Bradlee, was slapping together the organization, but most of it was self-starting. William Chapman of the *Washington Post* compared the process to a pickup baseball game, with kids seeing the game going on and asking if they could play.

Hoeh and Studds led the local effort in New Hampshire as an array of bright young political neophytes, mostly from East Coast colleges, came out of the woodwork to help, with little interference or direction from McCarthy.

According to speechwriter Jeremy Larner in his post-campaign book *Nobody Knows: Reflections on the McCarthy Campaign of 1968*, "these were the kids who reacted against the violent anti-Americanism of the New Left, whom they far outnumbered. Though they hated the war and the draft, they still believed that America could be beautiful—if it would live up to its own principles. American optimists at heart, immune in the long run to ideology, they were terribly grateful to have a chance to do something real. . . . The students enjoyed McCarthy's respectability and wit as the outer signs of solidity, courage and wisdom. They didn't miss his not directing them: he was the permissive father who is really wonderful but who has to be explained to outsiders."

Curt Gans, one of the few with political experience at the age of thirty, took on the task of delegate hunting, which did not seem at all promising at the start. Others included a thirty-year-old former Associated Press reporter named Seymour Hersh, who in due time was to play a major role himself in generating opposition to the Vietnam War. Sam Brown, a Harvard divinity student at twenty-four, headed up the college volunteers, soon to be know as McCarthy's Kiddie Corps. They shaved their beards and cut their long hair to be "Clean for Gene" and thus not alienate the straitlaced New Hampshirites. And finally there were Ann Hart, daughter of Senator Philip Hart of Michigan, a Johnson supporter, and McCarthy's own daughter, Mary, a freshman at Radcliffe.

* * *

While early McCarthy supporters in New Hampshire, Wisconsin and Massachusetts vied for national attention and for McCarthy's presence as their lead campaigner in their states, a home-grown effort in his own state of Minnesota was stirring, without much public notice locally and even less nationally.

Minnesota, unlike other states that held highly visible primary campaigns and elections, chose its delegates in a lower-key caucus-convention system. Voters on election night attended small party gatherings in homes, churches and other places in precincts throughout the state, barely covered by the local news media and essentially ignored by the national press. Although Minnesota was McCarthy's home state, it was the former senior senator, Humphrey, who commanded the loyalty of the state's regular Democratic (called Democrat-Farm-Labor or DFL) organization. So any significant challenge to the Johnson-Humphrey ticket there did not figure to get anywhere, and there was little thought of having McCarthy campaign there.

Soon after the McCarthy national headquarters opened in Washington, however, a young University of Maryland student named David Mixner wandered in offering to help. He was a fervent opponent of the war in Vietnam and had already been very active in antiwar protests, including the march on the Pentagon in October. Gans sent him off to Minnesota in late January with a thousand dollars and a short list of names of Minnesotans who were beginning to organize for the caucuses. Those precinct meetings in the state's neighborhoods would start the 1968 Democratic delegate-selection process on the night of March 5—a week before the first primary of the year in New Hampshire.

Mixner located the few Minnesotans interested in mounting a McCarthy campaign in the state, had two telephones installed in a small office in Minneapolis and went to work. He called friends from the antiwar effort and raised another $6,000. Then he went to several local college campuses and rounded up a handful of students willing to work the phones and canvass for McCarthy. A local nurse who worked at a Veterans Administration hospital, appalled at the influx there of American young men injured and maimed in Vietnam, quit her job and joined the effort. Soon two twelve-hour shifts were operating the phone bank and preparing card files. Mixner got the idea of soliciting help from Catholic convents, calling on the mother superior at each one and recruiting a host of antiwar nuns. One of his most fruitful trips was to St. Cloud, near St. John's College, McCarthy's old school.

"The McCarthy campaign was dropout," Mixner said later. "Dropout housewives, dropout nuns, dropout seminary students, dropout soldiers, nurses, students. Nothing seemed as important as what this man [McCarthy] was doing at this time, and what was happening in the nation."

Getting Minnesota voters to appreciate how their little-used precinct caucuses could be a weapon in stopping the Vietnam War was not easy. "You had to tell them it was their primary," Mixner said, "that this would probably be the only chance—at the time it looked like it would be—to vote against the war, to vote against Lyndon Johnson and to vote for Eugene McCarthy." The shoestring effort seemed on the face of it a fool's errand, but Mixner and his associates pressed on under a cover of obscurity.

*   *   *

More than any grassroots organization effort, however, events were working McCarthy's way, especially in Vietnam. There, a partial truce was in effect for the observance of the lunar new year, called Tet, when nearly 70,000 Vietcong and North Vietnamese troops on January 30 (January 29 in Washington) suddenly launched vicious attacks on 36 provincial capitals and 5 major cities across South Vietnam. They brought the war out of the jungles and rural areas into supposedly secure urban centers. The large American air base at Da Nang was hit; so were the ports of Qui Nhon and Cam Ranh Bay. Before the South Vietnamese and American forces could recover, Saigon was hammered the next day, with the American embassy itself invaded and held for several hours before the invaders were driven off. Can Tho, the major city in the Mekong Delta, My Tho, Pleiku and the provincial capital of Kontum were also attacked, as was the American air base at Bien Hoa not far from Saigon.

According to Stanley Karnow in *Vietnam: A History,* nineteen Vietcong in a truck and taxicab drove up to the embassy at about three o'clock in the morning, blasted a hole in the compound's wall and raced inside, firing automatic weapons. One American Marine guard and seven Army military police were killed in the attack.

64 JULES WITCOVER

General William Westmoreland boasted that the enemy's "well-laid plans went afoul" with the loss of many enemy lives. But the vulnerability of the American installations, and the embassy above all else, was a shocker to the American public, dashing the illusion that, as Westmoreland and other American leaders insisted, the war was being won. That night brought startling scenes of the carnage to American living rooms via television, the public relations battleground of the war.

*　*　*

It so happened that on the same day the American embassy in Saigon was attacked, Robert Kennedy was having breakfast with about fifteen political reporters at the National Press Club in Washington. As might have been expected, he was being interrogated aggressively about his political plans. Asked whether there were any circumstances that would make him change his mind about not challenging Johnson for the Democratic nomination, he answered, "No, I can't conceive of any circumstances." Later, he cautiously amended that to "any foreseeable circumstances." Maybe, one of his questioners suggested, Johnson after five grueling years in the presidency might not seek reelection after all. "You're talking," Kennedy broke in, "about an act of God."

He recited all the old barriers to his candidacy that were familiar by now to most of those around the breakfast table, including his fear that a challenge by him would only lead to the election of the despised Nixon. "If I ran I'd have to run in all the primaries," he added at one point. "I don't think I could win the nomination. I would have to win every primary." He said he thought he would have a "fair chance" in each one as it came along but sweeping every one would be like a horse finishing first in every start.

Yet the yearning clearly was there, born not only of his opposition to the war but his distress over the alienation and neglect of blacks, the young and the elderly at home. "The cause hasn't been analyzed and dealt with," he said. "There's affluence, yet a feeling of unhappiness in the country. If someone touched the heart of that, and how to bring the country back together—if he could bind the wounds, appeal to the generous nature of Americans . . ."

But working against this yearning was Kennedy's obvious sense of futility, of personal helplessness. A candidacy by him, he said, "would be very damaging to my trying to speak about any of these matters." And it could hurt the party in the end, he suggested. "If I ran, a lot of states would be split down the middle," he argued. "I not only would take the risk of weakening my opportunity to talk and have an effect on the issues, but I could bring down a good many Democrats as well."

As for McCarthy, he said, "his campaign so far has been very helpful to

President Johnson. . . . It could have been and still is to some extent an outlet to frustration about the war. The war is one of the great disasters of all time for the United States. But Gene McCarthy hasn't been able to tap the unrest in the country. You have to be able to touch this uneasiness. . . ."

Well then, somebody asked, why not support McCarthy yourself? "President Johnson would like for me to come out for McCarthy," he said. "Then it would be a 'Kennedy-McCarthy movement.' I don't think that would do any good." Furthermore, he suggested, "McCarthy has hurt me by his taunting, and he hasn't helped himself. He's made it impossible for any Kennedy people to work for him. A couple of months ago, he probably could have put something together if he had done it right."

As the breakfast approached its end, he repeated his frustration. "If there was anything I could do about it," he said, "I would do it." To Bruce Biossat, then a Scripps-Howard columnist, who heard Kennedy, "it was like seeing a man do battle with himself right before your eyes."

At one point, Peter Lisagor of the *Chicago Daily News* leaned over and passed a brief United Press International dispatch to Kennedy. It told of the outbreak of Vietcong attacks on cities and towns throughout South Vietnam. "Yeah, we're winning," Kennedy said with sarcasm. He did not seem to realize at that moment that something pivotal to his own future, and that of the other leading players in the drama of 1968, was now unfolding as the year's first month was ending and another, just as fateful, was to begin.

CHAPTER 3

February: Ominous Signs

Feb. 1 Unemployment rate reported at 3.7 percent for December; **7** Arthur Miller's *The Price* starring Pat Hingle opens on Broadway; actor Nick Adams (*The Rebel*) dies; **8** Roy Harris's *Eleventh Symphony* premieres at New York Philharmonic Hall; *Planet of the Apes* released starring Charlton Heston; **10** New York City garbage strike ends with 100,000 tons of trash on streets; Katharine Hepburn wins Oscar for *Guess Who's Coming to Dinner;* **11** playwright-actor Howard Lindsay (*Life with Father*), 78, dies; new Madison Square Garden opens in New York; **12** Justice Department sues Southern counties in desegregation cases; **13** AFL-CIO building trades to recruit blacks as apprentices; **21** bomb explodes in Soviet embassy in Washington; 13 midshipmen expelled at Annapolis for smoking marijuana; baseball players, owners agree to increase minimum season salary from $7,000 to $10,000; **23** novelist Fannie Hurst, 78, dies; **25** longest newspaper strike in San Francisco history ends; **29** Grammy Awards to Fifth Dimension for "Up, Up and Away," to Beatles for *Sgt. Pepper's Lonely Hearts Club Band,* to Glen Campbell for "By the Time I Get to Phoenix."

On the night of February 1, Richard Nixon's political aides put the finishing touches on a letter from him to New Hampshire households—150,000 of them—and dropped the letters into the mail. The exercise signaled a sharp departure from politics as usual, because it was Nixon's vehicle for announcing his candidacy for the presidency of the United States.

Telling the voters of New Hampshire in this direct and personal way that he knew they were "keenly aware of their special responsibilities, of the broad influence of their votes," Nixon informed them that "in 1968, your responsibility is greater than ever." They faced choices "beyond politics," he wrote, and "peace and freedom in the world, peace and progress here at home, will depend on the decisions of the next President of the United States."

Such circumstances, he went on, demanded both experience ("During 14 years in Washington, I learned the awesome nature of the great decisions a President makes") and a fresh look ("During the past eight years I have had a chance to reflect on the lessons of public office, to measure the nation's tasks and its problems from a fresh perspective. I have sought to apply those lessons to the needs of the present, and to the entire sweep of this final third of the Twentieth Century. And I believe I have found some answers.")

If the voters were led to believe by this letter that Nixon was ready and willing to provide those answers, especially on how to extricate the United States from Vietnam, they were soon to be disappointed. Nevertheless, the same basic message would soon be gracing posters of Nixon around the state that contrasted the new, cool former vice president with the frenzied Romney, without mentioning him: "You can't handshake your way out of the kind of problems we have today. You've got to think them through—and that takes a lifetime of getting ready."

The mailing of the letters was timed to coincide with Nixon's formal declaration of candidacy the next day. As they were delivered to the post office, Nixon—accompanied by speechwriters Pat Buchanan and Ray Price and personal aide Dwight Chapin—without fanfare boarded a plane in New York for Boston. They were met at Logan Airport by another general aide, Nick Ruwe, son of a prominent Detroit banker, who drove the party across the Massachusetts border to Nashua, New Hampshire, where they arrived unexpected and unannounced at a small hotel around midnight. They had a drink, dispersed and went to bed. Nixon had a news conference scheduled for early the next afternoon and he wanted to be well rested—a clear recognition that the lesson of quality over quantity learned in 1960 would be diligently applied in 1968.

Nixon luck prevailed from the start, in his arrival the previous night. The morning of February 2 dawned rainy and foggy, closing airports in New York and throughout New England. The rest of the Nixon party—the candidate's wife, Pat, daughters, Tricia and Julie, Nixon pals Bebe Rebozo and John Davies, and secretaries Rose Woods and Shelley Scarney—set out from New York in two cars. After an hour one broke down, so all except Davies, who was the telephone company's representative to the Nixon gubernatorial campaign in 1962, piled into the first car and headed on. Davies remained with the luggage and the disabled car. Reporters likewise were stranded at the New York area airports and some chartered a bus that arrived at the Manchester Holiday Inn barely in time for the news conference.

It was a new Nixon—yet another "new Nixon"—who presented himself from the very outset. "Gentlemen," he began, "this is *not* my last press conference." He broke into a smile, and laughter rippled through the room as the reporters immediately recalled his famous "last" press conference after that 1962 gubernatorial defeat in California. Since then, in fact, he had held more than 300 press conferences in which he had strived to live down that politically disastrous few moments of lashing out at his press critics.

Nixon got right to the point of the whole New Hampshire exercise, which for him was erasing his loser image. "I've given consideration to this problem, 'Can Nixon win?'" he said. "I want to be quite candid about it. . . . There is no one in this room or in the nation more interested in seeing the Republican nominee win this year. . . . The Republican Party must nominate a man who can win . . . a man who can do the job. Those who have lost elections in the past have come back to win. . . . I believe I am better qualified to handle the great problems of the presidency than I was in 1960. I recognize I must demonstrate to the American people . . . that I can win and that I can do the job. I am prepared to meet that challenge. I have decided that I will test my ability . . . in the fires of the primaries, and not just in the smoke-filled rooms of Miami Beach [where the Republican Convention would be held]. . . . I believe I am going to win the New Hampshire primary, come out the decisive winner of the primaries, go on to win the nomination, and if I do that, I believe I can defeat Lyndon Johnson."

Nixon pledged an "all-out, very intensive campaign" while planning even then to pace himself carefully, especially if the floundering Romney remained his only opponent. When asked about Romney's challenge to debate him, Nixon deftly dodged. "The great debate of 1968," he intoned, "should be between the Republican nominee and Lyndon Johnson. The only winner of a debate between Republicans . . . would be Lyndon Johnson."

That opening press conference was a model of decorum and good humor, in keeping with the modus operandi of this latest New Nixon. And that night, he presented himself in an even more surprising venue—a press party hosted by the candidate in a private bar at the New Hampshire Highway Hotel in Concord. As a bartender dispensed drinks, Nixon strolled among the assembled reporters, shaking hands, chatting amiably, renewing old acquaintances and making new ones. Then he jumped onto a chair in the center of the room and laid on the charm.

The horrible weather outside wasn't his fault, he said jokingly, but it did remind him of a state visit he had made to Morocco as vice president. The country had been experiencing a severe drought, but on the day he arrived there was a downpour. That night at the state dinner, he recalled, he was toasted as "The Man with Green Feet," which a translator told him meant, "Wherever you walk, grass grows." Later that night, in another bar in the hotel, we ungrateful press wretches fashioned a song to the tune of "The Wearing of the Green" that went:

Oh, your name is Richard Nixon, you're the newest ever seen,
You're speaking on the issues, but your feet have turned to green.
You're the party's elder statesman, there's no place you haven't been,
But who will buy a used car from a man with feet of green?

For many of the political reporters at the party, there had been too many New Nixons for them to accept easily this latest version of a friendly and candid one. Yet Nixon at the press party had made a specific point of assuring his assembled guests that this time around he would be making himself available frequently for briefings and interviews, and that reporters would not be kept in the dark about anything he was doing as a campaigner.

Early the very next morning, however, as the press corps slept, Nixon, Buchanan and a few other aides slipped out of the hotel. They drove over deserted roads to the nearby town of Hillsborough, where a small group of townspeople, farmers and college students handpicked by the local Nixon committee had gathered for an "entirely unrehearsed" discussion with the candidate at the Hillsborough Community Hall. A paid television crew recorded the scene for use in later television commercials. When word leaked out, Buchanan defended the slippery caper on grounds that the presence of reporters might "inhibit those people."

The goodwill generated by the press party didn't last very long in light of that episode. Nor was it restored the next day when the traveling press corps was taken by bus to another "entirely unrehearsed" meeting of preselected locals—but obliged to remain outside the hall as uniformed guards admitted the citizen props for another taping session.

What the press corps was seeing—or, rather, not seeing—was the second segment of a basic two-track campaign for the presidency that had been carefully thought out by Nixon and aides during the long night of his private citizenship after 1962.

The first track was the obvious and unavoidable public campaigning in the primaries—the speeches, the rallies, the handshaking walks through small towns—that was traditional in the presidential politics of the era. It could be physically grueling and politically hazardous as it unwound under the watchful eye of the news media, particularly the print reporters with their penchant for asking probing questions and putting the candidate's answers or nonanswers under a microscope. This track, because by nature it involved the spontaneous, was fraught with peril for a candidate who was not always surefooted and consistent. Yet it could not be abandoned entirely.

It could, however, be carefully controlled in what the candidate said and did and when he said and did it. Nixon in 1960 had campaigned nonstop, with events from morning to night daily that wore him into the ground in the process. In 1968 he would severely limit his appearances on the first, public, track. With television becoming increasingly dominant in presidential politics, Nixon would hold relatively few public appearances each day, almost always well scripted, and timed early enough in the day and located conveniently enough to major airports for television crews to ship their film of the events by air to the network shows in New York.

Meanwhile, on the second track, Nixon would be presented to the voters in the most positive light, in television commercials prepared by Madison Avenue wizards, fashioned sometimes from the closed-door meetings with preselected voters and sometimes carefully created in television studios. This second track, unlike the first, could be pursued out of easy scrutiny by the press, and in time it began to crowd out the first track as the view of the candidate actually seen by most voters. It was expensive, to be sure, but at the time there was no federal limitation on how much money could be contributed to or spent on a presidential campaign. And Nixon had a powerful fund-raising operation going that generated all the funds needed for the second track.

In New Hampshire, where all the polls had him far ahead of Romney, Nixon was determined to travel just enough on the first track to remind voters that he was running. And in the first days of his candidacy there, the startling events in Vietnam—the Tet Offensive by the enemy highlighted by the daring raid on the American embassy in Saigon—overshadowed all the presidential campaigning going on.

*   *   *

On February 1, as Nixon's announcement letters began flooding into New Hampshire, a singular incident occurred halfway around the world in Vietnam. Perhaps more than any other event before or afterward, it captured the brutality of the war and underscored why American public opinion was so ambivalent about the U.S. involvement.

The chief of the South Vietnamese national police, General Nguyen Ngoc

Loan, was a notoriously ruthless figure. Two years earlier, he had indiscrimi-
nately slaughtered or imprisoned hundreds of suspected military and civilian
critics of the regime taking refuge in Buddhist temples in Da Nang and Hue.
Now he was roaming Saigon with a small force of government troops. He was
looking for likely perpetrators of the devastating attack on the city in which
several of his men had been killed, including, according to writer Stanley
Karnow, one shot to death with his wife and children in their house.

Outside the An Quang Buddhist temple, suspected of being a Vietcong
command post, the troops had a prisoner in tow, his hands bound behind his
back. He seemed a fairly young man with a full head of black hair, wearing
black shorts and checkered shirt that hung outside the shorts. The soldiers
marched him over to Loan. Without hesitation, he extended his right arm
bearing a snub-nosed pistol against the man's head and fired. The man crum-
pled, blood gushing from his head. Not a word was said.

It was an execution that may have occurred many times during the war.
What made this one different was the fact that an Associated Press photog-
rapher, Eddie Adams, and a Vietnamese television cameraman for NBC
News, Vo Suu, happened upon the scene at precisely the critical moment.
They captured on film the chilling, willful killing in all its wanton brutality.
The execution photo hit front pages all over the United States and in many
other parts of the world the next morning, and ran on the NBC evening news
broadcast later that day.

The South Vietnamese vice president, Air Force General Nguyen Cao Ky,
dismissed Loan's action as a legitimate one against "a very high-ranking Viet
Cong officer." He declined, however, to identify him other than to say he was
a "civilian, a political officer." General Earle G. Wheeler, chairman of the
American Joint Chiefs of Staff, replying to an irate congressman, expressed a
"sense of revulsion at barbarous acts and summary executions," but then
added that the killing outside the Vietnam pagoda had happened "more in a
flash of outrage" than in an act of cold blood.

President Johnson meanwhile, ignoring the incident, told a news conference that the Tet Offensive was "a complete failure," psychologically as well
as militarily. It made him wonder, he said, "what would the North
Vietnamese be doing if we stopped the bombing and let them alone?" He
pledged to continue the bombing of the North "with a very precise restraint"
until there were "some better signs [that the enemy wanted negotiations]
than what these last few days have provided."

General Westmoreland meanwhile did his best to sugarcoat the whole Tet
Offensive. He dismissed the Vietcong attacks in Saigon and elsewhere in the
South as "a diversionary effort to take attention away from the northern part

of the country" where the U.S. base at Khe Sanh was under siege. While he expected the siege to continue for a few more days, he said, there were signs it was "about to run out of steam."

The next day, Westmoreland's headquarters put out this communiqué: "Although the enemy raided numerous cities and towns throughout the republic and achieved some temporary success, they have failed to take and hold any major installations or localities. Although some enemy units are still occupying positions in a few cities, they are rapidly being driven out." But the psychological impact of the invasion of the American embassy, of the multitude of other attacks around the country, and not insignificantly of the horrifying photo and television footage of General Loan's act of execution, deeply scarred American public opinion.

As always, Joseph Alsop also saw light where others saw darkness. "We are already engulfed in another spate of warnings that all is hopeless in Vietnam because of the attack on the U.S. Embassy and the other V.C. efforts in Saigon and other cities," he wrote. "In reality, however, this flurry of V.C. activities in urban centers will almost certainly prove to have just the opposite meaning in the end. The nearest parallel is probably the fruitless Japanese use of Kamikaze pilots in the Second World War's final phase."

Much later, after Johnson had left public life, he wrote in his memoir, *The Vantage Point:* "As I look back now, there is no doubt in my mind that the Tet offensive was a military debacle for the North Vietnamese and the Viet Cong. I am convinced that historians and military analysts will come to regard that offensive and its aftermath as the most disastrous Communist defeat of the war in Vietnam. . . . But the defeat the Communists suffered did not have the telling effect it should have had largely because of what we did to ourselves . . . I did not expect the enemy effort to have the impact on American thinking that it achieved. I was not surprised that elements of the press, the academic community and the Congress reacted as they did. I was surprised and disappointed that the enemy's efforts produced such a dismal effect on various people inside the government and others outside whom I had already regarded as staunch and unflappable. Hanoi must have been delighted; it was exactly the reaction they sought."

*   *   *

Elsewhere at home, there was no doubt that the Tet Offensive, whether a military success or failure for the enemy, was going to have an immense political as well as psychological impact on the presidential election of 1968. McCarthy on the stump chided the Johnson administration for "hollow claims of progress and victories," noting "that the enemy is bolder than ever, while we must steadily enlarge our own commitment." He reminded his audiences that "only six months ago we were told that 65 percent of the population was secure. Now we know that even the American Embassy is not secure."

Would the Tet Offensive be a factor in his favor politically? McCarthy was asked. "Give it three weeks," he replied, "time to sink in. By then it could make a difference." Already, however, McCarthy was moving up in the polls; one had him the choice of 18 percent of voters surveyed.

Robert Kennedy didn't need that long to conclude that Tet was a turning point in the war, as proof of the bankruptcy of Johnson's policies in Vietnam. The morning after his breakfast with reporters at which he had said he could not visualize "any foreseeable circumstances" that would make him a candidate for president in 1968, he was already having second thoughts about that phraseology. When Fred Dutton picked up the *Washington Post* the morning after the breakfast and read that phrase, he was astounded, because it conveyed to him a finality about Kennedy's decision that he knew from direct conversations did not reflect the senator's struggling indecisiveness. He phoned Kennedy and found that he too was chagrined about how final his thinking seemed in cold print.

In the next few days, Kennedy continued to agonize with aides, advisers, friends and even some reporters, second-guessing himself on the revised phrase he had used at the breakfast. He repeated his concerns about a candidacy of his own possibly egging Johnson on to further escalation of the war, about the damage it could do to other antiwar senators seeking reelection, and about helping to raise the prospects of the Nixon specter. He finally decided that if he couldn't bring himself to run, he could at least speak more forthrightly about LBJ's conduct of the war.

Kennedy had just had a book, *To Seek a Newer World*, published and he was invited to address the *Chicago Sun-Times* Book and Author luncheon on February 8. This time he pulled no punches. "Our enemy, savagely striking at will all across South Vietnam, has finally shattered the mask of official illusion with which we have concealed our true circumstances, even from ourselves," he said. Even if the Vietcong were driven from all the cities with terrible loss of life, he said, "they will nevertheless have demonstrated that no part or person of South Vietnam is secure from their attacks; neither district capitals nor American bases, neither the peasant in his rice paddy nor the commanding general of our own great forces."

The events of the Tet Offensive "have taught us something," Kennedy went on. "For the sake of those young Americans who are fighting today, if for no other reason, the time has come to take a new look at the war in Vietnam; not by cursing the past but by using it to illuminate the future.

And the first and necessary step is to face the facts. It is to seek out the austere and painful reality of Vietnam, freed from wishful thinking, false hopes and sentimental dreams."

The illusions that had to go, he said, were that the Tet Offensive had somehow ended as an American victory in turning back the attacks on the embassy and elsewhere; that the United States could win a war the South Vietnamese couldn't win for themselves; that victory at any cost was in the best interest of the United States or the people of South Vietnam; and that "the American national interest is identical with, or should be subordinated to, the selfish interest of an incompetent military regime."

Finally, Kennedy said, the United States had to stop thinking "this war can be settled in our own way and in our own time on our own terms." With no prospect of military victory, he said, "we must actively seek a peaceful settlement [giving] the Viet Cong a chance to participate in the political life of the country—not because we want them to, but because that is the only way in which this struggle can be settled."

To all this, Johnson predictably turned a deaf ear. Listening instead to his military leaders, he accepted their view that the Tet Offensive had indeed been essentially a diversionary action as a prelude to an all-out assault on Khe Sanh, in the hope of making it another Dien Bien Phu. The Joint Chiefs in a memo to LBJ from General Wheeler reported that the Marine base at Khe Sanh "could and should be defended." On February 9 at Johnson's instructions the bombing of Hanoi and Haiphong, after a one-month pause, was resumed. After the truces observing the new year on each side, it was business as usual again—although the week of January 28 to February 3 had brought a weekly record loss of 416 Americans killed and 2,757 wounded. The Pentagon said at the same time that an astounding 15,515 enemy forces had been killed in the same week. But that fact was not making most Americans feel any better.

Johnson continued to express confidence in Westmoreland, giving him another requested 10,500 U.S. combat troops in the wake of the Tet push, and to speak optimistically. On February 17 he flew to Pope Air Force Base in North Carolina and then on to the El Toro Marine Corps Naval Air Station in California to give personal send-offs to forces headed for Vietnam under the new call-up. He assured the troops in North Carolina that although the enemy was trying to win the war "now and this year" by shaking the Saigon government "to its foundation and destroying American will to fight on," that wasn't going to happen.

Westmoreland soon was saying that the enemy had actually "suffered a military defeat" in its Tet Offensive despite winning "some temporary psychological advantage." He said he didn't believe that North Vietnam "can hold up under a long war" but added that he would probably need "additional troops [to] more effectively deny the enemy his objectives, capitalize on his recent defeats . . . and clearly demonstrate to Hanoi our firm determination to prevent him from taking over any part of South Vietnam." (U.S. military sources soon were being quoted as saying the general was asking for 50,000 to 100,000 more troops.) He concluded by observing that "the time has come for debating to end, for everyone to close ranks, roll up their sleeves and get on with the job."

* * *

But the solidarity that such a response required was clearly not present at home. The war protest gained significant strength from the shock of the Tet Offensive and the major fighting that continued thereafter at Khe Sanh and in important cities like Hue. Activists in the protest had themselves been negotiating with Hanoi for the release of American captives. On February 16, Reverend Daniel Berrigan and Howard Zinn, representatives of the American Mobilization Committee Against the Vietnam War, hit paydirt. Three American airmen shot down in 1967 in raids over North Vietnam were handed over to them in Hanoi in what was described as a humanitarian gesture in honor of Tet. Little was made by the American government of the release, engineered by its most vocal critics on the war.

On the same date, Johnson made a decision that reverberated across the nation's college campuses. He eradicated as inequitable all draft deferments for graduate students except those studying medicine. Not only graduate students but seniors hoping to go on to graduate school the next fall suddenly faced the prospect of military service, and dispatch to Vietnam to fight a war many of them abhorred. Among them was Georgetown senior Bill Clinton, who only months earlier had been selected as a Rhodes Scholar for a year or two of graduate study at Oxford. At once, talk of the draft filled the conversations and thoughts of all the Bill Clintons around the country whose future had been abruptly clouded by Johnson's decision.

* * *

Other matters plagued or embarrassed the Johnson administration. More alleged confessions by crew members of the *Pueblo* came from North Korea as negotiations for their release dragged on. A senatorial report raised more questions about the alleged Tonkin Gulf attack on U.S. warships by North Vietnamese gunboats in 1964, which had been used by LBJ to extract a blank-check resolution from Congress on pursuit of the war. Fulbright, chairman of the Senate Foreign Relations Committee, accused McNamara of deception in his testimony before the committee on what actually had happened.

Also, rumors circulated that use of tactical nuclear weapons to break the siege of Khe Sanh was being considered when the Pentagon sent an expert in their use to South Vietnam. When McCarthy was asked about them, he observed that "there have been some demands already." White House press secretary George Christian branded McCarthy's remark as "false," adding that "the President has considered no decision of this nature. . . . Irresponsible discussion and speculation are a disservice to the country."

* * *

Also at home, war broke out again on the civil rights front. On February 8, attempts by students of all-black South Carolina State and Claflin colleges in Orangeburg to integrate a local bowling alley led to a confrontation. State police and National Guardsmen opened fire on a crowd in what came to be known as "the Orangeburg massacre." Three young blacks perished and thirty-four other individuals were wounded. Police first charged that students had opened fire but eyewitnesses said no weapons were seen in the crowd, and none was found afterward.

The Justice Department moved at once, forcing the desegregation of the bowling alley, but that action did not end the poisonous racial atmosphere. Democratic Governor Robert McNair, who had called out the National Guard, blamed the violence on "black power advocates who represented only a small minority of the total student bodies" at the two colleges. One of the wounded, twenty-three-year-old Cleveland Sellers, state coordinator for the Student Nonviolent Coordinating Committee, was arrested. But a later report by the Southern Regional Council said he had "little influence on the campus" and the state never brought him to trial.

February also saw other outbreaks of racial violence, North and South. White and black students clashed at two high schools in New Haven, Connecticut; Mississippi state troopers fired tear gas at 200 Alcorn A&M College students protesting against the dismissal of three students who had passed out campaign literature for black congressional candidate Charles Evers. In New Orleans, Rap Brown was arrested on a charge of threatening an FBI agent.

Other voices were being heard from black America. Grove Press published *Soul on Ice* by Eldridge Cleaver, a paroled Black Panther official who wrote about life in prison. In Atlanta, Martin Luther King in a regular Sunday sermon at his parish, the Ebenezer Baptist Church, told the congregation: "If any of you are around when I have to meet my day, I don't want a long funeral. And if you get somebody to deliver the eulogy, tell him not to talk too long. . . . Tell him not to mention that I have a Nobel Peace Prize—that isn't important. . . . I'd like somebody to mention that day that Martin Luther King Jr. tried to give his life serving others. I'd like for somebody to say that day that Martin Luther King Jr. tried to love somebody. . . . I want you to be able to say that day that I did try to feed the hungry . . . that I did try in my life to clothe the naked . . . that I did try in my life to visit those who were in prison . . . that I tried to love and serve humanity. Yes, if you want to, say that I was a drum major. Say that I was a drum major for peace . . . for righteousness." It would be his last sermon to his home parishioners.

* * *

In Pasadena, California, on February 15, a man named George Erhard sold a .22 Iver Johnson handgun that had been given to him by a neighbor to a man he knew only as "Joe" who worked at Nash's department store there, for $25. The man's real name was Munir Sirhan, who had come to the United States in 1956 along with his mother, sister and a younger brother whose first name was also Sirhan, as Palestinian refugees. The younger brother, slight of build, had worked around Southern California racetracks as an exercise boy and "hot walker" but at this time was employed at a local health food store as a salesman and delivery boy. He was a quiet young man, except on occasions when he got into heated discussions about tensions between Israel and the Arab world.

* * *

Two other events of moment began to unfold in February. In New York, Columbia University broke ground on a new gymnasium in a park bordering on Harlem that was a major recreational area for the local, overwhelmingly black, citizenry. And in Memphis, predominantly black sanitation workers struck the city for a pay raise, union recognition and other common labor rights. Police broke up a march with nightsticks and antiriot guns, leading to a call by a hundred black ministers for a boycott of all downtown businesses owned by members of the City Council.

On the same day as the Orangeburg confrontation, George Wallace finally announced that he would run for the White House again, this time as an independent candidate. His incendiary rhetoric, foretelling an era of anti-Washington politics, remained undiminished. If elected, he promised, he would "bring all these briefcase-toting bureaucrats . . . to Washington and throw their briefcases in the Potomac River." He pledged that he would "keep the peace if I had to keep 30,000 troops standing on the street . . . with two-foot-long bayonets." And he said he would work to have Congress change "the so-called civil rights laws," which he said were "really an attack on the property rights of this country and on the free enterprise system and local government." All the riots and civil disturbances plaguing the country, he insisted, were the work of "activists, anarchists, revolutionaries and Communists" who should, in a favorite Wallaceism, "be thrown under a good jail."

Although Wallace was a Democrat, it was not at all clear that his third-party candidacy would draw more support from his own party than from the Republicans. Law and order had been a Republican issue in the 1964 candidacy of Barry Goldwater and it could be expected to be part of the GOP platform again in 1968, especially if Nixon was the party's nominee.

Wallace had surprised the experts with his showing in the 1964 Democratic primaries but he knew he never could get the Democratic nomination. However, the independent candidate route, as he had noted to me in his Montgomery office in 1967, would give him a free ticket into the general election in November. Conceivably, he suggested, he could corral enough electoral votes in Deep South states to bar the election of the popular-vote winner—and set himself up for some sort of deal with him. Or so the speculation went at the time. Wallace added to it by saying in Chicago that if his candidacy resulted in a stalemated election, he would seek to make "a covenant" with either the Democratic or Republican nominee in exchange for support for some of his own policies.

* * *

Wallace's entry into the race, at any rate, assured that the issues of civil rights and racism would share the spotlight with Vietnam in the politics of 1968. For Robert Kennedy particularly, sensitized to both issues from his experiences in the Deep South as attorney general, there was a distinct linkage of the two. He preached along with King that black Americans were bearing a disproportionate burden of the fighting and dying, while at home their situation disintegrated.

More inner-circle meetings at Hickory Hill, his home in a northern Virginia suburb of Washington, only added to Kennedy's frustration, and indecision. The stronger rationalization for running continued to be the war, especially in the immediate aftermath of Tet. Old JFK hand Kenneth O'Donnell told another insider at the time: "If he's not going to do anything about the war, I'm not going to stay with him." And he said later he told Kennedy directly: "If you want to run because of the [war] issue, I'm with you. If you just want to get the White House limousines back, I'm against it."

Pierre Salinger produced a poll indicating that McCarthy could get 40 percent of the Democratic vote in New Hampshire and warned Kennedy: "If it's true, you have to announce before the primary." And Goodwin, also frustrated at the inaction, informed Kennedy: "As long as you're not running I think I'll go up to New Hampshire and work for McCarthy." At a meeting of the ADA, the old-line liberal organization voted to endorse McCarthy by a vote of sixty-seven to forty-five over the vociferous opposition of labor members. Among those voting for the endorsement were Schlesinger and Goodwin.

All these pronouncements from loyalists he trusted spun in Kennedy's head. The Tet Offensive had brought him closer to the edge, yet he couldn't bring himself to jump, although he continued to believe that McCarthy could not bring LBJ down. He "didn't understand that the movement was much stronger than one individual," Lowenstein said later, "and that given the strength of the movement, even McCarthy's odd conduct couldn't kill what was happening."

Then, in late February, came an icebreaker. Johnson after the 1967 race riots had appointed a special Commission on Civil Disorders headed by Governor Otto Kerner of Illinois to determine the root causes. In a leaked summary report, the commission proclaimed: "Our nation is moving toward two societies, one black, one white—separate and unequal." It blamed "white racism" at the core of the demoralized condition of blacks in the inner cities. "What white Americans have never fully understood—what the Negro can never forget—is that white society is deeply implicated in the ghetto," the report said. "White institutions create it, white institutions maintain it, and white society condones it."

The commission urged a "massive and sustained" national commitment to police, welfare, employment, housing and education reforms at the federal and local levels. Kennedy waited in vain for some positive response from the White House, and seethed.

* * *

February also brought intensified criticism of Johnson's conduct of the war, at home and abroad. In the Senate, Majority Leader Mike Mansfield joined the call for a bombing halt in North Vietnam; Senator Frank Church demanded an "agonizing reappraisal" of American foreign policy, calling the U.S. hope of restoring stability to "that half of the world that has just thrown off colonial rule . . . a grandiose dream of men who suffer from the dangerous illusion of American omnipotence." And former American Ambassador George F. Kennan labeled the U.S. policy in Vietnam "a massive miscalculation and error of policy, an error for which it is hard to find any parallels in our history."

In Europe, protest rallies against the American intervention in Vietnam drew thousands in West Berlin, Rome, Stockholm and London. British Labour Party members of Parliament passed a resolution calling on Prime

Minister Harold Wilson to withdraw British support of the U.S. policy. Sweden granted political asylum to six American soldiers who had deserted in West Germany in protest of their country's efforts in Vietnam.

All this criticism and expression of doubt about where Johnson was taking the United States in Vietnam led him to consult with old and trusted hands in both parties even before the man he selected to replace McNamara, Clark Clifford, was installed at the Pentagon. Among these old hands was Truman's former secretary of state, Dean Acheson. After having been given the customary rose-colored briefings by Defense Department and White House officials, Acheson was summoned to the Oval Office on February 27, obviously to reassure the president that his policies remained the wisest course.

According to Isaacson and Thomas in *The Wise Men,* Johnson informed him that in Westmoreland's view, "Tet had made the war 'a whole new ball game,'" and that the Joint Chiefs of Staff "wanted 200,000 [more] troops" sent to Vietnam. "For 45 minutes," Isaacson and Thomas wrote, "Johnson ranted on. As usual, three television sets were blasting away, aides rushed in and out, the phones rang incessantly. Acheson just sat there. . . . When it appeared to him that Johnson was more interested in delivering tirades than seeking advice, Acheson excused himself, walked out of the White House and returned to his law office. . . . The phone rang immediately; it was Walt Rostow [LBJ's national security adviser], asking why he had walked out. 'You tell the president—and you can tell him in precisely these words,' Acheson said evenly, 'that he can take Vietnam and stick it up his ass.'" Even the proper and diplomatic establishment was souring on the official line of optimism in the face of the reality in Vietnam.

On the same day, according to Clifford in his memoir, *Counsel to the President,* both Clifford and McNamara in another meeting with Dean Rusk reacted strongly to continued claims that the Tet Offensive had been an enemy defeat, and to pressures for a major increase in American forces in Vietnam. "Despite these optimistic reports," Clifford said, "the American people and world opinion believe we have suffered a major setback. How do we gain support for major programs if we have told people that things are going well? How do we avoid creating the feeling that we are pounding troops down a rathole? What is our purpose? What is achievable?" Clifford wrote that he then asked for a review of "our entire posture" in Vietnam, which Johnson soon ordered, under Clifford's direction.

At the same meeting, Clifford wrote, "as Rusk responded with a discussion of the need to intensify the bombing of North Vietnam, a remarkable event took place. Overcome with conflicting emotions, Bob McNamara's controlled exterior cracked. 'The goddamned Air Force, they're dropping more on North Vietnam than we dropped on Germany in the last year of World War II, and it's not doing anything!' he said. His voice faltered, and for a moment he had difficulty speaking between suppressed sobs. He looked at me: 'We simply have to end this thing. I just hope you can get hold of it. It is out of control.' We were all stunned, but, out of a shared pain and sense of embarrassment, we went on with the discussion as though nothing out of the ordinary had occurred. Everyone in the room understood what had happened: this proud, intelligent, and dedicated man was reaching the end of his strength on his last full day in office. He was leaving the Pentagon just in time."

* * *

While all this was going on, the committed antiwar McCarthy organization was writing a new chapter in presidential politics in New Hampshire. The polls continued to say that the senator from Minnesota stood no chance to upset an incumbent president. But college students by the carload streaming into the state on weekends, and many checking out of college for the duration of the primary, generated an almost joyful optimism in the ranks. It was not so much that this transfusion of youthful energy was changing the odds overnight. Rather, it was a sense among the hundreds of young volunteers, and some middle-aged activists against the war like movie actor Paul Newman, that they were finally doing something about their opposition, not simply talking or marching about it.

In mid-February, with midyear examinations over, Sam Brown, the young Harvard divinity student by way of his native Council Bluffs, Iowa, Redlands University in California and Rutgers, had a veritable army of eager contemporaries encamped in the state. They were working in church basements and sleeping in private homes, sometimes in beds, sometimes in sleeping bags on floors. The coed army was heavily recruited from nearby Ivy League schools like Dartmouth, Harvard, Brown and Yale, but with many others thrown in, some as far away as the Midwest. Every day and some nights they went out canvassing in the cold, their earnestness warming many usually distant, skeptical New Hampshirites.

Although the Johnson forces and regular Democratic leaders sought then and later to paint these young people as radical members of "the New Left" out to dismember "the system," they were hardly that. "They had been raised and schooled to believe in the promise of America," Todd Gitlin wrote, "and they hated the war partly because it meant that the object of their affections, the system that rewarded their proficiency, was damaged goods. They were the inheritors of the vision of a moral America, and they did not want their moral capital squandered. . . . Unswayed by the siren song of LSD, disaffected by cultural revolution, these straight insurgents wanted to rescue their country from its emergency."

Mary McGrory in the *Washington Star* described the young McCarthy recruits this way: "Their parents and professors might not recognize the cheerful, humble, willing volunteers who ring doorbells, sweep floors and lick envelopes for 16 hours at a stretch. . . . The 'straights' and the 'nonstraights' are separated. The 'straights' (clean shaven, neatly suited or modestly skirted) are allowed to go out in the wards with file cards and instruction sheets. The beards are put in the back room to fold and stuff literature, as Beatles music booms deafeningly out of the record player."

Ann Hart, screening the volunteers on arrival, McGrory wrote, would say to them: "Let me hear your accents. Talk to me." Advising them that the local folks didn't react well to harsh New York accents and manners, she counseled them to be low-key. McGrory wrote, "and one other thing. If you could say '*McCahty,*' it would help a lot."

In the streets of New Hampshire, "violet-eyed damsels from Smith are pinning McCarthy buttons on tattooed mill workers," McGrory reported, "and Ph.D.s from Cornell, shaven and shorn for world peace, are deferentially bowing to middle-aged Manchester housewives and importuning them to consider a change of commander-in-chief. . . . A kind of reconciliation process between the generations has begun to occur. McCarthy is leading the children back into the political process and thus willy nilly into communication with their elders."

The McCarthy effort became in a real sense a collective love affair, sometimes among the serious young men and women but always with the cause and with the candidate whose cool, dignified style impressed them, at least at this point, as worthy of their commitment. Johnson gave older students among them an added incentive with his end to draft deferments for those taking graduate courses.

In all that was being made of the McCarthy youth, the contribution of McCarthy himself was often overlooked, or downgraded. Goodwin wrote later in his book *Remembering America: A Voice from the Sixties* that McCarthy in New Hampshire "was not only an ideal candidate, but the most original mind I had ever known in politics. He understood the issues, and the politics that could transform popular discontent into votes. . . . He matched his personal conduct to the necessities of politics; perhaps because, in New Hampshire, his cause was pure, the issues cleanly drawn and unstained by personal ambition. It was easier to justify the raucous brawlings of politics for a cause than for himself." The judgment was one that others shared in New Hampshire, but less so later on down the road as unforeseen political events, and the personal animosities they unleashed, tarnished the purity of the candidate's effort.

All was not always smooth in the McCarthy camp in New Hampshire as disputes inevitably arose between the homegrown effort in the state and national headquarters operatives. Friction developed between Hoeh and Gans when Gans came into the state and objected to some of the free-form efforts that marked the McCarthy campaign there. About a month before the primary, for example, Hoeh said later, Gans objected strongly to a scheduled staff party at the Carpenter Hotel in Manchester on a late Saturday night. McCarthy was touring the city's ethnic clubs that night with reporters in tow and was scheduled to drop by, and the press would see the frivolity. Hoeh first ordered the party delayed, then changed his mind because the kids were "the ones who have a stake in this issue." McCarthy's appearance at the party, and his enthusiastic greeting from the student volunteers, generated favorable stories, Hoeh said, and was a general morale booster.

As McCarthy's Kiddie Corps toiled tirelessly at the headquarters and up and down the streets of New Hampshire towns, the opposition unwittingly began to contribute to their cause. The Democratic State Committee running the write-in campaign for Johnson committed a political blunder that McCarthy quickly seized upon. The committee sent out cards with three sections, each bearing the same serial number, to registered Democrats in the state asking them to pledge, with name and address, to vote for LBJ in the primary. One section was for the voter to keep. Another contained the pledge, noting that "as expression of your support, this card will be forwarded to The White House, Washington, D.C." The third went to the state party committee—an unsubtle way to determine who was with the president and who wasn't, with at least a sniff of intimidation.

McCarthy was quick to seize on the ploy to charge that, and worse. In a speech in Concord, he said the scheme came "closest to denying a people their right to a secret ballot of any suggestion I've seen in this country." Deftly, he played on the celebrated independence of the New Hampshire voter. At the same time, his young troops on their canvassing rounds politely suggested to local citizens that they were being asked to jump through a hoop for the remote man in the White House who did not deign to come to the state to ask for their support himself.

Johnson left any reply to his chief agents in the state, Governor King and Senator McIntyre. And as McCarthy's campaign appeared to be generating steam they assaulted him head-on as an unwitting agent of Hanoi. "Shall we continue to resist naked communist aggression with all the forces at our command," King asked in one speech, "or will we say the price is too high, the going is too rough, and we are ready to negotiate on terms laid down by Ho Chi Minh? That is why the people most interested in the results of this election are Ho Chi Minh and his communist friends. They will be scrutinizing the returns for signs of a breaking of the American will."

This was very heavy stuff for a compaign representing the president of the United States against a still-obscure senator from a small Midwest state who was not yet registering more than a blip on the nation's political radar screen. But without Johnson's presence in New Hampshire, his agents were beginning to panic.

LBJ, for his part, was telling the American people in a speech in Dallas that "we stand at a turning point" in the war in Vietnam, warning that any weakening of American resolve "would encourage the enemy and prolong the bloody conflict." There must be, he said, "no failing of our fighting sons, no betrayal of those who fight beside us, no breaking of America's given word or trusted commitments." That was the closest he was coming to campaigning for reelection in New Hampshire.

* * *

All this while, on the Republican side, Romney was sinking deeper into the hole he had dug himself. First it was his own indecision on what to do about Vietnam. Then, having finally stated his policy of "guaranteed neutralization," he had to convince New Hampshire voters that he was up to the presidency. Nixon's strategy of showing only a little leg in the state was succeeding in enticing loyal Republicans, and in leaving to Romney the broadest opportunity to stumble. While the determined Michigander's gaffes were only of a minor nature, they helped sustain the public perception that he was a bumbler.

Rockefeller continued pro forma support of Romney, praising him at a fund-raising luncheon in Detroit on February 24. But then in an exchange with reporters, he said that while he didn't expect a draft would come his way—Maryland Governor Spiro Agnew was still pushing one—he would accept it if it did. That statement of availability cast a further pall over the Romney effort in New Hampshire, especially because an amateur write-in campaign for Rockefeller had now surfaced in the state.

A few days later, an internal poll for the Romney campaign had Nixon at an astounding 75 percent, Romney at only 10 and Rockefeller at 8, and gaining. Being trounced by Nixon would be bad enough; losing to a write-in for Rockefeller, Romney's most important supporter, would be a disaster. The Romney strategists put their heads together, then called the candidate to say they needed to meet and consider a "proposal."

Later that same afternoon, with two weeks still to go before the primary,

Germond and I dropped by Romney's headquarters on Main Street in Concord to talk with an old friend, John Deardourff, who was running the Romney campaign in the state. We found him in what could only be described as the condition of a manager whose candidate had already lost. As he confided on a background basis how bleak the situation was, about the impossible poll numbers and about the mistakes that had been made, we realized that what we were hearing was the obituary of the Romney presidential bid.

As bad as the fact that he trailed Nixon by such a wide margin was polling data indicating that even with all he had said and done in the previous year, voters didn't have much sense of who Romney was. There was some thought, Deardourff told us, of asking Rockefeller to come back into New Hampshire, perhaps to channel the draft effort for him into the Romney column. Our conversation continued on through dinner, and after we left Deardourff it occurred to us for the first time that Romney might actually be persuaded to quit the race before even getting into the starting gate on the first primary day.

The next morning we drove to Hanover to talk to the Romney campaign's state chairman, Bill Johnson, who painted the same grim picture. At one point one of us asked him: "Is there any chance you might just pull out?" Johnson paused, then replied, obliquely, that "when you're lying awake in bed at night and you can't sleep, a lot of things go through your mind." We left it at that, but two days later, when we saw him again, he apologized. When we had walked into his office, Johnson said, he was working on a draft of a withdrawal announcement.

That night, Romney drove to Boston for a long radio interview in which he sought to downplay Rockefeller's remarks about his availability. He clung to the line that he would win in New Hampshire. Afterward, he motored back to Concord, where his staff confronted him with the dismal facts of his situation—and the recommendation that he quit. He said he would sleep on it and the next morning he agreed. It was decided that he would fly to Washington, where his fellow Republican governors were meeting, and break the news directly to them. There was some talk of his urging them to back Rockefeller, but it was felt that such a step would seem to confirm that he really had been, after all, only a stalking horse for the New Yorker.

As Romney headed for Washington, however, word of his plans leaked out. In mid-afternoon, Nixon was speaking to an audience of about 300 New Hampshirites in the Knights of Columbus Hall in Milford when Buchanan, then acting as his press aide, got a call from a friend in the press corps. At the same time, Mike Wallace of CBS News heard the news from his office. Both of them stood at the front of Nixon's podium waiting for him to finish so they could tell him. When Nixon finally stepped down, and before Wallace could get to him, Buchanan and Chapin hustled him into a nearby washroom. Chapin barred entry while Buchanan led Nixon into a stall and informed him: "Romney's pulling out of the race!"

Nixon couldn't believe his good fortune. He decided to say nothing about it until Romney had actually done the deed, and to continue on with his schedule, which had two more small towns to visit. When he came out of the washroom, Wallace rushed up and told him the news. Nixon feigned surprise, although it was clear he had just been briefed by Buchanan. "I don't believe it," he said. "I don't comment on rumors." As other reporters informed of Romney's plans crowded around him, Nixon coolly signed some autographs for a young boy. Then he proceeded to two more events, speaking calmly as if nothing had happened that would profoundly affect his political fortunes.

On his return to the Holiday Inn in Manchester shortly before Romney was to hold a televised press conference, Nixon instructed his key aides to watch it and report back to him. He himself, he said, never watched such things because he did not want to make a strategic judgment based on the emotional scene that certainly would unfold. He walked down the hall to his own room and closed the door behind him.

It was an upbeat, smiling George Romney who appeared on the nation's television screens. "It is clear to me that my candidacy has not won the wide acceptance with rank and file Republicans that I had hoped to achieve," he said. Therefore he was withdrawing now, he said, to give his fellow governors time "for meaningful consideration" of other candidates, and he pledged his "wholehearted support to the candidate" they chose. He did not recommend Rockefeller but thanked him, saying "he has asked nothing of me and has given more than I have asked . . . on his own initiative, without reservation."

Speculation was immediate, however, that Rockefeller would step quickly into the vacuum. Reagan a few days earlier had said it would be "arrogant" for himself to reach for the presidency after only a year in the governorship, and now in Sacramento he told reporters that Romney's decision didn't alter his own.

Moments after Romney's announcement, Rockefeller arrived at National Airport for the governors' meeting. On being told of the news by reporters, he observed: "It's a great loss for the party. He was my candidate. I don't have one now." He reiterated that "I'm not a candidate" but said also that if drafted he would respond.

Back in Manchester, John Sears, a young attorney from Nixon's New York law firm pressed into service in the campaign, had watched the Romney news conference on television. Immediately afterward, he walked down the corridor to Nixon's room to inform him of what had been said. He knocked lightly, opened the door and saw Nixon scurrying away from the television set. It was obvious to Sears that his boss had watched the conference himself in spite of saying he had no intention of doing so. Sears dutifully briefed him and Nixon listened with interest, as if he hadn't just seen and heard it all with his own eyes and ears.

Instead of appearing before the press, Nixon sent down a brief statement that commended Romney for waging "an energetic and vigorous campaign." There was no crowing, and in fact there lingered a suspicion in the Nixon camp that Romney really had been a stalking horse for Rockefeller all along. He was a cool one, this New Nixon. Or was there anything really new about him after all? Whatever the case, he clearly was in the driver's seat on the Republican side as the New Hampshire primary drew near.

Romney's sudden withdrawal sapped what little drama there was from the GOP contest in the state. It did serve, however, to throw the press and public spotlight at February's end more squarely upon the Democratic contest— if you could call the challenge of a little-known senator from Minnesota to a sitting president a contest.

CHAPTER 4

March: Eruption in New Hampshire

Mar. 1 Elvin Hayes of Houston named AP college player of the year; 4 Joe Frazier knocks out Buster Mathis for World Boxing Council title; 6 Former House Speaker Joseph W. Martin, 83, dies; National Book Award to Thornton Wilder for *The Eighth Day;* 7 Abe Bernstein, bootlegger and leader of Detroit's Purple Gang, 76, dies; 8 Terence Cooke named archbishop of New York; 9 convicts set Oregon State Penitentiary afire, take hostages; 14 Federal Reserve Board raises lending rate to 5 percent, highest since 1929; Neil Simon's *Plaza Suite* opens on Broadway; 15 Arthur Hailey's *Airport* published; 17 Villanova sets world two-mile relay record at 7:23.8; 18 *The Producers* released starring Zero Mostel; 22 expelled Congressman Adam Clayton Powell surrenders on criminal contempt charges; 23 novelist Edwin O'Connor (*The Last Hurrah*), 49, dies; UCLA beats North Carolina for NCAA basketball title.

On March 1, the day after George Romney bowed to the inevitable, Nelson Rockefeller issued this terse statement: "The Party must decide who it feels can best represent it and who it thinks can best command the confidence of the American people and best serve the country. The Republican Party has two objectives: a) It wants to be united; b) It wants to nominate someone who can get enough Independent and Democratic votes to get elected. I am not going to create dissension within the Republican Party by contending for the nomination, but I am ready and willing to serve the American people if called."

In other words, Rockefeller was saying: The party can't win with the super-partisan Nixon and needs someone like me, a moderate with appeal outside the party. I'm not going to fight for the nomination, but if you want to hand it to me, I'll take it.

One Republican who was more than willing to serve the nomination to Rockefeller on a silver platter was Governor Agnew of Maryland. He stepped up his efforts to get other Republican governors to join his draft-Rockefeller campaign, but nobody was biting. Governor Tom McCall of Oregon, whose state primary Rockefeller had won against Barry Goldwater in 1964, wanted Rockefeller to commit to run in it again. But if Rockefeller allowed his name to go on the ballot there, he would also have to run first in primaries in Wisconsin and Nebraska, both of which were solid for Nixon.

Nixon, in his usual transparent way, tried to egg Rockefeller on, confident that his late entry would be futile and would make Nixon look all the stronger. Also, having Rockefeller in the race might drive pro-Reagan conservatives who hated the New York governor into the Nixon camp. "Let me make one thing quite clear," Nixon said, "I'm not issuing a challenge. I'm not belligerently saying, 'Now, Governor, either come in or stay out.' . . . I take no pleasure, no gratification, in seeing him have to make this decision." And then the classic Nixon needle: "I admire men who get into the arena. Some of the others have not."

Nixon offered that Rockefeller "may think that it would be better for the kingmakers at Miami to select the nominee. . . . I would trust that Governor Rockefeller would get in and answer questions on Vietnam. . . . I think he has every reason not to answer them up to this point because he is not a candidate, but if he becomes a candidate, he could do so." Nixon's own unwillingness to discuss how he would end the war did not inhibit him in the slightest from making this comment.

The polls provided some perspective on why Rockefeller was unwilling to challenge Nixon in the primaries. *Newsweek*, for example, not only had Nixon far ahead of all other Republicans but closing in on Johnson. In New Hampshire, a write-in campaign had started up for Rockefeller, but it was an amateurish and underfinanced effort and the governor gave it a wide berth. Nevertheless, Nixon, in an attempt to paint what was now a shoo-in for him in the Republican primary as a critical challenge, proclaimed with a straight face: "New Hampshire becomes a very significant race with a massive, well-financed write-in for Rockefeller. He has the money and the men to do it."

Even without Rockefeller, Nixon argued, the primary would be an important event in "testing whether Nixon or Johnson gets the most votes." Left unsaid by Nixon were the facts that there were 149,000 registered

Republicans in the state and only 89,000 registered Democrats, and Nixon's name was printed on the ballot and LBJ's wasn't.

Still, looking ahead to the general election in the fall, some of Nixon's senior advisers, including Herbert Brownell, attorney general in the Eisenhower administration and a law partner of Thomas E. Dewey, insisted that Nixon had to craft a position on Vietnam that would clearly separate himself from the Johnson policy. Up to now, Nixon had gotten away with generalities, thanks largely to Romney's confusion on the issue and the news media attention it drew. But in a speech in Hampton, New Hampshire, on March 3, he suddenly blurted out: "If in November this war is not over, I say that the American people will be justified in electing new leadership. And I pledge to you that new leadership will end the war and win the peace in the Pacific."

The statement wasn't much in itself, since he had been criticizing Johnson's leadership on the war all along. But it marked the first time he had explicitly pledged to end the war. The question now arose: how? Did Nixon have a workable plan? If so, Democrats demanded with all the umbrage they could muster, he was obliged to inform the president at once, so that American armed forces would not die needlessly between then and the inauguration the next January. Or at least, reporters began to insist, he ought to say publicly what he would do so voters could make a judgment, rather than being asked to buy a pig in a poke.

Buchanan acknowledged long afterward, in a C-SPAN interview, what many of us who were traveling with Nixon and trying to draw him out on his Vietnam policy suspected—that there was no such plan. "That was a mistake," Buchanan said. "What Nixon had said was, 'I promise you that new leadership can find the diplomatic and economic ways and means to end this war in Vietnam. And I will end this war.' But the press immediately said he's got a plan. Nixon kept denying it and denying it and denying it. He didn't run on that. That was the worst mistake he made in the whole primary campaign."

Nixon, finally realizing that he had put himself in the line of fire, beat a hasty—and lofty—retreat. "People ask me, 'What will you give North Vietnam?'" he said in an interview in the *New York Times*. "Let me tell you why I won't tell you that. No one with this responsibility who is seeking office should give away any of his bargaining positions in advance. . . . Under no circumstances should a man say what he will do in January. The military situation may change, and we may have to take an entirely new look."

Nixon had no similar hesitancy, however, in coming down squarely on the matter of the recent violence in the cities at home. He assaulted the Kerner

Commission report on grounds that "it in effect blames everybody for the riots except the perpetrators of the riots. . . . That deficiency," he said in a radio interview in Keene, "has to be dealt with first. Until we have order, we can have no progress. . . . I believe we've got to make it very clear to potential rioters that in the event something starts next summer, that the law will move in with adequate force to put down rioting and looting at the first signs of it."

Two days later, he was even more emphatic. The government, he said, should meet "force with force if necessary," and make clear that "retaliation against the perpetrators and the planners of violence will be swift and sure." Having fed that red meat to Republican law-and-order conservatives, Nixon righteously observed: "On the other hand, we must move with both compassion and conviction to bring the American dream to the ghetto." But he offered no serious proposals to achieve that goal.

Martin Luther King, however, had his own approach. On March 4 in Atlanta, he announced firm plans for a "nonviolent poor people's march on Washington" in late April, at which time about thirty prominent black leaders would personally call on administration and congressional leaders to respond aggressively to the Kerner report. King said a "mule train" caravan of 3,000 blacks would set off on April 22 from Mississippi to Washington, gathering strength and numbers as it went north. Shortly afterward, he set June 15 as a special day of protest and said the demonstrators would "build a shanty town" in Washington and stay there until then. (The idea for this march, according to Robert Kennedy aide Peter Edelman much later, actually came from Kennedy. When Edelman's future wife, Marian Wright, told Kennedy she was going to Atlanta to see the civil rights leader, he said, the senator asked her to pass on the scheme to him.)

In Memphis, meanwhile, 121 sanitation strike leaders were arrested after a sit-in at City Hall on March 5, and other arrests followed. A week later, an estimated 9,000 blacks gathered for a pep talk from moderate black leaders Roy Wilkins, head of the NAACP, and Bayard Rustin, and two days after that, Martin Luther King dropped by, promising to attend another large demonstration on March 28.

* * *

In Washington, other pressures had continued to mount on Johnson. The Senate passed a civil rights bill with broad open-housing provisions, but its reception by civil rights groups was tempered by the fact it included antiriot provisions pushed through by two law-and-order senators, Strom Thurmond of South Carolina and Frank Lausche of Ohio. The *Pueblo* stalemate dragged on; LBJ received an open letter purportedly sent by the crew of the ship stipulating that "repatriation can be realized only when our government frankly admits the fact that we intruded into the territorial waters" of North Korea "and committed hostile acts. . . . " And above all the monkey of Vietnam clung to LBJ's back.

So tense, and even hostile, was the home front environment becoming that the president of the United States was finding himself a virtual prisoner within his own borders. Secretive to a fault under normal circumstances, Johnson began making almost furtive forays out of the White House with little or no advance notice to the press. He had been stung shortly before when his announced plans to attend a service at Burton Parish Episcopal Church in Williamsburg gave the rector enough time to change his sermon and denounce the president's war policies in his very presence. Thereafter, *Air Force One* took him mostly to secure military installations, such as Ramsey Air Force Base in Puerto Rico, where with family members in tow on March 3 he watched a simulated bomber alert and then escaped for a Sunday of golf. But there was no escaping the responsibilities entrusted to him, nor the growing rancor over his unyielding attitude toward Vietnam.

*   *   *

Antiwar protests were spreading in Western and Central Europe, and critics in the Senate, led by Fulbright, were demanding a voice in the dispatch of any additional forces to Vietnam. The demands were triggered by a report that General Wheeler, chairman of the Joint Chiefs of Staff, and Westmoreland had asked the president for a whopping 206,000 additional troops in 1968, despite assurances that Tet had been a resounding defeat for the enemy and that the coming year would see more of the same.

Secretary of State Dean Rusk was called before the Senate Foreign Relations Committee, where Chairman Fulbright told him that as a result of administration policies in Vietnam "the light of the American example burns dim around the world." Rusk for the first time acknowledged that "both sides suffered some severe setbacks" in the Tet Offensive, undercutting Westmoreland's claim.

Minnesota poet Robert Bly, on receipt of the National Book Award for his collection *The Light Around the Body* on March 6, declared that the Vietnam War had destroyed America's historic longing for "pure light, constant victory. . . . From now on," he intoned, "we will have to live with grief and defeat."

Finally, the Gallup Poll—which LBJ said he never paid attention to, but which was always at his fingertips—found that 49 percent of those interviewed now thought sending American troops to Vietnam had been a mistake. Also, 69 percent said they favored drafting and training more South

Vietnamese to take over the fighting and permit withdrawal of the Americans—in other words, the basic approach put forward by the discredited George Romney. Johnson met such findings of domestic unease with the observation that the United States had the power to deal with any adversary "anywhere in the world, except within our own boundaries."

In New Hampshire as well, Johnson suddenly was finding himself imperiled politically by his Vietnam policies—and by inept political strategists. As the grassroots efforts of McCarthy's Kiddie Corps and the senator's own low-key, rather disarming style of campaigning continued to touch a responsive audience, the Johnsonites resorted to rank jingoism. Governor King warned darkly that there would be "dancing in the streets of Hanoi" if McCarthy won. And as primary day approached, the state party regulars ran a newspaper advertisement that said: "The communists in Vietnam are watching the New Hampshire primary. . . . They are hoping for a divided America. Don't vote for fuzzy thinking and surrendering. Support our fighting men . . . by writing in the name of President Johnson."

Senator McIntyre, misrepresenting a McCarthy bill in the Senate, charged in a radio commercial that it would let "American draft dodgers . . . return home scot-free, without punishment. . . . To honor draft dodgers and deserters," he went on, "will destroy the very fabric of our national devotion. This is fuzzy thinking about principles that have made our nation great. Support the loyal men who do serve this country by writing in the name of President Johnson on your ballot."

The attacks on McCarthy's patriotism immediately backfired. A *Concord Monitor* editorial called them "little short of revolting" and the *Portsmouth Herald* deplored what it called "disgraceful political tactics." Five delegates running pledged to Johnson dissociated themselves from King's comments, saying they backed LBJ because he was the best candidate, not because he had "a monopoly on patriotism." McCarthy said "the affront to me is trivial [but] the affront . . . to the democratic process and to free debate is severe and wounding."

Even Kennedy came to McCarthy's defense—in his fashion. "The same kind of charges were made in 1960 against President Kennedy, and the present charges are as baseless now as those were then," he said. McCarthy "is setting forth his honest views of what is best for our nation," he said, but then added in maintaining his posture of neutrality, "just as President Johnson is carrying out policies which he believes are best for our nation. The motives of neither should be impugned."

A measure of the Johnsonites' nervousness as the primary approached was their prediction of how well McCarthy would have to do to claim any sort of success. They had started out saying he would be lucky to get 10 percent of the primary vote. A Gallup Poll of national sentiment in early March had Johnson running far ahead of McCarthy—70 percent to 18 in a two-man matchup. But now one of the local Johnsonites, a subcabinet bureaucrat in the Kennedy and Johnson administrations named Bernard Boutin, tried to persuade amused reporters that anything less for McCarthy than 40 percent against a write-in candidacy would be a disaster for him. "It would be a disgrace if McCarthy gets less than 40 percent," he said. "He's practically been living here. He's been campaigning with movie stars [referring to supporter Paul Newman] and beatniks from all over the Eastern seaboard, and he's spending money like Dick Nixon."

It was impossible, exposed to the runaway optimism and high spirits of the young McCarthyites in the state, not to sense that something electrifying was in the air. But Lyndon Johnson was, after all, the sitting president of the United States and Gene McCarthy was still barely known in New Hampshire. Many voters, indeed, revealed in interviews that they had him confused with Senator Joseph R. McCarthy of Wisconsin, the notorious witch-hunter of communists whose political philosophy had been diametrically opposite to that of the man from Minnesota.

* * *

Even before the voting in New Hampshire, McCarthy could claim a victory by default, when the Johnson forces decided not to enter the presidential preference primary in Massachusetts to be held on April 30. Failure to file LBJ's name or that of a prominent in-state stand-in by the March 5 deadline—Ted Kennedy obviously was not interested—appeared to cede the state's seventy-two convention delegates to McCarthy.

On the night of March 5, McCarthy added a real, if little-noticed, victory in his home state of Minnesota, where the assorted nuns, nurses, housewives and students opposing the war through his candidacy won the bulk of the 3,000 precinct caucuses. They carried every major city except Duluth and most of the delegates to the next level in the state's selection process. Neither McCarthy nor Johnson had campaigned in the state but the result was surprising nevertheless.

The regular Democratic organization leaders depended on party unity behind the president and Humphrey. "They would tend to say," McCarthy organizer David Mixner recalled, " 'Well, you're right on Lyndon, but we're gonna split the party, the Republicans will get in. And let's not embarrass Hubert. I mean, look what Hubert's done for us. . . . Why split the party in a fruitless attempt?'" But the Tet Offensive and stories from New Hampshire running in the Minnesota press about the LBJ campaign's gaffes, Mixner said, gave the McCarthyites ammunition with which to fire back.

Beyond that, there was the organizational work in behalf of McCarthy as the antiwar candidate. Mixner described the scene at one Minneapolis caucus when the chair called for the election of judges to oversee the tally: "Up came six of the nunniest-looking nuns you've ever seen for McCarthy. Who could vote against them? And they won, hands down. So here sit these six nuns up on the stage, sitting there, counting ballots. . . . There were nuns sitting next to New Left students, voting, yelling and cheering" as it was announced that "the Eighth Precinct has just voted 90 against the war, 2 for the war."

At the modest McCarthy headquarters in Minneapolis later, Mixner said, "I had one phone going to New Hampshire, yelling results in to the people in New Hampshire; I had one phone going to Washington. . . . The place was filled up. People were crying; girls were hugging each other. I just can't describe the emotion of defeating Lyndon Johnson, of defeating the war!"

The Minnesota vote did not, however, cause even a blip on the national political radar screen. But the McCarthy challenge to Johnson was stirring elsewhere as well. In California, the liberal California Democratic Council had already endorsed him, and on the same night of the Minnesota caucuses, more than 500 petition parties were held across the state to obtain signatures to put McCarthy's name and slate on the ballot for the June 5 party primary. The drive started at midnight of the first day petitions were authorized to be circulated, with notary publics and deputy registrars on hand at many of the parties, including one at The Factory, a popular discotheque in San Francisco at which more than a thousand McCarthy supporters signed up. By early in the morning, more than 30,000 names had been collected, assuring the candidate first position on the ballot.

Through it all, McCarthy resisted asking people outright to vote for him. "The people are prepared to make a judgment," he said as the New Hampshire primary date approached. "I'm not prepared to tell them what that judgment should be, but I've given my answers." Asked at one point to comment on his "lack of dynamism," he replied with customary whimsy: "I think that's a hard charge when you think we have dynamic fellows like Dick Nixon, and fellows like George Romney, setting fires all over the state. I don't want to be too different from the others."

* * *

The upbeat mood for McCarthy was not lost on Robert Kennedy. Up to this point he had declined to endorse McCarthy over LBJ, but now he defended him against charges of disloyalty, yet stopping short of an endorsement and reiterating his intention not to become a candidate himself. In fact, he had never stopped considering the possibility. When Romney dropped out, Kennedy was more convinced than ever that Nixon would be the Republican nominee, and the thought of him in the White House after defeating a vulnerable LBJ was a particular torture. And so the soul-searching had continued at Hickory Hill.

On March 5, a week before the voting in New Hampshire, Kennedy sent Dutton to sound out brother Ted, who had remained opposed to his running. It was strange on the face of it for Robert Kennedy to dispatch an emissary to discuss this most critical matter with his closest family member in politics. But he apparently wanted to be sure his brother would not be inhibited by familial loyalty in weighing the decision a final time and responding candidly. Dutton walked into Ted Kennedy's Senate office prepared to present all the latest pros and cons as conveyed to him by Robert Kennedy, when Ted told him: "Bob's just about made up his mind to run. The thing now is to make sense of it."

They walked over to Robert Kennedy's office and for three hours the three of them discussed over lunch not why he should run or why not, but for the first time in earnest and in detail when he should get in, and how. Should he announce before the New Hampshire primary results were in, or after? Here, the would-be candidate's longtime reputation as "ruthless," going back to his days as his brother John's iron-willed, curt and snappish "no man," was factored in. With reports from Kennedy loyalists in New Hampshire that McCarthy could be expected to do very well, Kennedy didn't want to appear to be pulling the rug out from under him.

Nor did he want to do anything that might undermine McCarthy's showing. After all, one of Kennedy's major inhibitions against challenging Johnson was concern that his action would be dismissed as mere personal animosity. If someone else could demonstrate LBJ's vulnerability, and a genuine desire in the country for another choice, Kennedy could with a clearer conscience join the fray.

So it was decided to delay until after the New Hampshire voting. In a modest effort to help McCarthy (and, to be sure, himself in the eyes of those who would resent his eventual entry), Kennedy again asked the amateur draft-RFK effort to desist. Also, on the morning before the vote, Kennedy supporters ran a half-page advertisement in the *Manchester Union Leader* making the same request, specifically urging voters to cast their ballots for McCarthy.

What of McCarthy himself? Kennedy wanted him to know not only that he was going to run, but that he was staying out of New Hampshire in deference to him. He asked Ted to tell him, but he wanted to wait until after the primary.

So the two brothers both told Dick Goodwin, now working for McCarthy, and asked him to pass the word. Goodwin told me later that Robert had asked him only to say that he was "thinking of running," and he did so.

"Manifesting neither surprise nor indignation," Goodwin wrote later, McCarthy "waited until I had finished, then: 'Why don't you tell him that I only want one term anyway. Let him support me now, and after that he can have it.'" When Goodwin suggested he didn't mean it, McCarthy told him: "I do mean it. I'm quite serious. I've given it a lot of thought, and it has nothing to do with Kennedy. The presidency should be a one-term office. It wouldn't be so dependent on the person."

Goodwin wrote later that in a phone conversation with Kennedy six days before the New Hampshire primary, Kennedy asked him how McCarthy was going to do there. "We're going to get at least 40 percent," Goodwin replied, "and if we had ten extra days we'd be over 40." Kennedy asked him: "How would I have done?" Goodwin told him: "You would have won 60–40." Later, Goodwin said, he learned that Kennedy had repeated the conversation to some friends, adding: "He's right. I would have won it."

By now, Kennedy was consulting with so many people, including old friends and acquaintances in the press corps, that it was obvious something was up. Among those he talked with was Walter Cronkite, the even-handed CBS television evening news anchorman who had just returned from Vietnam and had taken the unusual step for him of declaring on the air that the war was a disaster. At one point, Kennedy asked him if he was a Democrat. Cronkite told him he was an independent. What Kennedy had in mind was for Cronkite to run for his vacant Senate seat if he were to be elected president. Cronkite's immediate reply was thanks, but no thanks.

A tipoff to Kennedy's intentions came in a speech on the Senate floor on March 7. Fulbright had just made his demand that before LBJ sent 206,000 more Americans to Vietnam, the Senate should be consulted. Kennedy seconded the demand with a blistering attack. Every time there was a problem in Vietnam over the previous seven years, he said, "the answer has always been to escalate the conflict. It has always been to send more troops. And at the time we sent the larger number of troops, or increased the bombing, we have always stated that there would be light at the end of the tunnel, that victory is just ahead of us. The fact is that victory is not just ahead of us. It was not in 1961 or 1962, when I was one of those who predicted there was light at the end of the tunnel. There was not in 1963 or 1964 or 1965 or 1966 or 1967, and there is not now. . . .

"Moreover, there is a question of our moral responsibility. Are we like the God of the Old Testament that we can decide, in Washington, D.C., what cities, what towns, what hamlets in Vietnam are going to be destroyed? . . . Do we have that authority to kill tens and tens of thousands of people because we say we have a commitment to the South Vietnamese people? But have they been consulted, in Hue, in Ben Tre, or in the other towns that have been destroyed? Do we have the authority to put hundreds of thousands of people—in fact, millions of people—into refugee camps for their protection, or should these decisions be left to them?"

This time Kennedy did not shy away from criticizing Johnson. Citing corruption in the South Vietnamese military draft, he recalled that "when this was brought to the attention of the president, he replied that there was stealing in Beaumont, Texas. If there is stealing in Beaumont, Texas," Kennedy said, "it is not bringing about the death of American boys."

On Saturday, March 9, Kennedy flew to Des Moines with Peter Edelman for a fund-raising dinner for Governor Harold Hughes. Afterward, Hughes and three other Midwest governors—Robert Docking of Kansas, William Guy of North Dakota and Warren Hearnes of Missouri—and some Democratic congressmen met with Kennedy at a private reception. No one, according to some of the participants, pressed Kennedy to run. But they gave him an earful of gripes about LBJ. Their bottom line was that not only was the president in political peril himself; their own chances for reelection or for some other office were jeopardized by the prospect of having him at the head of the party ticket.

Back home on Sunday, March 10, Kennedy continued the endless conversations, in person and by phone, with friends and advisers. Among them was Ted Sorensen, his brother John's old speechwriter and alter ego who, as with several of the other old JFK aides, had been against him running. Sorensen again expressed his doubts and in the course of the conversation told Kennedy he had been asked to go to the White House the following day to see Johnson. Sorensen agreed to drop by Kennedy's office before going, and on arrival told Kennedy he had an idea that might yet dissuade the senator from running. He was going to propose to LBJ, he said, that he appoint a blue-ribbon commission to review the whole Vietnam policy. Kennedy listened.

According to Sorensen, when he was ushered into Johnson's presence he told him—clearly with Kennedy's permission—that the New York senator was seriously considering challenging him for the Democratic nomination. LBJ then asked him, Sorensen said later, whether he had any suggestions—presumably to avert that occurrence. Sorensen offered the idea of the commission on Vietnam and, according to Kennedy later, the president said "a similar idea had been advanced by a political leader," that he "welcomed the idea" and wanted Sorensen to suggest some names for the commission. The "political leader," Kennedy deduced, must have been Mayor Richard J. Daley of Chicago, who had mentioned the idea to him a few weeks earlier. Kennedy said later that Sorensen didn't get the idea from him, "did not propose me as a member and did not tie the idea in any way as to my prospective candidacy."

After the two-hour meeting, Sorensen called Kennedy and told him what Johnson had said. The commission idea was a slender reed that Kennedy could grab to pull him from the course on which he was now headed. Kenny O'Donnell told me later. "He really had a fetish about this idea that he would be breaking up the party. To suggest a commission on the war was the height of childishness. Commissions don't run wars. But he had to shut that last door." (That very day, some 50,000 American and South Vietnamese troops were launching what U.S. military authorities called the largest offensive of the war in the Saigon region.)

Still, Kennedy clung to the commission idea, even to the point of discussing with aides that day and the next—primary day in New Hampshire—the names of those who might serve effectively on it. Late that afternoon, before the polls closed in the Granite State, he boarded a plane for New York for another dinner, not knowing for certain what the outcome would be in the primary, but fairly sure it would be bad news for Lyndon Johnson—and who knew what for himself.

* * *

The morning of primary day had dawned in a typical New England winter snowstorm. In such weather, intensity of commitment usually is a major factor. The regular Democrats who were sticking it out with Johnson were no match in that regard for the zealous, upbeat McCarthy Kiddie Corps and other driven antiwar activists. At the McCarthy campaign headquarters they worked the phones diligently, urging voters out, arranging transportation for those who needed it. Meanwhile, the hardier young troops went out into the neighborhoods and towns and implored previously identified likely McCarthy voters to buck the blizzard and make the effort.

That morning in the *Union Leader*, voters had been greeted by a full-page ad that struck exactly the right tone. It said: "Think how great you'll feel tomorrow morning when you wake up and read that Gene McCarthy has won the New Hampshire primary!" A similar radio ad had been running across the state on the final two days. The McCarthy troops didn't wait until the next morning to feel great. Soon after the polls closed, it was clear that they had pulled off a political upset of immense proportions. At the Sheraton Wayfarer just across the Merrimack River from Manchester, young McCarthyites danced through the corridors declaring victory. The ultimate results were not quite that in terms of cold numbers: 49.4 percent for

Johnson on write-ins to 42.2 for McCarthy in the Democratic primary. But when Republican write-in votes for McCarthy were included, he trailed the sitting president by only 230 votes.

Beyond that, the Johnson campaign had foolishly permitted forty-five competitive filings among LBJ supporters for the twenty-four available national convention delegate slots, while the disciplined McCarthy campaign offered voters only a single slate of twenty-four. McCarthy walked away with twenty, to only four for Johnson. It was an astounding psychological blow to the president achieved by a soft-spoken, low-key senator from Minnesota who until the primary had been unknown to most New Hampshire voters.

McCarthy, for once, let some enthusiasm show when he walked into the Wayfarer's ballroom to chants of "Chi-ca-go! Chi-ca-go!" from his young campaign warriors. "People have remarked that this campaign has brought young people back into the system," he said when they had quieted down. "But it's the other way around. The young people have brought the country back into the system." He promised them that "if we come to Chicago with this strength, there will be no violence and no demonstrations, but a great victory celebration." With uncharacteristic humility, he told the kids who had worked their hearts out that "if I had failed, it would have been a great personal failure because I had the most intelligent campaign staff in the history of American politics—in the history of the world."

Johnson, addressing a Veterans of Foreign Wars dinner in Washington, dismissed the results with one-liners. He called the New Hampshire primary "the only race where anybody can enter and everybody can win . . . the only place where a candidate can claim 20 percent is a landslide and 40 percent is a mandate, and 60 percent is unanimous."

(On the Republican side, Nixon as expected won 79 percent of the vote and all eighteen national convention delegates at stake, to 11 percent for Rockefeller on write-in votes and the rest scattered among minor candidates.)

The next morning, Kennedy boarded a plane back to Washington with the full dimensions of McCarthy's remarkable accomplishment in New Hampshire just beginning to sink in. By previous arrangement, the Kennedy insiders were to gather later that afternoon at brother-in-law Steve Smith's Fifth Avenue apartment to consider any last-minute arguments against running. If none proved to be persuasive, they would set about the business of planning an announcement and the campaign kickoff. Kennedy was to return to New York for the later part of the meeting and until then keep his own counsel on his intentions. All in the Kennedy camp were sensitive to his reputation as ruthless and wanted to avoid if at all possible the appearance of horning in on McCarthy's moment of glory—a futile hope.

When Kennedy's plane arrived at National Airport, however, and the ever-diligent Sam Donaldson of ABC News accosted him with questions about how McCarthy's showing affected his own position, Kennedy inexplicably jumped the gun. "I am actively reconsidering the possibilities that are available to me," he said, "and I imagine that other people around the country are doing the same." But no one else was seriously in the picture, as Kennedy well knew.

McCarthy, flying back to Washington himself, enjoyed the congratulations of well-wishers aboard the plane—including Senator McIntyre, who had questioned his patriotism in an attempt to stem his New Hampshire surge. McCarthy accepted with a predictable coolness what the front-page headline in the *Boston Globe* on his lap proclaimed: MCCARTHY'S N.H. DREAM BECOMES LBJ NIGHTMARE. When the plane landed at National Airport, McCarthy's right-hand man, Jerry Eller, bounded aboard and handed the senator wire copy on Kennedy's remarks. "Bobby wants to see you," Eller said. "He's going to tell you he's going [to run]."

McCarthy got off the plane, into a phalanx of waiting reporters. He declined to comment on Kennedy's "reassessment." When asked whether he might step aside voluntarily if Kennedy got into the race, he replied curtly: "It might not be voluntary." Well, would he welcome Kennedy's entry? Earlier, he had indicated he would understand if that happened. Now he replied coldly: "Well, I don't know. It's a little bit crowded now." On the car ride to his Senate office, he saw a story about Kennedy's comments in one of the afternoon papers. "He wouldn't even let me have my day of celebration, would he?" he remarked. So much, at least in McCarthy's mind, for Kennedy avoiding the ruthless label.

Kennedy, back in his Senate office as the press corps set up a watch outside, began fielding some of the many phone calls and telegrams that were streaming in to him. He continued to take soundings, including some from reporters he knew and liked, who were ushered into his presence. One was Bruce Biossat, the soft-spoken Scripps-Howard columnist who was a Kennedy favorite. McCarthy's showing in New Hampshire, he confided to Biossat, had demonstrated that "the divisions in the Democratic Party are already there and I can't be blamed for creating them." There again was his concern that his candidacy would be read as a personal vendetta against Johnson, and his rationalization now that it could not, and would not, be interpreted that way.

Meanwhile, Cronkite had learned of what Kennedy had said to Donaldson and he prevailed on the senator to be interviewed for his evening news show. Again Kennedy went back to the same rationale. "I was reluctant to become

involved in this struggle because I thought it might turn into a personal conflict between President Johnson and myself," he said, "and that the issues that
I believe strongly in, and which I think are being ignored at the moment,
would be passed over."

The vote in New Hampshire, he said, had demonstrated there already was
"deep division in the Democratic Party." He also cited the administration's
stand-pat pursuit of the war, LBJ's lame reaction to the Kerner Commission
report, the prospect of Nixon's nomination and, in his view, certainty that
without drastic action the status quo would prevail.

Kennedy said that before he finally made up his mind about what he would
do, he wanted a chance to talk to McCarthy "about the future and about what
he's committed to—the policies. He's committed to bring about this change
that I think that both of us are interested in, and I would like to talk to him
about what he feels that perhaps I can contribute." Did that mean he might
just support McCarthy rather than run himself? Kennedy ducked. His insiders knew he had severe reservations about McCarthy as a candidate; that notion was the furthest thing from his mind.

A meeting was arranged in the Senate office of Ted Kennedy down the corridor from McCarthy's own. To avoid the reporters, McCarthy went to the
Senate gymnasium in the basement, then out a back door and up again to the
appointed meeting place, where Robert Kennedy was waiting. The meeting
lasted about twenty minutes and was distinctly cool. Kennedy did not explicitly say he was going to run, McCarthy said later, but it was clear enough.
Again he ticked off his justifications as McCarthy listened, not trying to
make it any easier for him.

Finally McCarthy told Kennedy he could do as he pleased; it would not affect what he himself would do. At one point, he said later, he told Kennedy
that he didn't believe he could actually win the nomination but if he did and
was elected, he only intended to serve a single term. Maybe it would be wiser
for Kennedy to wait until 1972. That one, predictably, fell on deaf ears. The
meeting broke up, according to Albert Eisele in *Almost to the Presidency*, his
excellent political biography of fellow Minnesotans McCarthy and
Humphrey, with McCarthy wisecracking: "Now at least three people in
Washington are reconsidering their candidacy."

McCarthy made clear that he had no intention of being chased out of the
race. Rather, he expressed a hope that Kennedy would "leave the primaries to
me," and to punctuate his determination said he would enter two additional
primaries, in Indiana and South Dakota. It was too late for Kennedy to file
for the Wisconsin primary, only two weeks away, but he could qualify for the
Indiana contest a month later, and McCarthy was making certain he would

have no free ride there. He did suggest, however, that if Kennedy did enter any primaries they possibly could make "joint appearances," and probably "some kind of settlement" might be worked out at the convention.

Kennedy returned to New York for the tail end of the "decision" meeting at Steve Smith's apartment. But the group gathered there, having watched the Cronkite interview, understood that the decision had for all practical purposes already been made. Or had it? Kennedy resumed calling around the country taking soundings with Democratic leaders. Mayor Daley, urging him not to enter the race, said he would call Johnson directly and try to persuade him to accept the idea of a Vietnam review commission. Daley phoned back shortly and told Kennedy, according to the senator's insiders, that the president was agreeable to the commission and was just waiting for Kennedy to submit names. Daley suggested that Kennedy contact Clifford, which he did through his brother Ted. Clifford agreed to a meeting and the next morning, Thursday, Robert Kennedy went to the Pentagon, accompanied by Sorensen.

* * *

The Kennedy strategists had decided by now that the best time for an announcement of candidacy was Saturday. It was usually a slow news day, so the event likely would dominate the front pages of the nation's big-circulation Sunday newspapers and insure offers from the Sunday television interview shows. Still, Kennedy clung to the possibility that the Vietnam commission might give him the rationale to let the cup of candidacy pass.

Clifford was as usual courtly and cordial. He listened as Kennedy and Sorensen restated the idea and Sorensen provided some blue-ribbon names: Edwin Reischauer, former ambassador to Japan; Roswell Gilpatric, former deputy secretary of defense; Carl Kaysen, former National Security Council aide to President Kennedy; General Lauris Norstad, former commander of NATO; General Matthew Ridgway, former United Nations commander in Korea; Kingman Brewster, president of Yale; and Kennedy himself. But the senator pointedly said, he reported later, that he would "willingly serve on such a commission, but I did not insist on that, and I stated that I should not be chairman."

Further discussion brought about added names—Senate Majority Leader Mike Mansfield and a Republican senator, either George Aiken of Vermont or John Sherman Cooper of Kentucky. Kennedy said later that Johnson's acceptance would signal to him "a clear-cut willingness to seek a wider path to peace in Vietnam," and thus "my declaration of candidacy would no longer be necessary. Ending the bloodshed in Vietnam is far more important to me than starting a presidential campaign."

Clifford, according to his memoir, told Kennedy directly that "it is my opinion that the possibility of your being able to defeat President Johnson for the nomination is zero," citing Henry Wallace's futile challenge to Harry Truman in 1948. He suggested that "the situation [in Vietnam] could change" before the Democratic convention, and even "if by chance you are able to gain the nomination, it will be valueless because your efforts . . . would so split the party that the Republican party would win the election easily."

Kennedy, Clifford recalled, said he had considered all that but had made up his mind. Clifford said he would talk to the president and get back to him. When Kennedy and Sorensen left, Clifford took Kennedy's recommendations to the White House. "I was never in any doubt that what it was, was an ultimatum," Clifford said later. "We talked the matter over at great length, and the president's attitude was that this is just an abandonment of his responsibility as President of the United States. The President of the United States can't select a group of citizens hand-picked by somebody else, and apparently agree in advance that these men could come in, study a problem, make a recommendation which would in turn be the president's decision. The president obviously was just as right as he could be. You wouldn't need a President of the United States if that's the way our government worked."

Johnson turned the proposal down cold. The idea of the commission, Clifford wrote later, "no matter how it was handled, in the eyes of the world it would appear to have been a political deal; second, it would give comfort to Hanoi; third, [Johnson] considered it an attempt to usurp presidential authority; fourth, the proposed membership of the commission was composed entirely of men whose opposition to the war was already known; the deck, he said, was stacked against the policy." Finally, LBJ said, according to Kennedy sources, he didn't want Kennedy on any such commission, although Kennedy had explicitly said he would not insist on being on it.

Kennedy saw no way out. It was then, he said later, that it "became unmistakably clear to me that so long as Lyndon B. Johnson was president, our Vietnam policy would consist of only more war, more troops, more killing and more senseless destruction of the country we were supposedly there to save. . . . That night I decided to run for president."

* * *

One of the first to be informed outside Kennedy's immediate circle was Lowenstein. "I can remember the conversation," Lowenstein said later. "He said, 'Al, baby, I've decided to take your advice,' And I said, 'You SOB,' I said, 'don't come around to me with your six-month late advice.' And he said, 'Oh, don't say that. That's what everybody else is saying. You can say something original. Think of something better than that.' I told him what I thought of what he had done, and he asked if I would come to see him and talk about it. And then I wobbled, and sort of stayed quiet for a minute, thinking about it. And then he said, 'You can keep me off your calendar, if you want.' Which was a reference to the fact that all during the dump Johnson period, whenever I would see Kennedy, I would be kept off his calendar, so nobody would know he had seen me. I'd always see him in an apartment or in a car going somewhere. In fact, that's one of the better illustrations of the peculiar kind of humor that made Kennedy as beloved as he was, 'Keep me off your calendar if you want.' So of course I had to laugh, and relent enough to go see him anyway."

When Lowenstein got to Hickory Hill the next night, he said, Kennedy and his strategists "weren't discussing whether he should run or not, they were putting together the announcement and the committees." Lowenstein felt that as a McCarthy supporter he should leave but Kennedy pressed him to stay, remarking, "That's stupid. We're all doing the same thing. We're trying to stop the war and beat Johnson."

According to Lowenstein, "a very vigorous argument" ensued when "many of his advisers insisted that the McCarthy candidacy would collapse, that people supporting McCarthy would switch to Kennedy right away. They never understood the depth of feeling on the issues, and therefore the depth of gratitude to McCarthy that he made the fight when Kennedy wouldn't. And they miscalculated so badly that it almost cost Kennedy the momentum he needed as a result of that miscalculation.

"They did not miscalculate about McCarthy's performance in many ways, that is to say, things about McCarthy that Kennedy said would make him an ineffective candidate; many of them were true. But the void was so great, and the gratitude was so great over someone taking on Johnson and the war, the people overlooked and concealed these problems and went on and worked for McCarthy."

A final chore before formally announcing his candidacy was for Kennedy to inform McCarthy directly, and make one last stab at accommodation. Conversations had been going on between Goodwin, still working for McCarthy, and Gans on the possibility of getting McCarthy and Kennedy to divide up the remaining primaries against Johnson rather than competing against each other at the same time. The scheme called for the two antiwar candidates to inflict all the political damage they could on LBJ and then face off against each other in the final major primary in California in early June. Gans said later that Blair Clark told him he had attained McCarthy's "assent."

At the same time, Goodwin, with his lines into the Kennedy camp, discussed the idea with Ted Kennedy and, he told me much later, with Robert Kennedy as well. "Bobby knew about it," Goodwin said. "It was fine with him." A meeting was arranged between the prospective candidate's brother and McCarthy in Green Bay, Wisconsin, that same Friday night, with Goodwin, Gans and Clark accompanying Kennedy on the plane—to the astonishment and chagrin of McCarthyites who saw them.

"I don't know how much we talked about it on the plane," Goodwin said later. "We all knew why we were going." En route, Gans said, there was more discussion over which states McCarthy and Kennedy would run in before meeting up in California for the showdown. Gans already had an organization going for McCarthy in Oregon but Ted Kennedy wanted that state for his brother, Gans recalled. Its primary immediately preceded the California primary and would have an important impact on it. Right there were the seeds of stalemate on the idea.

Airline connections were difficult and a weary Ted Kennedy and party did not arrive in Green Bay until long after midnight. McCarthy had gone to bed, leaving word, according to his wife, that he didn't want to be awakened. With Kennedy waiting in another hotel, Goodwin told Abigail and Mary McCarthy that he had had breakfast with Robert Kennedy that morning and that, since both senators wanted to oust Johnson, perhaps they could work together. Blair demanded that McCarthy be awakened and his daughter finally did rouse the reluctant candidate. While he dressed, Ted Kennedy was slipped into the hotel and the McCarthy suite by way of the freight elevator. But by this time the McCarthy press corps had smelled out the meeting.

The conversation, according to Jerry Eller later, began with some banter about the Green Bay Packers' football fortunes and the swapping of some St. Patrick's Day stories. A roomful of McCarthy insiders had assembled by now and observed the short and uncomfortable overture from Kennedy, begun with his report that his brother had decided to run.

Abigail McCarthy wrote later: "Senator Kennedy sat holding a briefcase on his knees as if he were about to open it like a lawyer or an insurance man, about to give documents to his client." Eller recalled McCarthy saying at that point, "You don't have to open that," in the fashion of an uninterested client cutting short the salesman's pitch. McCarthy told him later, Eller said, that he suspected Kennedy had a tape recorder in the briefcase.

In any event, McCarthy proceeded to tell Kennedy, Abigail McCarthy wrote, that he expected to do very well in Wisconsin and didn't need his brother's help. He said that he was committed to enter the primaries in Nebraska, Oregon and California, adding: "Of course, if we really want to challenge the president, there are primaries which have not been entered, and which it would serve a real purpose to enter"—specifically mentioning West Virginia and Louisiana, states where McCarthy was not entered.

Ted Kennedy did not pick up on the suggestion and the meeting soon broke up. "When they talked there wasn't anything to talk about," Gans said later. The matter of dividing up the primaries in the way that had been discussed on the plane "never made it into the dialogue," he said. "This was the non-meeting of the century," Eller recalled. If Kennedy had hoped to obtain McCarthy's agreement to a joint statement of conciliation and cooperation, McCarthy was having none of it.

Later, McCarthy expressed thanks to Robert Kennedy for his brother's "goodwill mission" but added that "there was no offer of any deal from him to me and certainly no response on my part except . . . that I don't intend to make any deals." When Ted Kennedy returned to Washington, Lowenstein said later he was told: "Your friend isn't interested in your plan."

* * *

The next morning, Saturday, March 16, Robert Kennedy announced his candidacy from the same ornate Senate Caucus Room on Capitol Hill from which his brother John had launched his successful 1960 bid for the presidency. It was a site doubly familiar and nostalgic for the new candidate, because it was here that he had gained public celebrity in his own right as a counsel for the Senate Labor Rackets Committee. With his wife, Ethel, and nine of their children in tow, Kennedy offered not only a statement of purpose but also another effort to combat the criticism that had already descended upon him for his entry into the race on the heels of McCarthy's success in New Hampshire.

"I do not run for the presidency merely to oppose any man," he said at the outset, "but to propose new policies. I run because I am convinced that this country is on a perilous course and because I have such strong feelings about what must be done that I am obliged to do all I can . . . because it is now unmistakably clear that we can change these disastrous, divisive policies only by changing the men who make them."

McCarthy's "remarkable New Hampshire campaign," he said, "has proven how deep are the present divisions within our party and country. Until that was publicly clear, my presence in the race would have been seen as a clash of personalities rather than issues. But now that the fight is one over policies which I have long been challenging, I must enter that race. The fight is just beginning, and I believe that I can win."

With his "ruthless" reputation clearly in mind, Kennedy sought to characterize himself as an ally rather than an opponent of McCarthy. Relating his brother's late-night trip to Green Bay, he said Ted had made clear to McCarthy "that my candidacy would not be in opposition to his, but in harmony." His objective, he said, was to "both support and expand his valiant campaign," and he urged his own friends and supporters to back McCarthy in the approaching Wisconsin and Massachusetts primaries—in neither of which had he himself qualified for the ballot.

Although he would enter the primaries in Nebraska and Oregon in May and in California in June, in all of which McCarthy was entered, Kennedy insisted that "in no state will my effort be directed against Senator McCarthy." He was running in California, he said, "in the belief, which I will strive to implement, that Senator McCarthy's forces and mine will be able to work together in one form or another." Translation: By that time, I hope McCarthy will have bowed out, throwing his support to me.

The question-and-answer session that followed revealed the skepticism, and cynicism, in the assembled press corps. Kennedy fended off a suggestion of "opportunism" by repeating that had he challenged LBJ sooner his action would have been misconstrued as personal. When it was suggested that he would so divide the party's opposition to Johnson as to insure his renomination "and make it easier for a Republican to win in November," Kennedy insisted that he would "broaden" the opposition. Well, he was asked, if that was the case why didn't he just choose "the alternative of putting your strength behind Senator McCarthy?" He said somewhat lamely that he didn't think "just supporting an individual" could generate the support that running himself could muster.

If the news conference underscored the reservations in the press corps about Kennedy's decision, the public response to the announcement seemed to bury them. Even as he and his family pushed their way through the crowds that pressed in as he left the Caucus Room, down a winding marble staircase and into a waiting car outside, it was clear that a political phenomenon had just been unleashed. In a scene full of electricity and magnetism, hands stretched out from all sides to shake the newly declared candidate's hand, to touch him, to grab some article of his clothing.

Roughly four years and four months after the flame of Camelot had been snuffed out in a Dallas motorcade, many saw an emotionally charged reigniting in Robert Kennedy's daring if late-starting candidacy. For Robert Kennedy was not the only American who saw Lyndon Johnson as usurper of a political dynasty. Never mind that Johnson had pledged to continue the JFK policies and had delivered on some important ones; he was the hard-edged, uncouth villain of the piece that went all the way back to that tragic day in Dallas that had brought him to power.

The family joined enthusiastically in reclaiming Camelot—all except Jacqueline Kennedy, who a few days later at a New York dinner party took Schlesinger aside and asked him: "Do you know what I think will happen to

Bobby?" Schlesinger, recalling the conversation in *Robert Kennedy and His Times*, said no. "The same thing that happened to Jack," she replied. ". . . There is so much hatred in this country, and more people hate Bobby than hated Jack. . . . I've told Bobby this, but he isn't fatalistic, like me."

Robert Kennedy hit the ground running. His motorcade raced from Capitol Hill to National Airport, where he caught a regularly scheduled flight to New York for the city's annual St. Patrick's Day parade. Passengers were startled to see him climb aboard followed by an unruly pack of reporters chasing the hottest political story of the day, or for that matter of recent years. On Fifth Avenue, he marched thirty-eight blocks, taking cheers from most of the crowd but also a fair smattering of boos and catcalls from onlookers who either supported the president on Vietnam or backed McCarthy and saw Kennedy, not LBJ, as the usurper.

In Green Bay, McCarthy watched the Kennedy announcement from a television station and was interviewed afterward by David Schoumacher of CBS, who asked him about a possible deal between the two antiwar candidates.

"I'm not really prepared to deal with anybody," McCarthy said. "I committed myself to a group of young people and, I thought, a rather idealistic group of adults in American society. I said I would be their candidate and I intend to run as I've committed myself to run. If a situation develops at the convention, of course, where I can't win, I will release my delegates. I don't have any other power over them anyway. I don't have a bloc of delegates whom I could trade with. If I did I wouldn't trade with them. So that, as far as I'm concerned, it will be an open and free convention. I'll run as hard as I can in every primary and stand as firm as I can at the convention. And then, if I find that I can't win, I will say to my delegates: 'You're free people, go wherever you want and make the best judgment that you can make.' "

McCarthy could not, however, resist sticking a sharp needle into his new opponent. He himself had challenged the sitting president, he said to Schoumacher, "when it seemed to me a lot of other politicians were afraid to come down onto the playing field. They were willing to stay on the mountain and light signal fires and bonfires, and dance in the light of the moon, but none of them came down. I'll tell you, it was a little lonely in New Hampshire. You were there. I walked alone. They weren't even coming in from outside; just throwing a message over the fence, you know."

In a rare observation of self-worth, McCarthy when asked about Kennedy's qualifications to be president offered that "I think I'm still the best potential president in the field." He said he thought he was "as qualified or better qualified" than John Kennedy was when he ran in 1960. Noting Robert Kennedy's association with Rusk and McNamara in the Kennedy administration, he remarked that "I don't see that association with those two members of the cabinet would particularly prepare one to deal well with the problem of Vietnam."

(Long afterward, McCarthy told me of Kennedy's entry into the race: "It changed the whole character of the campaign, especially when he almost immediately began campaigning against me. . . . If Bobby had said he was going to come in or might come in, we would have run a slightly different campaign, but we had a commitment from him that he wouldn't come in. He said it publicly, and he said it to me. We shook hands and that was it." Once Kennedy was in, McCarthy went on, "we realized we weren't going to be able to keep the campaign on the issue [of the war] the way we wanted to, and see what would happen on the issue rather than the question of getting nominated. Immediately the press said, 'Can he [McCarthy] beat Kennedy?' It really had nothing to do with the [war] issue. It just fouled up the whole campaign.")

Indeed, McCarthy's New Hampshire showing had generated an impressive transfusion of campaign money and student volunteers into Wisconsin for the next primary on April 2. To an offer from Kennedy to campaign for him in Wisconsin, McCarthy was notably disdainful. "I really don't think it would be very helpful," he told reporters. But he said he would accept the support of Kennedy backers as long as it was "not in his name, but under my banner." If Kennedy wanted to help, he suggested, it might have been better for him to enter primaries where McCarthy was not challenging Johnson, rather than contesting against McCarthy in Nebraska, Oregon and California down the road.

Later, wryly dismissing Kennedy's candidacy, McCarthy observed: "I don't need a stalking horse at this point. We don't need the money. We don't need organization. I just need running room." Asked in Milwaukee whether he had seen any evidence of defections from his staff to the Kennedy camp, McCarthy quipped that he had not, but "I notice that Dick Goodwin has a very large suitcase . . . he might have a change of clothes for another climate. But I am not sure. I haven't looked into it. It might be empty."

Johnson tried to toss the Kennedy challenge off with a quip of his own. "These are days when we have to take chances," he said. "Some speculate in gold—a primary metal—and others just speculate in primaries."

But in a conversation with Doris Kearns (later Goodwin), recounted in her book *Lyndon Johnson and the American Dream*, Johnson confided later that "I felt that I was being chased on all sides by a giant stampede coming at me from all directions. On one side, the American people were stampeding me to do something about Vietnam. On another side, the inflationary economy was booming out of control. Up ahead were dozens of danger signs pointing to another summer of riots in the cities. I was being forced over the edge by rioting blacks, demonstrating students, marching welfare mothers, squawking professors and hysterical reporters. And then the final straw. The thing I feared from the first day of my presidency was actually coming true. Robert Kennedy had openly announced his intention to reclaim the throne in the memory of his brother. And the American people, swayed by the magic of the name, were dancing in the streets. The whole situation was unbearable for me."

Still, in public, Johnson continued his trademark bravado. In a speech in Minneapolis, he vowed to fight on in Vietnam and to wage "a total national effort" against the enemy. "Make no mistake about it," he roared, "we are going to win. . . . We love nothing more than peace, but we hate nothing worse than surrender and cowardice. . . . We don't plan to surrender or let people divide our nation in time of national peril." Two days later, at a State Department conference, it was more of the same. "Today we are the Number One nation," he proclaimed. "And we are going to stay the Number One nation."

(McCarthy, reflecting much later on the impact of his showing in the New Hampshire primary, suggested that in a way doing so well had had an adverse effect in terms of shortening the war. "I thought that maybe a third of the Democrats didn't want the war and this would give them a chance to show it," he told me. Had he received only a third of the primary vote rather than nearly beating Johnson, he said, "it may have given [Johnson] a chance to make some compromises on the war. But when we beat him [sic], it was all in the pit." That is, Johnson then would have been perceived as acting out of political weakness at home had he made any concessions on his Vietnam policy.)

*   *   *

At approximately the time Kennedy was entering the race, halfway around the globe an incident was taking place unknown to him or most other Americans. It underscored in the most horrifying terms not only that the war was going to go on, but also that the conduct of some Americans in the field in Vietnam had sunk to stupefyingly barbaric proportions.

In the village of Son My in the coastal province of Quang Ngai, there was a small hamlet called My Lai but nicknamed "Pinkville" by the Americans for its suspected concentration of communists. There, on this day, more than one hundred unarmed Vietnamese inhabitants, including women and children, were slaughtered in cold blood—"wasted" in the common vernacular of the U.S. forces in Vietnam at this time. The Army issued a routine communiqué saying "128 enemy soldiers" had been killed in the operation, with no reference whatever to civilians. The figure was duly reported that way on the March 17 front page of the *New York Times,* which also chronicled Kennedy's entry into the competition for the Democratic presidential nomination.

The story from Saigon said "American troops caught a North Vietnamese force in a pincer movement on the central coast plain," and it described heavy artillery attacks against the area followed by the dropping of American troops by helicopter. "While the two companies of United States soldiers moved in on the enemy from opposite sides," the story went on, "heavy artillery barrages and armed helicopters were called in to pound the North Vietnamese soldiers. . . . It was not made clear how many of the enemy had been killed by the artillery and helicopter attacks, and how many were shot down by the American infantrymen."

Later the Army estimated that 109 civilians died, but survivors in Son My told American newsmen more than a year and a half later, when the atrocity came to light, that 567 were killed. The figure was arrived at by taking the known population of the hamlet and subtracting the number of survivors—132.

Survivors said later that after a one-hour artillery barrage on the suspected Vietcong stronghold, the American troops entered it. They dynamited or burned down all the houses, lined up the villagers in three groups about 200 yards apart and about twenty soldiers executed them with M-16 rifles and other weapons. South Vietnamese and American Army officials at first insisted that those killed were Vietcong or Vietcong ammunition carriers. But some American soldiers present eventually came forward and denied seeing any men of military age in the hamlet.

One of the soldiers, former Private First Class Michael B. Terry, told the *Washington Post* later that he had participated in the firing and that afterward "some of them were still breathing. . . . They weren't going to get any medical help and so we shot them. Shot maybe five of them. . . . I thought that was the best thing I could do."

Another participant, Paul D. Meadlo, said he had personally killed between thirty-five and forty women with his rifle upon orders from his platoon leader, First Lieutenant William L. Calley, and his squad leader, Staff Sergeant David Mitchell. Taking part, he told CBS-TV, "was the natural thing to do at the time. My buddies getting killed or wounded—we weren't getting no satisfaction from it, so what it really was, it was mostly revenge."

(Eventually Calley, commander of the First Platoon of Company C, First Battalion, 20th Infantry, 11th Infantry Brigade, and Mitchell, leader of the platoon's first squad, were indicted in the incident. Calley was charged with premeditated murder and Mitchell with assault with intent to kill. The investigation into the My Lai massacre resulted from a letter from a Vietnam War veteran named Ronald Ridenhour.

(The true nature of the episode did not come to the attention of the American public until November 1969, when an exclusive story was written for a little-known independent news service by Seymour Hersh, who at the time of the incident was McCarthy's press secretary. The Army, however, had heard about it a year earlier when a soldier in Calley's brigade named Tom Glen wrote a letter to the Americal Division headquarters providing some details. The division's deputy operations officer, Major Colin Powell, who had arrived in Vietnam three months after the episode, drafted the Army's official response. Without having interviewed the soldier, he dismissed the report as rumor.

(Calley insisted at the trial that his company commander, Captain Ernest L. Medina, had specifically ordered that all inhabitants be killed, which Medina denied. Calley said he had no regrets because "they were all the enemy. They were all to be destroyed." He eventually was court-martialed and sentenced to life imprisonment for the premeditated murder of at least twenty-two South Vietnamese civilians. Shortly after the verdict in March 1971, then President Richard Nixon said he would personally review the case "before any final sentence is carried out." Calley's sentence later was reduced and he was paroled in November 1974. Mitchell was acquitted of the charge against him in November 1970.)

* * *

Kennedy had no such single episode to justify his decision to challenge Johnson on the war. He needed none, so intense was his feeling against what was going on in Vietnam that he, and the American people at large, did not know about.

The next day, Sunday, March 17, after interviewers on NBC's *Meet the Press* pounded him for not having supported McCarthy in New Hampshire if his opposition to Johnson's Vietnam policies was so compelling, Kennedy went to Boston for another St. Patrick's Day parade. He was the senator from New York but this, everyone understood, was homecoming. The crowds along the route in South Boston were warmer than those the day before in his "home state."

Kennedy, returning to New York late that afternoon to start his first full-fledged campaign swing, was asked about a report by Roger Mudd of CBS News that he had finally entered the race because Johnson had rejected his Vietnam commission scheme. Then, and later aboard the commercial jet carrying him and his campaign party to Kansas, he patiently explained to reporters traveling with him his version of what had happened. Regular passengers gaped at the spectacle of a presidential candidate in shirtsleeves walking up and down the plane's aisle, perching on the arm of his seat as he fielded question after question from the press.

Contrary to any White House suggestion that he was trying to blackmail the president, Kennedy insisted that he had only responded to an LBJ initiative. "I didn't want to run for president," he insisted. "But when he made it clear the war would go on, that nothing was going to change, I had no choice."

Kennedy's decision gained immediate public support. In a Gallup Poll conducted before he took the final step and released on the Saturday of his announcement, he was the choice for president of 44 percent of all Democrats surveyed to 45 for Johnson in a two-man matchup. Among all voters polled, it was a dead heat between them, at 41 percent apiece.

Kennedy's arrival at the Kansas City, Missouri, airport that night, his first venture as a presidential candidate outside his Eastern seaboard backyard into heartland conservatism, was astonishing. The stop was to be only a transfer point, where he and Ethel Kennedy were to board the awaiting private plane of Governor Docking. Floodlights bathed Kennedy's taxiing plane as it came up to the terminal and a huge crowd surged past protective fences to the bottom of the ramp. When he emerged and started down the ramp, brushing one tousled forelock back from his eyes in a characteristic mannerism, the air was filled with shrieks, cheers and applause.

From a lower step, he addressed the crowd in words that were drowned out in the welcoming noise. With his chief advance man, Jerry Bruno, clearing a path, he and Ethel pushed their way toward the terminal, the senator grabbing or just touching outstretched hands. Finally he gave up, turned and pushed his way through more hands to Docking's small blue-and-white Cessna, his wife still in tow, for a short flight to Topeka, where it was more of the same.

There, an estimated crowd of 2,000 lined the airport fence and Kennedy walked along it, pumping hands, studying faces as he went, as if he were trying to read what his greeters were thinking. Was all this an outpouring of pent-up opposition to the war, or merely of nostalgia for the return of Camelot? Whichever, Frank Mankiewicz, his press secretary, alluding to Johnson's confining of his own trips around the country to secure military installations, grinned and remarked: "It sure beats those Army bases."

Kennedy, his shirtsleeves shorn of his gold cuff links by now, climbed an airline ramp and shouted into a bullhorn. "I come to ask for your help," he said, the word coming out "ahsk" in his New England accent. "We have a hard five months ahead and the odds are heavily against us. . . . I run just basically because I think the United States can do better. . . . We don't need to accept the divisions between races, between age groups, the divisions over the war in Vietnam. I need your help! I need your assistance!"

There was a plaintive quality to his appeal, delivered in a high-pitched voice as he pounded one fist into the palm of his other hand. He knew he was late in making his move, maybe too late. So he would make up for the tardiness with urgency, with energy, with an emotionalism that now came easily to him, after all the months of restraint and caution born of concern that his opposition to Johnson would be misunderstood—or politically self-destructive. All the past stops were pulled now, and it was all-out to end the war—and the presidency of Lyndon Johnson.

Along the fence in the chilly night, I asked a local farmer, Stan Mitchell, how he felt about Kennedy getting into the race on the heels of McCarthy's success. "I don't care how he got in," he said. "Just so he got in."

The next day, Monday, March 18, marked one of the most memorable and emotional days of the entire Kennedy campaign yet to unfold. It might have been expected that Kennedy would launch his campaign outside the East in some anti–Vietnam War hotbed such as San Francisco or Madison, Wisconsin. But before his declaration of candidacy, he had been scheduled to speak on this day at Kansas State University in Manhattan and Kansas University in Lawrence. The simplest thing to do in light of the lack of time to lay out a campaign schedule was to go ahead with the one already planned.

At the KSU field house, a crowd estimated by police to number 14,500 students and faculty jammed every available corner, with some college kids literally hanging from the steel rafters, their feet dangling over the side. At the outset, it was far from an all-Kennedy gathering. One sign asked: RFK: LEADER OF YOUTH OR REBELLIOUS OPPORTUNIST? Another proclaimed: GENE FOR INTEGRITY. And still others declared: RFK PROLONGS THE WAR and FATHER HO LOVES BOBBY. But there were pro-Kennedy signs as well, if not of the serious ilk that he hoped his candidacy would inspire. One said: I LOVE BOBBY; another, KISS ME, BOBBY; still others: BOBBY IS GROOVY; BOBBY IS SEXY; SOCK IT TO 'EM, BOBBY.

Kennedy started on the light side. The differences he had with Johnson on the Vietnam commission, he said, were minor: "I wanted Senators Mansfield, Fulbright and Morse, and the president, in his own inimitable way, he wanted General Westmoreland, John Wayne and [pro-LBJ movie actress] Martha Raye."

But it was all hardball after that. In a speech that would serve as a framework for the rest of his campaign, Kennedy laid bare not only all his arguments but also all his emotions regarding the political and moral calamity that had beset his country in the nearly five years since the death of his brother and the ascendancy of Lyndon Johnson. He did not dwell on Camelot Usurped except by implication. But the spectacle of another, younger Kennedy finally challenging the man who had taken his brother's place was not lost on the audience, or on the large contingent of national reporters who had signed on for what promised to be a political roller-coaster ride.

Clearly from the start, we were not going to be disappointed. Among Kennedy's traveling speechwriters were Walinsky and Greenfield, two impatient members of the tempestuous 1960s generation who had long urged Kennedy to run. They were now giving vent to their own pent-up sentiments by way of the texts they were writing for him.

"If in this year of choice we fashion new politics out of old illusions," Kennedy began, "we insure for ourselves nothing but crisis for the future— and we bequeath to our children the bitter harvest of those crises. For with all we have done, with all our immense power and richness, our problems seem to grow not less, but greater. We are in a time of unprecedented turbulence, of danger and questioning. It is at its root a question of national soul."

It was this national soul, he said, that was at stake in Vietnam. It was not his objective "to sell out America's interests, to simply withdraw, to raise the white flag of surrender," he said, to loud and sustained applause. "But I am concerned . . . that the course we are following at the present time is deeply wrong. . . . I am concerned that, at the end of it all, there will only be more Americans killed, more of our treasure spilled out, and because of the bitterness and hatred on every side of this war, more hundreds of thousands of Vietnamese slaughtered; so that they may say, as Tacitus said of Rome: 'They made a desert and called it peace.' I don't think that's satisfactory for the United States of America. I do not think that is what the American spirit is really about. I do not think that is what this country stands for."

Kennedy acknowledged up front his own early responsibility in helping to shape Vietnam policy in his brother's administration. "But past error is no excuse for its own perpetuation," he said, citing as misguided the call for sending 206,000 more Americans to Vietnam to assist a regime in which corruption was rampant. "The facts are that 18-year-old South Vietnamese are still not being drafted," he said to his largely draft-age audience, "though now, as many times in the past, we are assured that this will happen very, very soon. The facts are that thousands of young South Vietnamese buy their deferments from military service while American Marines die at Khesanh. I don't find that acceptable. If the South Vietnamese government feels Khesanh is so important, let them put South Vietnamese soldiers in there and let them take the American soldiers out!"

Kennedy shouted this last demand, pounding his fist, drawing a roar of approval from the crowd. The fact was that it was the American authorities who felt the Khe Sanh base was critical to defend and South Vietnamese forces who were involved. But Kennedy had a point to make, and he made it.

Recalling the American commander who had said of the village of Ben Tre that it was "necessary to destroy the town in order to save it," he thundered: "I'm responsible and you're responsible because this action is taken in our name. . . . We must ask our government, we must ask ourselves: where does such logic end? If it becomes 'necessary' to destroy all of South Vietnam to 'save' it, will we here in the United States do that too? Is that what we want? And if we care so little about South Vietnam that we are willing to see the land destroyed and its people dead, then why are we there in the first place?"

The field house was rocking with applause now as he called for an end to the bloodshed and a negotiated peace with the National Liberation Front, making a special and direct appeal to the students: "You are the people, as President Kennedy said, who have 'the least ties to the present and the greatest stake in the future.' I urge you to learn the harsh facts that lurk behind the mask of official illusion with which we have concealed our true circumstances, even from ourselves. . . . There is a contest on, not for the rule of America but for the heart of America. In these next eight months, we are going to decide what this country will stand for, and what kind of men we are. . . . I ask for your help!"

At the Phog Allen Field House at Kansas University, an even larger crowd of 17,000 awaited him—the largest political gathering in the school's history. He gave the audience a reprise of the earlier speech with the same thunderous reaction. Those of us who had heard the first version could see how he was deftly playing on the response that certain lines had generated, lifting the crowd to a higher level of emotionalism and in the process rising to it himself. Gone for the moment in all the fervor were the reservations and concerns about the late start, about the "personal vendetta" against LBJ, about the "ruthlessness" of jumping in on the heels of McCarthy's triumph. Maybe, in this conservative heartland, the votes would not be there for this liberal Democrat. But there seemed little doubt that Kennedy's deep feelings about the abomination of Vietnam were widely shared even here, and could provide the framework for an effective campaign everywhere in the country.

(Those feelings also were shared abundantly at Georgetown, where on March 20 student Bill Clinton was reclassified 1-A by his county draft board back in Hot Springs, Arkansas. His chances of completing a Rhodes Scholarship he had been awarded in England did not look good.)

* * *

Johnson, meanwhile, held firm on his war policy. In a speech in Minneapolis, the president was so harsh on his critics that one of his most faithful political advisers, James L. Rowe Jr., wrote him a memo telling him he was "shocked by the number of calls I received today in protest against your Minneapolis speech. Our people on the firing line in Wisconsin said it hurt us badly. A number of 'doves' called me to say they were against the president because of his Vietnam policy but were not resentful or bitter until the Minneapolis speech called them traitors."

Rowe wrote Johnson point-blank that "hardly anyone today is interested in winning the war. Everyone wants to get out and the only question is how." Rowe warned Johnson that he could lose the Wisconsin primary and he "must do something dramatic (not gimmicky) before the Wisconsin primary" to counter the impression that "McCarthy and Kennedy are the candidates of peace and the president is the war candidate."

When LBJ unexpectedly announced on the night of March 22 that the commander of all American forces in Vietnam, General Westmoreland, would be relieved and would become the Army chief of staff, columnist Joseph Alsop from Saigon hastened to blame Kennedy. "General Westmoreland has been replaced at a moment when a shameful, humiliating and quite irrational defeatism prevails at home, typified by Senator Robert Kennedy's talk of a war without end," he wrote. "Yet the facts—above all, the facts concerning the enemy's Tet offensive—point in just the opposite direction. . . . After touching every useful base, this reporter can state unequivocally that no seriously informed person in Saigon doubts that the Tet offensive was a play from weakness rather than from strength. Hanoi concluded that . . . Westmoreland was winning his 'war of attrition.' Hanoi therefore decided to go all out for short-range success."

* * *

As Kennedy took his case against Johnson to the country, there were new stirrings now on the Republican side. Ever since Romney's withdrawal and Rockefeller's statement of availability, moderate Republicans were conspiring to bring the New Yorker into the race. The conservative Goldwater, remembering Rockefeller's attempts to take the party nomination from him in 1964 and his subsequent refusal to support him against Johnson, declared that "I and fellow conservatives want no part of Rockefeller" and "I don't know how I could support him." But Reagan, who was no Rockefeller-lover either, took issue and he pledged he would support the party nominee. Goldwater then said he would do the same, but that he preferred Nixon.

On March 10, about thirty leading moderate Republicans had met with Rockefeller in New York, and the following week seventeen GOP senators had breakfast with him in Washington. The night before that meeting, Spiro Agnew, who remained Rockefeller's most enthusiastic cheerleader among the governors, met him at National Airport and took him to a dinner of the Order of Ahepa, a Greek society. The crowd mobbed the grinning, glad-handing Rockefeller, convincing Agnew, who preferred to be called by his middle name "Ted," not only that Rockefeller was going to run, but also that he could win regardless of his late start.

At the breakfast with the senators, however, Rockefeller got much less encouragement than he had hoped for. According to George Hinman, his chief political aide, the New Yorker "was rather chilled by their approach to the whole thing. The idea," Hinman related later, "was, 'Why, sure, go in and give Nixon a race. It will help him.' That wasn't exactly what the governor was looking for." After the second meeting, nevertheless, the *New York Times* reported that Rockefeller had decided to take the step and would announce his candidacy at a news conference in New York on March 21.

The timing was critical. If Rockefeller were to run, his best chance of beating Nixon would be in the Oregon primary in late May; he had after all won there over (absentee) Goldwater in 1964 and the state had a reputation for distinctly liberal-to-moderate politics. But before then, there was Nebraska, a Nixon stronghold whose last filing date was March 15, a week before Oregon's closing date. By waiting until March 21, Rockefeller would finesse Nebraska and still get under the wire in Oregon.

The alert Nixon strategists, however, tried to get Nebraska officials to extend the state's filing deadline. At first they refused, but when Kennedy's insiders decided they wanted to enter their man in Nebraska, they managed to get the Nebraskans to hold the rolls open an extra day for Kennedy, who was announcing on March 16, to qualify. Having done that, the Nebraska officials, on hearing that Rockefeller was about to announce his entry on March 21, felt they couldn't ignore it, so they agreed to keep open the deadline until Rockefeller was a declared candidate too.

Agnew, while being Rockefeller's most outspoken proponent among the Republican governors, was not an insider in the Rockefeller political camp. He knew little of the strategizing that was going on but he too recognized the potential peril of Nebraska. He told reporters he hoped Rockefeller wouldn't be forced to go into the state because it was "probably the top state for Nixon in the whole country." But whether he did or didn't go into the

Nebraska primary, Agnew was four-square for him, and he waited eagerly for Rockefeller's declaration, which was to be televised nationally.

That eagerness was soon to be a major unwitting factor in how the politics of 1968 would evolve. The cocksure Agnew, proud of the role he had played in bringing Rockefeller to the brink of presidential candidacy after long months of trying, decided to do a little crowing. He scheduled a news conference in his State House office in advance of the Rockefeller announcement, then invited the Annapolis press corps to stay and watch it with him on his office television set. He wanted to be sure they were present for his moment of triumph—and to duly report it in detail to the voters of Maryland.

At the end of his own news conference, Agnew was asked: "Governor, has Governor Rockefeller indicated to you what he plans to say at his press conference today?" Agnew replied: "No, he hasn't, and I'm just as glad, to tell you the truth. I haven't really placed any heavy pressure on him to let me know what his decision is because, at the moment, it's more comfortable to be in the dark."

As the Maryland reporters stood in a wide arc around him, Agnew sat before the black-and-white television set and watched a glowing Rockefeller enter the rear of the New York Hilton ballroom amid wild cheering from supporters. "I'm just as much in the dark as all of you," he repeated, but the way he said it suggested otherwise to the assembled newsmen.

Then, as he heard his hero proclaim his intentions, some of them thought they saw Agnew's jaw drop. Others thought a barely perceptible sick grin crossed his face for an instant. "I have decided to reiterate unequivocally," Rockefeller said to a disbelieving, groaning audience, "that I am not a candidate campaigning directly or indirectly for the presidency of the United States."

Agnew just sat there, frozen, as Rockefeller spelled out the reasons for his surprise decision. "Quite frankly," he said, "I find it clear at this time that a considerable majority of the party's leaders wants the candidacy of former Vice President Richard Nixon. And it appears equally clear that they are keenly concerned and anxious to avoid any such divisive challenge within the party as marked the 1964 campaign. It would therefore be illogical and unreasonable for me to try and arouse their support by pursuing the very course of action that they least want and most deplore."

Agnew was clearly dumbfounded as Rockefeller continued: "At precisely this time the Democratic Party, while in control of both the executive and legislative branches, threatens to be torn asunder. How should a responsible Republican act in a period of such crisis? I cannot believe that the Republican retort to the Democratic scene should be, 'Any din that you can raise, we can raise higher.'"

But Rockefeller wasn't closing the door entirely. "I have said that I stood ready to answer any true and meaningful call from the Republican Party to serve it and the nation," he declared. "I still so stand. I would be derelict or uncandid were I to say otherwise. I expect no such call and I shall do nothing in the future by word or deed to encourage such a call." And lest his good friend Spiro Agnew had any ideas about persevering, without mentioning his colleague from Maryland he added: "We live in an age when the word of a political leader seems to invite instant and general suspicion. I ask to be spared any measure of such distrust. I mean I shall abide by precisely what I say."

Rockefeller concluded by saying he had already sent telegrams to existing Rockefeller-for-President groups expressing "my deep appreciation to them for their faith and their effort and their work," but asking them "to desist." The crestfallen Agnew apparently never got his. "This comes as a complete surprise to me," he said to his assembled guests, who by now had concluded the same from the look on his face. "I must confess I am tremendously surprised. I also frankly add that I am greatly disappointed." Aides said later Agnew had elaborate remarks prepared spelling out how he intended to get Rockefeller nominated, but they were useless now.

How could Nelson have done this to him? Deciding after all the buildup not to run was one thing. But not giving Agnew warning so that he would not make a fool of himself before the Annapolis press corps was another. He told the reporters that he would comply with Rockefeller's wishes and close down the draft-Rockefeller operation he had launched in Maryland. What seemed to hurt as much as anything else was the fact that Agnew had learned of the decision the same way, and at the same time, as did millions of ordinary Americans. After the way he had gone out on a limb for Rockefeller, it was downright humiliating; downright insulting.

Agnew's secretary said later that two phone calls had come in from Rockefeller's office, one to alert him that Rockefeller would be calling him, and a second one saying Rockefeller was sorry he couldn't talk to him because he had too much to do. Agnew did get a phone call while he was watching Rockefeller on television. It was from waspish Governor Tom McCall of Oregon, another Rockefeller fan, who only added to Agnew's dour mood by ribbing him: "I'll bet your wattles are as red as an old turkey gobbler's!" But Agnew clearly was in no mood for levity.

The treatment he suffered was particularly galling because he was the designated head of a Rockefeller-for-President organization established by the New Yorker's political strategists after his March 1 statement of availability.

They had decided it would be wise to have some sort of unofficial organization to keep tabs on grassroots interest in Rockefeller while they appraised his chances. They chose Agnew to head it—but only after one other, former Governor William Scranton of Pennsylvania, declined and a second, Indiana businessman J. Irwin Miller, was considered and bypassed as too much of a political novice. So Agnew had reason to think he was special—while not knowing he was only the third choice for the job.

Agnew suddenly was a political jockey without a horse, and a bitter one at that. He was a man of immense pride, and he had been treated shabbily before the whole political world—and particularly in his own state of Maryland. Rockefeller's decision suddenly faced him with the possibility of losing control of his own national convention delegation. Representative Rogers Morton of Maryland was already solidly in the Nixon camp and an increasingly influential figure in the party.

The whole episode, however, was destined to have a most serendipitous effect on Agnew's already fortune-filled political career. It so happened that among those who recognized Agnew's political humiliation was John Sears, the young political operative from Nixon's law firm. At the time of Rockefeller's surprise withdrawal, Sears was in Alaska wooing Governor Walter Hickel to the Nixon camp. He immediately called Nixon and urged him to send an emissary to Annapolis to stroke Agnew while he was still seething at Rockefeller. Nixon agreed and dispatched his longtime associate in Congress, Bob Ellsworth of Kansas, to Annapolis, where Ellsworth persuaded Agnew to go to New York later in the month for a face-to-face meeting with Nixon.

Agnew had already indicated a certain receptiveness by saying at the time of Rockefeller's no-go decision that while "I don't have anyone who's running at the moment that I can support . . . I am not against Mr. Nixon. He may—may—even be my Number Two choice." A month earlier, he had told me much the same in an interview in his Baltimore office. "I don't have a thing against him," he said of Nixon. "I like him."

But Agnew did have an early bad impression. Back in late 1965, when he was still Baltimore County executive, according to former aide E. Scott Moore, Agnew wrote to Nixon trying to sound him out on his political plans, although he didn't know the man at the time. "He wrote him about November and didn't get an answer until maybe January or February," Moore told me later. "This was when Nixon was in his law firm. I can remember Ted yet, saying, 'That damn Nixon, he won't even answer your letters. No wonder he can't get elected.'"

* * *

Although Spiro Agnew in light of his very public courtship of Rockefeller had been widely identified as a fellow liberal, he was at this time displaying quite different ideological colors. His liberal image was largely based on the fact that in his successful race for governor in 1966 he had run against an ultraconservative, unreconstructed segregationist named George P. Mahoney who had won the Democratic nomination in a three-way race under the slogan "A Man's Home Is His Castle—Protect It." The motto advertised Mahoney's outspoken opposition to open housing, supported by his two opponents. In the racial unease of the day marked by white fears of integrated neighborhoods, it carried him to victory by less than 2,000 votes.

The Democratic nomination in Maryland was nearly always tantamount to election, but in this case appalled Democrats flocked to the only alternative standing between Mahoney and the governorship—Republican Spiro Agnew, the rather innocuous Baltimore County executive. Lost in the panic over the prospect of a Governor Mahoney was the fact that Agnew himself had specifically said that "if an open-housing bill affecting the right of the individual homeowner to sell to whomever he wishes is passed, I would veto it." He later backed off the statement, but the message went out to conservatives that while he was no Mahoney, he was no flaming liberal either. The fact that a liberal third candidate was in the race as an independent may have had something to do with Agnew's fuzziness on the issue, and a staff memo urged him simply to dodge open-housing questions from then on.

At the outset of the general election campaign, Agnew had pledged to stay on the high road, but he found that a flow of lofty position papers and dignity on the stump were getting him nowhere. His media adviser, Bob Goodman of Baltimore, wrote in an internal memo that "we are facing an opponent who has an emotional issue and we agree that the best way that we can overcome it is with an even stronger, longer, deeper, wider, even more emotional campaign than that of his opponent."

Goodman, taking note of a recent Ku Klux Klan meeting at which many Mahoney stickers were displayed, went on: "This issue is that of the KKK and the fanatical extremists who are supporting the candidacy [of Mahoney]."

Agnew seized the advice with zest. When Mahoney refused to debate him, Agnew said he was running a "yellow, skulking, slinky campaign" and suggested that a better campaign slogan would be, as in a popular toothpaste ad of the time, "I wonder where the yellow went." In a preview of things to come, Agnew called the Mahoney slogan against open housing "a veil of voodoo" and he told of "robed figures" and "fright peddlers" who had targeted him and his family with threatening letters and phone calls. He said

Mahoney's platform was "a two-pronged pitchfork based on incompetence and bigotry."

The voters of Maryland agreed, electing Agnew by just short of 82,000 votes, or 49.5 percent in the three-man race. The day after was his forty-eighth birthday and friends held a luncheon in his honor. An old friend, Bud Hammerman, presented Agnew as a man who one day would be introduced "as President of the United States," and everybody grinned, including the principal guest.

As governor, Agnew proved to be, in his first year, a man of modest goals and temperament, so much so that the Annapolis correspondent of the *Washington Post* wrote on his first anniversary that he remained "the possessor of an untarnished good-guy image . . . a good guy who wears a white hat that has barely begun to get dusty." And his championing of Nelson Rockefeller for the presidency had only embellished that image, especially in liberal eyes.

But there was one front on which Agnew's attitudes appeared to be taking an increasingly conservative turn—dealing with racial protest and civil rights. He was instrumental in watering down one open-housing bill, and when some black leaders began to speak out more forcefully against the Vietnam War he warned them that their comments were hurting the legislation's chances.

He greeted a call by Martin Luther King for a summer protest against the war by saying he had lost all confidence in him, adding that he never had any in Stokely Carmichael. The state's Interdenominational Alliance sent him a telegram saying his "intemperate and inconsistent pronouncements constitute an affront and a disservice to a cross section of the Maryland community which supported you in your bid for office when extremism was close to victory."

Agnew's new hard line was seen again when H. Rap Brown delivered a bitter and vitriolic antiwhite speech in Cambridge, Maryland, inciting his listeners "to get your guns" and "if you gotta die, wherever you go, take some of them with you." Police fired pellets at the crowd, slightly wounding Brown. A fire broke out in the black section of town and spread toward the white business section, with the all-white fire department declining to enter the black section and instead stationing itself at the business section. Only when the state attorney general, Francis Burch, climbed onto a fire truck and urged its driver into the burning area was official relief given.

Before daybreak, Agnew arrived in Cambridge and immediately ordered Brown's arrest, saying, "I hope they pick him up soon, put him away and throw away the key." Brown was charged with inciting a riot and inciting to burn, and a few days later was picked up by the FBI as a "fugitive felon" and released on bond. Whereupon Agnew announced that "it shall now be the policy of this state to immediately arrest any person inciting a riot and not to allow that person to finish his vicious speech." When civil liberties activists protested, Agnew backed off, instructing state police not to "abridge anyone's right to speak on any subject that he wants." But his developing law-and-order sentiments were surfacing increasingly.

As for accommodation and conciliation with protesting blacks, Agnew specified that "the violent cannot be allowed to sneak unnoticed from the war dance to the problem-solving meeting." When he submitted his 1968 legislative agenda, Agnew included bills that would give his office more power to deal with riots. He acknowledged that "intimidation" of lawbreakers was his objective. It was in this frame of mind that he tackled a confrontation to his authority in late March, two days before Rockefeller's withdrawal of availability that so jolted Agnew's political equilibrium.

A few weeks earlier, Agnew had received a letter from a young black man named Roland Smith, the student body president of Bowie State College, expressing the students' growing impatience with the dilapidated state of their dormitories and classroom facilities. An aide replied to Smith that the college's operating budget had been nearly doubled under Agnew and was at its highest ever. It was true, but the increase was required because enrollment had mushroomed.

On March 15, about forty students had met to air their gripes and a mood of tension built, finally triggered into open rebellion by the refusal of tenure to a particularly popular young history professor. On March 27, Smith led more than 200 students in a peaceable boycott that shut down classes and produced sit-in protests across the small campus. Some ninety students from predominantly black Howard University in Washington, D.C., which had just had a similar five-day strike, came to lend moral support. The protest leaders demanded that Agnew come and see the campus conditions himself.

But Ted Agnew was not one to be ordered about by a bunch of disruptive students. He sent an emissary, a fast-talking real estate developer and friend named Charles Bresler who only further ignited the situation. He responded to demands for Agnew's presence by pulling out a cigarette lighter and offering it to the students to burn the place down, as some of them were threatening. The college president, Dr. Samuel L. Myers, later told me Bresler's visit "was a fiasco [that] rubbed the students the wrong way." In a few days the campus takeover was complete, with Agnew still refusing to go there.

The Bowie State confrontation was much in Agnew's mind when he met Nixon in New York on March 29. For more than two hours, the two Republicans talked politics and issues. Afterward, Agnew said that while he still felt Rockefeller would be the party's best candidate, he admittedly was "discouraged" by his stated unavailability and said he had "a high regard" for Nixon. Nixon for his part told aides later than he had been impressed with Agnew's "strength." Some of them speculated that in the meeting, as one put it to me, "Agnew was so boiled about his treatment at Rockefeller's hands that he had some vengeance in him that he talked about."

At first the Nixon camp's interest in Agnew was to use him to reinforce the notion that Rockefeller was finally out of the 1968 nomination picture. "The effect of Nixon and Agnew even being seen together," Sears said later, "was to cause some people who had been behind Rockefeller to think twice before they started back on that path, and at least buy some time" against what the Nixonites thought was a distinct possibility—that Rockefeller might yet emerge from the ashes once again.

Indeed, Senator Thruston B. Morton of Kentucky disclosed on NBC News's *Meet the Press* that a new group of moderates called the National Coalition for a Republican Alternative was already active in sixteen states. He denied it was a stop-Nixon effort, but the name spoke for itself.

Columnists Rowland Evans and Robert Novak attributed Rockefeller's faintheartedness to "a case of tired blood on Fifth Avenue," observing that the same Rockefeller strategists who in 1960 had successfully persuaded the governor not to challenge Nixon for the presidential nomination had counseled him to drop out again. "Battered and wearied by ten years of rebuffs in national Republican wars," they wrote, "they had no stomach for another struggle," especially with the prospect of having to run against Nixon in Nebraska, which the columnists credited the Nixon campaign with arranging.

Conservative columnist William S. White, however, ever the defender of political orthodoxy and of his close friend Lyndon Johnson, wrote: "Nelson Rockefeller's effective withdrawal from the Republican presidential race is an act of high responsibility casting into sharp relief the savage national divisiveness with which another New Yorker, Senator Robert Kennedy, is opening his own campaign. Governor Rockefeller's measured words in abandoning any effort, direct or indirect, to seize his party's nomination will bring him eventual honor, however the cynical may now scoff at his motives. For they show honest concern for the integrity of the two-party system and are plainly intended to bring not further disunion but rather reconciliation to this Nation. Of him it can be said that nothing in his now dead semi-campaign had become him so much as the leaving of it." It was, as matters turned out, a premature elevation to sainthood.

From time to time thereafter that spring, Nixon would phone Agnew to keep him informed and to "ask" his political advice. It was a favorite Nixon tactic to make other politicians think they were on the inside, when he considered himself the supreme political tactician who didn't need the advice of less astute outsiders. Beyond that, however, there did seem to be a personal rapport between the two men of humble beginnings but burning personal ambition and the willingness and political toughness to do whatever it took to gain their objectives.

Also, Agnew's developing hard line toward racial protest raised eyebrows of approval among some Nixonites, particularly Pat Buchanan, the young press secretary and speechwriter who was emerging as the conservative ideologist in the campaign. He took particular note of Agnew's handling of civil rights matters, including the Bowie State boycott, and began sending Nixon newspaper clippings reporting on the Maryland governor's remarks and actions.

* * *

The discontent that had bubbled up on black campuses like Howard and Bowie State continued to seethe in pockets around the country, focused sometimes on civil rights injustices, sometimes on the Vietnam War, oftentimes on both. On March 23 and 24, hundreds of mostly young protesters, white and black, gathered at a YMCA camp outside Chicago. They discussed what to do at the approaching Democratic convention in Chicago in August, which was expected to crown Johnson despite the fervent efforts of the protesters to prevent that outcome. The discussion was heavy on proposed theatrics, ranging from talk of closing down the convention itself with disruptive tactics to conducting demonstrations of opposition to the war that would draw television coverage and touch the conscience of the country.

Antiwar movement strategy by this time was split among three main factions. The first, as David Dellinger noted in his book *More Power Than We Know*, favored concentrating on electing either McCarthy or Kennedy as the best means of ending the war in Vietnam. The second wanted to attack both Democratic liberals on grounds they supported the political system that sustained "special privilege" and the American military in its involvement in Vietnam. The third, which Dellinger came to embrace, was "to respect the right of individuals and groups within the antiwar movement to hold opposing views about the candidates and the electoral process, but not to let those differences stop the antiwar coalition from carrying out street demonstrations and the new forms of militant resistance." Dellinger and old SDS leaders Hayden and Davis proceeded to plan for the Democratic convention on the third track.

Hayden and Davis presented their plan for a "funeral march" to the convention hall on the night of Johnson's expected renomination, emphasizing to reassure the pacifists present that the march "should be nonviolent and legal." But new SDS leaders and others present, Hayden wrote in his memoir, "feared that instead of being on the cutting edge of change, the movement would be co-opted into liberal politics. Even worse, those in SDS and many others argued that lurking just behind Eugene McCarthy was the far more serious possibility of a Robert Kennedy candidacy. Wasn't the Chicago protest plan just a 'stalking horse' for the Kennedy interests, they wanted to know?"

Davis argued against blocking the convention delegates from the hall. "The delegates should be allowed to come to Chicago," he said, "so long as they give their support to a policy of ending racism and the war. I favor letting the delegates meet . . . and making our demands, and [letting] the actions behind those demands escalate in militancy as the convention proceeds." Dellinger reported that "we are not going to storm the convention with tanks or Mace. But we are going to storm the hearts and minds of the American people." No solid consensus emerged from the meeting.

On the same weekend, Abbie Hoffman and his cohorts, who on New Year's Eve of 1967 had gathered at his Greenwich Village apartment to rejoice about their recent "success" in shaking up the establishment at the Pentagon and giving birth to the Youth International Party, met again at Grand Central Station. In what they called the first "Yip-in," an estimated 3,000 young people jammed the terminal's central hall, climbing on the top of information and ticketing booths, chanting and waving signs that said PEACE NOW! A local disc jockey of radical bent observed over the air: "As H. Rap Brown said, 'Violence is as American as apple pie and cherry bombs.'" Demonstrators listening on transistor radios whooped at the remark. Soon New York police arrived and began to herd the crowd out of the terminal and onto 42nd Street amid much shoving and pushing. The scene was a mild prelude to what the Yippies already were planning for the Democratic convention in Chicago.

Also around this time, a group of black separatists met in Detroit under the sponsorship of the Malcom X Society to set up an independent government with a "black declaration of independence." The attendees voted to affirm "the principle that we are not citizens of the United States" and to establish a Republic of New Africa in five Southern states. A black militant living in Beijing named Robert F. Williams was chosen as president.

* * *

On March 28, Martin Luther King returned to Memphis as promised to lead another march in support of the sanitation strike. Police armed with riot clubs and tear gas and 4,000 National Guardsmen brandishing rifles and bayonets clashed with participants hurling sticks and bottles. King was whisked from the scene to a nearby motel, but more than 150 others were arrested and a sixteen-year-old black male was shot and killed. President Johnson proclaimed that, if necessary, federal assistance would be sent to Memphis to quell the rioting, while urging local law enforcement agencies to handle it with firmness.

For King, the episode was a calamitous refutation of his insistence on the weapon of nonviolent protest. He announced that he would soon lead another massive civil rights demonstration in the city in peaceful support of the striking sanitation workers, as well as his planned Poor People's March on Washington in late April.

* * *

Meanwhile, McCarthy having rejected Kennedy's offer of help in Wisconsin focused on the state himself as its April 2 primary approached. He was buoyed not only by the psychological boost his New Hampshire showing had provided, but also by other factors peculiar to Wisconsin. First, the state had a long tradition of political independence. McCarthy as a Minnesota neighbor was well known there. Opposition to the war had started early and strongly there, with the liberal faculty and student body of the University of Wisconsin in the vanguard. And tactically, the state permitted relatively easy crossover voting. With Rockefeller having dropped out of contention, McCarthy figured he could pick up a significant liberal or moderate Republican vote to add to the strong anti-Johnson, antiwar constituency in his own party.

The McCarthy organization was off and running in the hands of Wisconsinites well before the outcome of the New Hampshire primary had given respectability to the senator's candidacy. Students from campuses across the Midwest flocked to Milwaukee and Madison, more than enough to staff headquarters in every city and town of significance in the state. By this time, the organization skills tested in New Hampshire had been honed to a fine point by Curtis Gans and Sam Brown, and an aura of mission gripped the students as 13,000 canvassers set out to ring every doorbell in the state. Jeremy Larner recalled in his book on the campaign that "a mad joy prevailed. Kids on the McCarthy press corps worked all night on peanut butter, getting out transcripts and information. Managers held meetings all day long, researchers rushed up corridors in their underwear, everyone stayed up drinking and talking and fooling around. We were heady with history, which we knew was driving us on to win in Wisconsin."

By this time too McCarthy himself had fashioned a sort of understated charismatic quality in his own right. He was drawing large crowds to see the man who had humbled the haughty Lyndon Johnson while remaining, to more distant eyes and ears anyway, humble himself. His now public disdain for Kennedy's attempted usurpation pleased his loyalists no end, as when he observed that Kennedy's offer to campaign for him in Wisconsin sounded "like fattening me up for the kill" in later primaries in which the two would compete.

Lowenstein said later that Kennedy's abrupt entry into the race had a distinctly positive side for McCarthy. "It was Kennedy who turned McCarthy into a folk hero," he said, "which McCarthy would not have become to anything like the degree that happened, if Kennedy had not entered the [primaries] right after New Hampshire, giving the general sense that all of the worst images of Kennedy had been confirmed: that he was ruthless, opportunistic, indifferent to anyone but himself. And although that was a very gross misreading of what was going on in Kennedy's mind, because of the way that he acted at that time McCarthy emerged looking like the pure knight who had been put upon by this opportunist. And so McCarthy at that point not only has had the courage to take Johnson on when nobody would, but is also the victim of aggression by this opportunistic and ruthless figure, and . . . that made the McCarthy cult what it was."

Lowenstein for his part tried to keep his eye on his prime objective—to dump Johnson and end the war—and looked ahead to a time when the forces of McCarthy and Kennedy might come together in that cause. To him, the cavalier attitude in the Kennedy camp toward McCarthy and the corresponding bitterness among the McCarthyites both were detrimental to that objective. But he himself was viewed with suspicion on both sides because of his unwillingness to be a party to either sentiment. Although he continued to be openly aligned with the McCarthy side, he said, "there was a great deal of resentment directed at me, and suspicion, because I would never attack Kennedy."

In a speech for McCarthy to the California Democratic Council the day after Kennedy announced, Lowenstein pleaded for an end to the bitterness toward the new candidate. "I made a very emotional statement about where Dump Johnson had started, and what had happened," he recalled, "and what a calamity it would be if it was now poisoned and there were hate between people who agreed on the issues, and ended up with a statement that got used on television widely out there, that 'Bobby Kennedy is not the enemy.'"

The remarks were enthusiastically received by the anti-LBJ California liberal Democrats, Lowenstein remembered, "but the McCarthy clique . . . they were a small group of people who had developed a particular interest in the McCarthy candidacy, and their view of it was that this was of course an unacceptable heresy." Nevertheless, Lowenstein spent the next few weeks going around the country preaching this gospel. But even those who tried with him "to pull something less bitter out of the mess," he said, "pretty soon themselves decided that they would have to choose sides, and did, so that the middle position died fairly quickly, and, of course, got cremated after that in the primaries."

An element of "the mess" was the mutual low regard McCarthy and Kennedy had for each other. "During that period," Lowenstein recalled, "it became clear that McCarthy entertained what later came to be seen as obsessive hatred of Kennedy. Nobody had known that before. I had not any suspicion of it because he had suggested Kennedy as a candidate earlier on."

Lowenstein said he could only speculate "whether all of this hate was there, or whether it all came as a result of the New Hampshire behavior of Kennedy's after assessing his own candidacy more seriously than he had at the beginning. At the beginning . . . [McCarthy] suggested he might withdraw if his candidacy began to succeed and it looked like someone else could carry it further. Obviously that notion didn't survive very long. . . . It became very clear as it went along that he did have a very profound hate for Kennedy, which was shared.

"There was no less hate by Kennedy for McCarthy, but Kennedy, partly because of the original aggression he had committed and partly because a lot of us preached at him about it, behaved following his entrance into the race much better about McCarthy than his feelings would have indicated, and certainly better than McCarthy did about Kennedy."

In any event, in Wisconsin such matters were not a factor because Kennedy had missed the primary filing deadline and McCarthy had Johnson all to himself. Before the McCarthy canvassers were through, Goodwin reported later, 1.3 million Wisconsin homes had been visited by them.

* * *

The Johnson operation in the hands of the regular party apparatus in Wisconsin, meanwhile, was in a state of near-panic after New Hampshire. Leading Democratic officeholders in the state, starting with the two very popular senators, Gaylord Nelson and William Proxmire, were outspokenly critical of the war. Only one member of the Democratic congressional delegation, Representative Clement Zablocki, had publicly endorsed the president. McCarthy's campaign treasury had received a major lift from the New Hampshire result and now was poised to spend twice as much as the LBJ camp had budgeted for Wisconsin. Accordingly, the White House felt obliged to send high-profile shock troops into the state to try to avert another major embarrassment.

A string of cabinet members bringing assorted federal largesse, led by Secretary of Agriculture Orville Freeman, a former governor of Minnesota, and Attorney General Ramsey Clark, tried old-fashioned methods of persuasion on an electorate that was fixated on the war. Freeman was heckled so intensely at the University of Wisconsin in Madison that he had to halt his speech halfway through. Clark was hissed when he defended LBJ as "the greatest doer I have ever seen." When Vice President Humphrey paid a visit, he was politely but coolly received as he lectured the audience on heckling. McCarthy observed: "I'd like to see them come in as a group, rather than one by one. It's like a family reunion. A visiting uncle or two is all right. But when you get them all together, they don't look so good."

Les Aspin, then a Pentagon analyst and Wisconsinite who had run a Senate campaign for Proxmire, had been drafted to go back home and run the LBJ primary campaign. He had asked for the president to come himself, but said he was told that Johnson "is too busy in Washington." Of the eleventh-hour rescue team sent in, he observed rather forlornly: "It's not the president, but it helps."

A week before the primary, Larry O'Brien, the old JFK political mastermind who was now LBJ's postmaster general, was dispatched to assess the situation. He did not like what he saw and heard. Returning from a pro-Johnson rally in Milwaukee at which, O'Brien knew, the hall had been papered with federal employees, his car passed a darkened LBJ headquarters. Then, a few blocks away, it passed the McCarthy headquarters with, he wrote later, "perhaps a hundred young people hard at work inside. It was not a good sign."

* * *

As the Wisconsin campaign proceeded, Robert Kennedy, having entered the race too late to make the Wisconsin filing and having been rebuffed in his offer to help McCarthy in the state, looked elsewhere. He took his campaign to the South and then westward on a first major swing of nine days to the West Coast, the Rockies, the Midwest and Southwest before returning home. The trip had no particular bearing to the calendar of state primaries but served to demonstrate Kennedy's broad appeal. The obvious hope was to create the impression that his candidacy was a relentless force that would sweep aside the traditional calculations. In the fervor of public support it unleashed, it more than met the aspirations of its planners. On March 24, the Gallup Poll reported that Kennedy had edged ahead of Johnson, 45 percent to 44, as the choice of Democrats nationwide.

For Kennedy personally, the campaigning was a further release from the caution and restraint in expressing his feelings about Lyndon Johnson and the war that had held him a restless captive all those long months before his candidacy. At Vanderbilt University in Nashville, he said: "When we are told to forgo all dissent and division, we must ask: who is it that is truly dividing the country? It is not those who call for change, it is those who make present policy . . . who have removed themselves from the American tradition, from the enduring and generous impulses that are the soul of this nation." In a reference to his late brother's inspiration, he warned that the young were rejecting their "public commitment of a few years ago to lives of disengagement and despair, turning on with drugs and turning off America."

In California, Kennedy and his party hopscotched the state in two chartered jets. At city intersections he hammered at the war and LBJ's leadership in even harsher terms than he had on the campuses of Kansas and the South. Consciously or unconsciously, he played on the emotional appeal of his late brother's words and gestures and the undeniable family resemblance. "This is a time to begin again," he would say, "and that is why I *ahsk* for your help, and that is why I run for president." One sign at the Sacramento Airport read: CALL THE ROLL AT THE ROUNDTABLE. CAMELOT WILL COME AGAIN. ROBERT KENNEDY WILL BE PRESIDENT AGAIN [*sic*]. Another at a nearby shopping mall proclaimed: CONTINUE THE NEW FRONTIER.

There, after pushing through a mob of well-wishers straining to grab his hand, touch him, seize a cuff link, Kennedy climbed a ladder and tugged the heartstrings of a crowd that backed up into aisles of department stores that opened onto the mall. "Which of these brave young men dying in the rice paddies of Vietnam might have written a symphony?" he asked, his voice dropping. "Which of them might have written a beautiful poem or might have cured cancer? Which of them might have played in a World Series or given us the gift of laughter from a stage, or helped build a bridge or a university? Which of them might have taught a small child to read? It is our responsibility to let those men live."

(In composition, cadence and sentiment, the words would provide inspiration for controversial remarks by another Democratic presidential candidate, Senator Joseph Biden of Delaware, twenty years later that ultimately would contribute to his withdrawal from the 1988 campaign amid charges of plagiarism.)

The frenzy unleashed by Kennedy's highly emotional pitch, coupled with the nostalgia of Camelot Returned, at times spilled over into physical danger. As the crowds surged toward him, storefront windows seemed on the verge of shattering. Small children, stumbling along behind their parents, often slipped and risked being stepped on. Kennedy aides, trying to hold the crowds in check, would reach down and yank a child from peril, then move on as Kennedy worked his way toward the open convertible that inched him through all the adulation. Bill Barry, a former Kent State football star and FBI agent who now was a bank security official on loan to the campaign, would kneel next to Kennedy on the car's back seat, his arm wrapped around the senator's waist to keep him from being pulled into the mob. In time, his knees were rubbed so raw that Ethel Kennedy bought him a rubber kneeling pad to ease the pain. Often, he would look down and see that both his and Kennedy's hands were bleeding.

Along a picket fence at the Salinas-Monterey Peninsula Airport, Kennedy had to raise his hands and plead: "Ssssh. Just be quiet for a minute. Just clear a path for the children." With that, he reached down and pulled a small girl up, holding her until she and other children were led out of danger. On the madcap freeways of Los Angeles too, the frenzy continued. Motorists would speed up to Kennedy's car in the motorcade and the driver would take both hands off the wheel as he tried to snap the candidate's picture. At one point, Jerry Bruno, the trip's advance man, reached out, took a camera from a passing motorcyclist, snapped Kennedy's picture and handed it back to him.

The fevered temper of the crowd raised not only Kennedy's spirits but also the aggressive tone of his rhetoric. Speaking at the Greek Theater in Griffith Park in Los Angeles, Kennedy started with his familiar criticism of the Vietnam War but near the end went beyond it with a particularly biting commentary on Johnson. He charged that "the failure of national purpose" being seen at home and abroad "is not simply the result of bad policies and lack of skill. It flows," he said, "from the fact that for almost the first time the national leadership is calling upon the darker impulses of the American spirit—not, perhaps, deliberately, but through its action and the example it sets—an example where integrity, truth, honor and all the rest seem like words to fill out speeches rather than guiding beliefs. . . ."

To some ears, the allegation of "darker impulses" had gotten perilously close to the ugly, unspecific language that had marked McCarthyism more than a decade earlier. The distinguished and always fair-minded Washington bureau chief of the *Los Angeles Times,* Robert J. Donovan, wrote the next day that a lesson of Kennedy's early campaigning "is that when a war becomes a flaming issue, the line between debate and demagoguery becomes a thin one. A candidate can easily be carried across it in the ardor of the fight." Richard Harwood of the *Washington Post* wrote that the fervor of the crowds "has led at times to rhetorical devices" that even Kennedy staffers "regarded as bordering on the demagogic."

The way the crowd's energy affected Kennedy provided an interesting basis for comparison of the Kennedy brothers John and Robert. The late president had the same talent for firing up a crowd but its response seldom changed his detached manner; Robert for all his reputation as cold and calculating was a man much more touched and captured by the emotions his words set loose in others, and he often showed it.

In a sense, the "darker impulses" remark was the product of a presidential campaign that was being made up on the run. Unlike John Kennedy's campaign of 1960, which had been carefully planned over many months, Robert Kennedy's was being played by ear, day to day and sometimes event to event, with input from whomever happened to be at hand and had the candidate's ear. In this case, ironically, the inspiration came from Dick Goodwin, the Kennedy insider who had gone over to McCarthy when Kennedy first said he was not going to run, while Goodwin was still on McCarthy's staff. Goodwin now wanted to rejoin Kennedy but felt he had to stay with McCarthy until after the Wisconsin primary. He offered to write one speech in the meantime, and the "darker impulses" offering was it.

In any event, the press reaction served as an early warning to the Kennedy strategists that at a time passions were running deep, it would be prudent henceforth not to go overboard. But on the flight to California, Jesse Unruh had observed that "we can't just sit down at a table and expect to bargain for delegates. We've got to produce a groundswell in the country." Indisputably, Kennedy was well on his way to doing that, with the Gallup Poll now showing him leading Johnson, 44 percent to 41.

Other aides realized that voters who were not swept up in the emotionalism of the first days also had to be won over on more substantive grounds if Kennedy were to capture the nomination. Frank Mankiewicz later characterized what was going on in these first white-heat days as "the free-at-last syndrome" after Kennedy's months of procrastination. "It may have intoxicated everybody a little," he acknowledged.

The fact that Kennedy himself paid any attention at all to criticism from the press corps traveling with him was a commentary on the unusual symbiotic relationship that existed between them. Many of the reporters covering the campaign were contemporaries of Kennedy and knew him in Washington. Some were part of the mixed social universe that swirled around the Kennedy family; others shared an identity with the civil rights and antiwar issues that were at the heart of his candidacy. Some were unvarnished admirers, others had been disappointed in his earlier foot-dragging and had, at best, mixed feelings about his entering the race on the back of McCarthy's success. With most of them all, however, Kennedy enjoyed good-natured sparring through the course of the days that were now flying rapidly by in the frenzied game of political catch-up.

As always, Kennedy liked dark Irish humor as often served up along the way by the likes of Jimmy Breslin, the New York columnist. During a stop at an Indian reservation in the Southwest, after Kennedy had recited the inordinately high suicide rates among Native Americans, Breslin told him: "It's a good thing the rope broke for Jim Thorpe."

The one area where wisecracks were not appreciated was in any reference to the late president and revered brother. Even in private conversations at the back of the plane after a long day of campaigning, Kennedy's countenance would darken if a reporter referred to his brother as "Jack," and the senator himself in public would always speak of "President Kennedy" or "my brother."

Once, as Robert Kennedy stood in the aisle of his plane chatting with a couple of reporters, one noted that the senator was wearing, as usual, his *PT-109* tie clasp, the talisman of Kennedy insiders. The reporter took off his own tie clip, a pointed object with the side cut away to show wires within, and asked Kennedy if he knew what it was. Kennedy looked at it and shook his head no. "It's a torpedo," the reporter said. "I wear it when I travel with you just to show I'm staying honest." Kennedy's face froze. He handed the object back and walked down the aisle. Certain things were not funny.

* * *

In the McCarthy campaign in Wisconsin, the press's relationship with the candidate was more distant, by nature of the candidate himself. With a few exceptions, he held a low opinion of reporters as a group, finding them too often superficial, misinformed, lazy and clearly not near to being his intellectual equal. He had an imperial manner about him, not in the overpowering Lyndon Johnson mold but as if he fashioned himself an oracle. He delighted in feeding obscure literary or poetic references to the dirty-fingernail scribblers around him as well as the biting bits of sarcasm that not even they could fail to grasp. Yet, for all that, there was a considerable respect among reporters for what he had undertaken and for his diffidence toward the idea of aggressively questing for the presidency. His remarks seasoned with references to his "willingness" to serve made his campaign seem devoid of self-interest and laden with high purpose.

In a speech in Milwaukee on March 23, repeated two days later in Madison, McCarthy came about as close as ever to acknowledging he was actually seeking presidential power. And even then he was careful to cast himself as a representative of the public will. "This movement of which you are a part and which I, in a limited way, personify now by interaction of many circumstances," he said, "is not a movement which is carrying on a simple educational program in this country, as it was suggested we were going to do when we started. We are not really out trying to raise an issue for the attention of the people of this nation, because the issue has been raised and the people of this nation are aware of what that issue is. What we are doing is laying down a challenge to control the presidency of the United States of America.

"And I want to tell you that in pursuing this office I am not really fulfilling any boyhood dream of mine, and not even a late adult dream. I could not say that the first time I looked at the White House, I said, 'I want to live there sometime.' In fact, I thought it should have been made into a museum the first time I saw it."

McCarthy said once again that he did not believe men should seek the presidency out of personal ambition or by "succession"—a typical dig at Kennedy—but should respond to a public call. "The seeking of me as a candidate," he said, "came like the dew in the night. It was rather gentle, I must say, soft, but there were signs in the morning that something had happened during the night, and so here I am."

Don Peterson later had his own description. Young people from all over the Midwest, he said, came into Wisconsin "like ants at times . . . because they brought to the state and, I think, to the nation a clean kind of feeling about political life and the activity and attitude that people should have about it. You couldn't associate with these young people and the movement itself without feeling exhilarated, and you knew that no matter what happened that Senator McCarthy had provided people with something in American political life that never had been there in this degree before."

The McCarthy campaign, however, encountered some internal bickering in the final days in Wisconsin. Veterans of the civil rights wars and young idealists felt McCarthy was intentionally snubbing the predominantly black wards of Milwaukee, where the vote was minimal, in deference to more numerous white Polish-American voters who still reflected redneck attitudes. He finally took a highly publicized two-hour, eight-mile Saturday evening walk through the city's black ghetto during which his brisk pace and cool manner drew critical reviews.

Hersh, the campaign's oftimes abrasive and explosive press secretary, quit in the rhubarb but the organization was purring efficiently otherwise and the internal troubles caused hardly a ripple. A canvass of voters by McCarthy volunteers on the final weekend of the primary suggested that the Minnesota senator would get a staggering 63 percent of the vote. After McCarthy went to church with his family on the final Sunday morning and started on a round of college campuses, he allowed that "I don't wish to sound overconfident but I think the test is pretty much between me and Nixon now."

The observation conveniently overlooked Kennedy, who on March 28 had gone to Indiana barely in time to meet the filing deadline for the state's May 7 primary. McCarthy had already filed, as had Indiana's Democratic Governor Roger Branigin as a stand-in for Johnson. Kennedy had just received a poll showing him running close behind Branigin and well ahead of McCarthy. In an obvious effort to keep the focus of his campaign on LBJ—as opposed to McCarthy, whom he had said he would not run against—Kennedy told a large and boisterous crowd of supporters at the State Capitol in Indianapolis: "I am not here to oppose Governor Branigin. He is in no way responsible for the policies and actions I challenge this year."

McCarthy, campaigning in Oshkosh, said he would "have to conduct a very limited campaign in Indiana" because of limits on his time and resources, but was committed to "go down all the way, and the showdown of course will come in California."

Larry O'Brien meanwhile returned to Washington and informed the president that he was probably headed for defeat in Wisconsin—not just a moral victory for McCarthy as in New Hampshire but an out-and-out victory of humiliating proportions. "How bad?" Johnson asked him, O'Brien wrote later in *No Final Victories*. " 'Sixty-forty,' I told him. 'Maybe two to one.' "

The LBJ organization, devoid of public support, was a shell, and morale had hit bottom. On the final Saturday, I saw unmistakable evidence of the same conclusion myself when I dropped by the LBJ headquarters in Milwaukee to talk to Aspin, whom I knew in the course of reporting from the Pentagon several years earlier. Sitting alone in the spacious headquarters, he didn't try to deceive me. Barring a miracle, the president was going to lose the Wisconsin primary. "It's unlikely but possible," he said, "that the president could be shut out in the delegate race." (Ultimately, he nearly was; McCarthy won all but a handful of the state's fifty-seven delegates.)

* * *

On the same weekend, in Birmingham, Alabama, a man walked into the Aeromarine Supply Company, a gun shop, and purchased a Winchester rifle with telescopic sight and a box of soft-point bullets, using the name Harvey Lowmyer. The next day he returned and exchanged the purchase for a Remington 30.06 rifle, serial number 17350, with a Redfield telescopic sight. He was waited on by Donald Wood, son of the store's owner. It was, from all outward signs, a routine and insignificant transaction, but five days later it would prove to have been anything but that.

* * *

On Sunday night, March 31, President Johnson was scheduled to make a televised address to the nation. The widespread assumption was that it would be another appeal for support of the war effort geared to the voting in Wisconsin two days hence. Aides and advisers had held several meetings on the draft of the speech. Speechwriter Harry McPherson among others pushed for inclusion of a decision to halt bombing north of the 20th parallel in North Vietnam as an inducement for negotiations. Some wanted to end the bombing altogether and there was much opposition expressed, including that of Clifford, to reject the call of Westmoreland and the Joint Chiefs of 206,000 more troops to Vietnam.

Three days before the speech was to be delivered, Clifford and high-level State Department officials reviewed the speech draft again with McPherson. According to Townsend Hoopes, then undersecretary of the Air Force, in his book, *The Limits of Intervention*, "it was still essentially a defiant, bellicose speech written to be delivered between clenched teeth. It made a *pro forma* plea for negotiations, but said nothing whatever about a bombing halt, which was of course the prerequisite for talks."

Upon reading the draft, Hoopes wrote, "Clifford said: 'The president cannot give that speech! It would be a disaster! What seems not to be understood is that major elements of the national constituency—the business community, the press, the churches, professional groups, college presidents, students, and most of all the intellectual community—have turned against this war. What the president needs is not a war speech, but a peace speech.'"

Aware of likely resistance from Rusk, Clifford proposed that McPherson prepare two drafts for Johnson and let him choose. Rusk agreed, Clifford wrote later, and to Clifford's and McPherson's surprise and gratification, the president chose the one emphasizing the quest for peace. Meeting with Clifford, McPherson and others on March 30, Johnson finally agreed to the limited bombing halt and only a token increase in forces, and McPherson was instructed to prepare a final draft.

When the president looked at it, he saw no peroration and asked McPherson what had happened to it. "I didn't like it, Mr. President," McPherson replied, as he recalled later in his book *A Political Education*. "I'm going upstairs to write another. I'll make it short. The speech is already pretty long." Johnson, he recalled, smiled and answered: "That's okay. Make it as long as you want. I may even add one of my own." On that same day, the Gallup Poll reported that the president's favorability rating was down to 36 percent.

When LBJ had left, McPherson remembered, "I turned to Clifford, who was gathering up his papers. 'Jesus, is he going to say sayonara?' 'What?' 'Is he going to say goodbye tomorrow night?' Clifford looked at me with pity, as if I were too tired to be rational."

That Sunday morning, the president got up early to greet his daughter Lynda, who had just returned from California where she had seen her husband, Marine officer Charles Robb—later the Virginia governor and senator—off to Vietnam. There was a flow of tears, her mother wrote in *A White House Diary*, as Lynda pressed her father on why Americans had to continue to fight there. After they parted, Lady Bird wrote, she saw "such pain in his eyes as I had not seen since his mother died."

Later in the morning, Johnson went to the Washington apartment of Humphrey, about to leave in the afternoon on a goodwill visit to Mexico. The day before, LBJ's loyal vice president had told Virginia Young Democrats in Richmond: "I think most Americans know that there can be no true and lasting peace in Vietnam or Southeast Asia until militant and powerful Communist forces are convinced that aggression will not pay—and that they must turn to honest negotiation." There was no question whose side Hubert Humphrey was on.

Johnson took him into a room alone. "He read me the speech that he had in mind," Humphrey told Eisele later, "and he said, 'I've got two endings for this speech, and I want you to listen to them.' He read both of them to me. I said, 'Mr. President, you can't take that second ending. You can't do that. You just cannot resign from the office. Because that's what you would be doing.' He said, 'Hubert, I've got to tell you something. Nobody will believe that I'm trying to end this war unless I do that. I just can't get them to believe I want peace. And I don't think I can get any cooperation in this battle against inflation unless I do this. I've got to become totally non-political. I just don't see any way out of it.' He also said to me: 'I also have to tell you this. This is a terrible strain, and men in my family have died early from heart trouble. I'd like to live a little bit longer.'"

Johnson told him he hadn't fully decided to read the last sheet that night and swore him to secrecy. When Humphrey's wife, Muriel, asked him after Johnson had left what the president had said, her husband told her: "Nothing, Muriel, nothing."

Around five o'clock that afternoon, after more work on the speech with old Texas friend and adviser Horace Busby, the president phoned McPherson and told him he had written his own peroration. "So I had heard," McPherson wrote later he had replied. "Did I know what he was going to say? I thought so. What did I think about that? 'I'm very sorry, Mr. President.' 'Well, [Johnson replied] I think it's best. So long, podner.'"

Johnson also called Clifford and invited him and his wife, Marnie, to the

White House to witness the speech. On arrival, LBJ called him into his bedroom and showed him the final paragraphs of his speech. When he read them, Clifford said later, "you could have knocked my eyes off with a stick. I said, 'You've made up your mind?' He said, 'I've made up my mind.' . . . I said, 'All right, it's your decision, then it becomes my decision.'" Clifford went out and told his wife and Mrs. Walt Rostow, sitting together. "Neither one of them could believe it," he said. "They were absolutely and completely destroyed."

The president went before the television cameras, and a TelePrompTer, at nine o'clock that night, from the Oval Office. For about forty minutes, he talked about Vietnam, renewing his offer to stop bombing North Vietnam if Hanoi would enter "productive discussions" toward peace. In the meantime, he would unilaterally de-escalate by restricting much of the bombardment of the North. He insisted that there had been "substantial progress . . . in building a durable government" in the South and reported that the Saigon government would soon be drafting eighteen-year-olds—the absence of which was a sore point with Kennedy that he had been raising regularly in his speeches.

In addition, Johnson said, he would be sending 13,500 more American troops over the next five months, some of whom would be called-up reserves. He said $2.5 billion more would be spent to reequip South Vietnamese forces in the current fiscal year, and he made a special point of observing that he was carrying on with the mission of John F. Kennedy. "I believe now, no less than when the decade began," he said in the words of JFK's memorable inauguration pledge, "this generation of Americans is willing to pay any price, bear any burden, meet any hardship, support any friend, oppose any foe, to assure the survival, and the success, of liberty."

Then, recalling the traumatic circumstances of his ascendancy to the presidency in 1963 and the unity those circumstances bred in the nation, Johnson said: "What we won when all of our people united just must not now be lost in suspicion and distrust and selfishness and politics among any of our people. And believing this as I do I have concluded that I should not permit the presidency to become involved in the partisan divisions that are developing in this political year. With American sons in the fields far away, with America's future under challenge right here at home, with our hopes and the world's hopes for peace in the balance every day, I do not believe that I should devote an hour or a day of my time to any personal partisan causes or to any duties other than the awesome duties of this office, the presidency of your country."

In Mexico City, Hubert and Muriel Humphrey and aide Ted Van Dyk were at the residence of American Ambassador Fulton Freeman for dinner with

Mexican president Gustavo Díaz Ordaz. A few minutes earlier, the vice president had surprised his host and the Mexican leader by suddenly asking, "Do
you mind if we listen to the president's speech?" Van Dyk remembered thinking, "What terrible taste!"

The party retired to the library and tuned into the speech on a shortwave
radio. In the course of it, a phone call came to Humphrey from Johnson aide
Marvin Watson. "Mr. Vice President," Watson said, "the president says to tell
you it will be the second ending." Humphrey, he later told Eisele, replied:
"Oh, my God, he shouldn't do that." To which Watson answered: "We told
him that but he's made up his mind."

Humphrey returned to the library and listened somberly as Johnson reported he had decided to restrict sharply the bombing of North Vietnam.
Then, observing that he was determined not to permit any other interests, including political, to distract him from the search for peace in Vietnam, he
concluded: "Accordingly, I shall not seek, and I will not accept, the nomination of my party for another term as your president. But let men everywhere
know, however, that a strong and a confident and a vigilant America stands
ready tonight to seek an honorable peace, and stands ready tonight to defend
an honored cause, whatever the price, whatever the burden, whatever the sacrifice that duty may require. Thank you for listening. Good night and God
bless all of you."

As LBJ finished, Van Dyk burst into the room bent on congratulating the
man he thought had just become president. Because of the static on a radio
in another room, Van Dyk recalled later, he thought Johnson had announced
that he was resigning right then. Humphrey told him he had misunderstood,
then returned with his wife to the dinner.

McCarthy at this moment was addressing an overflow crowd in the auditorium of Carroll College in Waukesha, south of Milwaukee. As he finished,
some reporters ran into the hall, rushed up to the platform and told him what
Johnson had just said. He announced the news to the crowd amid much
cheering and turmoil and then quickly returned to his hotel in Milwaukee to
gather his thoughts. "I feel as if I've been tracking a tiger through long jungle grass," he told a friend, "and all of a sudden he rolls over and he's stuffed."

McCarthy finally emerged for a news conference, saying Johnson "now has
cleared the way for the reconciliation of our people." He said he didn't know
whether Humphrey would now enter the race, "but I think if you look
closely, you might see a slight cloud on the horizon tomorrow morning."
McCarthy said he would continue on, observing about Kennedy that "I have
not been seeking a knockdown, drag-out battle with him up to this point. On
the other hand, I have not been seeking an accommodation."

Kennedy was flying east from Arizona to New York as Johnson made his fateful speech. When the plane landed at Kennedy Airport, the New York Democratic Party chairman, John Burns, ran up the stairs and into the cabin, blurting to Kennedy: "The president is not going to run!" Kennedy was just rising from his seat when Burns's words hit him, sending him back down.

After a brief conference with Burns and Dutton, he and Ethel Kennedy left the plane and he silently and soberly pushed his way through a crowd in the terminal. "You're going to be our next president!" a woman screamed at him, but he did not reply. In the car going to Manhattan accompanied by his wife, Dutton and Dick Dougherty of the *Los Angeles Times*, he finally broke the silence. "I wonder," he said, "if he'd have done this if I hadn't come in." Later, he sent Johnson a telegram praising him for his "truly magnanimous" action.

According to Lady Bird Johnson in her later memoir, *A White House Diary*, the president actually had considered announcing his intention not to seek another term at the end of his State of the Union speech in January but had decided against it. That report lent credence later to the view that it was indeed Kennedy's entrance into the race two months after that speech that persuaded Johnson to withdraw.

Aspin insisted that LBJ's decision actually was bad news for McCarthy. "Lyndon Johnson with one speech has blown a big hole in the side of the McCarthy ship," he said. "He's taken away his issues. . . . The motivating force in his campaign is that he's an anti-Johnson candidate." McCarthy nevertheless would press on, certain now of a sweeping endorsement by Wisconsin's voters two days hence. Although Humphrey was saying nothing on this momentous night, the wide expectation was that it would be only a matter of time before he filled the vacuum as the regular party candidate left by LBJ's startling decision.

Among the many who called the White House after the president's disclosure and among the few who got through to him was Abigail McCarthy, the senator's wife, who had intended to call the first lady. "But the president was on the line almost at once," she wrote in her book, *Private Faces/Public Places*, "and I said what was in my heart at the moment, that I admired him profoundly for his decision and that I knew what it must have cost him."

Then she added: "I was almost immediately sorry because there was in the president's voice such a note of suppressed triumph that I could not miss it. It was the familiar voice of one who felt that he had once again stolen the march on everyone—the voice of a man who operated in the supreme confidence that he could outmaneuver anyone. 'Honey,' he said, 'I'm just one little person. It's not important what happens to me.'"

Johnson after a pause handed the phone to Lady Bird, who, after hearing the same comments from the caller, Abigail McCarthy wrote, commented: "When you have two boys out there [her sons-in-law], you know what Vietnam is about."

On the Republican side, Nixon had just concluded a successful rally in Milwaukee and was en route to New York on his chartered campaign jet when news of Johnson's withdrawal reached him. Upon landing, he was cool and collected. "This is the year of the dropouts," he said, always ready with the pithy phrase. "First Romney, then Rockefeller, now Johnson." He proclaimed Kennedy the Democratic front-runner along with his expectation that Humphrey would soon join the race. "I'd be very surprised if President Johnson lets Bobby Kennedy have it on a silver platter," he said.

At the same time, Nixon was already nervously looking over his shoulder again. "The Democrats are a divided party, but our game could change too," he went on. "Rockefeller will have to determine whether, after withdrawing from the race, he will enter it again." For now, though, Nixon was positioned to score another, essentially uncontested, primary victory in Wisconsin, with only perennial candidate Harold Stassen in "active" opposition.

Also on the ballot was Ronald Reagan, who had declined to sign a required affidavit that he was not and did not intend to become a candidate. He had indicated that because he expected to be California's favorite son as head of the state delegation he could not sign it. A group of Wisconsin backers bought some radio and television commercials touting him on the final weekend, but they were not expected to throw up any serious roadblock in the path of the Nixon steamroller.

So ended the tempestuous month of March—a shocking rebuke to the sitting president in the New Hampshire primary; an end to Robert Kennedy's private agony with a tardy declaration of candidacy; the barbaric slaughter at My Lai, not to be generally known for many months ahead; Rockefeller's march up the hill toward a candidacy and his abrupt march down again; the snub to Spiro Agnew, driving him into the open arms of Richard Nixon; ominous stirrings of racial violence once again in Memphis; finally, a prideful president known as a fierce combatant suddenly laying down his political sword. Certainly, the approaching month of April could not hold any jolts to the national psyche to match these.

CHAPTER 5

April: The Fire, This Time

Apr. 1 Supreme Court applies one-man, one-vote to local governments; **2** *A Dandy in Aspic* released starring Laurence Harvey; **3** Stanley Kubrick's *2001: A Space Odyssey* opens starring Keir Dullea; **5** John Updike's *Couples* published; **10** *George M!* opens on Broadway starring Joel Gray; **16** actress Fay Bainter, 74, Oscar winner in *Jezebel*, dies; novelist Edna Ferber, 82 (*Show Boat*), dies; **17** Gross national product rose at record annual rate of $20 billion for first quarter; **18** nationwide telephone strike begins; **21** Tony Awards to *Rosencrantz and Guildenstern Are Dead, Hallelujah Baby*, Robert Goulet, Leslie Uggams; **23** Methodist Church (10.3 million), Evangelical United Brethren Church (745,000) merge into United Methodist Church; **25** Justice Department brings first Northern desegregation suit against Cook County, Illinois; **29** *Hair* opens on Broadway.

Lyndon Johnson's electrifying announcement that he would not seek reelection was a bombshell to the business world as well as the political. Stocks shot up to record highs on Wall Street amid hope that his accompanying agreement to limit the bombing of North Vietnam might bring Hanoi to the negotiating table.

But it was in the political arena where the impact was most immediate and pronounced. The next morning, April 1, Kennedy held a news conference at the Overseas Press Club in New York and read his telegram to Johnson. Beyond expressing his "fervent hope" for the president's new efforts for peace,

Kennedy "respectfully and earnestly" requested a meeting with him at the White House "as soon as possible to discuss how we might work together in the interest of national unity during the coming months."

The request, in light of Kennedy's ferocious attacks on Johnson leading up to it, was breathtaking. But the senator in reading it seemed at least temporarily stripped of his aggressive emotionalism, and still somewhat stunned by the event of the previous night that had suddenly denied him his personal target. Johnson, for his part, also somewhat surprisingly responded quickly that he would "surely" honor Kennedy's request.

The news of LBJ's withdrawal did, however, swell Kennedy's crowds and their enthusiasm as he took his campaign to Philadelphia and Camden. Motorcading through the suburbs, the crush was so great and insistent that a car rolled over the foot of a child pressed against it. Everywhere, people lunged forward to grab Kennedy's hand or merely touch him, as the kneeling Bill Barry valiantly held his arm around the candidate in the open car. "Don't squeeze me so tight," Kennedy implored at one point, "you'll break my back."

But Kennedy's calmer tone belied the frenzy. Reverting to his posture toward the president that had marked his conduct before entering the race, he told one crowd: "We take pride in President Johnson, who brought to final fulfillment the policies of 30 years, and who yesterday sacrificed personal considerations to win the peace for which all Americans yearn. . . . The peace is above all what they want for the future. They will respect and honor President Johnson, who has sought to take the first step toward peace."

The political translation for Kennedy's effusive praise of LBJ was obvious: the man had been brought down, and there was no sense hammering at him any longer. But the praise brought political risks as well—chiefly the resurrection of Kennedy's own reputation as an opportunist, seeking somehow to win over voters who had stood by Johnson, in order to recapture Camelot. McCarthy was at no loss for his own analysis. "Bobby has to shoot straight pool now," he said. "When he was banking his shots off Lyndon, it was a different game." Larry O'Brien later put it another way, focusing on the need for pragmatism as well as the natural emotionalism: "He became a John Kennedy rather than a Bob Kennedy."

McCarthy reassured his backers that he would stay in the race, striving at the same time to cling to his position that he was more "willing" to serve as president than compelled by any personal ambition. He had told his followers earlier, he remarked the day after LBJ's withdrawal, that "I would . . . do as much as I could within the limits of my power and the time which was available to me to stand as their candidate, not aspiring to the presidency directly and by my own determination and by my own desire but rather because I thought there had to be some personification." He would continue, he was saying, in that vein.

(McCarthy, reflecting on the Johnson decision long afterward, concluded that in stepping aside, the president figured he would strengthen his hold on the war. "The Johnson withdrawal was kind of a psychological thing," he said. "I think Lyndon knew that if he stayed in, he might get nominated but he would in a sense have been beaten on the issue of the war. He would have lost control over the issue. So in a sense he gave away the office but retained power over the issue, because he was in a better position to force the Democrats to endorse the war by not running. He had somebody else [eventually Humphrey] carrying the ball."

(At the same time, McCarthy said Johnson's withdrawal should have, but didn't, bring Kennedy's position on Vietnam under closer scrutiny. "If you read his statements," McCarthy told me much later, "he really wasn't against the war; he was against the way it was being fought. What he brought to the campaign was pretty much the same proposition that he and McNamara [sic] and those guys had proposed to give to Lyndon, saying 'we won't run against you if you let us run the war.' But no one ever got down to reading what his proposition on the war was. It was that he was against Lyndon Johnson. [Henry] Kissinger [as Nixon's secretary of state] said what they used to settle the war was essentially the Kennedy platform, which was kind of progressive surrender not very different from Lyndon's. The press didn't sort it out, we couldn't sort it out. If the press had massively said, 'Look, this guy's not against the war, he's against the way it's being run,' or if we had had enough money to run a lot of ads, we might have been able to do it. But the whole projection was, 'He's against the war.'")

* * *

One of Hubert Humphrey's first concerns the day after the Johnson pullout was whether Kennedy had already filled the void among party regulars. Aides checked around the country, and by the time Humphrey arrived home from Mexico they were able to report to him that most of those contacted said they would hold off, awaiting his decision on running. He checked them himself, meanwhile meeting with his closest political advisers and friends to assess the political landscape ahead. He promised those he called he would have an answer for them soon.

Nixon, meanwhile, made it abundantly clear that in his mind Johnson's pullout and new moves to bring about negotiations had relieved him of the political burden of spelling out how he intended to end the war in Vietnam.

As was his style, he wrapped the politically beneficial in the words of self-sacrifice and high purpose.

"In light of these diplomatic moves," he intoned, "and in order to avoid anything that might, even inadvertently, cause difficulty for our negotiators, I shall not make the comprehensive statement on Vietnam which I had planned for this week." He did, however, urge Johnson to recall "the lesson of Korea," when most of the U.S. casualties were sustained after peace talks began, and warned against any settlement "that would encourage further aggression by its weakness." While it was a time "to explore every avenue toward settlement," he went on, in effect laying the groundwork for later criticism, it was also a "time to keep on guard against the temptations of a camouflaged surrender."

On April 2, as Wisconsin voted in its presidential primaries, McCarthy spent part of the day in Nebraska. He told reporters he had asked many Democratic leaders not to make any commitments until later in the campaign and had told them that whatever happened, he was "in the race all the way." He assured the leaders, he said, that he had "no arrangement" with Kennedy and there would be none. For that reason, he noted, he had withdrawn a week earlier from participation in a joint slate with Kennedy for the District of Columbia primary in May. He had been concerned at first, he said, that Johnson's pullout would start a stampede to Kennedy, "but I think that rush hasn't come." The Kennedy campaign, he said, "is like a grass fire. It will just burn off the surface. Mine is like a fire in a peat bog. It will hold on for six months."

McCarthy dismissed a possible Humphrey entry into the race as "irrelevant," saying it would "give some people, like labor leaders, a chance to hide for a while, but I don't think it will make much difference one way or the other."

By nightfall, the voters of Wisconsin had resoundingly expressed their agreement that Johnson had to go. They gave McCarthy 56.2 percent in the state's Democratic primary, and fifty-two of the sixty convention delegates at stake, to 34.6 percent for the sitting president. Write-ins for Kennedy totaled 6.4 percent and for Humphrey 0.5.

That night, according to Lowenstein later, Goodwin called him into his room at the Sheraton-Schroeder in Milwaukee and told him: "You and I can make McCarthy president. He's catching on. The things about him that are unattractive can be overcome. People don't know about them. He has a lot going for him because people are very angry at the way Kennedy's behaved. He is now the man who knocked off Lyndon Johnson. If we'll stay with him, we can win the primaries for him." Then, Lowenstein said, Goodwin "looked at me very solemnly and said, 'The question is, do we want Eugene McCarthy to be our next president'?'"

The question touched not only on the matter of loyalty to McCarthy— "Goodwin had quite properly said at the beginning that he would go to Kennedy if he entered, and I had not," Lowenstein recalled—but also on the doubts that were stirring within the McCarthy camp about its own candidate, as a result of his often arbitrary manner. Even before the New Hampshire primary, Lowenstein said, "McCarthy's behavior was so odd that a very serious Dump McCarthy movement began among the people who were for McCarthy. There were a series of meetings, very involved meetings, about that, whether he should be supported or not, whether another effort should be made to get Kennedy in." The concerns were cooled, he said, when McCarthy promised to step up "the amount of energy and time he would be willing to put in." But, Lowenstein said, "as people came to know him better, there was not always a consistency between statements made at one place and another, and therefore the feeling that a statement was a commitment was naive. . . ."

* * *

In the Republican primary, Nixon succeeded in topping his New Hampshire vote, getting 79.4 percent, to only 11 percent for Reagan and his absentee campaign that on the final weekend had run long television documentaries about him. Nixon, like Kennedy, was now also deprived of his prime target. But he confidently told aides that it would not be long before Humphrey would enter the race and could be attacked as the defender of the Johnson policies.

On April 3, Kennedy had his meeting with Johnson in the Cabinet Room. He brought along Sorensen, who had maintained a civil relationship with the president, and LBJ had Rostow and a political aide, Charles Murphy, on hand. The talk was stilted and proper, focusing not on the politics of the situation but on Johnson's plan for advancing peace talks with Hanoi. At one point Johnson read a teletype message, then handed it to Rostow, who passed it to Kennedy. It said that Hanoi was willing to start negotiations on stopping the American bombing of the North, and Kennedy expressed satisfaction at this "first step." LBJ pointedly advised Kennedy that he did not intend to take sides in the Democratic nomination fight.

After Kennedy left, the president summoned Humphrey and told him the same. It could not have been particularly bad news for the vice president, considering the low state of Johnson's popularity. Still, Johnson seemed in succeeding days to go out of his way to be impartial where Humphrey was concerned. When a luncheon was scheduled for the formal announcement of his candidacy later in the month and a number of Johnson cabinet members indicated their intention to attend, including fellow Minnesotan Orville Freeman, LBJ was outraged. According to Johnson White House aide Joseph Califano in his book *The Triumph and Tragedy of Lyndon Johnson*, the president phoned him and declared: "I can't have the government torn apart by cabinet officers and presidential appointees fighting among themselves about Kennedy, McCarthy and Humphrey." He instructed his aide, Califano wrote, to call the cabinet members and tell them to "stay out of the race or get out of the government."

Johnson, on the same day he met with Kennedy and then Humphrey, told a group of news editors that he was "very interested" in the Hanoi reply, but he could not limit the bombing further without risking "the lives of our boys and our security." He said he was ready to send a delegation "to any forum at any time to discuss the means of bringing this war to an end" and proposed Phnom Penh as the site. He also disclosed plans to go to Honolulu the next day to confer with U.S. military and diplomatic leaders in the Pacific.

* * *

Now the political battleground turned to Indiana. All things being equal, neither McCarthy nor Kennedy would have chosen the state for their first direct confrontation. In Birch Bayh and Vance Hartke, it did have two liberal senators as well as Democratic Governor Branigin. But Indiana was a place of generally conservative politics and outlook that conspicuously celebrated Americanism. The capital, Indianapolis, was national headquarters for the American Legion, and the center of town, with two huge war memorials, gave the city a distinctly military air. It seemed hardly the place to voice sharp criticisms of the use of American armed forces abroad.

Beyond that, Indiana was a state of enormous provincial pride. The locals always referred to themselves as "Hoosiers" almost as if the name connoted another country, and indeed out-of-state visitors sometimes felt they were in one. Favorite-son candidates seldom pose a real threat to national candidates in a presidential primary, but the presence of Branigin on the ballot, originally as a stand-in for LBJ but now an unofficial stand-in for the yet-to-declare Humphrey, muddied the picture. The Democratic Party organization in Indiana was a strong one on paper, bolstered by an old-fashioned patronage system that assessed state workers a percentage of their salaries for party activities.

Also, the readers of the *Indianapolis Star* and *News*, owned by archconservative Eugene Pulliam (grandfather of future Vice President Dan Quayle), received a daily dose of flag-waving Americanism, as well as sharp editorial criticism of liberals and antiwar activists that was not always confined to the editorial page. It was a fact that Kennedy particularly was soon to learn, to his consternation. Amid reports that the Kennedys were trying to buy the primary election—and they *were* pouring substantial amounts of money into the state to sustain strenuous canvassing efforts—the *Star* featured an editorial cartoon showing Robert and Ethel as the legendary Midwestern bank robbers Bonnie and Clyde racing through the state in an open roadster, tossing dollar bills with abandon.

Finally, there was a white ethnic, blue-collar mix to Indiana's population that posed a special challenge for a candidate who preached against racial injustice and inequities. Blacks constituted only 9 percent of Hoosiers statewide; there was a sizable white, blue-collar vote in heavily industrial Lake County southeast of Chicago and in other midsized cities that had given a heavy vote to George Wallace, preaching law and order, in the 1964 presidential primary. Kennedy somehow had to fashion a black and blue-collar coalition woven of both themes—racial justice and toughness on crime—that to many whites, convinced that crime disproportionately infected black ghetto life, seemed at cross purposes. The challenge would prove to be Kennedy's most difficult in Indiana, and his success in meeting it ultimately his most significant political achievement in the state.

The day after his meeting with Johnson, April 4, Kennedy made his first campaign foray into Indiana, where a downtown Indianapolis headquarters had already been opened over an old movie theater showing *Gone With the Wind*. He spoke at Notre Dame and Ball State Universities before sizable but not ecstatic crowds. At Ball State, a student asked about racial conflict and Kennedy replied that while there were extremists among whites and blacks, "most people in America want to do the decent thing."

* * *

That view, however, was being severely tested on this same day in Memphis, where Martin Luther King was again rallying the striking sanitation workers. On the day before, King had returned to the city and, learning that a federal injunction against a planned demonstration two days hence had been obtained, warned that "we are not going to be stopped by Mace or injunctions." He told reporters: "We stand on the First Amendment. In the past, on the basis of conscience, we have had to break injunctions, and if necessary we may do it. We'll cross that bridge when we come to it."

Defending the city's call for the injunction, Frank Gianotti, the Memphis city attorney, said it was motivated by a fear "that in the turmoil of the moment someone may even harm Dr. King's life, and with all the force of language we can use we want to emphasize that we don't want that to happen."

King was persuaded finally to delay the demonstration until the following Monday, in part to permit supportive labor union groups to get to Memphis.

That night of April 3, however, King had preached to a capacity crowd at Mason Temple about the climate of racial hatred and suspicion that was his routine lot to encounter. It was a cold and miserable night and he had not wanted to go to the hall, friends said later, suspecting that the turnout would be poor. He had in fact asked his chief lieutenant, Ralph Abernathy, to fill in for him, but Abernathy phoned from the hall to say it was jammed and that the crowd was expecting him. So he went, in what these friends recalled was a reluctant and somber mood that his words readily conveyed.

He told of the pilot on his plane from Atlanta that day telling his passengers over the public address system: "We're sorry for the delay, but we have Dr. Martin Luther King on the plane, and to be sure that nothing would be wrong on the plane, we had to check out everything carefully. And we've guarded the plane all night."

King had talked of the rumors, the death threats that always swirled around him. "Well, I don't know what will happen now," he had said. "But it really doesn't matter with me now. Because I've been to the mountaintop. I won't mind." The audience responded with "Amen" and other participatory calls as he went on: "Like anybody, I would like to live a long life. Longevity has its place. But I'm not concerned about that now. I just want to do God's will. And He's allowed me to go up to the mountain. And I've looked over, and I've seen the promised land."

In words that would soon seem to have been prophetic, King continued: "I may not get there with you, but I want you to know tonight that we as a people will get to the promised land. So I'm happy tonight. I'm not worried about anything. I'm not fearing any man. Mine eyes have seen the glory of the coming of the Lord!"

That same day, a man registering as Eric S. Galt checked into the New Rebel Hotel in Memphis. He was the same man who, under the name Harvey Lowmyer, had bought the rifle in the Birmingham gun supply shop the previous weekend. He checked out of the New Rebel the next day, April 4, and went to the York Arms Company, where he bought a pair of Bushnell binoculars costing $41.50 from Cordra York Sr. Then he moved to a rooming house at 424½ South Main Street, signing in as John Willard, and was given Room 5B, next to one occupied by a disabled veteran named Charles Stevens. The man reported later that "Willard" had made repeated trips to the bathroom, which overlooked Room 306 of the Lorraine Motel at 420 South Main, where King was staying.

King remained in his room at the Lorraine all afternoon, working on plans for his demonstration and march five days later, which would mark the first time he had ever actually defied an injunction. Early that evening, he and Abernathy were to go to dinner at the home of a local minister, Samuel Kyles. A few minutes before six o'clock, a chauffeured car arrived outside the Lorraine to pick up King, Abernathy and Kyles. Abernathy was not quite ready to leave so King pulled open the sliding glass door to the second-floor balcony and stepped out.

Just below, in the courtyard, the chauffeur, Solomon Jones, Ben Branch, a local musician, and two King aides, Andrew Young and Jesse Jackson, stood around talking. They were all going to another church rally after the dinner. Jackson called up to King: "Do you know Ben?" King replied: "Yes. Ben, be sure and sing 'Precious Lord, Take My Hand.' Sing it real pretty." Jones advised King to wear a topcoat for the chill night and the civil rights leader said he would.

Across the way, in the cheap hotel, "Willard" stood in the bathtub at the small window overlooking the Lorraine Motel, his arm braced against it, his eye sighting the telescopic lens on the rifle and his finger on the trigger. He squeezed it just once. The shot exploded the street's quiet and King fell to the floor of the balcony, one foot caught in the railing and blood gushing from a three-inch tear in his face. The time later was fixed as one minute after six o'clock, Central Standard Time.

Abernathy leaned over King, and then Young, who had sprinted up to the room. In later reconstructions of the scene, Jackson insisted that he also had bent over the body of his fallen leader and ministered to him, and he wore a shirt that he said bore King's blood. But others swore that Jackson was in the courtyard below at the time. Jackson's precise whereabouts became the source of a major controversy about Jackson, particularly in the black community, and one that lingered as he himself rose in prominence among America's black leaders and in national politics.

Abernathy got a towel from inside the room and applied it to the wound, and Young tried to find King's pulse. They rushed him to nearby St. Joseph's Hospital, where surgeons went to work, but he was pronounced dead at five minutes past seven. The rifle later was found against the door of the Canipe Amusement Company on South Main. A white Mustang in which "Willard" had arrived was nowhere to be seen.

Robert Kennedy was sitting in the cabin of his chartered plane at the airport in Muncie, about to take off for Indianapolis, when a reporter who had just talked to his office rushed aboard and up the aisle to Kennedy's side with the startling news from Memphis that King had been shot. "Oh, no," Kennedy said, grimacing. Before more details were available, the plane took off for Weir Cook Airport. En route, Kennedy instructed Dutton to find out immediately on landing what King's condition was, and what the mood was in Indianapolis's black wards, one of which was to be the site of a large street-corner rally for him that night. The moment the plane touched down, Dutton raced to the airport police office and came back with the feared news: King was dead.

The black wards were quiet, Dutton told Kennedy, apparently because word of the tragedy had not yet reached them. A nervous Ethel Kennedy wanted her husband to cancel the event but he declined. He sent her on to their hotel, the old Marott, with an aide. Then Kennedy and Dutton climbed into the back seat of an awaiting closed car, with Barry riding ahead in the lead police car. Kennedy asked Dutton what he should say, and Dutton mentioned the obvious—the need for nonviolence and reconciliation of the races, since it was already suspected that the assailant was white.

It was immediately clear upon arrival at the rally that the crowd did not know of King's fate. A festive mood governed the approximately 1,000 people in the audience, predominantly black. The cars drove directly to the platform, where Barry jumped from the lead car and hustled protectively to Kennedy's side. The candidate, hunched in a black topcoat against the night chill, climbed out and told the event organizer that he wanted to speak at once. After a perfunctory introduction, he began with a somber and wavering voice: "I have some bad news for you, for all our fellow citizens, and people who love peace all over the world. And that is that Martin Luther King was shot and killed tonight."

A gasp ran through the crowd, and some isolated screams of "No!" But not everyone grasped at once what Kennedy had said, and the mood of celebration continued among some, who applauded and cheered incongruously as he pressed on. Finally, by his own grave demeanor as well as by his words, he got through to them what had happened. The extemporaneous remarks, delivered from the few scanty notes Kennedy was able to assemble on the sober ride with Dutton from the airport, provided one of the most poignant moments of the eventful year.

"Martin Luther King," he said, "dedicated his life to love and to justice for his fellow human beings, and he died because of that effort. In this difficult day, in this difficult time for the United States, it is perhaps well to ask what kind of a nation we are and what direction we want to move in. For those of you who are black—considering the evidence there evidently is that there were white people who were responsible—you can be filled with bitterness, with hatred, and a desire for revenge. We can move in that direction as a country, in great polarization—black people amongst black, white people amongst white, filled with hatred toward one another. Or we can make an effort, as Martin Luther King did, to understand and to comprehend, and to replace that violence, that stain of bloodshed that has spread across our land, with an effort to understand with compassion and love."

In a personal reference that was almost unheard of from him, Kennedy went on: "For those of you who are black and are tempted to be filled with hatred and distrust at the injustice of such an act, against all white people, I can only say that I feel in my own heart the same kind of feeling. I had a member of my family killed, but he was killed by a white man. But we have to make an effort in the United States, we have to make an effort to understand, to go beyond these rather difficult times.

"My favorite poet was Aeschylus. He wrote: 'In our sleep, pain which cannot forget falls drop by drop upon the heart until, in our own despair, against our will, comes wisdom through the awful grace of God.' What we need in the United States is not division; what we need in the United States is not hatred; what we need in the United States is not violence or lawlessness, but love and wisdom, and compassion toward one another, and a feeling of justice toward those who still suffer within our country, whether they be white or they be black.

"So I shall ask you tonight to return home, to say a prayer for the family of Martin Luther King, that's true, but more importantly to say a prayer for our own country, which all of us love—a prayer for understanding and that compassion of which I spoke. We can do well in this country. We will have difficult times. We've had difficult times in the past. We will have difficult times in the future. It is not the end of violence; it is not the end of lawlessness; it is not the end of disorder. But the vast majority of white people and the vast majority of black people in this country want to live together, want to improve the quality of our life, and want justice for all human beings who abide in our land. Let us dedicate ourselves to what the Greeks wrote so many years ago: to tame the savageness of man and to make gentle the life of this world. Let us dedicate ourselves to that, and say a prayer for our country and for our people."

Among those in the crowd was John Lewis, a King aide and disciple who had been severely beaten as a leader of the Selma, Alabama, march of 1965. He had volunteered as a Kennedy worker in Indianapolis's black community. "People were stunned," Lewis recalled years later, when he was a member of Congress from Atlanta. "They could not believe it. They started crying; a lot of us stood there crying." Kennedy, he remembered, "spoke from his soul, he spoke from his heart. He appealed to the crowd not to be bitter. He referred to his brother being shot by a white man. That did more to keep the crowd together. And by speaking to that crowd he appealed to the nation not to be engaged in violence, but to remember Dr. King and what he stood for."

Leaving the audience of shocked and weeping men and women, Kennedy went back to his hotel and phoned King's widow, Coretta. He asked whether there was anything he could do, and she requested help in bringing her husband's body from Memphis to Atlanta. He said he would take care of it. He asked old Justice Department aide Burke Marshall to fly to Atlanta to be with her and had a chartered plane sent for the body—an action for which he was later criticized as seeking to extract political gain from the grim circumstance.

From the White House, President Johnson addressed the nation over television, calling on "all Americans . . . [to] search their hearts as they ponder this most tragic incident. . . . We can achieve nothing by lawlessness and divisiveness among the American people," he said. "It's only by joining together, and only by working together, can we continue to move toward equality and fulfillment for all of our people." He said he was postponing his trip to Honolulu to deal with the violence that already was erupting in cities around the country—including the capital itself from which he spoke.

Others, however, did not heed Johnson's plea for restraint. Floyd McKissick, national director of CORE, observed that night that King's philosophy of nonviolence had died with him, and that "white people are going to suffer as much as black people." In downtown Washington, looting and vandalism broke out in predominantly black business sections along 14th Street Northwest after Stokely Carmichael had led a group of young blacks calling on shops to close as a mark of respect for King. The *New York Times* reported him as urging a swelling crowd: "If you don't have a gun, go home. . . . When the white man comes he is coming to kill you. I don't want any black blood in the street. Go home and get you a gun and then come back, because I got me a gun."

At a news conference the next morning, Carmichael warned that "when white America killed Doctor King last night, she declared war" on black America and there could be "no alternative to retribution. . . . Black people have to survive and the only way they will survive is by getting guns." Roy Wilkins, executive director of the NAACP, pointedly rejected Carmichael's exhortations, saying that in all the "talk about 'Get Whitey' . . . the people who lose their lives are Negroes." And Whitney Young, the executive director of the National Urban League, observed that "the only thing more tragic" than King's assassination "would be that the only response would be black anger and white sympathy. What we need today is black determination and white action."

Rioting or racial disturbances that night or the next two days also exploded in Boston, New York, Newark, Trenton, Baltimore, Pittsburgh, Cincinnati, Detroit, Chicago, Nashville, Memphis, Kansas City and Oakland, as well as in more than a hundred smaller cities and towns. The *New York Times* eventually reported forty-six deaths and hundreds more injured. On April 5, Johnson called out 4,000 federal troops to quell the rioting in Washington, and before quiet was restored across the land more than 20,000 regular Army and 34,000 National Guardsmen had been ordered to antiriot duty. Attorney General Clark was dispatched at once to Memphis, where he reported that the FBI was seeking the assassin in several states, and that "all the evidence indicates that this was the act of a single individual."

Kennedy canceled the rest of his schedule except for a speech in Cleveland the morning after the assassination that he felt compelled to make. It proved to mark a turning point in his campaign, away from what seemed to so many a single-minded assault against the Vietnam War to a more comprehensive theme of racial and economic justice and reconciliation. Before the City Club of Cleveland, he talked somberly about "this mindless menace of violence in America which again stains our land and every one of our lives. . . . What has violence ever accomplished? What has it ever created? No martyr's cause has ever been stilled by his assassin's bullet. No wrongs have ever been righted by riots and civil disorders. A sniper is only a coward, not a hero, and an uncontrolled, uncontrollable mob is only the voice of madness, not the voice of the people."

He talked of "another kind of violence, slower but just as deadly, destructive as the shot or the bomb in the night. This is the violence of institutions; indifference and inaction and slow decay. This is the violence that affects the poor, that poisons relations between men because their skin has different colors. This is a slow destruction of a child by hunger, and schools without books and homes without heat in the winter. This is the breaking of a man's spirit by denying him the chance to stand as a father and as a man among other men. . . .

"We must admit the vanity of our false distinctions among men and learn to find our own advancement in the search for the advancement of all. We must admit in ourselves that our own children's future cannot be built on the misfortunes of others. . . . Surely we can learn, at least, to look at those around us as fellow men, and surely we can begin to work a little harder to bind up the wounds among us and to become in our own hearts brothers and countrymen again."

Even as Kennedy spoke, however, violence continued to erupt in cities across the country as black Americans expressed their rage at the killing of their most revered and charismatic leader. In Oakland, police engaged in a ninety-minute gun battle with members of the Black Panther Party, one of whom was killed and four other persons wounded, including Eldridge Cleaver, the Panthers' education minister, who was arrested.

On the morning of Sunday, April 7, a day after Johnson had viewed Washington's damage from a helicopter, Kennedy walked through the ruins of the capital's black neighborhoods. Everywhere, although he was white, he was greeted with gratitude for coming. A black woman came up, looked at him and then looked again and said, "Is that you?" Kennedy nodded. She grasped his hand and said: "I knew you'd be the first to come here, darling." It was a moment that crystallized the special empathy that joined this young white man of great wealth and prominence with impoverished city blacks.

"It was not so much what he said," Goodwin theorized much later, "but they detected the same intensity in him a lot of them had." Ted Kennedy told me much the same in a later interview: "People who have to live so much by emotions, who depend on their feelings, can see sincerity in others. He felt deeply about the things he talked about, and he showed it. They could tell he meant it. . . . The campaign personalized and intensified his concern. It happens in campaigns. I saw it happen before, with my other brother." And Dutton remarked: "He identified with people who hurt. Maybe it was because he hurt."

On the same day Kennedy walked Washington's black neighborhoods, Goodwin went to McCarthy's home and told him he now felt obliged to rejoin his old friend. McCarthy, as usual, took the news passively. The fires and looting continued in some other cities for another day or more. (Among the college students who joined relief efforts in Washington was Bill Clinton at Georgetown, who drove through burned-out black sections of the city delivering food and first-aid equipment to aid stations in neighborhood churches.)

One of the worst scenes was in Baltimore, where wholesale rioting had broken out on the city's overwhelmingly black east side on the night of April 5, the night after King's assassination. Moderate black leaders took to the streets in a vain effort to cool the situation and before police quelled the rioting, six people were dead, 700 were injured and 5,000 arrested. Governor Agnew declared a "state of emergency and crisis." He eventually requested about 5,000 federal troops along with 6,000 National Guardsmen to help deal with the violence and more than a thousand fires that raged in the city's predominantly black sections. Agnew seethed at the destruction and disorder, with eventual ramifications that once again would contribute to his unlikely rise to national prominence.

On April 8 in Memphis, Coretta King led the march her husband had scheduled in support of the striking sanitation workers. An estimated 42,000 people took part, about one third of whom were white. In front of City Hall, she urged the crowd to "carry on" but added: "How many men must die before we can really have a free and true and peaceful society? How long will it take?"

A nation that by now had been well schooled in the protocols of political assassinations showed the proper sensitivity to the circumstances—unlike the spectacle in the wake of President Kennedy's death in 1963, when the National Football League played its scheduled games on the same Sunday the nation was mourning its loss. The April 8 opening of the major league baseball season was postponed, as were the Stanley Cup professional hockey and the National Basketball Association playoffs, and the Academy Awards presentation in Hollywood. (Two nights later, the winner for best picture, somewhat ironically, was *In the Heat of the Night*, a drama of racial violence in the South, whose star, Rod Steiger, playing a racist Southern sheriff, won the award for best actor.) Schools, libraries, museums and stock exchanges closed their doors.

* * *

On April 9, McCarthy, who had heard of King's death while campaigning in San Francisco, and Kennedy went to Atlanta for his funeral, sitting a pew apart in King's Ebenezer Baptist Church, jammed to overflowing with dignitaries. Vice President Humphrey led the official government contingent. Also present was Richard Nixon, who was not indifferent to the violent act that brought the other notables to Atlanta—nor to the opportunity it provided him to embellish the theme of law and order that now would move to the forefront of his campaign, with Johnson no longer a prime target.

The service for King was long and the church sweltering as Abernathy orated at length. The departed's earlier request for brevity and simplicity was not honored, although a tape of his sermon embodying that request was rather incongruously played at the service. Afterward, King's coffin was hauled through the Atlanta streets on an old green farm wagon pulled by two mules for three and a half miles to Morehouse College, where another memorial service was held.

Most of the notables marched behind the casket. Kennedy again was criticized later for taking off his suit jacket under the broiling Georgia sun, although many of the other less notable marchers had done the same. McCarthy rode in a car in the procession because, his wife wrote later, "Gene was adamantly opposed to the idea of walking. He felt that it was not the kind of thing he would enter into a competition about." But later on, she wrote,

"Gene began to feel the simple emotion of the situation and he . . . decided to get out of the car and walk the rest of the way."

Dr. Benjamin Mays, president emeritus of Morehouse, expressed uncomfortable sentiments in his eulogy: "We all pray that the assassin will be apprehended. But make no mistake, the American people are in part responsible for Martin Luther King Jr.'s death. The assassin had [heard] enough condemnation of King and of Negroes to feel that he had public support. He knew that millions hated King. . . . Morehouse College will never be the same because Martin Luther came here; and the nation and the world will be indebted to him for centuries to come."

After the crowd had struggled through "We Shall Overcome," King's body was taken to Southview Cemetery, where a monument awaited proclaiming the most famous words from his historic speech on the steps of the Lincoln Memorial: FREE AT LAST, FREE AT LAST, THANK GOD ALMIGHTY, I'M FREE AT LAST. Abernathy observed: "No coffin can hold his greatness, but we submit his body to the ground."

The immediate product of King's death and the resultant riots was swift passage of a new civil rights bill prohibiting racial discrimination in the sale or rental of the bulk of the nation's housing, pushed energetically by Johnson. Included in the bill, and little noticed at the time, was the amendment by Senator Strom Thurmond of South Carolina making it a felony to travel across state lines with the "intent" of causing a "riot." (In March 1969, the only individuals ever indicted under the provision were the Chicago Eight charged with conspiracy to foment "actual or threatened" violence at the 1968 Democratic National Convention.)

No amount of legislation, however, could fill the void left in the hearts and hopes of millions of Americans, black and white, for the fallen civil rights leader. The dream of racial equality and harmony of which King spoke so eloquently seemed suddenly further beyond reach.

Barely more than three months into the stormy year of 1968, one national leader had been removed from the scene by what amounted to voter insistence, and another by a vicious act as yet unexplained. Still, those not content to dream pressed on with the two central public campaigns of the year that had driven Martin Luther King—to advance economic justice at home and to end the war in Vietnam.

Among the five most prominent presidential hopefuls remaining after Johnson's withdrawal, only one—Robert Kennedy—was widely perceived as an outspoken, aggressive champion of both causes embraced and led by King. McCarthy and Nixon campaigned as candidates who could and would end the war, but neither had a close and widely recognized identification with issues of racial equality; Humphrey, still publicly weighing his candidacy but widely expected to fill the vacancy left by Johnson, had that identification but continued to adhere to the LBJ line on the war. George Wallace opposed both causes in his own strident war against the Washington establishment.

Kennedy thus became the political inheritor of King's two-pronged dream. The black leader had never endorsed or expressed a public preference for any of the candidates, but according to Marian Wright Edelman as quoted in Schlesinger's *Robert Kennedy and His Times*, he was prepared to endorse Kennedy's candidacy when he was slain in Memphis. At any rate, the dreamers of peace abroad and racial harmony at home, who had had two clarion voices expressing their deepest felt sentiments, now had only one.

For Kennedy, however, that identification as seeker after and champion of racial injustice loomed as distinctly a mixed blessing as he moved toward his first direct challenge to McCarthy in the Indiana primary. The basic conservatism of the state, which in its southernmost counties especially was not far in racial attitudes from that of Dixie itself, did not promise an ideal forum for a campaign dedicated to lifting the lot of blacks and other minorities. The Ku Klux Klan, after all, had had early roots in southern Indiana. But King's associates made clear what they expected from Kennedy in a meeting in Atlanta the night their leader and friend was laid to rest, posing hostile questions about the depth of his commitment to their cause. He would have to tread carefully in Indiana, yet not surrender the almost worshipful support that black voters were demonstrating toward him in the urban tinderboxes across the land.

* * *

Johnson, in the wake of the riots, at first considered using them as a launching pad for new civil rights initiatives, just as he had done after the death of John Kennedy. As Doris Kearns Goodwin recalled much later, as a White House fellow at the Labor Department she helped draft a speech to a joint session of Congress with which Johnson "hoped somehow to capitalize on the emotions that were felt in the country [as a result of] the riots, as he had done in the great 'We Shall Overcome' speech in 1965 which brought about the voting rights act. . . . This speech hopefully would bring about some major step forward on economic justice.

"We worked on the speech for several days," she recalled, "but then the word came back from the White House that Johnson was realizing when he looked at the public mood that they were not seeing the riots in that sympathetic way, but were rather angry at the chaos and the disorder, and that there was no time and no chance for him to get popular opinion behind him by going to the Congress and asking for something for civil rights. So that what had been steady movement deeper and deeper at breaking apart the pieces of the civil rights problem, from the public accommodations act to the voting rights act to the open housing act of '68, this might have well been the next step, perhaps some sort of economic redistribution or the model cities in a fuller version.

"But the whole disorder of the society, and the sensed perception of chaos that the riots contributed to, had to do partly with the frustrations of the war and not being able to go forward with the hopes that the civil rights movement had generated. . . . The riots in some ways were another symbol of the turning of the popular tide against that forward progress."

* * *

In Montgomery, Alabama, George Wallace continued to cool his heels as his wife struggled at home to recover from yet another series of major operations and cancer treatments. Sitting behind the desk in the Capitol building of the Old Confederacy that once was his and now, legally anyway, was his wife's, he assessed for me one afternoon the impact on his own candidacy of the assassination of King and the aftermath riots.

"I don't think about it in terms of how it helps or hurts in politics," he said. "I just hope they catch the one who did it. I wish we could stop all this shooting." He flicked cigar ashes into a wastebasket, then went on. "Of course, any breakdown of law and order is going to support the position of anybody like me who is against a breakdown of law and order." He paused, then added, "Now, I don't want to be helped that way. I don't want to see any headlines that say Wallace is helped by the riots. All I say is they seem to be getting worse, and nobody wants to try to stop it. And that's all I want to say about that particular subject."

In the quiet of his office, or his wife's, Wallace was far from the sneering, incendiary haranguer of the campaign stump. He clearly recognized the situation had reached a point where it could backfire on him. Earlier, he had been quoted as saying if the first looter were shot there would be no more looting. Now he was more cautious. "This matter of just letting people shoot and burn with impunity has to stop," he said. "But I heard some government employees were looting in Washington. I'll tell you this: I think government employees who loot should lose their jobs so fast it would make their heads spin. . . . If you had strong policy, these things wouldn't get started."

Wallace at last was about ready to resume campaigning. By this time aides claimed to have him on the ballot in eight states and to be in the process of qualifying him in eighteen others. At a nearby campaign headquarters, women volunteers were tirelessly opening piles of envelopes bearing checks from, as Wallace liked to put it, "the little people," who were the heart of his independent effort.

He continued to talk of winning a popular plurality in enough states to win an electoral majority. But now he was suggesting he might get just enough electoral votes to persuade one of the two major-party candidates "to make a covenant with the American people—not a deal. That word," he said, "doesn't sound good." The "covenant," he hinted, would have to do with implementing the philosophy of states' rights so dear to his heart, especially in the area of civil rights. He flicked some more ashes into the wastebasket and smiled his tight, crooked little smile.

* * *

In Baltimore, there was another by-product of the King assassination and the riots it triggered that in due time would have significant political ramifications for the Republican Party, and eventually for the nation as a whole. On April 11, the same day Lyndon Johnson signed the new federal civil rights bill into law, Governor Agnew summoned about a hundred prominent black leaders to a meeting in the legislative council chamber of the State Office Building in Baltimore. It was only a week after the arrests of the Bowie State College students and a few days after the rioting and fires in Baltimore. Agnew's aides insisted later that the invitations had gone out before the Baltimore riots, but some of the leaders said they received them only after the rioting and looting were over.

An immediate catalyst for the meeting, according to Colonel Robert J. Lally, the superintendent of state police, was a report of a police undercover man. On April 3, the day before King's assassination, he had been assigned to keep tabs on Stokely Carmichael as he visited a tough black neighborhood to confer with local black figures in the community. While sitting in the next booth in a neighborhood café, he told Lally, he overhead Carmichael say at one point that "the only way to deal with the white man is across the barrel of a gun," and that riots were part of the struggle against the white power structure.

Lally said he sent a full report to Agnew. "This perturbed him no end," Lally said later, "and this was the thing that instigated the meeting. [Agnew believed] the black leaders with whom he was trying to work literally ignored his efforts to bring about peace in the community. He couldn't understand their dealing with extremists." There was no evidence that any of these black leaders had acted on Carmichael's words. But several of them pointed out later that for reasons of maintaining their own credibility in the black community, they could not simply snub a national black leader of such prominence.

In any event, Agnew was loaded for bear as he prepared to enter his own post-riot meeting with what was regarded as the mainstream black leadership of the city and state. About an hour before it was to begin, he called in his top law enforcement officials—Lally, Baltimore Police Commissioner Donald D. Pomerleau and Maryland National Guard General George M. Gelston among them, some dressed in riot uniform—and briefed them on what he was going to say. "He anticipated some sort of reaction from the black leaders," Lally told me afterward, "but he never actually expressed what he expected. He mentioned at one point that he was probably committing political suicide because of what he was going to tell them, but he felt it was necessary to bring about peace in the community."

Not everyone in public office in Baltimore agreed that Agnew's planned remarks would achieve that end. Mayor Thomas D'Alesandro, a Democrat but old Agnew friend, somehow got hold of a press copy of the speech and immediately telephoned him, urging him not to deliver it. Agnew aide Scott Moore said he heard later that the governor had received a death threat the day before and "I think that had an impact. The times were rough. But as a lawyer who would not want to be chewed out by a judge in open court," Moore commented, "you would have thought he would have been more sensitive to how the black leaders would feel."

As the black community figures arrived for the meeting, some were disturbed by the fact that a state police officer screened each one before admitting him. "I knew it was going to be a fiasco when I went over there," State Senator Clarence Mitchell, one of Baltimore's most moderate black voices, said later. "My instincts told me it would be, but I went." As the guests entered the room, whose arrangement took on the aspect of a court chamber, they saw three television cameras and crews in place to record the scene. Once seated, they were subjected to a warm-up talk by Agnew handyman Charles Bresler, he of the Bowie State fiasco. He proceeded to deliver a patronizing sermon about Agnew as the son of Greek immigrants and himself as the son of Jewish immigrants who had lifted themselves by their bootstraps. It was, said Christopher Gaul, then a *Baltimore Sun* reporter, "the most offensive thing I had ever heard north of Mississippi."

Bresler, the loyal Agnewite, himself described for me later the scene that then ensued: "In the midst of my speech, in they came. The door flung open, and by law, in front of the governor and behind the governor came state troopers. . . . You know what they look like—like an honor guard. . . . There was General Gelston in his paratrooper jumpsuit; you know, fatigues with his paratrooper boots, and he had a habit of carrying under his arm a crop, a riding crop. With his shaved—you know, crew-cut—head, typical military man all the way down the line."

Bresler described the entry of Agnew and all the law enforcement officials trailed by Agnew's human relations aide, Gil Ware, the only black man in the entourage, marching in and taking all the seats at a long head table. "Gelston puts his crop down there," Bresler continued, "I look for—there's no place for Gil to sit down, so Gil has to stand at the end. Now you look at this lineup. . . . You talk about a foreboding, all-white military lineup. It looked like the Gestapo was ready to interrogate you. . . ."

Agnew began reading the riot act to his black audience in a plodding manner, without looking up: "Ladies and gentlemen: hard on the heels of tragedy come the assignment of blame and the excuses. I did not invite you here for either purpose. I did not ask you here to recount previous deprivations, nor to hear me enumerate prior attempts to correct them. I did not request your presence to bid for peace with the public dollar." In his most insulting manner, Agnew was saying: Don't subject me to your bleeding hearts or expect me to buy you off.

By way of reminding his listeners that they were supposed to be in the mainstream, moderate leadership of the black community, he went on: "The circuit-riding, Hanoi-visiting type of leader is missing from this assembly. The caterwauling, riot-inciting, burn-America-down type of leader is conspicuous by his absence. That is no accident, ladies and gentlemen, it is just good planning. And in the vernacular of today—'That's what it's all about, baby!'"

Having thus identified the audience as the ostensibly responsible black leadership, Agnew proceeded to dress it down in the most pointed terms. He cited a "black unity" meeting held the previous month between moderates and black-power advocates after a split over inflammatory language by the latter. Agnew observed that many in the audience had "met in secret" with extremists "and you ran . . . you agreed, according to published reports that have not been denied, that you would not openly criticize any black spokesman, regardless of his remarks. You were beguiled by the rationalizations of unity," he said. "You were intimidated by veiled threats; you were stung by insinuations that you were Mister Charlie's boy, by epithets like 'Uncle Tom.' God knows I cannot fault you who spoke out for breaking and running in the face of what appeared to be overwhelming opinion in the Negro community. But actually it was only the opinion of a few, distorted and magnified by the silence of most of you here today."

That was enough for Parren Mitchell, a prominent Baltimore moderate and later a congressman. He walked out, announcing there would be a caucus of black leaders in the corridor. About a dozen others followed him out, and eventually a majority of the attendees. One of the first to leave with Mitchell was the Reverend Marion C. Bascom, a Republican who had been one of Agnew's first prominent black supporters when he ran for governor. Outside, he said of Agnew: "He is as sick as any bigot in America."

Agnew, undeterred by the walkout, droned on: "You know who the fires burned out just as you know who lit the fires. They were not lit in honor of your great fallen leader. Nor were they lit from an overwhelming sense of frustration and despair. Those fires were kindled at the suggestion and with the instruction of the advocates of violence."

Then, citing the report of Carmichael's visit to Baltimore on the day before King was killed, the governor observed: "The looting and rioting which has engulfed our city during the past several days did not occur by chance. . . . It is deplorable and a sign of sickness in our society that the lunatic fringes of the black and white communities speak with wide publicity while we, the moderates, remain consciously mute. I cannot believe that the only alternative to white racism is black racism."

Quoting incendiary remarks by Carmichael and Rap Brown, Agnew in his soon-to-be-famous alliterative style asked: "What possible hope is there for peace in our community if these apostles of anarchy are allowed to spew hatred unchallenged? . . . We cannot communicate and progress if the lunatic fringers are included in the problem-solving team. I publicly repudiate, condemn and reject all white racists. I call upon you to repudiate, condemn and reject all black racists. This so far you have not been willing to do."

One of the first blacks to respond to Agnew's harangue was Mrs. Juanita Jackson Mitchell, matriarch of one of Baltimore's most prominent black families and a civil rights pioneer in the city. As soon as she began to speak, Agnew went on the attack. "Do you repudiate black racists?" he shouted at the elderly woman. "Are you willing, as I am willing to repudiate the white racists, are you willing to repudiate the Carmichaels and the Browns?" The woman replied: "We have already done so. Didn't you read our—" A bullying Agnew broke in. "Answer me! Answer me! Answer me! Do you repudiate Stokely Carmichael and Rap Brown? Do you? Do you?"

It went on like that, incredibly, for another hour, by which time most of the invited black leaders had walked out. The black caucus moved to the Reverend Bascom's church up the street and finally issued a statement: "We are shocked at the gall of the governor, suggesting that only he can define the nature of the leadership of the black community. Agnew's actions are more in keeping with the slave system of a bygone era. At a time when the chief executive should be calling for unity, he deliberately sought to divide us."

Much later, Clarence Mitchell said of Agnew's performance: "I was shocked primarily because it had not been his pattern as governor. He had been open, listening to our problems. I have a tendency now to believe it was politically inspired. It was calculated to create a conservative image for political purposes. After Rockefeller insulted him, I believe Agnew decided he had to cast his lot with the conservatives. . . . You take a poll one day and you say, 'I'm going to move to bigger and better things.' You go with the breeze."

One who observed the same breeze, as noted earlier, was Pat Buchanan, who clipped newspaper stories about Agnew's tempestuous meeting with the black leaders and saw to it that they came to the attention of his boss, Dick Nixon. The transplanted Californian never would allow himself such blunt language; his own style favored furtive and suggestive code phrases, as in his standard campaign stump pitch on law and order: "Some of our courts have gone too far in weakening the peace forces as against the criminal forces, and we must restore the balance." If the listener wanted to apply a racial connotation to "criminal forces," he was free to do so. In any event, Agnew's harangue at the black leaders impressed upon Nixon that here was a philosophical soulmate—and a free agent from the Rockefeller camp to boot. He certainly bore watching.

* * *

Agnew was not, however, the toughest-talking white elected official in the wake of the riots triggered by the King assassination. In Chicago, where eleven blacks died, more than 500 whites and blacks were injured, nearly 3,000 persons arrested and 162 buildings entirely destroyed by fire, Mayor Daley on April 15 announced orders to city police to "shoot to kill" arsonists and to "shoot to maim or cripple" looters in any future rioting. Daley said he had been under the impression that these orders had been in effect during the recent riots, and was appalled to learn that police had been instructed to use their own discretion. He was going to make sure it wouldn't happen in the future.

The mayor's order came under immediate criticism from other public figures of both parties. Republican Mayor John Lindsay in New York observed: "We happen to think that protection of life . . . is more important than protecting property or anything else. . . . We are not going to turn disorder into chaos through the unprincipled use of armed force. In short, we are not going to shoot children in New York City." Attorney General Ramsey Clark called Daley's response "a very dangerous escalation of the problems we are so intent on solving," and even the FBI cautioned "against overresponding to disturbances."

In riots the previous summer, the agency warned, "persons thought to be looters were killed but it turned out upon later investigation that they were not looters." Daley later revised his order to say arsonists and looters "should be restrained if possible by minimum force." But he said at the same time they could not be given "permissive rights" to do as they chose.

* * *

Meanwhile, the hunt for King's killer had gone forward diligently by the FBI. On April 7, Attorney General Clark, turning aside speculation that the assassination might have been a conspiracy, had reiterated that "we have evidence of one man on the run. There is no evidence that more were involved." The gun was traced through its serial number and found to have been purchased in Birmingham by a man using the name Harvey Lowmyer. On April 11, the FBI impounded a 1966 white Mustang bearing an Alabama license plate that had been seen parked near a housing project in Atlanta since April 5, the day after the shooting.

It was soon established that "Galt" had bought the Mustang in Birmingham in the summer of 1967 and obtained a driver's license in that name. The FBI was able to discern that in the fall and winter of 1967 he had traveled between the West Coast and New Orleans, taking dancing lessons and a course in bartending in Hollywood, from which he was graduated in March 1968. Shortly after the assassination, unknown to the FBI, he moved to Toronto and by April 16 was living in a rooming house there, in a neighborhood containing a large colony of American men who had fled to Canada to escape the draft.

On that date, he went to the Kennedy Travel Agency on Bloor Street in downtown Toronto and ordered a twenty-one-day excursion plane ticket to Lisbon. When he told the agent, Lillian Spencer, that he was a Canadian but did not have a passport, she offered to help him get one—a routine travel agency service. He gave her a birth certificate, passport photo and affidavit of citizenship bearing the name Ramon George Sneyd, the name of a Metropolitan Toronto policeman, a stranger to him. It was learned later that he had managed to find out the real Sneyd's birth date and the names of his parents to obtain the birth certificate. The agent had the affidavit notarized for him as required by law and mailed it off to the Department of External Affairs in Ottawa.

Also on April 16, the FBI issued a federal fugitive warrant in Birmingham, charging "Galt," thirty-six years old, with having conspired with a man "whom he alleged to be his brother [to] injure, oppress, threaten or intimidate" King. On the same day, another warrant by the state of Tennessee was issued in Memphis charging him with first-degree murder. The FBI released two photographs of the man and on April 20 announced that "Galt" was an alias of James Earl Ray, actual age forty, who had escaped from the Missouri

State Penitentiary in a wooden crate in the back of a bakery truck on April 23, 1967, after having served seven years for armed robbery and auto theft.

Identification was made, the FBI said, after an extensive check of fingerprint records. Ray was said to have used numerous other aliases, including John Willard, the name for whom the room in Memphis was registered, as well as Lowmyer and Sneyd. The man was a tenth-grade school dropout who had joined the Army and was discharged in 1948 on grounds of "ineptness and lack of adaptability to military service." He had been arrested five times between 1949 and 1959. He was indicted within days in Tennessee on charges of murder and conspiring to violate King's civil rights.

At this time, Ray was still in Toronto awaiting his passport, which finally arrived in the mail in the name of Sneyd. His other aliases later were established to be the names of actual individuals living in the same Toronto neighborhood, some of them physically resembling the imposter, but none of them knowing him, or each other. The hunt for the King killer went on.

*   *   *

All this time that the nation focused on the escalating violence and racial conflict at home, the war in Vietnam raged on. On April 1, a force of 30,000 American and South Vietnam troops had launched a campaign called Operation Pegasus to relieve the besieged U.S. Marine base at Khe Sanh, surrounded by the enemy since January. Five days later, the siege had been lifted, and on April 8 South Vietnamese paratroopers undertook to recapture the Langvei Special Forces camp about three miles from Khe Sanh, even as Washington and Hanoi squabbled over a meeting place to open negotiations. Hanoi kept proposing sites within the communist bloc; LBJ kept rejecting them. Hope of agreement slipped as Defense Secretary Clifford on April 11 announced a call-up of 24,500 military reservists from thirty-four states for two years' service, 10,000 of whom would go to Vietnam. Clifford also announced a new troop ceiling of 549,500 American troops there.

The news appalled the war protest community, but it did nothing to depress a galloping stock market. For the first time since October 1929—the year of the great market crash—trading on the New York Stock Exchange exceeded 16.4 million shares. The Federal Reserve Board promptly raised the discount rate at which member banks could borrow from it to 5½ percent, the highest since that year, to curb inflation.

Federal Reserve Board chairman William McChesney Martin warned that "the nation is in the midst of the worst financial crisis since 1931." In a speech to the American Society of Newspaper Editors, he said the country was "faced with an intolerable budget deficit, and also an intolerable deficit in our international balance of payments." The United States, he said, could "face either an uncontrollable recession or an uncontrollable inflation," and he pleaded for a tax increase from Congress.

On April 16, President Johnson was in Honolulu for the meeting to assess the war situation that had been postponed as a result of King's death. From there he went on to South Vietnam and South Korea essentially to boost the morale of American troops and government officials in the two countries. Even as he attempted to do so, the American base at Khe Sanh underwent resumed shelling by the North Vietnamese, and the impasse over a site for peace talks dragged on. The notion that LBJ's withdrawal from the presidential race would produce a breakthrough on the war was quickly fading.

While Johnson was in Honolulu, a jury in the U.S. District Court in Baltimore was acting on one of the domestic ramifications of his war policies. The jury found the Reverend Philip Berrigan and three other war protesters guilty of destroying government property, mutilating government records and impeding the work of the Selective Service System by pouring duck blood on their records in their raid on the draft headquarters in Baltimore about six months earlier. The resistance at home also went on.

*   *   *

The presidential candidates, all of whom had broken off their campaigns in the wake of the King assassination, had resumed by April 10, with Kennedy plunging into Indiana. On the same day, self-starting McCarthyites in Connecticut pulled off a coup by winning 44 percent of the votes cast in two primaries that were permitted under an obscure election law. The law heretofore had been ignored under the firm hand of state chairman John Bailey, one of the last of the old Democratic bosses, elevated to Democratic national chairman in 1961 by his old friend John F. Kennedy. McCarthy had campaigned only a couple of days in the state, but the magic of New Hampshire was working its charm, particularly among party liberals. Some of them would have preferred Kennedy but rallied behind the available McCarthy as their vehicle to drive home the message that they wanted an end to the fighting in Vietnam.

On the campaign trail, however, all eyes were now on Kennedy as he mobilized for his first test of strength. Also on this same day, Larry O'Brien announced his resignation from the Johnson cabinet to take over direction of the Kennedy campaign. Goodwin also had joined, having left the McCarthy camp apparently on good terms with the candidate, if not with some of his campaign staff.

O'Brien and Goodwin shared the view that in order to win the Indiana primary, Kennedy would have to emphasize conservative positions, particularly in talking about crime and welfare, as he toured the state's smaller cities. "Some purists in our camp saw this as a sell-out," O'Brien wrote later in his political autobiography, *No Final Victories*, "but it was the only sensible politics by a man who was running a serious campaign for the presidency."

John Bartlow Martin, the author and an Indiana native who was now on the Kennedy staff, specifically counseled the candidate in the wake of the King assassination to condemn violence and rioting, but always to combine the condemnation with the observation that neither could racial injustice be tolerated. Kennedy readily agreed. In Fort Wayne, Columbus and Terre Haute the senator strummed the chords of law and order that were so familiar in the repertoire of Richard Nixon, though in much less strident tones. In short order, accompanying reporters were writing that Kennedy was turning conservative in what was simply a deft reading of the temper of the Indiana electorate, and of the public mood in black as well as white communities.

"To lead America one did not captain a guerrilla army or organize a coup," Goodwin wrote later. "So [Kennedy] set out to master the maze, made the necessary compromises, tailored his rhetoric to his audience as all politicians must. He talked of the need for law and order in a society increasingly streaked with lawlessness and disorder. He meant it, of course. No politician, no rational citizen, would advocate crime or violence. But he also knew that to many in his audience the phrase 'law and order' was a code phrase for opposition to black protests. It was not what Kennedy intended," Goodwin wrote. "It was not what he said. But if some of those listening gave it that interpretation, then the mistake was theirs."

The removal of Johnson from the competition clearly had created a different dynamic in the campaign. Kennedy struggled to reset his political compass, and his voice, to sustain the intensity that had excited the first days of his candidacy. Although he talked law and order, his continued focus on the inequities in American society, and his driving plea to audiences to accept individual responsibility for communal ills, kept the public fervor burning. Repeating his brother John's exhortation that "one man can make a difference" and providing visible evidence in his looks and manner of the resurrection of the magical days of Camelot, Robert Kennedy raced across the face of Indiana—and Michigan and West Virginia—like a political pied piper.

With Bill Barry clinging to him, kneeling behind as Kennedy stood on the back seat of an open convertible, the candidate literally offered up his body to adoring, often frenzied crowds reaching to shake his hand, to touch his arm, to grab a personal souvenir. His cuff links were the most expendable, but his shirt cuffs too often were ripped. In Kalamazoo, Michigan, a woman climbed into the seat with him and tugged off one of his shoes.

The campaign took on a carnival atmosphere as Kennedy from time to time stopped the motorcade to pop into a neighborhood bar, diner or coffee shop, for a snack and conversation with the eager, dazzled locals. Each time, the traveling reporters would pour out of the press buses behind him. On Dyngus Day, a Polish-American commemoration of the death of St. Stephen, Kennedy stopped at the West Side Democratic Club in South Bend, ate some kielbasa, drank a beer and sang a Polish song he had learned on his visit to Poland in 1963. "The Polish government refused to advise the people that we were there," he said. "It's sort of like the Indianapolis papers when I'm here."

The Pulliam papers indeed were mostly looking the other way, and pumping up the favorite-son candidacy of Governor Branigin, as Kennedy was creating political pandemonium across the state. One day, as he motored through the heavily industrial, heavily black city of Gary, crowds jammed the curbs for blocks on end as the motorcade rolled by. Kids of all ages on bikes tried to keep up with Kennedy's open car or ran pell-mell after it until exhaustion overtook them.

At one point Barry spied a boy of about ten, one arm in a cast, tugging his little sister, about four, behind him as he ran along. She tripped, whereupon her brother scooped her up onto his shoulders, hardly breaking stride, and continued after Kennedy's car. Barry drew Kennedy's attention to them and the candidate told his driver to stop—thus halting the whole motorcade behind him. He lifted the two kids into the convertible and parked one on either side of him. The little boy, who told Kennedy his name was Michael, reached over, took his sister's face in both his hands, turned it up toward the candidate's and said: "Look, here's Senator Kennedy."

The motorcade resumed, with Kennedy asking Michael every few blocks where he wanted to be let off. The boy would tell him not to worry; they'd find their way home later. Kennedy finally ordered his car out of the motorcade and back to the kids' home, a small frame house where their mother, in a housedress, hurriedly brought out iced tea. Kennedy sat on the front steps and talked while the long motorcade waited.

The days were not always unremittingly joyous. In Lansing, Michigan, Kennedy met with state party leaders at the Jack Tar Hotel on a corner directly across from the State Capitol. He was about to go to the airport when Barry came into his suite and told Dutton that local police had spotted a man with a rifle on a nearby rooftop. Dutton casually walked into the bedroom where Kennedy was changing his shirt and drew the curtains. Kennedy looked up. "Don't close them," he said. "If they're going to shoot, they'll shoot."

When it was time to leave, Dutton led the candidate into the hotel elevator, past the first floor and into the basement, where the car was waiting. When Kennedy asked what it was doing there, Dutton told him: "Well, we have a report—maybe serious." Kennedy frowned. "Don't ever do that," he said with annoyance, climbing into the back seat. "We always get into the car in public. We're not going to start ducking now."

The car roared up the exit ramp to the street, as the driver had been instructed to do. "Stop the car," Kennedy ordered. He jumped out and proceeded to shake hands with the crowd waiting outside the hotel, then climbed back in and the car headed for the airport. "He never said a word," Dutton recalled later, "but we got his message."

A few days later, Kennedy demonstrated his ability to joke about death as well as flirt with it. The entourage was packed into a small propeller plane at some nondescript airport, with Kennedy sitting in the rear with the reporters. The plane lumbered down the runway and, as it struggled to get airborne, the pilot finally jammed on the brakes and announced he would have to try again to achieve the required groundspeed. He turned the plane and went back to the starting point, revving the engines. As we all looked at each other with trepidation, Kennedy grinned and cracked: "I want to say in all modesty that if we don't make it this time, you fellows are going to be in the small print tomorrow."

Kennedy demonstrated the same dry sense of humor in the introductory remarks of his stump speeches. But invariably he would soon be imploring his audiences to consider their responsibilities to the less fortunate in the society, and to bearing the burden of the Vietnam War if it could not be stopped. He would begin by telling farm listeners that "I come from an agricultural state. I do more for agriculture than any other candidate. You should see my breakfast table every morning." His large brood, he would relate, consumed "more milk, more bread, more eggs" than the family of any other candidate. But in short order he would be off on his impassioned chronicling of the twin national ills of an unjust war abroad and racial division at home—imploring, cajoling, lecturing, at times scolding his audiences for their insensitivity or hypocrisy.

With Johnson out as a candidate and as a target, Kennedy did however moderate somewhat his rhetoric on the war, emphasizing that he was against unilateral withdrawal (so was McCarthy). At the same time, in preaching toughness on the crime that was plaguing America's cities, he focused on economic rather than racial factors. He reminded blue-collar white ethnic voters of the hardships and aspirations they shared with blacks who worked alongside them in the factories of the industrial cities like Gary and Fort Wayne. He cast lack of job opportunity rather than race as the core cause of inner-city crime, and set about building, without so labeling it, a coalition of economic have-nots against the haves of the society. And with an eye to rural and small-town conservatives, Kennedy championed private enterprise in job creation rather than "welfare handouts" as a means of bringing the voting segment into his coalition. (It was a recital that would not seem unfamiliar to many who twenty-four years later heard essentially the same message from another presidential candidate named Bill Clinton.)

The approach called for a delicate balancing act. Kennedy argued in private talks with reporters that there was a way to talk about being tough on crime that would not alienate blacks because, after all, they were the principal victims. As for rural whites, he told me during this period, "they don't want to listen to what the blacks want and need. You have to get them listening by talking about what they're interested in, before you can start to persuade them about other matters."

In Vincennes, for example, Kennedy told members of the local conservative Civitan Club: "I am part of an administration in which private enterprise and the people were freed from the cycle of boom and bust that had plagued this country for six generations. The profits of corporations after taxes rose during those years by almost 40 percent, and small business shared in this prosperity. . . . Today, business can extend its work to the unfinished business of our country. There is no commandment which says that government must undertake these tasks. . . . That is why I have introduced legislation to lower taxes to private enterprise which will undertake programs to wipe out hardcore unemployment and provide housing. That is why I believe the most important step we could take in ending poverty in America is our towns and farms, as well as in our cities, is to involve the private enterprise system. . . ."

On crime: "I was the chief law enforcement officer of the United States . . . the law has been my life . . . I don't believe in violence." And on local initiative: "I think it's a mistake for the federal government to decide where a school should be located. . . . We have to strengthen our police departments so they know how to cope with riots. . . ."

Inevitably, however, Kennedy the moralist was ever present. When a question came from this essentially conservative Republican audience about the waste of a federal program to cope with rats in the inner cities, he snapped back: "Do you know there are more rats in New York than people, and there are nine million people there? Children spend their nights trying to keep rats from biting them." A tittering went through the crowd and Kennedy froze. "You can smile," he said grimly, "it's true. . . . We're not going to tolerate the riots, we're not going to tolerate the lawlessness, we're not going to tolerate the violence. But we're going to do something about the conditions." The crowd seemed unmoved, but if practical politics dictated that he talk tough on crime, his personal sense of outrage against the neglect of children commanded that he address that too.

Such cool reactions, amid the constant sea of adoration that continued to flow over Kennedy from largely youthful street crowds, hinted at the scope of the challenge posed by the Indiana primary. He took to telling the Hoosiers, who had not held a significant presidential primary in many years, that just as the voters of West Virginia, another state off the beaten path of traditional presidential primaries, had been instrumental in 1960 in making his brother John the president, so could Indiana be decisive. But Kennedy knew that Indiana was not West Virginia; for one thing, the poverty that JFK had emphasized with adequate cause in West Virginia was not nearly so prominent in Indiana.

Above all, the Kennedy celebrity remained the candidate's most visible strength, and so the strategy continued to be to put him on display as widely as possible. On April 23, the Kennedy entourage undertook an old-fashioned whistlestop train trip through north-central Indiana. It followed the route of the old *Wabash Cannonball*, famed in country balladeering in a song popularized by baseball pitcher Dizzy Dean when he broadcast games on radio in the 1950s. At each stop, Kennedy would urge voters not to waste their votes on favorite-son Branigin, never saying much about McCarthy. Kennedy was trying his best to ignore the Minnesotan, who now was challenging Kennedy to debate the issues.

A distinctly lighthearted mood governed the day's events. At each stop, Kennedy would wind up his speech with a loose paraphrase of a line from Shaw's *Back to Methuselah* that his brother John had used in addressing the Irish Parliament in 1963: "As George Bernard Shaw once said, some men see things as they are and say, 'Why?' I dream things that never were and say, 'Why not?'" The line became a signal for reporters to scurry back onto the train before it began moving down the track. At one town, Kennedy didn't say it and several reporters found themselves looking at the rear end of the train as it pulled away. Kennedy was petitioned by his traveling companions from the press not to forget the Shaw line again.

As the long day drew on, the senator, his wife and children were invited into the press car to hear a new, many-versed version of "The Wabash Cannonball," written by a cabal of reporters and sung by guitar-strumming David Breasted, then of the *New York Daily News*. Identifying Kennedy as "the demon driver of the *Ruthless Cannonball*," the lyrics noted that "the blacks in Gary love him, the Poles will fill his hall, there are no ethnic problems on the *Ruthless Cannonball*." Another verse noted of Branigin that "he's riding for a fall; they're noted for long memories on the *Ruthless Cannonball*."

And of the other candidate, it went: "Now good Clean Gene McCarthy came down the other track, a thousand Radcliffe dropouts all massed for the attack; but Bobby's bought the right of way from here back to St. Paul, 'cause money is no object on the *Ruthless Cannonball*."

Kennedy, keeping a straight, even stern face, responded after the song was over: "As George Bernard Shaw once said—the same to you, sideways." When he asked me for a copy of the lyrics, I handed it to him and said, "Forget where you got it." He fixed his notorious "cold blue eyes" on me and said, "Oh, no, I won't." Ruthless Robert turned and started to walk away, then turned back, grinning, and added: "See, it keeps slipping out all the time."

Kennedy was focusing on Branigin in part because the Indianapolis newspapers were throwing their news and editorial columns behind him with gusto, while attacking Kennedy and McCarthy as interlopers. They reported a boomlet for Branigin as the vice presidential candidate on the Democratic ticket, although no out-of-state reporter seemed to be able to find any trace of it. Branigin took to telling fellow Hoosiers that Indiana had been "the mother of four vice presidents, and could be the mother of a fifth."

Branigin was endorsed by eighty-seven of the state's ninety-two Democratic county chairmen, but he was having trouble finding hands to shake on the campaign trail. Meanwhile, McCarthy was drawing adequate-sized audiences and Kennedy was continuing to be a magnet for large crowds. One page-one cartoon in the *Indianapolis Star* showed Branigin sitting at a dinner table with "Mrs. Indiana," who was busily warding off the advances of McCarthy and especially Kennedy, who seemed upon close scrutiny to have his hand on her left breast.

Branigin, for his part, sought to tap into the deep lode of Hoosier loyalty by urging his fellow citizens to "vote Indiana" and send an uncommitted delegation to the national convention, with himself at the head as favorite son. In the town of Marion, he told his audience of party workers that he was a serious candidate running "to keep Indiana an effective voice in party councils." While Kennedy and McCarthy were welcome in the state, he said, "a Hoosier should represent the Hoosiers in Chicago."

Kennedy, touring through the state's conservative southwestern corner, urged his listeners to "vote for one of the serious candidates for president. . . . Don't waste your vote in Indiana" and thus leave the decision "to the politicians to decide in Chicago." When a questioner suggested that Kennedy might run as the vice presidential nominee with Humphrey, for whom Branigin was clearly standing in, Kennedy dismissed the notion. "I'm not interested in being vice president," he said. "I'm running for president of the United States."

Kennedy, for all his efforts to present himself as more moderate than pictured by the Pulliam newspapers, did not hesitate to take the bully pulpit when confronted with attitudes he could not abide. On April 26, he spoke to students at the Indiana University Medical Center and was sharply challenged on his views regarding medical care for the poor. Questions were raised about the need to increase Social Security benefits and a student suggested that poor blacks weren't making use of the medical facilities already available to them.

"Where," one asked, "are you going to get all the money for these federally subsidized programs you're talking about?" Kennedy shot back at the would-be high-income doctors: "From you." Then came his lecture:

"Let me say something about the tone of these questions. I look around this room and I don't see many black faces who will become doctors. You can talk about where the money will come from. . . . Part of civilized society is to let people go to medical school who come from ghettos. You don't see many people coming out of the ghettos or off the Indian reservations to medical school. You are the privileged ones here. It's easy to sit back and say it's the fault of the federal government, but it's our responsibility too. It's our society, not just our government, that spends twice as much on pets as on the poverty program. It's the poor who carry the major burden of the struggle in Vietnam. You sit here as white medical students, while black people carry the burden of the fighting in Vietnam."

When a student interrupted, shouting, "We'll be going soon!" Kennedy answered: "Yes, but you're here now and they're over there. The war might be settled by the time you go." And when a black student called out to challenge Kennedy's premise that the medical school was lily-white, the senator replied: "I can see you, but you sure stand out."

The medical school exchange provided one of the rare occasions when the *Indianapolis Star* ran a page-one story regarding Kennedy. But predictably it was a negative one. It quoted Frank McHale, a former Democratic national committeeman and state party stalwart, accusing Kennedy of having "brought up racism by telling Indiana University School of Medicine students, most of them white, that Negroes carry the major portion of the struggle in Vietnam. 'The statement just isn't true, but it promotes racism, and that's apparently what he's trying to do,'" McHale said. "'We in Indiana haven't made distinctions counting our men who have died in Vietnam. The courageous Indiana Negroes who have died have died shoulder to shoulder with their white comrades. Why is King Bobby trying to downgrade the efforts of the white soldiers who have died?'"

A similar exchange took place a few days later at Valparaiso University, where Kennedy challenged heckling students questioning his defense of federal efforts to fight poverty: "How many of you spend time over the summer, or on vacations, working in a black ghetto, or in eastern Kentucky, or on Indian reservations? Instead of asking what the federal government is doing about starving children, I say, what is your responsibility, what are you going to do about it? . . . As Camus once said: 'Perhaps we cannot prevent this world from being a world in which children are tortured. But we can reduce the number of tortured children.' And if you don't help us, who in the world can help us do this?"

That call to conscience, issued even as Kennedy emphasized conservative themes in Indiana, was integral to his effort to construct and expand the black and blue-collar coalition in a state of both industrial and rural farm populations. In a side trip to Oregon, a state with little black population and a general sense of economic well-being and egalitarianism, Kennedy encountered a generally cool reception—and early warning of political problems to come that was largely overlooked at the time.

McCarthy meanwhile toiled in his low-key fashion in Indiana, but without the degree of news media attention that magnified his message in New Hampshire—and without the clear-cut, one-on-one confrontation with the sitting president that brought him the spotlight there and in Wisconsin. "Our candidate went on giving his stump speech and giving it well," Jeremy Larner wrote later, "but he did not react to the changing political climate, and in particular to the fact that he was no longer running against Lyndon Johnson and the war. . . . To his everlasting credit, our candidate never mentioned 'law and order'—but unlike Kennedy, he never addressed himself to the hatred and violence that made law and order an issue."

With Kennedy as well as Branigin as a favorite son competing in Indiana, McCarthy simply did not have the running room that had helped him in the two earlier primaries. Nor had his organization kept pace with his prominence; squabbles broke out between national and Indiana staff workers. Most significant, he came under attack from the Kennedy camp on aspects of his senatorial voting record, despite Kennedy's assurance in announcing his candidacy in mid-March that he was "not going to run against" McCarthy.

In his post-campaign book, *The Year of the People*, McCarthy displayed unvarnished bitterness toward Kennedy, noting specifically that Kennedy in his announcement "made special reference to his administrative experience in the executive branch of the government and especially in the National Security

Council. Since at that time President Johnson was still a candidate," McCarthy went on, "it was not possible that he was making this point to compare his qualifications with those of the chief executive who is also chairman of the National Security Council. The only possible interpretation was that he intended to use it against the man he was 'not going to run against.'"

But McCarthy had more pointed grounds to complain. A "fact sheet" was issued by a Citizens for Kennedy office in New York chaired by Dr. Martin Shepard, who briefly had tried to launch a draft-Kennedy effort in New Hampshire. It purported to list, McCarthy later wrote, "a number of what were alleged to be illiberal, somewhat hypocritical votes, ranging from a poll-tax amendment to rent control."

McCarthy compared the mailing to tactics he said Kennedy had used in defeating Republican Senator Kenneth B. Keating in New York in 1964, and said it had been circulated around the country. About two weeks after the list's release, the Citizens for Kennedy New York office said Shepard had been acting independently. But McCarthy subsequently wrote that he had been told that Pierre Salinger had been responsible for the attack on his voting record.

After the campaign, McCarthy told the *Boston Globe* that once Kennedy entered the race, "it was old politics pretty much. It wasn't really the challenge to the Johnson position; it got into the question of what's your record on civil rights, and why is your attendance record so bad? And all these other side issues that Bobby introduced. The question of my being for a guaranteed annual wage, stuff like that, that changed the whole context of it." McCarthy in Indiana found himself on the defensive for the first time, and much of the steam went out of his campaign.

In his post-election book, McCarthy wrote that his "student door-to-door effort in Indiana was blunted by the Kennedy canvassers who planted difficult questions ahead of the students' calls. We considered preparing the students to attack the record of Senator Kennedy," he wrote, "but rejected the idea. In Indiana . . . we sent them out to make the same kind of case they had made in New Hampshire."

According to Arthur Herzog in his book *McCarthy for President*, hostility between the Kennedy and McCarthy campaigns grew when the Kennedy camp tried to rent away the McCarthy campaign headquarters space in the ramshackle Claypool Hotel, quickly dubbed the Cesspool, and hire away young McCarthyites. Only a few defected. Within the McCarthy campaign, the young college kids took as their theme the Beatles song "Magical Mystery Tour," and in their dedication and optimism it remained that for them.

There were, for all that, growing reservations among the McCarthy workers about their candidate. Ben Stavis, in his book *We Were the Campaign: New Hampshire to Chicago for McCarthy*, wrote of their doubts about "whether we really wanted Eugene McCarthy to be president. What had previously been a jest was now a serious problem. I, with many others, was wondering whether McCarthy had the executive ability to be president. He seemed to pay no attention at all to his campaign. He viewed it as a spontaneous happening, which he should not try to control. He would arbitrarily cancel events on his schedule which had been painstakingly prepared by many people. He would ignore an audience or not make a promised speech. As for campaign administration, he permitted confusion at the top of his staff to demoralize the entire campaign. . . . In a major speech in Wisconsin, he promised a depersonalized, weak, lofty presidency and insisted he would not get tied up in the details of administration. He was, of course, attacking LBJ's style, but I was not sure that was the type of presidency we needed."

After King's assassination and the resultant riots, McCarthy spoke out more strongly on racial reconciliation, again in his fashion, and with an awareness that there was a political downside to doing so. Observing in one speech that American blacks were "mired in a cycle of poverty," he added: "Just as American Negroes are wearying of the demeaning conditions and the racist attitude which have now brought rioting to our cities, white Americans are tired of the riots these conditions cause." While the country "longs for reconciliation," he said, "[it] will come only with an administration which is prepared to commit itself to massive programs of correction."

(Nixon, cruising unopposed through the Indiana Republican primary, remained unmoved. For any politician "to tell the poor that right now the federal government is going to massively increase spending programs," he said, "is dishonest, a cruel delusion, and I am not going to join in the game, whether it costs the election or not." He knew, certainly, that such comments would not cost him the election or anything else, and in fact might help him win it by playing to white, blue-collar concerns.)

On Vietnam, McCarthy called for the firing of Dean Rusk and his replacement as secretary of state with Senate Majority Leader Mike Mansfield. And he challenged the further need of the North Atlantic Treaty Organization on grounds that "the Cold War in Europe is over. There is no need to go on fighting it." Such views delighted his antiwar followers but caused many other voters to regard him with skepticism or doubts about his appreciation of "the threat of communism," still a critical rallying point among conservative voters.

Beyond the war and the racial crisis, McCarthy sought to elevate his campaign to a broader crusade for a new politics that would engage voters out of the satisfaction that would come from playing an active role in the political life of their country. "It is a politics," he said in a sidetrip to Cleveland on April 22, "as old as the history of the country, because it's clearly consistent with what Adams described as the spirit of this country at the time of the American Revolution. He said that at that time there was abroad in the colonies what he called 'a spirit of public happiness.' He didn't use happiness in quite the same way we use it today. I think he used it in the same sense in which it's used in the great document . . . the pursuit of happiness. They were not talking about a kind of general joy or gleefulness or irresponsibility, but rather satisfaction. . . . The spirit Adams described as existing before 1776 is not dead in this country."

The direct primary confrontation between McCarthy and Kennedy in Indiana offered the first close-in opportunity for voters to experience and assess the campaign styles of the two combatants. Kennedy, with his endless laying-on of hands and exhortations to nobler purpose, resembled a political Elmer Gantry recruiting souls. McCarthy, with his laid-back, professorial approach to crowds, was the esteemed lecturer come to town for serious talk with serious listeners. Kennedy the evangelist would ask his audiences to "give me your help and your hand, and together we can turn this country around." McCarthy the explainer would calmly analyze the state of the nation and then merely ask for voters' "consideration" of what he had said, and of his candidacy.

Kennedy exuded a daredevil quality, plunging almost recklessly into crowds, leaving them aglow. BOBBY IS GOOD, one sign said, simply, along the way. McCarthy seemed indifferent to crowds and adoration, seldom going out of his way to shake hands or to prolong the exercise once started. Kennedy shouted, jabbed at the air, punctuated remarks with a single loud clap of his hands and milked applause lines. McCarthy spoke in a monotone of sober thought that cooled excited crowds into respectful listeners. He declined to pause for applause and seemed above all determined not to insult the intelligence of his audience, or his own.

Like Kennedy, McCarthy did not find Indiana to be ideal campaign ground. "There seemed to be a rather generalized defensiveness in Indiana against outsiders," he wrote in a whimsical vein in his campaign book. "In northern Indiana, especially Gary, people seemed worried about the prospect of being taken over by Chicago. In the south, they were threatened by Kentucky, in the west, by Illinois, and in the east, by Ohio. It was as though in Indiana they have to think Indiana for fear that if they do not, they will be absorbed by the outside world." And in Branigin, McCarthy noted, the Hoosiers had a vehicle for voting their provincialism.

The Minnesotan's best news in April thus came not from Indiana, but from Pennsylvania, where he was the only active candidate, spending two days in the state. His delegates won 71.6 percent of the Democratic vote in a non-binding primary, with only write-in votes for Kennedy and Humphrey. For David Mixner, who was involved there for McCarthy, the highlight was an appearance by actor Tony Randall, who helped open the McCarthy campaign headquarters in Philadelphia by telling the crowd: "I supported Lyndon Johnson in 1964. He promised us then he was going to end the war. And that son-of-a-bitch of a president lied to us!" In the end, however, when delegates were chosen by the state party led by Mayors James Tate of Philadelphia and Joseph Barr of Pittsburgh, both Humphrey men, McCarthy was given only twenty-one, to eighty-three for Humphrey.

* * *

As the combatants in Indiana approached the May 7 primary, Hubert Humphrey finally entered the race on April 27, too late to be placed on the ballot there and thus relying on Branigin as his stand-in. The *Indianapolis Star* promptly saw signs of a Humphrey-Branigin ticket. Two weeks earlier, Walter Mondale had opened a Washington campaign headquarters in Humphrey's behalf. In a nationally televised speech, Humphrey called for "a new American patriotism" and promised a leadership of "maturity, restraint and responsibility." Trying to walk a line of independence without giving offense to his benefactor, Lyndon Johnson, Humphrey said LBJ's record "will loom large in history for its dramatic leadership toward social progress, human opportunity and peace."

But it was Humphrey's own trademark effervescence that most marked his announcement. "Here we are," he rejoiced, "just as we ought to be, the people, here we are, in a spirit of dedication. Here we are, the way politics ought to be in America; the politics of happiness, the politics of purpose and the politics of joy! And that's the way it's going to be, all the way, from here on in!" The words sounded much like McCarthy's description of his new politics, but "happiness" and "joy" coming from the celebrated Happy Warrior had a much more personal connotation.

To those who saw little joy in a year in which young Americans were bogged down and being killed in the jungles and hamlets of Vietnam, in which generations were at war with each other at home and in which Martin Luther King had been assassinated with resultant riots in more than a hundred American cities, Humphrey's ebullience seemed particularly obscene. But from a purely personal political point of view, the man had ample reason to be upbeat. The presidency that he had sought and failed to achieve in 1960, and hopes for which had dimmed with the prospect of another full term for Johnson, suddenly seemed well within his grasp.

In the nearly four weeks after LBJ's decision not to run, Humphrey had been inundated with urgings from all segments of the party's establishment to pick up the standard. Two bedrocks of regular party support, organized labor and the American Jewish community, were in the forefront with checkbooks and political manpower at the ready. And in state after state where convention delegates were being selected by caucus and convention, as opposed to the handful choosing them in primaries, party leaders were lining up to deliver for the self-described Happy Warrior of countless old Democratic battles. Unlike 1960, when he failed in his bid against John Kennedy in the Wisconsin and West Virginia primaries, Humphrey would not in 1968 have to test his public popularity against anyone in the primaries. This time around he had proceeded with caution, taking his time to be sure he was on firm political ground before declaring his candidacy, and now he was happily on his way.

Yet, from the start, the Humphrey campaign had about it an aura of staleness. Although over the years he had built an admirable record of domestic social progress in his own right, as vice president he had become the superloyal courtesan of Lyndon Johnson, to the embarrassment and chagrin of many of his closest friends and supporters. Now he would be seen as the inheritor and caretaker of the Johnson policies, whatever he said.

As vice president, Humphrey had always been held on a short leash by Johnson and there was no reason for him to expect he would be treated otherwise as a presidential candidate. Van Dyk later recalled several occasions when Humphrey had been "absolutely excommunicated" by Johnson, denying him access to cable traffic and participation in National Security Council meetings, for having even suggested any modification of the policy of bombing North Vietnam. In 1967, when Humphrey returned from the inauguration of President Nguyen Van Thieu in South Vietnam, Van Dyk recalled, LBJ directed him to brief the cabinet, handing him a note that said: "Hubert: Brief upbeat presentation. Key in optimism and start. Sit down and shut up. Lyndon."

Humphrey well knew that he would have to walk a fine line between his continuing commitment to Johnson and establishing his own identity as a candidate. The day after his announcement, on NBC's *Meet the Press*, Humphrey proclaimed that while he would run on the Johnson administration's record, "I am my own man," committed to "speak out on what I think is necessary." From the outset, however, he was obliged to campaign in the long shadow of LBJ and "his" war in Vietnam, as he was destined to do throughout 1968.

If Hubert Humphrey the social reformer was the conservative Republicans' favorite "liberal, leftist" target, he also was a bona fide anticommunist who accepted Johnson's assessment that the Vietnam War was a logical extension of the Cold War. That view was to be defended out of principle as well as out of loyalty to his leader, who would continue to bear the responsibilities of governance as Humphrey campaigned for his party's nomination, and election in November.

*　*　*

Hubert Humphrey was not the only leading political figure who was persuaded to take another look at his political future in the wake of Lyndon Johnson's withdrawal from the 1968 race. In Albany, Nelson Rockefeller began to have second thoughts. The split in the Democratic Party that had already developed with the candidacies of Gene McCarthy and Robert Kennedy was certain to grow with Humphrey's entry into the race, suggesting that many disgruntled Democrats might be willing to cast a favorable eye toward a liberal Republican in November. Richard Nixon, a pariah among Democrats, certainly would not qualify. Perhaps the Republican Party, recognizing these same developments, would come to its senses and choose a nominee who could lure away those dissatisfied Democrats: Nelson Rockefeller.

Some of the New York governor's staunchest and wealthiest supporters shared this view. George Hinman, Rockefeller's able political lieutenant, phoned Al Abrahams, who had been manning the draft-Rockefeller office in Annapolis at the time Rockefeller inflicted his memorable insult on Ted Agnew, and asked him to come to New York to keep the flame burning. In Washington, meanwhile, Senator Morton on April 11—the day Agnew read the riot act to Baltimore's black leaders—announced formation of another draft-Rockefeller committee.

With Rockefeller having already taken himself out of the primary competition, convinced that Nixon had that route to the nomination locked up, a new strategy drove the reviving candidacy. As long as the beleaguered Johnson appeared destined to be the Democratic nominee, many Republicans felt even Nixon could beat him. But if the nominee were Kennedy, or Humphrey, they might not be sure. If the Republican Party could indeed be convinced that with LBJ out only a Republican who could appeal to Democrats could hope to be elected, Nixon might yet be stopped and Rockefeller nominated.

To demonstrate the governor's broader appeal, Rockefeller would "play outside Nixon's room"—beyond the party apparatus into the country at large.

Rockefeller and his publicists would undertake a mass communications effort, coupled with personal campaigning by him in key population centers, designed to lift Rockefeller so far over Nixon in the public opinion polls that the party would be persuaded to yield, to achieve its White House aspirations. If Nixon could be shown to be a sure loser, and Rockefeller a winner, then the party would go with Rockefeller; so went the theory.

The Rockefeller camp, in the governor's uphill reelection of 1966, had seen what a massive, imaginative and costly media blitz could do. Rockefeller had gone into that campaign abysmally low in the polls. But by trumpeting his achievements in one of the nation's toughest political jobs over television and radio and in newspaper ads, his media wizards had pulled him through. Why couldn't the same be done on the national stage?

A dry run before the American Society of Newspaper Editors on April 18 had not been encouraging. Rockefeller delivered a thirty-minute speech detailing a ten-year, $150 billion plan to cope with the urban crisis without a single interruption by applause. Nixon appeared before the same group the next day, and after having boned up for the question-and-answer session as if he were back at Duke Law School before examinations, he came off particularly knowledgeable and crisp, and even a bit humorous. Still, the Rockefeller camp remained convinced that Nixon was a loser and sooner or later the delegates to the GOP convention would come around to the same conclusion.

On the night of April 23, the day Kennedy's *Ruthless Cannonball* rolled through Indiana, Rockefeller and his wife went to the White House for a private dinner with LBJ and Lady Bird. The Rockefellers were first brought to the office of an aide, Joe Califano reported later in his book, and then escorted secretly to the presidential living quarters. Over dinner, Califano wrote, Johnson urged Rockefeller to run, in part because he was the best of the available Republicans and "if Kennedy turned out to be the Democratic candidate, Rockefeller was a good bet to beat him."

So, on the last day of April, Rockefeller reversed himself and entered the Republican race, pledging to fight for the presidential nomination "to the last vote on the convention floor. . . . I do this," he said, "because the dramatic and unprecedented events of the past weeks have revealed in most serious terms the gravity of the crisis that we face as a people. . . . In the new circumstances that confront the nation I frankly find that to comment from the sidelines is not an effective way to present the alternatives. . . ." He said he would enter no primaries and would discourage any write-ins, and made no mention of his media strategy, which soon would become obvious.

Nixon reacted confidently to Rockefeller's announcement, while administering an unsubtle dig. "I think I'm going to win," he said. "If I'd been advising Governor Rockefeller, I'd have told him to enter the primaries to prove [his] argument that he's more popular with the voters, and I'm preferred by the bosses. Now he's appealing to the bosses and I to the people." Then, mounting a higher road, he said it was "helpful to have another active candidate, even at this late date," and he was "glad to hear that he intends to address himself to the issues. That kind of a campaign will not divide the party. It will unite it at Miami."

On the same day, in spite of Rockefeller's stated disinterest in write-ins, Republicans in Massachusetts penciled him in for 30 percent of the vote to 29.5 for favorite-son Governor John Volpe, who had hopes of being Nixon's running mate, with Nixon running third with 25.8 on write-ins. But with Nixon far ahead already in delegates won nationwide, and with Rockefeller filed in no primaries, the result was meaningless. Rockefeller had chosen to play on the field of public opinion and he now had three months, until the party convened in early August, to make his case.

* * *

The politics of the nation was now in full cry—a laconic Midwestern senator throwing the Democratic Party into bedlam; a once-agonizing son of Camelot hell-bent on restoring the royal line; a sitting president forced to withdraw from the political battleground and his enthusiastic stand-in replacing him; the most prominent civil rights leader of his time slain; a one-time Republican standard-bearer left for dead rising from the ashes; a war halfway around the globe still tearing apart the fabric of the country.

As the final week of April began, more chaos was ignited at one of the bastions of American academia. It was initially driven by a singularly parochial issue but one that would soon become the vehicle for a broader generational protest. The bastion was Columbia University in New York and the issue was the planned gymnasium construction on the site of the thirty-acre public park situated between the university campus on upper Manhattan's Morningside Heights and the predominantly black adjacent enclave of Harlem.

The land had been leased by Columbia from the city in 1961 for $3,000 a year. The university after consultations with local residential groups had agreed to build two gyms, one for its undergraduates at a cost of $10 million and another, smaller facility for the Harlem community budgeted at $1.6 million.

Ground had actually been broken for the construction two months earlier, triggering complaints from Harlemites accustomed to using the site, known as Morningside Heights Park, for recreation. Because the land was publicly owned, Columbia needed state approval, and when the Harlem opposition had first surfaced, planners of the gym had agreed to include the new facilities for the neighborhood. But the foes were not placated. As their complaints gained wider airing in the community and spilled over onto the Columbia campus, two left-liberal student organizations—the local chapters of Students for a Democratic Society and the Students' Afro-American Society—took up the neighborhood fight.

Both groups had been engaged in various campus protests—against the Vietnam War, university defense contracts, and career recruitment on campus of Columbia upperclassmen by the Central Intelligence Agency and certain defense contractors like Dow Chemical. The SAS leader was a young black student named Cicero Wilson, and SDS was led by its chapter chairman, a twenty-year-old from northern New Jersey named Mark Rudd.

Rudd by this time had been identified by some university authorities as a radical troublemaker. Earlier in the year he had skipped three weeks of classes in Columbia College, the liberal arts undergraduate school, to visit Cuba. Prior to the protest against the new gym, Rudd had led a group of students in a demonstration at the offices of university president Grayson Kirk against the school's affiliation with the Institute of Defense Analysis, which conducted Vietnam-related weapons research. The protest was, intentionally, in violation of a new university prohibition on indoor demonstrations.

The assassination of Martin Luther King further fanned the Columbia unrest. During a memorial service for him in St. Paul's Chapel on the campus a few days later, Rudd abruptly walked up and took the microphone. He denounced the university for hypocrisy—memorializing King while disregarding the sensitivities and interests of the residents of Harlem in the gymnasium affair. Rudd walked out of the service followed by about fifty other students in a demonstration of the new hard edge of SDS.

Although some faculty members were in sympathy with Rudd and his cohorts, most university officials starting with Kirk pointedly rejected their complaints as none of their affair. One professor of government, Herbert Deane, summed up that attitude by remarking that "whether students vote yes or no on a given issue means as much to me as if they were to tell me they like strawberries." The flip remark later gave another Columbia undergraduate named James Kunen the title for a book that achieved a prominent place in the literature of the generational counterculture: *The Strawberry Statement*.

The Columbia unrest came at a time of growing student protest on other American campuses from Colgate in upstate New York to Tuskegee Institute in Alabama, and in Europe as well. On April 11, West Germany erupted upon an assassination attempt in West Berlin against Rudi (called Red Rudi) Dutschke, the twenty-seven-year-old leader of the Socialist League of West

German Students. He was wounded in an assault on Kurfürstendamm, the city's showplace thoroughfare, triggering demonstrations over the next four days in a dozen other cities. Two persons were killed in ensuing clashes between protesters and police. Student ferment was the order of the day on both sides of the Atlantic.

As the unrest on the Columbia campus mounted, Kirk, a man of sixty-four, in a speech on April 12 sounded an alarm for members of the older generation. "Our young people, in disturbing numbers, appear to reject all forms of authority, from whatever source derived," he declared, "and they have taken refuge in a turbulent and inchoate nihilism whose sole objectives are destructive. I know of no time in our history when the gap between the generations has been wider or more potentially dangerous."

Rudd responded in an open letter to Kirk that while "you call for order and respect for authority, we call for justice, freedom and socialism." Then he plunged into the vernacular of the young counterculture designed to outrage his target: "There is only one thing left to say. It may sound nihilistic to you, since it is the opening shot in a war of liberation. I'll use the words of [Black Panther writer] LeRoi Jones, whom I'm sure you don't like a lot: 'Up against the wall, motherfucker, this is a stick-up.'"

For his troubles, including the demonstration at Kirk's office, Rudd along with other participating SDS members was placed on probation, jeopardizing their education if they persisted in their radical political action. Such was the generational climate on April 23 when several hundred students gathered at a campus landmark, a sundial on the main quadrangle at West 116th Street, to address and listen to protests against construction of the new gym.

As the harangues filled the air, other hundreds stood around heckling. Wilson raised the specter of blacks on campus joining forces with Harlem residents to block the new building, violently if necessary. Warning of another long hot summer of revolt and rioting, he asked the crowd if it realized that "when you come back [for the fall semester] there may not be a Columbia University? Do you think this white citadel of hypocrisy will be bypassed if an insurrection occurs this summer?"

As tempers mounted, some of the demonstrators joined Wilson at the construction site and proceeded to tear down parts of a protective fence. Police moved in, breaking up the demonstration and arresting one white student. The students soon gathered again at the sundial and this time walked a short distance to Hamilton Hall, a principal classroom building for Columbia College, with Rudd in the lead. They took over the building and seized the acting dean of the college, Henry Coleman. They submitted a list of demands to him topped by a call to stop construction of the gym and end all affiliation with the nation's defense establishment.

Among those who got involved in an advisory capacity to the rebel students was Tom Hayden, who was considered insufficiently "revolutionary" by such Columbia SDS leaders as Rudd. "While I had gone through an intense intellectual development in formulating *The Port Huron Statement*," Hayden wrote later, "he [Rudd] considered 'SDS intellectuals' impediments to action. He was absolutely committed to an impossible yet galvanizing dream: that of transforming the entire student movement, through this particular student revolt, into a successful effort to bring down the system."

The Hamilton Hall occupation continued through that night, with black students joining and eventually the white students leaving the building to them at the blacks' urging. The whites in early morning went over to Low Library across the large open field in the quadrangle and occupied Kirk's office. Although Coleman was released after twenty-six hours, other bands of students occupied three other buildings over the next few days and classes were shut down.

University and city officials weighed the possibility of harsh police action but held off. Work at the construction site was halted at the request of Mayor Lindsay but the university rejected demands of academic amnesty for the rebels. In announcing the decision, Kirk said the university had "exercised great restraint in the use of police and security forces because, at almost all costs, we wish to avoid physical confrontation."

Before long the target became not merely the gym but the war in Vietnam, its morality and the disproportionate burden being borne by blacks. Black power leaders Brown and Carmichael met on April 26 with the black students holding Hamilton Hall. Brown, saying the protesters were "fighting against the racist policies" of the university, observed concerning the gym: "If they build it up, people in Harlem should blow it up."

A student group supporting the university position, calling itself the Majority Coalition, meanwhile tried to block the delivery of food and other supplies to the students holed up in Low Library. The school's board of trustees denounced the occupying students and instructed Kirk to deny amnesty and "maintain the ultimate disciplinary power" over their rebellious conduct. Labor mediator Theodore W. Kheel and eminent psychology professor Kenneth Clark were called in to confer with the occupiers, to no avail.

The confrontation continued until the early hours of April 30, when a thousand New York City police at the university's request poured onto the campus to remove the students from the five buildings. To the surprise and consternation of others in the siege, the black students holding Hamilton

Hall accepted arrest without a struggle. In the other buildings, however, the insurgents resisted the police with whatever they could throw at them, including the most incendiary language. In return, they got physical attacks from cops in antiriot gear who dragged them out and into police vans.

In the end, according to a later report of a fact-finding commission, 772 persons were arrested, 524 of them students hauled from campus buildings, and 148 injured including 20 police. It was not immediately determined what the university would do about Wilson, Rudd and the other rebellious students. Only hours after the police had moved onto the campus, a student strike was declared by campus leaders, who demanded the resignations of Kirk and university vice president David Truman.

So April had begun and ended like the other early months of 1968—in political and societal turmoil. The war in Vietnam and racial conflict continued to be the prime stimuli for the unrest, in the streets and on the campuses of America. On April 26, as many as a million college and high school students joined in a national student strike; the next day, an estimated 90,000 protesters marched in New York, and the day after that, Ralph Abernathy, King's close friend and successor as head of the Southern Christian Leadership Conference, led more than a hundred blacks to Washington as the vanguard of King's planned Poor People's Campaign and March on the capital. They met with cabinet and legislative leaders, pressing their legislative demands on them while warning that SCLC would be "more militant than ever" in its avowedly nonviolent campaign for equal rights.

But it was the Columbia campus rebellion that reflected a much broader generational upheaval taking place around the globe, and particularly in Europe—in Germany, as already noted, and in Italy, France and above all Czechoslovakia. There, student protests that had begun in the fall of 1967 had blossomed into "The Prague Spring" of courageous challenging of the dead-hand communist regime. A buoyant openness reigned that had not been seen since the iron fist of Stalinism had first come down across Central and Eastern Europe.

The assassination of Martin Luther King Jr. and consequent inner-city riots had cast a pall over early April at home, further dividing Americans along racial lines. "I thought the country was coming apart," Pat Buchanan said much later, in a C-SPAN interview. "Nixon was sort of riding through. . . . Were we helped by the Columbia demonstrations? You bet we were. The country did not like riots and they did not like the demonstrations."

The Columbia protest, and others of lesser intensity on other campuses, demonstrated, however, that a fierce determination to confront the established order remained in many quarters of the land, even as it flared abroad, and particularly among the rebellious young. "At a time when the radical movement was the most disheartened and dispirited," Rudd reflected later, ". . . the Columbia student rebellion broke through the gloom as an example of the power a radical movement could attain."

Nicholas von Hoffman, the Saul Alinsky disciple turned newspaper reporter and social critic, wrote in the *Washington Post* in the wake of the Columbia revolt: "The condition of youth has changed in important ways. College is no longer a voluntary business. You go to college or you go to war; you get your degree or you resign yourself to a life of low-paying jobs. Nor are the students the rollicking adolescents of the old rah-rah collegiate culture. At the best universities today, they enter freshman year with better academic training than seniors left with a generation and a half ago. They may not be mature, but they are serious people who take questions of war and peace, wealth and poverty, racism and emancipation personally and passionately. They do not agree with the way their universities deal with these questions. As a practical matter, they cannot leave the universities, so they are fighting for a part in the decision-making process. . . ."

The complacency of many in the generation that had come after the great civil rights battles of the late 1950s and early 1960s was rapidly falling away. If some of the dream had died with King's death, much of it remained in the minds and hopes of the protesters against the status quo—in Vietnam and at home, on campuses like Columbia and in the political process increasingly under scrutiny and attack.

CHAPTER 6

May: Passions Rising

May **1** Treasury sells two securities at 6 percent interest, lowest in 48 years; **2** *The Odd Couple* starring Jack Lemmon and Walter Matthau opens; Boston Celtics beat Los Angeles Lakers for NBA title; **3** 85 killed in Braniff Electra crash in Texas storm; **6** William Styron wins Pulitzer Prize for *The Confessions of Nat Turner;* James Michener's *Iberia*, Norman Mailer's *The Armies of the Night* published; **7** former U.S. Open, Masters golf champion Craig Wood, 66, dies; **9** cartoonist Harold Gray (*Little Orphan Annie*), 74, dies; **14** Rear Adm. Husband E. Kimmel, 86, removed as commander of U.S. Pacific Fleet after attack on Pearl Harbor, dies; **16** AFL-CIO throws out United Auto Workers in internal dispute; 22 killed in Mississippi Valley tornadoes; **18** Forward Pass wins Preakness; **19** Emmy Awards to *Mission: Impossible, Get Smart, Rowan and Martin's Laugh-In*, Bill Cosby, Don Adams, Lucille Ball; Wayne Zahn of Atlanta sets world bowling record of 4,043 pins in 18 games; **20** Supreme Court upholds equal treatment under the law for illegitimate children; **21** CBS News airs *Hunger in America;* **22** plane crash kills 23 on flight from Disneyland to Los Angeles; **27** San Diego, Montreal awarded National League baseball franchises.

Although President Johnson had removed himself as a target for Robert Kennedy's verbal attacks on American policy in Vietnam, Kennedy continued his criticism of that policy, albeit in less personal, less pointed terms. He turned to prodding Johnson to stop quibbling over such things as the site for negotiations with the North Vietnamese and get down to talking. Before an estimated 7,000 persons at Purdue University on May 1, Kennedy said the United States as "the strongest nation in the world" should not worry that it might "lose face" by agreeing to a site proposed by Hanoi. "The important thing—our responsibility to our own men and our own people—is to get the talks started," he said, "and try to reach an honorable settlement to this costly and divisive war."

That the war had by now demolished Johnson's contention that the country could have both guns and butter was acknowledged in his call to Congress to raise taxes. When it became clear to Johnson that Chairman Wilbur Mills of the House Ways and Means Committee was holding the tax bill hostage for deeper spending cuts, the president in a news conference on May 3 demanded that members of Congress "stand up like men" and stop "courting danger by this continued procrastination." Nearly two more months were to pass, however, before the bill—providing for more spending cuts as the price—finally would be passed and signed into law.

Also on May 3, with Kennedy's prodding certainly no factor, the United States and North Vietnam finally agreed on Paris as the site for negotiations, starting May 10 or shortly thereafter. Even so, North Vietnamese and Vietcong forces launched another major ground offensive against Saigon and other key cities on May 5 in an effort to improve their position in advance of the peace talks. The next day, a secret directive went out to American field commanders from the U.S. command in Saigon to undertake "an all-out drive" against the enemy, apparently for the same purpose.

No one watched the peace talks developments more intently than Hubert Humphrey. A declared candidate at last, he needed peace in Vietnam, or at least visible evidence that it was being conscientiously sought by the administration to which he belonged, as antidote to the venom that was already being spewed out against him. On May 4, on his first official campaign trip, about 150 members of war protest groups at Kent State University in Ohio walked out on his speech, and the next day a smaller group of students and teachers walked out on another at Bucknell University in Pennsylvania.

He told a labor audience in Washington that "you do yourself, your party and your president and your country a disservice by constantly downgrading your president, your party and your country." He pressed on diligently, and loyally to LBJ, as he consolidated his regular party strength. On May 9, the executive board of the United Steelworkers of America endorsed him and a day later the full Maryland delegation to the Democratic National Convention, representing forty-nine votes, agreed to back him.

Humphrey was aware, however, that his down-the-line support of Johnson on Vietnam jeopardized his hopes for a unified party behind him after the convention. For this reason, according to Van Dyk later, he went to the president around this time with a statement supporting a conciliatory convention plank on the war.

After an hour and a half in the Oval Office, Humphrey returned, dejected. "What happened?" Van Dyk asked. "I didn't see him," Humphrey said at first. "He had visitors." Van Dyk pressed him: "What happened?" Humphrey replied: "He said if I issued it he would denounce me. Then he said I would have the blood of his sons-in-law on my hands." Then, after a long pause, the vice president added, according to Van Dyk: "I've eaten so much shit in the last two years, I've almost gotten to like the taste of it."

*   *   *

Meanwhile the unrest continued at home, further gnawing at Humphrey's hopes for a unified party after the convention. On May 2 from the Lorraine Motel in Memphis where King had been gunned down, Ralph Abernathy conducted a memorial service and then led 1,500 followers on a walk across the nearby state line and on to the small town of Marks, Mississippi. From there, about 150 persons marched on to Edwards, Mississippi, where the "Southern Caravan" of the Poor People's March set out for Washington by way of Selma, Alabama.

On May 6, Abernathy led about a thousand marchers across the Edmund Pettus Bridge where three years earlier another group of civil rights marchers had been beaten and scattered by local and state police. Two days later the caravan arrived safely in Birmingham. (On May 6 too, the FBI reported later, a man traveling on the Canadian passport of one Ramon George Sneyd flew from Toronto to London and on to Lisbon the next day, where on May 16 he obtained a second passport at the Canadian embassy there, claiming the original had been spoiled. On May 17 he flew back to London, where he remained until early June.)

On May 8, a second group of about a thousand demonstrators set out from Marks in ten buses collectively called the "Freedom Train." And on May 13 a third group in fifteen mule-drawn wagons—the "Mule Train"—left Marks with about eighty people aboard. Similar bus caravans were departing for Washington during these days from Boston, Chicago, San Antonio, Los Angeles, San Francisco and Seattle. The first protesters against poverty arrived in Washington on May 11, a day after the National Park Service had issued a thirty-seven-day renewable permit to allow the march organizers to erect what they called "Resurrection City, U.S.A." in a park off the mall linking the Washington Monument and the Lincoln Memorial.

They set out building a sprawling encampment of canvas and plywood structures to house the multitudes expected. Abernathy in blue denim overalls drove the first nail and a "construction battalion" of some 500 blacks took up the work, shouting "Freedom!" as each nail was struck. Abernathy pledged to conduct a massive nonviolent protest "to arouse the conscience of the nation." Unlike previous Washington marchers, he said, "we will be here until the Congress of the United States decide that they are going to do something about the plight of the poor people by doing away with poverty, unemployment and underemployment in this country." He vowed to keep his people there until Congress adjourned, and then follow the legislators home if they still hadn't acted.

In New York, the trouble at Columbia continued. At a student rally on May 1, the day after police had extracted the occupiers of the five campus buildings and the consequent declaration of a student strike, police and students clashed again, with injuries to six students and five police officers. Although the police were withdrawn from the campus the next day, the strike continued and grew in numbers. The strike committee claimed that eighty student government officers and up to 5,000 of the university's 27,500 students were involved in demanding "the right to participate in the restructuring of the university"—and amnesty for all participants in the seizing of the buildings.

The strike effectively ended the spring semester at Columbia College. The faculty voted on May 5 to halt formal classes for the term and cancel final examinations. Individual faculty members were to assign grades for the semester. At the same time, the university's trustees announced that "consultations and negotiations with community leaders shall be held before decision is reached" on resumption of the gym's construction. Rudd, speaking for the strike committee, said his group would bypass Kirk as "too intransigent" and would deal directly with the trustees instead.

In Albany, the state Senate voted to bar state financial aid to any student convicted of a crime committed "on the premises of any college," leading Kirk to denounce the action, along with similar proposals before Congress. But normal academic life on the Columbia campus had come to a standstill, with more of the drama and confrontation still to be played out over the fate of Rudd and other prominent leaders of the insurgency.

* * *

During all this, Nelson Rockefeller in his on-again, off-again, on-again pursuit of the Republican presidential nomination searched for some way to block Nixon's seemingly clear path to it. It was too late to file for ballot position in any of the remaining primaries, and realistically he knew that write-in efforts in the Indiana and Nebraska primaries, and in Nixon's home state of California, would be futile. Only in Oregon, whose primary was on May

28, could a write-in have any hope. There, moderate and liberal Republicans in 1964 had given Rockefeller ("He Cared Enough to Come") a primary victory over no-show Barry Goldwater, and the state had strong antiwar currents running through it. He had four weeks before the Oregon primary to draw distinctions with Nixon and on May 1, the day after he stated his availability after all, he set out to do just that.

In a speech to the World Affairs Council in Philadelphia, Rockefeller struck a more moderate posture on the Vietnam War, insisting that there could be "no purely military solution" and calling for it to be "de-Americanized." He appeared to open the door for participation somehow in the Saigon government by a pacified National Liberation Front. The next day, at the University of Iowa, he proposed a drastic revision of the "arbitrary and inequitable" draft laws and use of a national lottery to replace the system whereby young men could obtain exemptions by attending college and other means. At the same time, he called for lowering the voting age to eighteen everywhere in the United States.

Rockefeller was sounding suspiciously like Kennedy as he moved to siphon off Nixon's moderate and any liberal support in the party. With Johnson out of the picture, Republicans who felt Nixon could have beaten the beleaguered incumbent might be thinking twice about his ability to hold his own with another Kennedy. They might be persuaded, the Rockefeller strategists hoped, that the GOP would have to have a liberal, charismatic nominee to cope successfully with a Democratic nominee who had the same characteristics.

Nixon, with his customary self-righteousness, met Rockefeller's remarks, and the news of an agreement on Paris as the site for peace talks, by reaffirming in Evansville that he would maintain his own moratorium on discussion of the war. Without specifically naming either Rockefeller or Kennedy, he added: "Let's not destroy the chances for peace with a mouthful of words from some irresponsible candidate. Put yourself in the position of the enemy. He is negotiating with Lyndon Johnson and Secretary Rusk and then he reads in the papers that not a senator, not a congressman, not an editor, but a potential president of the United States will give him a better deal than President Johnson is offering him. What's he going to do? It will torpedo those deliberations. It will destroy any chance for the negotiations to bring an honorable end to the war. The enemy will wait for the next man." (This observation would have a special ring later in the year, when reports would surface of a prominent Nixon supporter making just such a representation not to "the enemy," but to the South Vietnamese.)

On the home front, Nixon was quite willing to have Rockefeller pitch to the liberals, knowing they did not represent the true strength and sentiments within his party. He continued a hard conservative line, castigating the protesters at Columbia and cracking down harder on crime. "The role of poverty as a cause of the crime uprise has been grossly exaggerated," he said. Recent Supreme Court rulings putting restraints on the interrogation of suspects and use of confessions "seriously hamstring the peace forces," he said, and should be overturned by new anticrime legislation. His conservative and almost exclusively white audiences in Indiana mightily agreed, and approved, as he cruised unchallenged toward the state's May 7 primary.

* * *

On the Democratic side in Indiana, Kennedy sensed victory and campaigned with abandon in the final days before the voting, continuing to draw huge and enthusiastic crowds. As his motorcade moved through the town of Mishawaka in northern Indiana, he was yanked down, cut his lip and chipped part of a front tooth. He stopped off at a dentist, had it capped and plunged back into the madness, making jokes in a way that conveyed his optimism. Playing with his image as a ruthless politician, he told one crowd: "Make like, not war. See how careful I am?" And he confided to another that President Johnson had given him some sage advice: " 'Go west, young man, go west.' But I was in California at the time."

On the final Sunday before the Hoosiers would vote, Kennedy backtracked to the District of Columbia, which also was holding its presidential primary on the next Tuesday. Another mob scene ensued, but was marred when a lead car in his motorcade struck the dog of a twelve-year-old girl. Kennedy leaped from his car, kneeled down and stroked the animal while he tried to console the girl. On the flight back to Indiana, one of Kennedy's "body men," Los Angeles Rams football star Roosevelt Grier, strummed on a guitar and proclaimed of Kennedy: "This is the one the black man knows. He's the one who can do it."

The day before the primary, one of the most incredible outpourings of sentiment for a political candidate in all the annals of American campaigning unfolded. After a noontime rally at a jammed downtown intersection in Fort Wayne, Kennedy and party took a short flight to South Bend and began what was to be an afternoon of motorcading across the northwestern corner of Indiana to Gary and on into Chicago. It did not end until nine exhausting hours later.

The first event was a courthouse rally in the city of La Porte, hometown of one of the regular radio reporters in the entourage, Dan Blackburn, then of Metromedia News. He was a friendly and conscientious young man to whom Kennedy took a liking. From the platform, the candidate introduced the native son of La Porte in terms that advertised Blackburn as the nonpareil giant of American journalism. Kennedy's playfulness set the tone for what proved to be a remarkable motorcade marathon unmatched before or afterward in my own experience of more than forty years in political reporting.

Standing by the hour on the back seat of his convertible, with Barry holding on to him for dear life, Kennedy breezed through La Porte, Porter and Lake counties on the crisp and sunny spring day, shaking thousands of hands. They were outstretched to him in such numbers that sometimes he would simply extend his arm and meet them like Tom Sawyer scraping a stick along a picket fence. The crowds lined not only the streets of the towns through which the motorcade passed, but also along the highways that connected the towns. Kids ran breakneck or pedaled their bikes alongside his car for blocks, until fatigue forced them to fall away. His "old" friends Michael and his sister showed up again to greet him.

At one point, two young women in their twenties waved at Kennedy and jumped up and down as he passed, then turned and raced for their car. A mile or so farther down the road they appeared again, doing the same. Those of us on the press bus who noted their first two appearances began to look for them again, and sure enough, there they were another few miles down the road. Over the next few hours, we spotted them no fewer than thirteen times along the route, their enthusiastic greeting of Kennedy never waning. Finally some photographers in an open car behind Kennedy, also noting the phenomenon, invited them to join them, which they happily did, leaving their car for later retrieval somehow.

The motorcade pressed on into the early evening and dark of night with undiminished crowds lining the streets and highways. At another point, a young boy with a basketball ran alongside Kennedy's car, and when the candidate called for the ball, a game of catch ensued between the two of them for block after block. All this time, Barry on his aching and eventually bleeding knees clung to Kennedy's waist as the candidate brushed a forelock from his eyes and waved his free hand in a short, almost tentative manner.

When the motorcade passed through heavily black Gary and a particularly tumultuous reception and headed for Hammond, the mayor of that town climbed into the car with Kennedy. By this time the ride through Hammond seemed so endless to the candidate that afterward he referred to the day's motorcade as "Hammond, Hammond, Hammond." The schedule called for Kennedy to make a final speech in the town of Whiting, near the state border with Illinois, at five o'clock in the afternoon. The motorcade got there after ten at night.

Among the cars parked along the route was one with a mattress on the roof, several preschool kids stretched out on it in their pajamas, bundled in blankets against the night chill. Kennedy stopped the motorcade. "We tried to keep them awake," the children's mother told him, "but they fell asleep waiting for you." She woke them up and Kennedy and his wife held them and sipped coffee offered by neighbors. Meanwhile, we beer-guzzling reporters bounded off the press buses and raced desperately to private homes along the street with pleas for swift entry.

Beyond the sheer numbers and enthusiasm of the crowds was the composition of the neighborhoods through which the motorcade passed—from blue-collar white ethnic to black inner city to white and mixed suburban. Here was the black and blue-collar coalition that was at the core of Kennedy's political base, promising success in a state otherwise known for its deep conservatism. Even after Whiting, as the motorcade sped to Chicago's O'Hare Airport for a charter flight back to Indianapolis, the crowds lined the highway with Kennedy still standing and waving.

In Indianapolis, where an election eve reception had long since ended, the entourage staggered into the Weir-Cook Airport Holiday Inn for the night. Germond and I headed for the bar for a nightcap. We were sitting on stools at a small, high table when Kennedy came in and walked over. He didn't often do the bar scene after a day's campaigning as many other candidates of the time did, and he declined our invitation to sit down. He just stood at the table, reflecting on the incredible day.

"Well," he told us, "I've done all I could do. Maybe it's just not my time. But I've learned something from Indiana. The country is changing. . . ." He talked on about the crisis in the cities and the need for racial reconciliation. The old Democratic coalition of labor and the South, he said, wasn't the answer anymore; somehow whites and blacks in the North had to be brought together to break down the social barrier between them. More politicians and columnists in Washington, he said, should get out around the country and experience the intensity of feeling.

While he confessed to having been profoundly moved by the outpouring of positive sentiment toward himself over the long motorcade, Kennedy dwelled on one negative sign he had spotted en route that said: YOU PUNK. The man toting it, he told us, ran ahead of his car, then turned and grabbed his hand as it came by. "He squeezed my hand as if he were trying to break every bone in it," Kennedy said, incredulously. Well, one of us suggested, based on the outpouring of affection demonstrated toward him over this day and night, he might be the one politician who could effectively preach racial conciliation to whites and blacks alike. He said he hoped so, then turned, shook some more hands at neighboring tables and walked out of the bar.

Later, at dinner with his closest aides, friends and a few reporters at Sam's Subway behind the Marott Hotel where he was staying, Kennedy repeated the story that had stuck in his mind about the man who had squeezed his hand. But he talked also of the bright-faced kids who had greeted him, and he gradually relaxed and seemed to be enjoying himself. Then a man who had been drinking came over and made a derogatory remark about him. Kennedy just looked ahead and did not reply. When the man moved off, Kennedy sighed and said, "You get so tired sometimes. You have to restrain yourself." But the mood passed and he went back to enjoying the late dinner with his friends.

*   *   *

McCarthy meanwhile went through the final days of the Indiana campaign with what seemed to be a mood of resignation and some bitterness. Two days before the vote, he leveled an accusation that the New York office of Citizens for Kennedy had been falsifying his Senate record. Noting Kennedy's silence up to this point, he said, "I would have repudiated it at once and set the record straight." The next day Kennedy did disavow the New York group, saying he hadn't seen the material involved. If it was in error, he said, he would urge that circulation be halted and that "those responsible apologize forthwith" to McCarthy. At the same time, *Congressional Quarterly* reported that of twenty-nine key foreign and domestic policy votes since 1965, Kennedy and McCarthy had voted in agreement on twenty-two.

The McCarthy campaign in Indiana was geared to the small towns but did not have notable success against the high-balling Kennedy operation. In addition, the organization was no match for what it had been in New Hampshire and Wisconsin. One fiasco often cited later was a speech at Notre Dame, on paper likely to draw a large and enthusiastic audience for a candidate who was once a Benedictine novice. Little advance notice was given and McCarthy failed to fill a small hall of 350 seats. The campaign headquarters in Indianapolis, in the soon-to-be demolished Claypool, was in a state of continuous chaos and poverty. Many of the student workers on a subsistence allowance of seven dollars a day did not get paid for days on end; rental cars could not be used for want of gas money; campaign literature could not be mailed for want of postage. But the students' commitment to end the war, and belief in McCarthy, kept most of them going.

However, like the small rebuffed boy who says he didn't want to play anyway, McCarthy in expectation of a poor showing minimized the significance of the Indiana primary. He made a point of enjoying the Hoosier scenery and scribbling poetry along the way. In his post-election book, he wrote: "My schedulers seemed preoccupied with having me appear in every courthouse square in the state of Indiana. Still, these were rather pleasant stops, as stops go, especially in places like Greenfield, where an appearance could be combined with a visit to the home of James Whitcomb Riley. And in Franklin where the town turned out, and in Crawfordsville when the Baroque Quartet (harpsichord, cello, violin and flute) from nearby Wabash College played Vivaldi's *Four Seasons* at the meeting. This was the first time, I believe, that a candidate for the presidency had been accompanied by a harpsichord."

McCarthy, however, was a man with a sizable contempt for places, and people, he didn't care for. And Indiana obviously was one of those places, just as Robert Kennedy was one of those people. Speaking of the state later, he remarked: "They kept talking about the poet out there. I asked if they were talking about Shakespeare or even my friend Robert Lowell. But it was James Whitcomb Riley. You could hardly expect to win under those circumstances."

This attitude, according to Larner in his book, injected a frivolous quality to a campaign whose foot soldiers nevertheless remained deeply committed. With Goodwin going back to Kennedy after his entry into the campaign, McCarthy "had isolated himself from professionals," Larner wrote, "and from the beginning he had no interest in those who approached him in terms of their commitment to the issues. His only companions were hangers-on and specially sympathetic journalists who toadied to McCarthy and took precious pleasure in the atmosphere of contempt toward politics and politicians. The Dump Johnson people were out of favor now that Johnson had been dumped; and indeed their canvassing operation had lost some of its better people and ran less effectively from Indiana on."

McCarthy didn't expect to win in Indiana, and he didn't. On election night, it was all Kennedy. He won 42.3 percent of the vote to 30.7 for Branigin and 27 for McCarthy, and ten of the state's eleven congressional districts, the other one going to the favorite-son governor. Equally important for Kennedy, precinct samples showed that in addition to overwhelming support in black and blue-collar ethnic neighborhoods, he ran strongly in mixed racial and ethnic communities. As the parody proclaimed, there were no ethnic problems on the *Ruthless Cannonball*.

Nixon, running unopposed on the Republican ballot in Indiana, was the big vote-getter, rolling up about 508,000 votes compared to about 328,000 for Kennedy on the Democratic side. In the District of Columbia, in a head-to-head test against two Humphrey slates, Kennedy won 62.5 percent of the vote to 37.5 for Humphrey. McCarthy did not contest there after being part of a joint Kennedy-McCarthy slate for a short time, when Johnson was still in the race.

Still, McCarthy was not driven from the competition, which had been Kennedy's prime objective in Indiana. The Minnesotan's third-place finish was disappointing but he took some solace in the fact that his 27 percent was more than the polls had indicated he would get. "We have tested the enemy," he said on election night. "We know his techniques, we know his weaknesses." But on this night at least, he did not seem particularly well positioned to exploit whatever he perceived those weaknesses to be. Now that he had lost, he dismissed the Indiana primary as a mere "interruption" in the campaign because as a three-man race it did not offer a clear test between himself and Kennedy. "I think the direct confrontation that was denied us here in Indiana will be given us in Nebraska," he said.

Kennedy was interviewed on television, after which he appeared before his celebrating campaign workers at his headquarters hotel and then held a press conference—the pattern he was to follow after each of the succeeding primaries. The only unusual development at the press conference was a question from a very attractive blond woman who asked Kennedy whether, if elected president, he would appoint his brother attorney general. "No, we tried that once," he replied. Then he asked the woman whom she represented. She wouldn't say. It was Joan Kennedy, his brother Ted's wife.

Well after midnight that night, Dutton looked into the airport terminal coffee shop and found his candidate deep in conversation with two young McCarthy campaign college dropouts—Taylor Branch, then a twenty-one-year-old University of North Carolina student, and a young woman from Pembroke named Pat Sylvester. Branch, later the Pulitzer Prize–winning author of *Parting the Waters: America in the King Years, 1954–63*, and Sylvester, wearing McCarthy campaign credentials, were awaiting early morning flights home.

Branch, sitting on his suitcase, was dozing off, he recalled years later, "when somebody tapped me on the shoulder. I looked up and there was Robert Kennedy staring me in the face. He said, 'How are you? I see you're for McCarthy. Have you got a minute to talk? How would you like to have some breakfast?'" The airport coffee shop was closed but a Kennedy aide managed to get it opened. They sat in a booth eating a hurriedly prepared breakfast.

"We were awestruck," Branch remembered. "He talked politely with us. We must have stayed there until four or four-thirty in the morning. He asked why we weren't supporting him. He said he was concerned he was only getting the C students. He was getting the fraternity students. Did we understand McCarthy couldn't win?

"I remember being very impressed by the fact he had done this. . . . I thought, 'this guy has campaigned his ass off, he's finally won, he probably hasn't slept in three or four days, and here he is staying up talking to us.' It was amazing that he wouldn't even pause to absorb all this. We discussed why he hadn't opposed the war more forthrightly before, why he jumped in only after McCarthy did well in New Hampshire.

"We talked a lot about the war," Branch remembered. "My draft physical was coming up in Atlanta and I had decided that if I passed I would not serve. I would not go to Canada or [plead] conscientious objection against this particular war. I would refuse induction." Kennedy told him he should serve if drafted but added sympathetically, Branch recalled, "I'm against the war just as much as you are." (Branch subsequently flunked his physical as a result of a hip injury suffered in an earlier motorcycle accident.)

Because "my initial interest was in the civil rights movement," Branch said, "I had been canvassing for McCarthy in black neighborhoods," and he told Kennedy it had not been easy going. "That's not your fault," Kennedy said, according to an account in Richard T. Stout's book *People*, on the McCarthy campaign, which he covered for *Newsweek*. "Why wasn't McCarthy effective for you in those areas?" Sylvester interjected that Kennedy had "the name" that won over black voters. "Look, I agree I have a tremendous advantage with my last name," he said, "but let me ask you: Why can't McCarthy go into a ghetto? Why can't he go into a poor neighborhood? Can you tell me that he's been involved in those areas?" Kennedy told him, Branch recalled, that "McCarthy has no feel for poverty, for civil rights," adding that if Branch really wanted a candidate who did, and could win, he should back him.

"It never sounded like a campaign speech, he was so blunt," Branch said. "We were bowled over by him but at the same time proud of ourselves that we held to our position [of support for McCarthy]. We told him. He didn't like it. He was giving us the Kennedy version of the Johnson Treatment." While holding firm for McCarthy, Branch told me much later, he decided that as a result of the conversation at the coffee shop, he would never speak in opposition to Kennedy. He told Stout: "He kind of neutralized me. I still worked for McCarthy, but I was drawn to Kennedy because of his flair and passion for the black people."

Finally, the talkfest broke up in a friendly fashion, and Kennedy returned to the nearby airport hotel. Branch recalled that he and Sylvester "were so bowled over by him that we stayed up drafting a long letter to him rehashing all that was said. We told him of our respect for him but that we still felt loyal to McCarthy. . . . Our generation being power hungry, the one thing we admired about McCarthy was that he didn't seem to care about power. But we realized later that politics is about power, and we came not to appreciate [McCarthy's attitude] quite so much."

The two young students walked over to the airport Holiday Inn and slipped the letter under the door to Kennedy's room or that of an aide. Later, Dutton recalled about that night: "He had won in Indiana, but he couldn't win over those kids, and they really got to him. He had a lot of college kids with him, but he didn't have the super-activists, and he wanted and needed them, for himself. For days afterward, he talked about that boy and girl at the airport coffee shop—how great they were, in their idealism and determination."

Kennedy would now head for Nebraska and his second test against McCarthy a week later. This time it would be a straight two-man race, and he knew that the black segment of his black and blue-collar coalition would be largely a politically insignificant one in that farm state in the center of the nation's breadbasket.

Reflecting on the two young McCarthy workers, he knew that loss of their support, and of thousands like them, had been the price he paid for his long procrastination about running. Even on this night of triumph in Indiana, that fact gnawed at him and diminished his sense of achievement. As long as the Taylor Branches and the Pat Sylvesters endured for McCarthy, Kennedy knew he would have to persevere himself with only half an army of the generation of Americans that meant most to him. And he knew as well that McCarthy was not likely to fold his tent and leave the anti-administration Democratic vote to himself alone against Hubert Humphrey.

*   *   *

One other development on the May 7 primary day was worth noting. In Alabama, Democratic voters made their former governor, George Wallace, the recipient of their delegate votes to the party's national convention, although his intention was to run as an independent or third-party candidate in November. In an unprecedented circumstance, the state delegation would include two blacks who had run unopposed.

The day before the voting, Wallace's long-ill wife, Lurleen, the incumbent governor of the state, had died at forty-one, elevating the lieutenant governor, Albert Brewer, to the governorship. For the first time in a decade, state executive decisions in Alabama would no longer be made by George Wallace, but the state remained a loyal stepping-stone for him and his national ambitions.

With his wife departed, Wallace was now free to pursue his campaign in earnest, and he did. So concerned were supporters of the two-party system with Wallace's talk of striking a "covenant" with one of the major-party nominees that it was not long before the major parties were being urged by political scientists to enter into one between themselves. It was proposed that they agree in advance that in the event no candidate received a majority in the electoral college, the candidate with the highest number of popular votes would get the support of both parties for the presidency. Meanwhile, the specter of George Wallace continued to hang over the presidential politics of 1968 as he sought to make up for lost time on the campaign circuit with his political road show and provocative words and style.

*　*　*

Although McCarthy spoke optimistically on the night of his third-place finish in Indiana, something seemed to go out of him when he moved on to Nebraska. With only a week to campaign before the state's Democrats voted in their primary, instead of firing up his loyal troops and giving his all in the time available, he chose to sulk a good part of the week. He sniped at Kennedy as the interloper who, as he said in Omaha on May 9, had "poisoned the well in Indiana."

His young and gritty troops, exhausted after Indiana and handicapped by lack of campaign funds, were no match for the Kennedy operation that had now shifted into high gear. A plan to charter a train—*The Little Engine That Could* it would be called—to take the McCarthyites from Indiana through Nebraska spreading the word about their man to the state's small towns and farms had to be abandoned. And without Lyndon Johnson as a target, the message of change was muddled. Some dissension developed between the "old" hands who had steered the Children's Crusade through New Hampshire, Wisconsin and Indiana and a diminishing number of newcomers.

Hopes that McCarthy's Midwestern roots would give him an edge in this key farm state against the New England–accented New York transplant were not realized. Kennedy demolished the distinction with humor. When a single sheet of paper blew out of his hand while he was speaking at one rural stop, he blurted: "Give me that back. That's my farm program." In the town of Crete, when Kennedy spied a sign for Rockefeller, he asked the crowd: "Do you think Nelson Rockefeller understands the problems of the farmer?" "No!" the crowd shouted. "Does he care about Crete?" "No!" "When was the last time Nelson Rockefeller was in Crete? If he wants to be president, why doesn't *he* come to Crete?"

Kennedy said he was personally contributing to the farm economy by buying twenty-six bottles of milk a day for his ten children. "So I'm trying to do something about the farm problem," he said. "I'm working on it right now. Let any of *them* [the other candidates] match that by Tuesday."

At a stop in the small town of Beatrice, Kennedy suggested that if he lost in Nebraska, he might just settle there "and I'll bring Ethel and all 11 children," confirming a report on which his wife had declined to comment, that she was expecting again.

The farm vote was critical for Kennedy because the base that had sustained him in Indiana, his black and blue-collar coalition, was limited in Nebraska. The black population in the state was less than 5 percent and the blue collar only about 15, though both groups voted heavily Democratic, when they voted. On the downside, Nebraska was John Kennedy's worst state in his successful 1960 presidential bid. Also, Omaha had recently experienced riots, and racial animosity had been fanned by a visit from George Wallace. Kennedy benefited, however, from a good local organization sparked by Democratic Lieutenant Governor Philip Sorensen, brother of JFK's old speechwriter.

Having failed to knock McCarthy out of the race in Indiana, Kennedy wanted to accomplish that end in Nebraska. At the very least, he hoped to start gaining converts from the McCarthy army by inflicting a resounding defeat on him in a two-man race, and then confronting Humphrey alone. Some Kennedy strategists feared that McCarthy would hold on as long as he could simply to help Humphrey, whom he clearly preferred to Kennedy, on a personal basis at least.

The centerpiece of the Democratic primary was to be the state's annual Jefferson-Jackson dinner in Omaha on May 10. Humphrey was to be the featured speaker, with Kennedy and McCarthy invited and afforded an opportunity to address the influential party crowd. While Humphrey was not on the primary ballot, a write-in effort had been started in his behalf, and an electric performance at the dinner might possibly ignite it. A further complication was the fact that Johnson's name remained on the ballot, his withdrawal having come after the ballots had been printed.

The night before the dinner, two other reporters and I were in the dining room of the Blackstone Hotel in Omaha enjoying the state's celebrated steaks, when McCarthy sauntered over and sat down. He informed us, to our astonishment, that he was leaving Nebraska later that night for the West Coast, passing up the big Democratic fund-raiser. He had challenged Kennedy to debate once again in Nebraska and when Kennedy predictably declined, it had been expected McCarthy would want to make the most of his opportunity at the dinner to strike a contrast with him.

But the Nebraska primary really wasn't very important, McCarthy told us in his dismissive way. In fact, he said, none of the primaries really mattered all that much, possibly excepting California's. "Kennedy talks about me winning three primaries," he said. "I've won five." We knew of four he could claim to have "won," in one fashion or another—Wisconsin, Massachusetts and Pennsylvania, plus his moral victory in New Hampshire. What was the fifth? "The college primary," he told us with a straight face, referring to a recent nationwide poll of college students. "I'd rather win the college primary than the Indiana primary," he said, as we glanced at one another in disbelief.

The only real significance of the Indiana primary, he said, was that it had killed any chance Kennedy had for the nomination, presumably because he had not won decisively enough to convince the party that only he could save it from defeat in November. "All the cards are on the table now," he said. "It's just a question of playing them out."

The fact that he didn't have many delegates to the convention didn't matter either, McCarthy insisted. He was the only Democrat who could get enough independents and better-educated suburbanites to win, he said; any Democrat could do well among blacks and blue-collar voters against Nixon. He predicted that Kennedy would be kept under 50 percent in Nebraska, thus tarnishing him more, while he himself would exceed expectations by winning 30 percent. Having thus explained why Nebraska didn't warrant his further attention, McCarthy got up from our table and walked off, headed for California and for Oregon, the next state on the primary calendar.

The next night, Humphrey and Kennedy received enthusiastic but non-committal receptions from the dinner crowd, while the assembled Democrats buzzed about McCarthy leaving the field before the battle was over. Kennedy went first, before Humphrey's arrival, and dished up his usual indictment of the state of things, without mentioning Johnson or Humphrey. After Kennedy left the hall, Humphrey delivered one of his standard party pep talks, giving Nixon and the Republicans hell, and making only a veiled reference to the Kennedy campaign cyclone that was whirling through the state. "I do not think the American people want more frenzy," he said. "I do not think the American people will respond to leadership that exaggerates our difficulties to paralyze us with fear."

On the stump, however, Kennedy was enjoying the warm sunshine and friendliness of the people of Nebraska. In Wahoo on the day before the primary, he pointed to a theater marquee and cracked that "I hope that's what you will make me tomorrow." It read: THE HAPPIEST MILLIONAIRE. Then, down the road at Father Flanagan's Boys Town, the candidate whose wealthy and influential father devoted himself to giving his children the best of everything jokingly told the orphan residents who greeted him that "actually, I worked my way up the hard way." Apparently with their special condition in mind, he rather incongruously reminded them of the old saying, "I complained because I had no shoes, until I met a man with no feet."

Kennedy capped the final day with a huge noontime rally at the Creighton University quadrangle in Omaha. Peeling off his jacket and standing in shirt-sleeves in the hot sun, he started with a mild lecture to the students, telling them that college "gives you a license to remove yourself" from the problems that beleaguered the less fortunate. "You can take it as a free passage," he said, "or you can figure a college education gives you a responsibility and an opportunity to involve yourself."

In the question-and-answer period, the subject of the draft inevitably came up. Kennedy warmed to one of his favorite themes—the granting of student deferments while poor and undereducated blacks were drafted in great numbers. The remarks generated some boos and a question from one white student who asked: "Isn't the Army one way of getting young people out of the ghettos . . . and solving the ghetto problem?" Kennedy listened incredulously, then replied: "Here at a Catholic university, how can you say that we deal with the problems of the poor by sending them to Vietnam?"

Kennedy said there was "a great moral force in the United States" opposed to "the wrongs of the federal government and all the mistakes Lyndon Johnson had made, and how Congress had failed to pass legislation dealing with civil rights. And yet, when it comes down to you yourselves and your own individual lives, then you say students should be draft-deferred."

He asked for a show of hands by all those who favored the student deferments, and not surprisingly a majority went up. Visibly agitated, Kennedy said: "Look around you. How many black faces do you see here? How many American Indians? How many Mexican Americans? . . . The fact is, if you look at any regiment or division of paratroopers in Vietnam, 45 percent of them are black. How can you accept this? What I don't understand is that you don't even debate these things among yourselves. You're the most exclusive minority in the world. Are you just going to sit on your duffs and do nothing, or just carry signs and protest?"

The crowd, which had started out in a lighthearted mood, seemed stunned by the sharpness of Kennedy's challenge. His remarks were among his most pointed of the entire campaign, contrasting with the otherwise playful banter that marked the brief Kennedy drive for support in Nebraska.

McCarthy did return to Omaha on the day before the primary for a news conference. He again attacked Kennedy for "gross misrepresentations" of his Senate attendance record by his campaign workers. "It is not the kind of politics to which I would lend my name or allow to go on without repudiating," he said. In ten years in the Senate, he said, he had answered 79 percent of all roll calls, including one year in which he had a protracted absence because of illness, compared to Kennedy's 80 percent in three years. Nebraskans didn't seem to care.

On primary night, Kennedy did win a majority—51.5 percent—but again McCarthy exceeded expectations by receiving 31 percent. The write-in for Humphrey was a bust, giving him only 8.4 percent, and the inactive LBJ got 5.6. McCarthy blamed the involvement of Humphrey and Johnson, such as it was, for depriving him of the one-on-one confrontation he said he craved with Kennedy. He said he would go on to Oregon, voting two weeks later on May 28, and California a week after that.

For all of McCarthy's nonchalance about the Nebraska result, a staff shakeup ensued in which Washington lawyer Thomas Finney, who had helped McCarthy in his short-lived flirtation with Johnson over the 1964 vice presidential nomination, replaced Clark and Gans as chief operative. Gans after quitting was persuaded to head up the campaign in Southern California.

McCarthy in his post-election book dismissed his second defeat at Kennedy's hands this way: "Nebraska happened on the way west. After Indiana and before Oregon, I had only four days scheduled for campaigning there. Although I hoped that I would not do too badly in Nebraska, I had no real reason to expect that I would run very well. Oregon was the critical state and we had to concentrate our money, time and effort there, giving Nebraska little more than a quick once-over and hoping for the best." He also recalled that he liked to tell audiences that "in the history of the western movement it had been relatively easy to get the wagons to the Missouri, but after the crossing of the Missouri the real test took place on the Oregon Trail. I said we had the best wagons and horses and the best men, and we expected to win the West."

Kennedy, noting his strong rural support in a conservative state—roughly 60 percent of the farm vote—openly called on "those associated with Senator McCarthy" to make the move to his candidacy. The blatant nature of his pitch was bound to resurrect his reputation as ruthless in some minds but he had to shake McCarthy somehow. "I would hope perhaps we could work together . . . in Oregon and California," Kennedy said with little conviction that it would happen. He told reporters he had now proved he was the popular Democratic choice but "perhaps I'll have to go on and prove it again in Oregon, California and South Dakota," the three remaining state primaries in which he was entered.

Lowenstein, still supporting McCarthy but keeping his lines open to Kennedy as he himself ran for Congress on Long Island, later contrasted the attitudes in the two presidential campaigns. "The Kennedy campaign took the position that everybody was welcome," he said, "and they sort of solicited people. In many places they wooed people. In the McCarthy campaign, conversely, anybody that had anything kind to say about Kennedy was to be excluded and almost driven out. So the result was that the McCarthy campaign, through this particular paranoia, lost people all the time to Kennedy, and of course they tried to turn the Kennedy wooing of people into something disreputable. . . . The headquarters people would say, 'Ah, this is the ruthless Kennedy machine.'"

At the same time, Lowenstein said, "the Kennedy people made the stupidest mistake they could make in their wooing . . . so stupid that it hurt them much more than the McCarthy people's general paranoia hurt them at that time, which was that the Kennedy people used as their chief argument on the McCarthy people that McCarthy couldn't win. . . . And if there was one argument that was designed to make people stay with McCarthy and that was designed to make people furious, it was that. It was the one argument that, when I heard it, I blew up over. I said that I just could not believe anybody would say that. I said, 'We started a movement to stop Lyndon Johnson, when you people wouldn't have a damn thing to do with it. And the argument that you people made then was that we couldn't stop Lyndon Johnson. Now don't come back to us and use that same horseshit now. . . .' It was politically stupid because it had to make everybody angry. And until it was too late, they never stopped saying that. Pierre Salinger in Nebraska announced that McCarthy was finished in a tone suggesting that everybody had always known McCarthy was finished. Nothing could have made people decide more that they would go through Oregon, and California."

While his strategists thus dismissed McCarthy, Kennedy would focus increasingly on Humphrey. Kennedy said that his vote and McCarthy's taken together "quite clearly demonstrates dissatisfaction with what we're doing at the moment. . . . We can't have the politics of happiness and joy when we have so many problems in our own country." It was not quite time, however, for Kennedy to turn his back on Gene McCarthy, who in leaving Nebraska early had gotten a jump in Oregon, the next primary state.

* * *

Nixon once again breezed in the Nebraska Republican primary, receiving 70 percent of the vote to only 5 for absentee candidate Rockefeller on write-ins. Reagan, meanwhile, won a rather impressive 23 percent after supporters repeatedly ran a half-hour paid television documentary on his career. It was an essential ingredient in an almost secret bid for the Republican nomination that Reagan denied at every turn. In the now-lackluster campaign for that nomination, Reagan's showing got considerable attention from the news media as well as from the ever-watchful Nixon campaign. Ward Just, in the *Washington Post*, wrote that Nixon "must be America's only major political figure who can win 70 percent of a state's vote and still have the analysts talking about his opponent's 23 percent."

Perhaps it was because Nixon's largely unopposed primary "victories" never fully dispelled his image as tarnished political goods, or erased the intense hostility toward the man personally as well as politically from his critics, including important voices in the press. Would the Republicans really go into the general election in November with Nixon as their standard-bearer, when there was clearly a much more charismatic figure like Ronald Reagan in the wings? Reagan to be sure had his own image problems: he was indeed governor of California, but an old Grade B movie star for president? For many political professionals and analysts, that notion went down hard. And then there was still Rockefeller, with all that money and that bear-hug extroversion, who made Nixon seem an uncertain tea-dance wallflower by comparison, for all his transparent efforts to convey strength and self-confidence.

Rockefeller by now was going after Nixon daily as he traveled the country trying to make the case that he would be the stronger Republican candidate. Chiding Nixon for his generalities about dealing with crime and communism, Rockefeller said at Emory University in Atlanta: "It is not straight talk to issue resounding statements on crime control, which wholly omit the slightest mention of gun control . . . to place overwhelming blame on the national government for our sharply rising crime rate, when we all know that criminal law enforcement is overwhelmingly in the charge of state and local government."

Nixon at this time was talking about a "new alignment" in American politics that would "affect the future of all Americans for generations to come." He described it as including Republicans advocating individual freedom and enterprise and against "centralized and domineering" government—a theme that would echo long and undiminished into the future. He talked of a "new South" no longer tied to one-party Democratic politics. He spoke of black militants supporting black enterprise rather than "handouts or welfare," and "new liberals" advocating "more personal freedom and less government domination." Rockefeller assailed the concept, declaring it was "an exercise in political fantasy . . . to propagate notions of unity in terms of a 'new alignment,'" particularly in incongruously pretending to merge new Southern leadership and the new black militants.

But Nixon was certainly right about the emergence of a "new South" open to conservative Republican ideas, and in its courtship Rockefeller had no chance of outdoing Nixon. Part of Nixon's appeal to the "new South" was the

212 JULES WITCOVER

hard line he was taking toward protest, whether it was against racial injustice or the war. He pushed his case for "black capitalism" as the real answer to combating the former. While he had "compassion" for the Poor People's Campaign in Washington, he said, a massive federal spending effort "is not the road to bring people out of poverty."

Nor, he said, was campus protest the way to cope with racial injustice. He labeled the violence at Columbia "the first major skirmish in a revolutionary struggle to seize the universities of this country and transform them into sanctuaries for radicals and vehicles for revolutionary political and social goals." Columbia authorities, he said, should "rid the campus now [of its] anarchic students."

He warned that "if that student violence is either rewarded or goes unpunished, the administration of Columbia University will have guaranteed a new crisis on its own campus and invited student coups on other campuses all over this country." He declared that "academic freedom . . . dictates that the rationally committed stand up and resist the dictates of the emotionally committed. And academic freedom dictates that those engaged in the pursuit of knowledge and truth resist the encroachments of hotheads who assume they know all truth."

* * *

It was now barely five weeks since the assassination of Dr. King. The unrest on college campuses continued into May—at Princeton, the University of Chicago, Northwestern, Cheyney State College in Pennsylvania, Southern Illinois, Roosevelt University in Chicago and San Francisco State. Later in the month, there was further upheaval on the Columbia campus when Mark Rudd and four other students rejected an order to appear at the dean's office to face disciplinary charges and called for another rally. As passions were rekindled, students occupied Hamilton Hall again, police were summoned again and, after some peaceful arrests, the rioting and general mayhem broke out once more, lasting until the early hours of the next morning. In the end, police arrested 177 more participants and sixty-eight individuals were injured, seventeen of them police officers.

In New Orleans, a jury of nine whites and three blacks convicted Rap Brown of violating the Federal Firearms Act for carrying a rifle on a plane from New York to New Orleans in August 1967. The judge gave him the maximum sentence of five years in jail and a fine of $2,000. And in Baltimore on May 24, Philip Berrigan was sentenced to six years and two others got lighter terms for despoiling draft records. They also pleaded not guilty to charges that a week earlier they and six others including Berrigan's brother Daniel, also a Catholic priest, had stolen 600 individual draft records from the Selective Service office in Catonsville, a Baltimore suburb, and burned them in a nearby parking lot.

Ten days later the Supreme Court upheld an amendment to the draft law making it a criminal offense to burn or otherwise mutilate a draft card. In Boston, Providence and New York, federal officials began hauling draft evaders out of churches in which they had sought sanctuary. Meanwhile, in courts at all levels around the country, students and other protesters of the war were filing suits against General Hershey and the Selective Service System to bar their reclassification in the draft if they were found to be engaged in antiwar demonstrations.

At Resurrection City in Washington, about 1,500 demonstrators had arrived by mid-May and joined the encampment. Rains pummeled the temporary residents and the camp soon was mired in mud. But the Poor People's Campaign persisted and endured. Bayard Rustin, executive director of the A. Philip Randolph Institute and longtime civil rights and antiwar organizer, agreed to coordinate a massive Memorial Day demonstration, later changed to June 19.

On May 21, Jesse Jackson led a silent two-mile march of 300 Resurrection City campers from the campsite to Capitol Hill, but they were barred from admission to the House of Representatives' visitors' galley for lack of proper passes. By the time about forty were admitted, the House had adjourned. There were other marches and sit-ins over the next days at the Departments of Agriculture, Justice and Health, Education and Welfare and the Supreme Court, but their impact was undermined by dissension and controversy within the encampment.

On May 22, about 200 black youths, most of them members of Chicago and Detroit street gangs, were sent home. "They went around and beat up on our white people," explained the Reverend James Bevel, a Poor People's Campaign official. "They interfered with the workers and were hostile to the press. We had to get them out." On May 25, leaders of nonblack groups— Mexican-Americans, Appalachian poor whites and American Indians—bitterly complained they were being badly treated by blacks. And Rustin himself, who was black, soon came under attack within the campaign as "an outsider."

* * *

Although the Vietnam peace talks finally began in Paris on May 10, the news from the war zone continued to get worse. There were new intensified attacks by the Vietcong on Saigon and other cities in the South. In the week of May 5, a record 562 Americans were killed and another 2,153 wounded seriously enough to require hospitalization. The U.S. fatalities now had reached

22,951. Before the month was out, Johnson asked Congress for nearly $4 billion more for pursuit of the war as the peace talks dragged on with no substantial progress.

The Hanoi negotiators rejected the U.S. insistence on reciprocity in the halting of American bombing of North Vietnam, mockingly pledging to "refrain from bombing and all other acts of war on the entire territory of the United States." General Westmoreland meanwhile was telling Johnson that the enemy appeared "to be approaching a point of desperation" and its forces "deteriorating in strength and quality." While there would be more heavy fighting, he said, "time is on our side."

In Korea, the *Pueblo* continued in North Korean hands, with Secretary Rusk reporting to Congress that a stalemate had been reached in negotiations for its release. And there was more bad news for the U.S. Navy on May 29 when the nuclear-powered submarine USS *Scorpion* was reported missing, and subsequently declared "presumed lost" with ninety-nine men aboard during a return trip to Norfolk from the Mediterranean.

In Europe, Czechoslovakia's bold bid for a modicum of reform and breathing room within the Soviet sphere was under pressure from Moscow and other members of the Eastern bloc. The mild-mannered Alexander Dubček, who had replaced Moscow's man, Antonin Novotný, as Communist Party first secretary in January in a bloodless upheaval, was summoned to Moscow to explain the heralded Prague Spring. And on May 8, Soviet troops appeared ominously along the Czech border.

In France, left-wing student militants led by Daniel Cohn-Bendit—known as Danny the Red—seized a lecture hall at the Nanterre campus of the University of Paris on May 2. The act triggered occupation of parts of the Sorbonne campus and street fighting between students and police in the Latin Quarter over the next several days. President Charles de Gaulle warned the students against further violence but it continued, spilling over to several provincial cities. The numbers of demonstrating students swelled and were joined by striking labor organizations protesting against "police brutality" in suppressing the student demonstrations. Cohn-Bendit was ordered out of France but later in the month he returned in disguise and rejoined the protest at the Sorbonne.

On May 13, huge crowds estimated at up to 400,000 persons marched from Paris's Left Bank denouncing de Gaulle. And the next day, as Nebraskans voted in their primaries half a world away, students occupied the Sorbonne and sit-in strikes everywhere paralyzed the country. With de Gaulle in Romania on a state visit, Premier Georges Pompidou convened the National Assembly and warned that "our civilization is being questioned—

not the government, not the institutions, not even France, but the material-
istic and soulless modern society." He called the situation comparable to "the
hopeless days of the Fifteenth Century, where the structures of the Middle
Ages were collapsing."

De Gaulle rushed back to Paris as most French air and rail transportation
came to a halt. François Mitterrand, leading a noncommunist Federation of
the Left, called on him to resign, paving the way for a general election. The
Pompidou government barely survived an effort in the Assembly to oust it
and de Gaulle finally set a June referendum in which he would demand a vote
of confidence or resign. He acknowledged that reforms, particularly in university life that the protesting students found stifling, were needed, and he
pledged to institute them if he was given a resounding vote of support.
Instead, he was confronted with the worst street fighting and rioting up to
that time. De Gaulle finally dissolved the National Assembly, warning that
France was "threatened by dictatorship" and "totalitarian communism." He
vowed that "the Republic will not abdicate" and he set the referendum for
June 23 and 30.

All Europe, and the world, watched nervously at the prospect of France
falling to communism at the same time the valiant efforts in Czechoslovakia
to loosen its most repressive aspects seemed in dire jeopardy.

* * *

Back in the United States, the domestic version of protest against the established order—the competition between Robert Kennedy and Eugene
McCarthy to challenge Hubert Humphrey, the heir to the Johnson leadership
and establishment political structure—moved on to Oregon. Each had two
weeks before the May 28 primary to make his case in a state where opposition to the war in Vietnam and hospitality to those who voiced it were strong
and widespread. But because there would be only one week thereafter before
the critical California primary, both candidates felt obliged to shuttle between the two states in the period up to May 28.

Also campaigning in Oregon, against the Democrats and two phantom
Republican candidates if not against the established order, was Richard
Nixon. Unopposed on the Republican primary ballot, he nevertheless was
running against the prospect of write-in campaigns for Rockefeller and
Reagan. Rockefeller's feat of beating Goldwater in the state in 1964 was well
remembered in the Nixon camp. And his agents were well aware of reports
of heavy Reagan money being sent into Oregon, along with an updated version of the television biography aired in Nebraska.

Still, brimming with confidence, Nixon talked openly about possible running mates. David Broder interviewed him on May 16 and wrote afterward

that Nixon, impressed by Agnew's views on urban problems, had his eye on him. Agnew, who earlier had said "I am not standby material," now observed that "if it happened, it would be something I'd have to think about at that time." The next day in the *Los Angeles Times*, veteran reporter Don Irwin cited Agnew as "a man who has gained ground in recent months because of his strong stand on the cities."

Kennedy launched his campaign in Oregon with a speech to the Portland City Club on May 17. He recognized almost at once that he would be facing a much more difficult task in this state than those he had dealt with successfully in Indiana and Nebraska. Before the businessman's group, he warned that as long as the war continued "we will have to pay for the mistakes of the past" with a "moderate" tax increase and cautious budget cuts.

The audience was underwhelmed by such proposals, but that was the reaction he knew he would encounter from such a group. When he told of a business magazine's poll that found only one Kennedy supporter among 500 businessmen surveyed, he joked that "I'm the only candidate who can take all his business supporters to lunch." The crowd chuckled, but that was all.

A more ominous omen for his chances in Oregon came later the same day at Omark Industries, a chainsaw manufacturing plant where the workers were restrained and cool toward him. Next, at a nursing home, the elderly residents looked at the young man with the long hair and seemed unmoved. The crisis on Main Street America that Kennedy said had to be dealt with did not appear to be present in either the lives or the minds of Oregon listeners content with their own lot in this seeming paradise.

Back in his suite at the Benson Hotel in Portland that night, Kennedy quickly assessed that a major miscalculation had been made regarding Oregon. It had been assumed, after his victories over McCarthy in Indiana and Nebraska, where he had overcome natural conservatism, that he would be able to dismiss the McCarthy challenge once and for all in liberal and notably antiwar Oregon. And so it had been decided that the state could be left in the hands of second-stringers, with the leading first-team players going elsewhere—Larry O'Brien to New York, where delegates would be selected in June, and brother-in-law Steve Smith to critical California.

But McCarthy's earlier entry into the race against Johnson had earned him the respect and support of much of Oregon's large antiwar community, encouraged in its opposition to the American role in Vietnam by the state's two senators, Democrat Wayne Morse and Republican Mark Hatfield. Many antiwar Oregonians at the same time were resentful of Kennedy's late entry, only after McCarthy had cut LBJ down to size in New Hampshire. These war critics were not college students and dropouts either. Many were concerned

adults with considerable political experience who gave the McCarthy operation in the state a degree of professionalism it may have lacked elsewhere.
Beyond that, Oregon's organized labor had unpleasant memories of
Kennedy's role as a Senate rackets investigator focusing on vice and labor corruption in Portland among local Teamsters and others.

Kennedy picked up a phone and summoned O'Brien and Smith to
Portland, along with other old Kennedy hands. Oregon, Smith told me later,
"was something of a stepchild, and when you recognized the problem it was
almost too late." The first team grasped at once what Kennedy himself had
already seen—that the have-not coalition of blacks and lower-income white
ethnic workers that was his base was not present in Oregon in sufficient numbers.

When one late-arriving Kennedy strategist inquired, "Have we got the
ghettos organized?" Congresswoman Edith Green, the campaign's local political star, replied with obvious indignation: "There are no ghettos in
Oregon." The black population amounted to only 1 percent and what ethnics
there were had long since been largely assimilated into this comfortable and
affluent corner of the contented Northwest. "This state is like one giant suburb," Kennedy lamented at one point.

There was nothing to be done but to race Kennedy around the state in the
hope that once again his personal force and presence could carry the day. At
the same time, however, California and its 174 delegate votes at the national
convention could not be given short shrift. As for McCarthy, he later summed
up Kennedy's dilemma in Oregon by noting "there were no bloc votes" in the
state.

To drum up enthusiasm, Kennedy undertook another whistlestop train
trip, this time through the Willamette Valley from Portland to Eugene. The
crowds were good and the young people as usual responded to the candidate
with enthusiasm. He replied with the playfulness that had now become a pattern on the stump. Emphasizing the importance of Oregon to him, he would
hoke it up: "Can you imagine the conversation with my children at home?
They'll say, 'Daddy, you did well in Indiana and Nebraska, but how did it go
in Oregon?' If I have to tell them I lost, can't you see the tears coming to their
eyes and running down their little cheeks? You wouldn't want to do that,
would you?" Kennedy supporters in the crowds thought he was hilarious;
others thought he was trivializing an important civic duty in their hands. At
the final stop, when Kennedy referred to the city as "the Eugene I like best
in the country," the laughter was mixed with some boos.

Later in the day, Kennedy moved on to San Francisco to sandwich in some
California campaign time before his final push in Oregon. The detour under-

scored the difference in Kennedy's support in an urban setting as opposed to a suburban and rural one. The heavily Mexican-American crowds along Mission Street pressed in on the candidate with shouts of adoration and the customary grabbing for his hand that always marked his inner-city motorcades.

Late that night, as the Kennedy charter flew down to Los Angeles, Kennedy's mind obviously was still on bland Oregon. He roamed up and down the plane's aisle talking about the contrast between his reception in California and in comfortable Oregon. "Let's face it," he told Jim Dickenson, then of the weekly *National Observer*. "I appeal best to people who have problems."

That point was well illustrated as Kennedy continued campaigning in California, not neglecting huge suburban areas like the San Gabriel Valley but focusing on inner-city streets. On one three-hour motorcade through predominantly Mexican-American East Los Angeles, on four separate occasions he was physically hauled out of Bill Barry's grasp and almost out of the open convertible in which he stood.

At one point, as he touched a sea of outreached hands, a young boy climbed into the back seat and methodically removed one of Kennedy's shoes, and then the other, and was off in the crowd. The candidate borrowed Fred Dutton's shoes right off his feet. In a speech at a huge Los Angeles fund-raiser a few nights later, Kennedy started out by thanking his father for steering him into public life, his wife for her endless encouragement and "Fred Dutton, for his black shoes." No explanation of the remark was offered. It was another of the inside jokes that Kennedy loved, and felt no obligation to let others in on.

On the night he lost his shoes, Kennedy spoke at Temple Isaiah in Los Angeles. The *Los Angeles Times* reported the next day that he had "proposed a U.S.-Soviet agreement to stop the huge arms shipments to warring Jews and Arabs in the Middle East. . . . He emphasized, however, that he feels that until such an agreement was reached, the United States must fully assist Israel—with arms if necessary—so long as Russia continues sending arms to the United Arab Republic and other countries hostile to Israel." There was nothing new in the declaration of Kennedy's strong support of Israel, and standard fare for any Democratic candidate before a Jewish audience. But some others in the Arab community who read about the statement were not pleased.

On May 21, one week before the Oregon primary, Kennedy spoke to the local press club in San Francisco. When a reporter asked him what would happen if he lost there, Kennedy blurted out: "If I get beaten in a primary,

I'm not a viable candidate. I might be a nice man . . . I'd return to being un-ruthless if I lose in Oregon." Perhaps he was just being flip, but it was not the kind of acknowledgment that a prudent politician makes.

* * *

McCarthy meanwhile declined to describe Oregon as "crucial" while ex-uding a new sense of confidence. "I wish you people would stop talking about crucial primaries," he told inquiring reporters. "Whether you win or lose a primary or two isn't that important. Humphrey hasn't won any primary but people are calling him the front-runner." The distinction, however, was that Humphrey had the regular party establishment behind him controlling large delegations not selected by primaries; McCarthy, and Kennedy, were bucking the establishment and had to show their political strength in the primaries.

With Johnson no longer in the field, McCarthy made the office he occu-pied his target. In his lecturer's monotone, he would talk to audiences about ways the presidency had been used to erode the powers of Congress and even the Supreme Court, and how it had become excessively personalized by ruth-less men like Johnson. The clear implication was that in the hands of Robert Kennedy, that trend would surely continue and grow. Dwelling on the pres-idency itself was an intellectual's approach to campaigning; it sat well with well-educated, economically comfortable Oregonians as well as with loyal supporters elsewhere of McCarthy's view that American involvement in Vietnam was itself an abuse of presidential power.

On May 18, before launching his final drive in Oregon, McCarthy repeated at the ADA annual convention in Washington his intention to remain in the Democratic race through the party convention. The organization in turn reaf-firmed its endorsement of his candidacy, and the next night at a rally at Madison Square Garden in New York, antiwar backers pumped a reported $300,000 into his campaign.

Thus bolstered financially, and aware of the special peace-oriented con-stituency existing in Oregon enlisted for months in his ranks, McCarthy trav-eled the state with an air of confidence that belied his Indiana and Nebraska defeats. In a speech in Corvallis on May 21, the same day Kennedy was say-ing he would not be "viable" if he lost in Oregon, McCarthy made an im-politic if equally valid observation of his own. The public opinion polls, he said, "seem to prove that he [Kennedy] is running ahead of me among the less intelligent and less well-educated voters of the country. On that basis, I don't think we're going to have to apologize or explain away the results in the state of Oregon." He added: "I don't mean to fault them for voting for him, but I think that you ought to bear that in mind as you go to the polls here on Tuesday."

McCarthy's disdain for Kennedy was growing daily. Later that same day, asked by a television reporter on his plane whether he might lean to Kennedy or Humphrey if he himself were eliminated in the primaries, McCarthy said it was "not impossible" he could support the vice president if he were to change his position on Vietnam.

When word got around the McCarthy campaign, young staffers for whom Humphrey had replaced Johnson as the devil incarnate were deeply shaken. Phone calls poured in, campaign workers demanding to know whether McCarthy had indeed said he might support Humphrey and warning they would quit if he didn't retract it. By this time, more McCarthy foot soldiers had experienced or heard about his often disdainful attitude, and he seemed much less the White Knight he had been to them in the heady days of New Hampshire and Wisconsin.

McCarthy at first said he had been misquoted, but then "clarified" his remarks, insisting he was in a position of "absolute neutrality" between Kennedy and Humphrey. If Kennedy conducted himself properly, he said, he possibly could support him as well as Humphrey. This last was an obvious reference to the attacks on his Senate voting record that so grated on McCarthy, but it didn't make the young McCarthyites feel any better.

That "clarification" did not diminish McCarthy's obvious bitterness toward Kennedy. Painting him as the unruly brat of his famous family, McCarthy liked to tell audiences that "Bobby threatened to hold his breath unless the people of Oregon voted for him." Aides demanded that he criticize Humphrey as well, but when he did so it was restrained and devoid of the edge he applied to his remarks about Kennedy.

"At the very time when American foreign policy grew more disastrous, Vice President Humphrey became its most ardent apologist," McCarthy said. "Not merely did he defend the war; he defended every assumption which produced the war—America's moral mission in the world, the great threat from China, the theory of monolithic Communist conspiracy, the susceptibility of political problems to military solutions, and the duty to impose American idealism upon foreign cultures. All these myths—so damaging in their consequences—have had the enthusiastic support of Vice President Humphrey. And those who sought in the best American tradition to question those policies were subject all too often to his ridicule and scorn." McCarthy's main complaint against Humphrey seemed to be his unreasoning loyalty to Johnson.

* * *

Kennedy, for his part, tried his best to ignore McCarthy and focus on Humphrey. Through his friends in organized labor, Humphrey was pushing for a strong vote for Johnson, whose name remained on the Oregon ballot, as a means of undercutting Kennedy. Pro-Humphrey labor saw Kennedy, after his victories over McCarthy in Indiana and Nebraska, as the only barrier to Humphrey's nomination. An AFL-CIO phone bank had volunteers in Portland manning twenty phones for thirteen hours a day, reading from a card urging union members "to vote for President Johnson and Vice President Humphrey in the primary next Tuesday to show our support for them in the peace talks in Paris."

Kennedy told a crowd at Eastern Oregon College: "If I do badly in Oregon, the Vice President is going to be the major gainer. That's why his people, in his behalf, are having a telephone campaign in Oregon at the present time— to bring out the votes to see if he can defeat me here and in California. He is the major opponent." He called on Humphrey to come into the state and an- swer voters' questions—this at the time he was steadfastly turning aside McCarthy's taunting invitations to debate him. Kennedy wanted to do noth- ing that would remind voters that he had come into the race on McCarthy's back and was still trying to elbow him aside.

Edith Green summed up Kennedy's dilemma regarding Humphrey. "We're running against a ghost," she said. "The money is coming in, but the body isn't." There was, however, a very lively body in the state now, in the presence of Gene McCarthy. And Kennedy was learning he was no ghost, de- spite his earlier "deaths" in Indiana and Nebraska.

At midweek, Kennedy took a sightseeing boat on the Willamette River to be photographed "studying" harbor problems. It was a dank and grim morn- ing and Kennedy's mood matched it. As we were getting off the boat and walking up the pier, I asked him how Oregon was going. "I've got a problem here," he admitted without hesitation. When I pressed him to elaborate, he told me, quietly and without anger: "You're a political writer. You can look around and see what it is. I don't want to play games. I have my own analy- sis, but I don't think it would be useful for me to go into it." It was obvious that he understood that Oregon was lacking in his black and blue-collar coalition, "the people who have problems" who best responded to him.

On Friday, May 24, at the start of the final weekend before the primary, Kennedy toured Oregon's coastline. Walking barefoot with his wife and their dog Freckles along the beach at Astoria, he decided to take a quick dip in the Pacific. After obtaining agreement from the photographers with him not to snap pictures, he and Ethel walked another hundred yards or so down the beach, where he stripped to his shorts and plunged into the icy waters. This sort of thing was not done in Oregon, in May especially, and when the word got out, there was much local criticism of the caper.

More troublesome, however, was an intensified challenge from McCarthy to debate before primary day. McCarthy sent Kennedy a telegram telling him he had bought thirty minutes of television time in Portland for the purpose, chiding him that "campaign rallies and paid advertisements do not meet our obligation of conscience to give the people a fair opportunity to compare our positions."

The Kennedy staff was split on the wisdom of debating McCarthy. Younger members like speechwriters Walinsky and Greenfield argued that their boss was more disciplined than the often casual McCarthy. He could dispose of him in debate, they contended, in much the way that his brother John had cut Nixon down to size in 1960. But Kennedy was opposed to giving McCarthy the television exposure and to making himself look desperate in the process.

According to Larry O'Brien, another factor worked against the debate—a column by Drew Pearson. It said that Kennedy as attorney general in 1963 had ordered wiretaps on Martin Luther King that produced reports on a "Communist who was helping write King's speeches" and on "King's sex life." The column, appearing in several Oregon newspapers, quoted "a confidential informer as claiming that Dr. King 'has been having an illicit love affair with the wife of a prominent Negro dentist in Los Angeles since 1962.'" Salinger denied that Kennedy had ever authorized "eavesdropping of any kind" and would not comment "on individual cases," but there was concern McCarthy would raise the issue in a television debate. So Kennedy decided against one then.

Walinsky and Greenfield squawked and insisted on making one more pitch to the candidate. Their insistence only irritated him further, and when the two young speechwriters continued to discuss the matter loudly in the hotel corridor after they had been dismissed from his presence, he came storming out of his suite in his shorts.

"I thought we decided that," he barked. "Why are you standing around here making noise? If you want to do something, go out and ring doorbells. . . . Besides, I don't see why my speechwriters aren't writing speeches instead of playing the guitar all the time." And he turned and marched back into his room. His outburst was a delayed response to simmering irritation over their behavior on the campaign plane, playing and singing folk songs while he and other older aides not caught up in the music of their generation tried to work.

That night, McCarthy fired both barrels at Kennedy at a huge and boisterous rally at the Memorial Coliseum in Portland, painting him as nothing more than a man of the old politics practicing the old tactic of glueing minorities together. "He's not brought any new politics to the scene in 1968," McCarthy said. "We had something going and still have in new politics this year. But it doesn't consist of adding up somehow a consensus or a composite of minorities who have special problems and saying this is the new politics, because this is as old as the history of politics in this century."

McCarthy charged that Kennedy did little more than say what the problems were and bring back "all the Knights of the [Camelot] Roundtable," while saying "nothing about some of the old politicians who never left," like Rusk, McNamara, Selective Service chief Hershey and FBI director Hoover. He mentioned Freckles and Kennedy's Pacific swim. "I don't think this clarifies the issues very much. . . . This is all old politics. . . . But while he does take the cold plunge in the Pacific and brings the dog and does these other things, up to now he has refused to meet me in debate or in joint appearance." If Kennedy wouldn't debate him "when we're reasonably friendly [!!!] and of the same party," he wondered, would he debate Nixon in the fall if nominated?

The next day, Sunday, May 26, McCarthy almost got his "joint appearance" in a chance encounter at the Portland zoo, when the two candidates came within fifty yards or so of each other. Advised by Barry of McCarthy's approach, Kennedy ordered: "Let's get out of here." He climbed into his open convertible and raced away—amid cries of "Coward! Chicken!" from McCarthyites hoisting campaign signs and trying to block his way. McCarthy, seizing the opportunity, coolly climbed aboard the Kennedy press bus that had been left in the lurch, and in good humor invited the reporters aboard to join his entourage.

More significant in time was a speech that morning by Kennedy, a yarmulke on his head, at the Neveh Shalom Synagogue in which he again stated his position that "in Israel, unlike so many other places in the world, our commitment is clear and compelling. We are committed to Israel's survival. We are committed to defying any attempt to destroy Israel, whatever the source. And we cannot and must not let that commitment waver."

Later in the day, his words were carried elsewhere on television, including Pasadena, California, where in the home of a Jordanian family named Sirhan, a young man watched. According to his brother in a later report to an Egyptian correspondent, the young man became greatly upset at the sight and words of Kennedy in the temple. "He left the room putting his hands on his ears and almost weeping," the brother said of the scene.

* * *

On the final campaign day of the primary, Monday, May 27, Kennedy flew across southern Oregon in the hope of igniting the same spark of rural support that had rallied to him in Nebraska. As McCarthy in Portland spoke to a large and enthusiastic downtown audience and then walked through pressing crowds of supporters to his hotel, Kennedy was encountering yet other distressing events. His entourage was flying in two small planes and they narrowly averted crashing into each other as they approached the runway from different directions at the small airport in Roseburg. Nobody was hurt, but already taut nerves were a casualty.

Roseburg, in the heart of Oregon hunting country, confronted Kennedy with protests against gun control. One man in a lumberjacket complained that pending federal legislation supported by Kennedy was nothing more than a "backdoor bill for the registration of guns." Kennedy tried to reason with him. "All this legislation does," he explained, "is keep guns from criminals, and the demented and those too young. With all the violence and murder and killings we've had in the United States, I think you will agree that we must keep firearms from people who have no business with guns or rifles." He was greeted with boos for his trouble.

Back in Portland that night, Kennedy tried to keep up a good front at a final reception. But O'Brien and other strategists had told him that even in a friendly poll the outlook was close. O'Brien, known in the national press corps as a master of poor-mouthing, quipped to some of us: "It's a lot easier to poor-mouth when you don't have to."

Time pressures being what they were, Kennedy flew back to Los Angeles that night and spent the day of the Oregon primary campaigning to the north between Ventura and Santa Barbara. Late in the afternoon, a small sampling of Oregon precinct exit polls by CBS News brought Kennedy the first real indication that he was losing. At about 8:30 P.M., as his plane was about to take off for the return flight to Portland, Dick Dougherty of the *Los Angeles Times*, an old friend, was bringing the network projections aboard when Kennedy started down the plane's stair. "Bad news, Bob," Dougherty told him, simply. "Oh," Kennedy replied, "that's too bad." He turned and went back aboard the plane.

After twenty-six straight election victories, a Kennedy had lost. When a reporter tried to put the best face on the situation, Kennedy, sitting with shirtsleeves rolled up and tie pulled down from his open collar, would have none of it. "I've lost. I'm not one of those who think that coming in second or third is winning," he said, sipping a beer and eating a steak in his seat.

The one who gained the most in Oregon, he suggested, was not McCarthy, but Humphrey, who the night before had picked up two thirds of the 130-member Pennsylvania delegation in action by the state party committee, although McCarthy had beaten him by eight to one in Pennsylvania's April primary. Of McCarthy he said quietly, "I think what he wanted most was to knock me off. I guess he may hate me that much."

Kennedy had no illusions about the impact of his defeat. The regular party leaders, he said, "will use Oregon as an excuse for not supporting me"—not a surprising conclusion for a candidate who himself had said he would not be "viable" if he lost in Oregon. Finishing his dinner, he got up and walked down the aisle of the plane, thanking his staff, trying to buck up a disheartened Ethel. Meanwhile, Dutton wrote a congratulatory telegram to McCarthy—something McCarthy had never done after the Kennedy primary victories.

When the final numbers were in, Kennedy's defeat was clear-cut: 44.7 percent for McCarthy, 38.8 for Kennedy, 12.4 for Johnson—more than McCarthy's margin of victory—4 percent for Humphrey on write-ins, others 0.1 percent. Back in Portland, Bob and Ethel Kennedy walked through the lobby of the Benson Hotel wearing brave smiles, as onlookers quietly spoke encouragement or just gawked to see Kennedys in political defeat for the first time. In the hotel ballroom, he thanked his tearful followers and read the telegram to McCarthy that said "we can both take some satisfaction in the overwhelming expression of the Oregon voters for change."

In a lighter vein, Kennedy told the crowd he was going to shake up his organization—"I have decided to send Freckles home." A man shouted: "Don't do it!" Kennedy, smiling, said: "Not really." He concluded with gracious remarks of thanks to the voters of Oregon for making "a fair judgment" and to the state's news media for their fair coverage. He said he hoped that as a result of the discussion of issues in the primary the country "will move closer to peace at home and around the globe." Then he left the ballroom through the kitchen, skipping the press conference that had followed his earlier victories.

McCarthy, meanwhile, appeared before a jumping, cheering crowd of young and old campaign workers and supporters at an old Elks Club. A chant rolled through the crowd: "Gene in sixty-eight! The rest will have to wait!" The old McCarthy soft grin that had not been seen on election night since New Hampshire and Wisconsin was back again.

"In Nebraska, we discovered our weaknesses," he said. "In Nebraska, we discovered the weaknesses of the opposition and we were ready for the western movement." Then the old line heard in a less joyous context in Nebraska: "Every wagon train gets as far as the Missouri River, but the real test starts up the Oregon Trail. We know who had the best horses and the best wagons and the best men and women, and I think we proved that in Oregon." As more cheers erupted and hundreds of extended arms waved in the V peace sign, he added: "The next test is the California trail, and we're on to California. California, here we come!"

The victory would not have been complete for McCarthy, however, without some pointed tweaking of the press. "I haven't had any reporter ask me who I'm going to yield to in Chicago," he said. "I don't think we'll be asked that question again in 1968. I think we've answered it in Oregon. . . . It was just a question of finding our constituency. . . . Our campaign here didn't bridge the generation gap. It was solid all the way, and it will be solid all the way to Chicago."

In a conclusion that would prove to be less than clairvoyant, McCarthy exulted: "The President said we will have riots in the streets this summer. Instead of riots, we'll have singing and dancing in the streets. . . . We'll take the fence down around the White House and have a picnic on the lawn." A delirious crowd burst into singing "The Battle Hymn of the Republic" as the arms and fingers extended in Vs waved in time with the triumphant song.

* * *

In Kennedy's private suite at the Benson, there had been preparations for a victory party as had been held after the earlier, happier, primary results. Now, senior aides, friends and a few reporters were permitted in for a drink at the bar and quiet postmortems in the living room. Two bedrooms were off to the right and Kennedy sauntered in and out in shirtsleeves, wearing his *PT-109* tie clip long associated with Kennedy political clout, carrying a watered-down drink. He seemed more resigned than disappointed and not bitter—surprising for one so accustomed to winning and raised by his father never to settle for less. When a reporter joked that there was a movement afoot to eliminate the word "viable" from the language, Kennedy shrugged and said, "No, it's true." In small talk, he took full blame on himself.

At one point, he moved into one of the bedrooms for a more serious discussion with the older hands like Dutton, Sorensen, Salinger and Goodwin, and some of the younger aides who had not been part of the great Kennedy victories of the past. They did not dwell on Oregon but turned to California and what had to be done there to recover. One tactical issue was clear: Kennedy could no longer decline to debate McCarthy. The decision would be announced the next morning, on arrival in Los Angeles.

After the meeting, Kennedy strolled out into the living room again, sat on the arm of a chair and responded to questions from a small group of us who had overnight stories to write. Back on May 17, he said, he knew he was in trouble when the workers at the Omark plant didn't respond to him. Asked if he thought the Oregon defeat had hurt him, he laughed at the stupidity of the question. "It certainly wasn't one of the more helpful developments of the day," he said, grinning. It went on like that, with two other reporters and I continuing to question him. Kennedy responded for a while and then finally looked up and said, wearily, "We'll be having a press conference tomorrow. Can we hold off until then?"

We all agreed and the other two walked off. I was feeling unprofessionally sympathetic to what the candidate was going through, and curious about his willingness to linger over the defeat. I had known Kennedy since his days as counsel to the Senate Labor Rackets Committee and as campaign manager for his brother John. In those days he never suffered fools, gladly or otherwise, on occasion myself included. I asked him: "Why do you put up with all these questions at a difficult time like this?" He reached over and put his arm around my shoulder. "Because I like you," he said, and walked away.

At such moments, Ruthless Robert seemed an uncommonly inappropriate label for him. This softness beneath the hard shell he often showed, especially toward political adversaries, made those around him—even reporters not committed to him—feel a vulnerability about him that was incongruous with his favored station in life. It was so strong that even a hardened political skeptic like Dick Harwood of the *Washington Post* confessed to me on the Kennedy press bus in Oregon that he was going to ask his editors to take him off the Kennedy campaign because he was getting to like the candidate too much.

It was all part of the evolution of a private man—Robert Kennedy as his brother's tough and, yes, ruthless no-man—into a public man—a candidate himself and an elected public official—who was obliged to encounter the pains and hardships of everyday Americans. The emotional commitment he had made to his elder brother in time had been transferred to that special have-not constituency whose absence had been a major factor in his defeat on this night. And in that transferral, his harder edges seemed to round off in his dealings with many others who in one way or another came within his wider circle as the public man.

Of the Oregon experience, perhaps it was McCarthy who best summed up what had happened to Kennedy, the candidate of the "people who have problems," in the state that gloried in its seclusion from the troubles and inadequacies of the outside world. In his post-election book, McCarthy wrote of a man he had encountered in a town on the southern border of Oregon. He told the man he was going to California the next day, he wrote, "and the Oregonian said to me, 'Don't tell them we are here.'"

* * *

For Nixon, meanwhile, Oregon was another waltz. Both Rockefeller and Reagan chose to stay out of the state whose primary already appeared to be locked up for the front-runner. Their strategies in any event still depended not on primary results but on hopes that sufficient numbers of delegates at the convention would still believe that Nixon was a likely loser against the Democratic nominee and one or the other of them would eventually be seen as a more promising alternative.

Some eyebrows were raised when the governors of the two most populous states met privately for breakfast in New Orleans on May 20, but there was no clear evidence of any anti-Nixon collusion between them. Afterward, Rockefeller told reporters he saw no "ideological gulf" between Reagan and himself. But Reagan cooled any speculation of a deal by saying he would not agree to be Rockefeller's running mate—or anyone else's.

Each man did, however, send a surrogate into Oregon to speak in his behalf—former pro football quarterback Y.A. Tittle for Reagan and Mayor Lindsay of New York for Rockefeller. The latter caper prompted some unidentified Nixon supporters to write a newspaper ad that played on the 1964 Rockefeller slogan against the absent Goldwater: "He Cared Enough to Come." The ad said of Rockefeller in 1968: "He Cared Enough to Send Mayor Lindsay—So Write In Lindsay."

Nixon nevertheless was taking no chances. He spent most of the week after his primary victory in Nebraska in rural Oregon, making the most of absentee Rockefeller's 1964 slogan. He closed out the final week of the primary in Portland and Klamath Falls in what was his fifth visit to the state in six months. As the Reagan documentary continued to be aired in the state, Nixon concluded the primary campaign with a statewide telethon that triggered an estimated 31,000 phone calls. Just to be safe, Bob Ellsworth poormouthed, laughably, that Nixon would do well to get the 34 percent that Rockefeller had won in 1964.

In advance of the telethon, the Nixon campaign showed its own thirty-minute documentary whose title—*Nixon Now*—unsubtly conveyed the message that Nixon the onetime loser, the much-maligned Old Nixon, had since his 1962 defeat in California been reborn in the primaries as Nixon the present winner. The film was the summation of the primaries, complete with selected excerpts of his campaign speeches and appearances including the carefully staged "town meetings" that were open to invited Nixon supporters and closed to the press.

The telethon featured daughters Tricia and Julie taking phone calls with questions that were handed over to Nixon fan and former Oklahoma football coach Bud Wilkinson, who sorted out the softballs, tossed them Nixon's way and then marveled at the brilliant answers. At the time, evangelist Billy Graham, another Nixon friend, was preaching before turnaway crowds at a

Portland ball park and Nixon did not fail to mention him. He told this state of hunters that he relied on Senator Roman Hruska of Nebraska for advice on gun control, and favored a state-by-state approach. But the best way to control the sale of guns, he said, was to stop crime.

On primary eve, Nixon held a huge rally at a large arena in Portland. As a man who always insisted on labeling and categorizing things in historic terms—the "first" this and the "last" that—he began by saying to the crowd, his arms sweeping out grandly: "At this final event of the Oregon primary—" Suddenly he paused, and you could almost see his memory clicking in, telling him with its inner voice that he still had a breakfast reception on his schedule the following morning. Then he continued: *"as far as nighttime rallies are concerned . . . "* Those of us who had traveled long hours, days and nights with him howled, as others around us wondered what was so funny.

I got another good chuckle out of my exposure to Nixon the next day when I was ushered into his suite at the Benson for a private interview. It was Nixon's custom to grant such interviews on primary day to reporters traveling with him who represented the city in which he happened to be. One of the newspapers I was working for at the time was the Portland *Oregonian*, so it was my turn. Knowing Nixon's sense of precision and orderliness, I had prepared for the interview by jotting down the most important questions I wanted to ask him in logical order, in the hope that I would not have to waste the limited time talking instead of listening.

When I was led into the living room of the Nixon suite by aide Dwight Chapin, the candidate walked over, smiling, and shook hands with me. He invited me to sit on a long sofa and he sat in a large armchair and put his feet up on a coffee table between us. For all his cordiality, I could still sense the same wariness he had shown toward me when I had spent that week with him in the fall of 1966, when he had campaigned so successfully for Republican congressional candidates around the country.

After a few pleasantries, I asked the first question I had written down on my pad. He answered it fully, then continued on, expanding logically on that answer and in the process answering the second question I had jotted down, although I had not yet asked it. Without pausing, he went on in his narrative, answering the third and fourth questions I had prepared, again without my having asked them. He went along like that, providing answers to the other questions I had readied in logical order, until I could not suppress a grin. When I didn't, he seemed suddenly unsettled, so I remarked, joking: "Mr. Nixon, I believe you've peeked at my notes. I've written down my questions and you've answered most of them already." He froze, then said without a trace of humor: "Oh, no. I wouldn't do that." Realizing he thought I was serious, I told him I had only been kidding. He seemed embarrassed for a moment, then laughed in a self-conscious way, and the interview continued, a bit more stiffly now.

The conversation itself produced nothing new, but it did elicit from the candidate the calculated nature of the campaign that had brought him to the brink of the nomination. As was his manner, at one moment he denied any such calculation and at the next would provide an example of it. For openers, Nixon disavowed any master campaign plan. He had always said he was a fatalist and didn't have time to waste agonizing over the past. But this time he told me that "haunting this campaign is the specter of 1960." Then, he said, he was supported by the Eisenhower team and this time he didn't want to be saddled with "first-rate second-raters." He provided no names, but then he went on to talk about the "really first-raters" he had this time around, naming Buchanan and other members of his "entirely new, fresh team."

On the one hand, he denied that his campaign could have been carefully mapped out, what with the surprise decisions of Romney, Rockefeller and Johnson. After first focusing on the two Republicans, he said, he switched to LBJ and the Vietnam War, but when Johnson withdrew, "Vietnam went on the back burner" (where, in fact, it always had been as far as Nixon addressing it seriously was concerned). Then, however, he talked at some length about the carefully planned use of time, energy and, especially, television in this campaign as compared with 1960. Then, he said, "there was a frenetic quality about my campaign. Promising to go into all fifty states. We aren't going to make that mistake again."

He had learned, he said, "that the candidate should take time to think. Every three weeks I go to Florida for a few days." And he added: "That's how I keep the tan." Nixon did indeed have a glorious, deeply bronzed face—made to order for color television. "I take some of the boys with me," he said, "and we mix it; on the beach for a while, and then hours of going over ideas." (One of "the boys" told me later that the formula was much more sun than brainstorming. "We kept going back to Florida mainly so he could keep that tan," he said.)

One of the things he spent most time on there, Nixon insisted, was editing the speeches written for him. "The slowdown gives me a chance to do creative work," he said, painting himself as he had in other interviews I had had with him as an "intellectual," as he wanted the world to view him. "I'm basically more of an intellectual than I ought to be," he suggested at another point in the interview. After the Republican convention and before the start-up of the fall campaign, he said, "I want those ten days just to read and think." And what, I asked, would he be reading? "No politics," he said emphatically. "No mysteries either. Some good philosophy that makes the mind work." Sometimes it was hard to keep a straight face when you interviewed Dick Nixon the Intellectual.

More important, he talked of how he had come to realize that the set speeches were not as important anymore as how he handled himself on television. And to this end, although he didn't say so in this interview, his campaign strategists labored long and hard to present him on television only in the most carefully crafted and controlled circumstances. The Nixon that the viewing public saw was serious but not without folksy humor; surefooted on the issues—at least those he cared to talk about, like getting tougher on "the criminal forces"; above all, well-rested and confident, and never whiny. Burying the Old Nixon took more than merely winning primaries.

That, however, he did continue to do. In Oregon, he received more than 73 percent of the Republican primary vote to only 22 for Reagan in his neighboring state and 4 for Rockefeller. The Nixonites held a loud but orderly celebration in the lobby ballroom of the Benson even as Kennedy was pushing his way through the lobby to concede to McCarthy before his own disappointed followers. Nixon was jubilant, thrusting his arms over his head, the fingers of both hands waving the victory salute. Later, he joined a few old friends for a quiet victory dinner in the Benson's London Grill, taking congratulations from the stream of well-wishers coming to his table.

*   *   *

With California not to be contested on the Republican side because Reagan was holding the state delegation as its favorite son, Nixon knew that his only remaining obstacle to the nomination was countering Rockefeller's efforts to drive the Nixon ratings down in the polls, and his own up, to make the argument after all this that Nixon still could not be elected president.

A plan for Rockefeller had been drawn up by now by a New York advertising agency, Jack Tinker and Partners, and speechwriter and political adviser Emmett J. Hughes. The idea was to flood the major media markets with Rockefeller ads in thirteen "Northern Tier" states plus Texas that covered 60 percent of the nation's population. At an estimated cost of $3 million, 462 television spots a week were to be run on 100 stations in 30 cities, plus multiple advertisements in 54 newspapers in 40 cities.

At the same time, plans were laid in May to poll intensively in the largest cities in seven important states—Pennsylvania, Maryland, Ohio, Michigan, Illinois, Minnesota and Kansas—where the Rockefeller strategists believed the delegate situation remained fluid, and where their advertising was focused. Meanwhile, political pros like John Deardourff, who had worked in New Hampshire for Romney, urged party leaders to hold off on committing to Nixon until the Rockefeller-financed polls were completed indicating what a Nixon candidacy would mean to the political fortunes of other Republicans in those states.

At the same time, Rockefeller made the most of a few newspaper-financed polls in key states that helped make his point. He cited one in California for the *Los Angeles Times* that showed him beating Humphrey, Kennedy and McCarthy by margins ranging from 12 to 20 percent. He mentioned another in Ohio for the *Cleveland Press* that had him leading Nixon, 48.6 percent to 33.4, and a third in Minnesota for the *Minneapolis Tribune* that had it Rockefeller 45 percent, Nixon 38.

To counter the Rockefeller polling blitz, Nixon left Portland on May 29, the morning after the Oregon primary, on a swing through the Southwest and South—the conservative Sunbelt—to shore up his support there. He started in Phoenix with a pilgrimage to Mr. Conservative, Barry Goldwater, seeking election again to the Senate, and a conference with Republican Governor Jack Williams. Commenting on what he called a current "obsession" with public opinion polling, Nixon said "the idea that we are going to determine America's future by a few pollsters is ridiculous."

Having said that, however, he made clear he knew what Rockefeller's game was. He told Robert Semple of the *New York Times* that "the polls . . . will be the drill down in Miami. Rocky will come in with figures showing he can run better against the Democrats in such-and-such a state, and we of course will say that's not true. There will be polls flying all over the city."

From Phoenix, Nixon went on to Dallas, where he massaged favorite son Senator John Tower, who was ready to hold most of the fifty-six members of the Texas delegation for him. Then it was on to Atlanta for a meeting with the Republican state chairmen from thirteen border and Southern states on May 31. There was strong sentiment in a number of these states for Reagan, and Nixon merely asked the chairmen that they not commit to anyone else until he had a fair chance to demonstrate his strength at the convention. When several of the chairmen pressed Nixon for promises on federal patronage, about which they had been disappointed in the previous Republican administrations of Eisenhower (and Nixon), he reassured them.

Afterward, Georgia party chairman G. Paul Jones indicated a willingness to give party loyalist Nixon his shot. "The burden of proof is on the Reagan people," he said. "Up to now Nixon's main problem has been the question of whether he can win. He has always had tremendous support because he has worked so hard for us. But the Oregon results suggest that this man is also a winner." The North Carolina chairman (and later governor), James E.

Holshauser Jr., was already convinced. "You can feel the tide when it starts to run," he said, "and you can feel this is Mr. Nixon's year."

John Mitchell, Nixon's law firm partner and now campaign manager, claimed that 300 or more of the 348 border and Southern delegates represented by the thirteen state chairmen were now in Nixon's corner, already putting him over the 667 needed for the nomination. "The ball game for all intents and purposes is over," he declared. "And the people who work for Reagan are realists. Mr. Nixon has great rapport in the South over the years anyway. The people here all like Ronald Reagan, but they love Dick Nixon." Actually, Mitchell had it backward, but they had loved Goldwater in 1964 and went down to a crushing defeat with him in their ardor. This time, they really preferred winning with somebody they liked rather than risking losing again with one they loved.

For the Democrats, there could be no bypassing of California, where the final and very likely the most critical direct primary confrontation between McCarthy and Kennedy would come. Another defeat would end Kennedy's quest for the nomination and another setback for McCarthy would make his Oregon upset seem no more than an aberration.

The morning after the first Kennedy election defeat, May 29, as his campaign plane flew south to Los Angeles, the usually reticent Ethel Kennedy was open in her bafflement about what had happened in Oregon. She walked up and down the aisle, searching for some satisfying explanation, reaching for a comforting rationalization. "Such a small state," she lamented to several of us reporters, "and only 15,000 votes [the losing margin turned out to be nearly 20,000]. Do you really think it will make that much difference, if we win in California? That's the important state, more like the rest of the country."

In her estimate of the Golden State's political importance, the candidate's wife was certainly correct. Under state party rules, the winner of the June 7 primary would garner at least 172 of the state's 174 delegate votes and would send a powerful message to party brokers in other key states. Another demonstration of Kennedy's strength among the black and blue-collar coalition, with heavy ethnic support thrown in, would make a powerful argument for his ability to draw votes throughout key industrial states in the fall, where there was much greater concentration of "have-nots" than in idyllic Oregon.

In 1968, California had a population of 20 million, one tenth of the nation, with 7 million registered voters, 4.3 million in the Democratic Party. If Kennedy could combine California's huge delegate harvest with overwhelming strength from his own state of New York, which then was sending the largest single delegation of 190 votes to the convention, he would have 28 percent of the 1,312 votes needed for the nomination from these two states alone. That would still leave him a long way from a majority, but it might make a persuasive argument to those with reservations about limping into the November election behind the LBJ replacement, Humphrey.

Before the plane landed in Los Angeles, one critical piece of campaign business was being attended to at the mimeograph machines to the rear. They were grinding out copies of a Kennedy statement reversing himself on a debate with McCarthy and expressing his willingness to discuss the issues between them "separately or in joint appearances." On landing, Kennedy went to a small auxiliary terminal building and handed out the statement at a press conference. He called the California primary "a fair test of each candidate's appeal [and of] our differing philosophies, convictions and qualifications" and said "I will abide by the results of that test."

The press questions came thick and fast. Was he saying he would get out of the race if he lost in California? "I think the statement speaks for itself," he said. Well, why debate in California when he wouldn't in Oregon? "Because conditions have changed," he said candidly. "I'm not the same candidate I was before Oregon and I can't claim that I am." What about his statement about not being "viable" if he lost in Oregon? "I slept on it," he said. Would he take the second spot on the ticket if he lost in California? No, he said, he would go back to the Senate and stay busy "raising the next generation of Kennedys. It's a full-time job." How did it feel to lose for the first time? "I feel like the man Abraham Lincoln described who was run out of town on a steel rail and said, 'If it were not for the honor of the thing I'd rather have walked.'" He finally cut off the questions by saying "I've got to go because I have a lot of fans waiting—I hope."

Kennedy was not disappointed. His motorcade sped from the airport to downtown Los Angeles in time to catch the noon-hour crowds spilling out onto the narrow streets between business district skyscrapers. Advance men Jerry Bruno and Jim Tolan knew what they were doing. Ticker tape and torn newspapers floated down from office windows high above him as the motorcade inched through mobs of well-wishers, including a great many black and brown faces of his special constituency.

Anyone who had not heard the Oregon results could have taken the spectacle as a reception for a winner, not a loser, but it was as if a great collective bucking up was being administered to the candidate. Rafer Johnson, the Olympic decathlon champion from Los Angeles, was at Kennedy's side in the open convertible, helping him stand as he reached down to grasp or touch the sea of white, black and brown hands extended up to him. At one point, a woman in her fifties dressed in a garish gown of green sequins ran alongside the car shouting "Pooh on Oregon!" followed by a Bronx cheer.

Kennedy seemed ignited anew by the outpouring for him. He responded with the fervor that had marked the very beginning of his campaign, when his intense opposition to Johnson had fired him. "I need your help!" he shouted again and again, pounding his fist into his hand, as the motorcade halted every few blocks. The grasping hands stripped him of his cuff links and his tie clasp and yanked the tail of his shirt drenched in perspiration under the hot midday sun. But his spirits were undeniably lifted. "If I died in Oregon," he told campaign workers at the Beverly Hilton, "I hope Los Angeles is Resurrection City."

McCarthy meanwhile had flown to the San Francisco area, his plane decorated with colored balloons as his staff sipped champagne and reveled in the Oregon victory. Gerald Hill, leader of the liberal California Democratic Council and one of the campaign's California managers, in his exuberance declared Kennedy "eliminated" for the fight for the nomination. Kennedy's newfound willingness to debate was taken in the McCarthy campaign as the best of signs. His strategists were overjoyed because they knew their man needed the television exposure in this mammoth state and they were supremely confident that he would outshine Kennedy. McCarthy himself, however, seemed somewhat petulant now, complaining about the format in which three network reporters would pose the questions. "We'd rather have had a real debate confrontation," he told a radio interviewer. "He [Kennedy] just wants [us] to sit around the table and be nice to each other."

On Memorial Day, May 30, Kennedy took another whistlestop train through the Central Valley, as usual attacking Humphrey's "politics of joy" but this time going after McCarthy, whom he could no longer ignore. He told trainside crowds that he was "the first one of any of the present candidates who ever spoke out against the course we have been following in Vietnam." It was true, but he had not made the point in Oregon, where it might have helped him. The fact was, however, that it was McCarthy who first had put his political neck on the line for his Vietnam views, as the Democrats of Oregon well knew.

After the train trip and a reception in Oakland, Kennedy held an unscheduled, private meeting with about a hundred members of the Bay Area's Black Caucus, including some Black Panthers. The militants sounded off, calling Kennedy "a white bigshot" and worse. Kennedy just listened, as Rafer Johnson, who is black, seethed.

As for McCarthy, he simply continued his attitude of disdain toward Kennedy, in success as he had in failure. Commenting on Kennedy's indication that he would quit the race if he lost in California, McCarthy told his backers in Los Angeles: "Really, I don't have the right to withdraw. . . . Apparently there are some candidates who come into this campaign on their own and can go out of it. . . . No matter what happens here, we'll carry the issues to Chicago." He even ventured into heavily black Watts for a barbecue of questionable political benefit to him. As he spoke in defense of black power as a legitimate exercise of political clout, a local man remarked: "I'm eating his ribs, but I'm voting for Kennedy." From there, McCarthy, the candidate who would not give lip service to the conventional, went to a Jewish neighborhood and spoke of civil liberties and Israel.

On the final day of May, Kennedy escalated his direct attacks on McCarthy in a speech to the Commonwealth Club in San Francisco, complaining of distortion of his record in a campaign advertisement that said Kennedy "was part of the original commitment [in Vietnam] . . . participated in the decisions that led us to intervene in the affairs of the Dominican Republic . . . was directly involved in the disaster of the Bay of Pigs." McCarthy already was incensed over the earlier Kennedy attacks on his record. The stage thus was set for some bitter exchanges in the televised debate that was to be the opening event of importance as the presidential campaign moved into June.

On the evening of May 31, the Kennedy braintrusters were hard at work compiling ammunition on McCarthy's positions and records for use by their candidate in that debate on the following night. As for McCarthy, the old college first baseman, he was relaxing at Dodger Stadium, sporting a baseball cap and watching Dodger Don Drysdale survive a no-outs, bases-loaded situation in the ninth inning against the San Francisco Giants for his fifth straight shutout, tying a sixty-four-year-old record. Drysdale now had forty-five straight scoreless innings, only one and a half behind Carl Hubbell's National League record and eleven behind the major league record held by Walter Johnson.

Going to a ball game on the eve of a critical debate—that was Gene McCarthy; always unflappable, and by his own conduct conveying, whether intentionally or not, a sense of contempt toward his foes. At last he would have the confrontation with Kennedy he wanted, and his young supporters earnestly hoped he would make the most of it. But they could not be sure; that was Gene McCarthy too.

Perhaps McCarthy had his priorities straight, for the month of May had been a signal one in the world of sports. The winner of the Kentucky Derby, Dancer's Image, was disqualified two days later because traces of an anti-inflammatory painkilling drug were found in his urine specimen tested in

Churchill Downs's customary practice. (After an investigation, the Kentucky Racing Commission later declared Dancer's Image the official winner but ruled that his owner forfeit the purse.) In baseball, Catfish Hunter of the Oakland Athletics pitched a perfect game; in hockey, the Montreal Canadiens beat the St. Louis Blues for the Stanley Cup; at the Indianapolis 500, veteran Bobby Unser won with a record average speed of just under 152.9 miles per hour.

The political events of 1968 were proving to be so explosive, however, that what was happening on the racetracks, the playing fields and in the sports arenas was no match in dramatics for what was taking place on the nation's center stage. Demonstrations continued to break out everywhere.

In East Lost Angeles, for example, Mexican-American high school students staged massive walkouts in protest against discriminatory policies, launching a movement that spread beyond California. Eventually thirteen student leaders were arrested and indicted on conspiracy charges. There seemed no end to the turmoil. And the worst was yet to come.

CHAPTER 7

June: Murder of Hope

June 1 writer Helen Keller, 87, dies; 2 Stage Door Johnny wins Belmont Stakes; 4 actress Dorothy Gish, 70, dies; 7 actor Dan Duryea, 61, dies; 10 Supreme Court approves stop-and-frisk by police; 11 four convicts hold, release 25 hostages in Atlanta state penitentiary; 12 *Rosemary's Baby* starring Mia Farrow, Ruth Gordon released; 13 NASA puts 8 spy satellites in orbit; 17 Actors Equity strike shuts down 19 Broadway shows; pickets mar New York release of *The Green Berets* starring John Wayne; 24 Treasury reports $285 million drop in U.S. monetary reserves; 26 *The Thomas Crown Affair* starring Steve McQueen, Faye Dunaway released; trumpeter Ziggy Elman, 54, dies; 29 Detroit Tigers' Jim Northrup hits record third grand-slam in a week.

On the morning of Saturday, June 1, Robert Kennedy rose late in his suite at the Fairmont Hotel in San Francisco for an intensive two-hour debate preparation. Sorensen, Schlesinger, Mankiewicz and a few others took turns posing questions to him and suggesting how he could improve his answers. They broke off for lunch and went to Fisherman's Wharf for some handshaking recorded by accompanying television crews, then returned to the hotel for more cramming. At one point, in a discussion of ghetto problems, there was a casual mention of what the impact might be of moving blacks into ultra-conservative Orange County suburbs—a mention that Kennedy did not forget later that night. When the briefing was over, his aides left the suite and he took a ninety-minute nap to refresh himself for the debate.

McCarthy meanwhile was campaigning in his unruffled way up the coast from Los Angeles, arriving in San Francisco in the afternoon and also checking into the Fairmont. He too was presented with extensive briefing material and he reviewed it with Tom Finney, who hoped to keep his candidate focused on the debate as it drew near. Finney then left to allow time for McCarthy to rest or nap. Instead, poet Robert Lowell and some of McCarthy's other literary cronies including Shana Alexander and Mary McGrory—known disparagingly among the professional politicians in the campaign variously as "the McCarthy court" and "the astrologists"—drifted in with the apparent objective of helping him to relax.

Lowell didn't put much stock in all the formal preparations, obviously believing his friend was far superior in intellect to Kennedy, and he made light of them. Soon the McCarthy suite was ringing with the lilt of Irish songs, poetry and laughter. The merriment continued en route to the television studio for the early evening confrontation. Some of the pros were emphatic later in their belief that McCarthy's visitors had taken the competitive edge off him at a critical time. Tom Morgan, the senator's press man, said later that they had "castrated" him, to which David Garth, the New York consultant who had joined the campaign, replied: "No one is ever castrated if he doesn't want to be."

* * *

It had been a beautiful California afternoon during which many went to the beaches in Southern California and others took care of chores that had been neglected during the week or that demanded attention for the week ahead. Among the latter was a short, dark young man with black bushy hair who dropped by the Lock, Stock and Barrel gun shop in San Gabriel seeking armor-piercing .357 magnum ammunition of the sort used by state highway patrolmen. The owners of the shop, Ben and Dona Herrick, informed the customer that they didn't have it in stock because it was too powerful for sport shooters. Instead, they sold him four boxes of .22 caliber bullets for $3.99.

* * *

More than an hour before airtime for the Kennedy-McCarthy debate, 6:30 P.M. on the West Coast, 9:30 in the East, a predominantly pro-McCarthy crowd had gathered outside Station KGFO-TV, an ABC affiliate, awaiting the candidates. McCarthy arrived first, at about 6:10, relaxed and smiling, greeted by chants of "We Want Gene!" An aide dutifully informed reporters that an upbeat McCarthy had been "sitting around for an hour making funnies and singing Irish songs."

Inside the lobby, some local black newsmen complained to McCarthy about the all-white panel of ABC correspondents: Frank Reynolds, the moderator, Bill Lawrence and Bob Clark. The candidate brushed by, saying only a few words, and went inside. Kennedy arrived a few minutes later, also pushing past the protesters. When one of them again complained of the absence of blacks on the panel, Kennedy shot back: "Is there a Mexican-American on the panel? Is there an Irishman?" The questioner gaped. "It's obvious all you want is the votes, Senator," he finally replied. Kennedy moved on without further comment.

Going into the debate, the Kennedy strategy was not unlike that of his late brother John in his first, famous 1960 debate with Nixon. He wanted to demonstrate by a forcefulness and grasp of the issues that he was a match, or more than a match, for his older and presumably more experienced opponent. Like a boxer looking for an opening and attacking on seeing one, Kennedy seized on an aspect of McCarthy's first answer on Vietnam to throw him on the defensive.

To the opening question, what he would do "to bring peace to Vietnam" that Johnson wasn't doing, McCarthy observed among other things that a "new government in South Vietnam" would have to include the National Liberation Front "as a prerequisite to any kind of negotiations that might move on to talk about what the nature of that new government would be."

Kennedy pounced; while he too "would expect Saigon, the government in Saigon, would begin their own negotiations with the National Liberation Front," he said, "I would be opposed to what I understand Senator McCarthy's position is—of forcing a coalition on the government of Saigon, a coalition with the Communists, even before we begin the negotiations." He went on to insist on an end "to the official corruption" in Saigon and "a land-reform program that is meaningful, so that they can gain the support of the people themselves."

McCarthy replied rather lamely that "I didn't say I was going to force a coalition government on South Vietnam. I said we should make it clear that we are willing to accept that. . . . But I don't think there is much point in talking about reform in Saigon, or land reform, because we have been asking for that for five years and it hasn't happened."

Another question concerned the newspaper ads being run by the McCarthy campaign saying Kennedy had to bear part of the responsibility for the American involvement not only in Vietnam but also in the Dominican Republic, where Johnson had sent 22,000 troops in late April of 1965 in response to an uprising against the existing regime. Again Kennedy pounced; of the ad's reference to the Dominican Republic, he blurted: "I wasn't even in the government at the time!" Indeed, he had left the Johnson administration in 1964 to seek the Senate seat he then held.

Lamely again, McCarthy replied that he was referring "to a process, what was involved in our going into Cuba, involved in our going into the Dominican Republic, also into Vietnam, and I wanted to talk about the process. In any case, I had not seen the ad. When I saw it, I said, 'Stop it,' and they stopped it as soon as they could."

McCarthy tried to turn the exchange back on Kennedy by referring again to the leaflets that had been circulated earlier criticizing and, in McCarthy's view, distorting his Senate voting record. He also mentioned a prepared Kennedy ad featuring praise for him from former Secretary of Defense McNamara, whose Vietnam policy Kennedy supposedly deplored. With a straight face, Kennedy replied: "I don't know to what he is referring." Groans were audible in separate viewing rooms at the television station where traveling reporters with each candidate were watching.

Kennedy did not pass up any opportunity, either, to mention his experience: "While I was a member of the National Security Council for three and a half years . . . . As Attorney General I was the chief law-enforcement officer . . . . As a member of the Cabinet . . . ." And concerning opposition to the Vietnam policy: "When I spoke out in 1965. . . ." McCarthy's comparable comments went to his service on various congressional committees, less impressive-sounding although he had been in public life for twenty years, longer than Kennedy, and was ten years older.

Kennedy also deftly couched his replies on domestic issues in terms of California. As McCarthy talked of the need to cut the budget generally to meet the demands of the war in Vietnam, Kennedy spoke of having to cut $25 million from the Head Start program, "which is going to mean a thousand students already in the Head Start program here in the state of California will be excluded." He went on: "We can fight for freedom 12,500 miles away, but we must do something to deal with the quality of life here." Property taxes in California were "astronomically high," he said, and "problems of poverty" besetting the American people "must receive our first priority."

In that vein, Kennedy scored the heaviest points of the debate, and the most controversial, in an exchange over low-income housing and conditions and lack of economic opportunity in the inner cities. The answer, Kennedy said, was jobs in the ghettos where the poor, particularly blacks and other minorities, lived. "I think we have to provide jobs, with the government being the employer of last resort and bringing the private sector in, in a major way, and hiring people; doing away as much as possible with the welfare system, the handout, the dole, and getting people jobs, just by giving the private sector tax incentives and tax credits."

As McCarthy continued to emphasize the importance of public housing, Kennedy countered that federal programs had not "built the housing where it is necessary in the United States. I think a far less expensive way is to bring in the private sector and have them do it." It was an answer that might have come from a conservative Republican.

McCarthy then gave Kennedy, perhaps unwittingly, the opportunity to make his opponent sound threatening to the hundreds of thousands of white Californians living in lily-white suburbs. "I would say we have to get into the suburbs, too, with this kind of [public] housing," he said, "because some of the jobs are in the city and some jobs are being built there. But most of the employment is now in the belt line outside of the cities, and I don't think we ought to perpetuate the ghetto if we can help it, even by putting better houses there for them, or low-cost houses. What we have got to do is to try to break that up. Otherwise we are adopting a kind of apartheid in this country, a practical apartheid."

McCarthy said he agreed that private industry should build some housing in the ghettos, "but some of the housing has got to go out of the ghetto so there is a distribution of races throughout the whole structure of our cities and on into our rural areas." This was a notion that McCarthy had voiced as far back as the New Hampshire primary in a speech little noticed at the time, and embellished days earlier at the University of California at Davis.

Once again Kennedy pounced. "I am all in favor of moving people out of the ghettos," he said. "We have 40 million Negroes who are in the ghettos at the present time. We have here in the state of California a million Mexican Americans, whose poverty is even greater than [that of] many of the black people." And then he added pointedly to McCarthy: "You say you are going to take ten thousand black people and move them into Orange County."

Again there were groans in both press rooms. But to many conservative ears, the remark sounded like a warning that McCarthy would imperil their tidy and tranquil existence in that bastion of ultraconservatism. As Kennedy continued, he expressed his view more in the context of concern for the ghetto-dwellers who thus would be shunted into an impossibly competitive environment. Taking undereducated people and placing them "in the suburbs where they can't afford the housing, where their children can't keep up with the schools, and where they don't have the skills for the jobs," he said, "it is just going to be catastrophic." The answer, he said, was to train and employ them and "then they themselves can move out into other areas of the United States, and will be accepted and will find jobs and employment."

Intentionally or not, and even with his full remarks about how such a move would hurt those moved out of the ghettos, Kennedy's image of hordes of undereducated blacks descending on Orange County had all the earmarks of demagoguery. Even Peter Edelman, his issues man, acknowledged much later that the debate gambit "was not his most generous impulse. He turned a constructive, substantive view he had to an ill-advised political advantage."

McCarthy, however, did not call Kennedy on it. Again his response was bland and lame: "There are an estimated 250,000 jobs available [in the suburbs], but there aren't people within reach, and I thought when this question was first raised, that this was not your clear position, to concentrate that much on the ghetto."

Kennedy replied, again the champion of the ghetto-dweller rather than the protector of the white suburbanite: "I want to do things in the suburbs, but what I am saying is in order to meet the really hard-core heart of the problem, we have to face the fact that a lot of these people are going to live here [in the ghettos] for another several decades. And they can't live under the conditions that they are living under at the present time."

There was one other question in the debate that drew little attention from most viewers. One panelist about halfway through the hour noted that "many people think the Middle East will be the area of the next great confrontation between East and West," and that Kennedy had "this week proposed that we send 50 Phantom jets" to Israel. Did McCarthy agree? He said he did. Kennedy was not asked to respond, and didn't.

In terms of the substance of the debate, there was not much to choose between the two candidates. But in style Kennedy clearly was the more aggressive and engaged. McCarthy seemed content to parry and to get it over with. Afterward, Kennedy's aides were upbeat, knowing that their candidate had at least held his own, and had dealt with any impression that he could not stand up effectively to McCarthy. Most felt he had done so without appearing ruthless, although his answer about blacks in Orange County certainly showed a flash of political thuggery.

Many of McCarthy's aides felt let down by their candidate's inability or unwillingness to exploit Kennedy's vulnerabilities more tellingly. Jeremy Larner wrote later that while McCarthy scored points in the opening exchange on Vietnam, "Kennedy had had the guts to get up off the floor and fight it through, while McCarthy, dazed, was taking every punch." On the way back to the hotel, Albert Eisele wrote later, Finney was beside himself: "He flubbed it! Blew it! Threw it away! How can you get him elected?"

Kennedy pronounced himself "satisfied" with the debate; McCarthy dismissed it, all too characteristically, as "a kind of no-decision bout with three referees and sixteen-ounce gloves." Well, what did he think about a rematch? "No," he said. "We'd get tired of each other." Afterward, he joined a few friends for dinner at an expensive San Francisco restaurant. "I don't want to talk about politics," he told Gerald Hill, his California man. "I want to talk about Dante's Sixth Canto," and did so with the equally detached Lowell.

(The California debate continued to rile McCarthy years afterward. In one conversation with me, he called Kennedy's allegation that McCarthy wanted to send 10,000 blacks to Orange County "a complete fabrication," as was Kennedy's suggestion that McCarthy "would negotiate with the communists [in Vietnam] and he wouldn't." McCarthy also accused Kennedy of playing for the Jewish vote by having said earlier that he would approve sending American jets to Israel. In sum, he charged, Kennedy "appealed to three basic prejudices" in the California primary. Kennedy, he said, also "lied about" what was McCarthy's strong record in support of migrant workers by suggesting he opposed minimum wage legislation for them. As a result, McCarthy said, Kennedy swept the Hispanic vote in the state.

(Kennedy also benefited politically in California from the King assassination, McCarthy charged. "It didn't have any impact on Oregon, but I think it helped Bobby [in California]. He was playing the black thing against me. You can't really have a civil rights record that can stand against the attorney general's record on civil rights," he said. "He got practically all the black vote in California. I assume the King assassination helped him on that. It dramatized it and injected the race issue into that campaign.")

* * *

The next morning, Sunday, June 2, Kennedy in a taped television interview said he hoped that after the California primary he and McCarthy could "somehow join and try to bring together" all the anti-administration forces. To the McCarthy camp, this sounded like more of the wily fox eating the gingerbread man.

That impression was reinforced by efforts of Kennedy agents to persuade young McCarthyites to defect to their side if Kennedy won California on the next Tuesday. McCarthy, on another television show that morning, declared that "under no circumstances would I join with Kennedy to stop Hubert Humphrey."

The Kennedys went to Mass at St. Mary's Church just down Nob Hill from the Fairmont, at the edge of Chinatown. As we trudged back up the steep hill afterward, the pregnant Ethel insisting on it, she said of the previous night's debate: "Bob says McCarthy didn't do his homework. I can't get over it."

But McCarthy was not letting the business about Orange County go without a sharp reply, however tardy. He called Kennedy's remark "scare tactics" that "could increase suspicion and mistrust among the races." It was, he said, "a crude distortion" of his position and noted that Kennedy "incidentally" on that very Sunday was taking his campaign into Orange County. In Watts, black writer Louis Lomax joined McCarthy and endorsed him, saying Kennedy "may have won some votes in racist Orange County by what he said last night, but he lost mine and I suspect thousands of others." And in Bakersfield, McCarthy cracked: "Governor Reagan has been saying Senator Kennedy is talking more and more like him. I just didn't notice it until last night."

Kennedy did in fact go to Orange County that day, taking six of his kids to Disneyland in Anaheim. They were mobbed by tourists but did manage to get on one of the most popular rides, Pirates of the Caribbean, before retreating with Kennedy promising the kids to return another day, perhaps after Tuesday's vote, which would end the frenzied calendar of primaries. (Or, as Nixon might have said, "as far as direct primaries are concerned." There still remained the indirect primary in New York where convention delegates would be chosen but no candidates' names would be on the ballot.)

Monday, June 3, was another of those incredible days that marked the Robert Kennedy campaign as among the most emotional and exhausting in the annals of presidential elections. Determined to touch every important media market, Kennedy flew from Los Angeles to San Francisco for a noontime motorcade through Chinatown, down to Long Beach for another motorcade, on to San Diego for a rally and back to Los Angeles—about 1,200 miles in all. The final California poll had given him 36 percent to 31 for McCarthy and 15 for the pro-Humphrey slate headed by state attorney general Thomas Lynch. But there were 18 percent undecided in the survey. In earlier primaries, McCarthy received a lion's share of the undecideds, and if that happened in California there was no telling what the outcome would be.

Crowds lined up three and four deep to watch Kennedy inch through Chinatown, he and Ethel standing on the back seat of their convertible and waving. About three blocks in, just past an intersection, six sharp claps suddenly were heard. Ethel jumped down and sat on the seat, hunched over, but the candidate remained standing, waving and shaking outstretched hands, as if bracing himself. The claps turned out to be the sound of large firecrackers, like cherry bombs, much louder than what would have come from, for example, a .22 caliber revolver. At Kennedy's direction, a friend jumped into the back seat to steady Ethel.

Many in the entourage, including we reporters, were unsettled by the incident, not being able to distinguish between firecrackers going off and gunshots. To seasoned users of firearms, however, it probably would have been easy—for instance, to the short, dark young man with black bushy hair who at this hour was seen at the San Gabriel Valley Gun Club in Duarte, a suburb of Los Angeles, rapidly firing 300 or 400 rounds of .22 caliber bullets from a revolver. In doing so, he was violating the range's rules requiring shooters to pause between shots. For that reason, a college student and playground director named Henry Carreon, practicing about five feet to his right with a friend, David Montellano, asked the young man what kind of revolver he was using. When the fellow ignored him, he asked again. "An Iver Johnson," he said.

(Not everyone on this day was using a gun for target practice. In New York, artist Andy Warhol was shot in the chest and abdomen by a twenty-eight-year-old actress named Valerie Solanis whose movie script had been rejected by Warhol. She surrendered to police three hours later, saying, "I shot him. He had too much control over my life." After surgery and two months in a hospital, Warhol recovered. A year after the attack, Solanis pleaded guilty and received a surprisingly light prison term of up to three years.)

Kennedy's motorcade wound up on Fisherman's Wharf, where he spoke to a small gathering of Italian-Americans at DiMaggio's Restaurant. Referring to McCarthy's delayed reaction to the Orange County debate exchange, Kennedy with a trace of contempt observed that "he wanted to get me in a room with him. He got me in a room with him, and I thought he was very nice to me."

Kennedy and entourage then flew to Long Beach for a scheduled "walk in the park" and were met by 6,000 excited citizens. His talk was disjointed and his humor fell flat. When he got back in his car, Dutton asked him how he was feeling. "You had a little trouble with some words that time," Dutton observed. "I don't feel good," Kennedy said. Dutton decided to keep a sharp eye on him; the strain of the weeks of pressure, of being mobbed physically day after day, was showing.

The motorcade sped through Watts, taking sidestreets to make up time on a schedule slipping badly. But the route was taken also to dodge large, predominantly black crowds on the major streets whose usually welcome wild enthusiasm might unsettle white suburban voters watching the television coverage. As the motorcade raced down one deserted residential street, press secretary Dick Drayne on the press bus asked aloud: "What is this? Are we going house hunting?"

As the party headed for the airport and the plane for San Diego, Kennedy was feeling worse. He asked Dutton to get him a bottle of ginger ale. Dutton bought a six-pack and Kennedy drank a bottle every few blocks. Dutton got another six-pack to take on the plane. Another huge mob met Kennedy in San Diego and en route to an auditorium in the downtown El Cortez Hotel. This was to be the final event of the California primary and some celebrity friends, including singers Andy Williams and Rosemary Clooney, were there to entertain the crowd.

Kennedy decided to go right on. He raced through his standard speech, stopped abruptly and then walked to the steps leading from the stage and sat down on the top step, his face buried in his hands. At first, his aides thought he was merely reacting emotionally to the end of the hard direct primary trail. Rafer Johnson and Bill Barry hustled him down a corridor behind the stage and into a small dressing room. He leaned against a sink until his wife and Dutton joined him. In a few minutes he came out, went back and spoke to the crowd again in a more traditional windup. "For the benefit of my friends on the left," he said, looking at the press entourage, "I want to add, as George Bernard Shaw once said, 'Some men see things as they are and say, "Why?" I dream things that never were and say, "Why not?"'" Then he took a seat next to his wife and listened as Andy Williams sang.

The flight back to Los Angeles was subdued, the others in the traveling party taking a cue from Kennedy's obvious exhaustion, shared to a lesser degree by them. The Kennedys upon landing went to the beach home of movie director John Frankenheimer in Malibu to spend the night and primary day, resting and relaxing with the six children present. It would be their first full free day together in some time—at least until the California primary exit polls and returns started to come in.

The rest of the traveling party went on to the Ambassador Hotel, the Kennedy campaign headquarters for primary night. There, a bunch of us, reporters and staff aides, began an impromptu party in Drayne's room to mark the end of the California campaign. Before long there were impersonations of various celebrity figures and a songfest so loud that an unhappy hotel guest showed up complaining. Undaunted, we moved to the Kennedys' unoccupied suite and continued for another hour or so, doing considerable damage to their liquor supply. Primary day would be a relaxing one for all of us as well, until the polls and early returns would oblige us to go to work. We pinned a note of thanks to a pillow on the candidate's bed before departing.

* * *

The next morning, as McCarthy was flying from Los Angeles over to Phoenix for a meeting with supporters before coming back for the California returns, Kennedy slept late in Malibu. He rose about eleven o'clock and phoned Dutton at the Ambassador, still sleeping off our revelry of the night before, and Goodwin. Both agreed to drive out to Malibu a bit later. Kennedy and his wife had lunch with the six children and presidential campaign chronicler Theodore H. White and then they all repaired to the beach, although the day was chilly and overcast.

Kennedy stripped off his shirt and plunged into the ocean anyway, joined by some of the kids. Suddenly he saw twelve-year-old David being pulled by an undertow. He dove in and came up with the boy, who had a large red bruise on his forehead. The party went back to the Frankenheimers' pool for some safer frolicking and, later, a review of the early political intelligence with Dutton and Goodwin. The first exit polls were good, showing Kennedy running ahead with about 49 percent. He talked still of the possibility of getting together with McCarthy, noting how his brother John and Humphrey had been able to close ranks in 1960 after Humphrey's defeat in the West Virginia primary.

That night, the Kennedys gathered in their suite at the Ambassador with a horde of campaign aides, friends and a few favored reporters, awaiting the actual returns. Early in the evening, Dutton called South Dakota and was assured Kennedy was a comfortable winner. He was particularly bouyed by the vote in one Native American precinct: 878 votes for him, nine for McCarthy, two for Johnson. The final statewide totals were Kennedy 49.7 percent, native-son Humphrey 29.9, McCarthy 20.4.

But California was what mattered, and the early network projections were good for Kennedy. The first actual results, all from outside Los Angeles County, put McCarthy ahead. But the county, which had 38 percent of the Democratic registration in the whole state, was expected to be a Kennedy stronghold, so the Kennedyites didn't worry. Downstairs, Larry O'Brien told me: "I think we broke the pattern of the undecideds," referring to McCarthy's capture of most of them in Oregon. "I think the debate did it," he said. "Every survey of ours indicated two out of three came over to Bob after the debate. Our canvassers found that on Sunday and Monday."

O'Brien said he would be leaving Los Angeles the next morning for New York, where convention delegates would be elected in a June 18 primary in each of the state's forty-one congressional districts, without a preferential presidential primary bearing the candidates' names. The McCarthy campaign would be challenging Kennedy in most of the districts. The format demanded a higher level of political organization to educate voters on which delegates supported which candidate, and then to get voters to the polls without the pull of a direct vote for the candidate of their choice.

At the Beverly Hilton Hotel, meanwhile, McCarthy had seen the same network projections. Without challenging them, he did what he usually did when they indicated he was losing—he put down the significance of the primary involved. In an interview on CBS with David Schoumacher, the network's assigned reporter on the McCarthy campaign, the Minnesotan sought to slough off California.

"We made our real test in Oregon," he said, "where there were no [minority] bloc votes, and we made the case as clear as we could there, neglecting California in order to run in Oregon, and expected it would go about like this." Any Democratic nominee would do well with such blocs against Nixon in the fall, he insisted; the critical toss-up bloc was the independent voters. "We're demonstrating what we said we would," he told Schoumacher, "that I can get votes no other Democrat can get."

McCarthy had hardly neglected California; in saying so he was again engaging in denigration, this time of the large and professional campaign force that had toiled for him in what was then the nation's second most populous state.

At the Ambassador, Kennedy was holding off talking to the television networks as long as he could. He did not want to be premature in any expression of confidence based on the network projections as long as the actual tally, still awaiting returns from Los Angeles County, had McCarthy slightly ahead. In a conversation with Goodwin in the bathroom of his crowded suite, Goodwin wrote later, Kennedy urgently talked of the need "to get free of McCarthy. While we're fighting each other," Kennedy said, "Humphrey's running around the country picking up delegates. I don't want to stand on every street corner in New York for the next two weeks [beating back McCarthy's challenge there]. I've got to spend that time going to the states, talking to delegates before it's too late. My only chance is to chase Hubert's ass all over the country. Maybe he'll fold."

Sorensen joined them as Kennedy continued: "Even if McCarthy won't get out, his people must know after tonight that I'm the only candidate against the war that can beat Humphrey. That's what they want to do, isn't it, to end the war?"

At this point, Goodwin wrote, "taking me aside, Kennedy whispered, 'I think we should tell [McCarthy] if he withdraws now and supports me, I'll make him secretary of state." Goodwin wrote that he had suggested this step earlier but Kennedy had rejected it. "But now McCarthy could prove a fatal obstacle," he wrote. "The goal was well worth the price."

Kennedy finally could wait no longer to go downstairs. He did one interview with Sander Vanocur, then of NBC, and another with Roger Mudd, then of CBS. In both of them, he made conciliatory comments toward McCarthy and repeated his hope that their forces could unite—behind himself, he meant.

The Mudd interview provided the comic relief of the night. Kennedy was on his most congenial behavior, perhaps determined to take another step toward shedding his clinging image as ruthless, but Mudd wouldn't cooperate. "Well," he asked concerning Kennedy's hopes of uniting with his foe, "it ap-

pears, though, doesn't it, that you're not going to be able to shake Eugene
McCarthy?" Kennedy, obviously uncomfortable with that particular formula-
tion, replied: "I mean, he's going to have to make that decision himself. . . ."

Mudd seemed determined to cast Kennedy in combative terms, at least
against Humphrey. "You have no way now, between California and Chicago,"
he asked next, "to draw the vice president into a fight?" Kennedy winced at
the harsh implication. "No, I. . . . Do I have to put it that way?" he asked
Mudd. What he would like, he said, was to have a public discussion with
Humphrey around the country because "I don't think that the policies that
he espouses would be successful" in the country or the Democratic Party.

Kennedy was doing his best to sound reasonable, but Mudd was having
none of it. "Well, are you saying, Senator," he asked, "that if the Democratic
Party nominates the vice president, it will be cutting its own throat in
November?" Kennedy seemed to wince again, then smiled. "Well, again, you
use those expressions," he said. "I think that the Democratic Party would be
making a very bad mistake to ignore the wishes of the people and ignore
these primaries" (that Humphrey had declined to contest directly).

Kennedy next turned aside softly a suggestion of a Kennedy-Humphrey
ticket, then added that he didn't understand Humphrey saying that if
Johnson decided to run after all, he would bow out. Mudd put a hard edge
on that too. "You felt that was fairly shoddy politics, I take it?" he asked,
keeping a straight face. Kennedy was squirming now. "Well, again, I . . .
Roger, I, you know, I don't think . . . ." and stumbled on, trying to take the
high road. But Mudd persisted, smiling now as he clearly enjoyed the game.
Concerning delegates committed to or leaning to Humphrey, he asked
Kennedy, "Are they squeezable? Are they solid?" Kennedy finally grimaced
and said, in mock dismay, "Roger, your language! I don't like either of those
expressions." Well, Mudd retorted, laughing now, "isn't that the way you talk
about it?" Kennedy, also laughing at this point: "No, I don't go that far, I
don't, I don't. . . . Probably somebody else does." Mudd ended the interview
by promising Kennedy to "work on my language for the next time."

Kennedy was still laughing as he went down the corridor for two more interviews, one with Dan Blackburn of Metromedia News, whom Kennedy had
made a local hero on the campaign through his hometown of La Porte during
the Indiana primary and whom Kennedy always found time for. Then it was
back to Kennedy's suite for another assessment of the California results. They
seemed good enough now for him to go downstairs and greet his cheering
supporters in the Embassy Room, the hotel's main ballroom.

Kennedy had been trying to reach Al Lowenstein by phone at his home in
Long Island. He asked Goodwin to try again and tell him Kennedy would be

calling right after his victory speech to talk about the outlook in New York. Lowenstein was still with McCarthy but hopeful of coalescing the two forces. Before going down to the ballroom, Kennedy joked with John Lewis, who had teamed up with migrant workers' leader César Chávez in working California's minority communities for Kennedy. "John, you let me down today," Lewis remembered Kennedy saying to him. "More Mexican-Americans voted for me than Negroes." Then Kennedy added: "Wait for me. I'll be back in fifteen or twenty minutes."

* * *

For some time earlier, the short, dark young man who had been test-firing a handgun at the San Gabriel Valley Gun Club had been wandering around the Ambassador Hotel, dropping in on some election night parties for statewide California candidates and finally wandering into the Kennedy party. Outside the Venetian Room, drink in hand, he walked up to a hotel electrician named Hans Bidstrup and asked him if he was a Democrat. When Bidstrup told him he was, the young man thrust out his hand and said: "Shake hands with another Democrat." He sauntered about, making small talk with others in the crowd, wandering into the Colonial Room where members of the Kennedy press corps were working, and then into the kitchen pantry just beyond. It was near midnight when he asked a hotel busboy, Jesús Pérez: "Is Mr. Kennedy coming this way?" The busboy said he didn't know.

* * *

Kennedy, accompanied by his wife, Dutton and other aides, came down a service elevator into the hotel kitchen, shaking hands with kitchen workers, and out past a long serving table in a pantry corridor leading out to the ballroom. The time was about fifteen minutes before midnight, California time. Walking behind him, according to a Los Angeles fireman later who had been standing there, was a dark young man with black bushy hair gripping a rolled-up poster "who was looking all over all the area as he passed by."

Bob Healy of the *Boston Globe* and I were standing there in the pantry corridor as Kennedy came in, looking smart in a dark blue suit and striped tie. We congratulated him on his apparent victory and, in a buoyant mood, he invited us to join a celebration later at The Factory, a discotheque in which Pierre Salinger had a part ownership. I kidded "Ruthless Robert" about his interview with Mudd, remarking that I thought he had been "very ruthful." He laughed, walked on, then turned and said: "I'm getting better all the time."

Then, in a moment, he was out in the ballroom, on the raised platform jam-packed with friends and supporters behind the rostrum and a battery of microphones. Ethel, wearing an orange-and-white minidress and white stockings, was at his side. I squeezed onto the rear of the platform, next to

Dutton. He told me that when he informed Kennedy about our revelry in his suite the night before, "he was like a little boy who had missed out on something."

Kennedy was in a playful mood as he addressed the cheering crowd. He congratulated the Dodgers' Don Drysdale, who had just pitched his sixth straight shutout, a three-hitter over the Pittsburgh Pirates that ran his string of scoreless innings to fifty-four, eclipsing the previous National League record of forty-six by Carl Hubbell. (In his next outing five days later, Drysdale was to break the major league record of fifty-six by Walter Johnson, before yielding a sacrifice fly in the game's fifth inning against the Philadelphia Phillies.) Kennedy thanked brother-in-law Steve Smith for having been so "ruthless" in running his campaign, and others including "my dog Freckles—I'm not doing this in the order of importance. I also want to thank my wife Ethel." The crowd laughed with him.

Then he got down to his message. His victories in largely urban California and rural South Dakota on the same day, he said, made him confident "we can work together [to] end the divisions" in the country "between blacks and whites, between the poor and the more affluent, or between age groups or on the war in Vietnam. . . ." The country needed change, he said, and it would come about "only if those who are delegates in Chicago recognize the importance of what has happened here in the state of California" and in South Dakota—and New Hampshire.

The latter reference inferentially paid tribute to McCarthy and underscored Kennedy's continuing hope of bringing the McCarthy forces under his tent. He congratulated McCarthy and his followers for "breaking the political logjam" and making "citizen participation a new and powerful force in our political life." Then he asked the McCarthyites to join ranks "not for myself but for the cause and the ideas which moved you to begin this great popular movement." He added that he hoped "now that the California primary is finished, now that the primary is over, that we could concentrate on having a dialogue—or a debate, I hope—between the vice president and perhaps myself on what direction we want to go in" at home and in Vietnam. Again he expressed "my thanks to all of you, and on to Chicago, and let's win there."

* * *

As Kennedy finished and waved, the crowd crushed forward toward him. He was supposed to go out through the crowd and down some stairs to another spillover reception, where closed-circuit television had carried his remarks. But Dutton decided because it was already past midnight, 3 A.M. in the East, it would be best if Kennedy went right to the press room just beyond the kitchen pantry area, where we newspaper reporters wanted a short time with him before our last deadlines passed.

Barry and Dutton started down the steps off the platform and through swinging doors into the pantry corridor, believing Kennedy was behind them. But he was boxed in by the surging crowd shouting "We want Bobby! We want Bobby!" The hotel's assistant manager, Karl Uecker, took Kennedy by the arm and led him off the platform at the rear and directly into the pantry corridor, darkened at that end. By the time Barry saw that his candidate was not behind him, Kennedy had moved out ahead into the well-lighted end of the pantry area.

Rushing myself to get to the press room, I walked past a large floor-to-ceiling ice-making machine to my right and two stainless steel steam tables to my left. I saw only some kitchen hands to the left and didn't look right as I went by the ice-making machine, where a short, dark young man stood on a low tray stacker.

It was thirteen minutes past midnight when the senator reached approximately the spot where Healy and I had ribbed him about being "very ruthful" in the Mudd interview. Ethel Kennedy had been separated from him by the crowd and Barry and Dutton were only now catching up. Andrew West, a Mutual Radio reporter, had his tape recorder running at Kennedy's side and asked him how he was going to cope with Humphrey's delegate strength. Kennedy answered: "It just goes back to the struggle for it—"

As Kennedy turned to look for his wife, the young man standing on the tray stacker stepped down, raised his right hand high over the crowd and fired a snub-nosed revolver at Kennedy's head from only a few feet away. The first sound I heard, walking about ten or twelve feet ahead toward the press room with my back to Kennedy, was a quick "pop" like a firecracker or a boy's cap gun going off, then a pause and a rapid volley of additional pops—like the crackling noise when the firecrackers were set off the previous day in Chinatown. I turned and saw Kennedy already fallen on his back, his eyes open, arms over his bleeding head, his feet apart. He was conscious, but obviously very seriously wounded.

Uecker, the hotel assistant manager, grabbed at the assailant's arm, still holding the revolver, along with the two muscular athletes in the Kennedy entourage, Rafer Johnson and Rosie Grier, and then Barry and others. West, the Mutual Radio reporter, was still talking into his microphone as bedlam swirled around him, seemingly oblivious of the fact that he was recording history.

"I am right here and Rafer Johnson has hold of the man who apparently has fired the shot! He has fired the shot. . . . He still has the gun! The gun is pointed at me right at this moment! I hope they can get the gun out of his

hand. Be very careful. Get the gun . . . get the gun . . . get the gun. . . . Stay
away from the gun. . . . His hand is frozen. . . . Get his thumb, get his
thumb, get his thumb, get his thumb, get his thumb . . . and break it if you
have to . . . get his thumb! Get away from the barrel! Get away from the barrel, man! Look out for the gun! . . . Okay, all right. That's it, Rafer, get it!
Get the gun, Rafer! Okay, now hold on to the gun. Hold on to him. Hold on
to him. Ladies and gentlemen, they have the gun away from the man. . . ."

Finally the gun was wrenched free and it fell. Johnson picked it up as Grier
held the man in a headlock and others came up and began punching and cursing him. Shrieks of terror filled the air: "My God! He's been shot! Get a doctor! Get the gun! Kill him! Kill the bastard! No, don't kill him!" Jess Unruh
pushed forward, ordering: "I want him alive! If anything happens to this one,
you answer to me! We don't want another Oswald!"

In the hail of bullets, five others had been hit: Paul Schrade, forty-three, a
United Auto Workers official; William Weisel, thirty, associate director of
the ABC News Washington bureau; Ira Goldstein, nineteen, of Continental
News Service of California; Elizabeth Evans, forty-three, of Saugus,
California; Irwin Stroll, seventeen, of Los Angeles. All survived.

Young Stroll later told the grand jury that he had been shot in the left shin
when he "got in front of Mrs. Kennedy by accident" on his way to the kitchen
and pushed her down, possibly saving her from being hit. Goldstein later testified that after being hit in the left thigh he had staggered to a chair and
asked: "'How is Senator Kennedy? What happened to him?' And this woman
walked by, and she said to me, 'How dare you talk about my husband that
way?' and she slapped me across the face. And I said, 'I am sorry lady, but I
was shot too. I'd like to know how the senator is.' And she said, 'Oh, I am
sorry, honey,' and kissed me. This was Mrs. Ethel Kennedy. At that time she
was not in tears. She was a little hysterical, though, but she wasn't crying."

The fallen candidate's wife was brought to his side by a friend. "Oh, my
God," she said in a half whisper. She stepped across him, knelt and took his
hand. By now I had climbed up on a table and saw her below on both knees
on the cold concrete floor, whispering to him and stroking his brow. All was
pandemonium, but the still photographers and cameramen with their single-
mindedness pressed in. Drayne and another young press aide, Hugh
McDonald, shouted, "Get back! Get back! Give him air!" and Ethel Kennedy
looked up plaintively and said, "Please go, please go. Give him room to
breathe."

But most of the recorders of the bloody scene would not be deterred. One
woman photographer, on the verge of hysteria, put her camera down and
yelled to the others: "You can have it! You can have it!" When she tried to

pull one of them back he kept shooting, shaking her off and shouting: "Get away! This is history!" Other print reporters and I scribbled frantically in our little notepads. Later, when I looked at what I had written, it was all an indecipherable garble. But what I saw and heard in those terrible moments was etched indelibly in my mind ever thereafter.

As Kennedy lay there, a young kitchen boy named Juan Romero knelt next to him, took a set of rosary beads from his shirt pocket, placed it in the wounded man's hand and prayed. When young McDonald, overcome by it all, began to sob, Barry turned to him and said, quietly but firmly, "Stop crying and do your job." Somebody had removed Kennedy's shoes and McDonald was seen later wandering aimlessly, still holding the shoes. Ted Kennedy, learning the news as he watched television in his hotel room in San Francisco, immediately flew to Los Angeles.

After what seemed like an interminable time but actually only ten minutes after the shooting, two medical attendants finally wheeled in a low hospital stretcher and placed Kennedy on it. "Gently, gently," his wife said. "Oh, no, no," Kennedy said, in obvious pain, "don't." As the attendants strapped him onto the stretcher, he appeared to lose consciousness. A young kitchen worker took a white towel and proceeded to mop up the blood that had settled under Kennedy's head.

After an argument with the attendants about who would ride in the ambulance, Ethel and Dutton climbed in the back with the candidate and Barry and Warren Rogers, then Washington editor of *Look* magazine and a family friend, got into the front seat next to the driver. They took Kennedy to the Central Receiving Hospital a mile away where an emergency heart massage was applied, restoring his pulse.

Because Ethel did not know if her husband was dead or alive, the doctor reported later, "when we began to get a heartbeat, I put the stethoscope in her ears so she could listen, and she was tremendously relieved." A priest friend nevertheless administered the last rites of the Roman Catholic Church to Kennedy. He had taken one bullet in his head, in the mastoid area behind his right ear, on a path to his brain. He was moved at once to the Hospital of the Good Samaritan a few blocks away for surgery. Almost at once, a local television van had a spotlight on the entrance and police set up street barriers, behind which a massive vigil of shocked and concerned Angelenos had already formed.

Back at the Ambassador, Los Angeles police rushed into the pantry area, took the assailant from Grier and the others pinning him down, handcuffed him and led him out as stunned onlookers gawked, many of them sobbing. After they had left, Grier, an immense man, put his head down on the steam table and cried softly like a baby. A tough, hard-bitten veteran CBS television cameraman, Jim Wilson, who had just captured the whole bizarre scene on film, sat next to Grier and did the same.

Soon police came in and marked in chalk where Kennedy and Schrade had fallen, while the floor was swept and scrubbed clean of blood marks. Several overhead drywall panels were removed and searched for bullet fragments. On a wall just beyond the point where Kennedy had been hit, someone had put up a hand-printed sign that said THE ONCE AND FUTURE KING, a reference to the book from which the musical *Camelot* had been taken.

After watching the ambulance depart, I went back into the Ambassador lobby, where a sea of bewildered Kennedy supporters milled about, still unable to grasp fully what had happened. One woman stood on the edge of a large fountain and pool of water, waved rosary beads over her head and implored the crowd, "Kneel down and pray, say your rosary." Perhaps twenty people knelt, including a man who had been holding a drink and a cigarette and set them down on the carpet. As they all knelt, another man seized a chair and threw it into the fountain. Others grabbed and quieted him.

Up in the Kennedy suite, John Lewis, awaiting Kennedy's return, was watching the festivities in the ballroom on a television set when the news came. "We all dropped to the floor, crying," he said later. "I just wanted to leave Los Angeles then, to get out." He took the first flight he could get back to Atlanta, he remembered, "and I think I cried all the way back."

* * *

Over at the Beverly Hilton, McCarthy was in his seventh-floor suite with Clark and Finney drafting a telegram of congratulation to Kennedy. Mary McGrory was also there. The draft originally had talked of Kennedy's "splendid" victory but McCarthy changed it to "fine" because, McGrory recalled, he didn't believe the margin would be as large as the networks were projecting. He was correct. The final tally was Kennedy 46.3 percent, McCarthy 41.8, with the remainder for the pro-Humphrey slate.

As they labored over the telegram, Schoumacher rushed into the room. "Senator Kennedy has been shot!" he said, and ran out to get more details. As McCarthy's wife and daughters came into the room, McCarthy sat in a corner chair, put his hands over his eyes, then looked up and said, "Maybe we should do it in a different way. Maybe we should have the English system of having the cabinet choose the president. There must be some other way."

In Colorado Springs, Hubert Humphrey had just gotten to sleep in the VIP quarters of the Air Force Academy, where he was scheduled to deliver the commencement address the next afternoon. An aide, Dave Gartner, woke him with the news. He jumped out of bed, turned on his television set to verify what he had been told, then phoned Ted Kennedy at the Fairmont in San Francisco, who himself had learned only shortly before of the shooting of his brother. Humphrey asked what he could do to help. Kennedy asked him to arrange an Air Force plane to fly a renowned Boston brain surgeon, Dr. James Poppen, to Los Angeles. Humphrey did so, and also had another plane in Washington take other Robert Kennedy children and family friends there.

According to Van Dyk, however, while the first plane was headed to Boston to pick up the surgeon, Johnson phoned Humphrey, demanded to know what right he had to "commandeer" an Air Force plane and canceled the order. If that was so, Johnson must have changed his mind, because a government plane did take Poppen to Los Angeles, where he arrived after surgery had been completed.

The vice president told Air Force Chief of Staff John McConnell that he would be returning to Washington in the morning, and when McConnell protested that he had to deliver a speech at the academy, Humphrey told him: "General, I don't have to do anything. . . . Get yourself another commencement speaker." When Air Force Secretary Harold Brown protested to Van Dyk, the Humphrey aide related later, he told him that "the vice president's going back to Washington; it would be inappropriate for him to make the speech" because Kennedy had been shot. To which Brown replied, Van Dyk said, "What the hell difference does that make?"

* * *

The surgery on Robert Kennedy did not begin until nearly three hours after the shooting. It lasted three hours and forty minutes, as a team of neurosurgeons and chest surgeons labored over him. In addition to the bullet that had passed the mastoid bone and lodged in the midline of the senator's brain, the critical wound, another bullet had hit him in the back of his neck and a third had grazed his forehead.

Shortly before the surgery was completed, President Johnson issued a statement from the White House: "There are no words equal to the horror of this tragedy. Our thoughts and our prayers are with Senator Kennedy, his family and the other victims. All America prays for his recovery. We also pray that divisiveness and violence be driven from the hearts of men everywhere." Johnson also sent private messages to the family members and called Ted Kennedy, who had flown down to Los Angeles, and Steve Smith at the hospital.

After the King assassination, Johnson had asked Congress to authorize Secret Service protection for all presidential and vice presidential candidates, but no action had been taken. Now LBJ ordered that it be done on his own at once, then phoned the congressional leaders and asked them to pass the necessary legislation. The next day Congress did so. (Shortly afterward, Johnson appointed a presidential commission to study violence—with Senator Roman Hruska of Nebraska, a champion of the pro-gun lobby, as a member—and called for a much more sweeping gun control law, including national registration of guns and licensing of owners. The bill he finally got four months later included neither provision, successfully opposed by the gun lobby.)

As the news of the shooting of Robert Kennedy flashed around the world, Pope Paul VI in Vatican City told a large crowd gathered in St. Peter's Basilica that he was praying "for the life and health of this young man who was offering himself to the public service of his country." Elsewhere in Europe, where conspiracy theories still thrived over the assassination of John F. Kennedy, the news triggered more of the same. And outside the hospital in Los Angeles, the vigil continued as the crowds of silent well-wishers grew, many of them holding up hastily printed (and sold) bumper stickers in glowing orange on black that said: PRAY FOR BOBBY.

In the morning, McCarthy outside his hotel suite read a statement calling the shooting a tragedy for the nation as well as for the Kennedy family. "It's not enough, in my judgment, to say that this is the act of one deranged man, if that is the case," he said. "The nation, I think, bears too great a burden of the kind of neglect which has allowed the disposition of violence to grow here in our own land, or the reflection of the violence which we have visited upon the rest of the world, or at least part of the world. All of us must keep vigil with the nation in prayer, and hope that Senator Kennedy will recover. . . ."

McCarthy then stopped off at the hospital to pay his respects to the family before returning to Washington. The animosity that already existed between the two political camps was intensified when the police escorting McCarthy insensitively left their sirens on as they pulled up to the hospital entrance. McCarthy aides said later he had explicitly asked them not to do so, but they were rushing to catch a plane and traffic near the hospital was dense. McCarthy went in, talked briefly to Goodwin and Salinger, then left, not wanting to disturb the family.

On the flight to Washington, with Kennedy's condition still critical, McCarthy according to Richard Stout told Finney "it's all over" and it didn't matter much what the campaign staff did. "It's not going to make any difference," he said. "What we have to do now is cut down and just see what influence we can bring to bear on the situation between now and August."

* * *

Meanwhile in Los Angeles, Kennedy's assailant was identified at, of all places, a press conference by the ever-opportunistic Mayor Sam Yorty as Sirhan Bishara Sirhan, twenty-four, a Jordanian born in Jerusalem who had lived in the Los Angeles area since 1957. He was arraigned at 7:40 that morning and charged with six counts of assault with intent to murder, with bail set at $250,000.

Police said his identity had been traced through the revolver used and fingerprints taken when he applied for a job as an exercise boy at Hollywood Park racetrack. Two of his brothers confirmed his identity, police said, and a newspaper article critical of Kennedy was found in his pocket. Yorty also reported that two notebooks had been found in Sirhan's home in Pasadena bearing "a direct reference to the necessity to assassinate Senator Kennedy before June 5, 1968"—the first anniversary of the end of the six-day Arab-Israel war. (The exact words written were "RFK must die . . . RFK must be killed. . . . My determination to eliminate RFK is becoming . . . more an unshakable obsession. . . . Robert F. Kennedy must be assassinated before 5 June 1968.") The notebooks, Yorty said, also contained "generally pro-Communist writings" and pro-Arab, anti-Israel, anti-Kennedy references.

The day dragged on, with brief appearances by Mankiewicz in the press room conveying the sense that Kennedy was slipping away. The grimmest mandatory exercise of newspaper journalism, the advance preparation of an obituary, occupied many of us in these long hours, filled with public and private reminiscences of the man going back a decade or more, gleaned from professional and personal associations.

The press corps covering Robert Kennedy had been particularly close, often uncomfortably close, to him. In part it was a result of age and a shared generational outlook, in part it stemmed from respect for the man he was becoming more than the man he had been in his brusquer days. We had seen at close range his evolution from a rude, arrogant young brat as a favored brother of a prominent senator and a tough and abrupt campaign manager, to a wrenchingly troubled heir to a political legacy that had increasingly taken him out of himself and made him a public man, espousing the public good. As Dick Harwood had said, it was hard not to like him more the more you were exposed to him, and harder to maintain a professionally objective attitude toward him.

One day, one hour and forty-seven minutes after the bullets had struck down the junior senator from New York, Mankiewicz entered the press room and in a choking but controlled voice read without embellishment: "Robert Francis Kennedy died at 1:44 A.M. today, June 6, 1968. With Senator Kennedy at the time of his death were his wife, Ethel; his sisters, Mrs. Stephen Smith and Patricia Lawford; brother-in-law Stephen Smith, and Mrs. John F. Kennedy. He was 42 years old." Later he added the name of Senator Edward Kennedy.

Outside the hospital, many wept at the news. Johnson at the White House said: "This is a time of tragedy and loss. During his life, he knew far more than his share of personal tragedy, yet he never abandoned his faith in America." The president proclaimed the next Sunday a national day of mourning and ordered all flags on public buildings lowered to half staff.

(Even now, the bitter feelings Johnson felt toward Robert Kennedy clung and colored his judgment. According to Clark Clifford in his memoir, LBJ wanted at first merely to issue a statement on RFK's death and had to be talked into delivering it himself by advisers. The next morning, Clifford wrote, "I received a telephone call from the President that began one of the saddest experiences of my long friendship with him. He wanted to discuss whether or not Bobby Kennedy had the right to be buried in Arlington Cemetery. I was stunned . . . the regulations were irrelevant, and in any case could be suspended by the Commander in Chief. It seemed obvious that Bobby should be buried near his beloved brother on the gentle slope below the Custis-Lee Mansion; the politician in Lyndon Johnson understood this, but his personal bitterness continued even after Bobby's death.")

At the hospital, a six-hour autopsy was performed under California law—and to stem the kind of controversy that followed John Kennedy's assassination in Dallas. At the Los Angeles County jail, Sirhan's bail was revoked and he was held amid plans to seek a grand jury indictment against him for murder.

In the morning, I caught a plane to New York, where the slain senator was being taken on a presidential jet later in the day. Exhausted from the shock of what had happened and the long vigil at the hospital, I tried to sleep in my seat but couldn't. I decided to watch the in-flight movie to take my mind off all that was already engraved in my head. The film was a spy thriller. In an opening scene, the head of a very lifelike dummy was shattered by gunfire.

*   *   *

McCarthy, on learning of Kennedy's death, immediately ordered his campaign workers to suspend all political activity. Speaking of the family, he said: "Let us seek to comfort them by our quiet mourning, our rejection of violence and reprisal, and by offering renewed dedication to the cause of peace and reconciliation which Robert Kennedy served."

The slain senator's body and his family and closest friends were flown to New York aboard one of the presidential jets, the same model that had flown the body of John Kennedy to Washington from Dallas in 1963, though not the identical plane. Brother Ted sat with the casket through most of the trip with the widow.

I got to New York in time to meet the plane at a private terminal at La

Guardia Airport. The scene was reminiscent of the arrival of John Kennedy's body at Andrews Air Force Base from Dallas on November 22, 1963, except it was a warm spring evening. A host of political notables waited as the presidential jet landed and taxied over. Among them was McNamara, who had also greeted the plane bringing JFK to Washington for the last time.

As Robert Kennedy's casket was lowered, a stream of familiar Kennedy figures also descended, including his wife, and moved to awaiting limousines behind a gray hearse. When McNamara spied Jacqueline Kennedy on the opposite side of the motorcade, he leaped up, scrambled over the hood of her car and embraced her. Her face showed anguish but again not tears, as she relived the shattering moments of less than five years earlier. Her prediction to Schlesinger only three months earlier had proved to be devastatingly accurate.

Kennedy's body was taken to St. Patrick's Cathedral, there to be readied to lie in repose in a closed casket for public viewing. An honor guard was posted of relatives, friends and traveling reporters, with frequent rotations, that remained at the casket until it left the cathedral two days later. The viewing was not to begin until 5:30 the next morning, Friday, but already a line was forming outside. By sunrise, the line wound several blocks around and away from the great church on Fifth Avenue, and the wait to gain entry from the rear of the line was being estimated at as long as five hours.

Through the long day they came, white and black, young and old, many holding rosaries or crushed handkerchiefs, sometimes whispering a prayer as they passed the casket, or reaching out and touching it briefly. In due course, I took my brief turn in the honor guard, observing the depth of the grief expressed by those in the line that slowly passed by. The viewing was originally to end at ten o'clock that evening, but when the family saw the huge lines still forming, it was decided to continue it through the night.

Meanwhile, the Kennedy staff toiled to complete the funeral arrangements, which were to include a memorial train bearing the body and invited guests to Washington, for burial Saturday afternoon or evening, June 8, at Arlington National Cemetery. At a Solemn Requiem Mass Saturday morning attended by President Johnson, Vice President Humphrey, McCarthy and many other political luminaries of both parties, Ted Kennedy gave a memorable eulogy:

"My brother need not be idealized, or enlarged in death beyond what he was in life; to be remembered simply as a good and decent man, who saw wrong and tried to right it, saw suffering and tried to heal it, saw war and tried to stop it." His voice caught and broke slightly as he said these words, and he ended with his brother's familiar "Some men see things as they are and say, 'Why?' I dream things that never were, and say, 'Why not?'" That concluding reference carried particular poignancy for all of us who had traveled the eighty-five days of Robert Kennedy's presidential quest that was now ending. Then Andy Williams, without accompaniment, sang "The Battle Hymn of the Republic."

Afterward, about 700 invited guests were herded onto thirty buses for the short trip to Pennsylvania Station as massive crowds again lined the streets. The guests boarded a twenty-one-car train, with the last five cars reserved for the family and closest friends, and the casket in a special observation car with picture windows on each side. To make certain it could be seen from the railbed as the train went by, it was placed on chairs. For the next eight and a half hours, the train moved south past large and solemn crowds, bunched up at each station, stretched out along the tracks between them. Occasionally a high school band would stand playing a patriotic song; fathers would hold their infants high over their heads to see some passing history; boys in baseball uniforms stood at attention, their gloves over their hearts or their hands in salute at their baseball caps. Some women knelt in the hard gravel of the railbed as the casket rolled by.

The train trip, melancholy at the start, in time generated weariness but also some dark humor, as at an old Irish wake. As the hours dragged on, the trip far behind schedule, John Seigenthaler, the old Bob Kennedy associate at the Justice Department, remarked that if it lasted much longer, Kennedy would start "kicking the box." Later on, the late senator's eldest son, Joe, then fifteen, walked through the cars quietly and self-consciously, thanking the guests for coming. To the surprise of many, Ethel Kennedy did the same.

Mankiewicz took care that she was not in earshot when he briefed reporters about a tragedy that had taken place just past the Elizabeth, New Jersey, station. There, a four-car train coming north caught two trackside mourners in its path and killed them. He told the reporters also of an eighteen-year-old young man who had climbed onto a boxcar for a better view and was critically burned when he brushed against a high-voltage overhead power line.

At Arlington, a brief graveside candlelight service was held just below the grave site of John F. Kennedy in the summer darkness that had now descended on a scene also reminiscent of November 1963. Then, Robert Kennedy had been the strong, steadying shoulder on which the rest of the family, and particularly the grieving but stoic widow, leaned. This time it was the younger brother, Ted, at the side of Ethel Kennedy as she clutched the casket flag folded and handed to her, and walked off.

A gathering of the closest friends at Robert Kennedy's home went on as late as four in the morning, by which time a hundred or so mourners had taken positions at the cemetery gates to be the first to view the new grave. That next day, about 50,000 mourners, young and old, filed by the grave site, marked by a simple white cross, in stifling heat and silence. Party and partisanship held no place there; standing in line myself with my wife and three young children, I met a saddened Ben Wattenberg, then a speechwriter for Lyndon Johnson.

As tragedy, the assassination of Robert Kennedy was most obviously bracketed with the similar death by gunshot of his brother John in Dallas. But in terms of its impact on its time, the linkage was more significantly to the killing of Martin Luther King Jr. only two months earlier. Together, King and Robert Kennedy embodied the public protest of their times against a mindless war abroad and racial injustice at home.

King was best known as a civil rights activist, and he died pursuing that role; Kennedy's clearest identity was as an antiwar activist, and his death came as he pressed the case to end the American role in Vietnam. But each was involved at the same time in both causes, and together they represented a major segment of the national unrest in 1968, inspiring the most hope that the country could be brought to follow a more humane and just path at home and abroad. King and Kennedy, Marc Raskin wrote later in his book *Being and Doing,* "had been accepted as the symbols of American potentiality. It was thought that these men knew how to control violence in America and relate the white working class to the black poor." When first the one hero and then the other perished at the point of a gun, that particular American malady, shattered also was the dream of millions of an America that truly lived its principles and fulfilled its promise of a noble society.

That same Sunday, Arthur Schlesinger wrote in the *Washington Post:* "With the murder of Robert Kennedy, following on the murder of John Kennedy and the murder of Martin Luther King, we have killed the three great embodiments of our national idealism in this generation. Each murder has brought us one stage further on the downward spiral of moral degradation and social disintegration."

(Early in 1969, Sirhan was convicted of murdering Kennedy and of attempted murder in the other shootings. The jury voted for the death penalty, ignoring a letter from Ted Kennedy that observed: "My brother was a man of love and sentiment and compassion. He would not have wanted his death to be a cause for the taking of another life." The sentence was changed to life imprisonment when the state Supreme Court outlawed capital punishment.)

* * *

On the same day Robert Kennedy was being put to rest, Scotland Yard detectives climaxed an intensive manhunt at Heathrow Airport outside London by seizing and arresting James Earl Ray, sought for the murder of Dr. King. Ray, wearing eyeglasses and dressed in a light-colored raincoat, sports jacket and gray trousers, was about to board a plane for Brussels when apprehended, initially on charges of possessing a fraudulent Canadian passport and carrying a revolver without a permit.

The suspect had been tracked down through an exhaustive search by the Royal Canadian Mounted Police of more than 200,000 passport applications, and was placed under maximum security at London's Cannon Row police station. When he was arraigned on those charges two days later, the United States moved promptly, obtaining a provisional warrant for Ray's extradition to stand trial for murder.

Throughout the time that Ray had been at liberty, speculation continued that the assassin had been part of a conspiracy. The day after his arrest, however, Attorney General Clark reiterated that "we have no evidence of any other involvement by any other person or people." Concerning a theory that Ray had to have been "bankrolled" by someone to have traveled first to Canada and then to Europe, Clark said of him: "He is a person . . . who lived a life of crime, who obtained funds, money, through crime, and I think we can reason that there is a very plausible possibility as to the source of his funds."

(Ray at first insisted he was innocent, but on March 10, 1969, he pleaded guilty to murder in the first degree and was sentenced to ninety-nine years in prison. In a brief court appearance, however, in spite of his plea Ray said he did not agree with the prosecution's theory that there had been no conspiracy, but he did not choose to provide any information to support his disagreement. Judge W. Preston Battle commented that "it has been established that the prosecution at the time is not in possession of enough evidence to indict anyone as a co-conspirator in this case. Of course, this is not conclusive evidence that there was no conspiracy."

(Coretta King said she believed there had been a conspiracy and urged the state of Tennessee and the federal government to continue the investigation, which the Justice Department said it would do. Ray later denied he had shot King but appeals for a new trial were denied. Three times between 1971 and 1979, Ray tried to escape, actually getting out of the Tennessee prison that held him for fifty-two hours in 1977, but each time he was recaptured. The attempts fed the speculation that he had accomplices in the assassination. A Justice Department report released February 18, 1977, determined, however, that "the sum of all the evidence of Ray's guilt points to him so exclusively that it most effectively makes the point that no one else was involved."

(Still, speculation of a conspiracy continued, along with the major unanswered question: Why was King killed? A House Select Committee on Assassinations investigating both the John Kennedy and King assassinations reported on July 17, 1979, that it was "likely" that conspiracies were involved in both murders. Ray was interviewed eight times and provided three days of testimony before the committee but clung to his denial of guilt. He explained his travels prior to the assassination, and his admitted purchase of the murder weapon, as part of a gun-running operation in which he was involved with a mystery man he called "Raoul." The committee conjectured that the man was probably one of Ray's two brothers, Jerry or John, but failed to link either conclusively with the slaying of King.

(The committee after extensive investigations and interrogations concluded that while James Earl Ray's "lack of sympathy toward blacks and the civil rights movement would have allowed him to commit the assassination without qualms, his act did not stem from racism alone." And "while Ray's decision to assassinate Dr. King may have reflected a desire to participate in an important crime," the committee concluded, he probably did not act "solely from a need for recognition and ego-fulfillment." More likely, the committee said, "his predominant motive lay in an expectation of monetary gain," a conclusion that "necessarily raised the possibility of conspiracy."

(Further investigation by the committee uncovered reports that some segregationist businessmen in St. Louis in late 1966 or early 1967 had offered up to $50,000 for anyone who would assassinate King or arrange to have him killed. The committee suggested that Ray could have learned of the offer through his criminal associations and acted on it. Although he was found to be in dire financial straits when arrested in London, the committee speculated that his flight after the deed might have prevented payment, or that his prospective co-conspirators may have reneged on any payoff. In any event, the questions about collaborators and motives have persisted, without Ray shedding further light.)

* * *

Going into June, the fierce contest for the Democratic presidential nomination had eclipsed Richard Nixon's steady march toward the Republican nomination, despite the efforts of Nelson Rockefeller to sell the idea that he rather than Nixon offered their party the better prospect of a November victory.

On June 1, Nixon secured another anchor to his Southern base by meeting with Senator Strom Thurmond of South Carolina in Atlanta, then trotting him out to assure assembled GOP Southern and border state chairmen that they could count on Nixon to deliver the goods for them as president. Although Thurmond was aware of Nixon's pro–civil rights posture, the support of the old retired general was nailed down with a Nixon promise to maintain a strong national defense, specifically to make a start on an antiballistic missile defense system. Thurmond's support was regarded as an important element in thwarting inroads by George Wallace in the South.

But Rockefeller, in addition to his efforts to shape public opinion polls to make his argument against Nixon's electability, was seizing on any other opportunity that presented itself. So when Nixon's Southern campaign director, Howard "Bo" Callaway of Georgia, on June 1 told the Mississippi Republican convention in Jackson that independent candidate Wallace should join the Republican cause, Rockefeller demanded that Nixon repudiate the idea.

No Republican, the New York governor said, could win the presidency with Wallace "hanging around his neck or tied to him in any way." Wallace, Rockefeller went on, "is a racist and we don't need him." Callaway protested that his remarks had been taken out of context, and that all he was saying was anyone who wanted change should throw in with the Republicans. "What I said was maybe we can even get George himself on our side because that's where he ought to be" as someone who advocated change, Callaway explained.

Nixon moved swiftly to blunt Rockefeller's gambit. His own views and those of Wallace, he said, "are completely apart," and he didn't have, seek or want Wallace's support or that "of those who are racists." He elaborated that Wallace's appeal "is in the direction of racist elements, and that kind of appeal should not be made, and will not be made, by either of the two major-party candidates." Rockefeller responded that he was "very pleased" with Nixon's statement—a reaction doubted by those who saw it as effectively countering another Rockefeller attempt to sow seeds of doubt about Nixon.

Rockefeller nevertheless continued to radiate optimism, which was one of his trademarks. On June 3 in Milwaukee, he insisted that "the tide has turned," based on conversations he was having with convention delegates and party leaders who were expressing "their concern to win and a lingering uncertainty as to who can win." But if so, they were conversations that few Republicans outside the Rockefeller camp professed to hear. Even as Rockefeller spoke, Nixon was at his Key Biscayne retreat refocusing his campaign onto the August national convention and the fall campaign beyond, on the premise that he now had the nomination in hand.

By this time, Nixon law partner John Mitchell had moved into operational control of the campaign. It was decided that it wasn't necessary to spend all the time before the convention continuing to court delegates. Yet Nixon could not afford to look complacent either, or to snub important Republicans. So Nixon and his strategists decided simply to launch his fall campaign early, visiting key industrial states that would be hotly contested with the

Democratic nominee, such as New Jersey, Pennsylvania, Ohio and Illinois, and his own California.

In all the planning, the mistakes of the 1960 Nixon campaign were to be remembered and avoided. The first, obvious determination was not to exhaust Nixon by pledging to campaign in all fifty states. A strategy was devised based on a limited, carefully controlled daily schedule of appearances focused on states Nixon needed to fight for and could win.

Next, there was the matter of how to use his running mate. In 1960, there had been poor communications between Nixon and Henry Cabot Lodge, leading to some contradictory statements by Lodge that had to be ironed out. This time, the running mate would have assigned to his plane a politically astute Nixon loyalist to avoid the Lodge-type blunders. Selected for the job was John Sears, the quiet but brilliant young lawyer from the Nixon firm who was one of the candidate's chief delegate hunters. The plan was for Sears to shuttle between the presidential and vice presidential candidates' planes. But the identity of the latter would in time alter that scheme and sentence Sears to be the running mate's full-time watchdog.

The Nixon strategy in the remaining weeks before the Republican convention was to keep as low a profile as possible without seeming to be abandoning campaigning altogether. When the political world and the nation suddenly were jolted by Robert Kennedy's assassination, Nixon did not need to maintain a subterfuge. Like McCarthy and Humphrey, he shut down his campaign. So did Rockefeller, who could ill-afford lost time in his catch-up effort to head Nixon off.

Both Nixon and Rockefeller attended the Kennedy Requiem Mass in New York but Rockefeller was back on the stump three days later, telling a National Press Club audience that the country would emerge from the trauma "in a profoundly new mood," demanding "nothing short of a new government, a new party in power and a new leader at the head of the party." This longtime Eastern Republican establishment figure declared that "the men of the old politics do not understand change. They do not comprehend the new realities of American life. They do not appreciate the significance of emerging forces. They do not seem to care."

The next day, June 12, Rockefeller went to Watts and visited a predominantly black high school in an obvious bid to siphon off some of the minority support that had flowed to Kennedy. Nixon ignored him, as well as his challenge to debate, giving the standard front-runner's brush-off—that such a confrontation "would only serve the Democrats by promoting divisive tendencies among Republicans." He simply was not going to give Rockefeller even a toehold.

But the governor—and his money—persevered. He bought half an hour of national television time and plastered major newspapers with full-page ads proclaiming "Why I Run." Asked at one point what it all was costing, the multimillionaire replied: "I hate to think."

The strategy of generating support by showing public approval in the polls was not working out very well. As Rockefeller spoke at the Minnesota Republican state convention in Duluth, aides circulated a poll showing that he would beat either Humphrey or McCarthy in the state and Nixon would lose to both. Uncertain of whether Nixon could win the 60 percent of delegates to obtain the state party's endorsement, the Nixon lieutenants didn't push for it, and instead got the convention to conduct a straw poll, which Nixon won. He came out of the convention without an endorsement, but he didn't get damaged either, and Rockefeller wound up frustrated again.

The same was true as a result of a meeting of Republican governors in Tulsa on the weekend of June 15. Any hope that a gubernatorial bloc might line up behind the man generally regarded as the most impressive of their number faded and only Governor Raymond Shafer of Pennsylvania endorsed him. Several others, including former one-man Rockefeller draft leader Agnew, reiterated they would be favorite sons, which was fine with the confident Nixon camp. And so, as the Republican convention drew closer, Nixon was still on track.

*   *   *

Although Robert Kennedy's assassination did not set off the massive inner-city riots that had marked the slaying of King, the antiwar protests that had expressed his own revulsion to the war in Vietnam had continued. Some 800 delegates attended an SDS convention at Michigan State in mid-June amid much talk, eventually rejected, of transforming the loose federation of college chapters advocating radical reform into a tight revolutionary force.

In Boston, Providence and New York, federal agents dragged draft resisters from churches where they had claimed sanctuary and arrested them for violating draft laws. On June 14, a jury in Boston convicted Benjamin Spock, William Sloane Coffin and two others of conspiring to aid, abet and counsel draft dodgers, and each faced a maximum of five years in jail and a $10,000 fine. A fifth defendant, peace activist Marcus Raskin, was acquitted. Spock said he believed "a citizen must work against a war he considers contrary to international law. The court has found differently. I will continue to press my case."

In Washington's Resurrection City, the campers led by Abernathy pared their original ninety-nine demands for stronger federal action on jobs, housing, welfare, food for the poor and migratory workers' organizing rights.

About 250 of them marched on the Agriculture Department on June 12. Abernathy denounced Secretary Orville Freeman for planning to reduce "the price of food stamps to 50 cents a person for people with no income. He didn't [say] how a family with no income is supposed to find 50 cents per person for food stamps."

Meanwhile, the fourteen-wagon Mule Train from Mississippi, continuing its slow pilgrimage to the nation's capital, was halted by state troopers in Douglasville, Georgia, on June 14. All 130 riders were arrested for traveling on a busy expressway, on the order of segregationist Governor Lester Maddox, "to protect their own safety and welfare as well as the safety of motorists." They were subsequently released and drove on to Atlanta, where they were put on trains and trucks for the remainder of the journey.

In New York, a national convention of the Student Mobilization to End the War in Vietnam erupted in a power struggle between the student committee and members of the Young Socialist Alliance, with the student leaders walking out. The cauldron of the Vietnam War continued to boil.

* * *

McCarthy, meanwhile, seemed to have no fight left. On June 7, the day after Kennedy's death, he met with Humphrey at his own initiative for about an hour in the vice president's office next to the White House. According to Ted Van Dyk, who was called in by Humphrey immediately afterward, "it was clear that what Gene was doing was trying to find a reason to drop out. He wanted Humphrey to do something which would give him such a reason. He just had no more heart for it and quit campaigning." McCarthy-Humphrey biographer Al Eisele agreed. "A black mood descended on him," he said later. "He just kind of gave up."

Van Dyk recalled that Humphrey had the impression that "Gene was truly trying to help, that he was honestly and honorably trying to find some way to support Humphrey if Humphrey would just make some changes on Vietnam which don't look so major now, but they did then." When Humphrey said he couldn't, Van Dyk remembered, "there was no animus, they just agreed to disagree."

For his own part, Humphrey was not about to abandon Johnson to get McCarthy's support. That was clear in remarks he made at the U.S. Military Academy at West Point on June 8: "Our 'doves' must learn that there are times when power must be used. They must learn that there is no substitute for force in the face of a determined enemy who resorts to terror, subversion and aggression, whether concealed or open. . . . We must learn to meet and defeat our enemy on all, not just one, of the battlefields."

On June 11, McCarthy went to the White House for a briefing on national security and other issues with Johnson that was, understandably, formal and cool. The next day McCarthy held a news conference, saying "the issues remain essentially the same" as they were before Kennedy's death. He listed them as the need to reexamine not only U.S. policy in Vietnam but also "the militaristic thrust of American foreign policy," to pursue "the pressing domestic needs and particularly the problems of poverty and racism," and to continue "the test of the American political process." In the latter regard, he said, while he would find it difficult to back Humphrey as his party's nominee because of his support of the war policy, he would not lead any third-party effort against him. He intended, he said, "to work this out within the Democratic Party."

In the wake of Kennedy's death, Johnson, fearing some sort of conspiracy, advised McCarthy to go off someplace secure for a while with the Secret Service agents he had just assigned to him. Accordingly, McCarthy went into retreat for several days at St. John's Abbey, an adjunct of St. John's University, which he had attended, about eighty-five miles north of Minneapolis. Only Jerry Eller and the Secret Service unit accompanied him.

The Benedictine monks were thrilled to have the presidential candidate there, Eller recalled. They stocked their guest's room with liquor and they grilled steaks for him, creating a distinctly nonabbey atmosphere during his stay. McCarthy organized a softball team among the monks, some of them his old classmates, and they played the Secret Service agents each night. McCarthy with the monks' permission broke the customary silence with talks on politics to his hosts.

The abbey was considered an ideal safe haven for him, but McCarthy encountered a prominent priest-economist with whom he had not gotten along and who had a drinking problem. On one occasion, Eller said, the priest delivered a blackboard lecture to McCarthy that the candidate clearly resented. The priest left and sometime later, Eller said, there was an audible scuffling outside McCarthy's door. The priest had returned toting a pearl-handled pistol that another monk wrested from him. The Secret Service took the weapon but, Eller said, never prosecuted the monk, who had been drinking. Instead, after that, whenever McCarthy visited the abbey, Eller said, the priest was "paroled" to a nearby parish.

Although McCarthy resumed campaigning thereafter, he seemed even more remote than was his usual manner. His speechwriter, Jeremy Larner, wrote later: "McCarthy did not resign his candidacy; he left his lottery ticket in the big barrel to await the hand of God. But he never again addressed himself to the moment. . . . He stood all summer passive and self-absorbed in the winding-down of his campaign. . . . Now in the heat of a lost, hot, vacant summer, while millions hoped for him and waited, Gene McCarthy regressed to his balanced presentation of self, to the sacred ceremony of his personality."

While many Kennedy backers, out of their abhorrence of the Vietnam War, were now shifting their support to McCarthy, the Kennedy political organization itself was not. Sorensen said it would not switch either to McCarthy or Humphrey. Speculation that Ted Kennedy might be induced to step into the breach was cooled by associates, who also said he would not be interested in the vice presidential nomination.

McCarthy did not do his cause any good among many Kennedyites when he said at a news conference that while he favored federal registration of sidearms and "heavy guns," after twenty years in Congress "it's been my experience . . . that you really ought not to put through legislation under panic conditions." He apparently was referring to the pressure for action in the wake of the latest Kennedy assassination. "To say we'll need a different gun bill today than the one we needed yesterday or the day before," he said, "is not a good way to proceed."

The comment seemed to denigrate the significance of public opinion in forcing Congress to take tough action it might otherwise duck, and Larner later observed: "If he thought it over long and hard, he could not have chosen anything better calculated to alienate Kennedy people. The statement was more than just a political mistake, more than a random expression of McCarthy's procedural conservatism. Twist and turn it as you would, there was a kind of meanness beyond excuse or explanation."

Humphrey on the other hand shortly afterward called for immediate registration of all firearms. Congress finally passed a watered-down bill restricting the sale of handguns. Johnson signed it while calling it "only a halfway step" in the war on gun violence. A few days later, he called on Congress to require national registration of every firearm and licensing of every gun owner—a proposal that had little chance even in light of the "panic conditions" to which McCarthy had referred.

McCarthy meanwhile tried to raise the heat on Humphrey, who in the first Gallup Poll after the Kennedy assassination led Nixon by 42 percent to 36 and Rockefeller by 39 to 36. At the Idaho state Democratic convention in Idaho Falls on June 14, he challenged the vice president to debate him, saying flatly that "our party should take the most difficult issues to the people even if it destroys the party." The next day in Phoenix, he appealed to all delegates to "withhold final judgment" until the candidates had an opportunity to present their views directly to the convention—which would be a break with the tradition that a candidate should appear only to withdraw or make an acceptance speech.

Accused earlier of being indifferent to the plight of the poor and particularly of black Americans, McCarthy after first balking agreed to attend a rally for the Poor People's Campaign in New York on June 17. There, he said his agenda included "'a double challenge—first, to end the war and then to deal with the problems of the poor in America." But the plight of the poor was not a defining issue between him and Humphrey, who just two days earlier had also announced his support for the campaign. What continued to separate them was the war, and McCarthy was not going to let Humphrey easily remove the albatross of the LBJ Vietnam policy from around his neck.

As Humphrey insiders implored their man to put some distance between himself and Johnson on the war, former Johnson press secretary Bill Moyers predicted in an interview that Humphrey would "emerge on his own within a week" and spell out his differences with the president under whom he was serving. Moyers said he was speaking as a close friend of the vice president but only on a "hunch" and not "authoritatively." He added, however, that Humphrey "has to say publicly what he has been feeling privately, and that is that present policies are inadequate. . . . We must move away from where we have been, we must liquidate the war in Vietnam. . . ."

Coming from one of LBJ's closest former aides, the remarks sounded to many like a trial balloon floated to see how any kind of break by Humphrey from Johnson would play. Moyers went on to say that Humphrey had assumed the role of "public apologist" on Vietnam, defending "a policy that no one wanted to become as military as it did. He has always felt that relying on military power, instead of political solutions, is a mistake." Humphrey did not have to "campaign against the president" or shift his philosophy, Moyers said. "It is just a question of going back to what he was when he ceased to be an independent political figure."

McCarthy jumped all over that observation. "Mr. Moyers says the Vice President has private doubts about the war," he commented. "I think everybody has private doubts. There comes a time when the private doubts of a public man must become public doubts." It was basically the same taunting rejoinder McCarthy had made to Robert Kennedy's agonizing over the war before he finally entered the presidential race.

Humphrey, careful not to offend LBJ, completely sidestepped Vietnam in prepared remarks to the National Press Club on June 20. But he insisted he was "a man of change" who, if elected, would not try to "relive the Johnson administration." Referring to his son Skip in the audience, he said: "I don't ask him to live his father's life. I ask him to live his life. The President of the United States has not asked me to live his administration when I am privileged to have the Humphrey administration . . . with its own program, its own nuances, its own sense of direction, its own perspective, its own objectives."

At the same time, Humphrey said, "one does not repudiate his family in order to establish his own identity." In response to a question, he said he favored an immediate cease-fire to encourage the proper negotiating attitude in Paris but took issue with what he labeled a McCarthy call for unilateral withdrawal. Hanoi, however, brushed aside Humphrey's remarks.

McCarthy, although largely written off by now and campaigning intermittently in New York with an aloofness that crowded arrogance, got a lift there on June 18. Democratic primary voters gave him sixty-two of the state's 123 elected convention delegates, to thirty for Kennedy, only twelve for Humphrey and the rest uncommitted. Harold Ickes Jr., who led the impressive organizational effort for him in the state, observed afterward that "McCarthy didn't throw cold water on the New York primary—he pissed on it." Nevertheless, a McCarthy supporter, Paul O'Dwyer, won the Democratic nomination for the Senate in a three-way race, and in a Long Island congressional district, Al Lowenstein—"the man who dumped Johnson"—won the Democratic nomination.

If the hope was that the New York success would rejuvenate the campaign, it was soon dashed. On June 20, Curt Gans, Sam Brown and Blair Clark held a conference of McCarthy campaign leaders from around the country in Chicago, to map out a summer petition drive that would focus on generating grassroots pressure on the national convention delegates. After much talk, no conclusive decisions and a snubbing by McCarthy, the conference ended, and Gans was advised that there would be no more money for staff through the summer.

On June 22 in Minnesota, McCarthy and Humphrey separately addressed their home-state Democrat-Farm-Labor Party convention. Humphrey cited his career-long liberal record, familiar to Minnesota DFLers, and said the pursuit of peace in Vietnam was not a "cause for the timid," but rather "a lonely battle." McCarthy hit Humphrey's seeming complacency on the war, saying some party leaders "want to pretend there is nothing wrong." He said the time had come "to take the protection of our steel away from the nation which has been satisfied, for the most part, with thatched huts; to take napalm and flame throwers out of a country which has scarcely come to know the use of matches."

The stronger rhetoric didn't do McCarthy much good. Humphrey won the bulk of at-large delegates elected at the state convention. And the Vietnam plank McCarthy advanced, calling for an end to all bombing and an immediate withdrawal of 50,000 American troops, was rejected in favor of one advocating an immediate cease-fire, curtailment of the bombing of North Vietnam and participation of all parties in the political life of the unified nation.

The McCarthy forces didn't fare any better, either, at state party committee meetings in Connecticut, New York and Illinois. Their demands for delegate allocations on the basis of local primary and caucus results also were rejected, leading them to walk out in protest. In New York, where McCarthy had won at least sixty-two of the state's 123 votes elected in the primary, he was allocated only fifteen and a half by the state committee controlled by party regulars. McCarthy campaign leaders Clark and Lowenstein were specifically rejected as delegates.

Through all this politicking, McCarthy pressed his case on the war. On June 23, he suggested on a television interview show that "it might be a good thing for me, as a presidential candidate, to speak directly" to the North Vietnamese negotiators in Paris, "to find out what the possibilities for some kind of settlement and accommodation are." He said he wouldn't try to enter the negotiations but the suggestion predictably drew criticism that he would be meddling. Maybe so, he replied, "but it's official meddling. . . . This is what my campaign has been about. I've been trying to make some changes in our foreign policy with reference to peace." But ambassador to the United Nations George Ball argued that "interference of this kind would be mischievous" and would "confuse the situation and deflect the efforts" of American negotiators.

With the primaries over and the hot summer stretching ahead, McCarthy seemed to have lost a sense of perspective on the campaign. "It's as if someone gave you the football and you're running with it, but the field never ends," he said at one point. "There's no goal line. No opponent. You just run. And every time you reach a marker on the field it's always the 50-yard line."

Many in the McCarthy campaign also would have said there was no coach, or quarterback. The campaign's leadership was splintered between the original inspirers of the effort, like Curt Gans, and latecomers like Tom Finney, former Democratic National Chairman Steve Mitchell and McCarthy's brother-in-law, Steve Quigley; between the children's crusaders like Sam Brown and old professionals brought aboard after New Hampshire. The campaign was nearly a million dollars in debt and cuts had been made. Many of the young staffers were told they were being dropped—though many were working for nothing or on below-subsistence allowances. One old hand, Don Green, told Stout: "How could McCarthy fire them? He never hired them. They came when no one else would. It was as much their campaign as his."

McCarthy in his distant manner had a way not simply of ignoring his earnest and devoted young campaign workers, but of putting them down as if crediting them would take away from his personal achievement. Explaining the staff cuts to Gloria Steinem in a *New York* magazine article, he said: "It's a combination of things; partly an economy move, partly a normal cutback after primaries. And then, some of them are like ski bums in the summer. They ought to go home and get jobs. They just like to hang around." They weren't all like that, he added, "but they really should go home. Sometimes you have to get rid of a few good ones, too, because you can't just separate out the ones you'd like to go." Young staffers sent packing were left to wonder whether they were ski bums or part of the *few* good ones.

Humphrey meanwhile continued to resist pressures to put distance between himself and Johnson. "Anyone who would repudiate a government and a policy of which he has been a part in order to gain votes," he told the Oklahoma state party convention in Oklahoma City, "is not the kind of person you can trust to keep the promises he makes in a campaign and deliver on them in a general election."

Criticism of Humphrey mounted on the party's left, but so did his delegate count as he worked the nonprimary states and the party leaders who held the keys to much of the delegate selection in state caucuses and conventions. The *New York Times* reported that by its accounting Humphrey now had 1,600 delegates in hand, with only 1,312 needed for the nomination. On the stump, however, he was repeatedly plagued by antiwar demonstrations, which only served to draw more attention to his link with Johnson that he seemed unwilling or unable to loosen.

The frustration of the anti-administration forces produced a gathering of McCarthy and former Kennedy backers on June 29 and 30 in Chicago, calling itself the Coalition for an Open Convention. Organized by Lowenstein, it unanimously adopted a resolution opposing the nomination of Humphrey and laid plans for platform and credentials fights at the convention.

After declaring that "so far the democratic process has not worked," Lowenstein was asked about the possibility of a third-party effort. "We are Democrats," he said. "We are not potential troublemakers who won't accept the verdict of the people. We are the verdict of the people." But if his group failed to have an impact on the party convention, he said, "we will find some way to participate in the electoral process." Marcus Raskin, acquitted in the draft counseling case in which Spock was convicted, disclosed that one faction would work outside the coalition to put an independent party candidate on the ballot (in addition to Wallace).

Meanwhile, Tom Hayden and Rennie Davis held press conferences reiterating that there would be antiwar demonstrations at the convention. They enlisted Roger Wilkins, nephew of NAACP leader Roy Wilkins and head of the Community Relations Service in the Justice Department, to help negotiate with Mayor Daley's office for camping and march permits in Chicago, to no avail.

* * *

The peace talks in Paris dragged on throughout June, as did communist rocket attacks on Saigon and other South Vietnamese cities and towns. When General Westmoreland turned over the Vietnam command to General Creighton Abrams on June 10 to take up his duties as Army chief of staff in Washington, he frankly said that the American policy of "not expanding the war" made achievement of a military victory impossible "in a classic sense." Losses by attrition, however, could make continued fighting "intolerable to the enemy"—hardly an encouraging outlook to a nation growing ever wearier of the fighting in Vietnam.

Proponents of the war clung to small rationales for optimism. A joint session of the South Vietnamese National Assembly on June 15 approved the drafting of 200,000 persons by the end of 1968, answering a criticism repeatedly raised by Robert Kennedy. President Thieu, in signing the bill, said "we do not intend to ask the United States and our other allies for more troops, but we still need equipment and other types of help, of course." It was an overdue move, particularly with the U.S. command's report on June 20 that American combat deaths had now exceeded 25,000 since the beginning of 1961, plus nearly 83,000 wounded, and with the arrival in the previous week of a thousand more American troops, bringing the total in the country to an astounding 534,000.

Public opinion took a jolt on June 24 when a young correspondent in South Vietnam for the *Baltimore Sun*, John S. Carroll, reported that a decision had been made to abandon Khe Sanh, the military base earlier defended at great cost as a vital defense position below the old demilitarized zone between North and South Vietnam. The American command disaccredited Carroll indefinitely on grounds he had violated security regulations, but the reporter stood his ground. "The Marine privates knew about it [the withdrawal], the North Vietnamese knew about it and the only ones who didn't know about it were the people in the United States," he said. Military requirements dictated the decision, the U.S. command said, but the North Vietnamese called it the "gravest tactical and strategic defeat" of the war for the United States.

Driving home even more the frustration of carrying on the American commitment in Vietnam was Johnson's signing on June 28 of a new 10 percent income tax increase, a tangible refutation of his early contention that the country could afford both guns and butter. With half the year 1968 gone, the

United States seemed no closer to extricating itself from the military nightmare that was tearing the nation apart.

* * *

Richard Nixon, however, was content to keep playing to Vietnam hardliners in the Republican Party, who dominated its politics. In an interview on June 18, he said there was "no alternative to the war going on. We have to stop it with victory or it will start all over again in a few years."

Nelson Rockefeller sharply disagreed. "It is simply not true that the way to stop this war is to bomb on and on, and fight on and on, toward some imaginary military victory," he said. But in his party, Rockefeller was riding the wrong horse. Even his old ally Agnew now had harsh words for him. He said he was "puzzled by his lack of views" and said his own "gut reaction" was that polls suggesting that Rockefeller would make a stronger candidate than Nixon were mistaken.

Although on June 18 Rockefeller bested Nixon in the New York primary, winning seventy-seven convention delegates to five for Nixon, who contested for only eleven, the governor was no closer to stopping the Nixon steamroller. Even Senator Hatfield, one of the most outspoken Republicans against the Vietnam War, endorsed Nixon, on June 20. And on June 30, Senator John Tower of Texas, heretofore ostensibly running himself as a favorite son but in reality conducting a holding action for Nixon, endorsed the former vice president and released the fifty-six Texas delegates committed to him. Other favorite sons, openly or secretly, were poised to turn their delegates over to Nixon at the most politically propitious time.

Everything Rockefeller was doing seemed to cast him as a maverick outside the mainstream of his party—which he now was. The Republican Party that had twice nominated Tom Dewey in 1944 and 1948, Dwight Eisenhower in 1952 and 1956 and even Nixon in 1960 had begun a basic philosophical transformation with the nomination of Barry Goldwater in 1964. Nixon was not a new-breed conservative in the Goldwater mold, as for instance Ronald Reagan was. In comparison with George Romney and then Rockefeller, though, he was seen among the party's right-wing elements as much more acceptable, and malleable, to them.

One clear illustration of why Rockefeller was anathema to the Republican right came on June 26 when Johnson announced that Chief Justice Earl Warren of the Supreme Court was retiring at age seventy-seven, and that LBJ's close friend and onetime lawyer, Associate Justice Abe Fortas, would be nominated to replace him. Another old Johnson associate from Texas, federal appellate judge Homer Thornberry, would be named to take Fortas's seat, the president said.

Nixon immediately argued that because of the "transcendent importance" of the Court, "a new president with a fresh mandate" should be given the opportunity to make the choice of the next chief justice. In other words, Johnson should not fill the vacancy at the top but should leave it to his successor. Reagan and other conservatives agreed, seeing a golden opportunity to reshape the Court if Johnson delayed. But Rockefeller said it was the sitting president's "duty and responsibility under the law" to make the nominations.

Such observations were more telling among conservative Republicans than all the polls Rockefeller could muster to support his argument that he was the party's best hope for regaining the White House in November. So was a comment from Gene McCarthy on June 30 that if Humphrey failed to move closer to the McCarthy foreign and domestic positions and was nominated, "it is conceivable that I could support" Rockefeller. The prospective "endorsement" only convinced conservatives all the more that the New Yorker was not one of them. Nevertheless, he and his public opinion shapers continued their campaign, hoping enough Republican delegates would see things their way by convention time.

* * *

The other major effort to effect change by shaping public opinion, the Poor People's Campaign still mired in mud at the makeshift Resurrection City, pressed on, mounting a major protest march on June 19, proclaimed Solidarity Day. Two days before, the Supreme Court had given civil rights advocates a landmark victory by ruling, seven to two, that an 1866 Reconstruction era law barred all racial discrimination in housing sales and rentals. That ruling provided an optimistic backdrop as more than 50,000 supporters, about half of them white and including for a time both Humphrey and McCarthy, trooped from the Washington Monument to the Lincoln Memorial for speeches by Abernathy, Coretta King and other civil rights leaders.

The focus of the huge march was on the plight of the poor, but speakers including Martin Luther King's widow tied that plight to the struggle in Vietnam. She was cheered and applauded enthusiastically when she called for an end to "the most cruel and evil war in history" and the allocation of funds spent on it to a war on poverty. At one point, a group of antiwar marchers waded in the reflecting pool at the foot of the Lincoln Memorial, chanting "Hell, no! We won't go!"

Others, however, lolled alongside the long, shallow pool in a picnic atmosphere that smacked of quiet resignation. Signs like I HAVE A DREAM recalled King's famous speech at the same site five years earlier, but the more militant black power organizations were missing on the speakers' platform.

Still, a warning came from Whitney Young, the moderate black leader, that those present might be witnessing "the last march which is nonviolent and which brings blacks and whites together. . . . The nation and the Congress must listen to us now before it is too late," he said, "before the prophets of violence replace the prophets of peace and justice."

With the campaign's camping permit due to expire in four days, Abernathy vowed that "we will stay in Washington and fight nonviolently until the nation rises up and demands real assurance that our needs will be met. . . . I don't care if the Department of Interior gives us another permit to stay in Resurrection City. . . . I intend to stay here until justice rolls out of the halls of Congress and righteousness falls from the Administration. . . ."

The march itself was essentially peaceful, with only one arrest of an eighteen-year-old on a charge of carrying a loaded revolver, and the superficial stabbing of a fifteen-year-old by a band of juveniles when he refused to give them his camera. But that night police and campers outside Resurrection City clashed after six young men taunted the authorities with cries of "Gonna get me a whitey" and "Gonna get me a honky." Some townspeople joined the campers in throwing bottles at the police until Resurrection City marshals, in consultation with the police, quieted the protesters and got them back into the encampment for the night.

The next day, however, seventy-seven demonstrators were arrested when they tried to block the entrances to the Department of Agriculture. That night, some 300 campers outside Resurrection City threw rocks and bottles at police, who dispersed the crowd with tear gas. More demonstrations followed at the Agriculture and Justice departments, along with reports of more violence within the encampment. The expiration date of the permit passed with about 1,500 protesters still in place, down from a high of about 2,500. Interior said the permit would not be extended.

On June 24, as Abernathy and 260 other demonstrators were being arrested for unlawful assembly on the grounds of the Capitol, more than a thousand police surrounded Resurrection City and closed it down, peacefully arresting 124 occupants on the site. By late afternoon, Department of the Interior workers began dismantling the encampment, finishing the task the next day.

Later on June 24, another 150 demonstrators marched to the Washington headquarters of the Southern Christian Leadership Conference, where a riot of window-smashing and store-looting broke out. Police again used tear gas to disperse crowds over a twenty-block area, but the situation was soon out of hand. At eight o'clock that night, Washington Mayor Walter Washington called out 450 members of the District of Columbia National Guard and imposed an overnight curfew. When things settled down the next day, he lifted the curfew.

The Poor People's Campaign was in shambles. Abernathy was sentenced to twenty days in jail on June 25 and the others arrested with him got sentences of from two to forty-five days. When he wrote an open letter calling on the nation's clergy to demonstrate in his behalf the next day, fewer than two dozen answered his plea. And the day after the Mule Train finally arrived in Washington bearing about seventy-five protesters, the government impounded twenty-four mules on grounds that they were not being properly cared for. George Wallace, meanwhile, seized on the turmoil to call Washington "a jungle . . . where you can't walk safely with your wife and children in the shadow of the White House."

At home and abroad, violence continued to reign as the month of June drew to a close. A second popular champion had fallen victim to it when the country had not yet recovered from the shock of the assassination of the first. In London on June 27, Ray in an extradition hearing denied killing King or ever even meeting him, and Sirhan languished in a California cell. Much later, Humphrey told Albert Eisele: "This was just too much. It was like a mental breakdown for the American political community." Indeed, there was a growing sense now that America was out of control, wondering what new blow would come.

CHAPTER 8

July: False Hopes

July 5 Johnson signs flag antidesecration law; **8** Dusty Boggess, 64, National League umpire, author of *Kill the Ump!*, dies; **9** National League wins 1–0, at Astrodome, in first indoor All-Star Game; **13** Westbrook Van Voorhis, 64, film narrator who declared "Time marches on!" in *March of Time* documentaries, dies; **16** comedian Dick Gregory freed from Olympia, Wash., jail after 6-week fast protesting conviction relating to Indian fishing rights protest; **23** United Auto Workers, Teamsters form Alliance for Labor Action; **24** Pete Seeger, Joan Baez, Arlo Guthrie at Newport Folk Festival; **30** United Steelworkers Union, 11 producers agree to 3-year, 6 percent wage, benefits package; 87 Catholic theologians dissent from Pope Paul VI's rejection of artificial birth control; federal budget deficit of $25.4 billion for fiscal 1968 largest since World War II.

A month before the start of the great quadrennial national party conventions, twin exercises in self-deception were going forward in the camps of the underdog candidates of the two major parties: Gene McCarthy's in the Democratic and Nelson Rockefeller's in the Republican.

McCarthy, having contested the presidential primaries in his party and having faired surprisingly well despite setbacks, was arguing that the primary results demonstrated that he—or at least his position against the Vietnam War, shared by the late Robert Kennedy—reflected the true voice of Democratic voters, rather than Hubert Humphrey, who had not contested any primaries.

Rockefeller, having stayed out of all of the Republican primaries except his own state of New York, was alleging that they were not a true test of public sentiment or of the electability of Richard Nixon, who had swept the rest of them, because any Republican needed to attract millions of Democratic and independent votes to win in November, and Nixon could not.

In a "staff memorandum" in the first days of July that was released to the press, the McCarthy campaign argued that the fact Humphrey had received less than 20 percent of the total primary vote, largely as a write-in, marked him as a loser in the fall. On the other hand, the memo said, McCarthy in the primaries had run better in the middle-class suburbs where millions of votes were up for grabs "than any other Democratic candidate of modern times." It was an argument McCarthy had made even in the primaries he lost in Indiana and Nebraska, claiming they demonstrated he could win votes no other Democrat could get.

The McCarthy staff memo, obviously trying to buck up the troops, charged that the claim of the Humphrey camp that its candidate had as many as 500 more committed delegates than he needed for the nomination was "greatly exaggerated." The McCarthy plan was to use the remaining time before the Democratic convention to persuade delegates by demonstrating McCarthy's public appeal with highly visible rallies and town meetings, while also playing the inside game of contacting individual delegates.

The "Clean for Gene" army of young—and middle-aged—volunteers would ring doorbells to drum up public support and enthusiasm, while Steve Mitchell would plan the attack on Humphrey and credentials, rules and platform challenges at the convention in the hope of garnering delegate support.

Rockefeller meanwhile on the Republican side was pursuing a two-pronged attack of his own. The first part consisted of spending an uncounted fortune on extensive television and newspaper advertising in key states aimed at driving up his polling numbers to buttress his argument that he, rather than Nixon, could beat the Democratic nominee. The second was a frenetic personal travel schedule around the country in which Rockefeller sought to drum up impressive crowds and also court individual delegates. He too contended that his opponent's claims of having the nomination locked up were inflated, though he was having a hard time finding believers.

* * *

A third underdog had by now fired up his own campaign, feeding the public mood of unrest and contention with his special brand of rabble-rousing. George Wallace took his traveling political circus into Minneapolis on July 3 and stirred such a hostile reaction that he was forced to leave the platform. Wallace immediately blamed "anarchists" egged on by college professors. "A good crease in the skull would stop this," he said at one point. The turmoil led President Johnson on the Fourth of July to condemn "intolerance" and to urge all Americans "to communicate and reason together." But Wallace pressed on with his own particular brand of communication.

* * *

Before McCarthy could hope for any serious consideration among many Democrats, he had to climb in off a limb onto which his frustration with the war in Vietnam had perched him. His suggestion that he might go to Paris for direct discussions with the Hanoi negotiators had been perceived by many as what he himself had acknowledged it might be—meddling in a sensitive diplomatic endeavor that was the responsibility of American officials in power, not of a presidential candidate challenging the wisdom and positions of those officials. It did not require clairvoyance to foresee that if McCarthy persisted, his critics would soon be charging him with trying to scuttle the peace talks or worse—taking the side of the enemy against his own country. On July 7, on NBC's *Meet the Press*, he finally said he would forgo the Paris trip if he thought it would interfere with the negotiations.

Instead, he focused increasingly on Humphrey, at times chiding him, at times hinting there might be opportunities to narrow the differences between them—if the vice president moved away from rigid support of the policies embraced by the president under whom he still served. When Humphrey made a speech saying the United States could not be the policeman for the world, McCarthy countered in Seattle on July 12 that the statement "doesn't seem to quite square with the administration policy as it's been practiced over the past two or three years. Whether it squares with the earlier position of the vice president, I think is a question of when you define Humphrey's position."

McCarthy, drawing some very large crowds at his rallies now, insisted that his chances for the nomination were "50-50" and he pressured Humphrey to debate him. On July 19, McCarthy professed to see some movement on the war on Humphrey's part. He suggested a meeting to "clarify our differences, if there are any differences, and, if we find ourselves in agreement . . . some conflicts and some confusion within the party can be straightened out." On July 20, Humphrey agreed to a debate, but no date was set.

Humphrey meanwhile sought to give some personal identification to his own candidacy without seeming to put distance between himself and Johnson. He proposed an "open presidency" in which the views of average Americans would receive a greater hearing, through "Neighborhood Councils of Citizens" and creation of a National Domestic Policy Council on a par with the National Security Council. He called for a Marshall Plan for America's cities, starting with a pilot city as a model for the future. And in politics, he said that as far as he was concerned, all convention delegates bound to him by the unit role providing bloc voting by states were free to vote their individual preference.

But Johnson's hold-the-line position on Vietnam continued to cast a cloud over his vice president. On July 1, LBJ had resumed B-52 bomber raids on North Vietnam, amid official reports that American deaths in Vietnam in 1968 had reached 9,557, or more than recorded in all of 1967. Johnson held a high-visibility meeting with South Vietnamese President Thieu in Honolulu on July 19 and 20, at which each side vowed its resoluteness against the Hanoi regime. But it only served to remind voters that as matters then stood, a vote for Humphrey would be a vote to go forward with the LBJ war policy.

Hecklers confronted Humphrey at nearly every rally, chanting "Dump the Hump!" and competing with each other to compose the most outrageously insulting sign. One in Los Angeles was a serious contender for the honor. It said: HITLER, HUBERT AND HIROHITO. A Lou Harris poll in mid-July added to Humphrey's worries. It showed him barely edging Nixon, 37 percent to 35, while McCarthy ran ahead of the Republican front-runner, 42 to 34. Against Rockefeller, Humphrey trailed by 3 percent, while McCarthy led the New York governor by 4.

The old Happy Warrior could not seem to shed the public impression that he was a man hopelessly out of touch with the new rhythms of the day. Endorsed by black singer James Brown on a bandstand in Watts, Humphrey gamely tried to fit in. "You can do the boogaloo, man," the strutting Brown told him, "if you got soul." Humphrey, awkwardly attempting, wailed, "Oh, my goodness, Jimmy."

Humphrey nevertheless continued to roll up his convention delegate total, relying on regular party loyalists in nonprimary states. The manner in which his agents proceeded, Lowenstein said later, was contributing to his future woes. "They were acting as if every single vote they could get was important at a time when they could have acted with largeness of spirit," he said. "Some people believe that Humphrey's political stupidity began at the convention. It went way before the convention. Whether he was responsible by deciding these things or by not opposing them, his people all over the country in every [state] convention where they had an opportunity rode roughshod over the opposition in a way where what was building up was a feeling that no matter what happened, he's not going to get my vote—which feeling cost Humphrey the election."

That hardening of sentiment against Humphrey, and a growing sense among the strategists for McCarthy that, as Lowenstein put it later, "he didn't want to be nominated," had its manifestation in the Coalition for an Open Convention. "I decided fairly early in the summer," Lowenstein recalled, "that one had to be aware of the possibility that the candidate would not be McCarthy, that he would fritter away the opportunity, and that we could still stop Humphrey. . . . It is certainly true that the behavior of the McCarthy entourage and of McCarthy froze so many of the people who might have been for him and turned off so many more that had been for him, that by the time the summer had advanced a ways, it was impossible to take seriously the notion that McCarthy was going to emerge as the candidate. That was no longer a feasibility." So the focus among pragmatists like Lowenstein gradually shifted from pro-McCarthy to anti-Humphrey.

Beyond this development, "Johnson's war" remained Humphrey's main albatross. On LBJ's return from Hawaii, the president told a National Governors' Conference in Cincinnati that he would not impose a coalition government on the South Vietnamese nor would he permit "the totalitarians" in North Vietnam to force one. After the fiasco over a Vietnam resolution in support of Johnson during the 1967 "Ship of Fools" governors' conference, all he got out of this year's meeting was a general resolution praising his "long and devoted public service."

Humphrey's advisers pressed him ever harder to move away from Johnson's rigidity on the war. He had agreed to creation of a task force of fifteen experienced foreign policy and political associates to draft a Vietnam plank for the Democratic platform that would give him some breathing room without making a clean break. On July 25, the task force, headed by a Harvard professor, Samuel P. Huntington, met with Humphrey campaign aides and David Ginsburg, a Washington lawyer representing him at the convention. The prepared draft by Humphrey aide John Reilly called for an immediate halt to the bombing of North Vietnam, with hedges designed to assuage Johnson.

Humphrey was satisfied with the draft, and although Johnson had told him to clear any major statement on Vietnam with Rusk, he decided he'd better take it directly to the president. Later, he told Eisele: "I showed it to him, went all over it with him. His reaction was, in substance, 'Hubert, if you do this, I'll just have to be opposed to it, and say so. Secondly, Hubert, you ought not to do this because we have some things under way [in the Paris negotiations] now that can lead to very important developments. Thirdly, Hubert, I have two sons-in-law over there, and I consider this proposal to be a direct slap at their safety and at what they are trying to do.'"

Johnson's reply, especially the last part of it, took the wind out of Humphrey. He took the draft back to Reilly and Ginsburg and asked for a rewrite. When it was ready he took it home to Minnesota and worked it over himself in preparation for another review by Johnson. Heading into August, Humphrey still had not cleared the one major hurdle that he knew barred his way to party unity going into the Democratic convention.

* * *

On July 12, as Nixon leisurely holed up at his Park Avenue apartment in New York, he had an interesting visitor: Bui Diem, the South Vietnamese ambassador to the United States, who at the time was also doubling as a key observer for the Saigon regime consulting with American peace negotiators in Paris. He was accompanied by and introduced to Nixon by an enthusiastic supporter with a penchant for political freelancing named Mrs. Anna Chennault, the Chinese-born, naturalized American widow of General Claire Chennault of Flying Tigers fame. John Mitchell was also present. Later serving as co-chair with Mamie Eisenhower of the Women for Nixon-Agnew National Advisory Committee, Mrs. Chennault would boast that she had raised $250,000 for Nixon's candidacy and was forever thinking of other ways she could help.

A longtime supporter of the Nationalist Chinese regime on Taiwan, Madame Chennault was distrustful of American policy toward the communist regime on mainland China and suspicious of any American-negotiated deal between Hanoi and Saigon that might undermine the anticommunist South Vietnamese government.

In her book, *The Education of Anna*, she wrote that on meeting Bui Diem, Nixon told him: "Anna is my good friend. She knows all about Asia. I know you also consider her a friend, so please rely on her from now on as the only contact between myself and your government. If you have any message for me, please give it to Anna and she will relay it to me and I will do the same in the future." She is also quoted in *The Palace File* by Nguyen Tien Hung, a close adviser to President Thieu, and Jerrold L. Schecter as saying that Nixon at the meeting promised if elected to make Vietnam his top priority and "to see that Vietnam gets better treatment from me than under the Democrats."

Bui Diem, in his account of the meeting in his own memoir, wrote only that Nixon had said as he left that "his staff would be in touch with me through John Mitchell and Anna Chennault." The ambassador went on: "In the rush of flying back and forth between Paris and Washington, with side trips to Saigon . . . I soon forgot the Nixon meeting. Within a couple of months, though, it would come back to haunt me." (Chennault in her book said the meeting between Nixon and Bui Diem took place on a "snowy Sunday morning," but Bui Diem in a later interview said the July meeting was his only one with Nixon in 1968. He similarly was in touch with Democratic leaders during the campaign year, he said.)

* * *

The nation's governors of both parties, gathered in Cincinnati in an election year, were more focused on presidential politics this time around. On the Democratic side, there was much talk about the possibility of drafting Ted Kennedy to be Humphrey's running mate. Democratic Governors Richard Hughes of New Jersey and Samuel Shapiro of Illinois pushed the idea, and Mayor Daley joined the chorus. But on July 26 Kennedy, in seclusion at the family compound at Hyannis Port, squelched it. His reasons, he said, were "purely personal" and his decision "final, firm and not subject to further consideration."

As for the Republican governors, they now found themselves the objects of the affections not only of the two declared GOP presidential candidates, Nixon and Rockefeller, but also of one stealth aspirant—their colleague Ronald Reagan. While ostensibly only a favorite son for the purposes of maintaining unity in the eighty-six-member California delegation, Reagan was demonstrating the characteristics of a genuine national candidate, dropping in on Western states and schmoozing with their Republican delegates.

When Rockefeller, who seemed still to harbor visions of a "dream ticket" of Rockefeller and Reagan (in that order), suggested that Reagan was "working hard" for the presidential nomination, the Californian flatly denied it. He added that he wasn't interested in being anybody's running mate either. But in mid-July he visited and talked to Republican delegates in Texas, Arkansas, Virginia and Maryland en route to and from the governors' conference in Cincinnati. In Baltimore on July 21, he conferred with about 150 delegates and alternates from several surrounding states and the District of Columbia. His interest appeared to extend well beyond the borders of his own state.

* * *

As for Rockefeller, he picked up the endorsements of two more Republican governors, Claude Kirk of Florida and John Love of Colorado, and continued to focus on Nixon's electability. He proposed to party national chairman Ray Bliss that the party itself conduct a couple of polls, one in all fifty states and another in the big cities, matching himself and Nixon against McCarthy and Humphrey. His aides argued that the Southern states should be disregarded because Wallace was likely to siphon off their electoral votes—a contention that the Nixon camp challenged. In any event, Bliss flatly refused to get involved.

Rockefeller also pressed Nixon to debate him and fared no better. Nixon was cruising along, having just picked up the endorsement of former

President Eisenhower, recuperating from his fifth heart attack at a military hospital in Washington. The man who, in 1956, had suggested that Nixon not be his running mate for a second term told reporters he had "admired and respected" him "ever since I met him in 1952," and that any notion to the contrary had been "a mere misapprehension."

One of the problems for Rockefeller was that the more he attacked Nixon, the more he inadvertently solidified conservatives, who had no use at all for Rockefeller, behind Nixon. And given that attitude, the polls would have to show a very substantial margin for Rockefeller over Nixon to have any likely impact on party leaders and delegates. The Gallup Poll at this juncture showed Rockefeller running even against Humphrey while Nixon trailed the Democrat by five percentage points. Four months before the election, that difference was not enough to make conservative Republicans swallow hard and abandon Nixon for Rockefeller. But the governor kept pounding. When someone in a crowd in Springfield, Illinois, held aloft a NIXON'S THE ONE sign, Rockefeller shouted: "That's right, he's the one. He's the one who lost it for us in '60."

Toward the end of July, the Republican delegates began to gather at Miami Beach for the convention. As was the party's custom, platform hearings were held in the convention city during the week preceding the opening of the convention itself, and the Nixon camp made sure the hearings could not be used as a Rockefeller battleground on which to shake Nixon's grip on the nomination. Planks on Vietnam and crime, on Nixon's instructions, were sufficiently broad and noncontroversial to avert conflict.

Nixon, aware of the Rockefeller strategy, had said after the Oregon primary that "the polls . . . will be the drill down in Miami," and he was right. It was there, on July 29, that Rockefeller's balloon burst. After he had dutifully trooped to forty-four of the fifty states in the hope of driving up his public support, the *Miami Herald* that morning released the final preconvention Gallup Poll. It could not have been worse for the Rockefeller argument. It showed Nixon leading Humphrey by two percentage points and McCarthy by five, whereas Rockefeller was only running even with Humphrey and one point ahead of McCarthy. Among Republican voters, Nixon was the choice of 60 percent of those surveyed for the party nomination, to only 23 percent favoring Rockefeller.

Rockefeller's candidacy was mortally wounded—by a weapon of his own choosing. His camp was plunged into gloom, while the Nixonites gloated. "Experience in the primary elections," said Nixon campaign manager John Mitchell, "has shown that Richard Nixon runs far ahead of the polls when it comes to the actual election count. We, therefore, tend to discount the polls generally. But since it was Governor Rockefeller's suggestion that particular attention be given to public opinion surveys this year, additional interest must be centered on the Gallup Poll, which long has been looked upon as the most respected of the national polls." Then, anticipating efforts by the Rockefeller camp to try to squirm off the hook, Mitchell said he expected "there will be a separate series of gadgeteered polls, seeking to prove a specialized point of view. We predict that these will have no effect on the nomination."

Mitchell was right about the Rockefeller reaction. In near panic, the Rockefeller campaign a few hours later released a commissioned Crossley Poll indicating Rockefeller was beating Humphrey in eight heavily populated states—California, New York, New Jersey, Massachusetts, Michigan, Ohio, Pennsylvania and Maryland—and that Nixon trailed Humphrey in four of them—Massachusetts, Michigan, Pennsylvania and Maryland. Two days later another Crossley Poll commissioned by Rockefeller showed him leading both Democrats while Nixon led Humphrey but was tied with McCarthy.

Further muddying the waters was another poll by Louis Harris on July 31 that had Rockefeller leading both Humphrey and McCarthy by six points and Nixon trailing both, five behind Humphrey and eight behind McCarthy. Rockefeller aides frantically reproduced the Harris numbers and during the night slipped them under the hotel room doors of delegates and reporters. But Harris had a reputation as pro-liberal and his survey got short shrift. "To be on the low end of a Harris poll usually means to be on the high end of an election vote," Nixon publicist Herb Klein told reporters, contemptuously.

What Klein subsequently called a "pollsters' protective society" immediately swung into action. The credibility of the poll-taking business was having a rough year even before this incident, what with the wild unpredictability of the politics. George Gallup Jr., running his family's poll while his father, George Sr., was abroad, told me later: "I was under tremendous pressure to explain why we differed. Harris called me and suggested we could iron things out by showing the sequence [timing] of the polls. I jumped at the chance."

The result was a joint statement saying the "seeming differences" in their polls were "not as dissimilar as they might appear to the public at first glance" because of the times when the polling was done—Gallup's between July 20 and 23, Harris's between July 25 and 29—and "normal sampling fluctuations." Then, astonishingly, George Jr. agreed with Harris that all the findings taken together "firmly" indicated that Rockefeller "has now moved to an open lead over both possible Democratic opponents." A Nixon-Humphrey race, they said, "would be extremely close, hovering around the

50-50 mark, with Wallace perhaps holding the balance," but "the McCarthy vote has shown and continues to show the greatest amount of volatility among the four leading candidates."

Now the elation was on the Rockefeller side, but the whole business had descended to farce, and credibility was the casualty. Veteran pollster and pioneer Burns Roper said the Gallup and Harris polls indicated only that the four candidates "have roughly equal, though shifting, support among an electorate that shows something less than solid conviction." He added that while he had "the highest regard for the Gallup organization . . . it seems to me overly generous [for] Mr. Gallup to agree that . . . Rockefeller is in the lead in the absence of Gallup data that would support such a conclusion."

When George Sr. learned of the statement, he was concerned, primarily because it suggested that the Gallup organization was backing away from its own data. "It wasn't my intent to say the Harris figures were correct," George Jr. told me. "It was a gesture of friendship in a sense. It came out of all the harassment, not as a master plan to protect the polling industry."

Not since the polling fiasco of 1948, when Gallup and others stopped polling too early and reported that Thomas Dewey would beat Harry Truman, had the business of public opinion sampling suffered such a black eye. Since then, it had been a long uphill climb to credibility, but one that had been well earned thereafter, at least by Gallup in dealing with presidential and congressional elections. But the damage to the polling business was as nothing compared to what was sustained by the Rockefeller campaign. Publicists for the governor had rigged up floodlights that, when sweeping against the side of convention hotels at night, would proclaim the legend, several stories high, ROCKY CAN WIN. The Rockefeller agents went ahead with the stunt anyway, though it was now simply a reminder to arriving delegates of the conflicting polling evidence.

*   *   *

While the war remained Lyndon Johnson's preoccupation, and was a matter of personal involvement for him, another concern of both national and personal import in July was the Senate reaction to his decision to elevate his old friend, Supreme Court Associate Justice Abe Fortas, to chief justice of the United States. A bloc of sixteen Republican senators led by Robert P. Griffin of Michigan quickly formed in opposition, on grounds that Johnson had been motivated by "cronyism" not only in his decision on Fortas but also in his nomination of Homer Thornberry to take Fortas's seat.

The vocal opposition caused such a stir that retiring Chief Justice Warren said at a news conference that he would continue serving if the Senate failed to confirm Fortas "because the court is a continuous body and should have the leadership it is entitled to have." Critics of Fortas argued that no vacancy therefore existed, a contention that moved Attorney General Ramsey Clark to agree but to assure the Senate Judiciary Committee that Warren would retire "effective at such time as a successor is qualified." The Senate, he said, had an obligation to accept the Fortas nomination and "advise and consent" on it according to the Constitution's dictate.

Griffin charged on the Senate floor that Johnson had been guilty of "obvious political maneuvering to create a vacancy." He said that "such maneuvering at a time when people are in the process of choosing a new government is an affront to the electorate." He joined the chorus of Republicans who said Warren's retirement and replacement should await the inauguration of a new president in January.

The controversy came to a boil on July 16. Fortas, in an unprecedented appearance before a congressional committee by a sitting Supreme Court justice, disclosed that he had taken part in briefings and meetings at the White House on the Vietnam War and on the civil unrest it was generating in the United States. He acknowledged conversations with Johnson on the war and a telephone call he had made to a businessman friend chastising him for his criticism of the administration's spending for the war.

Fortas insisted that he had advised his friend the president only in "a few instances of national crisis" regarding the war and urban riots, and had limited himself at the White House meetings to recapitulating the views of others. He denied he had helped draft Johnson's message ordering federal troops to Detroit to quell the rioting there in the summer of 1967, acknowledging that "I did see it before it was delivered, but I did not write it."

Fortas insisted, however, that he had never "directly or indirectly, approximately or remotely," discussed with Johnson issues before the Court. Nor would he discuss any recent decisions, despite more than two hours of interrogation about such decisions by Democratic Senator Sam Ervin of North Carolina. Republican Strom Thurmond also pounded at Fortas to justify recent court decisions on the rights of criminal suspects and protest demonstrators. Fortas steadfastly declined to reply based on "limitations I believe the Constitution places on me."

In the matter of the telephone call, to Ralph Lazarus, president of Federated Department Stores, Fortas said he had called him "out of solicitude for the country as a citizen." Lazarus had publicly estimated that the Vietnam War was costing taxpayers $5 billion more than the administration was saying at the time—an allegation that proved to be correct. Fortas said he had called Lazarus in May of 1967 to tell him his estimate was "very exaggerated" and would give "an incorrect view to the American people of the . . . financial consequences of this nation's participation in the Vietnam War." He denied he had been "transmitting Lyndon Johnson's ire" in making the call, and cited eleven previous Supreme Court justices who had performed such extrajudicial services for presidents, including Chief Justice John Jay in the service of George Washington.

The propriety of these actions by a sitting member of the Supreme Court came under sharp questioning by Democrats as well as Republicans. When the Justice Department submitted a memorandum to the committee praising Fortas, Ervin denounced it as an attempt at "propagandizing the committee." The committee chairman, Senator James O. Eastland, said the department had been asked to comment.

Thornberry was also called and similarly declined to answer questions about positions he had taken as a lower-court judge. Thurmond for one refused to question him on grounds there was no vacancy and would be none until Fortas was confirmed as chief justice. The result was a suspension of the confirmation hearings on both men on July 23, with Fortas's fate much in doubt.

* * *

That night, another outbreak of inner-city violence of the sort about which Fortas had been interrogated occurred in Cleveland, in the overwhelmingly black ghetto of Glenville. A small group of militants who called themselves the Black Nationalists of New Libya, led by thirty-seven-year-old Ahmed (Fred) Evans, head of a local antipoverty project in Glenville, exchanged gunfire with police. Seven deaths resulted—three black nationalists, three police officers and one black man who had attempted to aid the police—and fifteen others were injured. Three more blacks were shot to death elsewhere in Cleveland that night as the violence spread, including burning and looting.

The outbreak occurred in a dispute over the right of Evans and his project to continue occupancy of their headquarters premises. Evans and his followers fired rifles on a police squad car maintaining surveillance on the headquarters and also on a city tow truck attempting to remove an abandoned car, wounding the driver. Police reinforcements armed with semiautomatic weapons arrived and returned the fire. Buildings were set afire by the nationalists as the melee spread.

Cleveland's black mayor, Carl B. Stokes, asked Republican Governor Rhodes to call out National Guard troops, and Rhodes ordered the first of 3,100 Guardsmen to Glenville. By the time they arrived early the next morning, however, the gunfire and rioting had ended amid heavy rains. In all, forty-eight people were arrested. Other black leaders from the Glenville and Hough sections of the inner city asked Stokes to have the Guardsmen and all white police removed from their areas. He complied, entrusting order to about 125 blacks on the Cleveland police force and several black citizens' patrols formed by local leaders.

When sporadic violence and looting recurred on the night of July 25, some Guardsmen were sent back in. Stokes ordered all bars and liquor stores closed and imposed a 9 P.M. to 6 A.M. curfew in the affected neighborhoods. Two days later, with order largely restored, the Guardsmen were withdrawn and the curfew lifted. Evans was arraigned on three charges of first-degree murder in the deaths of the three slain police officers.

The Cleveland outbreak was widely described as the first case of black extremists actually attacking police in a major city, although on July 15 Huey Newton, founder of the Black Panthers, had gone on trial on charges of shooting an Oakland patrolman to death. On July 27 in New York, the new program director of the Student Nonviolent Coordinating Committee, Phil Hutchings, called the Cleveland episode "the first stage of a revolutionary armed struggle." Such hyperbole had been heard before, but in the existing climate, his words could not be dismissed out of hand.

This concern was reinforced that night when more violence broke out in a black area of Gary, Indiana, as two police officers attempted to arrest two black rape suspects. Police said members of a black motorcycle gang, the Sin City Disciples, tried to prevent the arrests, and looting and arson ensued in the neighborhood. Another black mayor, Richard Hatcher of Gary, declared a state of emergency, ordered all bars, liquor stores and gas stations closed, and imposed a curfew as incidents of violence occurred over the next two days and nights. On July 30, Hatcher disclosed formation of a commission of fourteen black community leaders to work with city officials to restore peace. The news from Cleveland and Gary caused nervous officials of other major Northern cities to alert their police forces to be ready for another hot summer.

* * *

It seemed that the world, not just the corner of it called the United States of America, was becoming unglued. Beyond the continuing mayhem in Vietnam, the year of 1968 had already seen campus turmoil and violence in England, Italy, Poland, Spain, China and Japan; student protests and workers' strikes in France that had nearly toppled a government; left-wing riots and an assassination attempt against a protest leader in West Berlin. And then, starting in mid-July, came the worst of it—the end of the Prague Spring in Czechoslovakia.

In the fall of 1967, thousands of university students in Prague had marched on the Presidential Palace in protest of dormitory conditions and were brutally suppressed by police. The protests continued, spurring reform elements in the ruling communist regime led by Alexander Dubček to begin to challenge the rigidity of the party first secretary, Antonin Novotný.

In January 1968, the Dubček forces to the astonishment of the outside world had ousted Novotný and initiated a campaign to shed the shackles imposed by Moscow after World War II. It was the most daring bid for liberation within the communist bloc since the ill-fated Hungarian Revolution of 1956. Like a huge breath of fresh air, openness of political discussion and activity brought a sense of revival and renewal to the country, and especially in Prague.

The message of hope that spread out from Czechoslovakia—"socialism with a human face"—not only jolted the resignation of the people of the other captive countries of the Soviet bloc in Central and Eastern European countries; it also sent ripples of encouragement and boldness to restless students in France, West Germany and even the United States. A new generation weary of the oppression orchestrated by or acquiesced in by its elders had begun to take its fate, and that of its countries, into its own hands through political action. It ranged from rock-throwing and the occupation of buildings, conduct abhorrent to the political establishment, to grassroots organizing within it, or against it.

As the spirit of freedom was changing the face and mood of life in Czechoslovakia through the spring of 1968, anticommunist tracts became commonplace in the Czech press, though still within the general context of the socialist philosophy. The authoritarian regime in Moscow seethed. Its brutal crackdown of the revolt in Budapest in the fall of 1956 was supposed to have sent a sufficient message to all the Soviet satellites to keep the lid on.

In early May, the leaders of the other bloc countries were summoned to Moscow amid reports of Soviet troop movements toward the Czech border. Dubček gave personal assurances there of his country's loyalty to socialism. On May 8, Radio Prague had openly pleaded: "For God's sake, let us not repeat the tragic experience of Yugoslavia or even the Budapest events. . . . We know what we want and where we are going." Nevertheless, there were Warsaw Pact troop maneuvers in Czechoslovakia in June, and afterward Soviet forces remained, to the great consternation of the new Czech leadership and the populace.

Finally, a more specific warning signal came in an article on July 11 in *Pravda* drawing a parallel between the Budapest experience of 1956 and what was now going on in Prague. "There is nothing novel in these tactics," the article said. "Indeed, the counterrevolutionary elements in Hungary employed similar tactics when trying to hamstring the Hungarian people's Socialist gains in 1956. Now, 12 years later, the tactics employed by the people who seek to undercut the pillars of socialism in Czechoslovakia have become still more subtle and invidious."

On July 14 and 15, representatives of the Soviet Union, Poland, Hungary, East Germany and Bulgaria met in Warsaw to assess the rebellious development. Czechoslovakia declined to send anyone. The result was a letter of reprimand warning the Czech upstarts that their moves toward liberalization were "completely unacceptable" and a threat to socialism in Czechoslovakia, and demanding that they end.

At issue particularly was a manifesto signed by seventy Czech intellectuals and 40,000 average citizens calling for an acceleration of democratization. The Warsaw Pact leaders cited it in saying that while they did not "want to interfere in your affairs or infringe your sovereignty," they were disturbed about forces in Czechoslovakia that threatened "to push your country off the road of socialism, and that consequently it jeopardizes the interest of the entire Socialist system."

The Czech Party's Presidium replied that the fears were unfounded and that the steps being taken would actually strengthen support for socialism in the country. "We know that the situation is facilitated by the abolition of censorship in our country and the enactment of freedom of expression and of the press," the Warsaw Pact allies were told. "What had been spread in the form of 'whispered propaganda' etc. before can now be expressed openly." Such "assurances" were distinctly not, however, what the leaders of the closed societies wanted to hear. The Czech leadership also called on the Soviet Union to remove its troops as promised earlier.

As tensions mounted, Dubček appealed directly to the Czech people over radio and television. "All we wish to do is to create a socialism that has not lost its human character," he said. He pledged that his regime would continue on its course of democratization "to the end" and would not "depart by a single step" from that course. At the same time, he assured Moscow that it "does not threaten the interests" of socialism and in fact was "the only possible way to make our republic a really solid part of the Socialist establishment."

On July 19, however, Moscow demanded that members of the Czech Presidium meet with the Soviet Politburo on July 22 or 23 in Moscow, Kiev or Lvov for a showdown. The Czech leaders, in a gritty show of independence, replied they would be willing to meet, but only on Czech soil. Surprisingly, the Politburo acceded. At the same time, *Pravda* issued demands that Prague reinstate censorship, prohibit all anticommunist activities and restore Communist Party discipline. Also, Moscow, still not removing its troops that had taken part in the June maneuvers, demanded that Czechoslovakia permit the stationing of Warsaw Pact troops on the Czech side of its border with West Germany.

On July 23, stepping up the pressure, the Soviet Defense Ministry announced that greatly expanded maneuvers would be held along the Soviet Union's borders from the Baltic to the Black Sea, including its boundaries with Czechoslovakia. On July 27, Defense Minister Andrei Grechko publicly called on all Soviet forces to improve their readiness in light of an "attempt of international imperialism to make a breach" in the communist wall of unity.

The full Soviet Politburo and the Czech Party Presidium met in the Slovak town of Cierna on July 29 as Soviet mechanized forces in East Germany and troops in Poland were moved to the Czech border. For the next three days, the two sides argued, with Soviet Party General Secretary Leonid Brezhnev attempting in vain to shake the solidarity that Dubček had constructed among conservative and liberal factions of the Czech Presidium. At the end, the usual communiqué reporting on the "frankness and sincerity" of the exchanges did little to dispel the impression that the balmy climate of the Prague Spring was on the verge of being stifled in the hot summer of heavy Soviet disapproval.

* * *

At another time, the unfolding events in Czechoslovakia might have pushed all other news off the newspaper front pages and the television evening news programs across the United States. But the quadrennial showcases of American politics, the great party national conventions, were now about to get under way, first for the Republicans in Miami Beach and then for the Democrats in Chicago.

The conventions, for all their careful staging, still offered a glimpse of democracy in action that most Americans seldom saw. Millions of voters and nonvoters alike who ordinarily could take politics or leave it alone would spend several nights watching them unfold on television. And in 1968, they were in for an eyeful.

CHAPTER 9

August: Chaos

Aug. 8 Florida financier Louis Wolfson, 3 others found guilty of stock fraud; longest newspaper blackout in U.S. history, 267 days, ends in Detroit; **14** second Disneyland commuter plane crash in less than three months kills 21; **16** Mia Farrow divorces Frank Sinatra; 2 MIRVed nuclear missiles test-fired successfully; Federal Reserve cuts discount rate to 5¼ percent; Eisenhower suffers second heart attack in 10 days; **18** Jockey Earle Sande, 69, dies; **19** Tom Wolfe's *The Electric Kool-Aid Acid Test* published; **21** National Guard rescues 9 guards held at Ohio State Penitentiary, 5 convicts killed; **25** Arthur Ashe beats Bob Lutz in 5 sets for U.S. amateur tennis singles title; **26** actress Kay Francis, 65, dies; *Rachel, Rachel* released starring Joanne Woodward; **31** actor Dennis O'Keefe, 60, dies.

Nelson Rockefeller, having come this far in his bid to wrest the Republican nomination from Richard Nixon, was not going to be deterred by the unfortunate—for him—polling figures and controversy. On arrival in Miami Beach on August 3, he insisted that he had successfully blocked Nixon's chances of a first-ballot nomination. Nixon, he said, had only 550 of the 667 delegates he needed, to 350 for himself and 200 for Ronald Reagan. Where Rockefeller had come up with these numbers only he knew, and wasn't telling.

A first order of business for him was a meeting with his former chief gubernatorial supporter, Spiro Agnew, who came to Miami Beach as Maryland's favorite son. Together with two other governors, George Romney of Michigan and James Rhodes of Ohio, Agnew was part of a triumvirate of favorite-son candidates from states with a total of 132 delegates. By staying on the fence, the three could keep the Rockefeller candidacy alive or, by jumping to Nixon, could assure his nomination. It had to be, for Agnew, a delicious bit of irony, recalling how aggressively he had pursued Rockefeller until the New Yorker had slapped him in the face by announcing he wouldn't run—and by not giving him advance warning of his decision.

Now it was payback time. Agnew called the Maryland delegation into caucus and informed the delegates that he was bowing out as the state's favorite-son candidate and was endorsing Nixon, with whom, he said, he shared "deep ideological bonds." In the end, Nixon got eighteen of the state's delegates, to eight for Rockefeller. While that number did not clinch Nixon's nomination, it did have a major psychological effect on the convention, and on the Rockefeller camp.

When a reporter asked Agnew about the possibility that he might be chosen as Nixon's running mate, the governor brushed the question off, saying it was "not in the cards." And when the Nixon strategists asked him to place their candidate's name in nomination at the convention, the speculation was that Agnew was being thrown a bone in thanks for, in effect, thumbing his nose at Rockefeller.

There now remained only one other tactical hope for the New Yorker—a late candidacy by Ronald Reagan that could undercut Nixon's Southern base and keep him short of a convention majority on the first ballot. If he could be stopped then, supporters of both Rockefeller and Reagan reasoned, there was a possibility of a drawn-out convention in which the governors of the two most populous states, representing the left and right wings of the party, might slug it out on later ballots for the nomination. What this strategy underestimated, however, was Nixon's ability to hold the middle of the spectrum and to pull support from each extreme side if it appeared it might go over the top.

Rockefeller and Reagan each moved to stop talk that he would accept the vice presidential nomination on a ticket with Nixon, or with each other. Rockefeller said he wasn't built as "standby equipment" and that "under no circumstances" would he be Nixon's running mate, but he would be glad to "reciprocate such a possibility," since Nixon had "more experience at the job than I have."

On a television interview show, Rockefeller suggested that Nixon was telling Reagan backers: "Vote for me, Mr. Nixon, and then I'll leave it open to the convention and you can get Reagan as vice president." Nixon spokesmen called the suggestion "political fantasy." But just in case, Reagan sent a telegram to every state delegation saying he would turn down the vice presidential nomination even if the convention bestowed it on him.

Reagan, during a tour of eight states where he considered his potential support strong, was told by leading backers that they could hold very little for him unless he became a declared candidate. While he continued to insist he was only a favorite son, when asked at a news conference whether he would become "an active, full-fledged" candidate at the time his name went before the convention, he replied: "At that point you have no choice in the matter."

Soon Reagan was feeling the same pressure to get in or out from his own state delegation. On August 5, the California delegates caucused, after which former Senator William F. Knowland reported that the delegation had passed a resolution recognizing Reagan as "a leading and bona fide candidate for president." The old movie actor played the role of the political draftee with his customary aplomb. What could he say or do in the face of this genuine groundswell of support? "In keeping with the delegation's resolution," he intoned, "as of this moment I am a candidate before this convention." The word was flashed around the convention: Reagan was in.

It now became a question of whether the South would hold for Nixon, or Reagan could erode enough strength to deny him, in direct or indirect coalition with Rockefeller, a first-ballot nomination. As Reagan began working the Southern delegations, Nixon and strategists Mitchell, Thurmond and Harry Dent put their heads together. Nixon would have to give strong reassurances to the same delegations that he understood their needs, and would meet them if elected. What they wanted to hear was that Nixon would honor a reasonable pace for school desegregation, would appoint conservatives of their liking to the Supreme Court, would not cut and run in Vietnam and would choose a running mate with whom the South could live.

On the morning of August 6, Nixon met with two separate groups from Southern states. It so happened that a reporter for the *Miami Herald* obtained a tape recording of Nixon's remarks to the second group. That night, as the Nixon campaign held a lavish reception for all convention delegates, an account hit the streets of the convention city that for a time seemed to jeopardize his first-ballot nomination.

It was not so much what he said privately—he had made the same points publicly—as the language he used to flutter the Dixie hearts. Denying "some cockeyed stories that Nixon has made a deal" on his running mate, he proclaimed: "I am not going to take, I can assure you, anybody that is going to divide this party." The audience greeted that statement with heavy applause, because they knew it meant rumors that Nixon might try to jam Mayor

Lindsay of New York or Senator Charles Percy of Illinois down their throats were off base.

Asked whether he favored "forced busing of schoolchildren for the sole purpose of racial integration," Nixon replied that the problem existed in the North as well as in the South. "I don't believe you should use the South as the whipping boy, or the North as a whipping boy," he said. "I think that busing the child—a child that is two or three grades behind another child—into a strange community, I think that you destroy that child. The purpose of school is to educate." And on the Supreme Court: "I think it is the job of the courts to interpret the law and not make the law. I know there are a lot of smart judges . . . but I don't think there is any court in this country, any judge in this country, either local or on the Supreme Court . . . that is qualified to be a local school district and make the decision as your local school board."

Regarding his support of federal open-housing legislation, he bluntly gave a politician's answer to a group of politicians. Since Congress had to consider it, he said, it was better to "vote for it and get it out of the way . . . to get the civil rights and open-housing issues out of our sight so we didn't have a split party over the platform when we came down here. . . . Did you want to have it come down here to Miami Beach and fight it out then? . . .

"I want a united party. I know that when those Democrats meet in Chicago a couple of weeks from now, they're going to be hammering at each other. They're going to have majority planks and minority planks." That wasn't going to happen in Miami Beach, he said, because "some of us made those hard decisions and got some of these issues out of the way—maybe not the way we all like it, but out of the way, acted on, and now we can move in another direction." If Nixon's listeners wanted to conclude that he really wasn't all that strong for open housing, so be it.

That was one of Nixon's greatest appeals to fellow Republicans; he was flexible and accommodating, depending on the political imperative. The newspaper account of what Nixon had told the Southern delegates did him no harm; the important thing was that his remarks had fortified his delegates against the late efforts of Reagan to woo them away.

As usual, the Republican convention was essentially a lily-white, upper-middle-class affair that was more inclined to favor a tough law-and-order approach to street protest than to tolerate or seek to accommodate demonstrators. Nevertheless, the Poor People's Campaign brought its effort to Miami Beach on August 6 led by Abernathy. He declared his forces, arriving by symbolic mule-drawn covered wagon, "representatives of the 51st state—that of poverty." They demonstrated peaceably in front of the garishly ornate Fontainebleau Hotel, the convention headquarters, and some gained entry to the convention hall gallery.

Abernathy called Rockefeller "one of the last chances for the Republican Party to really win back the black vote." While stopping short of endorsing Rockefeller, he said Nixon "cannot bring about the type of victory for all Americans so desperately needed for the Republican Party."

The answer Abernathy got from the convention that night was not what he was looking for. Senator Everett McKinley Dirksen of Illinois, the platform chairman, railed against "the tyranny of the looter, the blackmailer, the arsonist" and asked: "Must this free people forever indulge lawlessness and violence? Must law-abiding citizens don bullet-proof vests safely to take an evening stroll? Must we avoid our great cities by night as if they were hamlets, guerrilla-infested, in Vietnam?"

House Minority Leader Gerald Ford pledged that a Republican administration would "meet the problems of the cities and depressed rural areas, the problems of welfare, the problems of unemployment and underemployment and crime." Former presidential nominee Tom Dewey, however, seemed to speak more directly to the street protesters in saying: "We are not a sick country, and it doesn't need a revolution or anarchy to cure its ills."

Nixon had already made clear through his lieutenants that he really didn't care all that much what was in the party platform. He just wanted it to be palatable enough to all factions in the party to insure passage without a unity-threatening squabble. As a result, the platform served up pabulum, including a Vietnam plank that pledged "peace in Vietnam, neither peace at any price nor a camouflaged surrender of United States or allied interests, but a positive program that will offer a fair and equitable settlement to all. " Even Senator Hatfield, one of the most prominent Republican doves on Vietnam, could swallow that as he prepared to second Nixon's nomination.

Agnew's speech nominating Nixon on the night of August 7 was no barn-burner. As Nixon's strategists labored to help the delegates forget the loser Nixon of 1960 and 1962, Agnew described him as "a man who had the courage to rise up from the depths of defeat six years ago and make the greatest political comeback in history."

Rockefeller by now was bowing to the inevitable, but Reagan continued to work the Southern delegations, spurred by his manager, F. Clifton White, a veteran of the 1964 Barry Goldwater nomination drive, in the hope of still blocking a first-ballot Nixon victory. Nixon was so confident by this time that he slipped out for a drive with his Secret Service men and a couple of wire service reporters. If either Rockefeller or Reagan had entered and beaten him in a single early primary, he told them, his loser image might have been resurrected and have cost him the nomination. But because neither did, he said, the race was all over on the night of the Oregon primary.

What Nixon did not see on a sheltered ride around Miami Beach was an explosion of the very lawlessness the party platform deplored, in a black section known as Liberty City several miles northwest of the convention hall, in Miami proper. The trouble reportedly was kicked off when a white reporter covering a black power rally refused to show his credentials. Police moved in, arrested fifty-two people and cordoned off an eight-block area. Abernathy and Florida Governor Claude Kirk left the convention hall and rushed to the scene, Abernathy pleading on television to the residents to "move now in constructive channels to put an end to this violence." Calm was restored by 10 P.M., but only temporarily.

Back at the hall, it was not until 1:20 A.M. on August 8 that the roll call of the states began. Nixon, in his hotel suite, kept score on a pad with his family and close friends and aides, and a CBS television crew observing the historic moment. The key state was Florida, which despite heavy lobbying by Reagan gave thirty-two of its thirty-four votes to Nixon. "If it hadn't been for Strom and Goldwater," Clif White said later, "Nixon never would have gotten the South."

New Jersey, supposedly holding for favorite-son Senator Clifford Case, gave eighteen of its forty votes to Nixon, and the dam was broken. Wisconsin put him over the top, and when it happened, the reaction in the Nixon suite demonstrated the confidence there. No champagne corks popped and no wild cheering ensued. Pat Nixon rose from her chair off to the side, walked over to her husband, patted him on the shoulder, then walked off. The final first-ballot tally was Nixon 692 votes, Rockefeller 277, Reagan 182, Governor Rhodes, Ohio's favorite son, 55, Romney 50, Case 22, others 55.

* * *

After taking a brief congratulatory phone call from Rockefeller, Nixon turned to the matter of selecting his running mate. In 1960, he had called in some three dozen party leaders and let them think they had convinced him to pick Henry Cabot Lodge—an obvious choice anyway. This time, the choice he had already decided to make was not by any measure an obvious one. But he wanted to create the impression again that he had consulted with a broad spectrum of party leaders, not because he felt he needed their advice but because he believed it was good politics to let them feel they were being listened to.

In advance of the convention, Nixon had sent letters to a host of party leaders soliciting their choices for his running mate. At the same time, he had his pollsters test the relative strengths of the various prospects to gauge which of them would be of most help to his election chances, or least damaging. "The vice president can't help you," he told his closest aides, "he can only hurt you." The internal polls, John Sears told me later, indicated that none of the prospective running mates would help Nixon. "Actually, we wanted to run without a vice president," he said, only half joking. Not being able to take that option, Nixon decided on the next best one—a nobody, someone not known nationally enough to do him much harm.

Having decided, Nixon now tested his choice by holding three meetings with different groups of staff aides and important political supporters. "The meetings were like the letters," Sears said, "to make everyone feel he was in on it." One faction, including speechwriter Ray Price, preferred Lindsay to appeal to Northern liberals, but that was out of the question in light of what Nixon had told the Southern delegations. Another faction, including Buchanan and Sears, wanted Reagan as a man who could counter the strength of George Wallace in the South and free Nixon to campaign elsewhere, but he would drive off liberal and moderate voters. Party unity was the goal that had to dictate the choice.

Nixon had already decided he wanted someone perceived as being in the middle, and a governor with some domestic experience, because Nixon himself expected to concentrate on foreign policy. And finally, he told Buchanan and others, he didn't want any "superstar" who might outglitter him. All those mentioned most often by the party leaders—Senators Percy, Hatfield and Howard Baker of Tennessee, Governors Romney, Dan Evans of Washington and John Volpe of Massachusetts, Congressmen George Bush of Texas and Rogers Morton of Maryland, John Gardner, the former LBJ secretary of health, education and welfare—had one drawback or another. And there was Robert Finch, California lieutenant governor and longtime Nixon confidant.

When Nixon met with the first group of staff people and party leaders, all the usual names came up. Finally, casually, Nixon asked: "How about Agnew?" Most said they didn't know much about him. Well, Nixon volunteered, he had made a hell of a nominating speech, which he hadn't. "The only reason Nixon said that," Sears told me later, "was to give the guy a credential." When nobody jumped on the Agnew idea, Nixon did not press it, instead commenting only that "your general advice is that I pick a centrist"—which he intended to do all along.

In the second meeting, peppered heavily with members of Congress, Agnew again was not mentioned until Nixon threw his name into the pot. According to Goldwater later, when the meeting broke up at around 5:30 A.M., Nixon walked him to the door and "put his arm around me. 'Could you live with Agnew?' he asked. 'Hell, yes,' I told him, 'he's the best man you could have. He's been firm, and so what if he's not known? No vice presidential candidate ever is.'" Goldwater knew whereof he spoke, having selected the forgettable William E. Miller of New York as his own running mate four years earlier.

After a short nap by Nixon, a third group was assembled of mostly congressional leaders, and again Agnew's name came up only when Nixon mentioned it. Nixon was disturbed that nobody had picked up on his suggestion when he threw it out. He called one more meeting of his six key advisers: John Mitchell, Los Angeles public relations man H. R. "Bob" Haldeman, former Representative Bob Ellsworth, Senator John Tower, Rogers Morton and Finch. The latter two were on Nixon's final list, along with Volpe and Agnew.

When Nixon asked their preference, one of the six pressed Finch on him, but Finch objected emotionally, shouting that "I won't put myself through it!" Nixon took him into an anteroom and the two talked for a few minutes beyond earshot of the others. Then Finch came out, composed, followed by Nixon, who turned to Morton and said: "Call Agnew." Rockefeller later told me: "I talked to Strom Thurmond that night, and he was describing how they had picked. He said the basis of the selection of Mr. Agnew was that he was the least worst of the candidates that were proposed by Mr. Nixon. That was his description."

Morton got Agnew on the phone and handed it to Nixon, who made the offer. Agnew immediately accepted, hung up, turned to his wife, Judy, and said, simply: "I'm it."

Nixon broke the news at a midday news conference at his hotel, milking his surprise for all it was worth. He said all the customary things—that he wanted "a man who was, first, qualified to be president; second, one who could campaign effectively; and third, one who could assume the new responsibilities that I will give the new vice president, particularly in the area of the problems of the states and the cities." When he finally said "Governor Agnew of Maryland," a gasp ran through the room, followed by unbelieving chatter as Nixon strode out, smiling. The question of the hour—and of many an hour thereafter—was born: Spiro who?

Agnew, who had been watching on television, went to Nixon's suite for a brief conference with him and then came down for his own news conference. The assembled reporters had been shocked, but they knew enough about Agnew's recent clashes with black leaders in Baltimore and his racially inflammatory statements to zero in on them.

"I am on record with many, many statements on civil rights," he said. "I am pro–civil rights. I am for implementation of civil rights, not just the elaborate programming and distribution of money which is intended to bring about the equal opportunity and the justice that everyone talks about. On the other hand, I expect fully that no civil rights can be realistically achieved without the restoration of order, without the abandonment of the condoning of civil disobedience." That latter remark dovetailed comfortably with Nixon's central law-and-order theme. Buchanan remembered later Nixon telling him: "I think we've got ourselves a hanging judge."

Agnew said he would "welcome the chance" to campaign in inner-city ghettos to help the ticket. He said he couldn't "analyze any strength I bring, and I agree with you that the name of Spiro Agnew is not a household name. I certainly hope that it will become one within the next couple of months."

The choice jolted party liberals who considered Agnew a turncoat against Rockefeller and assumed he had just been rewarded for the switch. Romney expressed concern that the selection would cost the party black votes, but party conservatives were satisfied. Reagan called Agnew "a darn good man" and Thurmond said he was acceptable "because he stands for the principles of the Constitution, and he stands very strong on what I think is going to be the number-one issue of the campaign—law and order."

That judgment was punctuated out on the streets of Liberty City that same afternoon, when crowds of blacks clashed with police at the site of a meeting at which Abernathy and Kirk were to speak. Neither showed up and the crowd rioted. A thousand National Guard troops were sent in along with a state highway patrol wagon and an armored truck spraying tear gas. Motorists were pulled from their cars and beaten; grocery and liquor stores were looted and fires were set, leading Kirk to impose a curfew over a 250-block area. Before order was restored, three black men were killed in gunfire with police, one of them a passerby caught in the crossfire, and disorder spread to within a mile of the convention hall. About 250 persons were arrested, then released amid charges of police brutality. The curfew remained in force for three days under a reduced National Guard presence.

Some party liberals were so distressed at the choice of Agnew that they tried to get Lindsay to agree to have his name placed before the convention on the final night. Lindsay, not willing to tilt at a windmill, declined and agreed to second Agnew's nomination, to be placed by Morton. Percy also agreed to second the nomination. Other liberals, however, turned to Romney and somehow convinced him to step into the breach. They thereby assured a second humiliation for the affable but explosive Michigan governor who had once been regarded as the front-runner for the presidential nomination but had been chased out of the race in New Hampshire.

Agnew won on the first ballot with 1,120 votes to only 186 for Romney, ten for Lindsay and one each for Senator Edward Brooke of Massachusetts and Governor Rhodes, who had sat on Ohio's large bloc of votes as a presidential favorite son to the bitter end. Romney moved to make the vote unanimous for Agnew, and it was. Agnew accepted, saying "I stand here with a deep sense of the improbability of this moment," about which few would have argued. "More important than words in this campaign and in the next administration will be action," said the man who was soon to wage a war of words that would in time make his own name, as he hoped, a household word.

Nixon's acceptance address was essentially a rehash of the speech he had been making over the past several years of his political resurrection, full of ominous references to fear and violence balanced with uplifting calls to patriotism, strength and, always, law and order:

"As we look at America, we see cities enveloped in smoke and flame. We hear sirens in the night. We see Americans dying on distant battlefields abroad. We see Americans hating one another, fighting each other, killing each other at home. And as we see and hear these things, millions of Americans cry out in anguish: Did we come all this way for this? Did American boys die in Normandy and Korea and Valley Forge for this?

"Listen to the answers to those questions. It is another voice, it is a quiet voice in the tumult of the shouting. It is the voice of the great majority of Americans, the forgotten Americans, the non-shouters, the non-demonstrators. They're not racists or sick; they're not guilty of the crime that plagues the land; they are black, they are white; they're native born and foreign born; they're young and they're old. They work in American factories, they run American businesses. They serve in government; they provide most of the soldiers who die to keep it free. They give drive to the spirit of America. They give lift to the American dream. They give steel to the backbone of America. They're good people. They're decent people; they work and they save and they pay their taxes and they care."

These forgotten Americans, he said, knew that "when the strongest nation in the world can be tied down for four years in a war in Vietnam with no end in sight, when the richest nation in the world with the greatest tradition of the rule of law is plagued by unprecedented racial violence, and when the President of the United States cannot travel abroad or to any major city at home without fear of a hostile demonstration, then it's time for new leadership for the United States of America."

Nixon got one of his greatest ovations when, in observing that "the first civil right of every American is to be free from domestic violence," he pledged that "if we are to restore order and respect for law in this country, there's one place we're going to have to begin: We're going to have a new Attorney

General of the United States of America!" Presidents-elect of an incoming party always replaced the head of the Justice Department, but Nixon made it sound as if he were leading a revolution. The delegates erupted in cheers as if they thought he was.

At the end of the speech, Nixon talked sentimentally of his life's journey in a way that seemed uncharacteristically genuine for this most artful of politicians. He told of a nameless child who "hears a train go by. At night he dreams of faraway places where he'd like to go. It seems like an impossible dream. But he is helped on his journey through life. A father who had to go to work before he finished the sixth grade sacrificed everything so that his sons could go to college. A gentle Quaker mother with a passionate concern for peace quietly wept when he went to war, but she understood why he had to go. A great teacher, a remarkable football coach, an inspirational minister encouraged him on his way. A courageous wife and loyal children stood by him in victory and defeat. And in his chosen profession of politics first there were scores, then hundreds, then thousands and finally millions who worked for his success. And tonight he stands before you, nominated for President of the United States of America. You can see why I believe so deeply in the American Dream."

It was indeed the stuff of which dreams were made: a man defeated for the presidency eight years before; that defeat compounded by the disappointment of another rejection when he bid to become governor of his state; a pronouncer of his own political death in his famous "last press conference" after that second defeat; the long climb back to political resurrection, first in the service of his party, then in a string of presidential primary victories that again had yielded him the nomination of his party. Most men in political life seldom got one shot at the presidency; here was Richard M. Nixon positioned for his second, with the opposition party in turmoil and division—a turmoil and a division about to be deepened as seldom before at another great national convention, in Chicago.

The day after the Republican convention closed, Nixon held a press party at his Key Biscayne hideaway. Speaking of his surprise selection of Agnew, he said: "There is a mysticism about men. There is a quiet confidence. You look a man in the eye and you know he's got it—brains. This guy has got it. If he doesn't, Nixon has made a bum choice." In due time the jury would be in on that one.

For all of Nixon's expressed confidence in his running mate, he was surprised at the intensity of the negative press reaction, emphasizing as it did Agnew's recent clashes with civil rights leaders in Maryland and painting him as a onetime liberal rapidly moving to the right. That reading disturbed

Agnew too, leading him to observe in an interview in his suite at the Eden Roc before leaving Miami Beach: "It's being made to appear that I'm a little to the right of King Lear, [who] reserved to himself the right to behead people, and by my definition that's a rightist position."

Defending his own civil rights record, Agnew said the criticism was "hard to take for a guy who passed the first local public-accommodation legislation south of the Mason-Dixon line. For the son of an immigrant who felt the sting of discrimination, it's hard to be referred to as a bigot. I think it should be completely obvious that if my civil rights position were what has been depicted, John Lindsay would never have seconded my nomination and neither would Chuck Percy. And since Mr. Nixon sees my role in the cities as vital during the campaign, I would never be effective in those areas. But this doesn't mean that I condone violence."

Agnew pressed on. He was not, he insisted, "one of the hard-liners who thinks people should be shot, who thinks property is more valuable than lives. I want to show you how ridiculous that is," he said, proceeding to offer the kind of justification for his thinking that in short order would only augment the image of himself he seemed so determined to dispel.

"When someone breaks and enters," he explained, "the police officer doesn't know whether someone has stolen a diamond ring, a loaf of bread, murdered the storekeeper or raped his wife. So, the policeman says 'Halt' or 'Stop,' and at that point the man runs away, and the police officer has to decide whether to stop him by whatever force is necessary, or not to stop him. The officer doesn't know what crime has been committed. If the law officer sees a grocery front broken and sees a ten-year-old kid with a bag of candy, he's not going to shoot him." But, Agnew went on, "I think it would be a tremendous deterrent if everyone who ran from arrest thought the police officer was going to decide it was a serious crime and that he's going to get shot."

If Agnew's intent in these remarks was to convince voters he was no hard-liner, it obviously failed, particularly among blacks. On August 11, for example, baseball Hall of Famer Jackie Robinson, then an aide to Rockefeller, resigned his post because, he said, he could not back the "racist" Nixon-Agnew ticket, which Rockefeller had pledged to support. Nixon, Robinson said, had "prostituted himself" to Southern Republicans to assure his nomination. Four days later, the only black on Agnew's personal staff, Dr. Gilbert Ware, resigned, saying he could "no longer accept an association, however peripheral, with positions with which I have fundamental objections."

Agnew felt obliged, as he took to the campaign trail in mid-August, to give repeated reassurances that, as he put it in a Seattle speech on August 19, "a man can be totally pro–civil rights and totally against civil disobedience."

And addressing a Veterans of Foreign Wars convention in Detroit two days later, he observed: "With law and order must come justice and equal opportunity. Law and order must mean to all of our people the protection of the innocent, not to some the cracking of black skulls."

Nixon's strategists nevertheless began to wonder what kind of tiger they had by the tail. Before long, however, they came to see the value of having a running mate who was so willing and able to hold the party's right flank, even as he professed that he was no right-winger, while Nixon himself strove to remain on the high road, above the battle. The only problem was Agnew's defensiveness; candidates of the party out of power had to be on the attack, and it wouldn't do to have a running mate spending his time explaining himself to critics. As Nixon had told his aides in considering the selection of the number two man on the ticket, "a vice president can't help you, he can only hurt you." It would not be long, though, before Agnew would go on the offensive, with a vengeance.

* * *

As the Democratic convention approached, Lyndon Johnson's Vietnam War policy, supported in all significant aspects by Hubert Humphrey, continued to splinter their party.

On August 1, the American command in South Vietnam announced that 4,500 men of the First Brigade of the Fifth Infantry Division had arrived in South Vietnam, bringing the American commitment to 541,000 troops. It was reported shortly afterward that American planes had now flown more than 107,000 attack sorties against North Vietnam, dropping 2,581,876 tons of bombs and rockets there over a period of three and a half years. The precision of the bookkeeping was a commentary on the statistical approach to waging war under the efficiency of former Secretary of Defense McNamara, who had presided over the American effort for all but a few months of that time.

The peace talks in Paris dragged on with little prospect for a breakthrough, as Hanoi continued to demand an unconditional halt to all American bombing of North Vietnam, without any reciprocal action. Johnson's patience seemed at an end. "The next move must be theirs," he told the VFW convention in Detroit. "Let's don't be hoodwinked. We are not going to stop the bombing just to let them step up the bloodshed. . . . This administration does not intend to move further until it has good reason to believe that the other side intends seriously to join us in deescalating the war and moving seriously toward peace. We are willing to take chances for peace, but we cannot make foolhardy gestures for which your fighting men will pay the price by giving their lives."

The murder of Robert Kennedy, to which Sirhan had pleaded not guilty on August 2, had deprived the antiwar forces of their most impassioned voice, but many of his followers continued on in the cause of extricating the United States from the war. On August 3, a Committee for a Democratic Convention was announced to rally support against Humphrey and the administration war policy. For a few days, according to Richard Stout, McCarthy, realizing his own chances of nomination were slim, considered seeking a truly compromise unity candidate such as Senator Edmund Muskie of Maine. But the idea never got off the ground.

The Coalition for an Open Convention meanwhile also hoped to find an alternative to Humphrey. If any notion remained that it could be a vehicle for McCarthy's nomination, it had faded by now and the coalition focused on various platform and credentials issues, with the long-shot objective of somehow thwarting Humphrey. At one point, Lowenstein said, he asked McCarthy to speak at the coalition's meeting in Chicago but "there were a lot of the Kennedy people and black people and others who simply would not come if McCarthy was to speak," on grounds the event would be seen as a McCarthy rally. So McCarthy was never really invited.

The coalition met in an indecisive conference and later in the month canceled its plans for a march and rally when city officials refused a request for use of massive Soldier Field downtown, along Lake Michigan. Such an event, Lowenstein said, would have provided a nonviolent channel for the mushrooming protest and anger. He lamented that the Democratic Party leadership "seems determined to have a confrontation that can only produce violence and disruption. . . . I cannot now view Chicago," he warned, "with anything less than a sense of dread." (Some members of the coalition subsequently joined the beginnings of a fourth-party movement at the conclusion of the Democratic convention.)

On August 10, Senator George McGovern announced his own candidacy for the Democratic nomination, essentially representing the forces that had worked for Kennedy's nomination. McGovern said he was committed to the "twin goals for which Robert Kennedy gave his life—an end to the war in Vietnam and a passionate commitment to heal the divisions in our lives here at home." While he did not claim "to wear the Kennedy mantle," he said, he hoped he might "serve as a rallying point for his supporters."

Three highly visible Kennedy associates—Salinger, Schlesinger and Mankiewicz—endorsed McGovern amid word that he would also have the support of Ted Kennedy, still in isolation after the assassination of a second brother. Mankiewicz said much later that "we sort of talked ourselves into the possibility that it [the nomination of McGovern] could happen. It was not clear to us that Humphrey had it on the first ballot. Our thinking was that George would be everybody's second choice."

As for McCarthy, he observed dismissively that "I would rather have had his endorsement." He suggested that the McGovern candidacy might provide a stopping-off point for Kennedyites not immediately ready to support his own campaign.

McGovern praised both McCarthy for his opposition to the war and Humphrey as a champion of social justice at home, and said that while he could support either one if he was nominated, he expressed reservations about both of them overall. He said he would fight for a strong antiwar plank at the party convention, including a call for an immediate halt in the bombing of North Vietnam, in a war that was "the most disastrous political, moral, diplomatic blunder in our national history."

McCarthy said he too could support Humphrey as the party nominee if Humphrey's views on the war became "reasonably close" to his own, but at this point they were far from that. Humphrey was laboring hard to win a modicum of breathing room on Vietnam from Johnson, to no avail. On August 9, the day after Nixon's nomination, Humphrey flew to the LBJ Ranch with yet another Vietnam speech draft. It included a Humphrey pledge to "not do or say anything that might jeopardize the Paris peace talks," and called for a bombing halt over North Vietnam only "when reciprocity is obtained from North Vietnam." Still Johnson balked.

"You can get a headline with this, Hubert," Humphrey later told Eisele Johnson had said, "and it will please you and some of your friends. But if you just let me work for peace, you'll have a better chance for election than by any speech you're going to make. . . ."

Humphrey told Eisele that as he read the situation, Johnson "couldn't help feel that here he was, a man that had given up the presidency, and here was his vice president, a man that was maybe going to get the presidency, and how could that vice president not endorse everything that the president had been for? . . . He had put so much into it and gone through so much pain and suffering for it, that there was just no way that he could disengage himself from it. And any retreat from his position that he didn't make himself looked like it was sabotaging his efforts."

Beyond that, Humphrey had a sense that Johnson, as he told Eisele, "was in the throes of feeling that maybe he shouldn't have resigned," and might have been thinking about going to the convention and being renominated by acclamation. While Humphrey said he didn't think that was much of a possibility, it was a thought. So he hung in with his president on Vietnam. "We are now at a point where, if we do not weaken our position with Hanoi by loose talk, that we have a better chance of gaining progress at the peace talks than at any point up to date," Humphrey said on a television interview show two days later.

* * *

The day after Humphrey's unhappy visit to the LBJ Ranch, Nixon as the new Republican presidential nominee paid a call. Clifford in his memoir wrote later of Johnson: "His anger at Humphrey led him toward his old adversary, Richard Nixon." Several weeks earlier, Clifford wrote, LBJ had told him: "I want to sit down with Mr. Nixon to see what kind of world he really wants. When he gets the nomination he may prove to be more responsible than the Democrats. He says he is for our position in Vietnam." After the meeting with Nixon, Clifford wrote, Johnson told him "that Nixon had said that as long as the Administration did not soften its position, he would not criticize us. I was as appalled as the President was pleased."

Clifford wrote that he told his closest civilian advisers at the Pentagon: "This is good news for Nixon. If I were Nixon, the development that would worry me the most would be an announcement that the bombing was being stopped in response to indications that progress was being made in Paris. Nixon's game plan is to offer us his support in return for inflexibility in our negotiating position, and thereby freeze poor Hubert out in the cold. . . . Nixon has outmaneuvered the President again, digging him in more deeply. Nixon is trying to hang the war so tightly around the Democrats' neck that it can't be loosened."

Around the same time, Nixon's good friend Anna Chennault visited South Vietnamese President Thieu in Saigon. The purpose, she wrote later, was "an informal presentation of credentials. I was delivering a message from Nixon requesting that I be recognized as the conduit for any information that might flow between the two." She also discussed the progress of the Paris peace talks, she wrote, and reported to Nixon and Mitchell upon her return that Saigon "remained intransigent" in its "attitudes vis-a-vis the peace talks."

* * *

McCarthy meanwhile continued to hint at a clean break with the Democratic Party. At a news conference in St. Louis on August 13, he said he would consider supporting an independent party movement against the war if he thought it had "substantial" voter support, but added he did not see one developing and in any event he would not lead it. Two days later, in New York's Madison Square Garden, a huge celebrity-studded rally, linked by closed-circuit television with others in about thirty other cities, sought to demonstrate that the McCarthy campaign still had vitality. But the impact on convention delegates was dubious.

Humphrey made what gestures he felt he could to conciliate his liberal antiwar opponents short of alienating Johnson. On August 17 he proposed a draft lottery confined to nineteen-year-olds to get rid of the onerous policy whereby student deferments benefited the well-off and penalized the poor and the black. He added that he would not keep General Hershey, the head of Selective Service who had wanted to target outspoken critics of the war for the draft.

Humphrey even compared himself to Robert Kennedy in a speech to the Liberal Party in New York, saying they "came to hold remarkably similar views on many, many questions, and, believe it or not, on one that seems to be in the forefront of people's thinking today, on Vietnam." He quoted Kennedy as saying he would "be opposed to forcing a coalition government on the government of Saigon, a coalition with the Communists even before we begin the negotiation"—a statement Kennedy had made in California to put some distance between himself and McCarthy. Such comparisons only earned Humphrey more contempt among antiwar Democrats, especially old Kennedyites.

Humphrey was also encountering a minor irritation from the party's right with the entrance into the presidential race on August 17 of Georgia's crackpot segregationist governor, Lester Maddox. He said he was running because "the void [in the party] has remained unfilled" and the party needed a voice for law and order. Any slight hope Maddox entertained to be taken seriously he dashed in a news conference two days later by expressing sympathy with the tenets of the John Birch Society, the extreme-right-wing group that had deeper connections in the Republican Party.

Another fringe candidate entered the presidential race on August 18 when the Peace and Freedom Party, meeting in Ann Arbor, Michigan, nominated Eldridge Cleaver, the Black Panther minister of information and author of *Soul on Ice*, as its candidate. Cleaver, on parole at the time of his arrest in the April shootout with police in Oakland, called in his platform for "the immediate withdrawal of U.S. troops from Vietnam." The delegates asserted "the right of armed self-defense [by] the oppressed peoples in America."

Among those at the Peace and Freedom convention was Marc Raskin, the one man acquitted in the celebrated draft counseling case in Boston. He dismissed the Ann Arbor convention as a "sectarian struggle among socialist groups on the left" and called McCarthy the only "credible candidate," urging support for him under the banner of a broader-based, independent new party.

*   *   *

Meanwhile, the national college student community seethed with the same afflictions over racism and the war that had infected the community of its elders. From August 17 to 26, the National Student Association held its annual convention at Kansas State University and fell immediately into rancorous debate. Black students comprising only a handful of the delegations walked out after a motion was defeated to discuss white racism before any other convention business was considered. Delegations from more than twenty major universities balked at the suggestion that they themselves represented "white racism institutions."

A convention report underscored the campus turmoil of the year, observing that students in at least 101 colleges and universities had conducted at least 221 major demonstrations involving nearly 39,000 students protesting against racism, the war and lack of student power. In fifty-nine of the demonstrations, the report said, one or more campus buildings had been seized and there had been 417 student arrests. Coincidentally, on August 24, Grayson Kirk announced his early retirement as president of Columbia to "help to insure the prospect of more normal university operations during the coming year."

* * *

The week before the formal opening of the Democratic convention, the party's credentials, rules and platform committees met to thrash out challenges and competing proposals. The anti-Humphrey forces hoped these deliberations and hearings would provide a wedge that somehow could break the vice president's hold on enough delegates to avert a first-ballot victory, and to open up possibilities to challenge his nomination. It was a long shot, but the intensity of the opposition to Humphrey fired the effort.

In one of the few demonstrations of convention unity, the forces of Humphrey, McCarthy and McGovern joined in support of a challenging Mississippi delegation led by black civil rights leaders Aaron Henry and Charles Evers and newspaper editor Hodding Carter 3rd. The convention credentials committee voted to unseat a pro-Wallace delegation headed by Governor John Bell Williams and replace it with the challengers. The result was a direct outgrowth of the challenge by the Mississippi Freedom Democratic Party at the 1964 convention that had produced a party rule requiring state organizations to open their activities to blacks.

Other credentials challenges, however, generated no such unity. The McCarthy forces after setbacks in the committee were obliged to take to the convention floor challenges essentially based on racial discrimination in Georgia, North Carolina, Alabama and Texas. No splitting wedge seemed likely in these.

In the rules committee, however, Humphrey appeared to give his opponents a tactical opportunity on August 21, when he wrote a letter to the committee chairman backing abolition of the unit rule for the 1968 convention and the call to the 1972 convention. This position was standard liberal fare and ordinarily would have been expected from Humphrey, except that he had privately assured Governor John Connally of Texas, in whose hands the unit rule meant convention power, that he would side with him on holding off its abolition. Connally was furious and said so. He hinted that not only would he deny Texas's votes to Humphrey but that Lyndon Johnson himself might be moved to come to the convention, saying he had changed his mind and wanted another term. Indeed, Johnson had his speechwriters at work crafting a speech he would deliver at the convention on his sixtieth birthday, with the expectation of those around him that he would go to Chicago.

Doris Kearns (Goodwin), then a White House intern and sounding board for Johnson on her antiwar generation, told Hayden later: "He wanted them to fete his accomplishments and, if the convention fell apart, crazy as it seems, he would be there, available." And any attempt by the convention to water down a plank supporting his Vietnam policy, she said, would have brought LBJ to Chicago. "He called me at the convention, where I was with my anti-war friends," she recalled to Hayden. "He wanted to come, was planning to come. He went on for 15 minutes about how the country was rejecting him." And she added to me later: "He said how horrible he felt, that he couldn't even come on his birthday, they hated him that much. He sounded so low. I thought, 'My God, he's been destroyed by this too.' I saw what the war had done to him."

The notion that Humphrey might accept a compromise peace plank further infuriated Connally. Larry O'Brien wrote later that the Texas governor told him: "If Humphrey thinks he's got the nomination locked up, he'd better count the delegates again, because all hell will break loose if we're kicked around. He'd better remember that we in the South can deny him the nomination if we withdraw our support."

The next day, O'Brien wrote, Connally "hinted that if Humphrey wasn't careful, Lyndon Johnson's name would be entered in nomination. I took that for the bluff that it was . . . but it underscored the uncertainty of Humphrey's position as he struggled for the presidential nomination that had eluded him since 1960." Humphrey was so uncertain, in fact, that he reacted to Connally's tantrum by assuring him he would support keeping the unit rule after all and would not deviate from Johnson's basic Vietnam policy.

Dick Goodwin recognized that here was a breach that might bear exploiting. He met with Connally and sounded him out about his availability on a McCarthy ticket as a way of punishing Humphrey. When McCarthy arrived in Chicago, the question was put straightforwardly to him. "You can take 24 hours to answer it," he was told. "Do you want to be president bad enough to have John Connally as a running mate?" McCarthy didn't wait for the deadline. "The answer is no," he said promptly. (McCarthy said later that while he could not recall this exchange, that certainly would have been his instant response.) So much for the McCarthy-Connally ticket.

* * *

As the opening of the Democratic convention approached, antiwar protesters who had vowed to change the party's Vietnam policy or disrupt it in the process began arriving in Chicago. In anticipation of trouble, the city's International Amphitheatre hard by the famous Chicago stockyards and near the heavily black ghettos of the South Side was encircled by barbed wire and a long, high chain-link fence. All entrances on one side were kept closed, to channel delegates and credentialed guests into the 12,000-capacity hall under tight security maintained by Chicago's iron-fisted Mayor Daley. Estimates of 100,000 or more demonstrators created an atmosphere of severe apprehension, although the actual numbers never came close to that figure.

McCarthy in advance of the convention had urged supportive students through their leaders not to come to Chicago, and a great many listened and stayed home. In the confusion and mayhem that followed, nevertheless, the young McCarthy workers who did come to Chicago were often lumped in, in police and press reports, with the relatively small number of New Left radicals who came bent on disrupting the convention, most of them still adherents to nonviolent protest.

Even the Yippies, according to Martin A. Lee and Bruce Shlain in their book *Acid Dreams*, "were preparing monkey-warfare hijinks and other street theater actions, but their plans did not call for organized violence or rioting on the part of demonstrators." The "Festival of Life" they were planning "would offer an enticing alternative to the 'death politics' inside the convention hall," Lee and Shlain wrote. "Plans for the festival included a variety of counterconvention activities: a nude grope-in for peace and prosperity, a joint-rolling contest, the election of Miss Yippie. . . .

"There'd be free food for everyone and workshops on drugs, communes, guerrilla theater, first aid and draft-dodging. It was an ambitious scheme for a group of dope-smoking misfits who had no political organization to speak of. But the Yippies knew they had the media at their beck and call, and they hoped hype would make up for what they lacked on a grassroots level. They tantalized reporters with visions of a Chicago inundated by a million stoned freaks who would force the Democrats to conduct their business under armed guard. . . . Of course, the Yippies realized that nowhere near a million people would turn up for the demonstration, but exaggeration was the crux of their organizing strategy."

Daley accordingly put the city's entire police force of more than 11,000 men on twelve-hour shifts, and at his request Democratic Governor Shapiro on August 20 called up 5,650 members of the Illinois National Guard. Another 7,500 regular Army troops were placed on standby call. The worst was expected, and before the convention was over, it would be realized.

Two major strikes further plagued the city. The International Brotherhood of Electrical Workers struck the Illinois Bell Telephone Company, complicating the task for the small army of phone and broadcast workers brought to the city to deal with convention communications. At the same time, about 80 percent of Chicago's taxicabs were put out of commission by a driver and mechanic strike, which also cut normal bus service almost in half.

Early arrivals to the convention city encountered a sea of blue-checkered police caps and blue-shirted police officers at virtually every downtown intersection, many toting menacing nightsticks. Dick Daley was not going to tolerate any nonsense from the long-haired hippies and yippies in tie-dyed shirts, miniskirts and all the other trademark fashions of the rebellious 1960s. As they camped out in city parks, with or without permits, the easily distinguishable scent of marijuana wafted over their gatherings as they sang war protest and civil rights songs, and chanted "Dump the Hump" and a variety of obscenities about Johnson. Tensions mounted on both sides of an invisible battle line between what Nixon at that other convention liked to call "the peace forces and the criminal forces."

* * *

In the midst of this growing apprehension in Chicago, as the first of the Illinois National Guardsmen were moving in to take up defensive positions against they knew not what, a contrastingly clear-cut confrontation of opposing forces exploded across the Atlantic on the night of August 20–21. Military troops of the Soviet Union and four of its communist satellite countries poured into Czechoslovakia to snuff out the freedom and democracy movement heralded in the West as the Prague Spring.

The invasion was swift and successful, with Alexander Dubček and other movement leaders seized and flown directly to Moscow. While there was no organized opposition, clandestine radio broadcasts spurred the Prague population to acts of resistance that were more notable in demonstrating public outrage than for effective response.

The use of overwhelming force came after three weeks of nervous hope in Czechoslovakia in the wake of the conferences in Slovakia between the Czech Party Presidium and the full Soviet Politburo. Dubček on his way back to

Prague on August 1 had assured his countrymen that "we have not taken a single step back." And in advance of another meeting of Eastern bloc leaders in Bratislava on August 3, he had told a nationwide television audience that "we promised you we would stand fast. We kept our promise." It had also been announced that all Soviet troops that had stayed in Czechoslovakia after the Warsaw Pact maneuvers in June had been removed.

At that second meeting, Dubček had been able to obtain a pledge that the Soviet Union and the other bloc countries would cooperate with his regime on the basis of "equality, sovereignty and national independence." But the communiqué also referred to "the subversive actions of imperialism" that had tried to challenge the communist philosophy in Czechoslovakia. It said all participants in the meeting "became convinced that it is possible to advance along the road of socialism and communism only by being strictly and consistently guided by the general laws of construction of Socialist society." At the same time, it noted that "every fraternal party, creatively solving the questions of further Socialist development, takes into consideration the national specific features and conditions." This latter phrase gave the Prague regime something on which to pin its hopes for survival.

Dubček on August 4 had assured the Czech people that "the principle of sovereignty is an indivisible part of our policy," and that "there is no need to fear for the sovereignty of our country." The liberalization that was under way in Czechoslovakia, he said, "will have far-reaching significance" throughout the communist world and "there is no other way, no other route" to continued cooperation within the bloc.

A week later, however, the nervousness returned with an announcement in Moscow that there would be more military maneuvers involving Soviet, East German and Polish troops in areas bordering on Czechoslovakia. President Tito of Yugoslavia was visiting Prague at the time as a show of support; Romanian President Nicolae Ceausescu, who had stayed away from the earlier Soviet bloc talks, was due shortly for the same purpose. Then, on August 16, the most ominous signal came in resumed criticism of the free Czech press in *Pravda*. The Bratislava agreement had been breached, the Soviet party paper said, by "fierce and slanderous attacks" on Czechoslovakia's communist neighbors.

The invasion jolted the nations of the West. President Johnson called his National Security Council into emergency session and went on national television. "The Soviet Union and its allies have invaded a defenseless country to stamp out a resurgence of ordinary human freedom," he said. "It is a sad commentary on the Communist mind that a sign of liberty is deemed a fundamental threat to the security of the Soviet system." He called on other members of the United Nations Security Council "to insist upon the charter rights of Czechoslovakia and its people." But with the Soviet Union possessing a veto on the council stronger action seemed fruitless.

Peace groups led by Benjamin Spock picketed the Soviet mission at the United Nations, but from Eugene McCarthy came the observation that LBJ had acted out of proportion. "I do not see this as a major world crisis," he said. "It is likely to have more serious consequences for the Communist Party in Russia than in Czechoslovakia. I saw no need for a midnight meeting of the U.S. National Security Council."

The remark generated much criticism from leading Democrats and appalled McCarthy's own aides. He sought to stem the furor by issuing a second statement that said "of course I condemn this cruel and violent action. It should not really be necessary for me to say this, but to make clear my attitude, I do." But his original observation was taken by foes as confirmation that he wanted to wish away the Cold War.

In any event, the invasion had two immediate political ramifications in the United States. It scuttled Johnson's plans for another summit meeting with Soviet leader Alexei Kosygin and it increased the likelihood that LBJ would insist on a platform plank at the Democratic convention saying the United States would hold firm in Vietnam.

Protests mounted in Prague as Czech citizens marched peaceably past a long row of Soviet tanks and soldiers with fixed bayonets on St. Wenceslaus Square. And there were isolated incidents of violence and sniper fire over the next few days as the Czech secret police began to seek out members of the resistance. On August 24, four young Czechs were shot and killed by Soviet soldiers after having been caught distributing anti-Soviet leaflets.

The next night, other young Czechs defied the curfew imposed by the Soviets and held an around-the-clock vigil at the statue of St. Wenceslaus in the square. Trains from the Soviet Union were derailed and train traffic so disrupted that Soviet troops were obliged to lift their equipment into Prague by helicopter. A host of clandestine radio stations blossomed as the invaders tried in vain to rally Czechs to help them overthrow "counterrevolutionary forces." The troops had come into their country, the Soviets insisted, "so that no one can take your freedom away from you." It was grim humor to the Czech people, who suffered twenty deaths and more than 300 persons wounded in the first four days after the invasion.

Dubček was summoned to Moscow, where what in effect were the terms of surrender were dictated, including the continued presence of Soviet troops in Czechoslovakia for an indefinite period. Dubček returned pledging to continue to pursue "the original aim of expressing humanistic socialistic princi-

ples" and the Czech National Assembly adopted a resolution calling the occupation "illegal" and calling for a specific date for troop withdrawal. But
there was no doubt that the flowering of the Prague Spring had come to an
abrupt end.

The United States, already bogged down in Vietnam, was not about to intervene, as the Soviet Union well knew. On August 22, Secretary of State
Rusk confirmed that the United States was planning no "retaliatory actions
or sanctions" against the invaders, but was merely calling on them "not to engage in punitive measures" against the Czechs and to withdraw the foreign
troops. Rusk emphasized that the United States had "no bilateral commitments to Czechoslovakia." The next day, the United Nations Security Council
did pass a resolution condemning the invasion, but it was vetoed by the
Soviet Union.

* * *

In Chicago, the cauldron continued to simmer. More demonstrators arrived
under the tough and watchful eye of the Chicago police. On the night of
August 22, a seventeen-year-old Native American in hippie garb named
Jerome Johnson was shot and killed near Lincoln Park by police who said he
had fired on them. The demonstrators were to be permitted to rally at the park
each day, but would have to clear it each night for an eleven o'clock city-
imposed curfew.

According to James Miller in his book, *Democracy Is in the Streets: From Port
Huron to the Streets of Chicago*, the army that was mobilized against the demonstrators included 12,000 Chicago police, 6,000 armed National Guardsmen,
6,000 U.S. Army troops and 1,000 intelligence agents from the FBI, CIA,
Army and Navy. Organizers of various aspects of the protest were placed under
electronic and direct personal surveillance and makeshift roadblocks barred all
avenues of entry. Jeeps with barbed wire on their bumpers, quickly dubbed
"Daley Dozers" by the demonstrators, took armed troops to expected trouble
spots.

On August 23, the Yippies led by Abbie Hoffman and Jerry Rubin caucused outside the Chicago Civic Center and nominated their own presidential candidate—a porker dubbed "Pigasus." Rubin walked him to the huge
Picasso sculpture known to locals as "the gooney bird," where a local reporter
asked him: "Why are you here?" Rubin replied: "We want to give you a
chance to talk to our candidate, and to restate our demand that Pigasus be
given Secret Service protection and be brought to the White House for his
foreign-policy briefing." In a minor scuffle, seven of the Yippies were arrested,
charged with disorderly conduct, and the pig was taken to a humane shelter.
Undaunted, the Yippies found another pig.

At the same time, they floated rumors that they were going somehow to inject LSD into the city's drinking water, send out "stud teams" to seduce the wives and daughters of the delegates and commit any number of other far-fetched schemes, all designed to unnerve the Democrats—and keep the Chicago police and investigative agencies busy chasing shadows.

On Saturday, August 24, more antiwar demonstrators moved into Lincoln Park, waving banners and shouting slogans in a relatively orderly fashion, as Chicago's finest watched. Allen Ginsberg, the beat poet, was on hand to chant his "Om" to pacify the crowd until curfew. On Sunday the crowds returned, in much greater numbers, to mill about, listen to freelance music and watch the Yippies go through their antics. The chant that was to be picked up and repeated endlessly over the next days—"Hey, hey, LBJ! How many kids have you killed today?"—was gaining voices by the hour.

Marshals from the National Mobilization Committee urged order and adherence to the curfew, but the Yippies preached confrontation, and that night about a thousand demonstrators defied the order to clear the park. An estimated 500 police weighed in with nightsticks swinging. Their predominantly young prey fled or turned and hurled rocks, bottles and profanities at the enforcers, as reporters and cameramen captured the scene. The convention itself was not to open until the next day, but a dose of what was in store had already been administered by the host city.

* * *

Harmony was in short supply on other fronts as well. On August 21, Humphrey backed out of his promised debate with McCarthy, citing the demands of McGovern and Maddox to be included. At this late date, the cancellation was all right with McCarthy. Also, at a breakfast meeting at Humphrey's apartment in Washington shortly before the convention, McCarthy made it clear he didn't want to be considered as Humphrey's running mate. He had already said publicly that "if I were to go on the ticket with Hubert it would be kind of like the captain of a ship getting in the first lifeboat and waving to those still on board, saying, 'I hope it doesn't sink.'"

The bitterness over Vietnam went on unabated. Also on August 21, Ted Kennedy chose to reenter the discourse on the war after more than two months of isolation after his brother's death. He proposed his own plan to end the war by halting all bombing of North Vietnam "unconditionally," negotiating with Hanoi the mutual withdrawal of all foreign troops from South Vietnam, promising economic and other nonlethal aid to Saigon thereafter, and "significantly decreasing" in 1968 "the level of our military activity and military personnel in the south."

Kennedy, while saying that "like my three brothers before me I pick up a fallen standard," reiterated that he would not be a candidate for the presidential nomination.

Kennedy's Vietnam plan quickly became the final basis for a compromise peace plank that had been in the making for most of the month by a behind-the-scenes coalition of McCarthy, Kennedy and McGovern strategists, in conjunction with Humphrey representative David Ginsburg. The idea, advanced energetically by Congressman John Gilligan of Ohio, a Democratic senatorial nominee, was to create a plank that Humphrey could swallow, then push it through the convention, thereby taking the decision out of Humphrey's hands and, therefore, beyond LBJ's direct retribution against him.

The principal stumbling block remained the antiwar coalition's insistence on a clear call for a halt to the bombing of North Vietnam. Dick Goodwin, who had now rejoined the McCarthy camp, and others agreed to minor compromises but would not yield on that critical point. The coalition's peace plank called for "an unconditional end to all bombing of North Vietnam," along with a phased withdrawal of all American and North Vietnamese troops from the South and an urging to the Saigon regime to undertake negotiations with the NLF with an eye to a coalition government.

Gilligan reviewed the plank with Ginsburg, who thought it acceptable, then called Humphrey in Washington and read it to him. The vice president also approved and in turn ran it by Rusk and Rostow, who raised no objections. Humphrey thought he finally was home free since Johnson previously had told him, he wrote later in his book *The Education of a Public Man*, to "just keep in touch with Dean Rusk" on dealing with the Vietnam issue. Appearing on NBC's *Meet the Press*, he again endorsed LBJ's Vietnam policies, believing the statement worked out did not give particular offense to them, and then left Washington for his home in Waverly, Minnesota, for a brief rest before going on to Chicago.

He was further relieved by a comment by Johnson in a weekend speech at his alma mater, Southwest Texas State College, after Connally had told reporters there was "a growing sentiment" within the Texas delegation to place LBJ's name in nomination after all. "I am not a candidate for anything," Johnson said, "except maybe a rocking chair."

But Humphrey was hardly out of the woods. When the president called congressional leaders to the White House for a briefing on Czechoslovakia, among them was Congressman Hale Boggs of Louisiana, who happened also to be the chairman of the convention's platform committee. Johnson produced intelligence reports and a cable from General Creighton Abrams in Vietnam indicating that a bombing halt would severely jeopardize the American military position there.

The president had an aide get from Ginsburg the full peace plank. LBJ insisted that instead of calling for an unconditional bombing halt it should read: "Stop all bombing of North Vietnam when this action would not endanger the lives of our troops in the field; this action should take into account the response from Hanoi." There was nothing unconditional about that.

Humphrey, back in Chicago for the start of the convention on Monday, got a phone call from Postmaster General Marvin Watson, one of LBJ's political right-hand men. The two met and Watson informed Humphrey that the peace plank was not acceptable to the president. Humphrey was crestfallen. "Well, Marvin," Humphrey wrote later that he told Watson, "I cleared this with the Secretary of State, and I've cleared it with Walt Rostow." Watson according to Humphrey replied: "That doesn't make any difference. It's been looked over again and it just doesn't meet with the president's approval."

An angry Humphrey phoned Johnson at his ranch in Texas. The president brushed aside Humphrey's report that he had run the proposed plank past Rusk and Rostow. "I don't want you to tell anybody that you're clearing any of these things with me," Johnson told him. "This plank just undercuts the whole policy and, by God, the Democratic Party ought not to be doing that to me and you ought not to be doing it; you've been a part of this policy." So much for any lingering hopes that a Vietnam plank compromise could be reached and a divisive floor fight diverted.

Humphrey wrote later: "Our choice was to stand and fight the president's emissaries or to give in to the inevitable. . . . Now I know, in retrospect, that I should have stood my ground. I told our people I was still for the plank, but I didn't put up a good fight. That was a mistake. I am not sure it would have made any difference in the election, but once we had arrived at that point, at some consensus with the Kennedy people, I should not have yielded."

* * *

The 1968 Democratic National Convention opened on Monday night, August 26, with a speech of welcome from Mayor Daley, whose thoroughly greased political machine billed Chicago as "The City That Works." He boasted that it was "an important sign of faith to the American people for this national political convention to be held here—not in some resort center, but in the very heart of a great city where people live and work and raise their families."

Daley lauded the diversity of voices and views in his party—up to a point. He did not refer, he said, to "extremists . . . who seek to destroy instead of to build, to those who would make a mockery of our institutions and values, nor do I refer to those who have been successful in convincing some people that theatrical protest is rational dissent. I speak of those who came because they know at this political gathering there is hope and opportunity."

But judging from the pessimism that already was plaguing the delegates, Daley was speaking of a relatively small segment of the convention. In an unvarnished warning to dissenters, he declared that "as long as I am mayor of this city, there's going to be law and order in Chicago." In the temper of the times, the use of those words that Democrats regularly charged were Republican code for racism was particularly jolting.

The convention keynoter, Senator Daniel K. Inouye of Hawaii, also took note of the mood of rebellion, particularly among the young and the black, but in more sympathetic and conciliatory terms. "Why, when we have at last had the courage to open an attack on the age-old curses of ignorance and disease and poverty and prejudice," he asked, "why are the flags of anarchism being hoisted by leaders of our next generation? Why, when our maturing society welcomes and appreciates art as never before, are poets and painters so preponderantly hostile?"

The Vietnam War was one answer, he acknowledged, and he agreed that the war had to be brought to an end. But "just as we shun irresponsible calls for total and devastating military victory," he said, "so must we guard against the illusion of an instant peace that has no chance of permanence."

As a Japanese-American, Inouye compared the relatively peaceful integration of citizens of his ancestry with the turmoil among black Americans. In addition to having all constitutional rights [after the regrettable World War II internments], he said, "neither my parents nor I were forced by covenants and circumstances to live in ghettos. . . . Unlike those of my ancestry, the Negro's unemployment rate is triple the national average. The mortality rate of his children is twice that of white children. . . . Is it any wonder that the Negroes find it hard to wait another one hundred years before they are accepted as full citizens in our free society?"

In a system that encourages social mobility and economic progress, he said, "it should hardly surprise us when the children of such progress demand to be heard when they become aware of inequities still to be corrected. Neither should we fear their voices. On the contrary . . . the marching feet of youth have led us into a new era of politics and we can never turn back."

At the same time, Inouye said, the tearing down of the system itself could not be tolerated. "To permit violence and anarchy to destroy our cities," he said, "is to spark the beginning of a cancerous growth of doubt, suspicion, fear and hatred that will gradually infect the whole nation." In seeming rebuttal of Daley, however, he added that neither could the country tolerate apathy and prejudice hiding "behind the mask of law and order," which could "only rest securely with justice as its foundation."

The convention then turned to the matter of the credentials and rules challenges that the anti-Humphrey forces hoped would provide a wedge with which they could pry some first-ballot support from the vice president. Despite Humphrey's pledge to Connally that he would oppose abolishing the unit rule at this convention, it was dropped by voice vote. But a challenge to Connally's Texas delegation on grounds of inadequate representation of blacks and Mexican-Americans was voted down.

A full-scale row was ignited, however, by a proposed compromise by the credentials committee chairman, Governor Richard Hughes, to split the Georgia delegation between regular party delegates under Governor Maddox and a challenging slate led by twenty-eight-year-old State Representative Julian Bond, a prominent black civil rights activist.

To start off, the regulars were seated with half the state's vote and the Bond slate was seated first in the balcony and then in an aisle while the full convention voted on its fate. Further attempts at compromise were rejected by the regular slate amid rancorous debate that finally culminated in a vote after midnight on seating the full Bond contingent. It lost, 1,413 votes to 1,041½, setting off angry demonstrations. One black delegate from California set fire to his credentials, and the bedlam forced a recess shortly before three o'clock in the morning with the Georgia question still unresolved.

When the convention resumed on Tuesday, August 27, the convention by voice vote approved the Hughes compromise to split the Georgia delegation, inducing more than twenty Georgia regulars to walk out. The others stayed and were joined by the Bond delegates. In another challenge, to the Alabama delegation by Humphrey loyalists who charged that some delegates supported the independent candidacy of George Wallace, sixteen delegates who declined to sign a "disclaimer of disloyalty" were tossed out and replaced by pro-Humphrey delegates. The convention also adopted a Hughes proposal for study of delegate-selection rules aimed at reform before the 1972 convention that would assure more "meaningful and timely opportunities" for participation by all Democrats. Given little attention at the time, this resolution would lead four years later to the injection of much greater "participatory democracy" in delegate selection, breaking the hold of party bosses and leaders on the process and radically changing the complexion of the next convention.

None of these actions, however, had provided the opening for a serious challenge to Humphrey's nomination. Nor did McCarthy's behavior. He continued to display a halfhearted attitude toward the whole business, agreeing to appear only before a handful of state delegations and refusing to extend himself in appealing for support. Eller said later that McCarthy always insisted on "dispassionate talk to delegates." He believed, Eller said, that "you can't incite the passions of the ignorant and uninformed and not expect consequences." For that reason, Eller said, Robert Kennedy's passionate style of speaking "really offended him." McCarthy believed, his close aide said, that the speaking styles of both slain Kennedy brothers aroused passions and led to the violent acts that cost them their lives.

In a reluctant appearance before the important California delegation immediately followed by Humphrey and McGovern, McCarthy was almost insulting. "I suppose," he said at the outset, "that this delegation needs to hear me less than it needs to hear any candidate in history. You know my stand on the issues. Senator Kennedy and I went up and down and across the state, and the results of that election are known to you, and what happened. . . . I do not intend to restate my case." That was his only mention of Kennedy, who had won his final and most significant primary victory in California. Instead, he focused on McGovern, who had inherited much of Kennedy's support, sniping at him for a remark he had made the previous day.

McGovern had observed that McCarthy "has taken the view that a passive and inactive presidency is in order, and that disturbs me. Solving our domestic problems will be much more difficult, and that will require an active and compassionate president." McCarthy now commented: "Well, I think a little passivity in that office is all right; a kind of balance, I think. I have never quite known what active compassion is. Actually, compassion in my mind is to suffer with someone, not in advance of him. Or not in public necessarily."

McCarthy declined to answer a question about Vietnam, saying his views were well known, and summed up by saying that "I suppose it must come to this—that one explain nine months in three minutes. But we expect to be put to rather severe tests. It is a little like building boats in a bottle. . . ." As a final kiss-off of Humphrey on Vietnam, he repeated that "I could not support a Democratic candidate whose views did not come close to what mine are."

When it was Humphrey's turn, he gave the Californians boilerplate. Asked about how his Vietnam policy differed from that of Johnson, he shot back: "I did not come here to repudiate the President of the United States. I want that made quite clear." The stalemate was the responsibility of Hanoi, he said. "The roadblock to peace, my dear friends," he said, "is not in Washington, D.C. It is in Hanoi, and we ought to recognize it as such." Taking on Humphrey thus fell to McGovern, who made the standard antiwar points while saluting Humphrey for his contributions to racial and social justice at home. The California delegation's "great debate" in the end amounted to nothing.

Later that day, McCarthy gave an interview in his suite to John Knight, publisher of the Knight Newspapers, and a few of his reporters. As

McCarthy's delegates continued to seek converts and thousands of his supporters in the streets faced the nightsticks of the Chicago police in Lincoln Park and elsewhere in the city, he blandly seemed to throw in the sponge. He volunteered that the presidential nomination "was probably settled more than 24 hours ago." Was he saying Humphrey had locked up the nomination? "I think so," he replied, to the surprise of his questioners.

McCarthy also said he thought Humphrey would "try to say that Nixon's position and [his own] on the war are the same, and try to neutralize that issue, and run on domestic issues. That was his pitch today. It looks to me that's the way Humphrey's going to try to play it." He said he wouldn't attempt to start a new party and would probably endorse Humphrey "after a couple of weeks" (in spite of what he had just said), but that Humphrey would probably lose to Nixon.

The report that McCarthy had surrendered cast a pall over his supporters, who still had hoped that an aggressive stand on the Vietnam peace plank might yet force Humphrey to move away from Johnson's embrace. McCarthy later said it was his understanding that the substance of the interview would not be published until after the vote on the presidential nomination, but his interviewers said no such stipulation was ever made.

Over in Lincoln Park that night, more occupants than ever refused to observe the eleven o'clock curfew. Police helicopters flew overhead, flooding the area with intermittent searchlights as loudspeakers warned: "If you do not leave the park you will be subject to arrest." Young girls walked in front of the line of guardsmen, Mixner recalled, "putting flowers in the barrels of their guns." Again the police poured tear gas into the park, eventually driving out some 3,000 mostly young protesters, arresting 140 of them. About sixty were injured in the melee. If McCarthy was giving up the fight, the street army—only a relatively small portion of which consisted of McCarthy campaign workers—was showing no sign of doing the same.

Reporters and photographers covering the park scene bore a heavy toll of the police action. Nicholas von Hoffman wrote in the *Washington Post:* "Police burst out of the woods in selective pursuit of news photographers. Pictures are unanswerable evidence in court. They'd taken off their badges, their name plates, even the unit patches on their shoulders to become a mob of identical, unidentifiable club-swingers. . . . The radical leaders have always said that cops' night sticks do the best recruiting for the left. But this is different. The Chicago police are radicalizing the Establishment." Seventeen members of the press and television reported having been beaten by the police on this one night.

At Grant Park, across Michigan Avenue from the Conrad Hilton, the chants of "Dump the Hump!" continued through the night to disturb the sleep of Humphrey and others, and to amuse many of his opponents watching from their hotel windows. What they saw eventually, however, was not amusing—the arrival, with sheathed bayonets and jeeps festooned with barbed wire, of 600 Illinois National Guardsmen who set up a line of protection between the demonstrators in the park and the hotel. The hotel itself had come under attack from stink bombs that had turned the lobby into an obstacle course to the banks of elevators.

Years later, Ken Galbraith, who was a Massachusetts McCarthy delegate and floor leader, recalled joining the demonstrators at one point, escorted by a National Guardsman. After counseling the young crowd to avoid violence, Galbraith quipped: "Just remember this is the National Guard and they're draft dodgers just as you are!" As he left, a National Guard sergeant took him aside. "May I have a word with you?" he said, as Galbraith recalled it. "I just want to thank you. That's the nicest thing said to me today."

Such comments, however, were not the order of the day. And as the resistance in the streets stiffened, the convention meanwhile had moved blandly on. Anita Bryant sang "Happy Birthday" to the most significant Man Who Wasn't There, Lyndon Johnson, celebrating his sixtieth—and monitoring events from Texas. Meanwhile, his speechwriters still toiled over his speech in case he decided at this late time to go to Chicago. He declared "I would go" if doing so could help "the presidency and the country," but he poked fun at those who were sure he would. They thought, he said, he would "hang on to the presidency to the end but it didn't come out that way. I suppose they think I would do the same thing about the convention."

Although Johnson finally did not go, Califano wrote later, he hoped to the end that the convention would offer him the nomination, at least so he could turn it down. In the meantime, his hand on the convention's procedures was so firm that Humphrey had no role whatever in the convention schedule. It was reported later he even had to send one of his sons to stand in line each day to pick up convention passes for his family and close friends.

Attempts by the Humphrey forces to bring the Vietnam plank to a quick vote shortly after midnight led to another wild scene, with antiwar forces demanding an adjournment so they could marshal their troops. House Majority Leader Carl Albert, the convention chairman, tried to ignore the call but the floor became so unruly, with shouts of "Stop the War!" echoing through the hall, that a red-faced Mayor Daley finally drew his finger across his throat in a signal to Albert, who then gaveled the convention into recess for the night.

* * *

Although it is doubtful that President Johnson took much solace in the fact, the night of his sixtieth birthday marked the end of the long political career of one of the most outspoken and recalcitrant critics of his Vietnam War policy. Democratic Senator Ernest Gruening, the tireless champion of Alaskan statehood who became one of Alaska's first two senators upon achievement of that goal in 1958, was defeated in his primary election by Mike Gravel. Gruening and fellow Democrat Wayne Morse of Oregon had been the only two senators to vote against the Gulf of Tonkin resolution that had given Johnson a free hand to escalate American involvement in the Vietnam War. After his primary defeat, Gruening ran an unsuccessful write-in campaign but continued to speak out against Johnson and the war.

Vietnam, Connally and Lyndon Johnson were not Hubert Humphrey's only headaches. Well before the opening gavel fell, Mayor Daley had begun to entertain severe doubts about Humphrey's electability. After discussions with many arriving party leaders, he had concluded that the convention was about to nominate a loser in Humphrey. On Saturday, August 24, he had phoned Ted Kennedy at Hyannis Port and urged him to become a candidate. Kennedy had declined, but told him that his brother-in-law, Steve Smith, was in Chicago as his eyes and ears and was available to him.

Former Governor Michael DiSalle of Ohio had already declared his intention to put Kennedy's name in nomination, despite Kennedy's express wishes that he not do so. Others interested in a Kennedy candidacy, including Lowenstein, had been holding informal conversations about the possibility when it had become apparent to them that McCarthy was not going to be nominated. They didn't think much of DiSalle's straightforward initiative, believing it would only generate resentment among diehard McCarthy supporters still holding out hope for their man.

But, as Lowenstein remarked sarcastically later, Humphrey "was a soaring figure in the polls. He was somewhere around 29 percent. So there was a certain sense of defeat in the air" that fed the Kennedy speculation, and eventually led many McCarthy delegates to see Kennedy as an escape hatch from the Humphrey nomination. Among them, and himself as well, Lowenstein said, "it was perfectly clear that we'd been with McCarthy quite faithfully, and that if he had any prospects of being nominated, it would be wrong not to support him. But that if he didn't, it was wrong not to do something to prevent the nomination of Humphrey."

Other loyal McCarthyites, Lowenstein said, pressed him to nominate Kennedy from the floor, thereby giving the move a certain sanction from the McCarthy campaign. "It was clear by then," he said, "that none of the big shots would do this without Kennedy's explicit approval. The issue then be-

came whether to do it . . . knowing that . . . it would set off so spontaneous
an eruption of enthusiasm that it wouldn't be necessary to have the big
shots." Lowenstein debated with himself, and waited.

The next morning, Sunday, Daley had breakfast with Jess Unruh, head of
the California delegation and a Kennedy loyalist. Unruh wanted Daley to
hold the large Illinois delegation in check while another candidate was found,
and they agreed that the obvious candidate was Kennedy. Daley caucused
with his delegation and announced that it would hold off making a commitment "to see if something develops."

The following morning, Monday, according to Goodwin in a later article
in *Look* magazine, McCarthy after a staff meeting inquired of him what was
going on with Kennedy. Goodwin said he hadn't talked to him but was sure
he didn't want the nomination, on the heels of his brother's death, and didn't
believe he would allow himself to be drafted in opposition to McCarthy. To
which, Goodwin said, McCarthy had replied: "Well, we might do it together.
After all, experience isn't really important in a president as long as he has the
right advisers. Character and judgment are the real thing."

Goodwin wrote that he wasn't sure McCarthy meant that he would support Kennedy for the presidential nomination until he added: "Of course, he's
young, but then those fellows in the Revolution were young too—Jefferson
and Hamilton. . . . Let's see how things develop."

Acting on these comments, Goodwin phoned Steve Smith and suggested
that he meet with McCarthy. The meeting took place the next day, Tuesday,
in McCarthy's suite at the Hilton. Goodwin wrote that Smith told McCarthy
that his brother-in-law was not a candidate and was not doing anything nor
was anyone else doing anything "that might be misinterpreted as a Kennedy
desire for the nomination."

According to Goodwin, McCarthy listened calmly and then spoke. "I can't
make it," he said. "Teddy and I have the same views, and I'm willing to ask
all my delegates to vote for him. I'd like to have my name placed in nomination, and even have a run on the first ballot. But if that's not possible, I'll act
as soon as it's necessary to be effective."

In an account of his own in *New York* magazine later, Smith said McCarthy
then added: "While I'm doing this for Teddy, I never could have done it for
Bobby." *Time* magazine subsequently reported that McCarthy's offer had
brought tears to Smith's eyes, to which Smith icily commented: "Somebody
mistook it for all the spit in them." McCarthy in his book, *The Year of the
People*, confirmed that "I did say, because of the campaign which had been run
against me, I could not have done the same for Senator Robert Kennedy."

Kennedy weighed the McCarthy offer and turned it down. And that, for all practical purposes, was the end of the Ted Kennedy boomlet. Emotionally, he did not have the stomach for the campaign right after the loss of his brother, and politically, he doubted whether McCarthy's delivering his delegates and help from Daley could stop Humphrey.

There was also a suspicion that the whole gambit was a plot by Daley to get Kennedy to take the vice presidential nomination; once he agreed to be a presidential candidate, it would be hard to reject the vice presidential nomination if held out to him in the interest of the party. Daley was quoted later as saying Jack Kennedy could add, Bob Kennedy could add but Ted Kennedy would have to learn. But perhaps he could add all too well.

"If there is such a thing as a draft," Smith said later, "that was it. If Edward Kennedy wanted to lift a little finger he could have been the nominee. But he could foresee Nixon throwing his age [then thirty-nine] and his family at him. And paramount was his determination that he didn't want to move on a wave of sympathy for his brother."

Talk of a Kennedy draft nevertheless swept the convention, with mixed reactions. Lowenstein, still hoping to block Humphrey, continued to toy with putting Kennedy's name in nomination himself. But he felt restrained by Kennedy's apparent unwillingness, and by his own commitment to McCarthy, from which he had not been released.

"I remember running into Charlie Evers [of the Mississippi delegation, brother of slain civil rights leader Medgar Evers]," Lowenstein recalled later, "and he said, 'What's wrong with you?' And I said, 'We're going to save the convention.'" And Evers asked, he recalled, "'Oh, how you gonna do that?' And I told him, and he got a very somber look on his face and said, 'Uh, uh. You're not going to do it to that family a third time.' I'm sure that's the first time in the history of the United States that a presidential nomination has in fact been determined or prevented by fear of assassination, and the consequences of nominating someone who is vulnerable to assassination. But that's part of the way we are." (Lowenstein himself later was shot to death.)

After he had decided not to enter Kennedy's name, Lowenstein recalled, a woman delegate confronted him, demanding that he do so. "You started this and now you're walking out on it at the critical moment," he remembered her shouting at him. "I just looked up at her," he recalled, "and I said, 'Nobody appointed me Jesus Christ. If you're so big on nominating him, you nominate him.'"

Lowenstein said later that had Steve Smith, sitting isolated in a Chicago private club and getting his information secondhand, understood the fervor that was building on the convention floor for Ted Kennedy, matters would have been different. "The essential conception that Steve Smith had at that time, though," he said, "is that without Daley and McCarthy, the nomination would not be possible, which was a total misconception, because it was very clear after you talked to the McCarthy delegates, that McCarthy could have stood like King Canute and not kept votes from going to Ted Kennedy."

In any event, Southern Democrats who wanted no part of another Kennedy began falling into line behind Humphrey. The next morning, Wednesday, Kennedy phoned Humphrey, Daley and Unruh and told them that he would not become a candidate or accept a draft. Humphrey was having breakfast with Daley in his suite when Kennedy's call came, and shortly afterward Governor John McKeithen of Louisiana arrived to assure him that the Southern governors were with him. Daley announced that Illinois would cast 112 votes for Humphrey, only three apiece for McCarthy and McGovern. At long last, the road to Humphrey's nomination seemed clear.

*   *   *

After lunching with black sports stars Jackie Robinson and Elgin Baylor in his suite, the vice president watched the convention proceedings on two color television sets as a steady stream of greeters came and went. The debate on the Vietnam plank was getting under way on the convention floor, and the scene was being interspersed with views of the street clashes of the previous night. At one point, according to Eisele, Humphrey said what he thought of television's role: "If that instrument would stop playing up the kooks and the rioters. They put them on only when the cops are fighting with them. That instrument just recruits trouble."

McCarthy too watched the Vietnam debate in his room two floors below, resisting pleas from key aides to go to the convention and join in it, in what would have been unprecedented at a national convention. Finney wanted him to agree to support the party's ticket if the peace plank was adopted, but he declined to do that too. Only if Johnson himself showed up in the convention hall to make the fight would he do so. "I've always been running against Johnson," he told Mitchell. "If Johnson goes, I'll go." But that wasn't in the cards.

Senator Muskie opened the debate in support of the Johnson-Humphrey plank with the soft and conciliatory argument that while there were "real differences" between the opposing planks, "the dividing line is not the desire for peace or war; the dividing line is limited to means, not ends."

The antiwar forces were not noticeably placated by Muskie's words, and a long demonstration broke out on the floor when Pierre Salinger proclaimed that had Robert Kennedy lived, he would have supported the so-called peace plank. The administration plank, Ted Sorensen added, was one "on which Richard Nixon or even Barry Goldwater could run with pleasure." Chants of

"Stop the War!" starting in the New York and California delegations spread to other delegations and into the galleries, and eventually had to be gaveled to an end. Further demonstrations erupted when Hale Boggs read the statement from General Abrams at the earlier White House briefing—that within two weeks of a bombing halt in North Vietnam, the enemy would be able to increase fivefold its military capacity in South Vietnam.

Three hours after the debate's beginning, the convention voted for the Johnson plank, 1,527¾ votes to 1,041¼ against. It was now about five o'clock in the afternoon, and word of the result quickly spread out of the convention hall to the streets of Chicago. Choruses of "We Shall Overcome" rose from the losing delegates, many of whom donned black armbands, as the convention recessed for dinner.

* * *

A crowd estimated as large as 15,000 persons meanwhile had moved into Grant Park for a rally by the National Mobilization Committee. Police monitoring the event distributed fliers that informed the crowd that "in the interests of free speech and assembly, this portion of Grant Park has been set aside for a rally" but then warned that "any attempts to conduct or participate in a parade or march will subject each and every participant to arrest."

Some rally organizers tried to hand fliers of their own to the police telling them: "Our argument is not with you. . . . This nightmare week was arranged by Richard Daley and Lyndon Johnson, who decided we should not have the right to express ourselves as free people. As we march . . . we will be looking forward to the day when your job is easier, when you can perform your traditional tasks, and no one orders you to deprive your fellow Americans of their rights of free speech and assembly."

Suddenly, a shirtless, long-haired young man began to lower an American flag—planning, it was said later, to fly it upside down in the international signal of distress. Something immediately snapped among the police tensely lined up along the rally's perimeter. They charged into the crowd, swinging their billy clubs with abandon. Demonstrators were seized by police, clubbed to the ground and thrown into awaiting paddy wagons.

After the police pulled off, the rally resumed. Leading Vietnam critics including comedian Dick Gregory and David Dellinger spoke and Ginsberg again delivered his "Om" mantra. Jerry Rubin, with his live pig "candidate" in tow, regaled the crowd and then Dellinger, after calling for a gathering of nonviolent marchers at one corner of the park, introduced Hayden. Reporting that Rennie Davis had been clubbed and was hospitalized, he called on the crowd to "avenge" him. "This city and the military machine it aims at us won't allow us to protest in an organized fashion," Hayden said. "So we must move out of this park in groups throughout the city and turn this overheated military machine against itself. Let us make sure that if our blood flows, it flows all over the city, and if we are gassed that they gas themselves."

Many in the crowd then tried to march from the park toward the Conrad Hilton, the downtown Loop and the convention hall, some waving Vietcong flags, but were blocked by police. Others, moving independently outside the park toward the Hilton, joined the Poor People's mule train led by Abernathy onto Michigan Avenue a mile or so from the hotel. The marchers converged on Michigan and Balboa, where blue-shirted Chicago police toting nightsticks barred the way. As the marchers began chanting "The whole world is watching!" the police fired tear gas into the crowd, then charged and started to club any convenient target.

What later was declared "a police riot" was under way before the eyes of thousands of unbelieving bystanders—and television cameras that would soon convey the bloody, wanton scene into the convention hall itself, and into millions of American homes across the land. In approximately half an hour, roughly from eight o'clock to 8:30 in the gathering dusk to dark, the complete breakdown of true law and order, and of the soul of the Democratic Party, was shatteringly exposed on Michigan Avenue. On this one night alone, at least 100 persons were injured, including 25 police officers, and more than 175 were arrested.

McCarthy, watching it all from his twenty-first-floor suite in the Conrad Hilton overlooking Michigan Avenue, described the scene to others in the room. "Look at them, the police have cut them off," he said of the cornered demonstrators in the park across the street, according to Richard Stout in his book *People*. "They told them they could march, and they've surrounded them. It's the way we treated the Indians. We always told them we were taking them to a happier hunting ground and then we surrounded them. The country is like that. Milling around, ready to march, and nowhere to go." He called the scene "a battle of purgatory" and turned from the window in disgust.

Among the demonstrators on the sidewalk outside the Hilton was Mixner, the twenty-three-year-old McCarthy organizer. He and others found themselves trapped against a huge plate-glass window looking into the hotel's Haymarket Lounge, where horrified patrons watched the mayhem by the Chicago police. "They started beating people, and they'd fall to their knees and they'd continue to beat them . . . as they fell on top of each other," Mixner said later. "All of us were yelling, 'Sieg heil! Sieg heil!' It was just spontaneous. It was everything that we had seen in the movies. It was bad. I saw a policeman rush up to a girl and beat her unconscious. And she fell to the sidewalk and he left laughing. I ran up to pick her up."

As he did so, Mixner said, "three policemen came and pushed us." Amid swinging police clubs, the window gave way and Mixner, his leg cut by the shattered glass, and the revived girl fell halfway into the lounge, then struggled out again. Cops pursued them, trying to club them as the paying customers in the lounge sat frozen at their tables or dashed for cover. Mixner and the girl fled to a nearby subway where other injured people were crouched in hiding. "The end result," Mixner said, "I was on crutches for about three or four months."

Hayden too was knocked through the picture window of the Haymarket Lounge. "The police leaped through the windows," he wrote later, "going right by me, turning over tables in the swank lounge, scattering the drinkers, breaking glasses and tables." (The lounge may have been "swank" by Hayden's standards, but it was an ordinary, slightly cheap gay-nineties motif saloon with waitresses in scant black costumes and high heels showing all the leg they had.)

As police tear gas wafted up to McCarthy's hotel floor and through the open window, he repaired to the fifteenth floor where his campaign had set up an emergency first-aid room. He pitched in to assist the injured and stunned who had staggered in or were brought there by McCarthy workers. "It didn't have to be this way," he was heard to say.

Stout in his book later presented a desperate teletype message sent by a young McCarthyite named Anne Jackson from the fifteenth floor to the McCarthy command post at the convention hall. Her anxiety came through as she typed erratically:

"This is Anne. The front of Hilton is bloody. People are being brought in here to first aid station which is across the hall from us and they have gashed gaps [sic] and God it cant be described. They are being pounded on. I[t] is the most unslightiest mess I have ever seen. . . . It is a scene that shows the true colors. The newsmen are getting it much worse than the demonstrators because they dont want them to publish or show this . . . sadistic or masochistic scene. You would never believe your eyes. Our staff is in hysteria. It is too much. I just dont believe that I see al[l] of this. God, please help us, please hurry up."

Pat Buchanan, staying at the Hilton as an observer for Nixon, had ventured into Grant Park the night before and, he said later, "taken some abuse" in his staid attire of tie and jacket. Now he watched the scene below, saw the police wade into the demonstrators and phoned Nixon in Florida with a report. "The police should have maintained discipline, but they were provoked," he said later. "There was no doubt that the police had enough, and deliberately went down that street to deliver some street justice."

* * *

Back in the convention hall, Albert, who had by now announced to the delegates that Johnson had informed him his decision not to run was "irrevocable," tried to move on to the roll call of the states for the placing of names in nomination for president. The galleries were now peppered with Daley retainers waving signs that said WE LOVE MAYOR DALEY. Trouble broke out on the floor as convention security guards tried to evict a New York delegate for McCarthy, Alex Rosenberg, when he declined to show his credentials.

The scenes of what had happened at Grant Park had not yet been shown live in the hall because of technical impediments resulting from the phone strike. But tapes and film now were being seen on television screens all over the amphitheater, triggering denunciations of the police from all corners of the floor. Anti-Humphrey delegates demanded a recess but Albert would not be deterred, and the roll call proceeded amid continuing bedlam.

McCarthy, after watching the mayhem in the streets and the turmoil in the hall on television, phoned Governor Harold Hughes of Iowa, who was to put his name in nomination. He asked him to desist, believing that action might have a calming effect. But Hughes told him it was too late to withdraw it, and doing so would not make much difference in the chaos now unfolding.

After speeches by Mayor Joseph Alioto of San Francisco placing Humphrey's name in nomination and by Hughes nominating McCarthy, Senator Abraham Ribicoff of Connecticut brought the convention to a new boil with his nomination of McGovern. "With George McGovern as president," he said, ". . . we wouldn't have to have Gestapo tactics in the streets of Chicago." The remark caused Daley to leap to his feet directly in front of Ribicoff, shaking his fists and, according to self-described lip-readers later, shouting a most crude accusation about Ribicoff's sexual proclivities.

Frank Mankiewicz, seconding the McGovern nomination, added fuel to the fire by referring to the "nightsticks and tear gas and the mindless brutality we have seen on our television screens tonight, and on this convention floor."

Back at the Hilton, the tear gas from below had also reached Humphrey's floor. At about ten o'clock, his eyes still watering from the fumes, he called reporters into his suite and told them he had been so busy he hadn't been fully aware of what was going on down on Michigan Avenue. He blamed the demonstrators. "They don't represent the people of Chicago," he said. "They've been brought in from all over the country. We knew this was going to happen. It was all programmed. It's a separate act to itself. A kind of side show."

Amid near-hysteria, the roll call for the nomination began at 11:19 P.M. Humphrey sat in his suite and kept his own scorecard. It was thirteen minutes before midnight when Pennsylvania cast 103¾ votes for him and gave him a first-ballot majority. He began jumping, rushing over to the television screen where his wife, Muriel, was shown in the hall, beaming. With typical buoyancy, he kissed her image, then rose and took two congratulatory phone calls, the first from Johnson, the second from Nixon, then a later one from McCarthy.

The final vote was Humphrey 1,761¾, McCarthy 601, McGovern 146½ and 67½ for the Reverend Channing E. Phillips of the District of Columbia, the first black ever placed in presidential nomination in a major party. Maddox had withdrawn before the balloting. At 12:03 Thursday morning, the Illinois delegation asked that Humphrey's nomination be made unanimous. Despite boos and catcalls, Albert called for a quick voice vote and declared Humphrey the convention's "unanimous" choice. Muskie's routine nomination for vice president was challenged only by a symbolic nomination of Julian Bond as the candidate of the dissenters, though he was not yet old enough to qualify.

McCarthy held a news conference in a ballroom below, saying he might support a fourth party but would not be its candidate. As he did, Marc Raskin was calling a caucus at the Drake Hotel at the foot of Michigan Avenue to consider just that step. The next day, about 500 dissidents of all casts met in a University of Chicago hall and formed the New Party, which after much diligent effort obtained ballot position in twenty-nine states.

"But we had a big hangup," Raskin said later. "Who would run?" McCarthy was solicited but, Raskin recalled, "he kept saying only that he was willing." In the end, comedian Dick Gregory became the candidate. The New Party, which its organizers saw as "the peace wing of the Democratic Party, a party of independents and the young alienated," Raskin said, became in the end a victim of "a sense of exhaustion. . . . Too much had happened."

After the presidential roll call at the convention hall, Ben Stavis wrote later, McCarthy workers young and old thanked each other "for hours of selfless labor. The senator was not there. I don't know when or whether he ever thanked any of the staff, young or old. Of course he did not need to. We had worked for peace, for burned children in Vietnam, for black children in ghettos; not for McCarthy."

Wearily making my way back to the Hilton from the convention hall after filing my last story to my newspapers, I joined some colleagues in the

Haymarket Lounge on the ground floor. The now-shattered glass window looked out on the scene of demonstrators still keeping their vigil and chanting "Dump the Hump!" and "Hey, Hey, LBJ? How many kids have you killed today?" The bar's waitresses scurried about the room waiting on tables amid the stench of stink bombs, as if it were just another night on the job.

In the McCarthy bedroom in the Hilton, Abigail McCarthy wrote later, "I listened in dread as the announcements from the police bullhorns [to clear the park] bounced against the hotel walls and the refusals echoed back. I sat up in bed as the tension mounted, wondering what to do, whom to call. I could hear the shouts from the park: 'You McCarthy people, you there in the Hilton, are you with us? Flick your lights if you are with us.' And then the approving roar as hundreds of lights in the hotel flicked."

Up in Humphrey's suite, the newly declared nominee buckled down to the task of selecting his running mate. Earlier in the day, he had made one more pitch to Ted Kennedy with a phone call to Cape Cod, and had again been turned down. Among the long-shot schemes considered, according to Eisele, was for Humphrey to announce in his acceptance speech the following night that he was resigning as vice president and flying to Kennedy's summer home to ask him to be his running mate. The perils of a likely rejection led to a quick dropping of the idea.

Now the choice narrowed to two senators—Muskie and Fred Harris of Oklahoma. After discussing the matter with close aides Van Dyk and Bill Connell and a group of Southern governors, Humphrey slept on the decision for a few hours, awoke and said it would be Muskie. When he informed Johnson, Humphrey wrote later, Johnson told him he didn't "know what political good this can do for you" and preferred Terry Sanford, the former governor of North Carolina. But Humphrey's mind was made up. He summoned Muskie and Harris, took Harris aside and told him he needed an older and more experienced man who as a Catholic would bring more strength to the ticket. Then he called in Muskie and told him he was the choice. Harris was the first to congratulate the winner, though friends said later he took the disappointment hard.

At an early afternoon press conference on Thursday, McCarthy told cheering supporters: "I think that the country has passed a judgment on the war. Our failure here was not with the people, not with reference to our not having accomplished our purpose, because we did accomplish that. It was only that the judgment of the people could somehow not be put through the procedures of politics in 1968. And I don't say we have altogether failed as yet. But in any case, we have tested the process and we have found its weakness."

What McCarthy seemed to be saying was that the future of the Vietnam

War was past, but the powers still in control did not know it yet. "I think we are on the way in 1968 to preparing the way for the judgments that need to be made, perhaps somewhat less clearly, perhaps with our getting less credit than we might have liked if we had the White House. But we are willing to share that, and to forgo it, if we can accomplish these things for the country.

"I think the outlook is one that must be reassuring; one of confidence and one of optimism, not really of our own making but by virtue of our having discovered it to exist in the minds and in the hearts of the people of this country. . . . I think we can say that we were willing to open the box and see what America was. We had that kind of trust and that kind of confidence. And when we opened it, we found that the people of this nation were not wanting."

From there, McCarthy walked across Michigan Avenue and into Grant Park, where National Guardsmen continued to stand watch. Addressing a die-hard group of supporters as "the government of the people in exile," he pledged to them that "I will not compromise" with the commitments he had made to them, and would not endorse either Humphrey or Nixon.

* * *

Although the major political decision of the convention had now been made, the demonstrations—and the violence—were not over. Another Grant Park rally sounded a dismal theme. Tom Hayden, as a National Mobilization Committee leader, told more than 2,000 supporters that "it may be that the era of organized, peaceful and orderly demonstrations is coming to an end, and that other methods will be needed." He exhorted his listeners to return home and create "one, two, three hundred Chicagos." His colleague, Rennie Davis, called for establishment of an American National Liberation Front under the slogan "There can be no peace in the United States until there is peace in Vietnam."

That night, Dick Gregory tried to obtain police permission for a march to the convention hall on the South Side of Chicago where he lived, but he was refused. Undaunted, he addressed the crowd with an ingenious proposal. As recalled later by Erwin Knoll, a longtime journalistic colleague of mine in Washington before becoming the distinguished editor of *The Progressive* magazine, Gregory said: "You're all invited to be guests at my house. Come walk with me. We're going to test in Chicago tonight whether I am free to invite you to come to my house, and whether you're free to walk in the streets of Chicago with me."

The police objected but finally told Gregory that he would be permitted to lead a march only to 18th Street and South Michigan Avenue, about ten blocks away. "Let's do it, and when we get there we'll see," he told the crowd.

Knoll and another Washington reporter, Stuart Loory of the *Los Angeles Times*, followed the slow-moving, orderly marchers, who were walking three and four abreast. When Gregory and the others reached the appointed intersection, they found, Knoll recalled, "a rather formidable display of national guardsmen and police. Blocking one street at that intersection was an armored personnel carrier which was parked crosswise in the street with machine guns mounted on it."Also blocking the way, Knoll recalled, were jeeps with "large barbed wire grills mounted on the front of them."

At the head of the march were a number of convention delegates "all wearing their convention credentials," Knoll said. Most of them were McCarthy delegates, he said, but also there was "a Humphrey delegate, a paraplegic in a wheelchair, a veteran of World War II who had been injured in the war and who said he had come and joined this march to demonstrate his revulsion against what the police had been doing in Chicago." A police official with bullhorn in hand announced that anyone who advanced would be "in an arrest situation." Gregory and others at the front stepped off the sidewalk and were immediately loaded into police vans and taken to jail—including the veteran in the wheelchair, and Knoll and Loory. When they asked the veteran why he had clearly invited arrest, he told them: "I just felt that I'd rather cross the street than turn around. You get to a point where you can do no less."

In the police van, a Catholic priest from Pontiac, Michigan, said to Knoll: "This is probably old hat to you, but I have never been arrested before." Knoll replied: "Father, you may not believe this, but I have never been arrested before either." The priest said: "Oh, I thought this sort of thing happened to you people all the time." To which Knoll countered: "Only in Chicago, Father." (Later, Mayor Daley said of the arrested journalists: "Many of them are hippies themselves, in television and radio and everything else. They're part of the movement.")

Inside the jail, Knoll's ballpoint pen was taken from him because, he was told, it was a "sharp implement." McCarthy campaign buttons also were confiscated, for the same reason. Bail was set at $300, of which Knoll and Loory had to post $30. Later, the city prosecutor offered them the chance to plead guilty to obstructing traffic and pay a fine of $15, but both refused and eventually the charges were dropped.

In all, more than a hundred marchers were arrested, including New York columnist Murray Kempton and Harris Wofford, one of the founding fathers of the Peace Corps, founding president of the State University of New York College at Old Westbury and later United States senator from Pennsylvania. In his book *Of Kennedys and Kings: Making Sense of the Sixties*, he subsequently wrote: "Spending the night in a Chicago jail was hardly the way I expected to mark the nomination of Hubert Humphrey. It may have been as good a way as any, however, to celebrate the end of an era. Sitting on a bench in a crowded cell, with a clogged toilet in the middle of the floor and a portable radio blaring the speeches from Convention Hall, I had a sense that the curtain was finally coming down on the decade of Martin King and John and Robert Kennedy."

* * *

In the final session of the convention, another McCarthy delegate—David Hoeh, the Dartmouth teacher who had been a leading force in his candidate's startling showing in the New Hampshire primary—confounded the security people by intentionally sticking a school identity card into the machine designed to verify official convention credentials, and having it work. He was handcuffed and hustled out of the hall, but later allowed to return—after he had made his point that the musclebound security was a joke.

Once again, as at the 1964 Democratic convention, a film of a fallen Kennedy brother, this time Senator Robert F. Kennedy, introduced on tape by the surviving brother, mesmerized the delegates and reduced many to tears. "If my brother's life, and death, had one meaning above all others," Ted Kennedy said, "it was this: that we should not hate but love one another, that our strength should not be used to create the conditions of oppression that lead to violence, but the conditions of justice that lead to peace." Here in Chicago at this time in this place, the message was particularly apropos.

For the next thirty-two minutes, the film spanned Robert Kennedy's career in public and private life, including the funeral of his brother John and then his memorable appearance at the 1964 convention, with his voice again flooding the International Amphitheatre as it had the hall in Atlantic City in the words that now had a relevance to himself as well: "When he shall die, take him and cut him out in little stars, and he will make the face of heaven so fine that all the world will be in love with night, and pay no worship to the garish sun."

As the image of Robert Kennedy strolling along the beach in Oregon only three months earlier froze on the screen at the film's end, applause burst and continued to roll over the hall for nearly five minutes, until Albert tried to gavel the convention to order. Kennedyites on the floor, many in tears, began to sing "The Battle Hymn of the Republic" as Albert stood by, frustrated. At a signal, Chicago political hangers-on who had been packed into the galleries began chanting "We love Daley!" turning the Kennedy demonstration into a contest, with the Kennedyites taking up another chant: "We want Teddy!"

So it went, until a black alderman from Chicago, Ralph Metcalfe, a Daley

man, was sent to the podium to deliver a totally unscheduled tribute to
Martin Luther King and call for a moment of silence. The maneuver stilled
the convention until Albert abruptly gaveled the silence to an end to get on
with the remaining business of the convention: Humphrey's acceptance
speech.

The demonstration for Robert Kennedy proved the political prudence of
LBJ in ordering earlier that the memorial film be shown after the convention
had nominated its presidential candidate, rather than before. According to
Califano, Johnson approved of its showing only after the nomination, out of
concern that if it were shown before, it might generate a move on the floor to
nominate Ted Kennedy.

Even in his moment of triumph, Humphrey was obliged to take note of
the turmoil in which it had been achieved. "One cannot help but reflect the
deep sadness that we feel over the troubles and the violence which have
erupted, regrettably and tragically, in the streets of this great city," he said,
"and for the personal injuries that have occurred. Surely we have now learned
the lesson that violence breeds counterviolence and it cannot be condoned,
whatever the source."

Never one even to hint at lack of gratitude, Humphrey in honoring his
predecessors as Democratic presidential nominees did not shy away from including at the end "Lyndon Johnson," setting off loud choruses of boos along
with the cheers. Then, speaking directly to the man who had plucked him
out of a political dead end and back into the party leadership, he added: "I
truly believe that history will surely record the greatness of his contribution
to the people of this land, and tonight to you, Mr. President, I say thank you.
Thank you, Mr. President."

The closest Humphrey would allow himself to come to putting distance
between himself and LBJ on Vietnam was to say that "if there is any one lesson that we should have learned, it is that the policies of tomorrow need not
be limited by the policies of yesterday. My fellow Americans, if it becomes
my high honor to serve as president . . . I shall apply that lesson to search for
peace in Vietnam as well as to all other areas of national policy."

* * *

There now remained one deplorable episode that unfortunately was in
keeping with the foul spirit that had cast a pall over the entire convention.
Long after the convention's adjournment that night, as demonstrators continued to prowl outside the Conrad Hilton, the loyal band of young
McCarthy workers, some of whom had been with the campaign all the way
from the New Hampshire primary, gathered in Room 1506A to drown their
sorrows, reminisce, sing songs and say goodby to old friends there. I wan-

dered in myself to see some of them, some for the last time, and to congratulate them on what they had done, and tried to do, to get the country off the course of endless war in Vietnam, and in the inner cities at home. Most were thoroughly exhausted, yet an air of quiet celebration governed among many who took comfort in the thought that they had supported a righteous cause and had done their best. I bid my own goodbys and went to bed.

I learned only later that sometime afterward, shortly after five o'clock in the morning, on the contention that objects had been rained down on police and National Guardsmen from the McCarthy staff room on the fifteenth floor, police raided it. They repeatedly clubbed the hapless young McCarthyites, including George Yumich, thirty-one, and John Warren, twenty-four, seized others and jammed them into elevators as part of an ordered evacuation of the floor, then assembled them like prisoners in the hotel lobby.

Knoll later described what happened next: "While these kids were sitting on the floor there in the lobby, a police officer, one of the many policemen milling about, lunged into the area, in the midst of these kids, and started beating one of them with his stick. I was standing right there, I could not have been more than seven or eight feet away, and saw no provocation whatsoever for this act. . . . Several other officers went in and pulled this one policeman out and attempted to subdue him." A field worker for Humphrey named Neal Gillen gave reporters his name and told them he was willing to testify to what he had just seen.

Yumich, bleeding from the brutal clubbing on the fifteenth floor, staggered up to the twenty-third floor, where he encountered McCarthy, leaving his room for an early morning walk. Yumich told him what had happened and the senator went to the fifteenth floor to see for himself. There, he found more bloody young workers amid screaming and general hysteria.

Down in the lobby, Goodwin found the young McCarthy workers herded together by the police. He demanded that the police back off and told them McCarthy and Humphrey were on their way, meanwhile dispatching a young aide to call them. McCarthy appeared, Humphrey did not; a Humphrey aide, apparently not comprehending the significance of what had happened, decided not to wake the vice president. McCarthy asked the police who was in charge. Nobody answered. He instructed his young charges to return to their rooms, facing down the nervous police.

Abigail McCarthy wrote later that earlier she had seen someone in the park signaling to someone on the roof of the hotel. "When objects supposedly thrown from the fifteenth floor were displayed later by police as reason for invading our headquarters," she wrote, "I remembered that signaling."

McCarthy had planned to leave Chicago later that morning. On the advice of his Secret Service contingent, he decided to stay until the afternoon, by which time most of his young staff and followers would be safely on their way home. As his chartered plane finally lifted off from the embattled city, the pilot's voice came on over the intercom: "We are leaving Prague." The staffers applauded, usually the playful reaction to a smooth landing, but this time a gesture of relief. So ended what the young workers and dreamers called "the McCarthy Magical Mystery Tour."

Daley meanwhile had held a news conference in which he denounced the demonstrators as "terrorists" who had invaded Chicago to "assault, harass and taunt the police into reacting before television cameras." His only concession to what had been seen on millions of television screens was an observation that "in the heat of emotion and riot, some policemen may have overreacted. But to judge the entire police force by the alleged action of a few would be . . . unfair."

Humphrey echoed Daley in denouncing the "planned and premeditated" violence by those who believed "all they have to do is riot and they'll get their way." It was time, he said, to "quit pretending that Mayor Daley did anything that was wrong" in maintaining the strong police presence that had tried to preserve order in his city. (Later, after Chicago police reported that 650 people had been arrested during the convention week, Daley added this revealing postscript: "I think you newsmen missed the point. No one was killed." He obviously wasn't counting Jerome Johnson, the Native American shot on August 22—four days before the formal opening of the convention.)

Writing in the *Washington Post*, von Hoffman, a veteran of other Chicago social wars, identified perceptively the attitudes that were at the core of the battle that had just been waged in the streets of his old city. "It is the cultural content of what the kids were doing," he wrote, "that explains the exact character of much of the police behavior. . . . The police are often called on to enforce youth's disenfranchisement from ordinary political processes. When Mayor Daley would not give them a parade permit or tickets to the convention, it was the men in the baby-blue helmets who had to back up these decisions on kids angered out of their heads at having tried to work 'within the system' but who felt they had been cheated out of their primary victories.

"The Mayor and his police department see it differently. They are lower middle-class Irish with a strong streak of puritanism who find the language and sexual behavior of upper-class kids from the better universities unforgivable. In times past, the Chicago police have protected Negro demonstrators singing 'We Shall Overcome' from white mobs although they don't like to do it. But the taunts and chants of the kids were simply too much. . . . For the Irish and Polish, such behavior is more immoral, more indecent, more infuriating than the Vietcong flags that were waved in the faces of the police. And Daley is the chief ethnarch of Chicago, a prototype of the lower middle class."

Thomas Finney said later of Humphrey's reaction to the mayhem outside the convention: "I think that what went on in Chicago, and Humphrey's failure to denounce it, was directly responsible for McCarthy not making some gesture of support or reconciliation at the convention itself. . . . Humphrey's own course of action contributed substantially to the attitude of many of the McCarthy people and McCarthy himself, and contributed to his eventual defeat."

Before leaving Chicago, Humphrey called in Larry O'Brien, who had agreed only to stay with the campaign through the convention, and pleaded with him to remain through the election. The fact was that Humphrey had only the barest of strategies pieced together for a general election campaign that was to begin in a few days. O'Brien had other, private commitments but Humphrey got those who held them to agree to give O'Brien a two-month reprieve. He reluctantly agreed, not only to take charge of the campaign but to assume the chairmanship of the Democratic National Committee, to assure maximum coordination.

It was a very short time for any candidate to assemble a winning effort. It was especially so for a candidate deeply wounded by his own convention, his party still in shreds over differences on the war in Vietnam, threatened in the South by the independent candidacy of Democrat George Wallace and still held on a short leash by his own president.

Factions, at the Democratic convention and thereafter, pursued their own strategies: the regular party establishment, behind Humphrey; the McCarthyites, essentially leaderless now; the Kennedyites, with McGovern as convention stand-in; the New Democratic Coalition of liberals still striving for reform within the party; the New Party, charting an independent course outside it; the SDSers and the Yippies, devising more radical, disruptive tactics; the Black Panthers and other black groups, going their own more militant way. Even for Hubert Humphrey, the happy warrior, the eternal optimist, it was hard to see the sun shining through.

CHAPTER 10

September: Running in Place

Sept. 1 Black Power Conference proposes organizing national black party; **2** record 688 killed in auto accidents over Labor Day weekend; Cardinal Patrick O'Boyle of Washington picketed for chastising priests in birth control controversy; **9** New York City teachers strike over black firings; Columbia University asks charges be dropped against students in spring protests; **10** Rockefeller names GOP Rep. Charles Goodell to RFK's Senate seat; Abernathy, Andy Young arrested in Atlanta sanitation strike; **11** Aleksander Solzhenitsyn's *The First Circle* published in U.S.; Helen MacInnes's *The Salzburg Connection* published; **15** St. Louis Cardinals clinch National League pennant; **16** Metropolitan Opera season opens with Francesco Cilea's *Adriana Lecouvreur*, Renata Tebaldi, soprano; **17** Detroit Tigers clinch American League pennant; Chemical Workers join UAW-Teamsters alliance; **18** actor Franchot Tone, 63, dies; **19** *Funny Girl* starring Barbra Streisand released; **20** country and western singer Red Foley, 58, dies; **26** *The Man in the Glass Booth* starring Donald Pleasence opens on Broadway; **28** Ford Foundation pledges $10 million to aid poor.

From the very start, when Hubert Humphrey arrived in New York on Sunday, September 1, to kick off his campaign in a Labor Day parade up Fifth Avenue, his chief problem smacked him squarely in the face. Several hundred antiwar demonstrators awaited as he tried to enter his hotel, shouting "Dump the Hump!" over and over again, forcing him to enter by a side door.

Earlier in the day, he had made a feeble attempt to neutralize the Vietnam War issue, calling on Richard Nixon to join him in telling the Hanoi regime that the presidential campaign "will not result in our granting . . . concessions which it cannot obtain through the legitimate processes of negotiation now under way in Paris. The time to negotiate is now, not later. The time to stop the killing is now, not later." The Nixon campaign dismissed the initiative as a political gimmick.

More heckling greeted Humphrey along the parade route Monday as he trudged twenty-five blocks at the side of AFL-CIO President George Meany, trying manfully to look like the happy warrior he professed to be, practicing the politics of happiness and joy. But any happiness and joy in the crowds was tempered by the hostility of the war protesters, often shouting obscenities at him as he passed by.

With the campaign against Nixon and Wallace now fully upon him and with no firm and comprehensive battle plan yet in place, Humphrey returned to Waverly that night. Larry O'Brien, pollster/consultant Joe Napolitan and Ira Kapenstein, O'Brien's chief aide, were aboard his plane to brainstorm en route. On arrival in Waverly, the three strategists immediately repaired to a guest cabin where they worked through the night fleshing out a plan that Napolitan had drawn up at the convention and on the plane.

Napolitan, an old O'Brien sidekick from western Massachusetts, had been called to the convention by O'Brien. He recalled later how campaign chronicler Theodore White had dropped by his Chicago hotel room one day and saw him busily laboring over a typewriter. "What are you doing, writing a speech?" White asked. "No, I'm writing the campaign [media] plan," Napolitan replied. "You're kidding," White said. "I wish I were," Napolitan said.

The campaign was without a plan at this late stage, he said later, because everybody was so busy with "damage control" at the convention that there had been no time to look ahead in any detail. "We were lucky to come out of Chicago alive, and I mean that almost literally," he said.

The culprit, Napolitan said, was Lyndon Johnson, who had insisted before he bowed out of the race that he be renominated on his birthday, August 27. By the time he pulled out, the date and other key convention decisions had been locked in, and the Humphrey campaign was obliged to plan on the wing. "If Lyndon Johnson had been born on the Fourth of July," Napolitan said later, "Hubert Humphrey would have been president. The country would not have had Nixon or Watergate or any of the rest."

Now, in Minnesota, other old Humphrey associates were brought in the next day to address questions of candidate scheduling and campaign financing. But as the demonstrators in New York had vividly reminded all of them, time and money were far from Humphrey's central dilemma. O'Brien well knew that unless and until his candidate could free himself of the albatross of Johnson's war policy in a way that would establish him as his own man, he was doomed.

Most of that first week, the imperatives of gearing up the campaign from a standing start occupied the Humphrey insiders. Where to run Humphrey consumed their attention rather than how he needed to be positioned. Humphrey being Humphrey, he would make up in energy, enthusiasm and his trademark propensity for nonstop talking for what he lacked in time, money and freedom from the yoke of Lyndon Johnson. Thus, by circumstance and personality, Humphrey would campaign for the next two months in the manner of a chicken racing, sometimes staggering, around the barnyard with his head cut off. It was not the ideal formula for a presidential candidacy, and unwittingly it offered the perfect contrast to the approach already conceived by the Nixon strategists.

*   *   *

Nixon launched his own campaign on September 4 with an extremely well-advanced and well-coordinated motorcade in downtown Chicago. It drew an estimated 450,000 onlookers and demonstrated the care and polish that had marked the Nixon operation through the Republican primaries and convention. He was smiling, confident and well rested, a candidate on cruise control compared to the frenetic pace that Humphrey was obliged to maintain.

While the Democrats were thrashing about in their divisions over the war all through August, the Nixon team after the GOP convention had made good use of a nine-day working convention at the plush Mission Bay resort near San Diego.

It was clear from the start that a few Nixon insiders, led by John Mitchell, would be in charge, with the Republican national chairman, Ray Bliss, instructed to attend to party "nuts and bolts" matters, the colorless details that were a good fit for his colorless personality and his valued efficiency.

Mitchell, a gruff and unsmiling take-charge sort, directed the campaign in close consultation with Nixon and Bob Haldeman, in a manner befitting his military background. Mitchell had been commander in World War II of the PT boat squadron in which a young lieutenant named John F. Kennedy had served heroically. He suffered few individuals gladly, fools or otherwise. He gave short shrift to young aides particularly, telling one of them, as the aide related it to me later, "I never deal with junior officers."

According to other Nixon aides, Mitchell wasn't impressed by senior officers either. When Admiral Arthur W. Radford, the former chairman of the Joint Chiefs of Staff, dropped by the New York campaign headquarters to offer his help, Mitchell instructed his secretary to tell him he was too busy to see him. He treated Republican members of Congress the same way; Nixon moved his old political adviser, Murray Chotiner, in as a deputy to Mitchell to massage the political figures whose presence Mitchell declined to tolerate.

Three issues were quickly identified as the keys to beating Humphrey: Vietnam, crime and violence, and inflation. Much was made during the Mission Bay meetings about issues, with Senator Tower assigned to oversee their development. But central to the campaign's issues strategy was a decision that Nixon as the front-runner would not spell out his positions in ways that would make him vulnerable on details. On the war particularly, one of the chief issues advisers told me later, "we had to be flexible. There was always the uncertainty of what Hanoi would do on the war, and there was Johnson. Nixon always was concerned that he'd pull a rabbit out of the hat. We knew he couldn't end the war, but we knew too he'd try a gesture sooner or later that might be interpreted that way."

The strategy was based on the premise that in a three-way race, Nixon would win merely by holding the strength he had. Even before the fiasco of the Democratic convention, the Gallup Poll had Nixon leading Humphrey, 40 percent to 38. The same approach that had proved so successful in the primaries, of Nixon campaigning "above the fray" as if he already were the party nominee, would be continued in the general election, as if he had already been elected president. Learning the lessons of his 1960 presidential defeat and the folly of exposing himself to numerous audiences daily in a pell-mell dash to every state in the union, Nixon would remain aloof, controlled, "presidential."

For the first time in modern American politics, a campaign was constructed not to acquire maximum exposure of a presidential candidate by traipsing him about the country in a breakneck, punishing schedule. Instead, he would be given optimum, quality exposure while treating him as the principal resource of the campaign, to be hoarded, protected and parceled out in the most constructively disciplined manner possible. And in this effort, the new technologies of mass communication, and the purveyors of them in the news media, would be deftly harnessed and exploited to present the candidate always in the best light, under the most ideal circumstances. The tired Nixon of 1960, the perspiring Nixon, the angry Nixon of that failed, frenzied campaign of eight years earlier would studiously be replaced by the rested, cool, serene Nixon of 1968, always on the top of his game—if not very specific in saying what he would do if he became president.

The knowledge that the Democratic Party was torn apart by the LBJ war policy reinforced the confidence among the Nixon strategists that they could successfully play this control game. Appearance was to take precedence over substance, and in the process the image-makers in the campaign—television experts like Frank Shakespeare, Harry Treleaven, Roger Ailes and Haldeman—stayed in the forefront over issues men like Ray Price, Pat Buchanan and Richard Whalen. In frustration Whalen left the campaign, and the image strategy pressed on unimpeded.

If serious issue discussion was not to be allowed to get in the way of presenting Nixon in the best light, neither was money. At Mission Bay, plans were drawn for a series of $1,000-a-plate dinners and direct appeals to party fat cats in the era before limits on campaign spending. The campaign finance chairman, banker Maurice Stans, vowed to raise $20 million (he actually raised $24 million), with more than half earmarked for television advertising. While Humphrey was obliged to pitch for money even as he campaigned, Nixon never had to lift a finger, or a telephone, to ask for financial help. "My approach as finance chairman," Stans told me later, "was to free the candidate from any money worries whatsoever. Ours was by far the most expensive campaign ever, and I never once had to go to him to ask him to do anything to raise money."

Finally, there was the question of how to handle Agnew. Again, the 1960 experience dictated the strategy. Communications between Nixon and his running mate, Henry Cabot Lodge, had been a sore spot, illustrated by Lodge's freelance "pledge" that there would be a black in the Nixon cabinet, a promise Nixon never intended to make. This time it was decided to have Nixon man John Sears shuttle between the presidential campaign plane, named the *Tricia* after Nixon's elder daughter, and the vice presidential plane, the *Michelle Ann II* after Agnew's granddaughter, to provide coordination, although at this time Nixon was expressing great confidence in Agnew. Herb Klein at Mission Bay had reported that Nixon and Agnew discussed plans to build "the most closely coordinated dual campaign in America's political history." It was not appreciated at the time, however, how much Agnew would need monitoring.

The Mission Bay strategy sessions also put to rest the 1960 folly of campaigning in all fifty states. Privately, the campaign decided to focus on seven key states that had 210 of the required 270 electoral votes to win the presidency—New York, California, Pennsylvania, Ohio, Illinois, Texas and Michigan. In 1960, Nixon had won only two, California and Ohio; this time, his strategists decided, he needed to win six of the seven. Nixon would concentrate on these seven and leave the rest to Agnew, with particular focus on the South and border states where Wallace would be a threat.

His strategy firmly in place, Nixon had then made quick visits to liberal Republican leaders who were outside his fold, notably including Rockefeller and Romney, again learning a lesson from presidential campaign history— Barry Goldwater's defiant pulling in of the welcome mat from liberals at the 1964 convention. Then it was on to Key Biscayne to enjoy via television the Democratic chaos in Chicago. Humphrey's nomination assured that Nixon would get a free ride on Vietnam; the Democratic nominee was in no position to challenge him on how he would end the war when Humphrey himself was tied in knots by Johnson.

Herb Klein was only stating the obvious after the Democratic convention in observing that "they are going to be spending the next four weeks picking up the pieces. Meanwhile we will be ready to go next week with a unified party." One of the pieces not being picked up by Humphrey, incidentally, was John Connally, courted ardently by Nixon agents in Texas upon his return from the Democratic convention. Connally, disgruntled, agreed privately to help Nixon win support from conservative Texas oilmen and politicians, with an unspoken prospect that he would be taken into the Nixon cabinet—if Nixon carried Texas.

As Nixon prepared to launch his fall campaign, he said he planned to make better use of television than he had in 1960. But he added: "I am not going to barricade myself into a television studio and make this an antiseptic campaign." This promise to campaign among the voters would prove to be technically kept, but tactically merely a facade behind which would be constructed the most controlled and protected candidacy in American political history. It would be a candidacy in an isolation booth that sought to make invulnerable a man with great vulnerabilities, but also, this time around, with great self-discipline.

How that candidacy would unfold throughout the fall became apparent on the very first stop in Chicago—a clever two-track strategy designed on the one hand to portray Nixon as a vigorous, energetic, accessible candidate, on the other to parcel him out in carefully contrived and controlled exposures that eschewed all spontaneity—and risk of political misstep.

By intent, Nixon arrived in Chicago precisely at the lunch hour, when office workers in the downtown Loop were pouring into the streets. Perched on the back of an open car with wife, Pat, at his side, Nixon took forty minutes to inch through nineteen short city blocks, with two recent Rockefeller backers, Senators Thruston Morton and Ed Brooke, in tow, signaling the unity in the party. Signs individually hand-painted but bearing the same legend,

NIXON'S THE 1, AGNEW 2, bespoke the careful coordination that had gone into the opening of the campaign.

That was the first track, providing an exciting and exuberant scene to feed the writing press and television cameras whose product would go out to the nation on the network evening news shows. The second track then proceeded in private. Nixon retired to the Presidential Suite at the Sheraton Blackstone for the rest of the afternoon. He had a long massage and then sat around talking with aides and studying the backgrounds of handpicked panelists who would question him that night on a three-state regional television hookup. The panel was carefully balanced—one housewife, one businessman, one "ethnic," one Jew, one black, one Chicago newsman, one downstate Illinois newsman.

The panel discussion took place a few hours later from Studio One at WBBM-TV, the very studio in which Nixon had debated John Kennedy for the first time in 1960—and had "lost" amid analyses that he had looked drawn or even sick, as he perspired heavily. That wasn't allowed to happen this time; Nixon was rested, hale and hearty, and the "opposition" was not the sharp, primed Kennedy. The candidate was his most relaxed and statesmanlike as he fielded soft questions about "the new Nixon," Agnew and law and order, while declining to make any partisan attack on the violence that had shaken the Democratic convention in this city. The 300 faithful Republicans herded into the studio dutifully and enthusiastically cheered and applauded each answer—as did the moderator, idolatrous Nixon fan Bud Wilkinson, the gung-ho former Oklahoma football coach. Reporters traveling with Nixon were obliged to watch through a window in an adjacent room.

The next morning, Nixon held a news conference carefully planned to give the Chicago afternoon newspapers an irresistible new lead. It would serve no useful purpose, he said, to criticize either the Chicago police or the demonstrators for what had happened during the Democratic convention. "What happened in Chicago was not the agony of Chicago," he said, dripping with understanding and sympathy. "It was not the agony of the Democratic Party. It was the agony of America. It could have happened in any other city."

* * *

It hadn't, however, happened in any other city, and Mayor Daley was still taking a pounding over the scenes of police brutality that had dominated television screens the week before. Humphrey on arrival in Waverly after the convention had been greeted by a handmade sign that urged him to GO BACK TO CHICAGO AND DALEY'S FASCIST COPS. He defended the mayor, saying "we ought to quit pretending that Mayor Daley did something that was wrong. He didn't condone a thing that was wrong. He tried to protect lives." But even Humphrey's running mate, Senator Muskie, observed on NBC's *Meet the Press* on September 1 that he had the impression the Chicago police had "overreacted." While no city could "tolerate anarchy" from "troublemakers," he said, police "should not assume that everyone in a crowd . . . is activated by the same thing." Shortly afterward, Humphrey himself conceded that the Chicago police had probably "overreacted."

The commission that Lyndon Johnson had appointed after Robert Kennedy's assassination to investigate the epidemic of violence announced it was looking into the Chicago experience. Daley quickly put out a report of his own saying his police had been provoked by out-of-town "revolutionaries" and that "only" sixty persons had required emergency hospital treatment. An independent Medical Committee for Human Rights made up of more than 400 medical caregivers in Chicago reported, however, that 125 persons had been treated in hospital emergency rooms, 425 others at medical aid centers for injuries from billy clubs, tear gas and Mace, more than 200 treated by roving medical teams and 400 given first aid in the streets. (The presidential commission, chaired by Chicago lawyer and later Illinois governor Daniel Walker, eventually attached the label "police riot" to what had happened. There had been 668 arrests made during the convention, the commission's report said, most of them of young Chicago men with no previous arrests, or credentialed reporters.)

Daley, in his first post-convention news conference on September 9, explained it all succinctly in classic Daley-ese: "Get the thing straight once and for all. The police isn't there to create disorder; the policeman is there to preserve disorder."

In the Senate, Stephen Young of Ohio, a fellow Democrat, charged that "democracy was clubbed to death by Mayor Daley's police." Conservative Senator Russell Long of Louisiana countered that television had presented a "distorted, one-sided, completely biased" picture, and he called Daley one of the "nation's finest mayors."

Defensively, Daley asked the three major television networks for an hour of prime time "for the purpose of balancing the one-sided portrayal of the controversial events that were telecast during the meeting of the Democratic National Convention." NBC and ABC countered with offers of time on their regular Sunday interview shows, but he rejected them. Metromedia and a Chicago station did offer him an hour, however, during which a defense of the police was aired, including a showing of the "weapons" used by demonstrators—bricks, broken glass, beer cans, a Molotov cocktail. Daley appeared briefly in a taped interview in which he said the use of the National Guard had been justified in light of the danger of assassination of the presidential candidates.

The American Civil Liberties Union immediately charged that Daley was trying to minimize the "illegal conduct" of his police force. But a Gallup Poll found that 56 percent of Americans sampled approved of the way the police had handled the demonstrators. Among blacks in the survey, however, only 18 percent supported the police action. In any event, one thing was certain: it would be a long time before either party would hold another convention in "The City That Works." An estimated 10,000 antiwar protesters marched down Michigan Avenue later in September to express, the organizers said, "outrage and shame" over what had happened during the convention, and to show that a peaceful protest could be held in Chicago.

(Chicago's police were not alone in coming under criticism. The growing militancy of the Black Panthers, and resultant police agitation and anger, produced serious clashes on both coasts. In Oakland, two officers were discharged and jailed after having fired more than a dozen shots into the Black Panthers' headquarters two days after the manslaughter conviction of Huey Newton in the shooting of the Oakland policeman. Other incidents of violence between Panthers and the police in New York and New Jersey were reported in September. On top of all this, threats and reports of gunfire marked the uneasy alliance of the Black Panthers and SNCC. And when the faculty of the University of California at Berkeley invited Eldridge Cleaver to speak, Governor Reagan denounced him as "an advocate of racism and violence."

(Violence of another sort also came under fire at the annual Miss America pageant in Atlantic City. Members of a new Women's Liberation Movement gathered on the city's famous boardwalk and proceeded to discard all manner of restrictive undergarments. Some burned their bras as a symbolic protest against the televised extravaganza that glorified the female form and, the protesters argued, demeaned the whole woman. One sign proclaimed WELCOME TO THE MISS AMERICA CATTLE AUCTION and another showed a kneeling nude woman with her body marked off as various cuts of beef. The beauty contest, deplored for producing a "degrading, mindless-boob-girlie symbol," selected eighteen-year-old Judith Ann Ford of Illinois, described by the Associated Press as "a striking platinum blonde with blue eyes," as the new queen. She accepted the crown without protest. Another group of blacks, meanwhile, picketed the contest as an exercise in "white racism.")

* * *

From Chicago, Nixon went on to San Francisco, where his motorcade took him through Chinatown. In 1962, as a candidate for governor of California, he had been greeted there by a large banner erected by Democratic prankster

Dick Tuck asking, in Chinese characters, WHAT ABOUT THE HUGHES LOAN?—a reference to a controversial loan to Nixon's brother from financier Howard Hughes. This time around, the Nixon campaign efficiency made sure there would be no repetition.

That night, Nixon spoke before a crowd of 30,000 in Houston, where it was feared Wallace strength would kill his chances in Texas. En route, Nixon told the pool reporters on his plane that he wasn't going to mention Wallace "but I am going to frontally say what is the difference, what is the diametric difference between Nixon and Humphrey." But in the speech, noting that Wallace was saying there was "not a dime's worth of difference between Nixon and Humphrey," he added: "There's not a dime's worth of difference between the policies Hubert Humphrey offers America and the policies America has had for the last four years. . . . It appears that the great debate this year is going to be Humphrey versus Humphrey, and I'm going to have to ask for equal time."

What the difference was between himself and Humphrey, he neglected to say, and as far as a debate with his Democratic opponent, Nixon wanted no part of any such confrontation. He remembered well what had happened to him in 1960, and besides, the polls had him comfortably ahead.

Morton and Brooke in a press conference gently prodded Nixon. "I feel sure that our candidate is not going to let this heady wine [of large and enthusiastic crowds] keep him from being definitive," Morton said. Knowing Nixon's reputation for negative campaigning, the two moderate senators understood that any campaign style that resurrected stories of the old Nixon would not be helpful. But the Houston speech was a minor deviation from the script. Defensively, the campaign ground out a statement in which Nixon boasted that he had "now taken positions, completely forthright positions, on 167 major issues in this campaign." The well-oiled machine kept humming, even as the Humphreymobile labored to get out of first gear.

* * *

Humphrey, though boxed in by his commitment to the Johnson policy on Vietnam, tried his best to argue that he was better suited than Nixon to make peace. In a press conference in Minneapolis on September 5 he observed that Nixon wasn't "known as a peacemaker" and that "his career has been noted for Cold War politics." A few days later, in a network television interview, he said Nixon was "more well known as a sort of Cold War warrior," and in Los Angeles he offered that Nixon took "a little harder line" than he did on Vietnam and the communist threat.

These were very mild observations, but not to Agnew. Asked his opinion by a reporter in Washington after Humphrey had pinned a "hard line" label on

Nixon, Agnew shot back: "If you've been soft on inflation, soft on Communism, and soft on law and order over the years, I guess other people look hard, I don't know. . . . When you see the similarities between now and before the war, Humphrey is beginning to look a lot like Neville Chamberlain [British prime minister and signer of the infamous Munich Pact with Hitler]. Maybe that makes Mr. Nixon look more like Winston Churchill."

The words "soft on Communism," and the Munich reference, raised signals with reporters who remembered the communist scare days of Senator Joseph R. McCarthy of Wisconsin. In the ensuing furor, Agnew was obliged to hold a news conference that day at which he dug himself an even deeper hole. Humphrey, he said, seemed to be for "peace at any price"—the charge made in the 1930s against Chamberlain. As for himself and Nixon, he said, they were "not going to be squishy soft as this administration has been" on crime and "knowing your enemies," and he was not about to turn the other cheek. "I guess by nature I'm a counterpuncher," he said. "You can't hit my team in the groin and expect me to stand there and smile about it."

Spiro Agnew was finally on the offensive, but in a way that caused more nervousness within the Nixon campaign hierarchy. Not only was Agnew emerging as a loose cannon on the otherwise carefully controlled Nixon ship; but he was also becoming a breathing reminder of the freewheeling, red-bashing Nixon his strategists hoped to erase from public memory. Agnew's words brought back the Nixon who had accused Harry Truman's secretary of state, Dean Acheson, of "color blindness—a form of pink eye toward the Communist threat" and, en route to his House and Senate elections, had called Truman, Acheson and Adlai Stevenson "traitors to the high principles" of their party. If the Old Nixon had been transformed into the New Nixon, Agnew was there to take up the slack. As Mary McGrory put it in the *Washington Star*, "the governor of Maryland has been attempting to prove that the old Richard Nixon is alive and well in Spiro T. Agnew."

Although Agnew cautioned reporters not to "get left with the impression that my campaign is going to be a communist hunt" or a "communist scare," or that he was "attempting to attract the support of those with whom such fear tactics have been successful in the past [presumably referring to Joe McCarthy, not Nixon]," all this did not sit well with certain other Republican leaders. Senate Minority Leader Everett Dirksen and House Minority Leader Gerald Ford said they knew of "no evidence" to substantiate Agnew's charge that Humphrey was "soft on Communism."

Agnew seemed genuinely perplexed about the furor his remarks had raised. If he feared a reprimand from Nixon, none came. As a vice presidential nominee himself in 1952, Nixon remembered how badly he had been treated by presidential nominee Dwight Eisenhower when the story of the "Nixon fund" had surfaced and threatened to knock him from the ticket. He was going to be more magnanimous than the famous general in whose shadow he had toiled for eight years.

Still, the remarks kept Agnew on the defensive and the next day, on the advice of Sears and other campaign aides, he decided to apologize—in his fashion. He said he was merely making a "comparison" in response to Humphrey's remarks about Nixon. "If I left the impression that I think the vice president was not a loyal American," he said, "I want to rectify that. I think he is a man of great integrity and I have high respect for him."

But Agnew did not let it go at that. "I don't agree with him on every issue, and the use of the comparison to Mr. Chamberlain and Mr. Churchill I think is a completely valid comparison. I think Mr. Chamberlain considered himself to be a very loyal Englishman. There were many people in England at the time he made his cry for peace at any price that believed this was a proper cry to make. He made it in good conscience and I think the comparison stands."

Agnew insisted that he wasn't aware that the expression "soft on Communism" had any particular resonance in American politics; had he known, he said, "I would have shunned it like the plague. My record is not one of sympathy to inquisitorial procedures. I have never been a particular admirer of former Senator Joseph McCarthy. I did not approve of the witch hunts at that time. I still don't approve of them. Had I known that my remark was to be related in some way to cast me as the Joe McCarthy of 1968, I would have turned five somersaults to avoid saying it."

That a forty-nine-year-old candidate for the vice presidency, who was a practicing lawyer in his mid-thirties in the McCarthy era and actively interested in politics, did not know the history of "soft on Communism" was remarkable—and hard to believe. Only a few days before he had used the term regarding Humphrey, Agnew had called for investigations into "a definite link" between campus protesters and communists, to be conducted in a way that wouldn't revive "events in our recent past." In so doing, he specifically observed that he had "no desire to go back to the Joe McCarthy witch-hunting days."

He also had charged that some student leaders had traveled to Moscow, Hanoi and Havana and "received instruction from active Communist leaders of the world." The *Baltimore Sun* quoted him as saying he was obtaining the names of sixty-two youth leaders with suspected communist leanings—reminiscent of McCarthy's infamous speech in which he said "I have in my hand" the names of fifty-seven communists in the State Department, never revealed. Agnew later demanded a retraction, insisting he had never made such a statement while conceding that the youth leaders, while given to "anarchy and disruption," perhaps weren't communists after all.

Agnew denied that his comments were part of any hard-line campaign strategy, or that he had been pressured by Nixon or any of his aides to retract them. "I have never been one to go the low road in politics," he said. "I want to get off the low road. . . . I said 'squishy soft' and I am not proud of it. The Vice President said 'wiggly and wobbly' [in referring to Nixon] and I doubt if he is proud of that."

Already, in the first week of the general election campaign, Agnew was well on the way to fulfilling his aspirations for making himself "a household name." His performance stood in sharp contrast to that of his Democratic counterpart, Ed Muskie, who had opened his own campaign at the Alamo in San Antonio on September 8 by calling on all Americans to "get our emotions under control" and on his fellow candidates to avoid "playing off one group of Americans against another" or "probing or irritating the sore spots which divide us."

Muskie a few days earlier had seemed to go beyond Humphrey's position on Vietnam. He indicated he would support halting the bombing of North Vietnam without conditioning it on reciprocal action by Hanoi, and later suggested that "calculated risks" would be in order to bring about a negotiated settlement. But in all this, he said, while candidates should offer voters "the thrust" of their thinking on Vietnam they should refrain from specifics in order not to "destroy the posture of our government" in the Paris talks. That was fine with Nixon. At the same time, the observation cast Muskie as a careful and responsible running mate, in contrast to the loose cannon from Maryland.

*　*　*

Wallace, meanwhile, had not yet selected a running mate. He finally approached former Governor A. B. "Happy" Chandler of Kentucky, a onetime commissioner of baseball. An announcement seemed to be set for September 10 but Chandler pulled out, complaining that Wallace aides had pressed him to change his liberal views on civil rights. He suggested that "Mr. Big," whom he identified as oil interests in the Southwest bankrolling Wallace, may have vetoed his selection. Wallace replied that "Mr. Big are the people of the country and they're very big"—and resumed his search.

Wallace was well aware that he was a burr in the side of Nixon's Southern strategy—his design to drive a deep wedge into the traditionally Democratic solid South by building on the toehold in Dixie grasped four years earlier by Barry Goldwater. In New Orleans on September 11, the Alabama governor charged that "both national parties look down their nose [at Southerners], calling us rednecks." While denying he was merely a "sectional" candidate, he called on "the soul of the South" to fall in behind him "so we can join together and go out to the rest of the country and win." With a solid bloc of electoral votes from Dixie, he said, "we don't have to win but three or four more states to be elected president."

At the same time, Wallace also took aim at Humphrey by pitching to blue-collar white ethnic voters in the Northern cities, but he encountered much hostility in that pursuit. In Milwaukee on September 12, NAACP "Youth Commandos," black and white, heckled him with shouts of "Fascist!" and "Bigot!" Jutting his jaw out, Wallace replied to the cheers of his backers: "You know who the biggest bigots in the world are? They're the ones who call others bigots." As always with Wallace rallies, a mood of impending violence gripped the crowd, although on this occasion none of any substance occurred.

Wallace was to have held a national convention at which his American Independence Party was to nominate him, but he announced it would not take place because, in a dig at Chicago and the Democrats, it would take "the armed forces of the country to make it possible to hold one in safety." Accordingly, on September 17, his party simply announced that he was its nominee—without, at this point, nominating any vice presidential candidate.

* * *

Humphrey at the same time was not coming off very well in comparisons with his own running mate. On a quick cross-country trip from Philadelphia to Denver, San Francisco and Los Angeles, he continued to encounter heavy heckling from demonstrators in crowds that were embarrassingly small for a presidential nominee. Always the optimist, he permitted himself in Philadelphia to tell reporters, without challenging the Johnson Vietnam policy, that "I think I can safely predict that unless there are any unusual developments . . . I would think that negotiations or no negotiations, we would start to be able to remove some of the [American] forces in early 1969 or late 1968."

In Denver, where more hecklers greeted and plagued him, Humphrey surprisingly said that the minority plank on Vietnam at the convention, which had called for an unconditional bombing halt, was so "mildly different" from the majority plank that he would have had "no trouble at all" accepting it. When the traveling press on his plane pressed him on the matter en route to Los Angeles, however, he backpedaled, saying he would still insist on some reciprocal action by Hanoi that would protect U.S. forces. Had the minority plank passed, he said, he would have accepted it as the expression of the party's will but would have "felt a right and indeed an obligation to make some interpretation and elaboration of my own." The minority plank, he said, had in some ways "papered over some of the real problems we have."

Even this temporary slip off the Johnson policy road was not tolerated in the White House. The next day, Rusk in a news conference observed acidly that "no one should suppose that a bombing halt is going to produce peace in a few days." And Johnson, addressing an American Legion convention in New Orleans, said concerning troop withdrawals that "no man can predict when that day will come."

Humphrey, though thus chastised, still squirmed for some breathing room on Vietnam. In Houston, asked about LBJ's comment, he said he had only "hoped" some troops "might be able to come home." Then, waving a copy of the *Houston Post* bearing the headline MARINE REGIMENT HEADS HOME FROM VIETNAM WAR, he observed that he had "just read in your morning paper that one of the Marine divisions is on its way home." But closer reading of the story showed that the Marine regiment had been in Vietnam on temporary assignment and replacements already had been sent. An embarrassed nominee was obliged to put out a statement acknowledging that the returning regiment "in no way indicates any general withdrawal of American troops." As a fitting ending to the day, when Humphrey returned to Washington that night, Clark Clifford called him from the Pentagon to tell him again he was wrong about what the Marine withdrawal signified.

* * *

All who knew Lyndon Johnson knew there was no good time to ruffle his feathers, but mid-September was a particularly bad one. Beyond the annoyance of having his vice president and his running mate flirting with going off the reservation on his war policy, Johnson had to deal with reports that his administration was ready to apologize to the North Koreans over the activities of the *Pueblo,* in return for release of the intelligence ship and its crew. And on top of that were new troubles with his nomination of his very good friend Abe Fortas to be chief justice.

The State Department flatly rejected the apology report and made public what it said were secret orders issued to the *Pueblo* nearly three weeks before its seizure, instructing the captain to remain at least thirteen miles off the North Korean coast, superseding a 1966 standing order permitting ships to go as close as three miles. Nevertheless, to Johnson's continued frustration and embarrassment, the ship and crew remained in North Korean hands.

As for Fortas, a witness before the Senate Judiciary Committee on September 13, B. J. Tennery, dean of the American University Law School, testified that Fortas had received $15,000 to conduct seminars at the school for nine weeks over the summer. The money came from a fund raised by Paul A. Porter of Fortas's old and prestigious law firm, Arnold and Porter, and contributed to by prominent businessmen. One of them had a son involved in a federal criminal case that could come before the Supreme Court on which Fortas now sat as an associate justice.

This testimony, on top of charges that LBJ was practicing cronyism at the highest judicial level, contributed to a split vote by the committee, eleven to six, to report the nomination to the full Senate with a recommendation for confirmation. Three conservative Southern Democrats joined three Republicans in voting against confirmation, suggesting more trouble ahead.

Humphrey tried to blame it all on Nixon, suggesting he had "made a deal with Strom Thurmond," a member of the committee, to block Fortas. Nixon, he said, "could have Mr. Fortas confirmed in a week if he'd say the word, because it's his troops in the Senate, his supporters, that are blocking that confirmation." Instead, he charged, "Mr. Nixon is going to play foot-loose and fancy-free by attacking the courts, attacking the Supreme Court and playing the game with Mr. Thurmond and denying Mr. Fortas the confirmation." Nixon replied that twelve Republican senators were supporting the nomination and suggested that Humphrey "look to his own party," which had sixty-seven senators. That fact, indeed, added to Johnson's frustration.

* * *

Nixon may not have had a deal with Thurmond on the Fortas nomination, but he had already delivered on another matter close to the South Carolinian's heart on his first post-convention swing into the South. On the night of September 11, in a taped interview in Charlotte with two local television newsmen and with the press again barred from the studio, Nixon threw a very large bone to Dixie, under arrangements that put the interview beyond the range of Northern television viewers. Traveling reporters were free to watch on closed-circuit television but the interview was not to be released until the next day, when it was to be aired in North and South Carolina. By that time, the Nixon entourage was off to other states, with other stories to be covered.

Nixon started out by saying he believed the Supreme Court's school desegregation decision was correct and that he could not condone "freedom of choice" plans that were really a subterfuge to perpetuate segregation. But then he got a question that enabled him to deliver the goods. Asked, in a classic example of objective questioning, whether he agreed with the withholding of federal funds to "bludgeon a local community into accepting an agency's doctrine" on desegregation, Nixon replied: "[To] say that it is the responsibility of the federal government and the federal courts to, in effect, act as local school districts . . . to use the power of the federal treasury to withhold funds or to give funds in order to carry [desegregation] out . . . that kind of activity should be very scrupulously examined and in many cases I think should be rescinded."

Nixon well knew that the threat of withholding federal aid had been the only really effective way to prod many Southern school districts to comply with the court decision. But he also knew what the Southern sentiment was, and no doubt recalled his reassurances to Thurmond when he was soliciting his support against the Reagan challenge in Dixie before the Republican convention.

Senator Brooke, who had dropped off the tour when it headed South, said, "I just wonder what he had in mind that would be more effective." So did the accompanying reporters, but when they sought a news conference with the candidate they were detoured by explanations from Nixon aides, not the man himself—a recurring pattern by now. One explanation not offered was the obvious one—that Nixon in addition to paying off a campaign debt to Thurmond was making a down payment on the South's vote in November, at a time it was being diligently stalked by George Wallace.

* * *

If there was one issue that shared Wallace's preoccupation with race it was the one he treated as a first cousin to it—crime. He gave no quarter either to Nixon or Agnew in playing the law-and-order theme on the blunt instrument that was the drawling voice from his snarling, pugnacious lips. His solution to crime, especially urban crime, was to seize every perpetrator and "put him under a good jail." He dismissed with contempt all the "pointy-headed intellectuals who couldn't park a bicycle straight" but wanted to coddle criminals because of their underprivileged childhood—because "their daddies never carried them to see the Pittsburgh Pirates."

* * *

Nixon was more subtle, if only a bit so. Sidestepping Wallace and focusing on Humphrey in Indianapolis on September 13, he called him "tragically naive" about "the crime crisis that grips America." Like LBJ, he said, Humphrey "has exaggerated and overemphasized poverty in this country as a cause of crime. . . . The war on poverty is not a war on crime and it is no substitute for a war on crime."

Humphrey said Nixon was "strong on jails" while he was "strong on building houses and enforcing the law where the law needs to be enforced. For every jail Mr. Nixon wants to build," he said, "I'd like to build a house for a family. And for every policeman he wants to hire I'd like to hire another good teacher. It isn't either-or, it's both. And if Mr. Nixon is going to play Fearless Fosdick, that's his privilege," he said, referring to a comic strip detective patterned after Dick Tracy. Humphrey said he'd prefer being president "of a country that wants to see both civil order and justice" than "the chief of detectives."

Agnew's use of law and order came under criticism from Ford, who urged him to talk about "order with justice under law." But Agnew pressed on, saying that "law and order . . . very possibly will decide the 1968 election," and that it would come "when government makes up its mind that the people and the Constitution, not the mob, will rule America."

Muskie offered at Wichita State University that while "some say the answer to crime is a policeman's nightstick . . . it won't work. The only way to have a secure society is to have enlightened individuals who have the opportunity to improve their lives and fulfill their potential." He noted that Wallace's Alabama had the highest murder rate in the nation and Agnew's Maryland the highest violent crime rate, but that only proved that "party labels are irrelevant when it comes to crime." Such reasonableness, however, was being lost in the thunder of the law-and-order candidates.

* * *

Agnew's law-and-order rhetoric, coupled with his recent civil rights encounters in Maryland, left him vulnerable to suspicions of racial bias. At a press conference in Chicago on September 13 in which he asked reporters to "drop the Communist thing—put it to bed," one of them awakened another slumbering vulnerability. Noting that there hadn't been many blacks in his crowds, the reporter asked Agnew whether it concerned him. "That hasn't occurred to me," he replied. "Very frankly, when I am moving in a crowd, I don't look and say, 'Well, there's a Negro, there's an Italian, and there's a Greek and there's a *Polack*.' I'm just trying to meet the people and I'm just glad that they're there and that they're friendly."

Reporters present weren't sure they had heard him correctly, or whether he was serious. "Nobody knew how to handle it," said Robert Shogan, then of *Newsweek*. "But here it came right on the heels of 'squishy soft.' It started to ooze out. It was a thrill a minute. This was a guy, we suddenly realized, who was saying anything that came into his head. And because there were no issues to speak of, we started to look for this kind of thing. It said something about him."

Agnew, according to aides, was mortified. Well on his way to becoming a household name, he was risking becoming a household joke. He took another step on the same path the next day during a television panel interview. After having condemned all kinds of civil disobedience, he was asked whether it wasn't true that "Jesus, Mahatma Gandhi, Henry Thoreau and Dr. Martin Luther King" all had been practitioners of it. Agnew replied: "Let me distinguish between those cases. The people you have mentioned did not operate in a free society," a bit of history that would have been a surprise to the latter two.

Agnew's freewheeling and often unthinking style troubled the Nixon strategists. Here they had meticulously laid out a strategy that would keep their presidential candidate on a carefully charted road, avoiding potentially hazardous spontaneity at every turn. And their vice presidential candidate was careening along, bouncing in and out of every pothole in sight, as if he were the Dick Nixon of 1960. Something had to be done.

The something was a new speechwriter named Stephen Hess, an Eisenhower administration veteran who had worked in Nixon's losing presidential and gubernatorial campaigns of 1960 and 1962. Hess proved to be too bland for Agnew's liking and later on Pat Buchanan volunteered to write speeches for him, in what would prove to be a marriage made in venom.

Agnew's relationship with the reporters traveling on his plane, several of whom had covered him in Annapolis, was cool at best. He seldom walked back to where the press sat, and when he did it was awkward. Even idle conversation seemed difficult. Once, as the plane headed toward Honolulu, a reporter asked Agnew whether he planned to go swimming there. Pinching a roll of fat on each side of his waist, he said he didn't want to reveal his "love handles." It was not the sort of remark the reporters had expected to hear from the aloof governor and they didn't know whether to laugh. Ted Agnew was, for sure, a strange bird.

* * *

Nixon, however, had more serious concerns than the idiosyncrasies of his running mate. By mid-September, word had come to him privately, "through a highly unusual channel," he wrote later in *RN: The Memoirs of Richard Nixon,* that Johnson was seriously considering ordering a halt in bombing North Vietnam—a move that might achieve a breakthrough in the Paris peace talks. The source was Henry Kissinger, Nelson Rockefeller's chief foreign policy adviser, who in 1967 had provided the Johnson administration, through French friends, with a secret back channel to Hanoi and subsequently had lines into the Paris talks themselves.

The Johnson negotiators were operating at the time on the premise that Kissinger was an unofficial member of their team. "Henry was the only person outside of the government we were authorized to discuss the negotiations with," Richard Holbrooke, then an aide to chief negotiator Harriman, told Walter Isaacson in his book *Kissinger: A Biography.* "We trusted him. It is not stretching the truth to say that the Nixon campaign had a secret source within the U.S. negotiating team."

As Johnson in mid-September considered offering the bombing halt, the development "came as no real surprise to me," Nixon wrote later, because "I had learned of the plan through a highly unusual channel," whom he then identified as Kissinger. He instructed John Mitchell, he wrote, to "continue as liaison with Kissinger and that he should honor his desire to keep his role completely confidential."

The arrangement was the beginning of a relationship that was to give Nixon a considerable tactical advantage in the remaining weeks before election day, as the status of the peace negotiations became increasingly critical in Humphrey's hopes to close the wide gap between himself and Nixon.

* * *

On September 14, meanwhile, Joe Napolitan sent a memorandum marked "Highly Confidential" to O'Brien telling him straight out that "it is my strong belief that if this campaign continues as it has started we will lose" unless Humphrey did something bold. He proposed that the vice president notify Johnson that he was going to Paris to meet with Harriman and the representatives of Hanoi, then announce "he is convinced that the first step on the road to peace is an immediate halt to the bombing." Then, Napolitan said, Humphrey should prevail on Harriman to resign, announcing "that he agrees with you [Humphrey], disagrees with the president and intends to spend the rest of the time before the election persuading the country that your position is right."

Napolitan's memo did not explain why he thought Harriman would go along, but it went on: "This would be a dramatic breakthrough that would put the stamp of leadership on the vice president. Obviously it requires a hard-nosed attitude to carry it off. But it would set to rest the fears of many persons that Hubert Humphrey does not have the courage to stand up to Lyndon Johnson. [Napolitan, in the understatement of the year, acknowledged that "the president will be unhappy."] Harriman is important to the operation, but not essential. The biggest plus is that the move would bring back to Hubert Humphrey millions of votes which should be his but which we cannot now claim."

Much later, Napolitan told me that he urged Humphrey directly to resign the vice presidency, saying he had some criticisms to make of the war policy and it would not be proper for him to make them as Johnson's vice president. "If it works you're president, if it doesn't, you still lose," Napolitan said he told the candidate. Humphrey replied, he said, that he was probably right but he couldn't do it, for three reasons: his loyalty to Johnson, the debt he owed LBJ for making him vice president, and the possibility that if something then happened to Johnson, aging House Speaker John W. McCormack [next in the statutory line of succession] would become president. "He said he liked McCormack," Napolitan recalled, "but didn't think he was the right guy to be president, considering the military situation."

Humphrey continued doggedly to fight the depression that gripped his campaign. At Canisius College in Buffalo on September 17, he told the faithful to forget the "premature funeral notices" and go out and work. The same day, he got a boost in the form of a telegram from Johnson to the Texas state Democratic convention endorsing Humphrey as a man who had the "courage, common sense and compassion" to handle the presidency.

But with every boost, it seems, came a knock. Unruh and Connally had snubbed his visits to California and Texas and Gene McCarthy was nowhere to be seen or heard. Other Vietnam doves, like McGovern and Ted Kennedy, did come his way, but only amid bitter heckling from antiwar diehards.

As Humphrey started a fifteen-day trip to fourteen states from Boston on September 19, Kennedy made his first public appearance since his brother Robert's death, at a jam-packed downtown intersection, but it made no difference. The hecklers had turned out in droves from Harvard and other highly charged antiwar campuses and blasted both the Democratic nominee and his prominent supporter. Shouts of "Dump the Hump!" were mingled with cries of "Shame on Teddy!" and "Sellout!" as Kennedy tried to introduce the nominee. Young protesters waved signs that said DON'T HUMP ON ME and MAYOR DALEY FOR HEART DONOR as Humphrey struggled to make himself heard.

"We will not move this country forward," he beseeched, "if it is plagued by those who deny freedom of speech, and who deny freedom of assembly to those who offer appeals to reason." But the crowd was not ready for a civics lesson. The reply came back in a distinct shout: "Bullshit!" In one of the most liberal Democratic cities in the country, the old New Dealer could barely contend with the hoots and howls, as Kennedy sat stolidly at Humphrey's side. At one point, when Humphrey lectured the crowd that "your actions here are going to disgust the American people," voices shouted back: "We are the American people!"

Humphrey was badly shaken by the Boston experience, and bitter. On the flight to South Dakota afterward, he noted that Boston was a major center of college protest. "We know it is going to happen," he said. "They will boo me, they will boo Teddy, they will boo the bishop." Asked to compare the protesters with the Goldwaterites of 1964, he replied: "The Goldwaterites were poor, misguided people. These people are intentionally mean anarchists. They do not believe in anything. This is the hard core. Take a look at them, filled with hatred, bitterness, bigotry. Look at their faces, filled with violence. They will never live long enough to run us off the platform because basically they are just cowards."

All this while, Nixon continued to enjoy the leisurely pace of the confident front-runner, doing his one or two daily events, always timed for maximum network television coverage that night. That usually meant a noontime rally at or near a major airport with flights to Chicago or New York, aboard which film could be rushed. Then he would take the afternoon off, and perhaps—but not always—do a no-pressure evening event at which the well-rested Nixon would bask in the adoration of the party faithful.

On September 18, in Fresno, he faced the first concentrated heckling against him of the campaign but he ignored it. Ronald Reagan dismissed the grape pickers who were razzing Nixon as a "noisy type of barbarians who will not follow orderly procedure." Most protesters, however, seemed to regard Nixon as a lost cause and turned their wrath on Humphrey.

In Cleveland on September 22, the vice president was unmercifully heckled by war protesters at an amusement park as he appealed to the crowd to vote against "the bitterness and nihilism and animosity" of the picketers. Unknown to him at the time was the fact that a local lawyer who worked for the Federal Aviation Administration had been stabbed as black and white youths fought behind the speakers' stand. It was just another misfortune befalling the man who continued to seem more and more the hapless warrior.

Still, Humphrey's natural ebullience could not be suppressed for long. On a tour of a farm near Buffalo, he was taken on an inspection of the spread of one Jim Cravens, who proudly showed off his large and impressive farm machinery. Humphrey, in his element, climbed aboard one after another of the large vehicles, admiring them vocally as he went. At the end, a microphone was set up on the rear of a beat-up old pickup truck for Humphrey's remarks. The vice president, thinking Cravens was still showing off his prize machinery, looked at the pickup, grinned and said: "Isn't that a dandy?" But there was nothing dandy about the prospects for his flagging campaign.

Had Humphrey been running against Agnew, his plight would have seemed much less hopeless. For a man who was selected because he was regarded as the next best thing to Nixon running alone, the governor of Maryland was attracting an inordinate amount of press attention as a vice presidential candidate.

In the context of the Nixon strategy on Vietnam to duck any specifics on how he might end the war, Agnew at lunch in San Francisco September 20 was asked why he and Nixon had not said how they intended to do so. "If we shot all our ammunition now," Agnew replied, "the whole campaign would collapse in boredom by the end of October." Well, he was asked, wasn't he engaging in a "deliberately delaying tactic"? He replied: "Isn't that the way you run a campaign?"

The remark led Nixon critics to demand that if he had an effective plan to end the war, he owed it to the men fighting in Vietnam to come forward with it at once, rather than hold it back for political gain. Agnew the next day was obliged to backpedal, saying "I never meant to indicate that there was a plan. . . . I simply indicated that as the campaign progresses, Mr. Nixon and I will be speaking out in increased detail on all the issues. And, of course, that includes the problem in Southeast Asia."

Here was another example of why Agnew needed an overseer from the Nixon campaign leadership. The next morning came another more egregious remark. As his plane headed out of Carson City, Nevada, after an Agnew speech and news conference in Las Vegas the night before—and some late hours at the gambling tables for some of the reporters—the candidate strolled back. He found one of the revelers, Gene Oishi of the *Baltimore Sun*, a stocky native-born Japanese-American who had covered Agnew in Maryland, dozing in his seat. Turning to Dick Homan of the *Washington Post*, Agnew asked: "What's the matter with the fat Jap?" Homan, surprised, said: "He was up all night in the casino." With that, Oishi awoke and said to Agnew: "That was a wicked city you took us to, Mr. Agnew." After some more pleasantries, Agnew strolled off.

Another reporter, Mike Weiss of one of the Baltimore papers, turned to Homan. "Did he say what I thought he said?" he asked. "Yes," Homan said. Others nearby vouched for the quote. They asked Oishi if he had ever been called that particular name in Annapolis, and he said he had not.

At first the incident became a matter of harmless bantering between the reporters and the Agnew staffers. Somebody sent a note up to the Agnew compartment that said: "Agnew is a thin-skinned, squishy-soft Greek with love handles." Oishi wanted to let the whole matter slide and at first that was what happened. But when he phoned his wife and told her what Agnew had said, she was furious. When several reporters pressed their colleague on the matter, he said he would not object if they wrote it. Homan, to protect himself competitively, mentioned it in the last paragraph of a story on another subject filed from San Francisco. "The fat Jap" first hit print four days after the remark was made, but it immediately became front-page news across the country.

Agnew again was stunned, and bitter. He had meant the remark as a light joke, and the reporters' reaction convinced him anew that the press was out to get him. In the hostility that increasingly marked his attitudes and comments about the news media, the "fat Jap flap" clearly was a milestone.

Beyond that, it fed the impression that Ted Agnew was a man who bore watching—by the reporters and by the Nixon campaign that had every other cog in the machine firmly in place.

The timing also could not have been worse. The story broke while Agnew was in Hawaii, heavily populated by Japanese-Americans and others of Asian ancestry. Democratic Representative Spark Matsunaga, a Japanese-American, observed on the House floor that "one does not win friends by insulting people of other racial backgrounds, particularly through mouthings of racial prejudice."

Incredibly, when the Agnew party boarded a smaller plane the next morning for a tour of the Islands, Agnew walked back, spied Oishi, and asked: "How's the fat Jap this morning?" As an icebreaker, or a labored effort to indicate he was only joking the first time, it wasn't very funny the second time either.

When Agnew asked other reporters if they really believed he had been serious, they told him that at the least he was insensitive in the remark to Oishi, and in the use of "Polack" as well. To explain himself—in his fashion—Agnew delivered a long and defensive discourse on insensitivity and racial bias at, somewhat incongruously, a festive luau in a large hut on the island of Maui.

"A funny thing happened on the way to Hawaii," he began. "Maybe it wasn't so funny after all. Those of you who read your local papers are going to find that this vice-presidential candidate, this son of a Greek immigrant, is being accused of an insensitivity to the national pride and heritage of other peoples." It was, he went on, "a rather ridiculous charge to make to a man who grew up in a neighborhood where his family was the only Greek family, a man who saw his father come home dead tired in the afternoon and climb down off a vegetable truck to be ridiculed by certain people who referred to us as 'those Greeks on the block.' Yes, we were sensitive in those days, but thank God the United States has passed that point where we're drawn up so tight that we can't communicate with each other, and where our sense of humor is beginning to disappear."

He then gave his version of what had happened, calling Oishi "a friend of mine . . . who happens to be Japanese [*not* Japanese-American]." He had, he said, "referred to him in certain slang, similar to the slang that people on athletic teams use affectionately among themselves, some of which wouldn't bear repeating." Oishi wasn't offended, he said, "but coming on the heels of another amplified statement that occurred a week ago in the campaign, where in designating certain ethnic groups—as I feel I have a right to do because I am part of one, and a very big part of one—I inadvertently used a slang expression for another ethnic group. . . . I confess ignorance because my Polish friends had never apprised me of the fact that when they called each other by this appellation it was not in the friendliest context."

Agnew, expressing his bafflement at the criticism that had come down on him, observed with an attempt at self-deprecation that "it's pretty hard for Zorba the Greek or Zorba the Veep, whichever you prefer, to really understand how the humor that's pervaded American life, that permits us as people of wide backgrounds to be free and easy in our expressions with each other, gets caught into such a desperate clutch that we must watch every expression we use."

Anger obviously rising in him and broadening his complaint, Agnew said he was "sick of sloganeering, I'm sick of people reading something different into law and order than what law and order really means. I'm sick of people attempting to put my thoughts into a context that they didn't exist in when I spoke them. And I say to you that when you stop and consider, how utterly ridiculous it is to think that a person who had felt the sting of unkind remarks that *were* uttered harshly in an ethnic or racial sense could say something that callous without meaning it in fun and jest. It just doesn't make sense to me."

Agnew said he was "not going to apologize for the spirit in which I said what I said to Gene Oishi. I *am* going to apologize to any who might have read in my words an insult to their Japanese ancestry, or to any who might have read into my words an insult to their Polish ancestry."

Then he launched into a long sermon on the perils of diverse America losing its sense of humor, pleading that "the camaraderie that exists among men, which allows them to insult one another in a friendly fashion, be not abolished in favor of the terrible and intense guarded atmosphere that seems to abound so freely in the dictatorships of the world. This is America; this is the melting pot of America! And if we are so ashamed of our background that a single word sets us into orbit, then the purpose of America, my friends, is beginning to fail."

Agnew concluded by saying "if I have inadvertently offended anyone I am sorry, I am truly sorry. To those of you who have misread my words, I only say you've misread my heart." Homan, in his account of the speech, observed that at its end, "Agnew's voice was choking with emotion and he dabbed his eyes with a napkin."

At a subsequent fence-mending party for the traveling reporters, Agnew again defended his remarks as no more than the kind of playful banter he had often heard in the locker room of the Baltimore Colts football team. Homer Bigart, the venerable veteran reporter of the *New York Times*, wagged his finger at the candidate and instructed him: "Governor Agnew, one thing you must remember. Locker-room humor should never be equated with running for Vice President of the United States."

(Agnew-watching by this time had become a sort of full-time spectator sport for the reporters covering him, appropriate in this year of notable sports achievements. As politics continued its roller-coaster ride through the year, there were still more historic diversions in sports. In September, Arthur Ashe became the first amateur to win a major open tennis tournament and the first black to win the U.S. Open when he beat Tom Okker of the Netherlands. And in baseball, the Year of the Pitcher continued with the Detroit Tigers's Denny McLain posting his thirtieth victory, the first player to do so since the famed Dizzy Dean performed the feat in 1934.)

Gene Oishi was more offended by attempts by Agnew and his staff to defend his remark, saying Oishi had always been called "the fat Jap" around Annapolis, than by the remark itself. When Agnew continued to say so, Oishi wrote him a note of complaint. He was called to the front of the plane, where Agnew told him, after all that had transpired: "I didn't know you felt that strongly about it. I'll never say that again." Oishi said later: "He kept his word. He never did." But for Agnew, often disparagingly referred to as "Spyro" by reporters, the damage was done, and no tortured explanation would change that.

Parody-writing by the traveling press corps covering the various candidates continued to be a boredom-chaser—for the lyricists if not for their captive audiences on the press planes. Agnew's antics inspired some of us on the Nixon plane to pen words for Nixon to sing to the chorus of "Can't Take My Eyes Off You":

Squishy-soft on communism, without much thought of realism,
Ted Agnew's got a way with words that Cabot Lodge did not.
I need you, Spyro, for putting Hubert down,
Keep swinging, Spyro, I'll try to calm them down;
You take the low road, I'll keep my moratoriums high.
So cool it, Spyro, don't knock the Polack vote,
And let the Jap sleep, he just got off the boat. . . .

If a vice presidential nominee best served his leader by being seen and not heard, Agnew was beyond that possibility now.

* * *

Humphrey's choice of Muskie as his running mate meanwhile looked better and better. Compared to Agnew, he was cool and reasonable, a healing figure who appealed for a lowering of rhetoric. But he could not help Humphrey in the two areas he most needed help—flushing Nixon out and at the same time freeing himself of Johnson's yoke. Stymied by Nixon's unwillingness to join the battle in a direct television debate or to say much that he could criticize, Humphrey at a rally in Portland, Oregon, took to calling Nixon "the Shadow"—another manifestation of his frustration. But about LBJ, he said nothing.

Instead, he made only the feeblest attempts to break out of the box on Vietnam in which Johnson had placed him. In a television broadcast from Toledo, he promised to "reassess the entire situation in Vietnam" and "take the action that that situation requires" if elected. Only hinting at freedom from Johnson, he observed that "men of independent judgment and strong conviction from time to time have different points of view," and that no president wanted only "yes men" around him. But Humphrey continued to come off as a classic example of one.

* * *

Nixon at the same time was ready to pounce if Humphrey did finally try to separate himself from the Johnson war policy. In an interview on September 24, he said it would be "very unfortunate if any implication was left in the minds of the American people that we were able to bring home our forces now because suddenly the war was at an end or about to come to an end." He said he did not "want to pull the rug out from under our negotiators in Paris by indicating now that we are going to start cutting back our forces and leaving the enemy encouraged to believe that if they just wait, that they don't really have to negotiate now."

As for himself, Nixon continued to adopt a wary stance toward the peace talks, for good reason. On September 26, Nixon wrote later in his memoirs, "Kissinger called again. He said that he had just returned from Paris, where he had picked up word that something big was afoot regarding Vietnam. He advised that if I had to say anything about Vietnam during the following week, I should avoid any new ideas or proposals."

* * *

Humphrey, after a dismal trip to California, was at the end of his rope. He hoped devoutly for a chance to debate Nixon, but the Republican nominee dashed any lingering hopes that he might agree by arguing in a St. Louis forum on September 26 that under federal equal-time provisions, Wallace would have to be included and that would only build him up, to the detriment of the two-party system. He would be willing to debate Humphrey, he said, but "I would not agree to a three-ring circus. . . . This is a two-party country, and if we are to avoid a constitutional crisis, both Hubert Humphrey and Richard Nixon should do everything to prevent" the election going into the House of Representatives (as provided in the Constitution if one candidate failed to achieve an electoral-vote majority).

The next day in Louisville, Nixon dismissed Humphrey's pressure for a debate as "kid stuff" and called Wallace Humphrey's "secret weapon" who could be built up in the South by a debate and thus undercut Nixon there. "I'm just not going to play that game," he said.

Why Nixon didn't want debates was no surprise. First, he had a clear lead over Humphrey and it was holding. Just as important, thanks to Stans, he had all the money he needed to buy television time of the sort he much preferred. He liked the kind where everything was carefully staged and controlled by his strategists and television handlers, with no opposing candidate matching wits (and physical appearances) with him, and no adversarial reporters throwing tough questions at him. The absence of formal news conferences made certain he didn't get any of those for weeks on end.

Another blow to Humphrey came on September 27, from McCarthy, just back—tanned and rested—from a ten-day vacation on the French Riviera. He told reporters in New York he would be campaigning for Senate candidates who agreed with him on the war and party reform—but not for Humphrey, because he didn't see any basic change in his allegiance to the Johnson Vietnam policy. Earlier, in Houston, Humphrey had said almost pleadingly of McCarthy that "it is inconceivable to me that we wouldn't be together when the choice is between Nixon and Wallace and myself." But all the comment revealed was that in spite of his long association with his fellow Minnesotan, he really didn't know him. While Humphrey was slowly expiring, McCarthy the old minor league baseball player would be covering the World Series for *Life* magazine.

Earlier in September, a collection of Democratic liberals active in the McCarthy and Kennedy campaigns had met in Washington—with McCarthy in attendance—to consider the possibility at that late date of a fourth-party candidacy, first raised by Marc Raskin. McCarthy said he would withdraw his name from the ballot wherever it was listed except in California, where he would not object if his backers succeeded in their self-starting effort to get the required 330,000 signatures. When the petition effort fell short, the directors of the liberal California Democratic Council voted to launch a write-in for McCarthy in the state, but it got nowhere.

The McCarthy statement of nonsupport for Humphrey was part of a double whammy against the vice president that day. He got an advance report on the latest Gallup Poll that had him trailing Nixon, 28 percent to 43, with Wallace only seven points behind him at 21. While Nixon remained at the same strength shown in the previous Gallup Poll early in the month, Humphrey had dropped three points and Wallace had gained two.

Later in the day, Humphrey was subjected to more heckling and a student walkout in Portland. With shouts of "Stop the War!" still ringing in his ears, he talked to O'Brien in Washington, who also had seen an advance copy of the Gallup Poll. "I thought this poll showed that it was imperative that Humphrey make a dramatic statement on Vietnam," O'Brien wrote later, "even if it meant running the risk that Johnson would denounce him. We simply had nothing to lose." Humphrey, after months of resisting, agreed.

O'Brien told his candidate he had pulled together $100,000, enough to buy half an hour of network television time for the critical statement. They agreed that the speech would be made on Monday, September 30, from Salt Lake City, where Humphrey was already scheduled to be.

George Ball, the distinguished former undersecretary of state, had just resigned as Johnson's ambassador to the United Nations to join the Humphrey campaign, and the candidate called him and asked that he meet him in Seattle the next night. A draft speech already written by Ted Van Dyk based on the work of Humphrey's task force on Vietnam in August was sent to Ball for his reading on the plane. He found it so unsatisfactory that he rewrote it en route, only to find on arrival that another version had already been written.

On Saturday morning, September 28, O'Brien also got a copy of the draft Ball had seen. "I read it and hit the ceiling," he wrote later. "It was weak; it begged the question—it was a disaster. I sent Humphrey a strong message, via telecopier, which said among other things that the speech was a waste of our $100,000." Those were very sharp words coming from the usually calming, diplomatic O'Brien. Humphrey called back, O'Brien said, and told him: "Larry, that was quite a telegram. But there's one problem—that wasn't any final draft you saw. The speech isn't even written yet. Why don't you fly out here and be with me, and we'll work on it?" O'Brien agreed to join the campaign entourage in Seattle the next night.

If Humphrey needed any further confirmation that the time had come to make the break with Johnson, he got it as he attempted to address a crowd of an estimated 10,000 people at the Seattle Center Arena. Protesters with bullhorns forced him to engage in a debate—or, more accurately, a shouting match—that was worse than any previous heckling he had encountered.

"Mr. Humphrey, in Vietnam there is a scream that does not end," one antagonist began. At first, Humphrey listened, telling the crowd that "one set of bad manners is enough." The man continued: "There is a wound that does not cease its bleeding. I'm talking about the scream of death and the wound of war. Why is the scream being heard in Vietnam by our soldiers and innocent Vietnamese people? Why is there this wound because of war—not a war for democracy but a war which supports a puppet government, a government where the now No. 2 man said his hero is Adolf Hitler? You have supported this man. You have supported Johnson. You have supported this war, this needless waste, this murder. We have come not to talk with you, Mr. Humphrey. We have come to arrest you."

When the man with the bullhorn asked the candidate, "What about democracy in Chicago?" Humphrey, his anger rising, shot back: "This is Seattle. Shut up!" But the man went on. "Mr. Humphrey, you are being accused now of complicity in the deaths of tens of thousands of Americans and hundreds of thousands of Vietnamese. This is not a joke to us, it is not a ploy. This is serious. We charge you with crimes against humanity. They did not escape. You shall not escape. Will you come to stand trial before the world, before the United Nations? Do you dare to do that? Do you dare to stand forth before the nations of the world at the United Nations and let them try you?"

Humphrey, flushed with anger now, shouted: "I shall not be driven from this platform by a handful of people who believe in nothing!" He pleaded again for quiet as the protesters were ejected from the hall, their followers chanting "Dump the Hump!" as they went out behind them. Humphrey now pleaded for civility. "We shall never settle our problems if we take them to the street in violence," he said. "We have a better way. We have the way of dialogue, of debate, of discussion, yes, even of open and honest dissent. Dissent in America, yes, but disorder in America, no."

Later, Humphrey told Eisele: "In many ways, Seattle was the low point of the campaign, but all it did for me was to make me more determined than ever that we were going to conduct our kind of campaign and not let a militant, noisy minority drive us off platforms. I think the outrage over that kind of thing may have helped us, too, because people just decided that was too damned much. It definitely was the turning point for me."

For the country, however, especially all those who wanted a new course in Vietnam, the Seattle episode was only another manifestation of the dissatisfaction with Humphrey's candidacy that he had to address head-on. Afterward, he sat up most of the night with Ball, O'Brien, Fred Harris and staff aides laboring again over a new draft of the speech he would make on television. The next day, the Humphrey party flew on to Salt Lake City, where again that night another session was held, in his suite at the Hotel Utah, to hammer out the final version.

The candidate sat in his bathrobe as a debate ensued between the doves—led by O'Brien, Harris and Van Dyk—and the hawks—led by old New Deal friend Jim Rowe and Bill Connell, Humphrey's closest staff aide. The doves insisted on a flat unconditional call for a bombing halt of North Vietnam; the hawks wanted a softener—conditioning the halt on the enemy's willingness to reestablish the demilitarized zone between North and South and warning that bombing would be resumed if the North Vietnamese acted in bad faith. Some of the hawks were, in fact, against any speech at all.

Rowe, according to O'Brien later, argued to Humphrey that "you can't expect to be elected president if you turn on the president you served under. You can't run on a ticket of disloyalty." Rowe and Connell, O'Brien wrote, "predicted that Johnson would denounce any Humphrey call for a bombing halt . . . and that it might be seen as undercutting the Paris peace talks. Personally, I found it hard to believe that Johnson, however angry, would denounce his own party's candidate." Ball, who had had earlier discussions with American negotiator Averell Harriman, called him again at one point and received assurances that he would not derail Humphrey over the language in the speech.

O'Brien recalled telling Humphrey: "You have to prove you are your own man. You're not going to be elected president unless the people are convinced you stand on your own two feet—and this is the issue you can prove it on!" Whereupon, according to O'Brien, "Humphrey exploded. 'Damn it, I'm on my own two feet. I'm sick and tired of hearing about how Lyndon Johnson will react or how Gene McCarthy will react. Let's start thinking about what Hubert Humphrey wants. This is my speech and I'll write it myself.' He grabbed a pen and began to work over the speech."

The debate nevertheless went on around him, into the early morning. The final draft was a compromise or, rather, a victory for the doves with a couple of sweeteners for the hawks. The key paragraphs read:

"As president, I would be willing to stop the bombing of North Vietnam as an acceptable risk for peace, because I believe it could lead to success in the negotiations and a shorter war. This would be the best protection for our troops.

"In weighing that risk—and before taking action—I would place key importance on evidence, direct or indirect, by word or deed, of Communist willingness to restore the Demilitarized Zone between North and South Vietnam.

"If the government of North Vietnam were to show bad faith, I would reserve the right to resume the bombing."

It was after five o'clock in the morning by the time the draft was finished and dictated for typing. After sleeping a few hours, Humphrey attended a breakfast with Utah Democrats and spoke at the Mormon Tabernacle, then went back to his suite to work on the speech again with Ball.

That night, fifteen minutes before airtime, Humphrey called Johnson at the White House and told him what he was about to say. Johnson listened and then, Humphrey wrote later, said: "I gather you're not asking my advice." Humphrey told the president that was so but assured him, he told Eisele later, that he had "sufficient protection in the language of this speech so that in no way will it jeopardize what you are trying to do" and had checked with Harriman and Ball. "Well," Johnson commented, "you're going to give the speech anyway," and hung up.

To make the point that he was speaking as his own man and not LBJ's vice president, Humphrey had the seal of the vice president removed from his lectern before he went on the air. In delivering the key paragraphs, he dropped the phrase "would be willing to stop the bombing" and instead said he "would stop the bombing." The language was not all that removed from LBJ's position, but it signaled that Humphrey was at last speaking for himself, even at the risk of alienating his patron.

This he did, according to Califano. "Johnson never forgave him for it," he wrote later, to the point that when Califano subsequently told the president "I was giving Humphrey ideas for his campaign, since we wouldn't need them for a legislative program in January, 1969 . . . Johnson flushed and snapped that those are 'my ideas from my staff and my task forces.'"

Nevertheless, on this last night of September, the Democratic presidential nominee told friends he felt liberated. But with only five weeks to go until election day, he knew it would take a combination of an extraordinary campaign effort and luck—and probably a breakthrough in the Paris peace talks—to catch the confident, unruffled New Nixon of 1968.

* * *

There remained also the question mark of George Wallace—would his strength hold or fade, and if it faded, would fellow Democrat Humphrey be the beneficiary, or fellow conservative Nixon? Wallace was in high gear now, taking his traveling road show North and South with all the brass, excitement and, yes, threat of explosion and violence that distinguished his performance on the stump. Urging voters to "Stand Up for America," he energized friends and foes alike, insuring that most Wallace rallies became shouting matches, and some of them vehicles for fistfights in the crowd and the throwing of bottles and beer cans. Wallace himself at times seemed to relish the near-mayhem, at others to be scared himself by it.

On September 30, he rode through Chicago's Loop during the crowded lunch hour waving from an open limousine as supporters and opponents exchanged words and waved rival signs. His partisans marched down State Street behind his car carrying placards that said WALLACE, DALEY AND THE PO-LICE and DON'T LET CHICAGO BURN, GEORGE. Young protesters, many of them black, toted others that read IF YOU LIKED HITLER, YOU'LL LOVE WALLACE. The police who were the constant object of Wallace's stated affection guarded him closely, some on motorcycles keeping the crowds at bay. Hecklers yelled "Wallace is a pig!" and "Sieg heil!" as they gave the stiff-armed Nazi salute.

After spending much of the afternoon at a second-rate Chicago hotel, Wallace and his entourage motored out to the notoriously conservative sub-urb of Cicero, lily-white and blue-collar. He held a street rally outside a Western Electric Company plant at quitting time, making his usual pitch on law and order. When a young girl held an antiwar sign aloft, it was ripped from her hands and torn up. And when, criticizing foreign aid, he started to say "there is one more thing we ought to do . . ." a white youth in a T-shirt broke in with ". . . Kill the niggers!" There was some laughter in the crowd but Wallace, unsmiling, pressed on as if he hadn't heard the comment. It was par for the Wallace course.

In a much less organized and efficient fashion than was the case in the Nixon campaign, Wallace tried to keep the inquiring traveling press at arm's length, but he never hesitated to use the reporters as props in his efforts to fire up his crowds. He would tell the assembled faithful that reporters from "The *Time* and the *Newsweek*" were out among them, and could be spotted by the way they scribbled in their little notebooks. The remarks always pro-duced turned heads and scowls, much to Wallace's delight. If any violence erupted in the crowd, he would urge his supporters to "let the police handle it, they know what to do."

Wherever George Wallace was, you could expect fireworks. But even he was about to outdo himself.

CHAPTER 11

October: Too Little, Too Late

Oct. 1 Cardinal O'Boyle relieves 39 rebellious priests of duties; **3** *The Great White Hope* starring James Earl Jones, Jane Alexander opens on Broadway; **7** Robert Conquest's *The Great Terror* published; Motion Picture Association adopts new rating system; **10** Broadway producer George White, 78, dies; **11** *Barbarella* starring Jane Fonda released; **14** United Mine Workers win 8 percent annual raise in 3-year soft coal agreement; **16** *The Boston Strangler* starring Tony Curtis released; **18** actor Lee Tracy, 70, dies; **22** Arthur Schlesinger's *The Birth of the Nation* published; *Star!* starring Julie Andrews released; **23** 9 Cuban exiles arrested in New York office bombings; **24** *The Lion in Winter* starring Katharine Hepburn, Peter O'Toole released; **25** daughter Lucinda born to LBJ's daughter Lynda Robb.

The inner glow that Hubert Humphrey felt in declaring a modicum of independence from Lyndon Johnson in the Salt Lake City speech had outward manifestations the very next day, October 1, in downtown Nashville and at the University of Tennessee in Knoxville. The hecklers who had plagued him almost daily since the Chicago convention were nowhere to be seen. In their place were supporters hoisting signs indicating that his new course in Vietnam had been heard. The most pointed said IF YOU MEAN IT, WE'RE WITH YOU, although another expressed reservations. It said: NO QUALIFICATIONS—STOP THE BOMBING.

In a local television interview, Humphrey sought to emphasize his modest declaration of independence from Johnson. Henceforth, he said, he would campaign not as vice president but "as the candidate and the leader of my party," and that was why he had ordered the vice presidential shield removed from his speaking stand. "I will have variances, there is no doubt, from time to time with the administration," he said. "I have some constitutional responsibilities as vice president, which I shall fulfill, [but] I don't want to confuse the positions."

There were other indications that Humphrey had turned a corner. O'Brien had had the wisdom to include a printed pitch for funds on the television screen at the close of the Salt Lake City speech. The money started to roll in— a quarter of a million dollars within a week. Compared to the Nixon campaign treasury it was peanuts, but it gave Humphrey a psychological boost and enabled his strategists to plan some modest television buys.

Nixon, in an obvious attempt to suggest that Humphrey was betraying Johnson with the proposed bombing halt, derided the vice president's remarks as the "fourth or possibly fifth different position" on it. He said it could "very possibly" be interpreted by the North Vietnamese as "offering a concession in January that they could not get now." If so, he said in a classic Nixonism, there was still time for Humphrey to recover.

"Because of the wide disagreement [over what Humphrey meant]," Nixon said in Detroit, "he ought to clarify it and say he is not undercutting the United States position in Paris." He said he hoped Humphrey would do so "and not pull the rug out from under the negotiators and take away the trump card [the bombing halt] the negotiators have."

At the same time, some antiwar Republicans were getting fed up with Nixon's pussyfooting on Vietnam. Senator Hatfield wrote an editorial in the moderate-to-liberal *Ripon Forum* asserting that "the Paris peace talks should not become the skirt for timid men to hide behind. In 1964," he wrote, "the American people—trusting the campaign promises of the Democratic presidential candidate—thought they were voting for peace, only to have their trust betrayed. Candidates at all levels are again expecting voters to accept their post-election intentions on faith, and they deal with Vietnam in terms of assurances not to 'sell out' our men in Vietnam and vague promises for 'an honorable peace.' This is not enough. In the democratic process, voters should not be forced to go to the polls with their fingers crossed; they should not be forced to rely on blind faith that the man they vote for will share their views on the most important issue of the election."

Nixon, though, was still comfortably ahead in the polls and was not about to be coaxed or shamed into saying anything about how he would end the war in Vietnam. He was getting nervous enough about the possibility that Johnson might pull off a diplomatic coup in Paris. So he was confining his observations to expressing support for LBJ's efforts, while being prepared to pounce on any deal that could be criticized as selling out America's stated objectives and her sacrifices in Vietnam.

In Paris, Xuan Thuy, head of the North Vietnamese delegation, quickly threw cold water on the Humphrey proposal. "This means," he said on October 2, "that Mr. Humphrey, like Mr. Johnson, still demands reciprocity." But the proposal had not been intended primarily for North Vietnamese consumption. The important question was what Americans opposed to the war, and the McCarthyites particularly, thought of it, and whether it would move them at last to Humphrey's side.

* * *

Johnson was still digesting the bitter pill slipped to him by his vice president when he had to swallow another one. On October 1, supporters in the Senate of his nomination of Fortas to be chief justice failed to invoke cloture to cut off an opposition filibuster. The vote was not even close. With fifty-nine votes required—two thirds of those voting—the president's forces managed to muster only forty-five and were defeated by a coalition of Republicans and Southern Democrats. Fortas promptly asked his old friend to withdraw his nomination, which Johnson did on October 2, calling the outcome "tragic." Judge Thornberry, LBJ's Texas friend who was to have taken Fortas's seat as an associate justice, also was blocked. Johnson smoldered.

* * *

On the same day on the other side of the Capitol, meanwhile, there were fresh reminders of the disastrous Democratic National Convention. Yippie leaders Jerry Rubin, dressed as a bead-bedecked guerrilla fighter toting a plastic toy M-16 rifle, and Abbie Hoffman cavorted in the packed hearing room of a House Un-American Activities Subcommittee investigating "subversion" behind the Chicago violence. As pro-Daley witnesses testified to the protesters' plans to aid "the policies of Hanoi" and "disrupt the total political process," Rubin and Hoffman chided subcommittee chairman Richard Ichord of Missouri until they were asked to leave, which they triumphantly did.

Another reminder of the violence of the stormy year came with the release of a 222-page report on the Columbia student rebellion by a five-man commission chaired by former solicitor general and Harvard law professor Archibald Cox. It found that although campus radicals had ignited the uprising, it was rooted in a "deep-seated dissatisfaction with Columbia life" among a much broader universe of students and faculty members.

While condemning the sometimes violent tactics of the insurgents, the commission rejected the allegation that the rebellion resulted from a well-planned conspiracy by SDS. "Part of the responsibility for the disturbances rests upon the revolutionaries consciously seeking to subvert and destroy the university," the report said, "but their total number was small—much less than the full SDS membership and their activities were only the catalyst that precipitated a deeper movement." Means should be found "beginning now," it said, "by which students can meaningfully influence the education afforded them and other aspects of the university activities."

(Young Bill Clinton by now had found a means to influence the Hot Springs draft board to enable him to continue the education at Oxford afforded him by his Rhodes Scholarship. On October 3, he boarded the liner *United States* in New York with other members of his Rhodes class, not yet having been called for induction. David Maraniss, in his excellent biography of Clinton, *First in His Class*, quoted Henry Britt, a Hot Springs lawyer and former judge, as saying he called the chairman of the draft board, a close friend, and asked him to "put Bill Clinton's draft notice in a drawer someplace and leave it for a while. Give the boy a chance.")

*　*　*

In the first days of October, Wallace continued his assault on the Midwest with a four-city swing through Michigan. Everywhere, he generated controversy: cheers from many blue-collar autoworkers concerned about blacks taking their jobs and the increasing violence and disintegration of heavily black Detroit; boos and shouted slurs from those who saw him as a dangerous demagogue.

In Kalamazoo, a college student repeatedly challenged him as he spoke by shouting "Racist!" Wallace supporters planted themselves in front of the young man, held up a Wallace sign to block him from the candidate's view and glared menacingly. He finally forced a rattled Wallace to stop his speech and observe, pointing at the youth: "You're never going to get promoted to the second grade if you don't behave." Wallace's faithful thought the remark was hilarious.

In Grand Rapids, when similar shouts threatened to drown him out, Wallace told the students: "That's all right, because you've gotten me a half million votes here today." That line drew cheers too, as did another staple in his repertory, telling "anarchists" of the sort who lay down in front of President Johnson's car in Los Angeles earlier that if they should try that with him, "that's going to be the last automobile they lie down in front of. And if you don't think I mean what I say about my automobile, I'm gonna come back here and you come and try me."

Nixon and Humphrey were becoming increasingly concerned about Wallace. He continued to show enough strength in the polls to threaten to siphon off sufficient votes from each to be critical in the election's outcome. He could undercut Nixon in his own region of the South and he could take the votes of white blue-collar voters in the North away from Humphrey.

Wallace was now playing the race card unabashedly in his television commercials. One showed a school bus rolling down a country road as the narrator intoned: "Why are more and more millions of Americans turning to Governor Wallace? Follow while your children are bused across town." The screen then showed acts of violence, after which Wallace was seen and heard saying, "As president, I shall within the law turn back to absolute control the public school systems within the respective states."

A second ad with the same lead-in showed a woman walking down a dark street as a street lamp was smashed, with the narrator inviting the viewer to "take a walk through your street or park tonight," and Wallace declaring, "As president, I shall help make it possible for you and your families to walk the streets of our cities in safety."

At the same time, a Nixon ad pictured the Republican nominee saying, amid scenes of street violence: "The first civil right of every American is to be free from domestic violence. So I pledge to you, we will have order in the United States."

Humphrey weighed in with an ad that sought to counter the Nixon implication that violence were a Democratic product—an impression fanned by the war protest demonstrations that were severely jeopardizing the vice president's election chances. His face filled the screen as he said:

"We have seen the terrible results of violence in this country. It would be intolerable if a handful of violent people, and that's what it is, just a handful, could harden us against the need to change. I've seen the hardening of violence too, and it perverts the very spirit of America. I saw it at the Republican convention in 1964, when Governor Rockefeller was shouted down. I saw it in Minneapolis when Governor Wallace, a man with whom I disagree, was heckled into silence. And it happened to me in Philadelphia. We must give notice to this violent few. There are millions of decent Americans who are willing to sacrifice for change, but they want to do it without being threatened and they want to do it peacefully. They are the nonviolent majority, black and white, who are for change, without violence. These are the people whose voice I want to be."

To combat Wallace especially, Nixon's strategists staged another of their controlled voter panels for him in Atlanta, beamed at considerable expense to forty-eight television stations in a dozen Southern states. As usual, the panel was constituted chiefly of Nixon supporters with a local newsman thrown in to provide a modicum of authenticity. He asked Nixon what he thought of

Humphrey's characterization of Wallace as an "apostle of hate and racism."
Nixon, appealing to potential Wallace voters, tread carefully at first.

"He's against a lot of things Americans are frustrated about," he began.
"He's against the rise in crime. He's against the conduct of foreign policy,
what's happened to American respect around the world. I'm against a lot of
those things. The difference is, I'm for a lot of things." Then, he added: "We
need policies at home that go beyond simply saying that, 'Well, if somebody
lies down in front of my presidential limousine, it will be the last one he lies
down in front of.' Now, look here. No President of the United States is going
to do that, and anybody who says that shouldn't be President of the United
States." Outside the studio later, Nixon told reporters that no one who would
make a statement like that "is even fit to be president."

Humphrey was tougher. He charged that Wallace was waging "a calculated campaign to divide this nation, to deliberately inflame the fears, frustrations and prejudices of our people, to bring this nation to the brink of
broad-scale disorder." He called Wallace "the creature of the most reactionary
underground forces in American life," including "groups dedicated to the
promotion of anti-Semitism." While he was at it, he got a few licks in on
Nixon, observing that while he was "surely no racist" he appealed to the
"same passions, the same frustrations which regrettably could unleash in this
country a torrent of unreasoning hate and repression."

                              * * *

Against this backdrop of hostility from both the Nixon and Humphrey
camps, Wallace made a move on October 3 in Pittsburgh that produced one
of the most bizarre scenes of the political year. It probably cost him whatever
chance he had to be a decisive factor in the election of 1968. At a press conference in a large ballroom of the Pittsburgh Hilton, he unveiled, or more
properly unleashed, as his choice to be his running mate retired Air Force
Chief of Staff General Curtis E. LeMay, the former commander of the
Strategic Air Command.

The scene was right out of the *Laugh-In* television show, though clearly not
by intent. As Wallace stood with LeMay on a stage in the ballroom, Secret
Service agents assigned to Wallace poked their heads out of large openings
high in the wall behind that was painted in a luminous psychedelic floral pattern. It was much like the set of that show wherein featured cast members
each week would pop their heads out to deliver funny one-liners.

The difference was that Wallace and LeMay were all seriousness throughout, although we reporters seated before them were first dumbfounded, then
appalled, then incredulous as LeMay, after Wallace's proud introduction, answered one pointed question. As the man once responsible for directing the

Air Force arm poised to deliver the nation's huge nuclear arsenal upon the Soviet Union or any other enemy, and in so doing invite nuclear retaliation on the United States, he naturally was asked about his position on the use of nuclear weapons.

"We seem to have a phobia about nuclear weapons," the general said, as Wallace stood by, not suspecting that his new running mate was about to drop a political nuke on him. "I think most military men think it's just another weapon in the arsenal," LeMay said. ". . . The smart thing to do when you're in a war—hopefully you prevent it. Stay out of it if you can." So far so good. But then he added:

"But when you get in it, get in it with both feet and get it over with as soon as you can. Use the force that's necessary. Maybe use a little more to make sure it's enough to stop the fighting as soon as possible. So this means efficiency in the operation of the military establishment. I think there are many times when it would be most efficient to use nuclear weapons. However, the public opinion in this country and throughout the world throw up their hands in horror when you mention nuclear weapons, just because of the propaganda that's been fed to them. I don't believe the world would end if we exploded a nuclear weapon."

We reporters covering the press conference looked at one another in amazement and watched for Wallace's reaction. He clearly was getting uneasy as his new sidekick blithely dismissed the potential for Armageddon in a nuclear exchange. As LeMay continued, Wallace got increasingly agitated, but said nothing at first.

LeMay dismissed as "propaganda" all the reports that nuclear explosions caused permanent and hereditary damage to human, animal and plant life. Citing tests at the Bikini firing grounds in the Pacific, he reported on motion pictures that had been taken after aboveground tests that made the blasts seem positively therapeutic.

"The fish are all back in the lagoons," he boasted, "the coconut trees are growing coconuts, the guava bushes have fruit on them, the birds are back. As a matter of fact, everything is about the same except the land crabs. They get minerals from the soil, I guess, through their shells, and there's a little question about whether you should eat a land crab or not." The rats on the atoll, however, were "bigger, fatter and healthier than they ever were before," he assured us.

Wallace continued to squirm as LeMay conceded that while nuclear war would be "horrible," there really was no difference between being killed by a nuclear weapon or by a "rusty knife" in Vietnam. "As a matter of fact," he said, "if I had a choice I'd rather be killed by a nuclear weapon." He offered no observation about the hundreds of thousands or millions who would go with him.

Wallace by now was beside himself. He stepped in, before the microphones, and tried to save his nuked and sinking campaign ship. "General LeMay hasn't advocated the use of nuclear weapons, not at all," he desperately insisted. "He's against the use of nuclear weapons, and I am too." Turning to LeMay, Wallace said, almost plaintively, "They said you agreed to use nuclear weapons; you didn't say it"—as if inviting LeMay to control the damage.

LeMay, irately, defended himself to the reporters. "I gave you a discussion on the phobia that we have in this country about the use of nuclear weapons," he said. "I prefer not to use them. I prefer not to use any weapons at all." But suppose, he was asked again, he found it necessary to use them to end a war? He did not retreat. "If I found it necessary I would use anything we could dream up—anything that we could dream up—including nuclear weapons if it was necessary." Here was the ultimate in a credible deterrent.

Wallace was in a panic. "All General LeMay has said, and I know you fellows better than he does because I've had to deal with you," Wallace said, implying trickery by the press corps along with naïveté on LeMay's part, "he said that if the security of the country depended on the use of any weapon in the future, he would use it. But he has said he prefers not to use any weapon. He prefers to negotiate. I believe we must defend our country, but I've always said we can win and defend in Vietnam without the use of nuclear weapons. And General LeMay hasn't said anything about the use of nuclear weapons."

Wallace at this point obviously wanted to roll the Mad Bomber back into the hangar, but LeMay persisted, more defensively this time. "Wait a minute now," he said in his stern commanding-general voice. "Let me make sure you've got this straight. I know I'm going to come out with a lot of misquotes from this campaign. I have in the past. And I'll be damned lucky if I don't appear as a drooling idiot whose only solution to any problem is to drop atomic bombs all over the world. I assure you I'm not. . . . But I'm certainly not going to stand up here and tell our enemies that I advocate that under all circumstances, that I'm not going to use nuclear weapons. We might as well bury them out at Fort Knox."

But LeMay was not going to be "damned lucky." His problem at this mind-boggling press conference was not "a lot of misquotes" but the verbatim transmission around the country of precisely what he had said. It was one of those uncommon moments in a campaign when we reporters could barely wait for the news conference to end so we could rush to the phones and to our typewriters to convey what had just been said.

The substance of LeMay's remarks was bad enough in itself. Just as damaging tactically for Wallace was the fact that it forced his campaign onto the defensive when its most effective posture was attack, attack and more attack against Nixon and Humphrey. Beyond the flap over nuclear weapons, LeMay also demonstrated his lack of political sensitivity as he told reporters why he had agreed to run with Wallace.

From reading about him in the press, he said, "you get the impression George Wallace is a bigot and a racist of the worst order," but after talking with him he found him to be "reasonable and practical" on racial issues. "I sometimes wonder what the real fuss is about," he said. Air Force units had been integrated smoothly, he said, by using "good solid-citizen colored people" to pave the way, and the same could be done for the country at large.

Wallace recognized at once that he had committed a colossal blunder in his selection of LeMay—and in putting him out front where he could unload his verbal megatonnage. He could not undo the selection, but he made certain in the next days to keep the bomber-in-chief's mouth shut.

From Pittsburgh Wallace and LeMay and the general's wife traveled together on the Wallace charter to Indianapolis and Dayton. At rallies in both places, Wallace merely introduced the general but gave him no opportunity to speak. As Wallace himself addressed the crowd, LeMay sat rather sullenly next to his wife without applauding any of the Wallace lines that pleased the crowd—and Mrs. LeMay, who laughed heartily at Wallace's quips. When he had finished in Indianapolis, she rushed up to him, eyes aglow, and congratulated him. Wallace looked at her uncomfortably, seemingly wondering what else he had wrought.

That night, LeMay got a taste of what he had bought into. In Toledo, at the Toledo Mudhens' ballpark, a television technician sitting in the stands was struck in the neck by a rock hurled from the center of a crowd of about a hundred Wallace dissenters. As the man bled, Wallace again told the crowd to "let the police handle it."

If LeMay also wondered whether in the Wallace rally he had stumbled into a performance of the Grand Old Opry, he couldn't have been blamed. The event, as they usually did, began with Sam Smith's five-piece band coming on stage and twanging out "Your Cheatin' Heart." Then the Taylor sisters, Mona and Lisa, dressed perkily in red and blue blazers and skirts, led the crowd in singing "God Bless America." Next, Dick Smith, an Alabama weekly publisher, warmed up the audience with a pitch for campaign contributions as "Wallace girls" including Mona and Lisa circulated through the crowd holding out yellow plastic pails.

Smith like Wallace reveled in taking on the inevitable hecklers. He would delight in telling them that "after November fifth, you're through." At one rally around this time, however, in his fervor he told the hecklers that "after November fifth, we're gonna do away with you!"

Such comments were appropriate introductions to the main act itself, the Wallace speech in which the candidate derided "pointy-headed bureaucrats who can't park a bicycle straight." Engaging the hecklers was a standard part of the show as Wallace would strut up and down the platform his chin jutting out pugnaciously, a curl on his lip. Chants of "Sieg heil!" against him would bring his observation that "I thought we got rid of the Nazis in World War II." Then, telling the crowd that Humphrey had compared him to Hitler, he would remark: "I'm a disabled American veteran [with a hearing disability]. I fought the Nazis and the fascists in World War II [as a tailgunner on a bomber]. When you see him, ask him what his military record is."

(Color blindness, a double hernia and later a minor lung calcification had kept Humphrey out of uniform. The issue had come up in the 1960 presidential primary in West Virginia when John Kennedy ally Franklin D. Roosevelt Jr. floated unsubstantiated rumors that Humphrey had dodged the draft. A forgiving man by nature, Humphrey "never fully forgave either Roosevelt or Robert Kennedy, whom he held responsible for the attacks," Eisele wrote later.)

Whatever else it was, a Wallace rally was a good show. But LeMay's remarks made it harder than ever for uncommitted voters to be more than amused by Wallace's candidacy. Nixon for one jumped on the LeMay fiasco. "We cannot put an irresponsible finger on the nuclear trigger and expect to avert the horror of a nuclear war," he said.

Before LeMay made his remarks, a Gallup Poll had Wallace getting the support of half of all union members surveyed in the South, to only 29 percent for Humphrey and 16 percent for Nixon. Nationally, Wallace was garnering 15 percent of labor's rank and file to 42 for Humphrey—very low for any Democratic candidate—and 35 for Nixon. Among the 16,000 members of the United Auto Workers at a Buick plant in Flint, Michigan, Wallace won 49 percent in a straw poll to 39 for Humphrey and 12 for Nixon. Now, however, the Humphrey and Nixon camps professed to see clear evidence that LeMay had eroded that Wallace support. "Bombs Away with Curt LeMay" became a favorite gag line for both campaigns.

Wallace, in a speech at the National Press Club on October 7, reiterated that he had no intention as president of using nuclear weapons in Vietnam. Asked about LeMay's earlier suggestion that the United States bomb North Vietnam "back into the Stone Age," Wallace dismissed the comment as "use of verbiage" and blamed the reporters covering his campaign for picking on his running mate. "He was questioned by some folks who are on our campaign trip for one purpose," Wallace charged, "and that's to discourage and disgrade [*sic*] and to slant and distort." (Repeatedly, he would tell audiences that the reporters accompanying him were on "a distortin' trip.")

As he spoke, LeMay sat at the head table, saying nothing. Although Wallace insisted that the general had been "unleashed" to campaign on his own, the head of the ticket clearly felt that his running mate had already said too much. The next day, in Los Angeles, LeMay, now flying solo on the campaign trail, told reporters he had joined the Wallace ticket because Nixon planned to pack his cabinet with "left-wingers." Asked to name them, he demurred. "I've only been in politics since last Thursday," he said, "and I'm not quite sure of my footing."

* * *

As the Wallace campaign continued to concern both Humphrey and Nixon, there was some closing of major-party ranks. The ADA finally endorsed Humphrey and Nelson Rockefeller announced his support for Nixon and campaigned with him on Long Island. Within a week, McCarthy also was heard from. He endorsed—Ed Muskie, but not Humphrey.

Muskie continued to encounter antiwar protesters although he seemed far more conciliatory to that group than did Humphrey. He called existing draft laws "unfair and unjust," and after a discussion of them at the University of Southern California on October 3 was reported to have smiled slightly as he watched three SDS members burn what they said were their draft cards. He said citizens unhappy with what was going on in the country could either work for change or break the law in protest, but "must be prepared to pay the penalty" for doing so. Those remarks didn't save him from more attacks from both sides of the argument.

Muskie, however, seemed in general to be a considerable help to Humphrey. The vice president's problem was Nixon—somehow to get him to join the campaign debate directly. Republicans in the Senate succeeded in shelving legislation that would have waived the equal-time requirement and have permitted a network-sponsored Humphrey-Nixon televised debate without Wallace. Still, Humphrey tried to shame Nixon into debating.

"Come clean like a man and debate," he said at a rally in Wilkes-Barre, Pennsylvania, on October 7. In Erie, he called on Nixon to debate "education, foreign policy, national security, human rights. . . . Let's talk about anything." He offered to split the cost of a debate between the two, and when Nixon didn't bite he offered to buy all of the airtime for a debate. Again the Nixon camp refused, calling the Humphrey offer "a phony deal and a publicity gimmick." Humphrey called Nixon "Richard the Careful" and then "Richard the Chickenhearted," but to no avail.

*   *   *

McCarthy and his principal followers continued to be another headache for Humphrey. Over the weekend of October 5–6, as McCarthy covered the World Series for *Life*, some of his old campaign lieutenants and their counterparts in the Robert Kennedy and McGovern campaigns met in Minneapolis and organized the New Democratic Coalition. Among those present were Gerald Hill, chairman of the California Democratic Council, and Jerry Eller, McCarthy's acid sidekick. After Humphrey's Salt Lake City speech, McCarthy had jotted down on the back of an envelope four conditions he required for his endorsement of Humphrey and asked Eller to phone them to Hill, which he did. Now Eller told Hill that McCarthy had said it was all right for Hill to release the conditions. He did. They called for an immediate and unconditional bombing halt, free elections in Vietnam with participation by the NLF, draft law reform and Democratic Party reform.

McCarthy listed basically the same conditions in a speech in New York on October 8, pointedly rebuking Humphrey. "We are not really satisfied by the grand intentions of free elections at some time in the future or qualified statements with reference to stopping the bombing," he said. ". . . We have to be willing to accept a new government in South Vietnam because that is what the war has been about."

He said the draft laws should permit conscientious objectors to "accept other responsibilities to prove the genuineness of their action," and the party nominating process had to be reformed "so that we shall not have another Chicago." He said the call for "party unity" now was the same as it had been all year and nothing had changed materially to warrant it. Translation: no Humphrey endorsement.

Humphrey, who had telephoned McCarthy just before he made the speech to urge him to endorse him, was clearly bitter. He was, he said, "not prone to start meeting conditions" laid down by McCarthy. "We would like to have had his support," he said, "but that's the way the ball bounces. Somewhere along the line, my friend will recognize this is a contest with George Wallace, who represents fear, and Richard Nixon, who represents regression."

*   *   *

Unable to get Nixon in his sights, Humphrey began to target Agnew as the weakness in the Republican ticket. In New York on October 9 to accept the Liberal Party's endorsement, Humphrey charged that Nixon's choice of Agnew as the man who would be a heartbeat away from the presidency if the Republicans were elected showed that his promise to make "responsible" appointments was meaningless. The next day, on Wall Street—Nixon Country—he asked a large noontime crowd to "consider the possibility of a

President LeMay, the possibility, if you please, of a President Agnew," or by contrast "the great possibility of a President Ed Muskie. . . ."

Often, Humphrey would assure crowds that "my co-pilot, Ed Muskie, is ready to take over at any time." Eventually my colleague, Jim Doyle, then of the *Boston Globe*, wrote a fake lead on his day's story that began: "Vice President Hubert H. Humphrey pledged today that if elected, he will resign immediately and let Senator Edmund S . Muskie become president."

Despite such disparagement, Agnew pressed on in his assigned role as the Republican ticket's basher of student protesters and Hubert Humphrey, and hard-liner alternative to George Wallace. On the south side of Milwaukee, he ridiculed the students as "spoiled brats who never have had a good spanking" and who "take their tactics from Gandhi and money from Daddy." In Chicago, he charged that Humphrey's proposed bombing halt "strengthened the hand of Hanoi." And when hecklers walked out on his speech in Portland, Oregon, on October 3, he resumed by saying, "Now that the delegation from Hanoi has left. . . ."

Several days later, Agnew charged that Humphrey and Muskie had a penchant for "fawning upon lawbreakers," taking note of Muskie's benign observation of the burning of draft cards as "inherent in the total permissive atmosphere . . . that allows irresponsible protest." Agnew was restrained, however, in remarks toward Wallace, not wanting to alienate his supporters, allowing only that LeMay's remarks on nuclear weapons made him nervous.

In Johnson's first clear-cut political speech of the campaign on radio on October 10, he joined in the criticism of the vice presidential selections of Humphrey's two foes by saying the choice was a "paramount consideration" and that Muskie was "fit in every way to serve a heartbeat from the presidency."

Johnson warned that Nixon if elected would "dismantle" the progressive domestic programs of the New Deal and in so doing would "pull America apart" by triggering greater alienation and protest from affected minority groups. Wallace, he said, was "a false prophet of fear" out to "divide our country and our people, to set them against each other in mutual fear and suspicion."

* * *

Amid the contentious presidential campaign, there were few bright spots. One was the first successful launching of an American manned space flight in nearly two years on October 11. Three astronauts—Navy Captain Walter Schirra, one of the original Mercury team, Air Force Major Donn Eisele and Ronnie Cunningham, a civilian, were aboard *Apollo 7* as it began an eleven-day trip that eventually orbited the earth 163 times in preparation for the

planned flight to the moon. The spaceship and crew splashed down safely in
the Atlantic on October 22 with the program director's boast that it had "accomplished 101 percent of our intended objectives," the 1 percent signifying
tests added after the liftoff.

Some of the new tests were denounced by Schirra as "idiotic" and at one
point he told ground control that "we are not going to accept any new games
like doing some crazy tests we never heard of." But all ended well and
Americans enjoyed one of the few moments of true exhilaration in this year
of shocks, disillusion and rancor.

*   *   *

It was now little more than three weeks to election day. Nixon, who had
been coasting along at a leisurely pace, taking off nearly every weekend to rest
at Key Biscayne and gliding through the weekdays on his light schedule of
limited and carefully controlled, staged events, was now going to sprint to
the finish. Or so he said. The last three weeks, he insisted at a rare news conference on October 15, would be "Operation Extra Effort." He had already
begun a nightly series of radio talks that would run for two solid weeks on
specific foreign policy and domestic issues—a way to trot out his carefully
scripted views and his credentials without subjecting them to press interrogation or heckling by the rabble.

The getaway press conference itself illustrated the sort of third degree that
Nixon wanted to avoid. He was peppered with questions about his refusal to
debate Humphrey and Wallace; he made it sound as if he were willing but
blocked by the equal-time law. Asked about Humphrey's expressed willingness to buy television time himself for a two-way debate, or simply a debate
without television covered by the press, Nixon said it wouldn't be "the best
use" of his and Humphrey's time, nor would it be a useful substitute for a
television debate "where the people themselves can judge." Once again, he
didn't want his views filtered through the news media—nor, it was clear,
compared with Humphrey's in any face-to-face setting with the risks that
spontaneity entailed.

His answers to these proposals provided a look at the classic Nixon. He obviously wanted to stiff a press corps he remained convinced was out to get
him. But never again, after his infamous 1962 "last press conference" following his gubernatorial loss in California, did he want to admit it or even show
hostility. "I don't mean to downgrade the writing press," he said in turning
aside a debate without television, "and I don't mean by that I think the press
would be unfair."

When he was asked whether he was retaining the option of increasing the
bombing of North Vietnam if Hanoi stepped up its military activity, Nixon

quickly replied, "No, I am not going to say that. The immediate reaction to any statement of that sort is that we are waving the bombing around, and I am quite aware how it would be played." Then, quickly, he added: "And I understand that, and I would not be resentful."

After saying he wasn't "going to engage in the kind of name-calling Hubert Humphrey is engaged in," he quickly added: "Incidentally, I'm not resentful of this." And in response to another question, Nixon started by saying, "I don't mean to correct you, understand," and then proceeded to correct the questioner. This man, so obviously reeking with resentments through most of his political career, especially toward the press, was going to be the New Nixon if it killed him.

Even this news conference, however, underscored Nixon's distrust of the news media and his fixation on achieving optimum control. Although he spoke on the record with all his comments directly attributable to him, no cameras or tape recorders were permitted. His handlers were not going to leave open the possibility that a spoken blunder by Nixon would be captured on film or tape. Many of us covering Nixon complained strenuously at the prohibition, but getting the candidate to hold any kind of news conference on the record was so difficult that in the end we swallowed hard and accepted Nixon's self-serving ground rules.

Nixon insisted in the news conference that "Operation Extra Effort" would be "the most intensive closing, the most intensive finish in campaign history," in terms of "people reached by radio and television, intensity of activity and speeches and issues covered." He was out not only to win election himself but to win control of Congress. "We're not going to play it safe," he said. "We're going all out on the issues, the appearances, the activities between now and the elections." This final "blitz," he said, would hit "the peripheral states" and then home in as never before on the target states that would be the key to the outcome—New York, California, Texas, Illinois, Ohio, Michigan and Pennsylvania.

Nixon's advertisement of "Operation Extra Effort" was half right. On the paid media track, the campaign indeed went all-out, thanks to the unflagging money-raising efforts of Maurice Stans and the creative efforts of Shakespeare, Treleaven, Ailes and the other Madison Avenue geniuses. On the in-person track, however, it was more of the same old evasion. In the first week of the "blitz," Nixon averaged fewer than two public appearances a day. Meanwhile a flood of position papers inundated the traveling reporters, giving us something to write—and readers something to make them think the Republican candidate was indeed engaged in "the most intensive finish in campaign history."

* * *

Wallace, in his fashion, also intensified his campaign. The first thing he did in these last three weeks of the campaign, however, was to get LeMay effectively out of range of the reporters for a few days by sending him to South Vietnam on a fact-finding trip. Even before his arrival in Saigon, the general said he was going to "blow the whistle" on the Johnson administration's "no-win policy" in Vietnam. On his return, he charged that the new bombing restrictions were "wasting" American lives by allowing "a tremendous flow of supplies moving South, at a higher rate than ever before because it is unhampered." Wallace obviously hoped that his running mate had more credibility as an expert on the conduct of war than on the health and happiness of the Bikini land crabs.

Wallace's voting strength remained uncertain, but on October 15 he demonstrated once more his remarkable ability to overcome the legal barriers to make himself a truly national candidate. The Supreme Court by a vote of six to three ruled that he had to be given ballot position in Ohio, the last of the fifty states he needed. Associate Justice Hugo L. Black, writing for the majority, said that new parties "struggling for their place" in the system had to be given a chance to meet "reasonable" ballot requirements. Neither Nixon nor Humphrey could take it for granted that Wallace's candidacy would not be a factor in the November outcome.

* * *

Agnew meanwhile was identifying himself more and more as the point man in the diligent Republican effort to undercut Wallace. Increasingly, he was emerging as Richard Nixon's Richard Nixon, providing a stern edge to the GOP campaign while Nixon himself labored to reinforce his new image as above-the-battle statesman. In a speech in Indianapolis on October 15, Agnew told the poor and the restless young: "We will listen to your complaints. You may give us your symptoms [but] we will make the diagnosis and we, the establishment, for which I make no apologies for being part of, will implement the cure."

The next day in Pittsburgh, a reporter asked Agnew at a rare press brunch why, if he was an urban expert as he said, he wasn't going into any urban ghettos. He replied that he didn't feel "there's any particular gain to be made by debating on street corners. . . . You don't learn from people suffering from poverty, but from experts who have studied the problem." Asked the same question two days later in Detroit, Agnew replied: "I've been into many of them and, to some extent, I'd have to say this: If you've seen one city slum, you've seen them all. . . . I don't think it's imperative that I conduct showboat appearances through ghetto areas to prove I know something about the problems of the cities."

Once again, Agnew found himself in the headlines. The fact was that he was not simply avoiding ghettos; he was avoiding any undue exposure, just as Nixon was, on the calculation that if they both just kept their heads down the rest of the way, they would win. The Pittsburgh brunch was Agnew's first meeting with the reporters traveling with him in nearly a month. They started to accuse the candidate's aides of playing "Hide the Greek," but the orders from the Nixon "mother ship" were clear: Don't make waves. "We sort of got locked in at this point," John Sears told me later; "to just try to ride it out; not do anything flashy, appear under very controlled circumstances, and let the Democrats do what they pleased."

On the Agnew swing that began in Pittsburgh, the candidate spent the night at the Pittsburgh Hilton, canceled a tour set for the next day and stayed in his suite. Reporters were told he was occupied with "staff work." Sears later described the Agnew schedule this way: "We sat all day in the hotel until night, then we got into a motorcade and motored way out of town to a rally. Then we came back, we went to bed, and the next morning left and arrived in the early part of the afternoon at the Detroit airport, where we made a fast move in the cars, a distance of about 500 yards over to the airport motel, where we sat until night, then went to Cobo Hall for a rally, gave a speech, got out and came back. We spent the night and then flew home for the weekend on Thursday—to take some rest."

The *Pittsburgh Post-Gazette* termed Agnew's visit a "non-day," and the reporters traveling with him burned as he sat for hours and days in the curtained-off front compartment of the campaign plane without making himself available to them. The reporters hammered at Agnew's old press secretary from Maryland, Herb Thompson, to produce the candidate. They were particularly irate when they learned on one occasion that the plane was headed for a quiet weekend in Corpus Christi, Texas, during which again there would be little or no access to Agnew.

Thompson conveyed the reporters' unease to Sears, the monitor assigned from the Nixon plane. Sears, with his customary sardonic humor, told him: "Herb, you go tell those bastards that if they want to come along with us, there's good food and drink on the plane, and we'll drop down once in a while and get a night's sleep at a good hotel. Tell them we've got a nice weekend planned in Corpus Christi. They'll have a nice fishing trip planned for them in the morning, and a picnic in the afternoon, and on Monday we may make a speech. Tell them that after the next stop we're going to get up in that plane and just fly around. If they want to come with the next vice president of the

United States, okay. Tell them we'll land after a while and then we'll all go into town and take a nap."

Faced with this prospect, the traveling reporters wrote that Agnew was hiding, and hoped that this non-news would get printed in their papers. To kill some of the immense quantities of time on their hands, they took to writing campaign parodies. The best of them, by Chuck Quinn of ABC News and others, was recorded and played on the plane's loudspeaker for all aboard, including Agnew. To the tune of "Love and Marriage," part of it went:

> Law and order, law and order, can't find "justice" on my tape recorder;
> I believe in let live, but please don't let it be permissive.
> Japs and Polacks, Japs and Polacks,
> Want to keep them on their own blocks;
> Then the press grows shrewish
> Though some of my best friends are Jewish.
> We don't go into the ghettos, they're not part of the nation,
> Besides, who ever heard of letting the patient do the operation?

The ditty concluded: "You can't have truth, you can't have peace, you can't have law—without the order."

* * *

One cloud continued to loom over the Nixon-Agnew strategy of killing the clock. Johnson was still frantically pressing for a breakthrough in the Paris negotiations that would enable him to claim with some credibility that peace at last was on its way in Vietnam. For all of LBJ's unhappiness with Humphrey's "declaration of independence" on a bombing halt, he did not want his anointed candidate, and in the process himself, repudiated by the voters. In addition to the obvious boost a breakthrough would give to Humphrey, it would inject an element of the unexpected into a Nixon campaign that avoided the spontaneous and the unplanned for at all costs. As long as the set strategy of substituting motion for substance and appearance for reality could be sustained, the Nixon masterminds believed, all would be well.

On October 12, however, a further warning came to the Nixon camp to prepare for a surprise. Kissinger, Nixon wrote later, phoned that "there was a strong possibility that the administration would move before October 23" on the bombing halt. Nixon, as he wrote later, had known for weeks that this move was under serious consideration, but it now seemed imminent.

Johnson, in fact, was on the verge of ordering a bombing halt but was not quite there yet, in part because he feared the move would be judged domestically as no more than a ploy to help swing the election to Humphrey. "I do not know what I want to do yet here," he told his Foreign Policy Advisory Group of Rusk, Clifford, Generals Earle Wheeler and Maxwell Taylor, CIA Director Richard Helms and Rostow, with press aides George Christian and Tom Johnson sitting in, on October 14. "This is not an easy decision for me. Many people will call it a cheap political trick," Tom Johnson had LBJ observing in his notes of the meeting.

Concerns also were expressed, according to the same notes, of political games by Nixon. "Electoral tricks we must watch for," Rusk said, recommending advance notice to Nixon of a halt. "Nixon has been honorable on Vietnam. We must give him a chance to roll with this. We must give him a chance to know about this." And, in a dig at Humphrey and his Salt Lake City speech, Rusk added: "He [Nixon] has actually been more responsible on this than our own candidate." Clifford chimed in: "As soon as the decision is made don't let the date of the election concern you. The weight of public opinion is for this [a bombing halt]. . . . I expect Nixon would play it fair with you. The security factor is so important."

That night, in another meeting with Rusk, Clifford, Wheeler, Rostow and Tom Johnson, LBJ reported on more speculation about the political ramifications of a halt. His friend—and Nixon's—Democratic Senator George Smathers of Florida, had told him, the president said, that "the word is out that we are making an effort to throw the election to Humphrey. He said Nixon had been told of it. Nixon told Smathers he did not want the president to be pulled into this, that wrong results could flow. Nixon said he is afraid we would be misled. Senator Smathers said he assured Nixon that the president would move if an opportunity for peace presented itself."

When Clifford responded, "I doubt it [a halt] would have any effect on the campaign," LBJ snapped: "Both sides think it would." Nevertheless, he said, he had to seize any real chance to stop the killing. "I do not want to be the one to have it said about, that one man died tomorrow who could have been saved because of this plan."

Two days later, on October 16, Nixon was called to a phone at the Union Station in Kansas City just as he was about to make a speech. Johnson was on the other end of the line, he wrote later, telling him that while rumors of a breakthrough "were wrong . . . there had in fact been some movement by Hanoi." Nixon the eternal plotter was astonished that LBJ would give him the warning, and in it the opportunity to soften the blow if it came. That night he prepared his defense and in Johnstown, Pennsylvania, the next day he covered himself.

"If a bombing halt can be agreed to in Vietnam," he said, "one which will not endanger American lives and one which will increase the chances for bringing a peaceful and honorable solution to the war, then we are for it. And the one man who can make that determination is the President of the United States. Let's let him make that determination, and if he makes it, we will support him because we want peace, and we do not want to play politics with peace." Ron Ziegler, the press secretary, denied that Nixon had received any inside information, and by attaching conditions for his support, he had left himself an out.

The possible breakthrough about which LBJ had spoken, however, did not come. The Saigon government continued to balk on grounds Hanoi had not indicated any credible willingness to de-escalate its military actions in the South. But by this time, the Johnson administration knew there were other reasons, having put the intelligence community to work tapping into the communications network of the South Vietnamese embassy in Washington. An intercepted cable from South Vietnamese Ambassador Bui Diem to President Thieu in Saigon, quoted later in Bui Diem's book, *In the Jaws of History*, suggested that the possibility that Saigon might get a better deal with Nixon in the White House also had dictated the foot-dragging.

On October 23, Diem, who had met Nixon in New York in July under the auspices of the shadowy Anna Chennault, cabled Thieu that "many Republican friends have contacted me and encouraged us to stand firm. They were alarmed by press reports to the effect that you had already softened your position."

Still, Johnson pressed the Saigon regime to agree to join the peace talks, in the hope of being able to announce a breakthrough before the election. And so the cloud of such a possible achievement continued to hover over Nixon, barely two weeks before the election. The latest Gallup Poll showed him still comfortably ahead with his stable 43 percent to 31 for Humphrey and 20 for Wallace. But the question was, would Wallace's strength hold up, and if not, where would it go? The Nixon camp nervously contemplated the answer.

That concern, however, did not intrude on Nixon's leisurely pace behind a facade of motion. On one late October Saturday, he flew about 1,600 miles to make one speech in an already solid Republican district in a Chicago suburb and another at a shopping center in Eatontown, New Jersey. Then, in spite of how late in the campaign it was, he took Sunday and most of Monday off, conferring with aides at his New York apartment and taping more radio talks.

*   *   *

One bombshell did explode in the faces of the American people at this time, however, unrelated to the presidential race. On October 20, on the private island of Skorpios off the coast of Greece, the memories and the myth of the American Camelot were shattered with the marriage of Jacqueline Kennedy at the age of thirty-nine to the sixty-two-year-old multimillionaire shipping magnate Aristotle Socrates Onassis.

Three days earlier, the country and the world had been jolted by the surprise announcement by the former first lady's secretary that she would marry Onassis, a man with a reputation for shrewd, even cutthroat, business deals and tempestuous relationships with women, most recently with opera star Maria Callas. The prospective bride flew to Greece with her two children and other family members hours after the announcement, and for a few days the fight for the American presidency now heading to a conclusion was almost eclipsed by the mystery of Mrs. Kennedy's decision. Comedian Bob Hope had one explanation. "Nixon has a Greek running mate," he said, "and now everyone wants one."

* * *

Nixon's lead in the Gallup Poll was not all that reassuring. While his support remained steady at 43 percent, Humphrey had gained slightly. And although the Nixon camp generally dismissed the Harris Survey as dependably favorable to Democrats, his latest numbers were unnerving: Nixon 40, Humphrey 35, Wallace 18. Nixon suggested that to avoid a constitutional crisis wherein Wallace could hold the balance of power if neither he nor Humphrey had a majority in the electoral college, the two front-runners agree that the winner of the popular vote would be declared president. Humphrey, confident that he would win if the failure of either front-runner to win that majority were to throw the election into the Democratic-controlled House of Representatives, would have none of it.

The very offering of that suggestion from the Nixon camp smacked of slipping confidence. Later, some Nixon insiders confided that they feared what one of them called "the Dewey syndrome." In hunkering down to protect his lead, Nixon was coming off as the incumbent when he should have been positioning himself as the "out" candidate against the incumbent party—a fatal failure of Tom Dewey in 1948.

Dewey, this insider said, "was so lofty in 1948 he lost his identity as the 'out.' Now Nixon, who had campaigned as though he already was president, already was 'in,' began to be regarded as the 'in.' He had to break out of that, to go on the attack as an 'out' is expected to do. But when it was that close to the wire, he had to consider how far he could go. We were positioned in the middle between Humphrey and Wallace, where the strong feelings did not reside, and where most of the country was. Politically we had to play it day by day—who's hurting you more, Wallace or Humphrey, and who's hurting you where you are. We tried to play them off, tried to expand the middle a little where it counted."

At this stage, the Nixon strategists knew that where it counted as much as anywhere else now was Ohio. Most blue-collar voters in the state were registered Democrats but many union members there had a record of voting Republican. If Wallace's strength in the state started to ebb in the closing days, it could well fall Nixon's way, especially if the issue of greatest concern to Ohioans at this point—crime, or law and order—was properly exploited, by attacking Humphrey, not Wallace.

A whistlestop tour of western Ohio starting in Cincinnati and moving northward on October 22 became the vehicle, and the Old Nixon was on hand to step in for the New when the chips were down. At a very large rally at the Cincinnati Garden in solid Taft Republican country the day before the train trip, Nixon excoriated Humphrey as a "do-nothing candidate on law and order," recalling that Humphrey two years earlier had said that had he lived in a slum as a youth, "I might have led a pretty good revolt." That attitude from a grown man, Nixon said, smacked of "adult delinquency not worthy of the Vice President of the United States." There was, he said, "no cause that justifies breaking the law," and he promised that "the wave of crime will not be the wave of the future" if he were elected.

The next day, as the train rolled north, Nixon hit Humphrey at every stop. At Dayton, he accused him of taking "a lackadaisical do-nothing approach to law and order" over the previous four years, watching "the United States become a nation where 50 percent of American women are frightened to walk within a mile of their homes at night. . . . Freedom from fear must be restored to the cities and towns of America," he said.

Nixon also attacked Muskie, who, he said, "stood and grinned while three scofflaws burned their draft cards. . . . This is a nation of laws, and as Abraham Lincoln said, no one is above the law, no one is below the law, and we are going to enforce the law, and Americans should remember that if we are going to have law and order."

As Law and Order Day on the Nixon campaign trail continued, the candidate methodically ticked off crime statistics at each depot, until the train finally rolled into the town of Deshler as darkness began to fall. There he recited a chilling scorecard of crime rampant: "In the 45 minutes it takes to ride from Lima to Deshler, this is what has happened in America: there has been one murder, two rapes, 45 major crimes of violence, countless robberies and auto thefts. . . ."

The whistlestop at Deshler would take on a certain irony when recalled by Nixon on the morning after the election in a distinctly different way.

The train rolled on into the night, with more such statistics, finally making a ninth and last stop at Toledo after ten o'clock. The day, indisputably, was the most intensive of the year for Nixon, a throwback to his frenetic pace of 1960 that he had vowed not to repeat.

* * *

Meanwhile, the specter of an "October surprise" from LBJ—achievement of a breakthrough on Vietnam peace talks that would benefit Humphrey—continued to hover over Nixon. A memo dated October 22 from political adviser Bryce Harlow, who like Kissinger had lines into the U. S. negotiating team, informed him that "the President is driving exceedingly hard for a deal with North Vietnam. Expectation is that he is becoming almost pathologically eager for an excuse to order a bombing halt and will accept almost any arrangement. . . . Careful plans are being made to help HHH exploit whatever happens. White House staff liaison with HHH is close. Plan is for LBJ to make a nationwide TV announcement as quickly as possible after agreement; objective is to get this done as long before November 5 as they can. . . . White Housers still think they can pull the election out for HHH with this ploy. . . ."

Nixon in his memoirs wrote later that he reread the Harlow memo several times and became "angrier and more frustrated" with each reading. He told Mitchell to check with Kissinger and asked Senators Everett Dirksen and Tower to "blast the moves by the White House." He instructed Mitchell, he wrote, to get Dirksen to call LBJ and "let him know we are onto his plans."

* * *

As Nixon was whistlestopping through Ohio, Wallace was making his own bid for the law-and-order vote in Wisconsin. At a rally in Oshkosh, student protesters threw eggs at him and chanted "Sieg heil!" as he spoke. That night at another rally he had to be hustled from the site by his Alabama bodyguards and Secret Service as a crowd of demonstrators surged toward him. Such reactions were becoming routine at Wallace rallies.

At another rally that nearly filled Madison Square Garden in New York two nights later, more than a thousand anti-Wallace protesters jammed the surrounding streets, requiring a force of 3,000 police to keep them away. Some officers on horseback rode into the chanting crowds to break up fights, clubbing some Wallace foes and arresting others. Inside, the former Golden Gloves boxer turned presidential candidate told his shrieking audience: "I've been waiting to fight the main event in Madison Square Garden a long time."

* * *

It seemed now that the whole country was brawling. In Philadelphia, for nine days in October, white and black students clashed in seven high schools;

in Washington, about 250 young blacks set fires, blocked traffic and had to be driven off by police tear gas after a white motorcycle cop shot a black pedestrian; in Berkeley, sit-ins and rock-throwing marked demonstrations over university restrictions on Eldridge Cleaver's campus appearance; another 250 blacks were arrested at the University of Illinois at Urbana for sit-in protests against discrimination in campus housing and financial aid. There seemed to be no end of protesting students, and of causes for them to protest about.

*   *   *

Not even the field of sports was immune. In Mexico City during the nineteenth Summer Olympics, two black track stars, Tommie Smith and John Carlos, the gold and bronze medal winners in the 200-meter dash, appeared on the victory podium wearing black stockings but no shoes, Smith with a black scarf around his neck. As "The Star-Spangled Banner" was played, each raised a fist gloved in black and bowed his head in a Black Power salute. Two days later they were suspended by the U.S. Olympic Committee for their political statement.

Still, the United States team shone, winning forty-five gold medals to thirty for the Soviet Union. The Americans also won twenty-eight silver medals and thirty-four bronze. One of the gold medalists was heavyweight boxer George Foreman, a black man not committed to Black Power. He paraded around the ring waving a small American flag after beating Iones Chepulis of the Soviet Union. (Foreman went on to win the world's professional heavyweight championship and, twenty years after losing the title, regained it at the age of forty-five in 1994.)

Whatever else was going on, sports was having a heyday. In the opening game of the World Series, St. Louis Cardinals pitcher Bob Gibson set a Series record with seventeen strikeouts in beating the Tigers's Denny McLain, who had finished the regular season with thirty-one victories. The Tigers, however, won the Series in seven games.

*   *   *

As for the turmoil off the fields of sport, J. Edgar Hoover and his agency had no doubt where the fault for all this trouble lay. An FBI report in October warned that the New Left, shifting from "passive dissent to active resistance," had "mushroomed into a major security problem" through such organizations as SDS, the National Mobe and the Yippies. Hoover wrote that it would be "foolhardy" to ignore what he called "revolutionary terror invading college campuses." The aim of the New Left movement, he said, was "to smash first our educational structure, then our economic system, and finally our government itself."

Tom Hayden, testifying before the president's commission on the causes and prevention of violence, had another view: the election of Kennedy in 1960, his creation of the Peace Corps and the public support for the great civil rights struggle in the South had raised the hopes of the young; then they were dashed by the government's failure to meet the needs of poor Americans at home, and by its "aggression" in Vietnam. Another witness, Yale president Kingman Brewster, succinctly warned that "the urge to violence rises in proportion to the frustration of peaceful change."

* * *

For Nixon, it was more attack politics at a less hectic pace the next two days in Michigan and Pennsylvania. The man who had deplored Humphrey's "name-calling" and had vowed not to answer in kind charged at an airport hangar in Saginaw, Michigan, that his Democratic opponent was imperiling Vietnam peace negotiations with "the fastest, loosest tongue ever in American politics." Those of us traveling with him who had noted the return of the Old Nixon after the Ohio whistlestop trip found more evidence in such remarks.

The Old Nixon surfaced in other ways too. The frustrated would-be athlete in him was hilariously on display at Saginaw when George Romney introduced him to two heroes of the 1968 World Series, Detroit Tigers Al Kaline and Jim Northrup. There and in Grand Rapids, Nixon talked animatedly, almost worshipfully, to the players, asking about how they felt when they got crucial hits. At one point, when some deaf mute schoolkids were brought over to meet the candidate, he pointed to the two baseball stars, swinging an imaginary bat as he did, and saying: "Kaline . . . Northrup . . . Detroit Tigers? . . . World Series? . . . Baseball?" The kids looked at him as if he had lost his mind, as Kaline and Northrup squirmed.

But there was little time now for such light moments. In 1960, John Kennedy had raised against Nixon the specter of a "missile gap" with the Soviet Union that he suggested had developed in the Eisenhower-Nixon years. Now, in a move reminiscent of that tactic, Nixon in a radio talk on October 24 charged that Kennedy and Johnson had permitted "a gravely serious security gap" to develop through "policies which now threaten to make America second best both in numbers and quality of major weapons." It had happened in large part, he said, by their failure to make proper use of the National Security Council, and he pledged to restore its importance in building "clear-cut" military superiority over the Soviets.

Nixon boasted that "during the eight Eisenhower years, there was not a Berlin wall, no Bay of Pigs, no Cuban missile crisis, no Americans fighting in Southeast Asia, no *Pueblo* piracy." Also during the Eisenhower years, he said, "we had a 50 percent advantage over the Soviet Union in the number of land-based intercontinental ballistic missiles—the crucial weapon. Today that advantage, so important during the Cuban missile crisis, has become only marginal. The trend is that even this slight edge will soon be gone.

"Eight years ago our numerical advantage over the Soviets in bombers was 30 percent. Now it's more than the other way around. Today the Soviets are 50 percent ahead of us." The same was true, he charged, concerning tactical aircraft and military stockpiles. It all stemmed, he said, from "a peculiar, unprecedented doctrine called 'parity' [that] meant America would no longer try to be first. We would only stay even. This concept," he said, "has done us incalculable damage."

All this, Nixon speechwriter William Safire wrote later in his book *Before the Fall*, was a "pre-emptive strike" against the Democrats to counter the feared "October surprise" of a bombing halt. Johnson promptly denounced what he called Nixon's "ugly and unfair charges" and Defense Secretary Clifford called a press conference at the Pentagon to report that the United States had a "substantial military superiority over the Soviet Union, including a margin of more than three to one in total deliverable nuclear warheads—by missile, bomber and submarine." Humphrey chimed in, accusing Nixon of "playing politics with national security [and] advocating an increasing militarization of American life and American foreign policy." But the Nixon camp hoped the allegations would do for their man what John Kennedy's "missile gap" charges—later proved to be unfounded—appeared to have done for him.

If Nixon's "security gap" accusations smacked of the Kennedy of 1960, Nixon's next gambit the following day, October 25, was pure Old Nixon. The campaign entourage had moved to New York and we in the press corps were ensconced in the Waldorf-Astoria for what shaped up as another leisurely weekend. That afternoon, Nixon spokesmen Herb Klein and Ron Ziegler walked into the press room with a statement from Nixon. It made clear how concerned the Nixon camp was about the possibility that Johnson would yank his Vietnam chestnuts out of the fire before election day.

"In the last 36 hours," it said, "I have been advised of a flurry of meetings in the White House and elsewhere on Vietnam. I am told that top officials in the administration have been driving very hard for an agreement on a bombing halt, accompanied possibly by a cease-fire, in the immediate future. These reports," the statement went on, "I have since learned to be true." Indeed they were.

But then Nixon added: "I am also told that this spurt of activity is a cynical, last-minute attempt by President Johnson to salvage the candidacy of

Mr. Humphrey. *This I do not believe* [italics added]." It was an old standard Nixon ploy—giving wide publicity to a serious charge and then knocking it down himself. It was also standard Nixon to give testimony to his own purity in not taking political advantage of the rumor, which he proceeded to do.

"This latest suggestion of presidential politicking with the Vietnam war is but one of many similar rumors and press speculations in recent weeks," he continued. "I think it is only appropriate, therefore, to reiterate the statement on this subject that I have repeatedly made in this campaign. At no time in the campaign have I found the president anything but impartial and candid in his dealings with the major presidential contenders about Vietnam. I know this has not been easy for him." Johnson, he said, "is profoundly concerned about our half million servicemen, including his two sons-in-law, in Vietnam. In every conversation I have had with him he has made it clear that he will not play politics with this war." Again, Nixon said he would "welcome a bombing halt" but again with the escape hatch: ". . . provided it will, in the long term, save American lives and not cost American lives."

Safire in his book later described the whole ploy as "a shot across Johnson's bow—a message couched in pious, I-just-can't-believe-it terms, that he had better not pull any fast ones on the weekend before the election; Nixon would label it 'cynical.'" Nixon himself in his memoir explained that "the only way to prevent Johnson from totally undercutting my candidacy at the eleventh hour was for me to make public the fact that a bombing halt was imminent. In addition, I wanted to plant the impression—which I believed to be true—that his motives and his timing were not dictated by diplomacy alone."

Those of us who had been traveling regularly with Nixon for the last several weeks wondered where Nixon had heard the report. Certainly there were suspicions that LBJ was pushing for negotiations in time to bail out Humphrey in the election, but it wasn't being suggested that was his sole "cynical" motivation. Nixon wasn't content with merely floating the rumor, he had to make himself a hero for not, as he claimed, taking advantage of it.

We pressed Klein and Ziegler to identify the "top officials" to whom Nixon had referred. "You've heard it at every stop," Klein said. "I'm not referring to any particular individual." Ziegler acknowledged that members of the Nixon staff were concerned but wouldn't say which ones. Klein wanted to know why we reporters were so concerned about which ones. "I'm concerned that you're trying to get a rumor in the paper by denying it," a reporter told him. Klein replied: "We don't participate in that sort of thing." Soon afterward, Congressman Mel Laird came into the press room, obviously assigned to gauge how the ploy was going over. He expressed surprise to be told by reporters who professionally had their ears to the ground that they hadn't heard the same report.

Much later, Sears told me: "It wouldn't have been proper for Nixon to make the accusation, but somebody else had to [in his name]. There's a hole in the dike, or three or four holes, and the water is gushing through, and you can feel the thing swaying, but you know in three or four days the water pressure will go down if you can hold on. Elections do get out of hand. You can't control them, but we did a pretty good job. At the end it's like riding a tiger; you hold on."

* * *

The other tiger on the Republican ticket meanwhile was getting his tail twisted again, and this time he twisted back by playing the unaccustomed role of wronged innocent. On October 22, the *New York Times* had run a story on an inside page reciting a number of old charges against Agnew when he was Baltimore County executive and governor of Maryland. They included allegations that he had used improper influence in a zoning case, in the purchase of land near a planned second parallel Chesapeake Bay Bridge site and as a director of the Chesapeake National Bank. Nothing substantial had come of any of the charges.

Four days later, however, the newspaper ran a harsh editorial based on the story, observing that Agnew in his county and state executive posts "has been the political ally and financial partner of a group of wealthy land speculators. These businessmen have made sizable fortunes out of developing land in suburban Baltimore over the past 15 years, in part because of favorable zoning and government decisions, and Mr. Agnew's financial net worth has also risen sharply."

The editorial charged him with "clear and repeated conflicts of interest" in his association with the bank. It said he had falsely claimed he had inherited bank stock when he had in fact bought it. The editorial concluded: "In his obtuse behavior as a public official in Maryland as well as in his egregious comments in this campaign, Mr. Agnew has demonstrated that he is not fit to stand one step away from the Presidency."

Agnew saw his chance to turn the tables on his oppressors in the news media. Nixon aide Steve Hess, riding shotgun for a time on the Agnew plane, told me later: "The *Times* was off base. The Agnew people felt, 'We've got them by the short hairs.'" The Nixon strategists apparently agreed, because Nixon himself kicked off the counterattack in an appearance on Sunday night, October 27, on CBS's *Face the Nation*—his first on a spontaneous network panel show in two years, after much criticism that he was hiding. He accused the newspaper of "the lowest kind of gutter politics that a great newspaper could possibly engage in." He called the charges "stale" and "inaccurate" and said a retraction would be demanded "legally," adding that he was certain it would be run "back with the corset ads or the classifieds toward the end of the week when nobody will pay any attention."

The next day in Houston, Agnew chimed in, accusing the newspaper of "having pulled the major blooper of the campaign." Its endorsement of Humphrey was well known, he said, and "the fact that the *Times* waited until a week before the election to distort the facts and make its inaccurate charges against me compounds the libel." He said it was "absolutely false" that his financial worth had "risen sharply" as a result of favorable treatment he gave friends while he was governor. He said that about half of his net worth came from funds given to him by his parents and that he had "voluntarily disclosed" his role in the Bay Bridge land purchase before his election as governor. He said the newspaper had misquoted him on the bank stock purchase; that he had bought the stock with inherited money. He joined Nixon in demanding a retraction.

Instead, the *Times* the next morning took the unusual step of reprinting the original editorial, adding that the fact some of the charges were old ones didn't make them any less valid. It did, however, then print another editorial backing away somewhat, noting that "nowhere in our [earlier] editorial comment did we accuse him of violating the law."

After a conference with an Agnew lawyer, the paper refused a retraction. Instead, another long story was run "clarifying" points at issue with Agnew. His campaign responded with a newspaper ad attacking the editorials, which spawned yet another one. "The fundamental issue is not over the details of shades of meaning," it said. "The fundamental issue is Mr. Agnew's apparent failure to comprehend the importance of the special standards of propriety that are rightly demanded of any holder of public office. It is his insensitivity to this problem of ethics of public servants that now stands revealed and reinforces our belief that he is a poor choice to be placed one step away from the Presidency of the United States."

(The *Times* had to wait five years for vindication, but it finally came. The Justice Department of the Nixon administration in which Agnew was serving developed solid evidence that he had been accepting payments from Maryland contractors as county executive, governor and even as vice president. To remove him quickly from the line of presidential succession, he was permitted to bargain down to one charge of federal income tax evasion, to which he pleaded nolo contendere and resigned the vice presidency in return for escaping a prison term.)

* * *

In addition to spearheading the attack on the *New York Times* over its editorial content on Agnew, Nixon on *Face the Nation* reiterated under sharp questioning his rationale for circulating the rumor that Johnson was cynically using the peace talks to elect Humphrey. He said he had been "consistent" in supporting LBJ on the war and that "Mr. Humphrey ought to get in line, agree with his president for a change." Only a few days earlier during the Ohio whistlestop, he had accused Humphrey of having spent "four years in Obedience School" as a Johnson yes-man. The New Nixon, in his inner struggle with the Old Nixon, was beginning to fray at the edges, observing at one point that "I only wish that Hubert Humphrey now would button up his lip and stick with the president on this."

The latest Gallup Poll helped to explain the edginess: Nixon 44 percent, Humphrey 36, Wallace 15, with Humphrey getting the bulk of Wallace slippage. Still, on his plane en route to Pittsburgh the next morning, Nixon professed not to be worried. "It finally came," he said of the Humphrey movement. "Humphrey picks up a little more in the North, I'll pick up a little more in the South. Over all, it's a wash." He predicted he would run 3 percent better than the final Gallup Poll and 5 better than the final Harris Survey.

Humphrey meanwhile jumped on Nixon's first appearance on a network panel show after a two-year absence, insisting he had at last "smoked out" his opponent with his insistence on debating. "This has been a hard fight," he said in Canton, Ohio, the day after. "We're on the upward trend. I finally got Mr. Nixon to talk. . . . It took some time to do it. His well-planned campaign is coming apart." And in Akron: "Anybody who can't face the reporters can't face the voters."

* * *

As the Nixon camp sought to encourage the impression that Johnson was pushing peace talks before the election to bail out the trailing Humphrey, more suspicious activities were going on strongly suggesting the Nixon forces were attempting just the opposite—to stall such talks. On October 27, in another intercepted cable quoted in his book, South Vietnamese Ambassador Bui Diem informed Thieu in Saigon: "The longer the present situation continues, the more we are favored. . . . I am regularly in touch with the Nixon entourage." By "Nixon entourage," he wrote later, "I meant Anna Chennault, John Mitchell and Senator Tower."

(While the full cable has never been made public, William Bundy, assistant secretary of state for East Asian and Pacific affairs at the time, said in a telephone interview much later that Benjamin H. Read, then executive secretary of the State Department and now deceased, took verbatim notes of it and read them to him. In his forthcoming book, *Tangled Web*, Bundy writes that Bui Diem in the cable further informed Thieu that he had "explained discreetly to our partisan friends our firm attitude" [not to go to the Paris peace talks] and "plan to adhere to that position," and that Johnson would "probably have difficulties in forcing our hand." Bundy, who elsewhere has referred to the cable as "the smoking gun" in tying the Nixon campaign to Saigon's action throwing a monkey wrench into the peace talks, writes that the cable also said that Bui Diem "had been informed that if Nixon were elected he would first send an unofficial emissary to Thieu and would consider going to Saigon himself prior to [his] Inauguration.")

Diem, in his memoir, observed defensively that while this and other quoted cables "constituted circumstantial evidence for anybody ready to assume the worst, they certainly did not mean that I had arranged a deal with the Republicans [through Anna Chennault]. . . . My impression is that she [Chennault] may have played her own game in encouraging both the South Vietnamese and the Republicans." Chennault, he wrote, had other contacts in the Saigon regime. "What messages went to what people during that hectic and confusing time are certainly beyond recovery at this point, and the so-called Anna Chennault affair will doubtless remain a mysterious footnote to history, though one that could easily have had greater consequences."

In an interview in 1995, Bui Diem acknowledged that he was in touch quite often in 1968 with Mitchell, Chennault and Tower but said he didn't remember getting into details about the Paris negotiations with them. He said they never asked him to convey any specific message to Thieu other than if Nixon were elected he would be supportive of Saigon, and he said he was never part of any deal to delay the Paris talks. But he volunteered that Chennault was a close friend of Nguyen Van Kieu, brother of President Thieu, who was then South Vietnamese ambassador to Taiwan, which she often visited, and that it was a possibility she had communicated with Thieu through him.

Clark Clifford for one suspected some such other Chennault line to Saigon. In his own book later, he wrote of Bui Diem's remarks: "Despite his disclaimers, I believe there were other messages, delivered through other channels; Diem correctly suspected he was under surveillance by American intelligence, and tried to fool watchers by using more secure channels." Besides, Clifford wrote, "Diem was not Anna Chennault's only channel to Saigon. . . . She took seriously Nixon's request that she act [as she boasted in her own book, *The Education of Anna*] as 'the sole representative between the Vietnamese government and the Nixon campaign headquarters,' and she certainly found other routes of communication with President Thieu."

Up to this time, LBJ seemed more concerned that he himself might be perceived as playing politics on the peace negotiations than worried about Nixon doing so. In another meeting with his foreign policy advisers on the same day as Bui Diem sent his cable reporting "I am regularly in touch with the Nixon entourage," Johnson observed, according to Tom Johnson's notes: "I would rather be stubborn and adamant rather than [a] ticky, slick politician. They think everybody is working toward electing Humphrey by doing this. This is not what motivates us. I want to take it slow."

But the intercept of the Bui Diem cable put the president in high dudgeon over Madame Chennault's high jinks. As a result of the cable, Califano wrote later, which "urged Thieu to block the peace process until after the presidential election, Johnson now suspected that Nixon had acted on Chennault's advice and treasonously, to his thinking, subverted his own government in order to win the election." James Jones, at the time a close LBJ aide and later an Oklahoma congressman and then American ambassador to Mexico in the Clinton administration, recalled in an interview that Johnson, upon intelligence confirmation of the Chennault overtures to Saigon, exploded: "This is treason!"

According to Safire in his book, Bryce Harlow got a phone call from Senate Minority Leader Everett Dirksen, "who said he had just been speaking with President Johnson and something had to be done in a hurry to cool him off. Johnson . . . was ready to blow his stack—and blow the whistle on the Nixon campaign's attempt to defeat his peace efforts by getting President Thieu to hold back. Anna Chennault's name was mentioned."

Harlow himself, now deceased, in an oral history interview later for the Lyndon B. Johnson Library in Austin, said the Nixon party was staying at the Century Plaza in Los Angeles at the time, and he ran up to Nixon's room and roused him from sleep, brushing past gatekeeper Bob Haldeman. "I told him 'You've got to talk to LBJ,'" Harlow recalled. "'Someone has told him that you're dumping all over the South Vietnamese to keep them from doing something about peace, and he's just about to believe it. If you don't let him know quickly that it's not so, then he's going to dump.'" Nixon, Harlow said, "got him on the phone and said there was absolutely no truth to it, as far as he knew."

In the oral history, however, Harlow said later that "I'm not convinced that it was not true. It was too tempting a target. I wouldn't be a bit surprised if there were some shenanigans going on."

In the same interview, Harlow acknowledged some political shenanigans of his own. When Johnson "started putting together this big statement about a bombing halt," he said, ". . . I knew all about that. I had a double agent working in the White House. I knew about every meeting they held. I knew who attended the meetings. I knew what their next move was going to be. I kept Nixon informed about the development of that, about my agent." When Nixon asked him, he said, "'Who are you dealing with?' I said, 'Dick, let's don't do that. This is too delicate.' He said, 'All right, okay.' It's the only way you can do this kind of stuff." Of his agent, Harlow said, "I rather doubt that his source in the White House was aware that he was keeping the Nixon forces up to date on what they were doing."

When Nixon was at a loss about what to do politically to counter the expected bombing halt, Harlow recalled, he tried to plant a damaging story with veteran reporter Merriman Smith of the United Press. "Smitty, what would you think if I told you," Harlow said he told the dean of the White House press corps, "that LBJ is going to dump on RMN in foreign policy at the time it would hurt the worst? . . . What would you say?" Smith replied: "I would say that's a damn lie. You're trying to plant a story. Is that what you're doing?" Harlow said he shot back: "Yes. That's what I'm trying to do. But I'm not trying to plant a lie. I'm trying to plant a story that's true, because that's what's going to happen. This will have to do with our relations with South Vietnam and North Vietnam, and it will be a blockbuster, and it will come from the president at a critical time in the campaign. . . . Why don't you just do a little prowling [at the White House] and see what you find? You might find something." Smith reported back later, Harlow said, that his information was wrong, but when Johnson finally announced the bombing halt, Smith called and apologized for doubting Harlow's word.

*   *   *

Suddenly what Chennault hoped would be a way to puncture Humphrey's best chance for an upset threatened to backfire on Nixon if Johnson were to report publicly that it was the Republican nominee who was playing politics with the Paris talks. Obviously unnerved, Nixon again phoned Senator Smathers and asked him to reassure Johnson on the matter.

Smathers called Jim Jones at the White House, who wrote in a memo that Nixon "understands the President is ready to blast him for allegedly collaborating with Tower and Chennault to slow the peace talks. Nixon says *there has been no contact at all* [italics added]." Nixon had told Smathers, Jones wrote, that he intended to go on television and "again back up the President and say he [Nixon] would rather get peace now than be President." Also, Jones wrote, Smathers told him Nixon "will say he will undertake any assignment the President has for him, whether that be to go to Hanoi or Paris or whatever in order to get peace. Nixon told Smathers he hoped the President would not make such a charge."

But Johnson at the same time was receiving more indirect reports of Nixon's conniving. In the early hours of October 29, the president held a series of meetings in the White House with key foreign policy and political advisers that lasted an exhausting five and a half hours. From it came his decision to declare the bombing halt after first warning Thieu to get in line and notifying the presidential candidates.

Before or during these meetings, White House national security adviser Walt Rostow passed on to Johnson a memo from his brother, Eugene Rostow, the Yale law professor who served as undersecretary of state for political affairs under LBJ. It told of a phone call "from an old friend in New York" who the previous day had "attended a working lunch" with two men "closely involved" with Nixon. "One of them explained to the group," the memo said, that Nixon "was trying to frustrate the president, by inciting Saigon to step up its demands, and by letting Hanoi know that when he took office 'he could accept anything and blame it on his predecessor.'"

A cover memo from Walt Rostow to Johnson identified the "old friend from New York." In it, Rostow said he had asked his brother "to go back to Alexander Sachs [a prominent New York economist], and see how much further detail he can get on the people involved and how close, in fact, they are to Nixon."

A second "Eyes Only" memo from Eugene Rostow elaborated that the speaker at the New York lunch "thought the prospects for a bombing halt or a cease-fire were dim because Nixon was playing the problem as he did the Fortas affair—to block. He was taking public positions intended to achieve that end. They would incite Saigon to be difficult, and Hanoi to wait."

Part of Nixon's strategy, he said, "was an expectation that an offensive would break out soon, that we would have to spend a great deal more (and incur more casualties). . . . These difficulties would make it easier for Nixon to settle after January. Like Ike in 1953, he would be able to settle on terms which the President could not accept, blaming the deterioration of the situation between now and January or February on his predecessor."

Getting together in the White House sitting room with Harry McPherson, Jim Jones, George Christian and Tom Johnson, LBJ showed the memos to them, then instructed them to make sure that Humphrey, Nixon and Wallace all would be reachable by conference call at five o'clock that afternoon. He clearly was nervous about what Nixon was up to. "Have a phone they can cram right up their butts," he ordered, according to Tom Johnson's notes.

Moving to the Cabinet Room, the president and the others were joined again by Rusk, Clifford, Taylor, Helms and Walt Rostow. LBJ read aloud the second memo from Gene Rostow, saying "this would rock the world if it were said he [Thieu] were conniving with the Republicans. . . . Can you imagine what people would say if this were to be known; that we have all these conditions met and then Nixon's conniving with them kept us from getting it?" He added a moment later: "I have no doubt there is some substance in this. This is [an] honest, reliable, prominent man who reports this."

Thieu continued to stall, declining to see American Ambassador Ellsworth Bunker in Saigon. LBJ instructed that Bunker demand to see Thieu and tell him that "we realize political forces are saying things to him and to Hanoi, but we are going to act in the best interests of South Vietnam. . . . Tell Bunker first that we have these intercepts from the political forces here. Next, say that we have sent orders out based on Thieu's clearance [for a start to the talks]. Tell him that we can delay those orders for a few minutes, but not for much longer. The question is whether we go with him or without him. . . . And tell him also that we are responsible for the conduct of the government until January 20th. . . ."

Immediately after this meeting, which ended shortly before 8 A.M., and as the president read the morning newspapers, showered and took a nap, Walt Rostow apparently got cold feet about the ramifications of charging Nixon with trying to sabotage the talks. In another memo to the president marked "Literally Eyes Only, Confidential—Sensitive" that specifically talked of having actual documentation of Republican collusion, he wrote:

"I have been considering the explosive possibilities of the information that we now have on how certain Republicans may have inflamed the South Vietnamese to behave as they have been behaving. There is no hard evidence that Nixon himself is involved. Exactly what the Republicans have been saying to Bui Diem is not wholly clear as opposed to the conclusions that Bui Diem is drawing from what they have said. Beyond that, the *materials* [italics added] are so explosive that they could gravely damage the country whether Mr. Nixon is elected or not. If *they get out in the present form* [italics added], they could be the subject of one of the most acrimonious debates we have ever witnessed.

"For the larger good of the country, you may wish to consider finding an occasion to talk with Mr. Nixon, making these points: 1. Here is the sort of thing we have been getting. 2. I do not believe that you personally have been involved in this. 3. It is not clear that some of your supporters have, necessarily, done anything out of line. 4. But what is clear is that this kind of talk is inflaming the inexperienced South Vietnamese who do not understand our constitution or our political life. 5. You might then tell him, assuming that we transit today's crisis, how difficult it has been and your feeling that the Vietnamese image of some of these conversations with Republicans may have played some part. Therefore, in the months ahead he may wish to caution his men to be exceedingly circumspect in dealing with inexperienced and impressionable South Vietnamese."

Intentionally or not, the last sentence seemed to assume that Nixon would be elected. The same assumption appeared to run through a lunch meeting at the White House later the same day attended by the president and all the major administration players, including note-taker Tom Johnson. With Thieu still standing aloof in Saigon, Clifford offered that "they [the Saigon regime] are trying to decide what is best—a Johnson administration or a Nixon administration to go on with. Bunker may not be putting it to them stiffly enough." Rusk jumped in. "What if Nixon's people say, 'Be tough.' They [the Saigon regime] read the polls. They are whipsawed too. They have a problem." Clifford again: "They have a moral obligation to go along with us. We said there were months of hard bargaining ahead. It is a matter of good faith. They think they will get a better deal from the next president. . . ." Rusk: "The GOP may be giving them advice. HHH has also scared them."

LBJ interjected: "They may just be testing HHH. . . . Nixon will double-cross them after November 5. All this publicity . . . all had an effect on Nixon. When the GOP could do it with us [presumably cooperate with the White House], they went to work on the [South Vietnamese] Embassy. They made Bui Diem think he could get a better deal from Nixon than us."

Regarded as a particular culprit in the Saigon foot-dragging was Vice President Nguyen Cao Ky, long a Thieu rival. "I think Ky is getting just as independent as Hubert," LBJ said at one point, reflecting his continuing pique at his own vice president as a result of Humphrey's Salt Lake City speech calling for a bombing halt. In another meeting with Rusk, Clifford, Rostow and the press aides that night, with Thieu still balking, the president seemed in fact to be doubting whether he wanted Humphrey to succeed him. "Saigon may see this as a political deal," Tom Johnson recorded him as saying. "They may think this would help HHH. They know the vice president would be softer. I do not want to help them put over a man who has this attitude toward us. . . . Look at the [McGeorge] Bundy speech, the vice president's Salt Lake City speech [both calling for the halt], and you see reasons for Saigon's concern. It may be better to wait. . . . I do not feel good about a quickie before the election."

Rusk pointed out the political peril of proceeding without Thieu. "If we go alone," he said, "the only conclusion is that we went ahead only for political reasons." And Rostow added: "Delay it one week. Get the election out of it." Johnson, though stopping short of that, said: "Let's don't go it alone. I know what forces are at work. I would postpone a day or two before I broke up the alliance. . . . [But] it is almost impossible with the people in our camp making these speeches. Thieu and the others are voting for a man they see as one who will stick with it: Nixon."

In another memo to the president marked "Secret/Sensitive," Rostow continued to give Nixon the benefit of the doubt. "Suppose Thieu does not go along today," Rostow wrote. "I suggest that you consider the following: First have in Nixon alone. *Give him the evidence—of which we have an important additional item* [italics added]—that the South Vietnamese are thinking that they can turn down the deal and get a better deal after the election. While sharing the information with Nixon, tell him flatly that you are confident that he has had nothing whatsoever to do with this."

Rostow then proposed that Johnson ask Nixon "to join in a private message to Thieu, with the other candidates," telling him they all supported LBJ's plan for the peace negotiations and "we believe it would be most ill-advised, under these circumstances for your government not to participate in the Paris talks promptly."

Johnson apparently ignored Rostow's suggestion. In a telephone interview much later, Rostow declined to comment further on the existence of physical documentation of intervention by the Nixon campaign with Saigon at the time to stall the Paris peace talks.

* * *

As all this consternation continued, Johnson ordered the FBI, in addition to its wiretaps on the South Vietnamese embassy, to put Madame Chennault under surveillance. The instructions went to Cartha "Deke" DeLoach, FBI director Hoover's liaison with the White House, and the wiretaps were quickly approved by Attorney General Ramsey Clark.

According to DeLoach in his book *Hoover's FBI*, "most of what we picked up over the wiretaps was garbage. . . . Then, at 7:30 a.m. on October 30, a curious conversation was recorded. A woman called South Vietnamese Ambassador Bui Dhien [*sic*] and the two of them spoke in English. The woman told the ambassador she was sorry she hadn't talked to him the day before 'inasmuch as there were so many people around,'" DeLoach wrote, and she asked him "what is the situation?" The ambassador told her that "something is cooking" and urged her to "drop by and talk to me. Time is running short." Whereupon the woman replied, "I'll see you right after the luncheon for Mrs. Agnew," leading listeners to conclude that the caller was Chennault, pursuing her efforts to stall the peace talks.

(A White House memo dated October 30 to Walt Rostow from "BKS" [presumably Bromley K. Smith of the White House staff] reported that "Mrs. Chennault entered the South Vietnamese Embassy at 3:26 this afternoon. She was still there at 4:30." Another memo, from Rostow to LBJ the next day, said simply: "The latest on the lady." Whatever information accompanied the note has not been declassified.)

In her book, Chennault wrote that "as the campaign neared its climax . . .

whenever I saw President Thieu I had to listen to his complaints about the steady pressure brought to bear on him by the Democrats to attend the Paris peace talks. 'Why should I go?' he would say. 'Why should I walk into a smoke screen?'" Thieu told her, she wrote, that "I would much prefer to have the peace talks after your elections. I think it would be good for both America and Vietnam."

Chennault wrote that "after hearing him out, I would ask him, to make sure, 'Is this a message to my party?' and invariably he would say, 'Yes, if I may ask you to convey this message to your candidate.'"

In *The Palace File* by former Thieu special assistant Nguyen Tien Hung and Jerrold L. Schecter, Chennault was quoted later as saying: "Thieu was under heavy pressure from the Democrats. My job was to hold him back and prevent him from changing his mind." Near the end of the 1968 campaign, the authors wrote, Mitchell called Chennault "'almost every day' to persuade her to keep Thieu from going to Paris for peace talks with the North Vietnamese. They knew their calls were being tapped by the FBI and she joked about it, asking Mitchell playfully, 'Who is listening on the other side?' Mitchell did not think it funny and told her, 'Call me from a pay phone. Don't talk in your office.' Mitchell's message to her was always the same: 'Don't let him go.'"

* * *

Now, one week from Election Day, Gene McCarthy finally dropped the other shoe. He issued a statement that was typically McCarthy—a grudging endorsement that only a happy warrior like Humphrey could rejoice about—and did. Humphrey's position on McCarthy's critical issues—ending the war, demilitarizing American policy, reforming the draft—"falls far short of what I think it should be," McCarthy said, but given the choice, he said Humphrey "has shown a better understanding of our domestic needs and a stronger will to act than has been shown by Richard Nixon." Also, under a President Humphrey, he said, "the possibility of scaling down the arms race and reducing military tensions would be much greater."

To his young army of followers, McCarthy said he would not ask them "to test the established political processes of the Democratic Party" again "unless those processes have clearly been changed," which he said he would continue to work to achieve. He concluded with a surprise: "In order to make it clear that this endorsement is in no way intended to reinstate me in the good graces of the Democratic Party leaders, nor in any way to suggest my having forgotten or condoned the things that happened both before Chicago and at Chicago, I announce at this time that I will not be a candidate of my party for reelection to the Senate from the state of Minnesota in 1970. Nor will I seek the presidential nomination of the Democratic Party in 1972."

Humphrey proclaimed himself "a happy man this morning" but he found it hard to hide his pique. Asked how he felt about the fact "that it took McCarthy so long to come around," he replied: "One of the qualities that a man that seeks to be president ought to have is forbearance and patience. And good will. I, of course, am pleased that the senator has come out . . . to help me. If he had done it a week ago, I would have been pleased. But I accept things as they are." Having said that, however, he said he sensed a definite pickup in support in the country and added: "I wish I had a few more days."

(McCarthy told me later that he had been prepared to endorse Humphrey in September at the time of the mixup over Marine withdrawals from Vietnam, when he talked about "withdrawing troops, [but] he took it back before we could even endorse him. We thought it was a sign of some concession but Johnson put the pressure on him and he took it back. If he had given us another day before he took it back, we probably would have endorsed him [then]."

(In any event, McCarthy said, "I endorsed him early enough. I don't think there was anybody who would have voted for Hubert if I had endorsed him a week earlier than I did. That was the only pressure we had on him. And it wasn't only a personal decision that I could have made. A lot of people had committed time, money and emotion to the campaign. I couldn't just say, 'Well, thanks, fellas, but I'm gonna leave you out there alone without making any fight.'")

* * *

In this final week, Humphrey played the card of party loyalty relentlessly. In midtown Manhattan on October 30, he told a moderate crowd hoisting many labor signs: "Four years ago this month, I came here to this very same spot to ask your help for Lyndon Johnson and Robert Kennedy, and they were elected, one to the White House, one to the Senate. I just don't believe you're ready to vote for Wallace in this city, and I can't believe you are ready to stand still while the world is moving on. . . . I don't believe that in the heritage and the tradition of a Franklin Roosevelt, and a Harry Truman, and a John Kennedy, and an Adlai Stevenson, a Lyndon Johnson and a Hubert Humphrey, you are not going to vote the Democratic ticket."

There was no running away from LBJ by Humphrey, and on the next night, Thursday, October 31, the same kind of patience he had shown in suffering McCarthy's delay in endorsing him was again rewarded. Johnson in a televised talk to the nation finally announced he had decided to halt the bombing of North Vietnam "on the basis of the developments in the Paris talks, and I have reached it in the belief that this action can lead to progress toward a peaceful settlement of the war." He expressed confidence that the

country "could now expect . . . prompt productive, serious and intensive negotiations in an atmosphere that is conducive to progress."

The Hanoi regime, Johnson said, had agreed to the participation of the
Saigon government at the talks in Paris and the United States had approved
a role for the National Liberation Front. Hanoi had been informed, he specified, that the approval "in no way involved recognition of the NLF in any
form, yet it conforms to the statements that we made many times over the
years that the NLF would have no difficulty in making its views known." He
added that Hanoi had to understand that "a total bombing halt must not risk
the lives of our men." He assured his listeners that the Joint Chiefs had told
him "that in their military judgment this action would not result in any increase in American casualties."

Prior to the airing of his talk, Johnson had placed a conference call to
Humphrey, Nixon and Wallace, informing them of what he was going to say.
In the course of doing so, Clifford wrote later, LBJ advised them that "some
old China hands are going around and implying to some of the embassies and
some others that they might get a better deal out of somebody who was not
involved in this. Now that's made it difficult and it's held up things a bit,"
Johnson said, "and I know that none of you candidates are aware of it or responsible for it. . . ." Incredibly, he was pointedly saying that he absolved
Nixon of any part in Anna Chennault's machinations—or warning Nixon in
a veiled way to desist.

A jubilant Humphrey called Johnson's decision on the bombing halt "very
wise and prudent" and said he had "been hoping for months that it would
happen." Nixon, at a major rally at Madison Square Garden that night, cautiously said he hoped the halt "would bring some progress" in the Paris talks.
Pointing to Agnew sitting behind him on the stage in one of their rare joint
appearances, he pledged that "neither he nor I will destroy the chance of
peace. We want peace."

Hung and Schecter, in their book, wrote that far from being deflated by
the development, Nixon "with his intimate knowledge of what Thieu was
contemplating in Saigon [apparently from Chennault] . . . was glad to see
the Democrats sinking into a self-created trap. Nixon knew that Thieu
would not go to Paris, yet the Democrats were inflating the prospects for
peace by linking the bombing pause to expanded peace talks scheduled for
November 6. . . . In a cunning move, Nixon turned the seeming disadvan-
tage to his favor. He inflated peace hopes even higher, knowing they would
be deflated by Thieu and he would benefit politically from the disillusion
and doubt over President Johnson's initiative."

Wallace, on hearing the news, said "I hope and pray" the decision would bring "an honorable peace," and "I couldn't care less who gets credit for it." But Richard Nixon's strategists certainly did. They labored hard to convince reporters that the development, if it held, had come too late to help Humphrey's election chances.

Chennault in her book recalled that on the night of Johnson's speech declaring the bombing halt and negotiations breakthrough, she was finishing dinner at the Sheraton Park apartment of celebrated Washington hostess Perle Mesta when a call came to her to phone Mitchell. She returned the call, she wrote, and heard Mitchell tell her: "Anna, I'm speaking on behalf of Mr. Nixon. It's very important that our Vietnamese friends understand our Republican position and I hope you have made that clear to them."

She wrote that "it was late, I was tired, and I wasn't sure quite what it was I was to make clear to the South Vietnamese. All I knew was that the instructions seemed to have changed from the ones I had been given, to keep Nixon informed of South Vietnamese intentions." She balked, she said, telling Mitchell: "Look, John, all I've done is relay messages. If you're talking about direct influence, I have to tell you it isn't wise for us to try to influence the South Vietnamese. Their actions have to follow their own national interests, and I'm sure that is what will dictate Thieu's decisions. I don't think either we or the Democrats can force them to act one way or another."

Mitchell, she wrote, "sounded nervous. 'Do you think they really have decided not to go to Paris?' [he asked]." "'I don't think they'll go,' [she replied]. 'Thieu has told me over and over again that going to Paris would be walking into a smoke screen that has nothing to do with reality.'" Mitchell, sighing, told her to "be sure to call me if you get any more news."

Chennault's version cast herself in the role of a mere message conveyor, while painting Mitchell as overtly attempting to pressure Thieu and interfere in the conduct of American foreign policy. She took note in her account that before she started talking to Mitchell, she had her frequent escort, prominent Washington lawyer Thomas "Tommy the Cork" Corcoran, listen in on another line. In any event, the notion of a political campaign meddling in peace talks to achieve domestic political ends would be, if true, dynamite in the hands of political opponents willing to use the information.

* * *

It was now five days until America went to the polls, but Humphrey believed he had reason on this last day of October to feel that things finally were beginning to turn his way. It was a feeling that was not to last very long.

CHAPTER 12

November: "Bring Us Together"

Nov. 4 Francis Russell's *The Shadow of Blooming Grove* published; Vern (Junior) Stephens, All-Star shortstop, 48, dies; **5** Democrat Shirley Chisholm of New York becomes first black woman elected to Congress; **8** *Pioneer* 9 interplanetary probe orbits sun; **11** 50th anniversary of armistice ending World War I observed quietly in U.S.; **13** *Yellow Submarine* (animated) featuring voices of the Beatles released; **14** *The Shoes of the Fisherman* starring Anthony Quinn released; **18** producer Walter Wanger (*Invasion of the Body Snatchers*), 74, dies; **20** actress Audrey Hepburn divorces actor Mel Ferrer; **25** William Manchester's *The Arms of Krupp* published; Upton Sinclair, Pulitzer Prize novelist, 90, dies; **26** FBI agents arrest 8 alleged Mafia leaders in upstate New York; white parents ask more integration in Little Rock schools; **27** Labor Department reports highest cost-of-living increase in six years; Alvin Karpis, former Public Enemy No. 1, paroled after serving 32 years for kidnapping.

On November 1, the morning after Johnson announced the halt in the bombing of North Vietnam, Nixon embarked on a two-day tour of Texas accompanied by Senator Tower. Nixon said pointedly in Fort Worth that he was "not going to say anything" about LBJ's action "to undercut him. Peace is too important for politics," he intoned, "and that's the way we're going to play it."

A local lawyer named J. S. "Tiny" Gooch who introduced Nixon to the crowd, however, hinted at sellout. "I sincerely hope we're going to have peace," he said, "but I just can't help but believe that Hanoi would much rather deal with Johnson and Humphrey than with President Nixon." Tower suggested that the timing of the halt "raises questions" about why immediate cessation was ordered when it was, when the broadened talks were not to start until the day after the election.

As for Nixon himself, Ned Kenworthy of the *New York Times* described his delivery of his speech as "almost dispirited." Nixon well understood that with Humphrey already closing the gap in the public opinion polls, the optimism about the prospects for peace generated by the bombing halt and a breakthrough in the Paris stalemate could do him in on election day.

In Saigon, however, South Vietnamese President Thieu was raising further objections with Ambassador Bunker. He conveyed certain new conditions that would have to be met for the Saigon regime to agree to participate in the broadened negotiations. Thieu had been negotiating with the Americans virtually alone on the talks, to preserve secrecy, and when others high in the regime got wind of what was going on, they balked. Bunker told him that it was too late for the United States to raise new conditions with the North Vietnamese because Hanoi had already accepted Johnson's proposals.

On November 2, the Saturday before the American election, an FBI tap on the South Vietnamese embassy in Washington intercepted a phone call from Chennault, again urging the Saigon regime to hold firm against participation in the Paris peace talks on the premise that it would get a better deal with Nixon in the White House. When Chennault was asked whether Nixon knew of her call, she replied: "No, but our friend in New Mexico does." It so happened that Nixon's running mate, Agnew, was in Albuquerque on that day.

On the same day, Thieu dropped a bombshell. He told a joint session of the South Vietnamese National Assembly that his regime was boycotting the Paris talks. Including the NLF, he declared, "would just be another trick toward a coalition government with the Communists in South Vietnam." He said Saigon would talk only to the Hanoi delegation.

The bubble of optimism that had hovered briefly over the Humphrey campaign burst at once. Nixon in Austin soberly observed that "in view of the early reports that we've had this morning, the prospects for peace are not as bright as we would have hoped a few days ago." He did not have to say the obvious: Saigon's refusal to play ball not only severely undermined hope for an early settlement but also made Johnson's boast of a breakthrough seem premature, if not contrived and intentionally misleading.

In the Nixon manner, the candidate said nothing more, but as his plane headed from Texas to California, Nixon aide Bob Finch approached two wire-service reporters, Bill Boyarsky, then of the Associated Press, and Dan

Rapoport of United Press International. He told them that based on what Johnson had told Nixon on the phone two nights earlier, "we had the impression that all the diplomatic ducks were in a row." The implication was equally clear—that LBJ had jumped the gun in ordering the bombing halt to bail out Humphrey's campaign. Finch declined to permit his name to be used, but there was no doubt he was acting as a conveyor belt from Nixon. That was obvious when, to get clarification on a point raised by Rapoport, he retreated to Nixon's private compartment and returned with a response.

Safire confirmed later in his book that Nixon, not wanting to float the implication himself, had sent Finch back on the plane to float it for him. For Nixon personally "to criticize a 'step toward peace,' even a phony one," Safire wrote, "would be bad because the step did not seem phony to mothers living on hope."

Appearing the next morning, Sunday, November 3, on NBC's *Meet the Press*, Nixon was asked by Herb Kaplow: "Some of your close aides have been trying to spread the word that President Johnson timed the Vietnam bombing pause to help Vice President Humphrey in Tuesday's election. Do you agree with them?"

Nixon answered: "No, I don't make that charge." Then he was off on the patented Nixon ploy of feeding an allegation by denying he was making it. "I must say," he added, "that many of my aides and many of the people supporting my candidacy around the country seem to share that view. They share it, I suppose, because the pause came at that time so late in the campaign. But President Johnson has been very candid with me throughout these discussions, and I do not make such a charge."

Well, Kaplow wanted to know, was it "conceivable" that an aide on his plane would put out the allegation "in disagreement with you?" Nixon replied: "Oh, altogether conceivable." He said that Finch, "who made this statement . . . completely disagrees with my appraisal of this. His appraisal of the situation around the country is that many people believe that the bombing pause was politically motivated and was timed to affect the election. I don't agree with him, but he is a man in his own right. . . . " Once again, as in Nixon's earlier, and pathetic, disclaimer of trying to float a rumor about a politically motivated bomb halt while professing to knock it down, there was a flash of the same Old Nixon.

To demonstrate his total support of, and willingness to cooperate with, Johnson, Nixon as he had promised through Smathers volunteered to go to Paris or Saigon "in order to get the negotiations off center" if LBJ or Rusk wanted him to. There had been, obviously, no such suggestion from either of them. Nixon hastened to add: "Let me make one thing clear. I don't suggest this as a grandstand stunt." Another flash of the Old Nixon.

Humphrey's hopes, for a fleeting moment so high, were deflated again. About the only thing that might now counter these latest suspicions that Johnson had been playing politics with the Paris peace talks was to come up with evidence that the Nixon campaign itself was doing so. Astonishingly, although information suggesting just such an outrageous gambit was in Johnson's hands, he wasn't making it public—surprisingly, considering Nixon's general reputation that he would probably do anything it took to win.

* * *

By now, Chennault as well as the South Vietnamese embassy had, in accordance with Johnson's instructions, been placed under surveillance by DeLoach. One FBI report from Director Hoover informed presidential aide Bromley Smith that Chennault on the day before the election was tracked by agents leaving her Watergate apartment, driving to the Vietnamese embassy, where she stayed about half an hour, and then going on to 1701 Pennsylvania Avenue, the address of Nixon's campaign headquarters, where she remained about an hour before returning to the Vietnamese embassy. The report, passed on to Walt Rostow as noted earlier, had no details on what she had said at either place, but her itinerary added to the conviction at the White House that Chennault was the Nixon campaign's agent in undermining the Paris peace talks.

Clark Clifford wrote later in his memoir: "What was conveyed to Thieu through the Chennault channel may never be fully known, but there was no doubt that she conveyed a simple and authoritative message from the Nixon camp that was probably persuasive in convincing President Thieu to defy President Johnson—thus delaying the negotiations and prolonging the war. . . . The activities of the Nixon team went far beyond the bounds of justifiable political combat. It constituted direct interference in the activities of the executive branch and the responsibilities of the Chief Executive, the only people with authority to negotiate on behalf of the nation. The activities of the Nixon campaign constituted a gross, even potentially illegal, interference in the security affairs of the nation by private individuals."

Yet Johnson still declined to blow the whistle publicly on Nixon. "It was an extraordinary dilemma," Clifford wrote afterward. "On the one hand, we had positive evidence that The Little Flower [Chennault] and other people speaking for the Republican candidate were encouraging President Thieu to delay the negotiations for political reasons. On the other, the information had been derived from extremely sensitive intelligence-gathering operations of the FBI, the CIA and the National Security Agency; these included surveillance of the Ambassador of our ally, and an American citizen with strong political ties to the Republicans."

Johnson failed to disclose what he knew, Clifford wrote, because he still hoped Thieu would cooperate and hence "seriously underestimated the harm the Chennault channel caused to the negotiating efforts," because he didn't want to undermine American public support for Thieu, and because Rusk feared "revealing the Chennault channel would reveal to Hanoi the strains between Saigon and Washington, stiffen Hanoi's position and [further] disrupt the negotiations." And, finally, Clifford wrote, LBJ was ambivalent about whether he really wanted Humphrey to be elected. "What mattered to President Johnson at that moment," he wrote, "was not who would succeed him, but what his place in history would be. . . .

"Perhaps in the wake of a decade of post-Watergate revelations about intelligence activities," Clifford went on, "the decision not to go public may seem fussy and old-fashioned. . . . Had the decision been mine alone, I would either have had a private discussion with Nixon, making clear to him that if he did not send a countervailing signal to Thieu immediately, he would face public criticism from the President for interference in the negotiations; or I would have allowed the incident to become public, so that the American public might take it into account in deciding how to vote. Had he been the candidate himself, this is what I believed Lyndon Johnson would have done."

Jim Jones later offered another reason for Johnson not having gone public with what he knew or suspected about the Chennault affair. LBJ realized, Jones said, that if it was true that Nixon had been involved in attempting to undermine the Paris peace talks for political gain and subsequently was elected, "it was treason perpetrated by a presidential candidate, and it would throw us into a huge constitutional crisis if he were elected."

* * *

Johnson was further irked when some eleven members of the South Vietnamese Senate, on the same day Thieu boycotted the talks, said they wanted to see Nixon elected. On Sunday afternoon, after Nixon's television appearance in which he had been asked about Finch's remarks, Johnson phoned Nixon at his suite at the Century Plaza in Los Angeles. What the hell was going on? he demanded to know. Nixon repeated that he had nothing to do with Chennault's machinations. Well, LBJ, sputtered, "who is this guy Fink" making veiled accusations of political shenanigans in his behalf?

Califano wrote later: "Now Johnson was certain in his own mind, whatever the evidence he could uncover to prove it, that Nixon had betrayed his country and enlisted Thieu to torpedo the arrangement. Nixon's denials, when

Johnson phoned him, did nothing to undermine the president's conviction. At last, now in the final hours, Johnson desperately wanted Humphrey to win the election. . . .

"Instead of just getting mad, Johnson had a way to get even. He offered Humphrey the information on the activities (as he saw them) of Anna Chennault and Nixon, which included a wiretapped phone call from Chennault to the South Vietnamese embassy in Washington, to use in the final days of his campaign. Humphrey didn't want to do it. Johnson was furious, thinking it was 'the dumbest thing in the world not to do it.' Humphrey thought it would be 'terrible to do that sort of thing' when he wasn't absolutely sure of the facts. Johnson thought it would be worse to have as president a man so consumed with power that he would betray the country's national-security interests, undermine its foreign policy and endanger the lives of its young soldiers to win the office."

Larry O'Brien confirmed later in an interview for the LBJ oral history archive that Humphrey at that time had "expressed deep concern" over the information and "made a couple of references to Nixon personally: 'What kind of a guy could engage in something like this?' He was, I guess you'd have to say, shocked. But now, in the context of what knowledge he had," O'Brien recalled, "I think what came across to me was his concern about utilizing it—whether it was justified, whether there was enough evidence so he could hold his head high and not be accused of playing cheap politics at the end in a desperation effort to win an election. . . . He let it hang there. If he'd discussed this in detail with me and I'd really focused on it, I would have pressed him hard to go [use it]. I think he knew that and he wasn't prepared [to do it]."

Here was a chance to turn the tables on Nixon by exposing Chennault's activities and letting the public and press draw its own conclusions about whether the Nixon campaign was behind them. Given Nixon's history and reputation for political gamesmanship, there was more than a fair chance that enough undecided voters would believe the charge, swing away from him and over to Humphrey if the story surfaced in the final two days before the election.

What may have seemed to be an obvious political call was further complicated in Humphrey's mind, however, by a concern voiced by some of his advisers that airing any allegation of attempted interference with the American election by the Saigon regime would have totally destroyed any chance of getting its representatives to the peace table quickly.

Besides, Van Dyk said much later, Humphrey had now edged ahead of Nixon in the Harris Survey (but still trailed slightly in the more prestigious and usually reliable Gallup Poll). "The last thing we wanted was to come up with a charge like that," he told me. "It would have looked like a last-minute wild thing." If Chennault's actions had occurred two weeks earlier, Van Dyk said, "Humphrey might have accused her. Besides, we couldn't explain how we got the information, which was from a CIA or FBI tap." Still, Humphrey was seething. "The China Lobby is going to deny me the presidency," he complained to Van Dyk.

So Humphrey said nothing about the caper of "The Little Flower." Instead, according to Van Dyk, he ordered his aide to release a statement saying that if elected, he would withdraw American support from the government of South Vietnam. Van Dyk, deciding to save his boss from himself, said in the statement only that if the South Vietnamese refused to go to the peace table, the United States should go without them.

Humphrey went on ABC News's *Issues and Answers* and declared that the United States "had every right to expect" that the Saigon regime take part in the Paris talks. The American people, he said, "have paid a heavy price in men and matériel and in many other ways for the defense of South Vietnam, and I think it is fair to expect that government will recognize the sacrifices that we have made and will respond to what is an honorable effort to bring about a cessation of hostilities."

Humphrey's refusal to use the Chennault information against Nixon, Califano wrote later, "became the occasion for a lasting rift" between Johnson and his vice president. That refusal, Califano added in a later interview, "really tore it. Johnson thought Hubert had no balls, no spine, no toughness. But he did all he could for him. He really hated Nixon, going all the way back to [Nixon's senatorial campaign against] Helen Gahagan Douglas." Johnson believed, at the same time, that Humphrey's comments on withdrawing American troops from Vietnam were "inhibiting his chances to end the war on his watch," which was LBJ's paramount goal, Califano said.

* * *

With Humphrey's crowds growing larger and more enthusiastic as he campaigned through New York, Pennsylvania and Ohio and with labor working diligently to pry blue-collar voters from Wallace, he felt he could not risk the injection of another bombshell into the campaign. Only the traditional windup parade through Chicago's Loop was disappointing; the after-affects of the August convention had not yet worn off, and Mayor Daley was visibly pessimistic about Humphrey's chances.

Humphrey did seize on the bombing halt to declare the Democratic Party finally united on Vietnam. He told the Chicago crowd that "those brave men who led dissent last spring have made their mark on policy . . . they have helped the search for peace . . . they are coming home [to the party]." He spoke confidently that "many thousands of the young people who went door to door in New Hampshire, in Indiana, in Nebraska and Oregon and California [for McCarthy and Kennedy], will go from door to door next Monday for that same cause—for our party, for Ed Muskie and me, but most of all for justice."

On the final Saturday of the campaign, Humphrey attended a rally in a Maryland suburb of Washington and took then the occasion to call on Johnson. What ensued reflected the degree of disintegration between the president and Humphrey in the wake of the Salt Lake City speech. It had been raining and Humphrey stopped off at his home to change clothes. As a result, he wrote later, he was "running about ten minutes late. During that time, Jim Jones, the president's aide, called my office and said, 'If the vice president isn't here in five minutes, the president is leaving for the weekend.' . . . As I got out of my car at the White House, Jim Jones approached and said, 'The president is not going to see you. The meeting is canceled.' I told Jones in a fury that I was trying to run a presidential campaign as the Democratic nominee, and if Lyndon Johnson didn't care, that was fine with me. Then I asked Jones if he would carry a message from me to the president. He agreed. And I described in terms that the president would understand what they could do with their meeting."

On the next afternoon, Sunday, the candidate nevertheless joined Johnson in Houston for a rousing, star-spangled rally before 58,000 people at the huge Astrodome, featuring Frank Sinatra and other show business supporters. The public LBJ before his fellow Texans proclaimed that Humphrey, "my friend and co-worker for 20 years, is a healer and a builder and will represent all the people all the time. Hubert Humphrey has worked all his life not to generate suspicion and not to generate fear among people, but to inspire them with confidence in their ability to live together."

Humphrey, loyal to the end despite the personal affronts he had suffered at Johnson's hands, called him "one of the truly great men of our country for all times" and said "I have been, at least I've tried to be, his faithful friend, and in all the months of the campaign his loyal vice president—and proud of it."

Among the prominent Texas Democrats present was Governor Connally, who had been playing ball with the Nixon campaign in the hope and expectation of landing a high cabinet post. But Humphrey was coming on now in Texas and LBJ was openly in his corner, so Connally, apparently fearful of being left in the cold in his own state, decided to stay in the Democratic ranks. Later, during the Nixon White House years, John Sears told me: "If the fellow had had a few more guts, he'd be Secretary of Defense today."

The news from the polls on that final weekend was astounding from Humphrey's point of view. The Gallup Poll, released Sunday, reported that he had surged into a virtual tie with Nixon, trailing only 42 percent to 40, with Wallace down to 14. The Harris Survey, suspect always of favoring Democrats, came out Monday and actually had Humphrey ahead, 43 percent to 40, with Wallace at 13 in an election Harris deemed "too close to call."

Humphrey was campaigning at last as the true happy warrior, in spirit as well as in upbeat rhetoric. In Los Angeles on Sunday morning, in a late televised bid for the peace vote, he talked tough in prodding the Saigon regime to join the talks. "The foreign policy of the United States and the fate of young Americans in Vietnam should and will be determined by the U. S. and not by any foreign government," he said. "That policy and those young Americans should not be placed at the mercy of domestic considerations in another country."

Then Humphrey and Muskie rode in an open convertible through an uproarious crowd in the downtown Los Angeles business district, matching the delirious one that had greeted Robert Kennedy the day after his primary defeat in Oregon. Mexican-Americans and blacks surged against the motorcade, just as they had done for Kennedy. To the end, Humphrey was going to the people in his trademark person-to-person tireless style, hoping by sheer energy, endurance and conspicuous optimism to stagger across the finish line ahead. An authoritative California poll had him a mere percentage point behind in Nixon's home state, which the Humphrey forces only weeks before had all but written off.

Muskie's presence was the final effort to remind voters of Nixon's choice of Agnew. The campaign also ran a thirty-minute biography of Muskie at considerable expense to make the same point, along with an ad in which the sound of a thumping heart was heard, and then a voice intoning: "Imagine Spiro T. Agnew a heartbeat away from the presidency." Another ad for television had a long soundtrack of laughter followed by the simple question: "Agnew for President?" But according to Larry O'Brien later, "we canceled it after getting protests from our own people that it was too tough and might backfire."

For the same reason, he said it was decided not to rerun films of Nixon's famous "Checkers" speech of 1952 and his "last press conference" of 1962, for fear they might evoke sympathy for Nixon. Napolitan said later he watched a film of the 1962 meeting with the press after Nixon's gubernatorial defeat in California and recommended against using it. "If you watched that whole thing you couldn't help feeling sorry for him," he said. "What he said he didn't say sarcastically. He said it as a beaten man."

* * *

While Humphrey and Muskie were basking in the adoration of the Los Angeles street crowds, Nixon was following his own standard script elsewhere in the city. He stood on a chair before fifty or so workers in the local campaign headquarters and cautiously played to the disappointment over the intransigence of the Saigon regime—without, obviously, mentioning Chennault.

"Developments of the past few days clearly indicate that the American people need fresh new ideas, new men and new leadership if we are to bring an end to the war," he said. "When we consider the fact that it was only three days ago that the hopes for peace were tremendously high as a result of the bombing pause, and that now those hopes are quite discouraging because of the developments since then, it is clear that if we are going to avoid what could be a diplomatic disaster, it is going to be necessary to get some new men and a united front."

Having thus provided the television networks with a compact, flawless clip for use on their evening news shows, Nixon hopped down off the chair and retired to his suite at the Century Plaza to rest for a final telethon on election eve. Klein tried to persuade reporters that spot phone calls to 300 persons around the country had found only 2 percent—six individuals—who said the bombing halt might change their vote. At the same time, Mitchell dismissed the latest polls, especially the Harris results, which he called "a gratuitous concoction."

Some Nixon insiders, however, were in a sweat. "By Sunday night I thought we were finished," Buchanan told me later. "The bombing halt really had the women moving to Humphrey. I thought then we were down the tube. But when the South Vietnamese indicated they hadn't been plugged in, it started back. It knocked the hell out of the euphoria about a peace breakthrough. But the boss stayed remarkably cool through all of it. He checked the polls and watched TV. He was as calm as he could be. The old fatalism was operating then."

An unsigned memo in the White House files dated that Monday, November 4, sized up the likely thinking in the Nixon camp at the eleventh hour. "The object of the exercise [casting doubts on a peace breakthrough] was to nullify the political impact of the President's decision by making it dubious," the memo said. "They think that goal has been achieved. They think the political effect of the bombing halt has been reduced by 25%-33%. The damage was done via Thieu in Saigon, through low-level Americans. They think the damage has been done. Thieu, in their judgment, will continue on his present line until it becomes impossible. Mitchell's strategy is for Nixon now to be a statesman. He can't do any more mischief politically at home, although his troops will continue to use the line here. He regards any further steps by him as counter-productive."

In another memo on November 4, from Rostow to LBJ and marked "Sensitive Eyes Only, Deliver Direct to the President," Rostow reported on an hour's meeting with Secretaries Rusk and Clifford "on the China matter," presumably an allusion to Madame Chennault. The meeting was called at LBJ's request, Rostow wrote later, "to consider the question of whether the story should be made public." An unsigned White House memo of the same date reported that "Saville Davis of the *Christian Science Monitor* is upstairs. He said they are holding out of the paper a sensational dispatch from Saigon (from their Saigon correspondent), the first para [*sic*] of which reads: 'Purported political encouragement from the Richard Nixon camp was a significant factor in the last-minute decision of President Thieu's refusal to send a delegation to the Paris peace talks—at least until the American presidential election is over.' He said he will await WWR's [Walt W. Rostow's] comments." The writer of the memo was instructed not to comment, and did not, and the story was not published.

Rostow's November 4 memo observed, in part, that "the information sources [presumably U.S. intelligence agencies] must be protected and not introduced into domestic policies. . . . Sec. Rusk was very strong on the following position: we get information like this every day, some of it very damaging to American political figures. We have always taken the view that with respect to such sources there is no public 'right to know.' Such information is collected simply for the purposes of national security.

"So far as the information based on such sources is concerned, all three of us agreed: (A) even if the story breaks, it was judged too late to have a significant impact on the election. (B) the viability of the man elected as president was involved as well as subsequent relations between him and President Johnson. (C) Therefore, the common recommendation was that we should not encourage such stories and hold tight the data we have."

The memo then proceeded to report more travels of Madame Chennault that morning—from her apartment to the Vietnamese embassy, thence to the building in which the Nixon headquarters was based, back to the Vietnamese embassy, to the Chinese embassy and then to her own office.

* * *

Although, as Buchanan suggested, Nixon's "old fatalism" may have been operating then, the deep nervousness among others on his staff was evidenced in the release of a statement by Eisenhower that the Nixon campaign said was written by him from his room at the Walter Reed Army Hospital in

Washington (but that a hospital spokesman said came from the old general's Gettysburg home). "Opinion polls this morning suggest to me," the statement said, "that the American people may have been swayed by President Johnson's recent order to stop our attacks on North Vietnam. If that interpretation is correct, I feel an urgent obligation to offer these observations.

"First, Richard Nixon deserves the plaudits of the American people for his extraordinarily responsible conduct of his campaign respecting Vietnam. His outspoken support of the president throughout the campaign in major measures on the war gave the president the freedom to take his action.

"Second, even though the president's action, taken just before the election, seemed likely to have political repercussions adverse to his own fortunes, Nixon resisted all pressures to challenge the action on political grounds. In the circumstances, this must have taken extreme self-restraint. . . .

"Third, the adversities that have developed in the president's program since the bombing halt was announced have suggested to many people that the president acted hastily, perhaps seeking to influence the election. But again Nixon withheld criticism. I suggest that his statesmanlike conduct warrants national commendation."

The Eisenhower statement read like a page out of the Old Nixon playbook, like Nixon's earlier airing of the rumor that Johnson was timing a bombing halt to benefit Humphrey, his companion observation that he himself didn't believe it, and the Finch implication that LBJ had jumped the gun in announcing a peace breakthrough to help Humphrey. Eisenhower's statement succeeded in repeating the allegations while crediting Nixon for disavowing them. The hope obviously was that coming from the revered Eisenhower, the statement would not be seen this time as merely the Old Nixon at work. For maximum impact, the statement was also read during the telethon by grandson David Eisenhower.

The Nixon telethon, in two one-hour segments, one for Eastern audiences, one for Western, was a fitting conclusion to the most controlled, contrived presidential campaign up to this time. Nixon daughters Tricia and Julie were part of a team that answered phones in the studio and wrote down questions for Nixon that were called in. The questions were then passed on to Nixon staffers, who put them aside and substituted others written by the staff on the same subjects in ways that would best serve the candidate. The substitute questions were then presented on the air by friendly moderator Bud Wilkinson, attaching to them the names of the posers of the original questions. Nixon not surprisingly handled the fake questions easily, as a carefully screened studio audience applauded his answers. Traveling reporters again were shunted to another studio with television monitors to watch.

Humphrey's own telethon in the ABC television studio a dozen miles away was a sharp contrast, with unrehearsed questions and answers and a distinctly more relaxed mood. Movie and television stars, including old McCarthy stalwarts Paul Newman and Joanne Woodward, dropped in. McCarthy himself called in unexpectedly, commending what Humphrey a few hours earlier had said about the Vietnam situation and saying he hoped "I've cleared the way so my friends are free to vote for you—not only free but a little moved by what I've said." For McCarthy, the comment was a ringing rallying cry.

The four-hour telethon was marked by a tribute on film from Ted Kennedy. It concluded with a documentary of Humphrey's life showing him with a mentally retarded granddaughter, tearfully telling how dealing with her problem had affected his own life, teaching him "the meaning of true love." Later, Napolitan wrote that "there is no doubt in my mind that this film did more to help Humphrey . . . than any other single thing we did in the campaign."

Throughout the telethon, Muskie was at Humphrey's side, as he had been all day in Los Angeles. Agnew meanwhile was out of sight, shipped out to Virginia, one of Nixon's safest states—clear evidence that he was regarded at best as an uncertain element in the Republican campaign.

So concerned was the Nixon camp about late attacks on Agnew's qualifications by Humphrey and his paid television ads that the Nixon strategists made certain their candidate was asked leading off each segment of his telethon whether, if he had the choice to make again, he would still pick Agnew. "I most certainly would," he insisted. "I'm not unaware of the fact that Agnew has been the subject of some pretty vicious attacks by the opposition," he said, "but he's a man of great courage. He doesn't wilt under fire. . . . If he had to hold the highest position in the country, he'd be cool under pressure."

Later, Nixon observed that "to show you how really low they got, Humphrey three weeks ago said that we have to remember that there is one chance in three that the next man we elect won't live out his term in office. If anything should happen to me," he said, "Agnew will be a strong, compassionate, good, firm man." The reason for this stout defense of Agnew, Sears told me later, was that internal polling was finding that Agnew, for all the criticism and ridicule of him, was cutting into the Wallace vote in the South. "Nixon wanted to be darned sure," Sears said, "all those people who might be viewing from all those places would understand that right off the bat, before they got to any other questions, he thought Agnew was one hell of a good guy."

Nixon also took one final opportunity in the telethon to argue that

Johnson's bombing halt had backfired, and had been damaging to American interests. He offered "a very disturbing report" that since the halt "the North Vietnamese are moving thousands of tons of supplies down the Ho Chi Minh Trail, and our bombers are not able to stop them."

There was no word about whether Eisenhower had heard this bald attempt to exploit the situation by the man he had just commended for having shown "extreme self-restraint" and "statesmanlike conduct" in discussing the bombing halt. But Humphrey was advised while he was conducting his own telethon what Nixon had just said, and answered him directly on the air in what was the closest the two men came to a debate in the 1968 campaign. He had checked with Washington, Humphrey said, and "there is no indication of increased infiltration, Mr. Nixon. And let me say that it does not help the negotiations to falsely accuse anyone at this particular time."

Nixon ended his orchestrated telethon with his hands held high over his head as the handpicked audience applauded, until the last television camera red eye went off. Then he dropped his hands, stepped back, did his version of the Jackie Gleason "Away we go" shuffle and strode quickly out of the studio and into the back seat of his car. There he sat, chin in hand and staring straight ahead, a reading light over his head, tense to the last.

At the end, not even the remarkable discipline of the fully scripted campaign of Richard Nixon could veil an aura of uncertainty about how it would all play out against a loose-knit, seat-of-the-pants Humphrey ramble that had ended on a note of genuine enthusiasm and hope. At about two o'clock in the morning of election day, November 5, David Eisenhower was rousted out of his bed at the Century Plaza by Nixon aides. They got him to cut a radio tape quoting his famous grandfather to the effect that Nixon was right on Vietnam and if elected would end the war. The tape was processed in haste and transmitted to radio stations in about forty states for airing as voters went to the polls. For all the pinpoint planning and public expressions of confidence, this exercise demonstrated the gnawing fear in the Nixon camp that once again, as in 1960, defeat could be snatched from the jaws of victory.

Joe McGinniss, in *The Selling of the President 1968*, summed up the Nixon effort: "The image campaign had done all it could within its limits. But its limits were the man. Richard Nixon. Who had as his best friend a man named Bebe Rebozo, who dealt in real estate in southern Florida. Whose daughter would be married in a ceremony performed by Norman Vincent Peale. To a grandson of Eisenhower. Richard Nixon, whose authorized biography, a part of the literature of the campaign, said 'Nixon belongs to impressive in-town clubs—Metropolitan, Links, Recess—and fashionable country clubs—Blind Brook in Westchester, Baltusrol in New Jersey.'

"We had seen the mules in the hot Atlanta street and heard the sobs of children inside the crowded church as they buried Martin Luther King. And watched Bob Kennedy's life spill across the gray hotel kitchen floor, and taken the train ride and seen black men cry again, and we had cried with them. And now this Nixon came out of his country clubs which he had worked so hard to make and he waved his credit cards in our face."

* * *

Humphrey meanwhile went from his telethon to a party in Beverly Hills at the home of old friend Lloyd Hand. There, he lost himself in a dancing, drinking, chattering crowd of about 300, doing a fair Charleston at one point before boarding his chartered jet at about 2:30 A.M. for a red-eye flight back home to Minnesota. "We've done the best job we could," he told awaiting reporters at Twin Cities International Airport on arrival just before eight o'clock on election day morning. "The American jury is out now. We hope things come out well. We shall see." As he spoke, more demonstrations were already under way or planned for this election day by SDS and Mobe chapters in New York, Washington, Boston, Ann Arbor and numerous other locales.

Humphrey and wife Muriel were driven directly to their polling place in the Maryville Township Hall about a mile from their home in Waverly, where they cast their paper ballots and went home for breakfast and sleep. That afternoon, the candidate awoke and drove over to the village of Buffalo where he dropped off a suit at his cleaners and had some hot chocolate at a local restaurant. Early election night, the Humphreys drove to the Minneapolis suburban home of old friend Dwayne Andreas for dinner before heading for the Leamington Hotel in Minneapolis to await the election returns.

Nixon stayed over at the Century Plaza on election eve, rose early as voters in the East had already begun to vote and phoned a number of political associates to thank them for their help. He also called Mamie Eisenhower and then headed to Los Angeles International Airport with his wife and daughters for the trip home aboard the chartered campaign plane *Tricia*. For some weeks now, a small portable piano had been aboard the plane for Nixon's pleasure, and he had entertained staff and press from time to time at the keyboard. But on this momentous flight, only one reporter, Anthony Day, then of the *Philadelphia Bulletin*, was permitted aboard and Nixon for most of the time sat in his sheltered front compartment, summoning aides to field and analyze reports on voter turnout in key states obtained by Bob Ellsworth over the air-to-ground telephone.

Nixon lunched with old friend Bebe Rebozo and then strolled once through the cabin, thanking his staff but completely ignoring Day, who sought an interview in vain. The snub was a fitting commentary on the year-long Nixon campaign of isolation and insulation on which America's voters were even now casting their judgment in cities and towns 35,000 feet below the streaking jet.

It was a quarter past six on election night when the plane landed at Newark Airport. Nixon made no comment as a black limousine pulled up directly to the plane's ramp and, after waving briefly, he climbed in. The limousine sped to Manhattan and his election night headquarters at the Waldorf-Astoria, where the briefings from staffers continued in his thirty-fifth-floor suite.

Wallace meanwhile wound up his campaign on the steps of the Georgia State Capitol in Atlanta with Governor Lester Maddox at his side. While campaign master of ceremonies Sam Smith declared that 1968 would mark "the first time a medicine show ever elected a president," the Taylor sisters, Mona and Lisa, sang one more chorus of "Are You for Wallace?" and "Those Old Cotton Fields Back Home." Wallace called on "the people of all races" to turn back the "attack by the liberal left-wingers of both parties" against him. Obviously taking note of polls showing Nixon strong in the state, Wallace ended his campaign on a characteristically high note by telling the crowd that the Republicans "wouldn't spit on a Georgian except for your vote."

* * *

The Nixon election night operation was as efficient and disciplined as all that had preceded it in this year. Ellsworth in his capacity as political director worked out of an operations command post, feeding state-by-state results to Nixon and Mitchell. Chotiner, shunted aside at the top but given fourteen key states including five of the Big Seven—California, Illinois, Ohio, Michigan and Pennsylvania—was summoned personally to the presence from time to time for his reports. His access, however, was not widely advertised by the rest of the staff, given Chotiner's reputation for unsavory politics.

Elsewhere in the hotel, special rooms set up for television viewing—and drinking—by fat-cat contributors were jammed. Key campaign aides moved in and out with inside information about the trend of the election. And in the Grand Ballroom, the party faithful and the press watched other television sets and waited as Lionel Hampton, a loyal Republican, and his band entertained. In a press conference room behind the ballroom, Klein and Ziegler popped in occasionally to report on Nixon's confidence and high spirits. No opportunity was permitted any reporter, however, to verify the state of the candidate, who was said to be relaxing after having soaked in a warm tub to ease any tensions it might be admitted he had.

The first notable result came from Connecticut. Humphrey won its eight electoral votes, 49.5 percent to 44.4 for Nixon and 6.1 for Wallace. Then, unnervingly to the Nixon insiders, three of the Big Seven went to Humphrey—New York (43 electoral votes), Pennsylvania (29) and Michigan (21). The story, as feared, was prospective Wallace voters in the Democratic ranks going home to Humphrey.

Nixon meanwhile was benefiting from the Wallace falloff in the South, capturing North Carolina (13), South Carolina (12), Kentucky (9) and Tennessee (11). An observation by General LeMay on election eve that he would resume bombing of North Vietnam immediately "if I were in control" was not seen by the Wallace camp as helpful. But it was clear by now that this election night would hardly be easier for Nixon than the previous one in 1960.

Humphrey at the Leamington in Minneapolis was buoyed by the early results. Before midnight, with half the votes counted, NBC reported that he was now 600,000 popular votes ahead. But soon it was clear that Nixon had won or was likely to win most of the remaining six key states—California (40), Illinois and Ohio (26 each), Texas (25), New Jersey (17) and Missouri (12)—and win at least a plurality of the electoral college vote. Only Texas was holding up for Humphrey, and his only chance now was for Wallace to capture enough electoral votes to prevent Nixon from winning the requisite 270 and thereby throw the election into the House of Representatives. But what Wallace was taking away from Nixon in Dixie was being countered by what he was taking from Humphrey in the blue-collar Northern states, although other Democrats were returning to the party in droves, making the election exceedingly close.

By two o'clock in Minneapolis, however, it was apparent that the Democratic machines in Chicago and Cleveland had not delivered sufficient votes to overcome suburban and rural Republican votes in Illinois and Ohio. Mayor Daley, reflecting the concept that all politics is local, went on television and proclaimed the night one of the greatest victories in the history of the Democratic Party—because the party had carried Cook County!

"When word finally came that Chicago and Cleveland weren't coming through and it was clear that he had lost," Van Dyk said later, "Humphrey stood up, hitched up his pants and said: 'Well, sir, the American people will find that they have just elected a papier-mâché man.'"

Humphrey went down to the hotel ballroom to thank his campaign workers. He did not concede defeat, calling the race still "a donnybrook," and he urged them to get some sleep, as he intended to do. When he awoke shortly before nine o'clock that morning, it was clear that his last hopes—California and Illinois—were gone and that Nixon had been elected.

Nixon meanwhile had decided by 3 A.M. Eastern time that he had won. He called in his closest aides to review the numbers and, according to Theodore White, wanted someone to go down to the Waldorf ballroom and proclaim victory then and there. The reason, it turned out, was that eight years earlier at precisely this time, he himself had conceded the 1960 election to John Kennedy. The man who dwelled on his past failures and slights toward him wanted to cancel out that unhappy memory. But Haldeman prevailed upon him to hold off, arguing that his victory was not yet clear to the American television audience and it would not redound to his credit to look too eager to claim it. Nixon finally agreed, settling for an informal victory celebration with close aides and supporters in his suite.

Officially, California and Illinois were still out. Illinois was of particular concern to Nixon because he had long contended privately that Daley had stolen the election from him in 1960 by holding out Chicago precincts and then voting in just sufficient numbers to carry the state. This time, the Nixon campaign had hired a former FBI agent, Lou Nichols, to organize a special poll-watching operation in Illinois. Also, several Republican stronghold counties held back their votes until Chicago's vote could be gauged and only then were they reported, giving Nixon the state in the early morning.

Before retiring, Nixon made a few calls, to Agnew, Rockefeller and a few others, and then slept briefly, awaking in time to see the networks finally conceding the election to him. He decided to await a concession call from Humphrey, which came shortly before 11 A.M. The final results were Nixon 31,770,000 popular votes or 43.4 percent of the total, Humphrey 31,270,000 or 42.7 percent, Wallace 9,906,000 or 13.5 percent, with 0.4 percent for others. Nixon won 302 electoral votes—32 more than he needed to keep the election out of the House—to 191 for Humphrey and 45 for Wallace. All of Wallace's electoral votes came from the Deep South, suggesting Nixon would have won by a wider margin had Wallace not been in the race.

* * *

In Johnson's 1971 memoir, *The Vantage Point*, he insisted without mentioning Anna Chennault by name that her intervention had defeated Humphrey. He wrote that "people who claimed to speak for the Nixon camp began encouraging Saigon to stay away from Paris and promising that Nixon, if elected, would inaugurate a policy more to Saigon's liking. Those efforts paid off. On November 1, after previously indicating they would go to the Paris peace talks, the South Vietnamese leaders decided not to participate. That, I am convinced, cost Hubert Humphrey the presidency, especially since a shift of only a few hundred thousand votes would have made him the winner. I am certain that the outcome would have been different if the Paris peace talks had been in progress on Election Day."

Humphrey himself in his book *The Education of a Public Man* recorded his thoughts on election day as he awaited the outcome of his grueling campaign. "I wonder if I should have blown the whistle on Anna Chennault and Nixon," he mused. "He must have known about her call to Thieu. I *wish* [his italics] I could have been sure. Damn Thieu. Dragging his feet this past weekend hurt us. I wonder if that call did it. If Nixon knew. Maybe I should have blasted them anyway."

Theodore H. White, in his *The Making of the President 1968*, bought completely the Nixon camp's assurances that Nixon was not involved in Chennault's maneuverings. "The fury and dismay at Nixon's headquarters when his aides discovered the report of Republican sabotage in Saigon were so intense that they could not have been feigned simply for the benefit of this reporter," he wrote confidently. White concluded that Humphrey had thus acted "morally" in not making political use of the information. "What could have been made of an open charge that the Nixon leaders were saboteurs of the peace one cannot guess," he wrote; "how quickly it might, if aired, have brought the last 48 hours of the American campaign to squalor is a matter of speculation. But the good instinct of that small-town boy Hubert Humphrey prevailed. . . . I know of no more essentially decent story in American politics than Humphrey's refusal to do so."

Much later, Joe Napolitan, reflecting on Humphrey's decision not to use the reports of the Chennault intervention to derail Nixon, spoke not only of Humphrey's laudable character but of the political practices of the time. In that pre-Watergate era, he said, most politicians were much more wary about making charges of misbehavior against their opponents, especially if they did not have solid proof. Napolitan's remarks were a commentary on how attitudes have changed regarding the use of negative campaign tactics—and the willingness to make campaign issues of their use.

Historians thereafter argued whether Chennault's activities had been endorsed by Nixon, whether they had been decisive in Saigon's rejection of the Paris peace talks and whether they had determined the outcome of the American election. Stephen E. Ambrose in his Nixon book covering this period wrote: "Nixon knew that Thieu would not go to Paris, with or without that rather silly woman whispering in his ear the promises John Mitchell was passing along from Richard Nixon. Being Nixon, he worried, and could not keep himself from trying to influence Thieu through Chennault, so he was guilty in his motives and his actions, but he was not decisive. It was not

Nixon who prevented an outbreak of peace in November 1968. He merely exploited a situation he did not create."

Herbert Parmet in his book *Richard Nixon and His America* noted: "It may be argued that Thieu did not need Nixon to tell him to resist going to Paris, but how could Nixon be sure? He wanted to win, and the dynamics of the campaign overwhelmed any other consideration."

Clifford in his memoir later rendered his own judgment: "All this raises a critical question: what did Richard Nixon know and when did he know it? No proof—in the terminology of the Watergate era, no 'smoking gun'—has ever turned up linking Nixon directly to the secret messages to Thieu [although William Bundy subsequently described Bui Diem's October 27 cable as such]. There are no self-incriminating tapes from the campaign, and the whole incident has been relegated to the status of an unsolved mystery.

"On the other hand, this chain of events undeniably began in Richard Nixon's apartment in New York, and his closest adviser, John Mitchell, ran the Chennault channel personally, with full understanding of its sensitivity. Given the importance of these events, I have always thought it was reasonable to assume that Mitchell told Nixon about them, and that Nixon knew, and approved, of what was going on in his name."

There was no doubt that the speculation about Chennault's role worried the Nixon camp, before and after the election. Nixon communications director Herb Klein, in his later book *Making It Perfectly Clear*, wrote of concerns that he would be asked about the matter in a post-election interview on CBS News's *Face the Nation*. Reviewing the factors involved in LBJ's rejected bombing halt, he said, "was a delicate area because we did not want to offend the president [Johnson] at this time and I did not want to leave an opening for a discussion of whether or not Anna Chennault . . . had privately exerted any influence on South Vietnam to reject the bombing halt. I was reasonably sure that Mrs. Chennault had at least attempted to urge the South Vietnamese to ignore the Johnson move, but I was not certain of the answer. . . . There fortunately was no Anna Chennault question."

Safire in his book acknowledged that he didn't know what the truth was about Chennault's role. "The question," he wrote, "is: Did Anna Chennault act as an agent of Candidate Nixon to urge South Vietnam's leaders to refuse to come to the Paris peace table under the terms offered by President Johnson just before Election Day? Dammit, the answer appears to be yes and no. I cannot positively assert that she did so, or if she did, that it was at the direction of Mr. Nixon or his aides." Safire then went on to document her efforts to set up the earlier meeting between Nixon and Bui Diem. He insisted that Chennault, while "in close touch with the Nixon campaign and in close touch with the South Vietnamese Ambassador . . . was not able to reach the top of the campaign for authorization to my knowledge." There was "no evidence" that Nixon had instructed her "to get the South Vietnamese to hang back," he wrote; "he only did not discourage her."

(Nixon obviously was sensitive to any appearance that he was dealing with the South Vietnamese authorities. On a "Top Secret" memo to him from foreign policy adviser Richard Allen suggesting a meeting with Bui Diem, Nixon wrote: "Should be [top secret] but I don't see how—with the S.S. [Secret Service]. If it can be, RN would like to see—if not—could Allen see for RN?")

Safire also noted, however, that "when people later wondered why Nixon thought so highly of President Thieu, they did not recall that Nixon probably would not be president were it not for Thieu. Nixon remembered." He concluded with an observation later to become familiar from the Nixon camp in the Watergate scandal—that it all was just politics: "Should Democrats be proud of the manipulation of foreign policy for political ends against a political deadline, and should Republicans be proud of letting supporters, once removed from the campaign itself, seek to frustrate those manipulations? No. It was not one of American politics' finest hours."

After the American election, South Vietnamese Minister of Information Ton That Thien held a press conference in Saigon. A cable from the American embassy informed the White House that when the minister was "asked whether Nixon had encouraged GVN [Government of Vietnam] to delay agreement with the U.S., Thien replied that, while there may have been contacts between Nixon staffers and personnel of the SVN [South Vietnamese] Embassy in Washington, a person of the caliber of Nixon would not do such a thing." Walt Rostow sent the cable on to LBJ, observing that this comment "will certainly interest you."

* * *

Several weeks after the 1968 election, my colleague Tom Ottenad phoned Walt Rostow and asked him point-blank about Chennault's preelection activities. Rostow refused to comment but immediately sent an "Eyes Only" memo to Johnson quoting "the exact text" of his conversation with Ottenad, indicating he had recorded it, and observing that "the Lady is about to surface."

He was correct; Ottenad duly reported the Chennault contacts in his paper, the St. Louis Post-Dispatch, based on information from "informed diplomats as well as [Johnson] administration sources and a number of Republicans including some within Nixon's own organization." An official of the South Vietnamese embassy in Washington denied that Mrs. Chennault had urged his government to "go slow in joining the Paris peace talks" but acknowledged that she had been an occasional visitor to the embassy.

In an interview at the time with Ottenad, she told him: "You're going to get me in a lot of trouble. . . . I can't say anything. . . . Come back and ask me that after the inauguration. We're at a very sensitive time. . . . I know so much and can say so little." With the possible participation of the Nixon campaign in mind, Ottenad asked Mrs. Chennault whether others had made contact with the South Vietnamese. She replied, he reported: "I certainly was not alone at that time."

Ottenad was not able to contact her thereafter, but in the process of writing this book I located her twenty-six years later at an office she maintained in Georgetown. She told me she was writing a book herself and could not discuss the matter. When pressed on whether she had acted on her own in contacting the Saigon regime, however, she told me: "The only people who knew about the whole operation were Nixon, John Mitchell and John Tower, and they're all dead. But they knew what I was doing. Anyone who knows about these things knows that I was getting orders to do these things. I couldn't do anything without instructions. I knew Nixon for many years, and Mitchell, and in 1967 [sic] I was responsible for Asian affairs in the campaign. I was constantly in touch with Mitchell and Nixon."

DeLoach, a right-hand man to Hoover and the FBI's liaison with the White House at the time, informed me in an interview that Mrs. Chennault had made basically the same comments to him. He confirmed that the White House had learned of her urgings of the Saigon regime to boycott the Paris peace talks through a National Security Agency intercept of a message from the South Vietnamese embassy in Washington to the Saigon authorities.

Johnson aides, DeLoach said, instructed him to put Chennault under "physical surveillance" and wiretap. She was watched but the wiretap was rejected by the FBI, he said. According to an FBI memorandum by DeLoach quoted in a 1975 Senate committee report on intelligence operations, the FBI balked at the wiretap because "it was widely known that she [Chennault] was involved in Republican political circles and, if it became known that the FBI was surveilling her, this would put us in a most untenable and embarrassing position."

After the election, according to DeLoach in his Senate committee testimony and in his 1995 book, *Hoover's FBI*, Johnson continued to pursue his suspicions. Three nights after the election, DeLoach wrote, Jim Jones called to tell him Johnson wanted information that same night on a suspected phone call between Nixon in Albuquerque and Chennault on November 2, three days before the election, "in connection with a previous conversation between Mrs. Chennault and Ambassador Dhien [*sic*], asking the South Vietnamese to honor a request to delay participation in the Paris Peace Talks."

When DeLoach balked because of the lateness of the hour, he said later, Johnson "came on the phone and proceeded to remind me that he was Commander in Chief and he would get what he wanted and he wanted me to do it immediately." Checks over the next few days, DeLoach wrote, found that Nixon had never stopped in Albuquerque at that time but that Agnew had. Five phone calls were made from there by his staff during a brief Agnew stop, DeLoach reported, none of which involved Chennault or the South Vietnamese Embassy.

Another "Eyes Only" memo in the White House files dated November 12, 1968, from Walt Rostow to Johnson, however, listed phone calls on November 2 from Albuquerque to "the Lady . . . at 1:41 p.m. EST and to Secretary Rusk at 1:55 p.m. EST" along with the times of arrival (1:15 P.M. EST) and departure (4 P.M. EST) of "the gentleman in Albuquerque." Rostow noted that "these new times . . . suggest he had ample time to make the telephone calls to the Lady and Secretary Rusk while in Albuquerque, before departing for Texas."

Rostow, in a telephone interview much later, did not refute the conclusion that "the gentleman in Albuquerque" was Agnew but said it would be improper for him to comment further on material in the Johnson White House files reflecting on the Chennault matter, in light of a fifty-year embargo in effect on that material at the Lyndon B. Johnson Presidential Library in Austin, where the documents were kept.

(On June 16, 1973, Rostow sent a sealed envelope to Harry Middleton, director of the LBJ Library, containing "a file President Johnson asked me to hold personally because of its sensitive nature" to be consigned to the library. "The file," Rostow wrote, "contains the activities of Mrs. Chennault and others before and immediately after the election of 1968. At the time President Johnson decided to handle the matter strictly as a question of national security; and, in retrospect, he felt that decision was correct." Rostow himself "recommended" that the files be shielded from public scrutiny for fifty years. Sometime thereafter, Middleton reported in a 1995 telephone interview, the fifty-year embargo was lifted and the material was sent to the appropriate federal agencies for clearance. Some but not all of the papers have been released, he reported, but no telltale cable definitively confirming intervention by the Nixon campaign has been made public.)

Another Nixon campaign insider, Melvin R. Laird, later Nixon's secretary of defense, told me that to his knowledge Nixon probably had met with Mrs.

Chennault only twice during the campaign, once to discuss fund-raising and once to hear her recommendation that her friend John Tower be made secretary of state. But, he said, "she had no influence" and was "freelancing entirely" in any overture to the South Vietnamese. Putting her up to urging Saigon to hold off for a better deal from a President Nixon, he said, "was not a strategy of the campaign."

If Johnson's worst suspicions were well-founded, however, and Nixon had intervened in the conduct of a critical foreign policy matter explicitly to preserve his election to the presidency—indeed, even if those suspicions were not well-founded—Humphrey's refusal to use the report may indeed have cost him the election. It was true that prior to the election Mrs. Chennault had not said she was acting on Nixon's or Mitchell's instructions in advising the Saigon regime that it would get a better deal with the Republican nominee if he were elected. But politically speaking, that was almost beside the point. Considering Nixon's general reputation for shady politics—especially in the eyes of Democrats—it seems incredible even today that Humphrey would elect not to use the report to try to pull out the election.

*   *   *

In a postscript to the Anna Chennault story twenty-six years later, H. R. Haldeman's posthumously published diaries disclosed that President Nixon in 1973 had tried to enlist John Connally to persuade former President Johnson to have the Democratic-controlled Congress's investigation into the Watergate affair derailed by threatening to disclose (inaccurately) that LBJ had bugged a Nixon campaign plane in 1968 to find out what Chennault was up to.

At this suggestion, Haldeman wrote in his White House diary entry for January 12, 1973, Johnson "got very hot and called Deke [DeLoach]" at the FBI. Johnson, Haldeman wrote, warned DeLoach "that if the Nixon people are going to play with this, that he would release (*deleted material—national security*), saying that our side was asking that certain things be done"—that is, blackmailing him into trying to get the Watergate investigation curbed. Nixon, according to Haldeman, dropped the whole idea.

(The italicized notation in the Haldeman diary entry was the only such indication of a deletion, strongly suggesting that LBJ was referring to some hard evidence, such as another intercepted cable from the South Vietnamese embassy to Saigon, that Chennault had been acting on the instructions of the Nixon campaign in urging that Thieu balk at participating in the Paris talks. DeLoach, in his book published in 1995, wrote that Johnson had called him only a few days before his death asking whether he had ever ordered surveillance on Anna Chennault "because of some request she supposedly made to the South Vietnamese ambassador." DeLoach wrote that LBJ added: "I never did a thing like that, did I?" When DeLoach replied, "Yes, you did, Mr. President. I vividly recall the matter," Johnson "gave a long, audible sigh," DeLoach wrote, and said: "Well, if you say I did, there must be something to it. But if they [the Nixon White House] try to give me any trouble, I'll pull out that cable from my files and turn the tables on them." [Inquiries at the LBJ Library failed to produce any such cable but, as already noted, portions of Johnson's special file on Chennault have never received federal agency clearance for release.] Walt Rostow, in a "Literally Eyes Only" memo to Johnson dated three days after the election, wrote: "First reactions may well be wrong. But with this information I think it's time to blow the whistle on these folks." But Johnson did nothing.

* * *

In Congress, the Republicans gained five seats in the Senate and four in the House on November 5, leaving both bodies in Democratic hands, and the GOP picked up five governorships. Among the new Republican senators were Bob Dole of Kansas and Bob Packwood of Oregon, who would later achieve greater celebrity, and Barry Goldwater of Arizona, recapturing a Senate seat four years after having given it up to seek the presidency.

In Minneapolis, Humphrey thanked his tearful supporters and tried to buck them up. He said he intended "to continue my dedication to public service and to the building of a responsive and vital Democratic Party." He concluded: "I shall continue my personal commitment to the cause of human rights, of peace, and to the betterment of man. If I have helped in my campaign to move these causes forward, I feel rewarded. I have done my best. I have lost. Mr. Nixon has won. The democratic process has worked its will, so now let's get on with the urgent task of uniting our country."

In New York, Nixon also sought to strike a unity theme. Before cheering partisans in the Waldorf ballroom, he seized upon something he professed to have seen during his October whistlestop trip through western Ohio that he said would mark "the character of the new administration."

He recalled that he had seen "many signs in this campaign. Some of them were not friendly and some were very friendly," he said. "But the one that touched me the most was one that I saw in Deshler, Ohio, at the end of a long day of whistle-stopping—a little town, I suppose five times the population was there in the dusk—but a teenager held up a sign, BRING US TOGETHER. And that will be the great objective of this administration at the outset, to bring the American people together.

"This will be an open administration, open to new ideas, open to men and women of both parties, open to the critics as well as those who support us.

We want to bridge the generation gap. We want to bridge the gap between the races. We want to bring America together. . . . "

This reference to Deshler took on a particularly ironic twist when it was recalled, as many of us did standing below Nixon at that moment and reporting in our newspaper stories the next day, what he had said from the rear of his railroad car at that stop only two weeks earlier: "In the 45 minutes it takes to ride from Lima to Deshler, this is what has happened in America: there has been one murder, two rapes, 45 major crimes of violence, countless robberies and auto thefts. . . . "

On that October afternoon, Nixon the candidate had been grasping desperately for white backlash votes he feared Wallace was taking from him, threatening the loss of critical Ohio. But now Ohio was safely in his pocket and now he was president-elect, sounding a message of conciliation that the country undoubtedly wanted and needed to hear.

(Bill Safire, in *Before the Fall*, all but confirmed that Nixon never saw the celebrated sign in Deshler that day. He wrote that fellow speechwriter Richard Moore at the Deshler stop "stood in the twilight in the midst of the crowd observing the signs, as he always did, picking up the local color that the candidate could work into his speech at the next stop. Moore boarded the train with that mystic look a writer gets when he has something delicious to work with, some piece of color that could be more than a gimmick."A few days later, Safire wrote, Nixon mentioned the Deshler teenager and her sign in a routine speech but "it didn't get much of a pickup in the papers the next day. . . . I tucked it away—it was one of those things that could come in handy someday.")

Nixon was not the only one who decided it was time for a fresh start. The next morning, the editorial page cartoon by *Washington Post* cartoonist Herblock, long a scourge of Nixon who regularly drew him with a heavy and sinister stubble of beard, pictured a striped barber pole over Herblock's sketching desk, and a shaving mug bearing the presidential seal on a table amid containers holding sharpened pencils. Pasted on the wall above the table was this printed announcement: THIS SHOP GIVES EVERY NEW PRESIDENT OF THE UNITED STATES A FREE SHAVE. H. BLOCK, PROPRIETOR.

* * *

Nixon the candidate also had talked about going to Saigon if elected, in an unconvincing reprise of Eisenhower's "I shall go to Korea" pledge in the 1952 campaign that had helped put him in the White House. Now Nixon the president-elect announced on November 7, through spokesman Ziegler, that in spite of an explicit invitation by cable from South Vietnamese President Thieu "to make an on-the-spot assessment of the war and the situation,

[Nixon] plans no foreign trip and will make no such trip unless President Johnson suggests that it would be helpful in furthering the negotiations towards peace."

On November 8, Humphrey and Muskie flew to Florida to meet with the vacationing Nixon and pledged their support "in matters that relate to our national security and our foreign policy." Nixon replied that he would call on Humphrey for his advice, counsel and assistance, "particularly in matters of foreign policy." Humphrey knew, however, not to waste his time waiting for his phone to ring.

In another of Nixon's quests to relive history, he said at one point regarding Humphrey's visit that "in 1960 after [Nixon had lost] a very close election, President-elect Kennedy called on me when I was in Florida. That visit, too, came on the Friday after Election Day." He did not point out that Kennedy the winner had gone to him and that he as the winner let Humphrey come to him.

Aware that even before he could take office he had an "Agnew problem," Nixon met with the vice president–elect on November 9—for the first time since their election. He announced that he would be giving Agnew "some new duties beyond what any vice president previously has assumed," particularly in the international field. Agnew, already on the defensive as a result of the sharp editorial criticism that had come his way, said he was "terribly heartened" at the indications that he would be "interjected into the mainstream [of the new administration] to a degree beyond my expectations." At first, Nixon would have cause to congratulate himself on his choice of a vice president; later, he would have much more cause to regret it.

For Humphrey, it was what might have been. His family and friends were supportive, and then there was Gene McCarthy. In a post-election interview with Ned Kenworthy, he called the day after the election "a day for visiting the sick and burying the dead. It's gray everywhere, all over the land." Then, in a last comment that surely warmed Humphrey's heart, he added: "If he'd said a month ago what he said last week, he would have won." McCarthy could well have reflected on the same possibility concerning his own tardy endorsement.

Johnson, however, remained convinced that it was Humphrey's Salt Lake City speech that had done him in. In his memoirs later, LBJ wrote that "part of Saigon's foot-dragging about attending the Paris talks, I believed, stemmed from [that] speech." It was, he wrote, "widely interpreted as a refutation of the administration's Vietnam policy, particularly with respect to bombing." While Humphrey had called to tell him "it was not intended to be a major departure from our current policies," he said, such an interpretation "was not discouraged by several Humphrey aides who briefed the press after the speech." Johnson concluded: "I am certain that the outcome would have been different if the Paris peace talks had been in progress on Election Day." (While he was at it, Johnson added: "I am convinced that if I had run again I would have been reelected.")

Joe Napolitan reported later, in his book *The Election Game and How to Win It*, that Humphrey's campaign advertising agency, Lennen and Newell, returned $318,000 in unspent funds to the Democratic National Committee after the election. "They weren't trying to steal anything," he wrote. "They just wanted to make sure they weren't holding the bag [for unpaid bills] after the election. If their accountants and time buyers had used a sharper pencil, and had not allowed so much for contingencies, we would have had another quarter of a million or three hundred thousand dollars additional to spend on media in the final week of the campaign." Had only 36,000 voters in three states—Alaska, Delaware and Missouri—switched their votes from Nixon to Humphrey, he said, the election would have been thrown into the House of Representatives, where the Democratic candidate would have prevailed. But the Humphrey campaign managers didn't know the money was available, and their man fell just short of what would have been a remarkable comeback.

* * *

Richard Nixon was president-elect only four days when the perils of holding the nation's highest office, or simply being poised to hold it, were underscored in a chilling reminiscence of the political violence that had already scarred the year. Secret Service agents and New York City police swooped down on three men in Brooklyn and charged them with plotting to assassinate him. They were identified as Ahmed Raget Namer, forty-three, a naturalized citizen from Yemen, and his two sons, Abdo Ahmad Namer, nineteen, and Hussein Ahmed Regah, twenty-one. An unidentified informant was immediately taken into protective custody.

The next day the three suspects were indicted on four counts—conspiracy in the first degree to commit a murder, criminal solicitation in the first degree involving murder and two counts of possession of dangerous weapons. They were arraigned, pleaded not guilty and bail was first set at $100,000, then reduced to $25,000—surprising in light of the alleged crime. But Brooklyn prosecutors almost at once expressed doubts about the informant's credibility.

Even before taking office, Nixon was at the center of a foreign policy controversy. Yemen on November 11 charged the United States, in the three arrests, with deliberately trying to discredit the Arab world, hinting that the story was a Zionist hoax to undercut Arab relations with the incoming Nixon administration. All three men eventually made bail and were set free, and their trial was set for January. (In July 1969, they were acquitted of the most serious charges but convicted of the minor charge of possessing switchblade knives.)

Also on November 11, Nixon paid a cordial call on Johnson at the White House. He grandly allowed afterward that the president and Rusk could speak "for the next administration" on all major matters concerning foreign policy until he took office on January 20. Regarding Vietnam specifically, he observed that progress in the peace talks could be made "only if the parties on the other side realize that the current administration is setting forth policies that will be carried forward by the next administration." So much for Nixon's campaign insistence that the country required new leadership and new directions.

* * *

With the time pressures of the election behind him, Johnson persevered in trying to get the Paris peace talks moving again. On November 8, Thieu had offered to end his boycott with a proposal for a two-sided conference to replace the planned four-sided arrangement. His Saigon regime and the United States would be teamed but with Saigon in the lead role against a team of the Hanoi regime and the NLF, with the Hanoi government in the lead role. This unsubtle effort to downgrade both the United States and the NLF was promptly rejected by Hanoi.

Johnson wasn't going to play that game either. On November 12, Defense Secretary Clifford warned Saigon that if it continued its boycott the United States might go ahead and negotiate with North Vietnam alone. The objective of such talks, he said, would be to "work out steps that could lead to a diminution in the level of combat" in South Vietnam, leaving "a political settlement" to be worked out later by Saigon and Hanoi. The message to Saigon in that notion was not subtle either—join the talks or face American military abandonment. Clifford strongly insisted that Saigon could not be given "a veto on the plan" worked out with Hanoi for talks. By this time, 29,184 Americans had died in Vietnam.

Saigon's information minister, Ton That Thien, shot back that "the U.S. can do what it likes. It is clear we cannot win the war without the U.S. But the U.S. cannot win the war without us. That also applies to making peace."

With the election over, President-elect Nixon was now just as eager as Johnson to have the Saigon regime join the peace talks. Such a development would not threaten him politically any longer, and in fact would promise to lighten his burden as the new president. According to Bui Diem in his book, on November 9 Senator Dirksen called on him, saying he was there on behalf of both Johnson and Nixon. "South Vietnam has got to send a delegation to Paris before it's too late," he said. "I can also give you firm and unequivocal assurances that under no circumstances will the United States recognize the National Liberation Front as a separate entity. I absolutely affirm that the United States does not contemplate a coalition government between the two sides in Vietnam."

Further evidence that Nixon was singing a different, post-election tune came in a meeting with Mitchell to which Anna Chennault was summoned in New York on November 13. "We need to do something about our friends in Saigon," Mitchell told her, according to her book. " 'Do what about our friends in Saigon?' I asked, not yet understanding. 'Well, persuade them to go to Paris.'" She replied: "You must be joking. Two weeks ago, Nixon and you were worried that they might succumb to pressure to go to Paris. What makes you change your mind all of a sudden?"

One obvious conclusion was that Nixon, aware that Johnson knew before the election of Chennault's activities, was demonstrating his gratitude to LBJ for not having used the knowledge of them against him publicly—or was moving to make it less likely Johnson would now do so.

Later that same night, according to Chennault's book, Herb Klein phoned her and told her bluntly: "Anna, I'm not going to beat around the bush. You must promise to say to the press that our friend [Nixon] does not know about our arrangement with President Thieu." She answered: "What arrangement are you talking about? I know of no arrangement; I never made any arrangement." To which Klein replied, she wrote, "We know you're a good soldier, we just want to be sure our friend is protected." Dirksen also contacted her the next day, she wrote, telling him he just wanted to "make sure that I would not let my anger get the better of me by talking to the press."

Weeks later, Chennault received a visit from Robert Murphy, a former high State Department official just named to be Nixon's personal foreign policy representative with Johnson. "Mr. Nixon asked me to come by and see you in order to let you know how much he has appreciated everything you've done for him," Murphy said, she recalled in her book. "He certainly has strange ways of showing it," she said.

Only later after Nixon was inaugurated, did he thank her directly, she wrote, "when Nixon took me aside and, with intense gratitude, began thanking me for my help in the election." Apparently referring to all the speculation and criticism that she had helped block the peace talks, she replied, "I've certainly paid dearly for it." To which Nixon said, she wrote, "Yes, I appreciate that. I know you are a good soldier." She continued to hint in later interviews, however, that she had not been a freelancer, but had operated with Nixon's knowledge and approval—if not his genuine gratitude.

Much later, in his memoir, Clark Clifford saw in what he called "the Chennault–Bui Diem channel" an early indication of what was to come four years later in the Watergate scandal. "It revealed a general behavioral and moral pattern," he wrote, "that, once given the power of the presidency, would lead to actions, some illegal, that were far more blatant than the secret messages to Thieu."

Walt Rostow too, in the 1973 memo he inserted in the White House files on the Chennault matter, saw in it the seeds of Watergate. "I am inclined to believe the Republican operation in 1968 relates in two ways to the Watergate affair of 1972," he wrote. "First, the election of 1968 proved to be close and there was some reason for those involved on the Republican side to believe their enterprise with the South Vietnamese, and Thieu's recalcitrance, may have sufficiently blunted the impact on U.S. politics of the total bombing halt and agreement to negotiate to constitute the margin of victory.

"Second, they got away with it. Despite considerable press commentary after the election, the matter was never investigated fully. Thus, as the same men faced the election of 1972, there was nothing in their previous experience with an operation of doubtful propriety (or, even, legality) to warn them off, and there were memories of how close an election could get and the possible utility of pressing to the limit—or beyond."

William Bundy was another who agreed. "You see Watergate writ large in this one," he said in a telephone interview much later. "I haven't the slightest doubt that Nixon ran it from a distance. From the smarmy way he behaved that last weekend, I believe he was in it up to his hips. And when a presidential candidate becomes indebted [to a foreign leader] it is not a very healthy situation. Thieu felt he was owed a debt by Nixon. Thieu digging in his heels was decisive [in stalling the peace talks until after the election]."

* * *

On the ground in Vietnam, other developments were threatening productive talks. On November 13, Washington charged Hanoi with conducting military operations in the demilitarized zone in violation of the agreement that had halted the American bombing of the North. Hanoi replied by accusing the United States of increasing its "aggression" in the South and continuing reconnaissance flights over the North behind a "smoke screen" of false charges regarding activity in the DMZ. It all sounded like the same old stalemate. Walt Rostow suggested that Saigon was balking because it feared it was being forced into joining a coalition government with the NLF. He reiterated that the Johnson administration "has always been opposed to a coalition government in South Vietnam. We are never going to use our leverage [to force one]," he said, "and I dare say the next administration will take the same view."

This picture of the old and new administrations walking in lockstep, however, led to confusion, at least in parts of the press, when Nixon on the same day announced the foreign policy appointment of Murphy. Nixon emphasized that it would be "essential that there be prior consultation and prior agreement" between himself and Johnson on key foreign policy decisions. For the arrangement between the outgoing and incoming administrations to be "viable," he said, it was "necessary that there be such consultation and that the president-elect not only be informed but that he be consulted, and that he agree to the courses of action."

That remark sounded as though Nixon expected to be a co-president with Johnson on foreign policy until he took over the whole job on January 20. Johnson called a news conference the next day and disposed of any such expectation. He alone, he said, would "make whatever decisions the President of the United States is called upon to make between now and January 20." Nixon, who as vice president had been so careful not to presume anything or step on the presidential prerogatives of Dwight Eisenhower during the general's illnesses, looked to many to be excessively impatient to grab the nation's foreign policy reins.

Beyond this minor flap, it was now smooth sailing for Richard Nixon. He began to make key appointments, starting with his White House staff. His first appointee was Bryce Harlow as his assistant for legislative and congressional relations. Next, he named Haldeman as his general administrative assistant, later known as White House chief of staff, John Ehrlichman as counsel, Ron Ziegler as press secretary and Pat Buchanan and Ray Price as speechwriters. Other staff appointments quickly followed, including chairmen of ten task forces dealing with various domestic matters.

Nixon also informed FBI Director Hoover in a November meeting that he would be kept on. Hoover, having no trouble transferring loyalties, quickly informed the president-elect in Haldeman's presence that Johnson had ordered the FBI, according to Haldeman, "to bug Nixon's campaign airplane and this had been done," as well as wiretaps on Anna Chennault.

Hoover had some advice for his soon-to-be new boss. "When you get into the White House," Haldeman recalled him saying, "don't make any calls through the switchboard. Johnson has it rigged and little men you don't know will be listening." After Hoover departed, Haldeman wrote later, Nixon said: "We'll get that goddamn bugging crap out of the White House in a hurry." The LBJ apparatus was removed "as one of our first actions when he took office," Haldeman wrote, but a better one, completely automatic, was installed in February 1971, with eventually cataclysmic consequences.

Nixon's cabinet posts were to be announced in December, a procedure guaranteed to fill the relatively quiet days remaining in the month with press speculation. Among the most prominently mentioned were Nelson Rockefeller, to be United Nations ambassador, a distinct comedown from the governorship of New York, and the Senate's only black member, Edward Brooke of Massachusetts, to be secretary of housing and urban development. Each of them met with Nixon in New York and said later he was not interested.

Disclosure of the Rockefeller meeting came only after Ziegler had told reporters the two men had not met. Later, when word of the meeting got out, Ziegler said he hadn't known about it when asked. When a reporter pointed out that Ziegler had held a press briefing after finding out and still didn't report it, Ziegler admitted: "Well, yes, I was aware of it at that time. [But] I was not asked the question." Besides, he said, "it was a private meeting." So indeed were all the others Nixon was having, but the presence of other visitors was announced.

It was a small matter, but an early sign that the same passion for control and secrecy that had marked the Nixon campaign would govern in the Nixon administration. Herb Klein had made a point of assuring reporters that the new administration was determined to close the "credibility gap" that had existed between Johnson and the press. It was a telling start.

(Even as president-elect, however, Nixon personally swung from deep bitterness, resentment and suspicion of the press to attempts to be friendly and personally helpful. At the time I was covering the Nixon transition at the posh Pierre Hotel in New York, the publishers of a book I had just written about the Robert Kennedy campaign prevailed upon me to give a copy to Nixon, obviously in the hope that it would generate some publicity. I reluctantly agreed but took the precaution, to guard against the predictable jeers and ribbing of my colleagues, of putting the book in a plain envelope and slipping it to the president-elect just as he was getting onto the hotel elevator to go to his suite. Whereupon he pulled it out of the envelope and, grinning broadly, turned and held it over his head as cameras rolled. I was mortified—and my publishers delighted. A day or so later, when a few reporters were permitted into Nixon's suite for the first time, the book was placed conspicuously on his desk, as if he had been reading it. That sighting also was duly reported—though not even this boost from the next president of the United States could squeeze it onto the bottom of the *New York Times* best-seller list.)

* * *

In the November lull, other events that had been crowded out of the news by the election captured attention. A group of Yippies was held in a bombing in Detroit; a warrant was issued in California for Eldridge Cleaver for parole violation; a court in Arkansas threw out an old "monkey law" on the teaching of evolution; an unmanned Soviet spaceship circled the moon and returned safely. Amid new anti-Soviet demonstrations and a student sit-in strike in Prague, a nervous NATO Council of Ministers warned the Soviet Union against further intrusions in Europe, and Rusk pointedly specified that any Soviet attack on Austria or Yugoslavia would have NATO implications.

In the continuing Vietnam War protest, singer Joan Baez began a drive to collect draft cards; more demonstrations and sit-ins closed down San Francisco State; the Catonsville Nine were found guilty in Baltimore of their draft records burning episode in May. A teachers' strike of more than two months finally ended in New York; Black Panthers staged another shoot-out with police; a crisis hit the American money market; miners were trapped in a West Virginia cave-in; a Mississippi judge fined the Ku Klux Klan and three members a million dollars for killing a black man. A Jimi Hendrix concert drew an overflow crowd at New York's Philharmonic; Yale went coed; a running back from the University of Southern California named O.J. Simpson won the Heisman Trophy. And a nation of television sports watchers flooded the phone switchboard at the NBC network when a close professional football game between the New York Jets and the Oakland Raiders was cut off with the Jets holding the ball and leading, 32–29, with a minute to go—for the airing of the movie *Heidi*. In that last minute, the Raiders recovered a fumble and scored twice, winning 43–32. Bettors and bookmakers alike went bonkers when they learned the outcome later.

None of these various events, however, provided more than a temporary and minor distraction from the impasse in the Paris peace talks. After intensive American arm-twisting and cajoling but no substantial change in the arrangement agreed to by Washington and Hanoi, the Saigon regime on November 26 finally announced that it would abandon its boycott, claiming to have won its points. The United States assured South Vietnam that its sovereignty would be intact and that the United States would oppose any attempt to impose a coalition regime on it.

The next day, however, the Hanoi regime flatly rejected the idea of the Saigon government playing a leading role. "In settling the Vietnam problem," Hanoi radio announced, "we will talk only with the United States." Hanoi suggested that the talks proceed without Saigon.

Meanwhile, the fighting had intensified, with violations of the DMZ on both sides and casualties mounting again. On November 29, Hanoi radio broadcast an order to Vietcong troops to launch a new offensive to "utterly destroy" American and South Vietnamese forces. The optimism that had marked the start of the American bombing halt on the first day of November had already faded.

Johnson now had only fifty days to achieve the peace for which, exactly eight months earlier, he had sacrificed the chance to remain in power for four more years. He was still president and would be until January 20, as he had so emphatically noted, but Nixon's election had already eclipsed him. All eyes now were on the winner as he proceeded to shape the presidency that would bear his personal mark—in ways not then remotely forecast.

CHAPTER 13

December: Fly Me to the Moon

Dec. 1 *Promises, Promises* starring Jerry Orbach opens on Broadway; **6** William Eckert fired as baseball commissioner; **7** *Stargazer* satellite orbited; **11** Arthur H. Sulzberger, *New York Times* publisher, 77, dies; unemployment at 3.3 percent, lowest in 15 years; **12** Ethel Kennedy has 11th child, daughter Rory; actress Tallulah Bankhead, 65, dies; **14** Mississippi beats Virginia Tech, 34–17, in Liberty Bowl; **15** Jess Willard, who won heavyweight crown from Jack Johnson in 1915 and lost it to Jack Dempsey in 1919, dies at 86; **16** FBI reports crime up 19 percent in last nine months; **18** *Chitty Chitty Bang Bang* starring Dick Van Dyke released; **19** socialist leader Norman Thomas, 84, dies; **20** novelist John Steinbeck, 66, dies; **22** Senator Strom Thurmond, 66, marries Nancy Moore, 22-year-old South Carolina beauty queen; **28** U.S. tennis team captures Davis Cup from Australia; **29** Baltimore Colts rout Cleveland Browns, 34–0, for NFL championship; New York Jets beat Oakland Raiders, 27–23, for AFL title; **30** Missouri beats Alabama, 35–10, in Gator Bowl; no executions in U.S. first time since data kept in 1930.

As Richard Nixon addressed the task of assembling his administration, a group of one hundred American and foreign intellectuals gathered at Princeton University on December 1 for what was loftily referred to as a summit conference to assess "The United States, Its Problems, Its Image and Its Impact on the World" on the eve of that new administration.

The outlook from these assorted deep thinkers was sobering for Nixon. George F. Kennan, the former American ambassador to the Soviet Union, declared that the Nixon administration "must be given a fair opportunity to show what it can do" and that "a general movement of national unity" would be widely welcomed. But he warned of "a great cultural gap between the established outlooks of our society and the hopeful approach to the solution of some of our greatest problems." It was, he said, "a gap which is not likely to be filled either by the traditional postulates of American liberalism or by the angry flamboyant demands of student mobs and black militants."

Concerning the latter, American playwright Lillian Hellman replied: "God knows many of them are fools and most of them will be sellouts . . . but they're a better generation than we were. . . . Since when are youths not allowed to be asses?"

A more confrontational attitude was expressed by Roy Innis, director of the Congress of Racial Equality, the increasingly militant black organization. "The American way is a white way and has nothing to do with black people," he charged, arguing for racially separate societies. "Why can't we also have our own way?"

These and other comments reflected the scope of the challenge to Nixon in his pledge to "bring us together." John Kenneth Galbraith, the author, economist and former American ambassador to India in the Kennedy administration, predicted another pitfall. "Mr. Nixon's vulnerability," this prominent liberal Democrat said, "will not be in his opposition to the welfare state or to the new economics. It will be in his subordination to organization. . . . He is, almost too patently, the organization's man."

It was a view that called for close examination not only of the Nixon cabinet, still being selected in private, but also of the staff already chosen, headed by Haldeman and Ehrlichman, two of the most dedicated of the Nixon loyalists who had demonstrated their organizational skills—and penchant for rigid control—in the successful campaign just concluded. Added to them on December 2 was Professor Henry A. Kissinger, the Harvard foreign policy expert, as Nixon's national security adviser, who Nixon announced would start reorganizing "the entire White House security planning machinery." This administration, clearly, would run a tight ship on its own carefully charted course.

One exception, many suspected, would be Agnew, who had demonstrated often in the campaign a talent for navigating into troubled waters, or for stirring up the calm. It didn't take long for that suspicion to be reinforced. To underscore the new administration's stated intention to work in partnership with the nation's Republican governors, Nixon and Agnew went to Palm

Springs, California, for the group's annual conference. In a private meeting, Agnew, still smarting from the story and editorial about his Maryland land deals in the *New York Times* and also *Newsweek*, labeled them "executionary journals" that, he added, fit neatly "into the bottom of a bird cage."

When word of Agnew's remarks leaked out, he was asked about them at a news conference. At first he said he had been speaking in a "humorous" vein and was not going to elaborate. But in a formal speech to the governors he assumed an aggressive posture. "I was a controversial governor," he told his old colleagues. "I have been a controversial candidate for vice president. There is no reason to believe that I will be any less controversial as vice president. I do not intend to play games with the secret meaning of words nor practice the gentle art of the platitude. I do intend to rely on dictionary definitions and to call the shots as I see them. I think this is what Richard Nixon selected me to do [and] what the American people elected me to do." The nation was thus forewarned.

About a week later in New Orleans, Agnew demonstrated again he would not be a shrinking violet in his new job. In a discussion of the Nixon administration's approach to combating inner-city poverty before a National League of Cities conference, Agnew observed that the poor should participate "when they can be effective." But then he added: "All too often participation of the poor has been construed to mean playing both patient and doctor; when all too often the unhappy result has ranged from protracted delay at best to extravagant boondoggling at worst." Mayor Henry Maier of Milwaukee commented: "If I had any stock in the Office of Economic Opportunity [the federal antipoverty agency], I'd sell it."

*   *   *

In these first days of December, there also was much looking back, particularly by the Democrats, at the defeat that had befallen them. December 1 also brought the report of Johnson's National Commission on the Causes and Prevention of Violence, focused on the conduct of the Chicago police during the Democratic National Convention. It charged that it had amounted to a "police riot" that dwarfed any violence committed by the demonstrators. While sometimes provoked by some demonstrators, the report said, the response was "unrestrained and indiscriminate violence . . . often inflicted upon persons who had broken no law, disobeyed no order, made no threat."

The report specifically cited Mayor Daley's order to police to "shoot to kill" after the rioting triggered by the assassination of Martin Luther King. Daley surprisingly called the report "an excellent study" but said if only the summary and not the full report was read it would "mislead the public." Chicago

Police Superintendent James B. Conlisk said use of the term "police riot" was
a distortion.

In any event, there was little disagreement among Democratic leaders with
a judgment that the convention in Chicago had dealt a devastating, if not
fatal, blow to Humphrey's chances of election. He said himself on December
2 that he had tried in advance to have the party convention moved from
Chicago, but that he had little to say in an operation that was tightly controlled by the Johnson White House. The *Washington Post* reported that the
Justice Department in advance of the convention had sent a team to Chicago
headed by Deputy Attorney General Warren Christopher to urge Daley to negotiate with the antiwar forces on arrangements for demonstrations, but that
Daley had refused.

Countering the presidential commission's report in early December were
more hearings on the Chicago violence conducted by the House Un-
American Activities Committee. While the earlier hearings in October had
been picketed by demonstrators including Rubin and Hoffman, on this occasion Tom Hayden, one of the founders of SDS involved in Chicago, said he
and his supporters weren't bothering because in terms of discrediting the
committee "the job's already been done against HUAC."

Hayden, along with Rubin, earlier had publicly burned their HUAC sub-
poenas at a rally on the Berkeley campus of the University of California. But
Rubin proclaimed that he definitely would appear, so that he could collect
travel money from the committee and use it "to finance the revolution." In
Washington after having been indicted by a Cook County grand jury on
charges of solicitation to commit mob action during the convention, Rubin
showed up wearing a Santa Claus suit. "It's a circus in there," he explained.
"Why not treat it as a circus?" When he refused to take off the costume, he
was not permitted to testify.

Hayden in his testimony and peace activist David Dellinger acknowledged
that they had met with representatives of North Vietnam and the Vietcong
prior to the Chicago convention but insisted that the demonstrations had not
been the result of those meetings. They, and Rennie Davis, all said they had
had no intention of disrupting the convention and had tried to avoid violence. Hayden said the explosion in Chicago could have been avoided had
Daley issued the requested permits to march and rally.

Nixon's election did nothing to curb the domestic turmoil, in the streets
or on the campuses. December brought: a firebomb attack on a Black
Panthers headquarters in Newark, with the victims blaming the police; a
week of demonstrations and vandalizing by high school students in New
York in the wake of a teachers' strike, resulting in 123 arrests; the closing of

a school in the heavily black Boston suburb of Roxbury because of rioting triggered by the beating of a teacher by students. Five black schools in Worth County, Georgia, also were closed after boycotts by black students, protesting the transfer to a juvenile detention center of two of their number trying to attend an all-white school. As many as 3,000 students staged a strike at San Francisco State College over demands for an autonomous black studies program and closed down the school. Its new acting president, S. I. Hayakawa, declared that an "utterly irresponsible and rebellious body of student officers" would have no role in disciplining the protesters. "I will not try to come to terms," he said, "with anarchists, hooligans or yahoos."

Other December disturbances broke out at the College of San Mateo, Wisconsin State University, New York University, the University of Connecticut, Brown, Pembroke, Cornell, Coppin State, Washington University, Cheyney State, Reed, Harvard and Radcliffe, usually involving disputes over racial policies, the Vietnam War, or both. An SDS convention at Ann Arbor further heightened campus tensions and unrest.

In Chicago, the FBI arrested thirty-two persons charged with obtaining illegal draft deferments by using false identification with the Illinois National Guard. Along the Atlantic and Gulf coasts, a dock strike of 75,000 longshoremen threatened to paralyze much of the nation's commercial shipping abroad. In Remo, Virginia, a witness in a labor rackets extortion case was assassinated in a duck blind while hunting with two protective federal marshals. In Newark, eight Paterson, New Jersey, police were indicted on charges of tear-gassing a black civil rights meeting. On and on it went, leaving no doubt that Richard Nixon would have a lot of bringing together to do to live up to his pledge. The FBI reported in mid-December that nationally reported crime in the first nine months of 1968 had gone up 19 percent over the corresponding period in 1967, with violent crime up 21 percent.

* * *

The popular music world that in 1968 had helped chart the restlessness and rebellion of youth, white and black, had a brief reverie in December, with the first appearance before a live audience in eight years of Elvis Presley on an NBC television special. His return came after a period in Hollywood marked chiefly by bad movies and records that were, in the words of critic Peter Guralnick, "devoid of even a semblance of commitment."

His account of the Presley appearance in the *Rolling Stone Illustrated History of Rock and Roll* talked of "having the opportunity to see our idol outside his celluloid wrappings for the very first time, knowing that we were bound to be disappointed. The credits flashed, the camera focused on Elvis, and to our utter disbelief, there he was, attired in black leather, his skin glistening, his hair long and greasy, his look forever young and callous." Presley didn't disappoint, either, in his opening comment: "If you're looking for trouble, you've come to the right place."

The music of 1968, like the year itself, had been a roller coaster that ranged from protest and defiance to romance and resignation and back again. James Brown in "Say It Loud—I'm Black and I'm Proud" sang about critics who complained about malice and arrogance among many restless blacks of the time, and responded to them by declaring that with the treatment his race had received its people were not going to be shunted aside in their pursuit of social and economic justice: "It takes two eyes to make a pair, brother, we can't quit until we get our share."

The Beatles, in "Revolution," seemed to many to have become disheartened, even disillusioned, with the counterculture of protest they had come to symbolize. They sang of the desire to change the world they shared with their generation but declared they wanted no part of tearing down the system with resort to violence, support of hate groups or communism: "But if you go carrying pictures of Chairman Mao, you ain't gonna make it with anyone anyhow . . ."

Yet the Beatles in 1968 also had one of their all-time hits with "Hey Jude": "Hey Jude, don't make it bad; take a sad song and make it better." It was a year in which they, like millions of other young people, searched for ways out of the maelstrom in which they lived. In February they had gone to India hoping to find answers from the Maharishi Mahesh Yogi, only to abandon the quest shortly afterward.

The Rolling Stones likewise seemed frustrated at the lack of effective outlet for their own rebelliousness in "Street Fighting Man." They sang of summertime protests in the streets of London and yet a sense of their own helplessness to play an important role in response to injustices they saw: "But what can a poor boy do except sing for a rock 'n roll band."

And in a commentary on the escalation of violence in the society, Mick Jagger sang in "Sympathy for the Devil" of the devil reminding his audience of everyone's complicity in the tragedies of the time: "I shouted out, 'Who killed the Kennedys?' when after all it was you and me . . ."

There also was Paul Simon's lament for ready uncomplicated heroes in the immensely popular "Mrs. Robinson" from the Dustin Hoffman movie *The Graduate*, in which Simon lamented: "Where have you gone, Joe DiMaggio? A nation turns its lonely eyes to you . . ."

Other artists reflected the range of what by now had come generally under the rock and roll rubric, from the traditional to the turbulently experimental. There were Jerry Lee Lewis, Little Richard and Chuck Berry; the folk rock of Bob Dylan and the rhythm and blues of Ray Charles and B.B. King; the Beach Boys and the Motown sounds of the Temptations and Smokey Robinson and the Miracles.

There were Creedence Clearwater Revival, the Byrds and the Doors; the acid rock of the Grateful Dead and Jefferson Airplane; Jimi Hendrix and the early punk rock of Sly and the Family Stone. There was the jazz rock of Blood, Sweat and Tears and the art rock of Simon and Garfunkel and Frank Zappa and the Mothers of Invention, and, on the cutting edge, the Velvet Underground. The names alone, aside from the music often so discordant and confusing to older ears, drew a distinct generational line between the now generation and its parents, who had so easily glided to Glenn Miller's "Moonlight Serenade" and swung, in their fashion, to his "In the Mood."

* * *

Richard Nixon, one of America's most conspicuous squares when it came to such matters, had neither the time nor the disposition now to sort out the mysteries of the angry younger generation. The situation in Vietnam and at the Paris peace talks commanded his attention, and was similarly discouraging. Perhaps for that reason, Nixon greeted coolly a suggestion by Harriman that he send an observer to the Paris talks. When Harriman told reporters after briefing Nixon in New York that he "got the impression" the president-elect would do so, Ziegler was quick to say Harriman must have "misinterpreted" Nixon.

For a time, the prospects for serious talks seemed to increase with the arrival in Paris of South Vietnamese Vice President Nguyen Cao Ky and his staff. But discussions between Harriman and Ky, and between the U.S.-Saigon side and Hanoi and the NLF soon became bogged down in ludicrous proposals and counterproposals on the shape of the conference table. The sticking point remained basically whether the negotiations would be two-sided or, as Hanoi insisted, four-sided with the NLF as a full partner. When Clifford on a weekend interview show on December 15 said the United States was "ready to sit down at any kind of table," Ky chastised him for having "shown a gift for saying the wrong thing at the wrong time."

Turning up the heat, Clifford noted that the United States had no "obligation to keep 540,000 troops in South Vietnam until a political settlement was achieved." Ky complained that "I have to fight not only my enemies but also my so-called friends. . . . I think we on our side have many irresponsible people who ought to keep their mouths shut." It occurred to more than one observer that Ky was stalling, awaiting the inaugural of Nixon. On December 23, he returned to Saigon, saying his government would talk directly with the NLF only after Hanoi withdrew all troops from the South and the war had ended.

On the battlefield, even as American bombers slacked off over North Vietnam, they intensified air strikes on North Vietnamese infiltration routes and base camps in Laos. Clashes between the two sides continued in the DMZ and American and South Vietnamese forces were placed on alert in Saigon in anticipation of another major enemy attack, with American bombers hitting suspected communist staging areas just north of the capital city.

Meanwhile, American casualties mounted steadily. By mid-December, the U.S. total of combat deaths had exceeded 30,000 since the beginning of 1961. In the same period, the U. S. command reported, enemy deaths had totaled more than 425,000. But most Americans had had enough of such comparisons; they looked to the new president to do as candidate Nixon had indicated he would, and end the war.

The one prominent observer on Vietnam who continued to see light at the end of the tunnel was columnist Joseph Alsop. He had this to say in his column: "For months after the Tet offensive, the American public was inundated by torrents of hogwash about the situation in Vietnam. . . . There is the undoubted fact that the hogwash had a powerful political impact in the United States. But . . . militarily, every informed person now agrees that Hanoi's three 1968 offensives were almost unqualified disasters. . . . The really central fact [is] that Hanoi's options have now been cruelly narrowed."

* * *

At home, the spotlight was on the team Nixon was assembling to lead the country in the new direction that he had also promised in the campaign. On the night of December 11, amid much carefully staged fanfare, Nixon disclosed his full cabinet and introduced the members en bloc on television. For all the hoopla, the new cabinet was a pedestrian collection—twelve white men, all Republicans of the party establishment. Leading the pack were his old lawyer friend, William P. Rogers, as secretary of state, old congressional colleague Melvin R. Laird as secretary of defense and Wall Street banker David M. Kennedy as secretary of the treasury.

Nixon picked cronies John Mitchell to be attorney general, Maurice Stans to be secretary of commerce and Bob Finch as secretary of health, education and welfare. This was to be Nixon's bold new start. In a transparent, minor sop to blacks, he announced at the same time that he would reappoint Walter

Washington, a black, as mayor of Washington, D.C., and for the Democrats, he said he would pick one to be ambassador to the United Nations—hardly a plum.

Of his cabinet, Nixon told reporters, "I have picked big men, strong men, in my opinion. We are not going to have a cabinet that will be basically of yes-men. . . . I will encourage them to speak out. . . . " In time, that promise too would wither.

Mitchell, asserting himself as the political voice of the new administration, said Nixon intended to clean house—no great surprise with a change of parties in the presidency—by removing bureaucrats who weren't up to snuff, while keeping the strongest of the incumbents. The remarks served to reinforce a no-nonsense aura as Nixon prepared to take over.

On December 16, the presidential electors in all fifty states—the members of the invisible electoral college—met in their state capitals, cast their ballots and gave Nixon 301 to 191 for Humphrey and 46 for Wallace. That was one less for Nixon and one more for Wallace than the voters had cast. A single "faithless" elector in North Carolina, Dr. Lloyd W. Bailey of Rocky Mount, declined to be bound by the popular vote in his state, which went for Nixon, and cast his vote for the Alabamian. It didn't matter. For all the speculation that this election might wind up in the House of Representatives, it had followed the usual course. The final indignity for Humphrey was that it would fall to him as vice president when the new Congress convened, just as it had to Nixon in 1961 in that same capacity as presiding officer of the Senate, to announce the results of the election he had lost, and declare the man who had beaten him the next president of the United States.

As Nixon thus geared up to assume office the next month, conditions at home and abroad underscored the challenge he faced after one of the most destructive and divisive political years in the nation's history. There were, however, some causes for optimism. The nation's unemployment had dropped to 3.3 percent, the lowest in fifteen years, the upside of a country being at war. Johnson predicted a modest surplus in the federal budget for the next year.

On December 21, the *Apollo 8* spacecraft blasted off bearing astronauts Frank Borman, Jim Lovell and William Anders en route to what would be the first orbit of the moon. The next day, the crew of the American intelligence-gathering ship *Pueblo* was finally freed, and, in a matter of great personal pride, Nixon saw his second daughter, Julie, wed to David Eisenhower, grandson of the former president.

The conclusion of the *Pueblo* drama was bizarre. The crew was turned over to American authorities only after the United States first repudiated the North Korean charges that the ship had intruded illegally into North Korean waters and had engaged in espionage, then signed a "confession" prepared by the North Korean regime. Commander Bucher also denied the charges in a press conference in Panmunjom at the time of his release. Secretary Rusk called the release arrangements insisted upon by the North Koreans "a strange procedure. . . . If you ask me why these two contradictory statements proved to be the key to effect the release of our men," he said, "the North Koreans would have to explain it. I know of no precedent in my 19 years of public service."

(Bucher later received a court-martial for permitting the North Koreans to board the ship, and so did his intelligence officer for having failed to destroy sensitive manuals. A third officer received a letter of admonition for failing to provide leadership to the crew, but Secretary of the Navy John Chafee threw out the findings, saying of the three officers: "They have suffered enough.")

On December 24, Christmas Eve, the three men of the *Apollo 8* crew became the first human beings to orbit the moon. "Please be informed," said Lovell, "that there is a Santa Claus." On that same night, a Christmas truce was observed in Vietnam. But three days later, as the spacecraft returned safely to earth, the American command in Saigon reported that the truce had been violated by 140 enemy engagements, forty-seven of them resulting in casualties. When the enemy declared it would also observe a truce for the New Year holidays, American and South Vietnamese officials said they would not participate, in light of the Christmas truce violations.

The Nixon family flew to Key Biscayne for Christmas. Reporters covering the transition were given an opportunity to bring their families along aboard a special charter, which I did. We landed at Homestead Air Force Base just outside Miami in advance of Nixon's arrival aboard a small presidential jet put at his disposal by Johnson. A large crowd of military personnel and their families lined a fence to greet the president-elect. Getting off the plane, he walked over to the fence to greet them and shake hands.

Then, seeing the traveling reporters standing to one side with their families, he came over, and when he came up to me I introduced him to mine. He shook hands with my daughter Amy, then eight years old, and just looked at her, saying nothing. She looked at him, saying nothing. It went on like that for a long moment, until Nixon finally said to Amy: "I guess you're glad I got elected president, so you could come to Florida for Christmas!" And he moved on. Amy looked up and, with the wisdom and insight of an eight-year-old, said: "Gee, he was embarrassed, wasn't he? He didn't know what to say to me." It was another example of Nixon's chronic unease, even with a child, and his inability to engage in all but the most trite small talk. The gesture was appreciated, but the execution was comic.

Nixon spent Christmas and saw the New Year in at his favorite retreat in Key Biscayne, with family and old friend Bebe Rebozo. On Christmas Eve, the president-elect went to nearby Coral Gables to visit Barbara Jane Mickle, the daughter of a wealthy builder who had been kidnapped and buried for more than three days in a "tomb" equipped with food, water, a fan and battery-powered light. She was rescued by FBI agents who heard her rapping her knuckles on the box. Many had given her up for dead—just as had the political future of Richard Nixon been consigned before his remarkable resurrection.

A year laden from start to finish with the disastrous and the bizarre nevertheless marked, for Richard Nixon, the triumph of his life. The historic orbiting of the moon by three Americans and their safe return provided a fitting companion piece to his personal rise in the political firmament.

But to many other Americans, the year 1968 had been one of incredible, even unprecedented disappointment and heartache. Couriers of hope like Martin Luther King and Robert Kennedy were gunned down, Eugene McCarthy, carrying the dreams of a generation to end a hated war and recapture a government and a country gone wrong, had faltered and failed; a president, Lyndon Johnson, had been broken and in the process broke his faithful servant, Hubert Humphrey. The Democratic Party was so shaken that near year's end two leading liberals announced their decisions to challenge incumbents in key congressional leadership posts—Representative Morris K. Udall of Arizona against House Speaker John W. McCormack of Massachusetts and Ted Kennedy against Senate Majority Whip Russell B. Long of Louisiana. (In the party caucuses in January, Udall lost; Kennedy won.)

Racial division wracked the nation and American cities, and campuses alike were aflame with protests against the war. On December 27, the Justice Department added the names of Robert Lowell, McCarthy's poet friend, and five others as members of "the same conspiracy" for which Spock had been convicted. Humphrey, at home in Waverly on New Year's Eve, Eisele said later he was told, "got up at the stroke of midnight, went into his bathroom and flushed the toilet, as his way of saying what a terrible year it had been."

Not all Americans, to be sure, saw 1968 that way. Richard Nixon, after all, had become president by the will and votes of the people, not as the result of some banana republic coup. Many, repelled by what they saw as excesses in the movements that brought dissent to the nation's streets, saw in him new hope for an end to the war and for restoration of law and order at home.

But for all that—the dismay of those who lamented the year as a disaster and the guarded optimism of the others—the ramifications for the future of what had happened in 1968 were not yet imagined.

CHAPTER 14

After the Dream Died

On the twentieth day of January 1969, the newly elected president, Richard M. Nixon, performed the traditional ritual of oath-taking that had eluded him eight years earlier in his failed bid for the White House. Standing behind him on the steps of the United States Capitol as he was sworn in were the departing president and vice president, Lyndon B. Johnson and Hubert H. Humphrey—one of them the man Nixon was replacing and the other the man he had defeated. The election campaign of 1968 had been the occasion of sharp differences and bitter words between the two Democrats leaving power and the Republican assuming it. But now there was little said that reasonably could be cited as a cause of serious friction or dissent among them.

"We are caught in war, wanting peace," Nixon in his first address as the nation's thirty-seventh president said. "We are torn by division, wanting unity. We see around us empty lives, wanting fulfillment. We see tasks that need doing, waiting for hands to do them. To a crisis of the spirit, we need an answer of the spirit. To find that answer, we need only look within ourselves. When we listen to 'the better angels of our nature,' we find that they celebrate the simple things, and the basic things—such as goodness, decency, love, kindness."

The new president went on: "Greatness comes in simple trappings. The simple things are the ones most needed today if we are to surmount what divides us, and cement what unites us. To lower our voices would be a simple thing. In these difficult years, America has suffered from a fever of words: from inflated rhetoric that promises more than it can possibly deliver; from angry rhetoric that fans discontent into hatreds; from bombastic rhetoric that postures instead of persuading. We cannot learn from one another until we stop shouting at one another; until we speak quietly enough so that our words can be heard as well as our voices."

In so lecturing the nation, Richard Nixon understandably made no mention of the fact that his own voice, and that of the new vice president standing behind him, Spiro T. Agnew, had been two of the angriest and most bombastic raised to shouting level in the bitter political campaign only recently ended. Inaugural ceremonies are times of national hope and courtesy at which disbelief traditionally is suspended, at least for the moment.

That mood, however, was destined not to last much beyond the echoes of Nixon's remarks over the crowd of thousands gathered before him in the plaza of the Capitol, and the millions of others who had heard them over the national radio and television networks. Although the Paris peace talks had resumed four days before Nixon took the oath of office, and ten days afterward he ordered that a plan be drawn to end the draft and institute a volunteer army, the turmoil went on at home. Protests and student strikes continued on such campuses as San Francisco State, Wisconsin, Minnesota, Duke, Brandeis and Harvard. And when in March a new communist offensive was launched in Vietnam the new president declared that there was "no prospect for a reduction in American forces in the foreseeable future."

By April of 1969, the number of Americans killed in Vietnam, 33,641, had surpassed the 33,629 who died in the Korean War. Public support for Nixon on the war had dropped to 44 percent. In June, he announced that 25,000 Americans would be withdrawn from Vietnam in the following two months and projected that 100,000 would be out by the end of the year as his plan for "Vietnamization" of the war went forward. Still the protests continued.

Republican Representative Paul "Pete" McCloskey of California, a vocal war critic, declared in July that he would challenge Nixon for the 1972 GOP nomination, and in October the Vietnam Moratorium Committee held massive antiwar demonstrations in Washington, New York and Boston. Meanwhile, members of the Weatherman movement and other radicals conducted a rampage of trashing and violence against police in Chicago dubbed the "Days of Rage."

Agnew stepped up his divisive rantings against "radical liberals," decrying the "carnival in the streets" by "a strident minority who raise . . . intolerant clamor and cacophony." In a widely publicized speech in Des Moines, he turned his vitriol onto television news commentators who had, in his view, the effrontery to analyze a televised Nixon defense of his Vietnam policies. Shortly after that, Agnew added "the liberal establishment press" to his indictment. (Agnew's coinage of "radical liberals," Vice President Al Gore commented later, was "an Orwellian construction designed to merge the two concepts liberal and radical in voters' minds. It was an embodiment of the coordinated effort by Republicans to use the extremes on the left as a way of unfairly characterizing the vast majority of Democrats who were moderate but deeply concerned about the war.")

In mid-November, the New Mobilization Committee to End the War in Vietnam drew an estimated 250,000 protesters to a demonstration in Washington. About 40,000 participated in a silent "March of Death" past the White House carrying placards bearing the names of Americans killed in Vietnam and villages destroyed there.

When Nixon sent American forces into Cambodia at the end of April 1970, the campuses exploded again, and the flames were fanned by the slaying of four students by trigger-happy National Guardsmen at Kent State University in Ohio. The "New Mobe" held another protest in Washington marked by the bizarre spectacle of Nixon making a post-midnight visit to demonstrators at the Lincoln Memorial, during which he sought to find common ground with them by talking about football.

In the 1970 midterm election campaign, he was booed and subjected to near-misses by egg-throwers as he and Agnew stumped for Republican congressional candidates who stood by him on the war. As had become commonplace by now, Agnew assumed the hatchet-man role for which Nixon earlier had become infamous. In a speech in Belleville, Missouri, in late October, Agnew declared in response to antiwar hecklers: "It's time to sweep that kind of garbage out of our society."

Although Nixon continued to draw down the American presence in Vietnam through 1971 and 1972, the protests went on. In April of 1971, a "Dump Nixon" rally was held in Providence, Rhode Island, addressed by McCloskey and Allard Lowenstein, "the man who dumped Johnson." Publication of the Pentagon Papers, chronicling the folly of American policy in Vietnam, kept the fires of disaffection burning, though by August 12, 1972, the last U.S. ground combat troops were withdrawn. Public protest continued as well as a result of heavy bombing of North Vietnam and the specific targeting of Hanoi and the port of Haiphong by American planes, as communist forces moved in greater numbers into the South.

By this time, the scandal of the Watergate break-in at the Democratic National Headquarters by agents of the Nixon-Agnew reelection committee had broken on the political scene. But Nixon and other high-ranking administration officials denied knowledge or complicity, and in the fall of 1972 a hapless George McGovern as the Democratic presidential nominee was unable in spite of valiant efforts to turn the affair to his political advantage in his campaign against Nixon.

Nixon as president, with the antiwar demonstrations intensifying, had continued to exploit his winning law-and-order theme of 1968, broadening his support among voters fed up with violence and disorder in the streets—and ready to blame the Democrats in general and antiwar candidate McGovern in particular.

When White House National Security Adviser Henry Kissinger on October 26 declared that "peace is at hand" in the Paris talks for an end to the fighting in Vietnam, Nixon was on the verge of a landslide reelection. A week after his inauguration for a second term he could bask in the achievement of a peace treaty, though on terms that critics said could have been reached four years and thousands of American deaths earlier. And by late March of 1973 the last American military personnel were withdrawn from Vietnam. There was by this time, however, another monkey on Nixon's back—the unraveling of the Watergate affair that sixteen months later drove him in disgrace from the presidency.

* * *

The specific events that brought about Nixon's resignation on August 9, 1974, had occurred in 1972, but in the liberal view at least, the condition the nation had reached by then could be traced back to circumstances of years before, culminating in the cataclysm of 1968. "It was like a tornado year," Tom Hayden said in an interview much later. "There were a lot of forces and they became like a vortex. Everybody was turned around and changed, for better or worse. But you have to understand that 1968 was determined by what went before."

After the eight years of postwar normalcy experienced in the two administrations of Dwight D. Eisenhower, the election of John F. Kennedy in 1960 had ushered in a spirit of renewal in the country. This spirit was personified in the young and stylish new president who talked of "getting this country moving again" and literally reaching for the stars with an action plan to put a man on the moon and return him safely to earth before the decade was out.

Kennedy's triumph over early foreign policy failures with his dramatic staring-down of bullying Soviet leader Nikita Khrushchev in the Cuban Missile Crisis of 1962, and his launching of the Peace Corps, rekindled American confidence and pride. "The sixties began," according to Hayden, "with a kind of moral awakening that was translated into direct action by a new generation seeking to be central to our country's history, and the world's history. John Kennedy's election was a sign of that, but not the cause of it. While he was in office he accelerated that consciousness among young people. His death was a tragic interruption that set the stage for greater divisions in the country, leading to 1968."

In the view of Rick Stearns, who as a young man was the McCarthy coordinator in Fresno in 1968 and in 1972 tracked delegate selection for the McGovern campaign, "much of the generational attitude that manifested itself in the schisms [of 1968] was planted in the early 1960s." The civil rights movement, he said much later when he had become a federal district judge in Boston, had an "enormous impact . . . in fanning people to attack conventions" across the spectrum of the society. "It forced a lot of people to confront, for the first time, race and social relations and social justice."

The movement, he said, had broader implications as well, forcing the country "to be more inclusive in its politics," most notably in the universities in demands for student participation in their governance. "Long before the [height of the] Vietnam protest," he noted, "there was debate over the democratization of the university power structure and attacks on the hierarchy of authority," as seen in the Free Speech Movement at Berkeley in 1964. "A lot of the political styles and modes didn't spring full-blown in 1968," he said. "And the student radicalization wasn't simply a function of Vietnam and the reaction of privilege to the draft. It all began much earlier, before many had ever heard of Vietnam."

The sexual revolution, and the emergence of feminism as a potent political force in the mid-1960s emphasizing the economic as well as social impediments to equal rights and opportunity, also fed the dissatisfaction with the status quo. But it was the war in Vietnam, building on the drive for civil rights in the South in the early 1960s and later for economic justice toward minorities in the inner cities of the North, that broadened the protest movement well beyond America's campuses.

The assassination of John Kennedy in 1963, Gore said much later as a member of the 1960s generation, "was in many ways the beginning of an enhanced cynicism that has premised our politics since then." Yet, he went on, "there was a lot of hope in 1964 [with the defeat of hawkish Barry Goldwater]. But in 1965, at least from the standpoint of a young person in those years, the Vietnam War policy began to erode confidence in government. The government's way of communicating what that policy was did further damage, and the net result was to reawaken the disaffection and alienation [felt] in the aftermath of President Kennedy's assassination." By 1968, he said, "the healing had not completely occurred."

The death of John Kennedy had indeed jolted the country, and the younger generation especially. But the manner in which Lyndon Johnson picked up the Kennedy agenda, and carried it to objectives Kennedy himself probably never envisioned, encouraged the nation's spiritual recovery—until LBJ's accelerated conduct of the Vietnam War in 1965 intervened.

"Johnson promised not to send American boys to fight in Asian land wars and he did it," Hayden said. "Those of us who were in the civil rights movement were still sufficiently part of the system to be trying to reform the Democratic Party, to even be willing to vote for Johnson in 1964. [But] the period of betrayal from the Mississippi Summer Project of August 1964 [when the LBJ-dominated national convention rejected an attempt to seat an alternate, integrated Mississippi delegation] to March 1965, when Johnson sent in 135,000 troops [to Vietnam], was just a disaster which led to a deep division from which we have not recovered."

Another prominent member of that generation, former Senator Gary Hart of Colorado, observed that in spite of the John Kennedy assassination, by the time 1968 arrived "we were willing to give [the political process] another try, but with a lot more fatalism than in 1960" about what could happen. Hart said he "felt eerie when Robert Kennedy got into the race. He was such a lightning rod, because he was a polarizing force." Then, when King and Robert Kennedy were assassinated, he said, "we thought, 'What the hell can you expect?' People didn't think that before then."

Still, going into 1968, there remained among a substantial number of Americans the sense of the "moral awakening" of which Hayden spoke. "America was struggling to handle the big problems it had in race relations," Fred Dutton, the veteran of the John and Robert Kennedy forces, recalled much later. "You still had the buoyancy that had come with JFK; you had Lyndon Johnson's very substantial legislative accomplishments; there was considerable prosperity; the country was rather upbeat."

The progress in legal rights for black Americans over the previous decade, while not satisfactory to many of their leaders, had been remarkable, to the degree that the movement was advancing by that time from the pursuit of social justice to broader economic goals. The civil rights acts barring discrimination and requiring equality in housing, voting and other areas, championed by King in the streets and by Johnson in the government, were now on the books.

As a result, both King and Robert Kennedy now were focusing increasingly on the economic disparity between whites and blacks. At the same time, however, the war continued to intrude as a major racial issue: blacks were being sent in disproportionate numbers to Vietnam to fight and die there. Both King and Kennedy recognized this circumstance and preached against it. They came to understand that the two causes, civil rights and protest against the war, were or should be interwoven.

King had come to realize as early as 1966 that the linkage of the civil rights and antiwar movements was critical, and he underscored it in his celebrated speech at Riverside Church in April of 1967. In making that linkage, however, King's relationship with Johnson changed critically. According to Doris Kearns Goodwin, who was a confidante of LBJ at the time, "once the turn was made on King's part, Johnson as president began to view King and the civil rights movement as potential enemies rather than embracing them. When the two hooked up together, that's when real change was able to take place—King pushing from outside and the Selma demonstration getting [white] people's sympathy behind the black marchers because of the dogs, etc. Johnson's 'We Shall Overcome' speech meant the government embracing an outside movement." With the march on Selma generating public support and Johnson getting the Voting Rights Act passed in six weeks, she said, "the synergy worked." But that harmony of purpose fell away with King's increasingly vocal opposition to the war.

While the instrument of street demonstration remained an essential weapon in the civil rights and antiwar arsenals, the McCarthy and then the Kennedy candidacies in 1968 provided vehicles for channeling protest through the existing political process.

The McCarthy effort, as a direct outcome of the Lowenstein/Gans Dump Johnson initiative spurred essentially by opposition to the war, likewise concentrated on the conduct of foreign policy. Although McCarthy had a strong record on civil rights, Kennedy had the more conspicuous allegiance to the cause through his very public actions as attorney general and as inheritor of the family legacy, which included overwhelming support among black voters. So Kennedy's campaign evolved, in the public perception at least, as more of a two-pronged protest than did McCarthy's.

Kennedy as a candidate came to embody the linkage of the civil rights and antiwar protests, but his personal and policy differences with Johnson hindered any long-term possibility of reconciliation. Along with King, Kennedy had the kind of following in both protest movements that offered the hope, as did McCarthy, that the country might yet right itself at the ballot box. Many protesters believed that electing either Kennedy or McCarthy could end the war in Vietnam and permit new advances in the cause of economic justice for blacks and other minorities, and for women.

As long as George Romney remained a possible Republican nominee, and Nelson Rockefeller after him, there was some hope as well among some of the protesters that there could even be deliverance from the war abroad and racial and social injustice at home in the election of a Republican. Instead, Nixon, clinging to Cold War rhetoric on foreign policy, including Vietnam, and embracing the law-and-order code words of the Goldwater campaign of 1964, acted as a catalyst for more street protest against the war.

With long-haired, foul-mouthed radical youth often grabbing the attention of the television news cameras, Nixon speechwriter William Safire said long afterward, "certainly Nixon exploited the scruffiness factor." The Nixon strategists, he said, "hoped that the people who showed up shouting obscenities" would come to the Nixon rallies. "We didn't hire any," he said. "We didn't have to." Their presence and demeanor were elements that in 1968, and again in 1972, played to Nixon's political advantage, yet in the long run they furthered the bitter polarization that would mark his presidency.

*   *   *

In preaching law and order, Nixon had a political competitor in George Wallace, but the Alabamian was also an ally in the stirring up of public resentment. Wallace lashed out not only against the war protesters but also against the Democratic establishment in charge, in the beginnings of the antigovernment crusade that was to mark the eventual rise of the new American conservatism. Wallace's presence in the race clearly took votes from Nixon and prevented him from winning decisively over Humphrey. At the same time, however, he gave voice to a cultural rejection of liberalism and political elitism that flowered thereafter in the critical Republican success in courting blue-collar Democrats.

Historian Alan Brinkley of Columbia, in an interview much later, argued that while most perspectives on 1968, from veterans of the antiwar movement, "are always viewed in terms of what it meant to the left," the events of the year really were more significant in "how they mobilized and engaged the right." Wallace's vote combined with Nixon's—a total of 56.9 percent—was the real measure of what happened, he said, with the Democratic vote dropping from the 61.1 percent for Johnson in 1964 to only 42.7 for Humphrey. It was an emphatic statement, he said, "against the antiwar movement, against the counterculture, against violence and for law and order."

Nixon, Safire said later, "sensed at that time a depth of feeling in the American psyche" that was turning against the turmoil in the streets and yearning for a society of law and order, embodied in what Nixon called the Silent Majority. "The clean-cut American, the crew-cut American, was coming into his own," Safire said, "and in the labor movement, the construction trades, the hard-hats, identified with Nixon on the war."

Not only the political voices of the left but also the mainstream news media misinterpreted what had gone on among voters in 1968, Brinkley said. For example, he said, when then Senator Abe Ribicoff chastised Mayor Daley for "Gestapo tactics" by his police during the Chicago convention, "everybody [in the press and television] thought he spoke for the nation. But it very quickly became clear that the public reaction to the televised violence on the streets of Chicago was not against the police but against the demonstrators." Thereafter, he noted, Ribicoff had a tough campaign for reelection.

In all this, Brinkley said, "there was a real disjunction between what the conventional wisdom of elites thought was going on in 1968 and what much of the electorate thought was going on." Also, he said, "I think the election to some degree was misinterpreted. Wallace's strength was viewed by most people, and by most commentators, almost entirely in terms of race and racial backgrounds, even though that was not what he talked about in his campaign. Very few people were willing to take literally what he was talking about, which was law and order, long-haired demonstrators, pointy-headed intellectuals and bureaucrats—a cruder form of the right-wing rhetoric of the next twenty-five years. Race was certainly part of that message, but it wasn't the whole message. Similarly, Nixon played the race card subtly too, but it wasn't race alone."

Brinkley argued that Americans "have been much too preoccupied with what the left was doing in 1968 and not attentive enough to the bigger story of a kind of counterrevolution occurring." People of the generation that protested in 1968, he said, "see it as a revolutionary year, when in fact it was much closer to being a counterrevolutionary year."

The assassinations of King and Kennedy as well played into the mood of voter hostility, he said. "The violence that was unleashed [after King's slaying] came to be seen to many people as the vision of America's future, and gave salience to law and order as an issue. . . . The '68 riots, the campus uprisings reinforced that fear, that anxiety in 1968." Whereas the assassination of John Kennedy five years earlier had largely been viewed at the time as an isolated episode "by a single crazed gunman," Brinkley said, the latter two slayings "had in many ways a more profound effect on the larger American view [that they were] a symptom of a deep sickness in American life."

These shocks to the nation's system, and all the other jolts of 1968, he said, "far from radicalizing America created a real political reaction which the right was able to begin to exploit. Not that Nixon was an authentic figure of the right by 1968, but it certainly was a defeat for the Democrats from which they never really fully recovered."

Nixon speechwriter and adviser Pat Buchanan, in an interview much later, basically agreed. "Nineteen sixty-eight was two sides of the same coin," he said. "Everything came apart for the Democrats and together for the Republicans. It seemed like we moved serenely through the eye of the hurricane to the nomination. We went to New Hampshire on the night of the Tet

Offensive, won Wisconsin as Johnson was dropping out, Indiana when King was assassinated and had the nomination when Kennedy was shot. Then, after the election, we moved to consolidate the Wallace vote. Nineteen sixty-eight was the last-ditch stand of the New Deal and the beginning of the whole Republican era.

"We went on to create a new majority coalition built on the ruination of the Great Society," he said. "It was the same coalition Reagan had. What he added was tax cuts and a positive economic growth theory, along with a funny disposition and optimism. But Nixon was its architect, and that coalition continues today. It's getting bigger and bigger."

Also, Buchanan said, "the values war started then. People thought drug-taking and the sexual revolution were wrong, but the liberals wouldn't stand up for their own values. They could not say no when the demonstrations got out of control. . . . The American people saw it [in Chicago] and were revolted. And on the campuses, the liberals wouldn't stand up to the academic thugs. . . . I can't see Harry Truman ever condoning the riots, but the liberals had no backbone for standing up to them."

Kevin Phillips, in *The Emerging Republican Majority* in 1969, had already seen 1968 in the same vein. "Far from being the tenuous and unmeaningful victory suggested by critical observers," he wrote then, Nixon's election "bespoke the end of the New Deal Democratic hegemony and the beginning of a new era in American politics. . . . This repudiation visited upon the Democratic Party for its ambitious social programming, and inability to handle the urban and negro revolutions, was comparable in scope to that given conservative Republicanism in 1932 for its failure to cope with the economic crisis of the Depression."

Phillips went on: "The great political upheaval of the Nineteen Sixties is not that of Senator Eugene McCarthy's relatively small group of upper-middle-class and intellectual supporters, but a populist revolt of the American masses who have been elevated by prosperity to middle-class status and conservatism. *Their* revolt is against the caste, policies and taxation of the mandarins of Establishment liberalism. . . . The emerging Republican majority spoke clearly in 1968 for a shift away from the sociological jurisprudence, moral permissiveness . . . welfare and educational programming and massive federal spending by which the Liberal (mostly Democratic) Establishment sought to propagate liberal institutions and ideology—and all the while reap growing economic benefits."

Hayden, asked about the view that the excesses of the radicals of 1968, of whom he was a leader, fueled the rise of conservatism and the resurrection of the Republican party after the Goldwater debacle of 1964, sharply rejected it. "When an election is decided by one or two points, it's fallacious to blame the outcome on a single faction," he said later. "The climate that was created had nothing to do with the actual outcome of a very narrow election. But the climate was a response to the sixties that is with us still . . . a law-and-order climate, and the order is the status quo.

"Law and order meant the status quo at that time against the perceived threat of the blacks, the students, the women, the antiwar demonstrators," Hayden said. "You still see that today. It very much animates Gingrich's consciousness when he talks about rescuing American civilization, or rescuing Western civilization. He's talking about rescuing his version of the status quo from what he perceives to be the Visigoths and barbarians at the gates, who are all these people from the sixties.

"But there's quite another way to look at it, a better way," he said. "The United States never should have been involved in the war in Vietnam. That's the root cause, because it created a sea of blood that created lasting emotions, feelings and resentments. It prevented the possible completion of the antipoverty effort and the urban agenda which led directly to the conditions for the black riots, the insurrections, further bloodshed and creation of a climate of law and order.

"If there's blame, and I'm only responding to those who want to blame the New Left, the root responsibility was the decision to continue escalating the war in Vietnam in 1963, 1964, 1965. . . . If you want to place a date when it all went wrong it was the Gulf of Tonkin decision in August 1964. That was it. So all the conservatives, the people who blame the New Left, are doing is focusing on a later set of events that brought about the beginning of a Republican ascendancy. . . .

"If you go back four years earlier, if you want to get down to what really divided the country, what caused the reform-minded students to become revolutionaries, what caused a breakdown of trust, what caused the racial violence, it was the escalation of the war in Vietnam. . . . If Johnson had acted on the recommendations of his advisers who wanted to emphasize the Great Society and deal with the unrest in the cities, [the riots] might not have happened."

Finally, Hayden said, "there's a big what-if over the sixties that should keep people from casting blame or causality, and that is the assassinations. What that robbed us of, and caused us to feel, has to be factored in. I don't know if you want to call that the tragedy factor or the catastrophe factor. . . . It makes it impossible to single out a single cause, because the cause they [conservatives] are singling out is self-serving. They want to blame the radicals. But who knows what would have happened if King and Kennedy were alive? It could have launched a liberal period of governance. I have no idea. . . .

"They lost the sixties and they're trying to regain it through history," Hayden said. "[They try to] prove that the sixties created this climate of permissiveness, because they're the puritans. . . . They were all against the civil rights movement and they were all for the Vietnam War, and they lost the civil rights issue and the war issue, and are somewhat more successful in the historical touch-up. It doesn't matter, because the sixties produced a climate of equal rights, advancement of voting rights, greater opportunities for minorities and women, the first appreciation of the environment, the beginning of environmental laws, the downfall of the imperial presidency, the expansion of participatory democracy and all that they're against. But they can't really be against that frontally, so they pick the alleged excesses of the sixties."

* * *

In any event, taking to the streets to advance civil rights and to try to stop the killing in Vietnam clearly had its distinct political downside for the participants, in 1968 and thereafter. While the opposition to the war was loud and conspicuous, going into 1968 polls indicated it did not approach majority sentiment in the country. Millions of Americans, themselves frustrated by the casualties and duration of the U.S. engagement in Vietnam, continued to believe that the best course was to stand by the president. They thought so either out of pure patriotism or because to do otherwise would lend aid and comfort to the enemy in Hanoi, by signaling lack of American will and staying power.

These attitudes generated not only disagreement with the demonstrators but hostility to them—and to their ragged, often irreverent, appearance and lifestyles. In opposing the war, they seemed to be opposing America itself, and many of the radicals said as much, to the great consternation of many others on Main Street America viewing their antics on television.

William Bennett, the conservative theorist who served in high posts in the Reagan and Bush administrations, said in a C-SPAN interview years later that a "cultural revolution" occurred in 1968 when "it became quite fashionable, acceptable, indeed even desirable on the part of many people to be in opposition to any tradition, to any practice or anything that's an inherited American custom or idea. . . . I know people whose lives were changed by this because they fell into the belief in 1968 that this was a horrible country. . . . Their lives have been changed, mostly for the worse." In the aftermath of 1968, Bennett said, "I was very worried about this country. I thought we might come apart. I learned it was a very strong and resilient country."

Still, he said, "that strand or dimension of thinking has persisted to today."

As a young man who started out as a liberal, he said, "I went to the right when I saw the protest moving way beyond reasonable protest [against the war] . . . to what I perceived as a real hatred of America."

In a separate interview, Bennett recalled a scene at Harvard Law School when fellow students, learning of the bombing of a military installation in Massachusetts at which some American soldiers were killed, cheered at the news. "I said, 'What the hell are you cheering about?' . . . The country was coming apart. . . . When I saw people not just opposing the war but calling for victory for the Vietcong, I got off the boat. Remember 'Amerika' with a 'k'?"

On the civil rights front as well, growing numbers of whites, males particularly, came to look less and less sympathetically at the civil rights movement as demonstrable gains were made but the protests continued, increasingly under the leadership of militant, threatening blacks. This attitude became a critical obstacle to Johnson's drive for racial equality, and for economic assistance and justice for blacks and the poor of all races.

According to Harry McPherson, one of Johnson's chief speechwriters and political advisers, the civil rights acts of 1964 and 1965, culminating the long fight to end segregation, "were backed by a great majority of the American people. Southerners, however, were angry because they [the laws] did pick out the South. They also thought that was about it; Johnson had solved the worst of the domestic ills. We had rid ourselves of centuries of guilt by ridding ourselves of bigotry."

But Johnson was not content with that, McPherson noted. He cited an LBJ speech at Howard University in June 1965, "in which he said we'd ended segregation but the Negro had a long way to go. You don't just strike the shackles from a man who has been shackled for a long time and tell him to run a foot race. He had to be educated, given the chance to build a strong family. Johnson was signaling to the world he was going to do a lot of things beyond just ending discrimination. He was going to have affirmative action, he was going to tax Americans to provide funds for programs of benefit to blacks. He had to do it because of two centuries of mistreatment for which whites were guilty. A fair-minded person couldn't say this analysis was wrong. We had to make this effort. But we didn't have any idea how bad it was going to be. Soon there were riots by those for whom these efforts had been made."

So the political impact of the antiwar and civil rights protests was in the eye of the beholder. The demonstrators in the years up to and including 1968 saw their activities as the legitimate exercise of their rights in the quest to move society, in the case of civil rights, and the government, in the case of the war in Vietnam, to do what was right and just. Success in civil rights encouraged them that similar success could be achieved with similar methods to try to end the war. At the same time, foes of civil rights, or those who believed the movement had gone far enough, and supporters of the Vietnam War saw the street protests as distasteful, disruptive, disloyal, even disgusting.

"The mistake the Democrats made," Buchanan said, "was not stopping at desegregation. Everybody was for that. The country came to feel segregation was wrong. The liberals should have stopped there instead of endorsing busing, set-asides and all that. And then, on Vietnam, the best and brightest marched us in—500,000 Americans there when we went into the White House—and they all ran out on us. They called it Nixon's War. Everybody knew the liberals got us in, and they wouldn't stand with us when we were getting our troops out."

Ben Wattenberg, a Johnson speechwriter at the time who eventually became a prominent neoconservative, observed later that "the [Democratic] convention was not just a liberal revolt. There was a tremendous amount of resentment against everything people were seeing on television, and in many ways properly so. A lot of the so-called social issues, the erosion of order, and some of the sexuality, were personified by the events—the drugs, the nudity, all that kind of stuff—that people saw on television for the first time."

John Ehrlichman, Nixon's campaign aide in 1968 who became the chief of domestic affairs in the Nixon White House and later was convicted and jailed on charges growing out of the Watergate coverup, agreed. "An element of noncivility was involved that was not present eight years before [when Nixon ran for president the first time]," he said in an interview much later. "Heckling, rock-throwing, vegetable-throwing came into play. It was almost impossible for the candidate to speak without screening the crowd in advance."

(This, Ehrlichman said, was accomplished in the Nixon campaign several times by extraordinary efforts. At the Nixon-Agnew rally in Madison Square Garden in late October of 1968, he said, "we issued tickets broadly, and anyone who presented a ticket who didn't look right, was carrying a sign [critical of Nixon] or was a hippie, was referred down one hall, and the others dressed right were sent down another hall." Those routed to the first hall, he said, "were led to a door that let out onto the street, where there was a 'cop' standing. When they came back around the front and complained, they were directed to go get another ticket a block away in a storefront. There, a Nixon man would stand on a table and report that the fire marshal had just announced that no more would be allowed in." The storefront, he said, was rented just for the purpose of diverting potential hecklers.)

By the narrowest of margins in an election complicated by the presence of a third, independent candidate, those who held the view of an America being trashed by rabble in the streets prevailed in 1968, and Richard Nixon, who along with his running mate had encouraged that view on the stump, moved into the White House. Nevertheless, both street campaigns, for justice at home and peace abroad, went forward, to Nixon's vexation and opposition. Both "wars" continued to be waged, now often in more radical hands after the deaths of King, the latter-day apostle of nonviolence, and Kennedy, who had come to share the same conviction, as most eloquently expressed in Indianapolis on the night of King's assassination.

Because the major legal goals of the civil rights movement had already been achieved, that movement eventually went into eclipse, despite—or perhaps because of—the refocus on black power and separatism. The struggle for economic justice that King had begun to undertake in Chicago and Memphis went on, but without the same biracial sense of moral imperative that the fight against segregation had generated among many white as well as black Americans.

Arthur Schlesinger Jr. said in an interview later that King had been challenged by Kennedy to move into the North to improve the economic condition of blacks, but that his earlier successes "on the moral and legal sides of the civil rights movement" were not being duplicated as he moved into this new dimension.

Ron Walters, a political scientist at Howard who has been a political adviser to Jesse Jackson, had a harsher observation: "By 1968, the civil rights part of the sixties movement was all but moribund. What had taken over was the black power movement, far more aggressively."

Dick Goodwin agreed. "The civil rights movement had really reached its peak in 1965," he said later, "with the end of legalized apartheid in the South, securing the right to vote for blacks, which was to change forever the face of American politics. Now the issues were much more resistant—the economy, jobs. Where did you protest? City Hall or the First National Bank? The hopes of blacks had been so raised by the victories, and then they ran into this blank wall of the cities of the North."

At the same time, the cause of racial justice at home was overshadowed after 1968 by the protest against the war. But the antiwar effort too was robbed by the events and political outcome of 1968; many of the young and idealistic foot soldiers in the campaigns of Eugene McCarthy and Robert Kennedy gave up on the political process they had hoped would deliver their country from the turmoil that had gripped it. Ken Galbraith later observed that many of them "retained a commitment to active politics but eventually, with the passing of time, careers and family, they became absorbed in other areas, and others became radicalized."

Curt Gans, who eventually became the director of the Committee for the Study of the American Electorate, cited important members of the Clinton administration who had come out of the McCarthy campaign and had maintained their confidence in the political system—Harold Ickes, John Shattuck, John Podesta, Eli Segal among them. "You could scratch 90 percent of the people who worked in the McCarthy campaign," Gans said, "and they would be continuing, with the same hope, to be in service to society."

Al Lowenstein saw the McCarthy campaign not only as a vehicle for channeling protesting young America into constructive action but also as one that built a cadre of idealistic political activists for future tests. "Certainly it defused the trend towards radicalism among the young, at least for a year," he said in an oral history later. "It didn't stop campus protest. Columbia was boiling over in the spring of 1968 when all the ads in the papers [were saying] 'McCarthy's brought our children home.' He never brought these children home. The children who got involved weren't the violent activists in the first place. They were approaching that, maybe, in many cases and might have gone there faster had they not had the outlet of the campaign. So it did calm that for a while, and it left a residue of who knows how many politically trained young people."

McCarthy himself expressed to me later a somewhat more cynical view. "It's a mixed thing," he said. "Some of them are still involved in non-national political efforts. And some of them have become regulars, like Sam Brown [also in the Clinton administration]." McCarthy cited a newspaper advertisement signed by former members of the 1968 McCarthy campaign "denouncing me for supporting Humphrey." In 1976, he said, some of the same former McCarthyites "signed an ad denouncing me for not supporting Jimmy Carter." The latter ad, he observed wryly, was "kind of a ticket to appointment" in the Carter administration, and some of the signers later got jobs in the Clinton administration, "so it was a lasting endorsement."

Others of his supporters of 1968, however, "just dropped out," McCarthy said. "They thought it was a great experience but they were disillusioned with politics altogether. Some of them said the political effort we made wouldn't work anyway, was a distraction, and they felt the campaign proved they were right, that you couldn't work it through the political process. We said they ought to try. They resented us, some of the radicals; they picketed us a couple of times and said we were betraying the revolution. It got more violent in the seventies."

Some young McCarthyites acknowledged later that they had become disillusioned not only with politics, but with McCarthy himself, because of his often contrary manner, especially toward the end of his 1968 campaign. A more mature McCarthy supporter at the time, Professor David Riesman of Harvard, who was chairman of Social Scientists for McCarthy, observed later that he had warned his students about their candidate: "McCarthy has one fine quality. He doesn't respect generals. But he's not a nice man. So don't idealize him. He's important for this trip only." But Erwin Knoll, the editor of *The Progressive* magazine, later observed of the criticisms of McCarthy: "We have to come back to the point that he did what he did, and it was a dazzling achievement in its way. I heard someone recently refer to Senator McCarthy as a man for one season. Perhaps he was, but it was a hell of a season."

* * *

The radicals who came to dominate much of the antiwar movement after 1968 pursued their objectives with rhetoric and tactics that only hardened the opposition, making them susceptible to the harangues of Nixon and Agnew. "With the exception of one period during the bombing of Cambodia," Gans noted later, "most of the time from the spring of 1968 to the spring of 1974, a majority of people still supported the war. There was a resonance against the war, but the antiwar movement became more strident and hence less effective. And Nixon barricading the White House helped create the existence of the Silent Majority against the extremists, and to that extent the antiwar movement played into it."

That phenomenon of Nixon and Agnew exploiting hostility toward the war protest in radical hands, and the linking of radicals and liberals as "radic-libs," worked for them not only through their first term but in the 1972 re-election campaign. McGovern noted later that "I was able to tap into the concern of the sixties and direct it into winning [the Democratic nomination] in 1972. I captured most of the McCarthy and Kennedy people and got control of the party." But Nixon and Agnew then played effectively on the vulnerability that the antiwar protest also brought to McGovern's candidacy. "A lot of young people figured the political process was hopeless," McGovern said. "Their behavior fed images of our wing of the party being countercultural, anti-establishment and anti-American. It was a twist on the 1960s that really didn't fit the idealism and methods of the McCarthy, Kennedy and McGovern campaigns." Nevertheless, this image helped seal McGovern's fate.

Buchanan contended much later that the hostility toward the Nixon administration from liberals after 1968 not only backfired among voters who were already turned off by the protests, but also inspired conservatives to take on the liberals, and the news media they saw as liberal-dominated, for control of the country.

Many liberals thought Robert Kennedy would have beaten Nixon had he lived, Buchanan said, and felt that somehow "the Nixon campaign and the Republican victory was, the way Lyndon Johnson's [assumption of the presidency in 1963] was, illegitimate, that they really didn't deserve it." The Nixonites felt, he said, that the liberals thought Nixon had become president "because some assassins had murdered their leaders. . . . That sense of hostility and bitterness [on the part of liberals] toward conservatives, Republicans and the right certainly has endured," he said.

In the face of criticism of the Nixon administration in the news media, Buchanan said later, he went to Nixon and told him: "This is about your presidency. . . . They hate us. We might as well use their hostility against them." He urged Nixon to arouse "the Silent Majority" against the hostile press and to use Agnew as his tool. Nixon assented and assigned Buchanan, and Safire, to help write Agnew's slashing speeches against network television and the press. Nixon, Buchanan said, "did with the press what FDR did with Wall Street."

Buchanan contended that "the best thing that came out of this was a much more self-confident Republican Party and conservative movement which thought, 'Okay, they don't like us very much, but we can take over this country, we can rule this country, and we can defeat the whole liberal establishment.'" It was, however, an attitude finally reflected in excess in the Watergate break-in and other administration adventures beyond the law that brought down the Nixon presidency.

Until then, though, the increasingly hard edge of the protest movement played into the hands of Nixon and Agnew and stiffened the determination of conservatives to rout the liberals. Hayden observed later that "after 1968 the protest didn't lose steam, but it became more militant. It became more bitter, confrontational, both ways, from the establishment and from the student and black communities. The possibility of reform was the glue that had held it all together going into the late sixties. As that unraveled, it just became an ugly confrontation between an unreasoning establishment and protesters who had become radicals because we had given up any basis of hope for reaching the establishment."

As a result, Hayden noted, "the classic demonstration was bigger than ever, but the tone had changed. People like myself who were on the radical edge had concluded that the possibilities for reform were slim to none. I was more in the category of those who thought there was still a slim hope, as opposed to the Weather Underground who thought there was no hope."

Even before the disillusionment of 1968, Hayden said, the Students for a Democratic Society of which he had been a founder and intellectual voice "was cracking up. The first wave of radical reformers like myself had gone. . . . A new, more disillusioned radicalism was sprouting, from 1965 to 1968, and in the wake of 1968 you had a further splintering into what became the Weather Underground, which had concluded that only by violent disruption [could change be achieved].

"This was not a completely mindless approach," he said. "The new leaders of SDS who became the Weather Underground were the younger brothers and sisters of the people who had started SDS in a rosier time. You know how you get into fights in a family. Well, they felt that our generation had failed. By that they meant reform had not occurred. In fact, more people were getting killed in Vietnam, and people trying to reform the system in Mississippi had been denied, and in Chicago had been beaten up with clubs. So they took the leap from that to the conclusion that the establishment didn't listen to reason, or morality or to marching feet or even to votes. The change would only come about if the establishment faced a continual low-grade, violent headache at home.

"And so you started to get these bombings of power lines, ROTC buildings. But never before, in many years, [except] maybe in labor strikes, had there been this much violent disruption in America. If you look at it amorally as a historian would, you'd have to say they had some effect. They may not have brought about reform and they certainly didn't bring about the good society or the blessed community. But they did add, just as they thought they would, to the burden of the establishment going on with the Vietnam War. It became clearer and clearer that if you went on with the Vietnam War, you were creating more and more of this chaos at home."

While many of the young McCarthy and Kennedy workers dropped out in disillusionment, some did persevere as relative moderates. In Hayden's view, 1968 "also created a new group of mainstream reformers to arise who became the Bill Clintons—the Bill Clinton–Al Gore generation. They wouldn't choose sides with the radicals; that was too far off the edge of respectability, but they shared our moral critique of the war and the establishment. So you started to see in the student governments, the student body presidents, a more moderate antiwar movement symbolized by Sam Brown, David Mixner. People like Bill Clinton and Al Gore happened to emerge in that same time frame."

It was Brown and Mixner, Hayden noted, who began organizing the Moratorium march in 1969 as "a more moderate channel. . . . Obviously they were fundamentally disoriented, even profoundly damaged by the deaths of that springtime and the defeat of McCarthy. But they didn't give up. They formed a new mainstream antiwar tendency and continued to try to find ways to reform the Democratic Party."

In the process, Hayden said, both at the Chicago convention of 1968 and thereafter, "we shattered the viability of the old Democratic Party, the one that chose delegates in back rooms long before the primaries. That created the space for a new, reformed Democratic Party which brought about McGovern and created a new home for the Mixners, the Browns and ultimately the Clintons and Gores. So only after the crack-up and collision, what the reporters described as the chaos of 1968, came reform. It was only when the old party was rendered hopeless."

Todd Gitlin, the University of California sociologist who was an early Hayden colleague in SDS, argued in a later interview that "given Johnson's commitment to the war on the one hand and the passions of the antiwar and black movements on the other, some kind of collision was in the works, was fated. Whether Johnson had run or not, whether the assassinations had taken place or not, the Democratic Party was on its way to being ripped apart. The police were looking for a fight, a lot of the left was looking for a fight, and combined with the Wallace campaign, whatever form the collision would have taken, it meant among other things the rupture of the Democratic Party, from which it hasn't recovered. In some ways it was a foreordained conclusion. It would have taken miraculously shrewd politics to avoid it."

At the same time, Gitlin said, the assassinations of King and Kennedy heaped on top of this internal rupture in the party were "absolutely devastating," what he called in *The Sixties* "The Decapitation of the Heroes." Until then, he said, "it was possible to believe that there were great men who could bootstrap their way out of the swamps, even after the assassination of Jack Kennedy. Precisely their importance would have been to cement together a new majority coalition, which would have been made up of the old New Deal coalition minus the Dixiecrats, with some important cement remaining between Northern blacks and white ethnics, without fatally estranging the white guys. And then finding a strong thrust of nonviolence, which, although embattled, might have outlasted the destructiveness of the Black Panthers."

* * *

One of the outcomes of 1968 not attributable directly to the protest was the success of Democratic Party activists in bringing about reforms in delegate selection for the 1972 and subsequent conventions. A commission mandated by the 1968 convention and headed by McGovern achieved liberal reforms that opened the process to greater voter participation and reduced the influence of entrenched party officials who had delivered the 1968 nomination to Humphrey. Had those reforms been in place in 1968, indeed, Kennedy had he lived quite probably would have been the party nominee. "If it accomplished anything," Hayden said later of the 1968 convention, "it reformed the system so people can choose the nominees."

Some old-line, regular Democrats later argued, however, that this greater "participatory democracy" contributed to the party's defeat in 1972 when McGovern himself was the Democratic nominee, and to the nomination and election in 1976 of Jimmy Carter, who became a one-term president. What was a more open, democratic process to the party activists who favored it was seen too often by nonactivist voters as chaotic and the turning over of the party to its more radical elements. In any event, in the scheme of the events of 1968, this party reform was small consolation to many Democrats.

Nor did party reform notably resurrect the confidence in the political process among the young who had worked for McCarthy or Kennedy and continued to deplore the war. For them, the year 1968 and particularly the deaths of King and Kennedy, the failure of the McCarthy campaign and the election of Nixon and Agnew signaled the shattering of their dream that they could bring about change through the system. In good faith, they had turned in hope to it, and what they got was not fulfillment of their dream, but a nightmare. Although the process was opened somewhat by the rules changes, they had come too late for McCarthy and Kennedy, and voting in succeeding years fell among the young, as it did among the population generally.

* * *

One who experienced that nightmare in a manner more personal than most was Joseph P. Kennedy II, eldest son of Robert Kennedy, who later became a member of Congress from Massachusetts. "As a member of the generation caught up in those two great struggles of civil rights and the Vietnam War," he said much later, "it did seem that 1968 brought an end to a certain kind of idealism and hope that the country could heal itself; that we could have people of different backgrounds come together on a mission that meant that regardless of color of skin or views on the threat of communism, we would work together as a people. That sense of the destruction of a mission for America culminated in 1968. There was a real them-against-us mentality; long hairs against short hairs; blacks, browns, yellows against this other America—very much the white middle class who wanted to pull the safety ladder up rather than extend it down to include those people too in the hopes and dreams of America.

"There were signals that came out of the year, in my own family in particular, that were severely brought home. [Afterward], it was just a decade with no direction—nobody to help, not just my family, but a whole group of people to help make sense of all the things the country went through. Nobody to turn to, to let you know everything was going to be okay, that you ought to keep working, you ought to stay with it, that there was a cause and a reason to hope. Without that kind of leader and that kind of hope, it became a very confused, nonproductive and very self-destructive time in both the country's life and in my family's individual lives."

John Lewis, who knew both King and Kennedy well and later became a congressional colleague of Joe Kennedy, shared his assessment. "Something died in America in 1968," he said much later. "It was that sense of hope, that sense of optimism, a sense of what could be. The sense of possibility died in all of us. I'm not so sure as a nation, as a people, those of us who came through that period have been able to get over that, really. It was the worst of times to see two young leaders cut down like they were cut down, and the violence that occurred, especially after the assassination of Dr. King, and what we have come to as a people. It was a dark year for America."

Vice President Gore, addressing the twenty-fifth reunion of his class at Harvard in 1994, observed: "The year before our graduation, our hopes were once again briefly raised by the political insurgency we helped inspire and that we hoped might somehow end our national nightmare [of the war]. Then, months later, those hopes were cruelly crushed by the assassinations of Martin Luther King Jr., renewed race riots, this time nationwide, and then the assassination of Robert Kennedy—and what seemed like the death of any hope that we might find our way back to the entrance of the dark tunnel into which our country had wandered. All of this cast a shadow over each of our personal futures."

To Dick Goodwin, who had labored in both the McCarthy and Kennedy campaigns, "Nineteen sixty-eight at least symbolically marked the end of postwar America. The year itself began in such hope and ferment; the kids in New Hampshire, a very healthy kind of ferment and debate in this country. And when the year ended the major leaders, King and Kennedy, were dead and the past was in the saddle, with the election of Richard Nixon. Everything that people had been fighting against in a sense took over. We were probably, in retrospect, reaching a profound turning point, the end of that whole postwar experience of hope, growth and opportunity that one historian called the golden age of the West, and approaching the seventies with the turmoil of a gradual slowdown of economic and social welfare and justice."

* * *

Central to the 1968 protesters' dashed hopes for a better America, obviously, was the loss of King and Kennedy, because the two men so clearly embodied their vision of racial and class reconciliation through nonviolent means at home, and an end to the use of violent means to achieve peace in Vietnam. As a result, many of those interviewed for this book expressed the conviction that had King and Kennedy lived, the nation would have taken a much less divisive course.

Ted, brother of the slain candidate, observed that "in 1968, civil rights was the unfinished business of the country, with a peaceful movement coming to grips with perhaps the most painful issue that the country was facing." His brother together with King, he said, provided "the outside support for the recognition that this was something the country had to deal with. They were gone after 1968 and a good deal of the outside force that impacted on the political process was gone. Still, they left a powerful motivation inside the political institutions and outside in the landscape that continued to reverberate, and has to an extent to the present time."

Kennedy said that while specific aspects such as affirmative action can be debated, "on the overreaching issue of civil rights [it cannot be denied that] this country became a fairer country, a more just country, a more decent nation and set a more powerful example around the world as a result of their [King's and Kennedy's] work." Had they lived, he said, "their petitions to the American people in terms of bringing them together would have been utilized to energize the center, in coming to grips with the nation's problems."

Both King and Kennedy, he said, "appealed to the nobler side of human nature," but when Nixon and Agnew took over they "appealed to the darker side, and what changed the political dialogue was this change to the darker side." In a time when Americans came to challenge "not only their political institutions but the institutions of the church, of education and of family," Ted Kennedy said, "Nixon was able to take some advantage of that."

Of King particularly, Todd Gitlin observed: "When you realize that King was only thirty-nine when he was killed, he would have been a central figure if he could have survived. He would have been the embodiment of the old dream of assimilation and integration as the ideal. He would have gone through all kinds of difficulties. . . . It was a rough time for universalist ideas, for color-blindness and for political coalitions. There certainly was a wave of cultural separatism, cultural distinctiveness that had to express itself. It was nothing new. It tends to express itself most vigorously when the prospects for biracial or cross-racial politics are poor. There would have been bad years for the kind of politics King represented, but I don't think he would have gone away. He would have been there. And when the Panthers by way of political revolutionism burned out, and when some of the wilder and more extravagant elements of the cultural black movement reached their limits, I think he could have been there. At thirty-nine years old he had a long way to go. . . . He would have been mau-maued from the left, but he would have been a force.

"And Bobby Kennedy—he was the last white politician who could aspire to creating a majoritarian, basically class-based coalition. I think he would have been the consolidator of a new political majority, which would have been a sort of modernization of the welfare state. . . . He was forty-three; he had a lot of races ahead of him. He was magic. . . . The magic he had was not only the edge of tragedy and of self-transcendence; he was so appealing to the American love of the self-made, self-saved, that he had this capacity not to invoke compassion in the sense of noblesse oblige but to invoke solidarity, a sense of the common condition. The chance of him being nominated was remote but not negligible; the chance of him playing a significant part in American politics from then on? A fighting chance."

A few, however, like Wattenberg, suggested the country wouldn't have been much different had Kennedy survived, and Ehrlichman postulated that had Kennedy been the Democratic nominee, his candidacy "would have become a focal point for [even more] strife. I was sitting with Nixon when Bobby announced [his candidacy]," Ehrlichman recalled, "and he [Nixon] predicted that 'this is going to bring violence into the campaign.' The stridency and passion of a Kennedy candidacy at that time would have been very divisive."

Most others interviewed, however, contended that Kennedy, and King, would have been effective vehicles for channeling the civil rights and antiwar protests into more moderate and conciliatory avenues; their leadership thus could have commanded broader public support and diminished the militancy in both movements that invited increased public hostility after their deaths.

Peter Edelman later called King and Kennedy "bridge figures," King with his roots in the traditional civil rights movement and Kennedy with his in the traditional Democratic Party, both with "the reach and breadth to connect to the old and the new" as the focus of their efforts shifted from the old battles for political rights to the new fights for economic justice. (Edelman said King and Kennedy shared mutual respect but not close personal friendship. "Kennedy disapproved of King in some personal ways [relating to the wiretaps of King by Kennedy's Justice Department] and King probably mistrusted Kennedy for some historical reasons [presumably his early conservatism]," Edelman told me.)

Brinkley also said he saw Kennedy particularly as "a real bridge figure of the sort we haven't really had since." While Brinkley said he did not believe he would have been nominated or elected had he lived, "he was the only political figure of that era who could inspire passion both among all groups on the left in the Democratic Party—the minorities, the poor, young people—but also inspire passion among low- and middle-class working people. One of the things lost when he died was not so much the likelihood of getting elected to the presidency but the possibility of finding a way to bridge the deep and probably lasting divisions in the Democratic Party."

If Kennedy, and King, had lived, Lewis said later, "a lot of the problems we have in America today wouldn't be—the violence, the cynicism would have been avoided, maybe eradicated. I could see the two of them together, one white, one black, more than any other figures they had the ability to bring people together across racial, ethnic and religious lines . . . to move toward what Dr. King called 'the beloved community,' a truly interracial democracy." This sort of speculative optimism was widespread among the King and Kennedy faithful, enhanced by their martyrdom.

* * *

Some conservative Republicans, however, also recognized the loss. Jeffrey Bell, a political theorist, wrote in his book *Populism and Elitism: Politics in the Age of Equality* that Kennedy's campaign was an effort "to counteract the mounting liberal demoralization caused by domestic violence and social breakdown. He was willing to acknowledge liberal failures on issues ranging from welfare to education to crime, and to structure new answers in a way that would keep intact the Democratic alliance between blacks and conservative-trending whites. His bridge between these two groups was not Vietnam dovishness but domestic populism. . . . Kennedy's assassination on the night of the California primary put an end to that effort, not just for 1968 but in large part for the decades since. No subsequent liberal leader has made an effective effort to develop a form of left populism, and no liberal leader has come close to uniting blacks and Northern working-class whites. . . . "

Sharing the view that the losses of King and Kennedy were mortal blows to liberalism is Speaker of the House Gingrich. "Looking backwards," he said in an interview, "you could argue that '68 was the year that liberalism lost its two most powerful articulators in King and Kennedy, and that its third potential leader, Humphrey, was drowned in the collapse of the Johnson presidency; he just couldn't escape it as the vice president. . . . You lose the two constructive personalities who had the charisma to command the left, who had the attachment to American idealism to allow themselves to remain responsible, and with their disappearance you have a dramatic shift towards a sort of irresponsible antisystems behavior pattern that ends up ultimately being very nihilistic and self-destructive."

While it is "unequivocally true" that the Democratic Party left itself open to exploitation by Nixon and Agnew by not disavowing its most radical elements, Gingrich said, "with the death of Martin Luther King and Bobby Kennedy there was no liberal left that had the moral authority to do it. Humphrey by being Johnson's vice president had lost the stature and you have nobody to fill that vacuum. Gene McCarthy is simply not a serious person in that sense, and you have to have moral authority to define things. Once those two were killed, there was nobody on the left who could do that."

Whereas Goldwater in 1964, like McCarthy in 1968, was a loser, Gingrich said, Goldwater unlike McCarthy remained "an integrated part of [his party's] system" and helped to keep his supporters in the ranks, to be picked up by Ronald Reagan. "The fascinating thing after '68 is that the left finds nobody who is a serious person inside the system around whom they can rally," Gingrich said. "And you could make an argument that that remains true to today, that in Carter and Clinton they've gotten terribly flawed leaders from their perspective."

In the vacuum in Democratic ranks created by the deaths of King and Kennedy, Gingrich said, "Nixon does in fact, to his considerable credit, weave together a populist conservatism which by '72 draws blue-collar whites back into the political structure and they resubmerge themselves into American normality, which is probably Nixon's greatest domestic contribution."

Circumstances, Gingrich said, prevented what would have been a true ideological test in 1968 between Kennedy and Reagan for the presidency. "Nixon retained control of the Republican machinery and postponed the rise of Reagan for twelve years," he said. In doing so, he went on, "instead of having a clear choice of which way we were going, you had a sort of compromise conservatism [in Nixon] versus a compromise liberalism [in Humphrey], with 13 percent of the country opting out of the choice and going for George Wallace in repudiation of both of them.

"You had a deadlock," Gingrich continued, "which then in the absence of Bobby Kennedy allowed the irresponsible left to seize control of the Democratic Party, something which it has not fully recovered from today. And you allowed an exhausted traditional conservatism to retain control of the Republican Party. . . . I see a period from '68 to '92; Reagan almost breaks through, but the fact is the world that is shaped by '68, the Great Society domestically and a cautious containment policy internationally, basically sustain themselves until the present.

"I think for most Americans, the imagery of the Chicago riots, the sense of things falling apart, led to a demoralization which was then compounded by Kent State and by Watergate. And in a real sense we have not regained [our bearings]. . . . My guess is if you went back to '67, you'd find a kind of general broad optimism which disappeared sometime during the crucible of '68 and from which we have not to this day fully recovered, although Reagan almost broke through, almost reestablished an optimistic American model."

* * *

Most of those interviewed also speculated that King would have blunted the excesses of the black power movement and probably would have followed the same basic course traveled in succeeding years by Jesse Jackson, but with greater acceptance among whites, for stylistic reasons. At the same time, most of those interviewed were convinced that Kennedy, if nominated and elected, somehow would have soon extricated the United States from Vietnam. "He would have done something about the war immediately upon being elected," Edelman said. "There would have been a sense that the protest had provided something in the way of a constructive outcome within a reasonable period of time. The protest wouldn't have unraveled and turned violent the way it did."

That was what the Kennedyites hoped would have happened had their man been elected to the presidency in 1968. There was no clear consensus among them, however, on whether he actually would have become president had he not been gunned down in Los Angeles. Most of his key campaign strategists and aides interviewed for this book were uncertain whether Kennedy would have been nominated. But most thought that had he been, he could have beaten Nixon.

Schlesinger for one contended later that Kennedy would have taken the Democratic nomination and gone on to defeat Nixon. The growing disenchantment of the McCarthy youth with McCarthy, he said, "would have made it very easy for them to go with Bobby," especially with prominent McCarthy supporters like Lowenstein and Galbraith "prepared to shift to Kennedy." And in the general election, he said, much of the vote that went for Wallace would have gone to Kennedy, enough to beat Nixon.

Other activist Democrats of the time, like Rick Stearns, who later made a detailed study of the possibility for a graduate thesis, concluded however that Kennedy never could have received the nomination because "Johnson controlled 70 to 75 percent of the delegates [for Humphrey]. . . . There was no way," he said, "any kind of stampede would have pushed the nomination to anybody Johnson didn't want."

Buchanan also contended later that the cards would have been stacked against Kennedy in a race against Nixon because of LBJ's bitterness toward him. "Humphrey would [still] have been the strongest Democrat," the former Nixon aide said. "Connally and LBJ would have given Texas to us [had Kennedy been the candidate]."

Historian Garry Wills, who covered the 1968 presidential campaign as a young magazine writer, is another who thought Kennedy never would have been elected. "His own realism would have made him cast his lot with Mayor Daley," he said much later, "and that would have angered the kids so much that his whole movement would have fallen apart. . . . Bobby couldn't have gotten the South, and the Democrats haven't been about to win without it." Talk of a Robert Kennedy presidency had he lived, Wills said, "is all myth, all part of the Kennedy nostalgia."

McCarthy had his own view of what might have been had Kennedy survived. "It would have been some convention," he said. "Lyndon might even have supported me. I don't know what would have happened, but if Kennedy had gone to work in the nonprimary states, where he had more strength than I did, and had picked up other primaries, he'd have been in a very strong position, with a compromise position on the war, to ask for my support. We would have had a hard time saying no under those conditions. If he'd done what we said [divided up the primaries with McCarthy against LBJ], I could have done it [supported him]."

McCarthy observed that if Kennedy had taken this course, "I assume he wouldn't have done the kind of campaign against me that he'd done. If he wanted to run against Lyndon's civil rights record and these other things, why, that was all right. I would have had no real grounds, except a general suspicion of him I guess, if he had done that. After he saw the strength we had, he would have been in a good position to have done that." Then, McCarthy suggested, Kennedy could have built his own delegate strength and have come to him and his people for their support at the convention. "Maybe the McCarthy people would have gone to him anyway, some of them, whether I wanted them to or not," he said. Either he or Kennedy could have beaten Nixon, McCarthy said.

Gans for one dismissed the notion of McCarthy yielding support to Kennedy at the convention. "My personal belief is that Kennedy would not have won the election, but he might have gotten the nomination, although McCarthy would have done anything to prevent it," he said. "He felt betrayed by Kennedy."

One prominent Democrat who said he believed Kennedy would have been nominated and elected was Senator Bob Kerrey of Nebraska, the decorated Vietnam veteran who became one of the war's most outspoken critics. When I asked him on what he based his belief, he smiled and replied: "Hope." But so emphatically were Kennedy and King seen as leaders with the unique ability to harness and constructively channel the dominant political and emotional forces of 1968 that Kerrey's answer spoke for millions of other

Americans who lived through, and were psychologically wounded by, the events of that year.

Regarding civil rights, Hayden said, "Martin Luther King's death seemed to me to completely undermine what remained of the possibility of a broad-based, class-based, integrationist civil rights effort that could have reformed the Democratic Party, that could have focused on reforming the country. In his absence, in that vacuum, black nationalism and separatism spread.

"Robert Kennedy's campaign could have rescued us from the cliff," Hayden went on. "He had a good chance to defeat the Humphrey-Johnson forces at the convention. If he had been at the convention, there would have been a larger protest rally outside, but out of deference to his possibilities I don't think it would have been revolutionary or confrontational. If he had won the nomination, I think he would have had a better chance to beat Nixon after the disaster of that convention.

"If Bobby Kennedy had been president, in my judgment knowing him, he would have been very unlikely to continue the war for the next four or five years, which led to this deep, almost violent pathological confrontation within families, between peace protesters, Cold War elements, civil strife and the levels of violence that were breaking out. There would have been no Nixon presidency; there would have been no Watergate."

Dick Goodwin said Kennedy's nomination and election were "doubtful," and even had he become president "I don't know whether any leadership could have restored the hope and ebullience of the sixties. But I think Bobby would have made a difference," he said. "If you don't believe that, you can't believe that politics matters at all. He surely would have tried like hell. I remember saying to him, 'You'll either be a great president or a disaster.'"

One result of a Kennedy election about which Schlesinger was certain was that he would have extricated the country from Vietnam quickly. "He hated the war," he said later. "He was determined to end it, and 30,000 Americans now dead would be alive." (That many already had died in Vietnam, however, by the time he would have taken office.)

* * *

If Kennedy had not been nominated and elected, it seems probable, had Kennedy lived, that with Humphrey's loss and Nixon's victory he would have come out of 1968 as the clear leader of the Democratic Party. And in that capacity he doubtless would have continued to pressure Nixon to get out of the war and to take steps to advance economic justice for minority Americans. As such, he would have been well positioned to capture the Democratic presidential nomination in 1972.

"He would have been a powerful figure to break Nixon," Dutton said, "to channel the forces that were stirring on the left to challenge him in '72. You would still have had the radicals, but they would not have had the space and attention that the vacuum [of Kennedy's absence] created." Kennedy and King together, Dutton said, "would have been able to act as safety valves. With cities burning, you would have had somebody saying, 'Stop that!' What we lacked when King and Kennedy went," Dutton said, "was leadership with the capacity to direct, moderate and more successfully institutionalize what the new forces stood for; 1968 was a great opportunity to avoid the divisions, the mediocrity, the basically third-rate politics we've had since then.

"How often does a big society like America get to a high energy level to attack its real problems?" Dutton asked. "The important dimension of both King and Kennedy was they were always trying to build a broader political base. King was trying to involve whites as well as blacks in civil rights; Bob in his kind of mainstream politics wanted to reach out to kids, but he was also prepared to tell the docile white middle class, 'You've got to get off your ass, you've got to be involved, you've got to stand for something.'"

Dutton acknowledged at the same time that Kennedy "was a high idealist but a hard-nosed pragmatist, somewhat of a polarizing figure and no one should blink at that." For this latter reason, Wattenberg argued later, Kennedy might have been the Democratic presidential nominee in 1968, but he would not have beaten Nixon.

"He was way out of the loop of mainstream political ideology," said Wattenberg, who was a strategist for Senator Henry M. "Scoop" Jackson of Washington in 1972 on the party's right. Wattenberg recalled "all the stories about the frenzy [around Kennedy], the jumpers and the screamers and the grabbing of his cuff links, and everybody writing as if that stuff were this wonderful, incredible sensation. But a whole lot of people were sitting back watching it on television and saying, 'Whoa, hold on there. These are not the people we want running the country.' There was something a little leftist, crazed, trendy about both the Kennedy and McCarthy things."

This view, however, did not deter the more optimistic opinions of the supporters of Kennedy, and of King, on what might have been. Edelman, later counsel in the Department of Health and Human Services under Clinton, mused that while he thought Kennedy would have been elected, "even if he was not president, he stood for a new approach to problems in the country that we then lost, though recaptured to some extent in Bill Clinton's New Democrat thinking. Kennedy did it a lot earlier in a way that reflected a real inventive understanding of the importance of strengthening communities and neighborhoods, but with the appropriate involvement of the federal government."

Instead of taking this approach, Edelman said, the Democratic Party "got off track. Democratic politics went backward in a sort of Hubert Humphrey way toward the federal program mentality, and then a George McGovern way in the entitlement mentality. Both ways moved away from a community development, jobs emphasis."

In what happened in America's inner cities after Kennedy's death, Edelman said, was his loss particularly felt. Chances for revitalization on the scale of the Bedford-Stuyvesant project in New York that was a great Kennedy interest "all stopped with the election of Nixon. Nixon was totally uninterested in all that except in a sort of cosmetic way," Edelman said.

"What happened is, you get a kind of crime counterpart of the movement violence. . . . What you get instead is random street crime. You get kids who instead of being engaged in politicized violence, what started with a revolution of rising expectations [in the inner-city riots in places like Watts, Newark and Detroit], the political element just disappears and they become criminals. . . . The politics is long gone and these kids don't even understand that when they're killing each other that it has some connection to the fact somebody didn't do anything to deal with the problems of that neighborhood almost thirty years ago."

Had Kennedy lived and even if he had not been elected in 1968, Edelman obviously was suggesting, thereafter he would have addressed the revolution of rising expectations with inner-city solutions that might have curbed the violence. Again, here was more speculative optimism culled from the direction in which Kennedy seemed to be heading at the time of his death.

* * *

The violence and rebellion of 1968 was hardly confined to the United States. It flared in Europe and Mexico, among blacks, whites and Mexican-Americans, Hayden noted, "and in Latin America the priests and nuns had invented liberation theology as a way to begin to stand on the side of the poor instead of the oligarchies in those countries. A huge awakening had been occurring for a number of years, and now the violent counterreaction, the grim reaper of the status quo had cut down all of these leaders. What happened that year was very much like, in the biblical sense, the forces of light and darkness clashing and creating chaos."

For all that, the events of 1968, and the protest against authority that marked them, did produce some results. A president conducting a war was forced to withdraw from a bid for a second term. And although the war continued, official talk of winning it waned to the point that the central debating point was not winning but getting out—when, how and on what terms. And eventually the United States did get out, with the voices that were raised against the war before, during and after 1968, assailing officialdom until it happened.

John Sears, the Nixon and later Reagan campaign strategist, recalled that Nixon "stopped talking about winning the war and starting talking about ending it on grounds that were honorable. In the earlier sixties, we'd talked about winning it; we were going to win it next week, six months from now, or if we put another 500,000 troops in, we'd win it. That all stopped. When Nixon came in, he wanted to get the war over. His tactics may have been debatable—bombing Haiphong harbor, bombing Laos and all that, but he was trying to end the war. When he got in, he began to pull ground troops out to stop the [American] casualties. The protests had a lot to do with that."

"By 1970," Kerrey noted, "the argument was settled. It was just a question of time. You could protest Cambodia, this act or that. But it was inevitable that American forces were going to be gone from Vietnam, because of the way the protest brought the war home. It was like we were tearing each other apart in anger and frustration. It didn't seem to have any purpose any longer. The country was devouring itself over the war. We were fragging each other, blacks and whites were at each other's throats in '71 and '72.

"The effort had disintegrated into a civil war between Americans, and the same thing was going on on the nonmilitary side, the civilian side. It wasn't just the war," Kerrey said, "it was the way the war ended, the way we got out. There was no honor permitted to those who went and no relief permitted to those who were involved in trying to figure out what we should do.

"I was extremely hard on Nixon. I hated Nixon. I choose the word carefully. He was the only human being at the time I hated." But after reading the history of the war from 1968 through 1972, Kerrey said, "I forgave Nixon. I saw this was a guy trying to figure things out. He had a Cold War mind-set, believed in it, instituted I think a very bad policy of Vietnamization and gradual de-escalation. But for me to hate him was wrong. It didn't change his life any and it didn't change mine, to hate him. But I don't think that was unusual in the seventies, for people to hate one another."

Dick Goodwin, who said he believed that if Johnson had run and been reelected "he would have invaded North Vietnam," also agreed that the protest of 1968 turned the issue from winning the war to getting out. "Some of the steam went out because the prospect of an ever-widening war disappeared," he said later. "When Nixon came in, he couldn't do that [invade the North] at that stage in history. But on the other hand it was impossible to bring it to an end. So the war lost some of its mass support."

Riesman argued that Americans were not so much against the war as that "people thought it should have been fought better," and when it was clear finally that it couldn't be won, it was best to get out. And the American failure for the first time to win a war, Gans contended, "totally changed the character of our politics. It circumscribed what we could do nationally and internationally. People weren't going to be interested in similar adventures. There were limits to our power and resources."

* * *

The Democratic Party, too, sustained wounds in 1968 from which it has not yet recovered. On the most obvious level, the year marked the end of Johnson's Great Society and began the gradual assault on liberalism that had its fruition in the eras of Reagan, George Bush and Gingrich. "We will never know if the Great Society would have worked," Gans said. "A lot of things that Johnson did were good, if he hadn't gotten bogged down in Vietnam."

Doris Kearns Goodwin recalled later how Johnson in retirement would compare his Great Society to "this beautiful, voluptuous woman who was made fatter by laws he had put on the books and everybody would love so much, they would remember him even more than they did FDR. He had this image in his mind that the Great Society programs under Nixon were being cut, little by little, and that the woman was becoming skinnier and skinnier; she was going to be thrown in a closet because nobody would want to look at her because she'd become so old and wrinkled. And that when she died, he too [Johnson] would die."

After 1968, Dick Goodwin said, the Democratic Party "made the mistake of getting into interest-group politics, whether it was gays or minorities, instead of developing ideas and a coherent purpose and ideology that went beyond civil rights. While the party continued to hold control of Congress [after 1968]," he said, "the last great issues of the Democratic Party were the issues of '68. Since then, the Democratic Party has been brain-dead. Meanwhile, the right wing and conservative groups were developing a coherent purpose and ideology. They won the battle for words, and eventually for office."

In another basic way, the Democratic Party may have severely wounded itself, not simply for the political outcome of 1968 but ever since. The images of radicalism that flashed so conspicuously across the nation's television screens in the riots following King's assassination, at the Chicago convention and in the antiwar demonstrations all tarnished the party's reputation on Main Street America.

"The angry white male syndrome harks back to that," Representative Barney Frank of Massachusetts, a liberal Democrat, said long afterward. "The whole notion that violence and rudeness was the way to go," he said, "just angered the majority. That was the point at which the Democrats began to lose their fundamental identification with working-class white people. Cops used to vote Democratic, and then they heard kids saying, 'You're a motherfucker and your wife's a whore,' and they saw the liberals defending their right to say those things. . . . We got beyond political disagreement to a cultural war. These were not people saying your policies were wrong. These were people saying you're rotten, terrible people, you're hateful, you're pigs and racists, and we're going to destroy you. And while we were prepared to say this policy or that policy was wrong, we weren't prepared to think of ourselves as racist butchers."

At the same time, Frank said of his fellow liberal Democrats, "we got caught in the middle, because we were their defenders. That did more to break the bond that had been there [with working whites] since Roosevelt and Truman. It was such a terrible period for us because it traumatized us. Too many Democrats at that point became morally intimidated by the [far] left. For a long time afterward, fear of a left walkout became a real inhibition. Partly it was because many liberals felt that the left was right about some issues. Blacks had been treated horribly in the cities. Yes, the Vietnam War was a big mistake, as it evolved. And it's very hard sometimes to separate out substantive agreement with people from disagreement with their tactics and rhetoric. But we were more tolerant of excess than we should have been."

Before long, Frank said, "Democrats wouldn't say criminals were bad people who should be locked up, that anybody who hit somebody else on the head was a rotten person. We had to say work was better than welfare, that the United States was better than Russia. But from the beginning of the late sixties until fairly recently, sensible liberal Democrats were afraid if they said any of these perfectly noncontroversial things by any rational standard, they would be yelled at by the left." Wattenberg, too, observed of the plight of liberal Democrats at that time: "By not disagreeing, they were perceived to have agreed with all of that raucous stuff. It was the all-American guilt trip. They didn't say, 'This is alien to our tradition.'"

*   *   *

Gitlin strenuously disagreed that the mistake of the Democratic left was in a failure to disavow the most extreme elements in the party or in the antiwar and civil rights movements. "What would it have gained the left of the Democratic Party to have denounced more strenuously the Yippies, or Leary or SDS?" he asked. "I don't know who would have been impressed."

Nearly thirty years later, Gitlin asked: "What does it avail the right to try to dissociate itself from its crazies? Given smart leadership on the other side [the Democrats], it might not work, just as Nixon was very shrewd in playing this [extremism] in '68. . . . Once a dynamic of the sort you have in '68 gets rolling, then the room to maneuver on the part of liberals is relatively small. They're in a precarious position. If they renounce whatever crazies they choose, who is that supposed to impress? In a polarized dynamic, the part of the electorate that is impressed is probably not decisive. This theme that the country is going to the dogs and civilization is breaking down [goes back to] Goldwater. . . . What was necessary for left liberals to do was to win. They couldn't win. So they didn't have the credit to isolate the crazies."

If the liberals are to be faulted, Gitlin said, including himself in the indictment, it was in their failure to support Humphrey as the alternative to Nixon. But, he remembered, "it was psychologically almost unthinkable" at his age, which was twenty-five. "I knew almost no one who voted for Humphrey, anybody I heard of or had any respect for," he recalled.

"The war was the primary catastrophe," he said, agreeing with Hayden. "The liberals had forfeited a good deal of their capacity to lead the more alienated forces in the society by stupidly failing to begin to understand the Vietnam War. That was even more important than their mistakes at the convention, which arguably were plausible.

"On the war, '68 was very late to try to recoup those losses. Bobby Kennedy could have done it with his kind of magic. . . . The odds were against the stabilization of some sort of left-of-center majority, but the odds did not foreclose it. It would have taken a lot of luck to squeak out of the sixties with some remnant of an ecumenical Democratic Party with a strong left. It probably would have taken Bobby Kennedy as a candidate, it probably would have taken considerable wisdom from both the [radical] left wing of the party and the liberals essentially to recognize they needed [each other]."

Still, he said, "if Humphrey was the nominee, what it would have taken to win was for Humphrey to get off Lyndon Johnson's lap." The Democrats, after all, were still in power, Gitlin noted, and in control of the House, which would have decided the election in Humphrey's favor if the result had been only a bit closer and Nixon had been denied an electoral majority.

Even as the Democratic left was failing to hold its old coalition together, Gitlin noted, the Republican right and Nixon were stealing away elements of it. Their racial strategy appealed to Southern conservatives, and the theme of law and order captured Northern blue-collar whites alienated by the excesses of the radicals of the left, and by the growing economic threat from blacks. In this sense, he said, "part of the untold story of the sixties is the right."

Bennett observed: "In 1968, the Democratic Party underwent a kind of cultural brain transplant [as part of] the radicalization of the American left. . . . The word 'traditional' became synonomous with 'wrong.' All authority was wrong. The bumper stickers said QUESTION AUTHORITY. . . . The Democratic Party for twenty years has been carrying the baggage of [being described as] lightheaded, soft, radical. The Democratic Party became the Democratic Party with a fringe left."

The sexual revolution, the drug culture, feminism all were part of the phenomenon, he said. "Feminism—not women's rights—did more harm than good. Women were liberated from the kitchen to victimhood in the bedroom." Bennett cited as evidence the growth in teenage pregnancy, single motherhood, attacks on the concept of family and open marriages.

In the realm of civil rights, Rick Stearns said later, black leaders after Kings death "used the guilt of liberal whites as a lever. They were intimidated by the supposition they were not pure enough, and it was not simply a rhetorical problem, it was substantive. . . . Liberalism tried to get more context to its vision of racial justice. They tried to engineer absolute equality," Stearns said, leading to remedies like school busing and affirmative action that bred racial discord rather than harmony.

In the antiwar protest, Galbraith for one dismissed extremist groups like SDS and the Weathermen as being "very much at the margin." But Nixon and Agnew were not hesitant to exploit the general public repulsion toward the excesses of the Democratic radicals to portray them not as extreme elements of the party, but as its soul. "It played into Nixon's paranoia that the country was under siege, that the White House was under siege," Hayden said, "and therefore they had to use any means necessary."

From the siege mentality came more polarizing attacks on "radical liberals" by Agnew, the burglary of the office of Daniel Ellsberg's psychiatrist after the leaking of the Pentagon Papers, and, ultimately, the attempted break-in of the Democratic National Committee headquarters at the Watergate complex.

None of these episodes prevented the reelection of Nixon, but in time his zeal to cement in the public mind the negative image of the Democratic Party conveyed by the turmoil of 1968 contributed greatly to his undoing. The Watergate cover-up was the supreme manifestation of Nixon's siege mentality, and in the end it drove him from the White House in disgrace. At the same time, it extended public distrust to the Republican Party as well as to the Democratic, further undermining voter confidence in all politics and government.

* * *

Nixon's successor, Gerald R. Ford Jr., quickly proclaimed that "our long national nightmare is over" but then gave the American people a reprise of it in his pardon of his predecessor. Whatever was left of public respect for authority sustained yet another blow. Six years after the deaths of Martin Luther King and Robert Kennedy, the country seemed not yet to have regained its bearings. Nearly three decades later, many Americans, and particularly the disciples of the two men who perished in 1968, still look back at that year as the time something went out of the nation's optimism and self-confidence, and its promise.

"A whole generation of young people grew up believing anybody who is involved in government is crooked or up to no good," Edelman said. And Galbraith observed: "The year changed the power of the United States on the world scene. That it was no longer a reliable source of military intervention was deeply ingrained in political thought." Dick Goodwin argued that 1968 was more a turning point for the nation than 1963 with John Kennedy's death because "in 1968 there was hope of a return to what JFK represented and was still alive, and after '68 it was gone."

After 1968, Joe Kennedy said, "the sense of hopefulness became a sense of hopelessness, and people became more and more radicalized. A lot of people in 1968 gave up, they just plain gave up. They went into their own little worlds and some of them have never really come out of it. Others went into business or became doctors or lawyers, but the sense of hopefulness that President Kennedy, Martin Luther King, my dad and other leaders too brought about, of joining the Peace Corps, being involved in giving something back to your country, that all just ended. Then there was all this politics of making money and disdain for working-class people, a callousness toward vulnerable people that took over the mood of America, that was very discouraging."

Civil rights historian Taylor Branch, who as a college student for McCarthy encountered Kennedy in the Indianapolis airport the night of his Indiana primary victory, also cited the disappearance of common civility in politics and social contact in the wake of 1968. He traced the beginnings to 1964, with the campaign that year of George Wallace in Northern states, not preaching segregation but rather a contempt for a federal government that "can't solve every problem." It was a message Wallace continued in 1968 and in time was adopted by the Republicans as a "very blunted states' rights message," he said. It amounted to running "a velvet race campaign," he said, because blacks were most prominently seen as the beneficiaries of federal programs, and served to pit whites against blacks.

Branch said he was dismayed at the "almost overnight" disappearance after 1968 of the American "ethos to hold out hope for and contact with one's enemies," manifested not only between the races but between factions of liberals against the war and in the civil rights movement "over who was purer. It was just craziness." Gone, he said, was "the sense of emphasizing what we had in common, an appeal to the conscience of one's opponents. Everybody was eating each other alive." Kennedy's somber speech to the shocked crowd in Indianapolis on the night of King's death, Branch said, was one of the last expositions of that sort. "You didn't hear that kind of speech in Chicago," he lamented.

John Lewis said: "The election of 1968 set in motion all the wrong things. So many well-meaning people, after Chicago, dropped out. People literally gave up and many of these people have not returned. Individuals I knew who came to the movement were like soldiers in a crusade. People came out with scars, not just physical scars, and they have not recovered from the scars of '68. We lost some good minds, good organizers who just said they didn't want to hope again, because of the loss of Martin Luther King Jr. and Robert Kennedy. Maybe those who lived through that period are afraid now to place their hopes, their longings for a better future, in mortal men. They don't want to be let down again. That is what 1968 did to us."

Hayden wrote later that 1968, "the watershed year for a generation . . . started with legendary events, then raised hopes, only to end by immersing innocence in tragedy. . . . Rarely if ever in American history has a generation begun with higher ideals and experienced greater trauma than those who lived fully the short time from 1960 to 1968. Our world was going to be transformed for the good, we let ourselves believe not once but twice, only to learn that violence can slay not only individuals, but dreams."

Much of what is said by those who fought in 1968 against racial injustice and the war in Vietnam is heavily coated with nostalgia and romanticism. To them, 1968 was truly the year the dream died, dashing hopes for a speedier reconciliation of all Americans at home and peace at last abroad. Gitlin commented later however, referring to the Kent State shootings, that "a lot of people say this is where the innocence died. Americans love to re-create innocence. They're always looking for some moment when it died. But it would be hard to kill. After hundreds of years of bloody history, people still think that the day before yesterday we were innocent. . . . But it's certainly true a lot of people felt that way about '68. . . .

"What all these moments concerned were the progressive breakdown in the belief of patching together the salvation or the resurrection or the improving of the world. . . . It's not that these breakdowns of innocence are terminal. . . . The crucial thing is that in each of these moments, a significant number of people who believe in the possibility of rational, cogent, deliberate action to improve the world diminishes. We're living in a backwash. . . . So that now nobody believes in a goddamned thing." Even in the absence of

assassinations, he noted, "a lot of people feel the same way. . . . It's not because of assassinations. It's because of the failure of government to deliver."
But '68, he concluded, was certainly "a year when believers felt like [they
wished they were] falling into a hole."

Many others who believed that civil rights by 1968 had achieved all that
was legitimate or necessary and deplored the antiwar demonstrations in the
nation's streets will look back on the year with entirely different sentiments.
They saw in the election of Richard Nixon an end to the overreaching of
Democratic liberalism as manifested finally in Lyndon Johnson's Great
Society, and a reaffirmation of America's role as a steadfast foe of communism
in Vietnam and around the world. To many of them, 1968 marked a turning
toward greater self-interest, as individuals and as a nation, demanding stricter
standards of behavior and performance from all those, at home and abroad,
vying for the help of the world's most bountiful government.

From either perspective, however, 1968 was a political and societal maelstrom of unprecedented intensity. Nearly three decades later, the nation remains divided, though no longer so sharply on the issue of America's role in
world affairs. The threat of communist ideology and power that dictated U.S.
foreign policy in 1968 is in ashes, and the country struggles chiefly to find its
proper role in the post–Cold War world.

Today's divisions are chiefly over issues among Americans on those matters
of economic equity and justice with which Martin Luther King and Robert
Kennedy were beginning to grapple in 1968. Race continues to be central to
the discussion and debate, on issues ranging from affirmative action to welfare dependency, as the role of the federal government is under severe examination in meeting the needs of the American people.

The liberalism that had its zenith in the Great Society, and at the same
time sparked much of the struggle for civil rights and against the Vietnam
War in 1968, is a severely retrenched and embattled political ideology. The
conservatism that abhorred the domestic handiwork of Lyndon Johnson but
generally supported his pursuit of the war in Southeast Asia has been in the
ascendancy since then.

So much of what happened in 1968 colors the politics of today. What
might have happened, meanwhile, remains the stuff of tantalizing speculation. Consider:

• What if Robert Kennedy in 1967 had agreed to challenge Johnson for
the Democratic presidential nomination? Gene McCarthy almost certainly
would not have entered the race and Kennedy would have had the antiwar
sentiment solidly behind his candidacy. Observing how close McCarthy came
to beating Johnson in the New Hampshire primary, it is reasonable to spec-

ulate that Kennedy would have defeated LBJ outright there and gone on to win the Democratic nomination.

• What if Kennedy had endorsed McCarthy at the outset rather than running against him? The antiwar sentiment in that event would have been unified behind McCarthy and the chances were strong that he too would have defeated Johnson outright in New Hampshire. Had he failed to win the nomination, he might well have thrown his support to Kennedy for the nomination in Chicago, as he himself acknowledged later.

• What if Kennedy had lived to run against Nixon? He almost certainly would have laid claim to at least as much Democratic support as eventually went to Humphrey, and probably enough of the Northern blue-collar Wallace vote to defeat the Republican nominee. There was every indication from his actions and words before and during the 1968 campaign that as president he would have moved with dispatch to achieve peace negotiations with North Vietnam and extricate the United States from the war.

• What if Martin Luther King had lived? Although his efforts to move the civil rights protest into the quest for economic justice for blacks were enduring great difficulties at the time of his death, he would have been a still-young and vigorous bulwark against black power, separatism and abandonment of nonviolence as the centerpiece of the movement. King and Kennedy together as strong nonviolent voices for civil rights and against the war might well have succeeded in stitching together a winning black and blue-collar coalition that would at least have postponed the advent of the new conservatism in the country.

• What if McCarthy had endorsed and campaigned early and energetically for Hubert Humphrey as the Democratic nominee? Given the closeness of the 1968 election, and abandonment of the Humphrey candidacy by many liberal antiwar Democrats, such visible support from McCarthy might well have enabled Humphrey to beat Nixon—and give aspects of the Great Society at least a four-year lease on life. And with no President Nixon, there would have been no Watergate and its destructive legacy to public confidence in all government.

• Finally, what if Humphrey had made public in the final days of the campaign the information Johnson offered to him from FBI and other government cable intercepts and wiretaps regarding the Chennault affair? Provable or not, the allegations could well have turned enough votes from Nixon to Humphrey, or energized enough disgruntled liberal Democrats to cast ballots for Humphrey, to put the Minnesotan in the White House.

Engaging in might-have-beens, however, no matter how tantalizing, is a futile exercise. The reality was that the events of 1968 delivered a death blow to the old Democratic coalition that had produced and sustained the New Deal, Fair Deal, New Frontier and Great Society, and left a new conservatism a-borning in its place.

Since then, it is beyond dispute that the nation has experienced a major transformation. It has gone from being a country in which Americans looked to their government to confront and solve the social ills facing it, to one in which Americans put little faith or trust in their government to do either.

The transformation has been the result not of the events of any single year alone. But for millions who participated with deep commitment in the stormy events of 1968, and for other millions who observed the same events in heartbreak, dismay, disbelief and revulsion, the year was a seismic explosion. Its aftershocks are still felt, not only in the country at large but particularly in the lives of these millions, and in their memories of a year that rocked a bitterly divided nation to its core—and set it on a new course that keeps it divided still.

NOTES

Most quotations not otherwise attributed in the notes below are from the author's personal reporting or from the following sources: Associated Press, United Press International, the *Washington Post*, the *New York Times*, the *Washington Star, Time, Newsweek* and *Facts on File.*

Introduction

ix "We'll never laugh again." Arthur M. Schlesinger Jr., *A Thousand Days: John F. Kennedy in the White House*, p. 1,028.

CHAPTER 1: *Ring Out the Old, Ring in the New*

3 "Johnson unlike Kennedy . . ." Interview with Tom Hayden, San Francisco, 1994.

3 "If in good conscience . . ." Interview with Marcus Raskin, Washington, 1994.

4 "One impulse . . ." Todd Gitlin, *The Sixties: Years of Hope, Days of Rage*, p. 285.

5 "The effect of these disclosures . . ." Thomas Powers, *The War at Home.*

6 "I feel as though . . ." Interview with Mark Satin, Toronto, 1967.

10 "I'm against the war . . ." Author interview, Kentucky, 1967.

10 "I've always been a Democrat . . ." Interview with R. C. Smith, Kentucky, 1967.

12 "It's a device, of course . . ." Interview with Richard M. Nixon, New York, 1966.

12 "In order to make a decision . . ." Ibid.

13 "When Johnson returned . . ." Joseph Califano, *The Triumph and Tragedy of Lyndon Johnson*, p. 291.

16 "I wouldn't be human . . ." Interview with Nelson A. Rockefeller, aboard S.S. *Independence*, 1967.

16 "I still say if he's drafted . . ." Interview with Spiro T. Agnew, aboard S.S. *Independence*, 1967.

20 "I believe strongly . . ." Lyndon B. Johnson, *The Vantage Point,* p. 576.

21 "He couldn't look . . ." Interview with Fred Dutton, Washington, 1968.

23 Kearns, it so happened . . . Interview with Doris Kearns Goodwin, Concord, Mass., 1995.

24 "all the worst little blandnesses . . ." Allard K. Lowenstein, McCarthy Historical Project Archive, Georgetown University, Washington, D.C.

24 "the idea of dumping Johnson . . ." Interview with Curtis Gans, Washington, 1995.

24 "My position was always . . ." Lowenstein, McCarthy Archive, Georgetown.

25 "He took it as seriously . . ." Interview with Lowenstein, Washington, 1968.

26 "We are not out to dump Johnson . . ." Interview with Eugene Daniell, Franklin, N.H., 1967.

26 "The notion that the students . . ." Lowenstein, McCarthy Archive, Georgetown.

26 "If you can get him . . ." Interview with Lowenstein, Washington, 1968.

27 "I think Bobby should do it." Interview with Lowenstein, Washington, 1968.

28 "The way he said he would do it . . ." Lowenstein, McCarthy Archive, Georgetown.

28 "Mary, I know that somebody . . ." Abigail McCarthy, *Private Faces/Public Places*, p. 294.

30 "This is like a small boy . . ." Interview with Ronald Reagan, aboard SS *Independence*, 1967.

33 "I was just about ready . . ." David Hoeh, McCarthy Archive, Georgetown.

33 "When I talked to him . . ." Don Peterson, McCarthy Archive, Georgetown.

34 "Arthur, when was the last time . . ." Arthur Schlesinger, *Robert Kennedy and His Times*, p. 825.

34 "Your position has worsened . . ." Richard Goodwin, *Remembering America*, p. 478.

35 "continuing on our present course . . ." Robert S. McNamara, *In Retrospect*, p. 307.

36 "retard the possibility . . ." Johnson, *The Vantage Point*, p. 375.

36 "I've been watching you . . ." Walter Isaacson and Evan Thomas, *The Wise Men*, p. 680.

36 "the Nicodemas Society." Interview with Eugene J. McCarthy, Washington, 1995.

36 "would be regarded . . ." Interview by Albert Eisele with George Ball.

37 "When he came out . . ." Hoeh, McCarthy Archive, Georgetown.

38 "Johnson was abusing the Senate." Interview with Eugene McCarthy, Washington, 1995.

39 "as soon as I had word . . ." Lowenstein, McCarthy Archive, Georgetown.

40 "This was a godsend . . ." Peterson, McCarthy Archive, Georgetown.

41 "It was very cold . . ." Lowenstein, McCarthy Archive, Georgetown.

42 "He argued that maybe . . ." Interview with Dutton, Washington, 1968.

42 "This looks like a government . . ." Hoeh, McCarthy Archive, Georgetown.

43 "There we were, all stoned . . ." Report of the National Commission on the Causes and Prevention of Violence, 1968.

CHAPTER 2: *January: The Volcano Rumbles*

48 "the kind of people . . ." Joseph Alsop in the *Washington Post*, Jan. 3, 1968.

50 "Dave, I've decided . . ." Hoeh, McCarthy Archive, Georgetown.

51 "All across the national . . ." William S. White the *Washington Post*, Jan. 10, 1968

53 He confided how . . . Interview with George C. Wallace, Montgomery, 1968.

60 "as old guard . . ." Tom Hayden, *Reunion: A Memoir*, p. 259.

61 "these were the kids . . ." Jeremy Larner, *Nobody Knows: Reflections on the McCarthy Campaign of 1968*, p. 37.

63 "The McCarthy campaign was . . ." David Mixner, McCarthy Archive, Georgetown.

64 "No, I can't conceive . . ." Notes of Bruce Biossat of Scripps-Howard, 1968.

CHAPTER 3: *February: Ominous Signs*

72 "We are already engulfed . . ." Joseph Alsop in the *Washington Post*, Feb. 1, 1968.

72 "As I look back now . . ." Johnson, *The Vantage Point*, p. 383.

76 "If any of you are around . . ." David L. Lewis, *King: A Critical Biography*, p. 377.

77 In Pasadena . . . Dan E. Moldea, *The Killing of Robert F. Kennedy*, p. 80.

78 "If he's not going to do anything . . ." Author interview, Washington, 1968.

78 "If you want to run . . ." Interview with Kenneth O'Donnell, Washington, 1968.

79 "As long as you're not running . . ." Interview with Richard Goodwin, Washington, 1968.

79 He "didn't understand . . ." Lowenstein, McCarthy Archive, Georgetown.

80 "Tet had made the war . . ." Isaacson and Thomas, *The Wise Men*, pp. 686–87.

80 "Despite these optimistic reports . . ." Clark Clifford, *Counsel to the President*, p. 485.

81 "They had been raised . . ." Gitlin, *The Sixties*, p. 295.

82 "was not only an ideal . . ." Richard Goodwin, *Remembering America*, p. 492.

83 "the ones who have a stake . . ." Hoeh, McCarthy Archive, Georgetown.

CHAPTER 4: *March: Eruption in New Hampshire*

90 "That was a mistake." Patrick J. Buchanan, in interview for C-SPAN series, *1968: The Year and the Legacy*.

91 The idea for this march . . . Interview with Peter Edelman, Washington, 1995.

94 "They would tend to say . . ." Mixner, McCarthy Archive, Georgetown.

96 "Bob's just about made . . ." Interview with Dutton, Washington, 1968.

97 "thinking of running . . ." Interview with Richard Goodwin, Washington, 1968.

97 "Manifesting neither . . ." Richard Goodwin, *Remembering America*, p. 508.

97 At one point, Kennedy asked . . . Interview with Walter Cronkite, Chicago, 1968.

98 when he was ushered . . . Interview with Theodore C. Sorensen, Washington, 1968.

99 "He really had a fetish . . ." Interview with O'Donnell, Washington, 1968.

101 "Bobby wants to see you . . ." Albert Eisele, *Almost to the Presidency*, p. 299.

101 "He wouldn't even let me . . ." Ibid., p. 300.

102 "Now at least three people . . ." Ibid.

103 "it is my opinion . . ." Clark Clifford, with Richard Holbrooke, *Counsel to the President*, p. 504.

104 "I was never in any doubt . . ." Clark Clifford, Oral History Collection, Lyndon Baines Johnson Library, Austin, Tex.

104 "no matter how . . ." Ibid., p. 505.

104 "I can remember . . ." Lowenstein, McCarthy Archive, Georgetown.

105 "Bobby knew about it . . ." Interview with Richard Goodwin, Concord, Mass., 1995.

106 "Senator Kennedy sat . . ." Abigail McCarthy, *Private Faces/Public Places*, p. 372.

106 "You don't have to open . . ." Interview with Jerry Eller, Arlington, Va., 1995.

106 "Of course, if we really . . ." Abigail McCarthy, *Private Faces/Public Places*, p. 373.

107 "When they talked there . . ." Interview with Gans, Washington, 1995.

107 "Your friend isn't interested . . ." Lowenstein, McCarthy Archive, Georgetown.

108 "Do you know what . . . " Schlesinger, *Robert Kennedy and His Times*, p. 857.

110 "It changed the whole character . . ." Interview with Eugene McCarthy, Washington, 1995.

110 "I felt that I . . ." Doris Kearns (Goodwin), *Lyndon Johnson and the American Dream*, p. 343.

111 "I thought that maybe . . ." Interview with Eugene McCarthy, Washington, 1995.

113 Tom Glen wrote a letter . . . *Newsweek*, September 11, 1995.

114 "It sure beats those Army bases." Conversation with Frank Mankiewicz, Topeka, 1968.

115 "I don't care how he got in." Interview with Stan Mitchell, Topeka, 1968.

118 "shocked by the number . . ." Memorandum from James L. Rowe Jr. to Johnson, 1968.

118 "General Westmoreland has been . . ." Joseph Alsop in the *Washington Post*, March 26, 1968.

119 "was rather chilled . . ." Interview with George Hinman, New York, 1969.

121 Agnew's secretary said later . . . Telephone interview with Alice Fringer, 1971.

121 "I'll bet your wattles . . ." Telephone interview with Tom McCall, 1971.

122 "I don't have a thing . . ." Interview with Agnew, Washington, 1968.

122 "He wrote him . . ." Interview with E. Scott Moore, Towson, Md., 1971.

123 "we are facing an opponent . . ." Memorandum from Bob Goodman to Agnew, 1966.

125 "was a fiasco . . ." Interview with Dr. Samuel L. Myers, Bowie, Md., 1971.

126 "Agnew was so boiled . . ." Author interview, 1968.

126 "The effect of Nixon . . ." Interview with John Sears, Washington, 1969.

126 "a case of tired blood . . ." Evans and Novak in the *Washington Post*, March 1968.

126 "Nelson Rockefeller's effective . . ." William S. White in the *Washington Post*, March 1968.

128 "feared that instead . . ." Hayden, *Reunion: A Memoir*, p. 262.

129 "a mad joy prevailed." Larner, *Nobody Knows*, p. 47.

130 "It was Kennedy . . ." Lowenstein, McCarthy Archive, Georgetown.

130 "I made a very emotional statement . . ." Ibid.

132 "is too busy in Washington . . ." Interview with Les Aspin, Milwaukee, 1968.

132 "perhaps a hundred . . ." Lawrence F. O'Brien, *No Final Victories*, p. 228.

135 "It may have intoxicated . . ." Interview with Mankiewicz, Washington, 1968.

137 "like ants at times . . ." Peterson, McCarthy Archive, Georgetown.

138 "How bad?" O'Brien, *No Final Victories*, p. 229.

138 "It's unlikely but possible . . ." Interview with Aspin, Milwaukee, 1968.

139 "it was still essentially . . ." Townsend Hoopes, *The Limits of Intervention*, p. 219.

139 Aware of likely resistance . . . Clifford, *Counsel to the President*, p. 520.

139 "I didn't like it . . ." Harry McPherson, *A Political Education*, p. 437.

140 "such pain in his eyes . . ." Lady Bird Johnson, *A White House Diary*, p. 642.

140 "He read me the speech . . ." Eisele interview with Hubert H. Humphrey, 1971.

140 "So I had heard . . ." Ibid., p. 439.

141 "you could have knocked . . ." Clifford, Oral History Collection, LBJ Library.

142 "Do you mind . . ." Interview with Ted Van Dyk, Washington, 1994.

142 "the president says to tell you . . ." Eisele, *Almost to the Presidency*, p. 324.

143 "I wonder if he'd have done this . . ." Interview with Dutton, Washington, 1968.

143 the president actually . . . Lady Bird Johnson, *A White House Diary*, p. 616.

143 "But the president . . ." Abigail McCarthy, *Private Faces/Public Places*, p. 256.

CHAPTER 5: *April: The Fire, This Time*

147 "The Johnson withdrawal . . ." Interview with Eugene McCarthy, Washington, 1995.

148 "You and I can make . . ." Lowenstein, McCarthy Archive, Georgetown.

150 "I can't have the government . . ." Califano, *The Triumph and Tragedy of Lyndon Johnson*, p. 291.

153 "Do you know Ben?" Lewis, *King: A Critical Biography*, p. 388.

155 "People were stunned . . ." Interview with John Lewis, Washington, 1995.

158 "It was not so much what he said . . ." Interview with Richard Goodwin, Washington, 1968.

158 "He identified with people who hurt." Interview with Dutton, Washington, 1968.

159 "Gene was adamantly . . ." Abigail McCarthy, *Private Faces/Public Places*, p. 397.

161 he was prepared to endorse . . . Schlesinger, *Robert Kennedy and His Times*, p. 873.

161 "hoped somehow to capitalize . . ." Interview with Doris Kearns Goodwin, Concord, Mass., 1995.

162 "I don't think about it in terms . . ." Interview with Wallace, Montgomery, 1968.

163 "This perturbed him . . ." Interview with Col. Robert J. Lally, Baltimore, 1971.

164 "I think that had an impact." Interview with Moore, Towson, Md., 1971.

164 "I knew it was going to be . . ." Interview with Clarence Mitchell, Baltimore, 1971.

164 "In the midst of my speech . . ." Interview with Charles Bresler, Annapolis, 1971.

167 "I was shocked primarily . . ." Interview with Mitchell, Baltimore, 1971.

170 "Some purists in our camp . . ." O'Brien, *No Final Victories*, p. 238.

171 "To lead America . . ." Richard Goodwin, *Remembering America*, p. 530.

172 "Don't close them." Interview with Dutton, Washington, 1968.

178 "Our candidate went on . . ." Larner, *Nobody Knows*, p. 76.

178 "made special reference . . ." Eugene McCarthy, *The Year of the People*, p. 117.

179 "student door-to-door effort . . ." Ibid., p. 132.

180 "whether we really wanted . . ." Ben Stavis, *We Were the Campaign*, p. 51.

181 "There seemed to be a rather . . ." Eugene McCarthy, *The Year of the People*, p. 133.

182 "I supported Lyndon . . ." Mixner, McCarthy Archive, Georgetown.

183 "absolutely excommunicated . . ." Interview with Van Dyk, Washington, 1994.

185 "if Kennedy turned out to be . . ." Califano, *The Triumph and Tragedy of Lyndon Johnson*, p. 290.

187 "whether students vote . . ." Charles Kaiser, *1968 in America*, p. 158.

189 "While I had gone through . . ." Hayden, *Reunion: A Memoir*, p. 275.

190 "I thought the country . . ." Buchanan, C-SPAN interview, 1993.

191 "The condition of youth . . ." Nicholas von Hoffman in the *Washington Post*, June 16, 1968.

CHAPTER 6: *May: Passions Rising*

194 "What happened?" Interview with Van Dyk, Washington, 1994.

199 "Well, I've done all I could do." Conversation with Robert F. Kennedy, Portland, Ore., 1968.

200 "My schedulers seemed . . ." Eugene McCarthy, *The Year of the People*, p. 132.

201 "had isolated himself . . ." Larner, *Nobody Knows*, p. 78.

202 "when somebody tapped me . . ." Telephone interview with Taylor Branch, 1995.

203 "That's not your fault." Richard T. Stout, *People*, p. 237.

203 "It never sounded like . . ." Telephone interview with Branch, 1995.

203 "He kind of neutralized me." Stout, *People*, p. 237.

203 "were so bowled over . . ." Telephone interview with Branch, 1995.

204 "He had won in Indiana . . ." Interview with Dutton, Washington, 1968.

206 "Kennedy talks about me . . ." Interview with Eugene McCarthy, Omaha, 1968.

209 "Nebraska happened . . ." Eugene McCarthy, *The Year of the People*, p. 139.

209 "The Kennedy campaign took . . ." Lowenstein, McCarthy Archive, Georgetown.

217 "was something of a stepchild . . ." Interview with Stephen Smith, New York, 1968.

217 "Have we got the ghettos . . ." Interview with Dutton, Washington, 1968.

218 "Let's face it." James Dickenson interview with Robert Kennedy, 1968.

221 "We're running against . . ." Ibid.

221 "I've got a problem here." Conversation with Robert Kennedy, Portland, Ore., 1968.

222 another factor worked . . . O'Brien, *No Final Victories*, p. 241.

222 "I thought we decided that." Interview with Dutton, Washington, 1968.

224 "It's a lot easier . . ." Interview with O'Brien, Portland, Ore., 1968.

224 "Bad news, Bob." Conversation with Dick Dougherty, New York, 1968.

226 "It certainly wasn't . . ." Conversation with Robert Kennedy, Portland, Ore., 1968.

227 "Why do you put up . . ." Ibid.

227 a man he had encountered . . . Eugene McCarthy, *The Year of the People*, p. 151.

229 It was Nixon's custom . . . Interview with Nixon, Portland, Ore., 1968.

233 "Such a small state . . ." Conversation with Ethel Kennedy, California, 1968.

235 The militants sounded off . . . Interview with Dutton, Washington, 1968.

CHAPTER 7: *June: Murder of Hope*

239 "No one is ever castrated . . ." Stout, *People*, p. 272.

243 "was not his most generous . . ." Interview with Edelman, Washington, 1995.

243 "Kennedy had had the guts . . ." Larner, *Nobody Knows*, p. 117.

243 "He flubbed it!" Eisele, *Almost to the Presidency*, p. 320.

244 "I don't want to talk about politics." Ibid.

244 "a complete fabrication . . ." Interview with Eugene McCarthy, Washington, 1995.

244 "Bob says McCarthy . . ." Conversation with Ethel Kennedy, San Francisco, 1968.

246 "You had a little trouble . . ." Interview with Dutton, Washington, 1968.

248 Kennedy stripped off . . . Theodore H. White, *The Making of the President 1968*, p. 180.

248 "I think we broke . . ." Conversation with O'Brien, Los Angeles, 1968.

249 "to get free of McCarthy . . ." Richard Goodwin, *Remembering America*, p. 536.

251 "John, you let me down . . ." Interview with Lewis, Washington, 1995.

251 "Shake hands with . . ." Moldea, *The Killing of Robert F. Kennedy*, p. 29.

251 "Is Mr. Kennedy coming . . ." Ibid, p. 30.

251 I kidded "Ruthless Robert" . . . Conversation with Robert Kennedy, Los Angeles, 1968.

252 "he was like a little boy . . ." Conversation with Dutton, Los Angeles, 1968.

256 "We all dropped to the floor . . ." Interview with Lewis, Washington, 1995.

256 "Maybe we should do it . . ." Stout, *People*, p. 280.

256 Humphrey had just gotten to sleep . . . Eisele, *Almost to the Presidency*, p. 331.

257 while the first plane . . . Interview with Van Dyk, Washington, 1994.

258 "it's all over . . ." Stout, *People*, p. 283.

260 "I received a telephone call . . ." Clifford, *Counsel to the President*, p. 545.

263 "had been accepted . . ." Marcus Raskin, *Being and Doing*, p. 288.

263 "My brother was a man of love . . ." Moldea, *The Killing of Robert F. Kennedy*, p. 123.

269 "it was clear that what Gene . . ." Interview with Van Dyk, Washington, 1994.

269 "A black mood descended . . ." Interview with Eisele, Washington, 1995.

269 "Gene was truly trying . . ." Interview with Van Dyk, Washington, 1994.

270 The Benedictine monks . . . Interview with Jerry Eller, Arlington, Va., 1995.

270 "McCarthy did not resign . . ." Larner, *Nobody Knows*, p. 124.

271 "If he thought it over . . ." Ibid., p. 132.

273 "McCarthy didn't throw cold water . . ." Eisele, *Almost to the Presidency*, p. 340.

274 "It's as if someone . . ." Eugene McCarthy, in the *New York Times*, June 1968.

274 "How could McCarthy fire them?" Stout, *People*, p. 304.

275 "It's a combination . . ." Interview by Gloria Steinem in *New York*, June 1968.

280 "This was just too much." Eisele interview with Humphrey, 1971.

CHAPTER 8: *July: False Hopes*

284 "They were acting . . ." Lowenstein, McCarthy Archive, Georgetown.

285 "I showed it to him . . ." Eisele, *Almost to the Presidency*, p. 336.

286 "Anna is my good friend . . ." Anna Chennault, *The Education of Anna*, p. 175.

286 "to see that Vietnam gets . . ." Nguyen Tien Hung and Jerrold L. Schecter, *The Palace File*, p. 23.

286 "his staff would be in touch . . ." Bui Diem with David Chanoff, *In the Jaws of History*, p. 237.

286 "snowy Sunday morning . . ." Chennault, *The Education of Anna*, p. 175.

286 said the July meeting . . . Interview with Bui Diem, Rockville, Md., 1995.

289 "I was under tremendous . . ." Telephone interview with George Gallup Jr., 1969.

290 "It wasn't my intent . . ." Ibid.

CHAPTER 9: *August: Chaos*

302 "If it hadn't been for Strom . . ." Conversation with F. Clifton White, Washington, 1969.

303 "Actually, we wanted to run . . ." Interview with John Sears, Washington, 1969.

303 "How about Agnew?" Ibid.

303 "put his arm around me." Interview with Barry M. Goldwater, Washington, 1969.

304 "I won't put myself . . ." Interview with Sears, Washington, 1969.

304 "I talked to Strom . . ." Interview with Rockefeller, New York, 1969.

305 "I think we've got . . ." Buchanan in C-SPAN interview, 1993.

310 "there were a lot of the Kennedy . . ." Lowenstein, McCarthy Archive, Georgetown.

310 "we sort of talked ourselves . . ." Interview with Mankiewicz, Washington, 1994.

311 "You can get a headline . . ." Eisele, *Almost to the Presidency*, p. 337.

312 "His anger at Humphrey . . ." Clifford, *Counsel to the President*, p. 563.

312 "an informal presentation . . ." Chennault, *The Education of Anna*, p. 184.

315 "He wanted them to fete . . ." Hayden, *Reunion: A Memoir*, p. 293.

315 "He said how horrible . . ." Interview with Doris Kearns Goodwin, Concord, Mass., 1995.

315 "If Humphrey thinks he's got . . ." O'Brien, *No Final Victories*, p.251.

315 "You can take 24 hours . . ." Eisele, *Almost to the Presidency*, p. 349.

316 "were preparing monkey-warfare . . ." Martin A. Lee and Bruce Shlain, *Acid Dreams,* p. 216.

320 the army that was mobilized . . . James Miller, *Democracy Is in the Streets*, p. 295.

322 "just keep in touch . . ." Hubert H. Humphrey, *The Education of a Public Man*, p. 388.

323 "Stop all bombing . . ." Eisele, *Almost to the Presidency*, p.347.

323 "Well, Marvin . . ." Humphrey, *The Education of a Public Man*, p. 389.

323 "I don't want you to tell . . ." Ibid.

323 " Our choice was to stand . . ." Ibid., p. 390.

325 "dispassionate talk to delegates." Interview with Eller, Arlington, Va., 1995.

327 "was probably settled . . ." Eisele, *Almost to the Presidency*, p. 354.

327 "putting flowers in the barrels . . ." Mixner, McCarthy Archive, Georgetown.

328 "Just remember this is . . ." Interview with John Kenneth Galbraith, Cambridge, Mass., 1995.

328 he hoped to the end . . . Califano, *The Triumph and Tragedy of Lyndon Johnson*, p. 322

329 "was a soaring figure . . ." Lowenstein, McCarthy Archive, Georgetown.

330 "Well, we might do it together." Richard Goodwin, in *Look*, 1968.

330 "While I'm doing this for Teddy . . ." Stephen Smith in *New York*, 1968.

330 "Somebody mistook it . . ." *Time*, 1968.

330 "I did say, because of the campaign . . ." Eugene McCarthy, *The Year of the People*, p. 211.

331 "If there is such a thing . . ." Interview with Smith, New York, 1968.

331 "I remember running . . ." Lowenstein, McCarthy Archive, Georgetown.

331 "The essential conception . . ." Ibid.

332 "If that instrument . . ." Eisele, *Almost to the Presidency*, p. 356.

332 "I've always been running . . ." Ibid., p. 357.

334 "Look at them . . ." Stout, *People*, p. 363.

334 "They started beating people . . ." Mixner, McCarthy Archive, Georgetown.

335 "The police leaped . . ." Hayden, *Reunion: A Memoir*, p. 319.

335 "It didn't have to be . . ." Eisele, *Almost to the Presidency*, p. 357.

335 "This is Anne." Stout, *People*, p. 366.

335 "taken some abuse . . ." Buchanan, C-SPAN interview, 1993.

337 With typical buoyancy . . . White, *The Making of the President* 1968, p. 303.

337 "But we had a big hangup." Interview with Raskin, Washington, 1994.

337 "for hours of selfless labor." Stavis, *We Were the Campaign*, p. 190.

338 "I listened in dread . . ." Abigail McCarthy, *Private Faces/Public Places*, p. 425.

338 Among the long-shot schemes . . .Eisele, *Almost to the Presidency*, p. 359.

338 "know what political good . . ." Humphrey, *The Education of a Public Man*, p. 391.

339 "You're all invited . . ." Erwin Knoll, McCarthy Archive, Georgetown.

340 "a rather formidable display . . ." Ibid.

341 "Spending the night . . ." Harris Wofford, *Of Kennedys and Kings*, p. 427.

342 Johnson approved of its showing . . . Califano, *The Triumph and Tragedy of Lyndon Johnson*, p. 319.

343 "While these kids were sitting . . ." Knoll, McCarthy Archive, Georgetown.

343 "When objects supposedly . . ." Abigail McCarthy, *Private Faces/Public Places,* p. 427.

345 "I think that what went on . . ." Thomas Finney, McCarthy Archive, Georgetown.

CHAPTER 10: *September: Running in Place*

347 "What are you doing . . ." Interview with Joseph Napolitan, Washington, 1995.

348 "I never deal . . ." Author interview, 1969.

350 "My approach as finance chairman . . ." Interview with Maurice Stans, Washington, 1969.

363 "Nobody knew how to handle it." Interview with Robert Shogan, Washington, 1971.

364 "love handles." Ibid.

364 "through a highly unusual channel . . ." Richard Nixon, *RN: The Memoirs of Richard Nixon*, p. 23.

364 "Henry was the only person . . ." Walter Isaacson, *Kissinger,* p. 131.

365 "it is my strong belief . . ." Memorandum from Napolitan to O'Brien, 1968.

365 "If it works . . ." Interview with Napolitan, Washington, 1995.

368 "What's the matter . . ." Interview with Gene Oishi, Washington, 1971.

368 "Agnew is a thin-skinned . . ." Ibid.

369 "How's the fat Jap . . ." Ibid.

370 "Governor Agnew . . ." Interviews with Oishi, Shogan, Washington, 1971.

371 "I didn't know you felt . . . " Interview with Oishi, Washington, 1971.

372 "Kissinger called again." Nixon, *RN*, p. 323.

374 "I thought this poll . . ." O'Brien, *No Final Victories*, p. 259.

374 "I read it and hit the ceiling. . . ." Ibid.

374 "Mr. Humphrey, in Vietnam . . ." Eisele, *Almost to the Presidency*, p. 374.

375 "In many ways, Seattle . . ." Ibid., p. 376.

376 "you can't expect to be elected . . ." O'Brien, *No Final Victories*, p. 260.

376 "You have to prove . . ." Ibid.

376 The key paragraphs read . . . Ibid, p. 261.

377 "I gather you're not asking . . ." Humphrey, *The Education of a Public Man*, p. 403.

377 "sufficient protection . . ." Eisele, *Almost to the Presidency*, p. 377.

377 "Johnson never forgave him . . ." Califano, *The Triumph and Tragedy of Lyndon Johnson*, pp. 325–26.

Chapter 11: *October: Too Little, Too Late*

382 "put Bill Clinton's draft notice . . ." Maraniss, *First in His Class*, p. 119.

388 "never fully forgave . . ." Eisele, *Almost to the Presidency*, p. 147.

390 McCarthy had said it was all right . . . Ibid, p. 383.

395 "We sort of got locked in . . ." Interview with Sears, Washington, 1971.

395 "We sat all day . . ." Ibid.

395 "Herb, you go tell those bastards . . ." Ibid.

396 "there was a strong possiblity . . ." Nixon, *RN*, p. 324.

396 Johnson, in fact, was on the verge . . . Notes of Tom Johnson, LBJ Library.

397 "Electoral tricks . . ." Ibid.

397 "As soon as the decision . . ." Ibid.

397 "the word is out . . ." Ibid.

398 "many Republican friends . . ." Hung and Schecter, *The Palace File*, p. 244.

399 "the Dewey syndrome." Author interview, 1969.

401 "the President is driving . . ." Nixon, *RN*, p. 326.

404 "pre-emptive strike . . ." William Safire, *Before the Fall*, p. 85.

405 "a shot across Johnson's bow . . ." Ibid., p. 86

405 "the only way . . ." Nixon, *RN*, p. 327.

405 "You've heard it at every stop . . ." Conversation with Herb Klein, New York, 1968.

406 "It wouldn't have been proper . . ." Interview with Sears, 1969.

406 "The *Times* was off base. . . ." Interview with Steve Hess, Washington, 1971.

408 "The longer the present . . ." Diem, *In the Jaws of History*, p. 244.

408 (While the full cable . . . Telephone interview with William Bundy, 1997.

409 "explained discreetly . . ." Bundy, *Tangled Web*, draft chapter 5, p, 26.

409 he was in touch . . . Interview with Diem, Rockville, Md., 1995.

409 "Despite his disclaimers . . ." Clifford, *Counsel to the President*, p. 582.

410 "I would rather be stubborn . . ." Notes of Tom Johnson, LBJ Library.

410 "urged Thieu to block . . ." Califano, *The Triumph and Tragedy of Lyndon Johnson*, p, 327.

410 "This is treason!" Telephone interview with James Jones, 1995.

410 "who said he had just been speaking . . ." Safire, *Before the Fall*, p. 93.

410 "I told him, 'You've got to talk . . .' " Bryce Harlow, Oral History Collection, LBJ Library.

411 "understands the President . . ." James Jones, White House memo dated Nov. 3, 1968.

412 "from an old friend . . ." Memorandum from Eugene V. Rostow to Walt W. Rostow, LBJ Library.

412 "to go back to Alexander Sachs . . ." Memorandum from Walt Rostow to Johnson, LBJ Library.

412 "thought the prospects . . ." Memorandum from Eugene Rostow to Walt Rostow, LBJ Library.

412 "Have a phone they can cram . . ." Notes of Tom Johnson, LBJ Library.

412 "this would rock the world . . ." Ibid.

413 "we realize political forces . . ." Ibid.

413 "I have been considering . . ." Memorandum from Walt Rostow to Johnson, LBJ Library.

414 "they are trying to decide . . ." Notes of Tom Johnson, LBJ Library.

414 "They may just be testing . . ." Ibid.

414 "I think Ky is getting . . ." Ibid.

414 "Saigon may see this . . ." Ibid.

414 "If we go alone . . ." Ibid.

415 "Suppose Thieu does not go along . . ." Memorandum from Walt Rostow to Johnson, LBJ Library.

415 "most of what we picked up . . ." Cartha "Deke" DeLoach, *Hoover's FBI*, p. 402.

415 "Mrs. Chennault entered . . ." Memorandum from "BKS" to Walt Rostow, LBJ Library.

415 "The latest on the lady." Memorandum from Walt Rostow to Johnson, LBJ Library.

415 "as the campaign neared . . ." Chennault, *The Education of Anna*, p. 186.

416 "Thieu was under heavy pressure . . ." Hung and Schecter, *The Palace File*, p. 23.

417 he had been prepared to endorse Humphrey . . . Interview with Eugene McCarthy, Washington, 1995.

418 "some old China hands . . ." Clifford, *Counsel to the President*, p. 593.

418 "with his intimate knowledge . . ." Hung and Schecter, *The Palace File*, p. 26.

419 "Anna, I'm speaking . . ." Chennault, *The Education of Anna*, p. 190.

CHAPTER 12: *November: "Bring Us Together"*

421 "No, but our friend . . ." Seymour Hersh in the *New York Times*, June 27, 1973.

422 "we had the impression . . ." Conversation with Bill Boyarsky, New York, 1968.

422 "to criticize a 'step . . .'" Safire, *Before the Fall*, p. 87.

423 One FBI report . . . FBI cable in LBJ Library.

423 "What was conveyed . . ." Clifford, *Counsel to the President*, p. 582.

424 "it was treason . . ." Telephone interview with James Jones, 1995.

424 "Now Johnson was certain . . ." Califano, *The Triumph and Tragedy of Lyndon Johnson*, p. 328.

425 "expressed deep concern . . ." O'Brien, Oral History Collection, LBJ Library.

425 Humphrey had now edged . . . Interview with Van Dyk, Washington, 1994.

426 "became the occasion . . ." Califano, *The Triumph and Tragedy of Lyndon Johnson*, p. 926.

426 "really tore it . . ." Telephone interview with Califano, 1995.

427 "running about ten minutes . . ." Humphrey, *The Education of a Public Man,* p. 404.

427 "If the fellow had had a few more guts . . ." Interview with Sears, Washington, 1969.

428 "we canceled it . . ." O'Brien, *No Final Victories*, p. 263.

428 "If you watched that whole thing . . ." Interview with Napolitan, Washington, 1995.

429 "By Sunday night . . ." Interview with Patrick Buchanan, Washington, 1969.

429 "The object of the exercise . . ." Unsigned memorandum, LBJ Library.

430 "to consider the question . . ." Memorandum from Walt Rostow for the Record, LBJ Library.

430 "Saville Davis . . ." Unsigned memo in White House files, LBJ Library.

430 "the information sources . . ." Memorandum from Walt Rostow to Johnson, LBJ Library.

432 "Nixon wanted to be darned sure . . ." Interview with Sears, Washington, 1971.

433 "The image campaign . . ." Joe McGinniss, *The Selling of the President 1968*, p. 127.

436 "When word finally came . . ." Interview with Van Dyk, Washington, 1994.

437 wanted someone to go down . . . White, *The Making of the President 1968*, p. 393.

437 "people who claimed to speak . . ." Johnson, *The Vantage Point*, p. 548.

438 "I wonder if I should have . . ." Humphrey, *The Education of a Public Man*, p. 8.

438 "The fury and dismay . . ." White, *The Making of the President 1968*, p. 381.

438 reflecting on Humphrey's decision . . . Interview with Napolitan, Washington, 1995.

438 "Nixon knew that Thieu . . ." Stephen E. Ambrose, *Nixon: The Triumph of a Politician*, *1962–1972,* p. 216.

439 "It may be argued . . ." Herbert Parmet, *Richard Nixon and His America*, p. 520.

439 "All this raises a critical question . . ." Clifford, *Counsel to the President*, p. 584.

439 "was a delicate area . . ." Herbert G. Klein, *Making It Perfectly Clear*, p. 40.

439 "The question is . . ." Safire, *Before the Fall*, p. 88.

440 Nixon obviously . . . Ibid., p. 89.

440 "when people later wondered . . ." Ibid., p. 88.

440 "asked whether Nixon . . ." State Department cable, LBJ Library.

440 "will certainly interest you." Memorandum from Walt Rostow to Johnson, LBJ Library.

440 "Eyes Only" memo . . . White House memo from Rostow to LBJ dated Nov. 8, 1968, LBJ Library.

441 "You're going to get me . . ." Interview by Tom Ottenad with Anna Chennault, 1968.

441 "The only people who knew . . ." Telephone interview with Anna Chennault, 1995.

441 the same comments to him. . . . Telephone interview with Cartha De-Loach, 1995.

441 "it was widely known . . ." Senate Committee Report, 1975.

441 "in connection with a previous . . ." DeLoach, *Hoover's FBI*, p. 404.

442 "came on the phone . . ." Senate Committee Report, 1975.

442 "the Lady . . . at 1:41 p.m. . . ." Memorandum from Rostow to Johnson, LBJ Library.

442 did not refute . . . Telephone interview with Walt Rostow, 1995.

442 "a file President Johnson . . ." Letter from Walt Rostow to Harry Middleton, LBJ Library.

442 the fifty-year embargo . . . Telephone interview with Harry Middleton, 1995.

443 "she had no influence . . ." Interview with Melvin R. Laird, Washington, 1995.

443 "got very hot . . ." H. R. Haldeman, *The Haldeman Diaries*, p. 567.

443 "because of some request . . ." DeLoach, *Hoover's FBI*, p. 413.

444 Walt Rostow, in a "Literally . . ." White House memo from Rostow to LBJ dated Nov. 8, 1968, LBJ Library.

445 "stood in the twilight . . ." Safire, *Before the Fall*, p. 82.

446 "part of Saigon's foot-dragging . . ." Johnson, *The Vantage Point*, p. 548.

449 "South Vietnam has got to send . . ." Diem, *In the Jaws of History*, p. 245.

449 "We need to do something . . ." Chennault, *The Education of Anna*, p. 193.

449 "Anna, I'm not going . . ." Ibid.

449 "make sure I would not let . . ." Ibid., p. 194.

449 "Mr. Nixon asked me . . ." Ibid., p. 196.

449 "when Nixon took me aside . . ." Ibid., p. 196–97.

450 "It revealed a general . . ." Clifford, *Counsel to the President*, p. 596.

450 "I am inclined to believe . . ." Memorandum from Walt Rostow for the record, LBJ Library.

450 "You see Watergate writ large . . ." Telephone interview with William P. Bundy, 1995.

451 "to bug Nixon's campaign . . ." H. R. Haldeman, *The Ends of Power*, p. 40.

451 "We'll get that goddamn . . ." Ibid.

CHAPTER 13: *December: Fly Me to the Moon*

462 "For months after . . ." Joseph Alsop in the *Washington Post*, December 1968.

465 "got up at the stroke . . ." Interview with Eisele, Washington, 1995.

CHAPTER 14: *After the Dream Died*

469 was "an Orwellian construction . . ." Interview with Vice President Albert A. Gore Jr., Washington, 1995.

470 "It was like a tornado year . . ." Interview with Hayden, San Francisco, 1994.

470 "The sixties began . . ." Ibid.

471 "much of the generational . . ." Interview with Richard Stearns, Boston, 1995.

471 "was in many ways . . ." Interview with Gore, Washington, 1995.

472 "Johnson promised . . ." Interview with Hayden, San Francisco, 1994.

472 "we were willing . . ." Telephone interview with Gary Hart, 1995.

472 "America was struggling . . ." Interview with Dutton, Washington, 1994.

473 "once the turn was made . . ." Interview with Doris Kearns Goodwin, Concord, Mass., 1995.

474 "certainly Nixon exploited . . ." Telephone interview with William Safire, 1995.

474 "are always viewed in terms . . ." Interview with Alan Brinkley, New York, 1995.

474 "sensed at that time . . ." Telephone interview with Safire, 1995.

475 "Nineteen sixty-eight was two sides . . ." Telephone interview with Buchanan, 1995.

476 "Far from being . . ." Kevin Phillips, *The Emerging Republican Majority*, p. 31.

476 "The great political upheaval . . ." Ibid., p. 470.

476 "The emerging Republican majority . . ." Ibid., p. 471.

477 "When an election is decided . . ." Interview with Hayden, Sacramento, 1995.

478 "it became quite fashionable . . ." William Bennett in C-SPAN interview, 1993.

479 "I said, 'What the hell . . .' " Interview with Bennett, Washington, 1995.

479 "were backed by a great majority . . ." Interview with Harry McPherson, Washington, 1994.

480 "The mistake the Democrats made . . ." Telephone interview with Buchanan, 1995.

480 "the [Democratic] convention . . ." Interview with Ben Wattenberg, Washington, 1995.

480 "An element of noncivility . . ." Telephone interview with John Ehrlichman, 1995.

481 "on the moral and legal sides . . ." Interview with Arthur Schlesinger Jr., New York, 1995.

481 "By 1968, the civil rights . . ." Ron Walters in C-SPAN interview, 1993.

481 "The civil rights movement . . ." Interview with Richard Goodwin, Concord, Mass., 1995.

481 "retained a commitment . . ." Interview with Galbraith, Cambridge, 1995.

482 "You could scratch . . ." Interview with Gans, Washington, 1994.

482 "Certainly it defused . . ." Lowenstein, McCarthy Archive, Georgetown.

482 "It's a mixed thing . . ." Interview with Eugene McCarthy, Washington, 1995.

483 "McCarthy has one fine quality . . ." Interview with David Riesman, Arlington, Mass., 1995.

483 "We have to come back . . ." Knoll, McCarthy Archive, Georgetown.

483 "With the exception . . ." Interview with Gans, Washington, 1994.

483 "I was able to tap into . . ." Interview with George McGovern, Washington, 1995.

484 "the Nixon campaign . . ." Buchanan in C-SPAN interview, 1993.

484 "This is about your presidency . . ." Telephone interview with Buchanan, 1995.

484 "after 1968 the protest . . ." Interview with Hayden, Washington, 1994.

486 "given Johnson's commitment . . ." Interview with Todd Gitlin, Paris, 1995.

486 "it was possible to believe . . ." Ibid.

487 "If it accomplished anything . . ." Interview with Hayden, Washington, 1994.

487 "As a member . . ." Interview with Joseph Kennedy II, Washington, 1994.

488 "Something died in America . . ." Interview with Lewis, Washington, 1995.

488 "Nineteen sixty-eight at least symbolically . . ." Interview with Richard Goodwin, Concord, Mass., 1995.

489 "in 1968, civil rights . . ." Interview with Sen. Edward M. Kennedy, Washington, 1995.

489 "When you realize . . ." Interview with Gitlin, Paris, 1995.

490 "would have become . . ." Telephone interview with Ehrlichman, 1995.

490 "bridge figures . . ." Interview with Edelman, Washington, 1995.

490 "a real bridge figure . . ." Interview with Brinkley, New York, 1995.

491 "a lot of the problems . . ." Interview with Lewis, Washington, 1995.

491 "to counteract the mounting . . ." Jeffrey Bell, *Populism and Elitism*, p. 142.

491 "Looking backwards . . ." Interview with Rep. Newt Gingrich, Washington, 1995.

493 "He would have done . . ." Interview with Edelman, Washington, 1995.

493 "would have made it very easy . . ." Interview with Schlesinger, New York, 1995.

493 "Johnson controlled . . ." Interview with Stearns, Boston, 1995.

493 "Humphrey would [still] have been . . ." Buchanan in C-SPAN interview, 1993.

494 "His own realism . . ." Telephone interview with Garry Wills, 1995.

494 "It would have been some convention . . ." Interview with Eugene McCarthy, Washington, 1995.

494 "My personal belief . . ." Interview with Gans, Washington, 1994.

494 "Hope." Interview with Sen. Bob Kerrey, Washington, 1995.

495 "Martin Luther King's death . . ." Interview with Hayden, San Francisco, 1994.

495 "I don't know whether . . ." Interview with Richard Goodwin, Concord, Mass., 1995.

495 "He hated the war." Interview with Schlesinger, New York, 1995.

495 "He would have been a powerful . . ." Interview with Dutton, Washington, 1994.

496 "He was way out of the loop . . ." Interview with Wattenberg, Washington, 1995.

496 "even if he was not president . . ." Interview with Edelman, Washington, 1995.

497 "and in Latin America the priests . . ." Interview with Hayden, San Francisco, 1994.

498 "stopped talking about winning . . ." Interview with Sears, Washington, 1995.

498 "By 1970 the argument . . ." Interview with Kerrey, Washington, 1995.

498 "he would have invaded . . ." Interview with Richard Goodwin, Concord, Mass., 1995.

498 "people thought it should have been . . ." Interview with Riesman, Arlington, Mass., 1995.

499 "We will never know . . ." Interview with Gans, Washington, 1994.

499 "this beautiful, voluptuous woman . . ." Interview with Doris Kearns Goodwin, Concord, Mass., 1995.

499 "made the mistake of getting . . ." Interview with Richard Goodwin, Concord, Mass., 1995.

499 "The angry white male . . ." Interview with Rep. Barney Frank, Washington, 1995.

500 "By not disagreeing . . ." Interview with Wattenberg, Washington, 1995.

500 "What would it . . ." Interview with Gitlin, Paris, 1995.

501 "In 1968, the Democratic Party . . ." Interview with Bennett, Washington, 1995.

502 "used the guilt of liberal whites . . ." Interview with Stearns, Boston, 1995.

502 "very much at the margin." Interview with Galbraith, Cambridge, 1995.

502 "It played into Nixon's paranoia . . ." Interview with Hayden, San Francisco, 1994.

503 "A whole generation of young people . . ." Interview with Edelman, Washington, 1995.

503 "The year changed the power . . ." Interview with Galbraith, Cambridge, 1995.

503 "in 1968 there was hope . . ." Interview with Goodwin, Concord, Mass., 1995.

503 "the sense of hopefulness . . ." Interview with Joseph Kennedy II, Washington, 1994.

503 cited the disappearance of common civility . . . Telephone interview with Branch, 1995.

504 "The election of 1968 . . ." Interview with Lewis, Washington, 1995.

504 "the watershed year for a generation . . ." Hayden, *Reunion: A Memoir*, pp. 254, 326.

504 "a lot of people . . ." Interview with Gitlin, Paris, 1995.

BIBLIOGRAPHY

Ambrose, Stephen E. *Nixon: The Triumph of a Politician, 1962–1972.* New York: Simon & Schuster, 1989.

Armbrister, Trevor. *A Matter of Accountability: The True Story of the Pueblo Affair.* New York: Coward-McCann, 1970.

Avorn, Jerry. *University in Revolt.* London: MacDonald, 1969.

Bell, Jeffrey. *Populism and Elitism.* Washington: Regnery Gateway, 1992.

Bernstein, Irving. *Guns or Butter: The Presidency of Lyndon Johnson.* New York: Oxford University Press, 1996.

Califano, Joseph A. Jr. *The Triumph and Tragedy of Lyndon Johnson.* New York: Simon & Schuster, 1991.

Caute, David. *The Year of the Barricades.* New York: Harper & Row, 1988.

Chennault, Anna. *The Education of Anna.* New York: Times Books, 1980.

Chester, Lewis, Hodgson, Godfrey, and Page, Bruce. *An American Melodrama: The Presidential Campaign of 1968.* New York: Viking, 1969.

Christian, George. *The President Steps Down.* New York: Macmillan, 1970.

Clifford, Clark, with Richard Holbrooke. *Counsel to 'the President.* New York: Random House, 1991.

Dean, John. *Lost Honor.* Los Angeles: Stratford Press, 1982.

Dellinger, David. *More Power Than We Know.* New York: Anchor Press, 1975.

DeLoach, Cartha D. "Deke." *Hoover's FBI.* Washington: Regnery, 1995.

Diem, Bui, with David Chanoff. *In the Jaws of History.* Boston: Houghton Mifflin, 1987.

Eisele, Albert. *Almost to the Presidency.* Blue Earth, Minn.: Piper, 1972.

Frady, Marshall. *Wallace.* New York: New American Library, 1968.

Frank, Barney. *Speaking Frankly.* New York: Times Books, 1992.

Gitlin, Todd. *The Sixties: Years of Hope, Days of Rage.* New York: Bantam, 1987.

Goldman, Eric. *The Tragedy of Lyndon Johnson.* New York: Knopf, 1969.

Goodwin, Richard N. *Remembering America.* Boston: Little, Brown, 1988.

Guthman, Edwin. *We Band of Brothers.* New York: Harper & Row, 1971.

Halberstam, David. *The Odyssey of Robert Kennedy.* New York: Random House, 1968.

Haldeman, H. R. *The Haldeman Diaries: Inside the White House.* New York: Putnam, 1994.

Haldeman, H. R., with Joseph DiMona. *The Ends of Power.* New York: Times Books, 1978.

Hayden, Tom. *Reunion: A Memoir.* New York: Random House, 1988.

Hersh, Seymour M. *The Price of Power: Kissinger in the Nixon White House.* New York: Summit Books, 1983.

Herzog, Arthur. *McCarthy for President.* New York: Viking, 1969.

Hoopes, Townsend. *The Limits of Intervention.* New York: McKay, 1969.

Humphrey, Hubert H. *The Education of a Public Man: My Life and Politics.* Garden City, N.Y.: Doubleday, 1976.

Hung, Nguyen Tien, and Schecter, Jerrold L. *The Palace File.* New York: Harper & Row, 1986.

Isaacson, Walter. *Kissinger: A Biography.* New York: Simon & Schuster, 1992.

Isaacson, Walter, and Thomas, Evan. *The Wise Men.* New York: Simon & Schuster, 1986.

Johnson, Lady Bird. *A White House Diary.* New York: Holt Rinehart Winston, 1970.

Johnson, Lyndon B. *The Vantage Point.* New York: Holt Rinehart Winston, 1971.

Kaiser, Charles. *1968 in America.* New York: Weidenfeld & Nicholson, 1988.

Karnow, Stanley. *Vietnam: A History.* New York: Viking, 1983.

Kearns (Goodwin), Doris. *Lyndon Johnson and the American Dream.* New York: Harper & Row, 1976.

Klein, Herbert G. *Making It Perfectly Clear.* Garden City, N.Y.: Doubleday, 1980.

Koning, Hans. *1968: A Personal Report.* New York: Norton, 1987.

Larner, Jeremy. *Nobody Knows: Reflections on the McCarthy Campaign of 1968.* New York: Macmillan, 1969.

Lee, Martin A., and Shlain, Bruce. *Acid Dreams: The CIA, LSD and the Sixties Rebellion.* New York: Grove Press, 1985.

Lewis, David L. *King: A Critical Biography.* New York: Praeger, 1970.

Lukas, J. Anthony. *Nightmare: The Underside of the Nixon Years.* New York: Viking, 1976.

Maraniss, David. *First in His Class.* New York: Simon & Schuster, 1995.

McCarthy, Abigail. *Private Faces/Public Places.* New York: Doubleday, 1969.

McCarthy, Eugene J. *The Year of the People.* New York: Doubleday, 1969.

McGinniss, Joe. *The Selling of the President 1968.* New York: Trident Press, 1969.

McNamara, Robert S. *In Retrospect: The Tragedy and Lessons of Vietnam.* New York: Times Books, 1995.

McPherson, Harry. *A Political Education.* Boston: Little, Brown, 1972.

Miller, James. *Democracy Is in the Streets: From Port Huron to the Streets of Chicago.* New York: Simon & Schuster, 1987.

Moldea, Dan E. *The Killing of Robert F. Kennedy.* New York: Norton, 1995.

Napolitan, Joseph. *The Election Game and How to Win It.* New York: Doubleday, 1972.

Nelson, Jack, and Bass, Jack. *The Orangeburg Massacre.* Cleveland: World, 1970.

Newfield, Jack. *Robert Kennedy: A Memoir.* New York: Bantam, 1969.

Nixon, Richard M. *RN: The Memoirs of Richard Nixon.* New York: Grosset & Dunlap, 1978.

Oberdorfer, Don. *Tet!* New York: Doubleday, 1971.

O'Brien, Lawrence F. *No Final Victories.* New York: Doubleday, 1974.

Obst, Lynda, and Kingsley, Robert. *The Sixties.* New York: Random House/Rolling Stone, 1977.

Parmet, Herbert. *Richard Nixon and His America.* Boston: Little, Brown, 1990.

Phillips, Kevin P. *The Emerging Republican Majority.* New Rochelle, N.Y.: Arlington House, 1969.

Powers, Thomas. *The Man Who Kept the Secrets: Richard Helms and the CIA.* New York: Knopf, 1979.

————. *The War at Home: Vietnam and the American People, 1964–68.* New York: Grossman, 1973.

Raskin, Marcus. *Being and Doing.* Boston: Beacon, 1971.

Rolling Stone Illustrated History of Rock and Roll. New York: Rolling Stone Press, 1980.

Safire, William. *Before the Fall: An Inside View of the Pre-Watergate White House.* Garden City, N.Y.: Doubleday, 1975.

Sann, Paul. *Angry Decade: The Sixties.* New York: Crown, 1979.

Schandler, Herbert Y. *The Unmaking of a President: Lyndon Johnson and Vietnam.* Princeton: Princeton University, 1977.

Schlesinger, Arthur M. Jr. *Robert Kennedy and His Times.* Boston: Houghton Mifflin, 1978.

———. *A Thousand Days: John F. Kennedy in the White House.* Boston: Houghton Mifflin, 1965.

Solberg, Carl. *Hubert Humphrey.* New York: Norton, 1984.

Stavis, Ben. *We Were the Campaign.* Boston: Beacon, 1969.

Stout, Richard T. *People.* New York: Harper & Row, 1970.

U.S. House of Representatives. *Report of the Select Committee on Assassinations.* New York: Bantam. 1979.

Viorst, Milton. *Fire in the Streets: America in the 1960s.* New York: Simon & Schuster, 1979.

White, Theodore H. *The Making of the President 1968.* New York: Atheneum, 1969.

Wills, Garry. *The Kennedy Imprisonment.* Boston: Atlantic-Little, Brown, 1981.

———. *Nixon Agonistes.* Boston: Houghton Mifflin, 1970.

Witcover, Jules. *Crapshoot: Rolling the Dice on the Vice Presidency.* New York: Crain, 1992.

———. *85 Days: The Last Campaign of Robert Kennedy.* New York: Putnam, 1968.

———. *The Resurrection of Richard Nixon.* New York: Putnam, 1970.

———. *White Knight: The Rise of Spiro Agnew.* New York: Random House, 1972.

Wofford, Harris. *Of Kennedys and Kings: Making Sense of the Sixties.* New York: Farrar, Straus & Giroux, 1980.

INDEX

Gitlin on, 489–90
hunt for killer, 168
and Johnson, 473
Lewis on, 491
and march on Washington, 91, 129
in Memphis, 91, 128–29, 151–53
speculation on, 493, 494, 496, 506
as third party head, 24, 27
and Vietnam, 5, 8–9, 472
wiretaps on, 222
Kirk, Claude, 287, 302, 305
Kirk, Grayson, 187–90, 195, 314
Kissinger, Henry, 364, 365, 372, 396, 456, 470
Kitt, Eartha, 58
Klein, Herb, 289, 350, 351, 404, 405, 429, 435, 439, 449, 452
Knoll, Erwin, 339–40, 483
Knowland, William F., 299
Ku Klux Klan, 123, 161
Kunen, James, 187
Ky, Nguyen Cao, 13, 19, 71, 414, 461–62
Kyles, Samuel, 153

Laird, Melvin, 405, 442–43, 462
Lally, Robert J., 163, 164
Larner, Jeremy, 61, 129, 178, 201, 243, 270, 271
Latin America, 497
Lausche, Frank, 91
Law and order. See Crime
Lazarus, Ralph, 291
Lee, Martin A., 316
LeMay, Curtis, 384–89, 391, 394, 436
Lennen and Newell (co.), 447
Lescaze, Lee, 49
Levinson, Sanford, 23
Lewis, John, 155, 251, 256, 488, 490, 504
Liberalism, 491–92, 505
Liberty City (Miami), 302, 305
Lincoln Park (Chicago), 327
Lindsay, John V., 8, 167, 189, 303, 305, 306, 308
Lisagor, Peter, 65
Loan, Nguyen Ngoc, 70–71, 72
Lodge, Henry Cabot, 267, 302, 350
Lomax, Louis, 245
Long, Russell, 353
Loory, Stuart, 340
Love, John, 287
Lowell, Robert, 239, 465
Lowenstein, Allard, 39, 107, 273, 274, 310, 469
dump Johnson movement, 23–28, 130
and/on Humphrey, 275, 285

and Kennedy (Robert) candidacy, 25, 28, 34, 104–5, 130–31, 209–10, 250–51
and Kennedy (Ted) candidacy, 329–30, 331
and/on McCarthy, 40–41, 482, 130–31, 148–49, 209–10
Lowmyer, Harvey. See Ray, James Earl
Lynd, Staughton, 27

Maddox, Lester, 313, 321, 325, 337, 435
Mahoney, George P., 123–24
Maier, Henry, 457
Mankiewicz, Frank, 34, 114, 135, 259, 262, 310, 336
Mansfield, Mike, 79, 180
Maraniss, David, 382
March on Washington. See Poor People's March/Campaign
Marshall, Burke, 156
Martin, John Bartlow, 171
Martin, William McChesney, 169
Maryland, 122–24
Massachusetts, 94
Matsunaga, Spark, 369
Mays, Benjamin, 160
McCall, Tom, 89, 121
McCarthy, Abigail, 28, 106, 143–44, 338, 343
McCarthy, Eugene J., 15, 24, 27–29, 33, 36–43, 310–12, 465
arbitrary manner, 149, 180
attacks on patriotism, 93
on blacks, 180
in California, 239
campaigning, 72–73, 76, 93
and civil rights, 473
on Connally, 315–16
on Czechoslovakia, 319
at Democratic convention, 316, 321–23, 325–27, 329–32, 336–39, 343–45
disillusionment with, 482–83
Gingrich on, 492
on gun control, 271
and/on Humphrey, 220, 269–73, 281–83, 327, 373, 390, 416–17, 432–33
on issues, 180–81, 270
and Johnson's decision not to run, 142, 146–47
and/on Kennedy (Robert), 64–65, 93, 96–97, 100–102, 105–10, 130, 131, 148, 178–79, 200, 220, 235–36, 249, 252, 494
and Kennedy (Robert) assassination, 256, 258, 260
Kennedy (Robert) debate, 239–44
at King funeral, 159–60